Magical Nominalism

SERIES EDITOR

Darrin McMahon, *Dartmouth College*

After a period of some eclipse, the study of intellectual history has enjoyed a broad resurgence in recent years. The Life of Ideas contributes to this revitalization through the study of ideas as they are produced, disseminated, received, and practiced in different historical contexts. The series aims to embed ideas—those that endured, and those once persuasive but now forgotten—in rich and readable cultural histories. Books in this series draw on the latest methods and theories of intellectual history while being written with elegance and élan for a broad audience of readers.

Other Books by Martin Jay

The Dialectical Imagination: A History of the Frankfurt School and the Institute of Social Research, 1923–1950 (1973 and 1996)
Marxism and Totality: The Adventures of a Concept from Lukács to Habermas (1984)
Adorno (1984)
Permanent Exiles: Essays on the Intellectual Migration from Germany to America (1985)
Fin-de-Siècle Socialism and Other Essays (1988)
Force Fields: Between Intellectual History and Cultural Critique (1993)
Downcast Eyes: The Denigration of Vision in Twentieth-Century French Thought (1993)
Cultural Semantics: Keywords of Our Time (1998)
Refractions of Violence (2003)
La Crisis de la experiencia en la era postsubjetiva, ed. Eduardo Sabrovsky (2003)
Songs of Experience: Modern European and American Variations on a Universal Theme (2004)
The Virtues of Mendacity: On Lying in Politics (2010)
Essays from the Edge: Parerga and Paralipomena (2011)
Kracauer l'exilé (2014)
Reason after Its Eclipse: On Late Critical Theory (2016)
Splinters in Your Eye: Frankfurt School Provocations (2020)
Trois Études sur Adorno (2021)
Genesis and Validity: The Theory and Practice of Intellectual History (2022)
Utopía y Dialéctica: Ensayos sobre Herbert Marcuse (2023)
Immanent Critiques: The Frankfurt School under Pressure (2023)

Magical Nominalism

THE HISTORICAL EVENT, AESTHETIC REENCHANTMENT, AND THE PHOTOGRAPH

Martin Jay

The University of Chicago Press CHICAGO AND LONDON

The University of Chicago Press, Chicago 60637
The University of Chicago Press, Ltd., London

Published 2025
Printed in the United States of America

34 33 32 31 30 29 28 27 26 25 1 2 3 4 5

ISBN-13: 978-0-226-83721-5 (cloth)
ISBN-13: 978-0-226-83722-2 (e-book)
DOI: https://doi.org/10.7208/chicago/9780226837222.001.0001

Library of Congress Cataloging-in-Publication Data

Names: Jay, Martin, 1944– author.
Title: Magical nominalism : the historical event, aesthetic reenchantment, and the photograph / Martin Jay.
Other titles: Life of ideas.
Description: Chicago : The University of Chicago, 2025. | Series: The life of ideas | Includes bibliographical references and index.
Identifiers: LCCN 2024019036 | ISBN 9780226837215 (cloth) | ISBN 9780226837222 (ebook)
Subjects: LCSH: Nominalism. | Photography—Philosophy. | Events (Philosophy) | Scholasticism.
Classification: LCC B731 .J39 2025 | DDC 149/.1—dc23/eng20240501
LC record available at https://lccn.loc.gov/2024019036

♾ This paper meets the requirements of ANSI/NISO Z39.48-1992 (Permanence of Paper).

For Cathy, one last time

Contents

Preface

The concept of a "late style," proposed by Theodor W. Adorno in a 1937 essay on Beethoven and given wide currency by Edward Said in his 2006 book *On Late Style*, may be an appropriate point of entry into the origins of *Magical Nominalism*.[1] Advancing age and approaching mortality, so its proponents suggest, leave their marks on the final efforts of writers, composers, and visual artists, who abandon the vital holism and harmonic coherence sought in their earlier creations and unflinchingly register the tensions that persist within their work and between it and the culture out of which it emerges. Displacing the tropes of exhaustion and decay developed in the familiar idiom of civilizational "decadence" from the macro to the micro level, the idea of late style stresses the ravages of time rather than the warm, retrospective glow of putatively golden years. Taken to an extreme, it implies the alienation of the artist from his or her community, the frustrations of thwarted communication, and the futility of trying to synthesize fragments into a meaningful whole. Paraphrasing Adorno, Said writes that "the power of Beethoven's late style is negative, or rather *it is negativity*: where one would expect serenity and maturity, one instead finds a bristling, difficult, and unyielding—perhaps even inhuman—challenge."[2]

Until now, late style has been attributed almost exclusively to creative artists, and as the example of Beethoven indicates, primarily to those among them who have earned the right to be called geniuses. To introduce it at the beginning of an exercise in intellectual history may thus seem inappropriate, even pretentious, and indeed on more than one count. Intellectual history is, after all, typically identified with synoptic content analysis and the paraphrastic simplification of difficult texts to spare an audience the trouble of dealing with them directly. Even those who pursue a social history of ideas are often taxed with reducing them to mere symptoms of their contexts of genesis or reception. These condescending characterizations may well be challenged,[3] but it is undeniable that intellectual history is a second-order discipline dependent on the imaginative efforts of thinkers and artists whose legacy is being analyzed, evaluated, and re-presented by commentators who know full well they are not themselves creative geniuses. What we do may be tallied up in a lengthy CV, but it is not likely to be called an oeuvre.

And yet, as Hayden White in particular has made us all aware, intellectual historians, like historians in general, do have imaginative styles of thought that depend on underlying rhetorical patterns of expression and ideological investments, whether acknowledged or not.[4] There is, in other words, no hard and fast distinction between fictional narratives and those that purport to represent the historical past, nor an absolute difference between a visual artist's portrait and a metaphorical one "painted" by the descriptive powers of a historical biographer. Thus, although the stakes are certainly lower, it may not be entirely idle to wonder if intellectual historians, like the people they study, will also display the signs of a late style in the projects they tackle and the ways they approach them as their careers near their inevitable end.[5]

What nonetheless may still seem unacceptable is the application of the category of late style by the intellectual historian to his or her own life's work. It might be thought instead that periodizing a scholar's trajectory, assuming different periods are there to be discerned, would be better left to the disinterested gaze of posterity, should it care to cast it at all. Unless you have undergone a dramatic conversion experience from one ideological or methodological investment to another, you may not be the best judge of the stages of your career, or even aware of them. It is, however, difficult to suppress the self-reflexivity that comes with spending a lifetime grappling with the provocations of innovative thinkers, who unsettle the traditional protocols of academic comportment. And so if you have survived long enough, scribbled with sufficient frequency, and read Adorno and Said with enough sympathy, it is hard at least not to wonder if your own work has also come to exhibit some of the same traits that betray "lateness" in a creative artist's style.

Indeed, the willingness to address such concerns in public may well be a mark of that very outcome, as a younger scholar—and here I speak from experience—would be loath to indulge in such self-referential ruminations. When you write the doctoral dissertation that can launch an academic career, the last thing you are encouraged to do is focus on your own quivering sensibility or what in the jargon of our day is called your subject position. Get on with it, the aspiring historian is taught, and tell the tale in the voice of an omniscient, disinterested narrator who follows the sources where they may lead. Only when you have been around for a while are you given grudging permission to pull down the curtain, at least a bit, and expose the perspiring ventriloquist behind the anonymous, disembodied voice. There may even come a time to turn your own life story into the stuff of historical reconstruction and venture a memoir or even full-fledged autobiography.[6]

The readers of this preface will be relieved to know I have no such ambition. But it may still be instructive to think of *Magical Nominalism,* which is very likely to be my final sustained project, as expressing certain marks, for good or for ill, of "lateness." At the beginning of my academic career, I observed the convention that urges apprentice historians to frame their efforts in ways that conform to prefabricated rubrics. That is, when I wrote my dissertation on the history of the Institute of Social Research from 1923 to 1950, I did not have to invent the temporal boundaries of my study, which were set by the founding of the Institute and its return to Germany after its American exile.[7] Nor did I have to select the protagonists of my group portrait, who were all collegially connected, or even fashion a common intellectual position for the Critical Theory that had inspired most of their work. Although there were challenges in measuring the congruence between the Institute and what became known as the Frankfurt School, and figuring out how to integrate sui generis figures like Walter Benjamin into my narrative, by and large the story I was seeking to tell was more to be discovered than invented. In fact, I felt an obligation to tell it in ways the still surviving members of the Institute would recognize as accurate to their own experience, a challenge that seems to have been more or less met.[8]

Several of the projects that followed—modest intellectual portraits of Siegfried Kracauer and Adorno[9]—also by and large observed the temporal and spatial conventions of the traditional biography form, which rely on the contours of an individual's life and work for the guardrails that keep them on track. At virtually the same time, I began the first of a series of studies that oscillated between conceptual history (*Begriffsgeschichte*), the history of discourses, and what I came to call cultural semantics.[10] Their focus was on concepts like totality, whose "adventures" I traced in *Marxism and Totality*; experience, whose "variations" I followed in *Songs of Experience*; and reason, whose afterlife following the "eclipse" of its emphatic, objective version I limned in *Reason after Its Eclipse*. The more diffuse "discourse" of anti-ocularcentrism was the subject of *Downcast Eyes*, while *The Virtues of Mendacity* reconstructed debates about the role of lying in politics from Plato to Hannah Arendt.[11] In all of these cases, the object of inquiry—concept, discourse, or debate—was found in the historical record rather than my post facto concoction, and would have been likely recognizable to the figures who had originally adopted or developed it.[12] What, of course, they could not have fully known—and this is true of all historical actors—was the longer narrative context in which their work might be located, only made visible in hindsight and through historical reconstruction.

In addition to being grounded in the prior existence of the concepts or discourses whose fortunes were being followed, these studies also often depended on taking seriously the contextual limits set by the cultures, large or small, suggested by the approach of cultural semantics. In the case of totality, this meant that the twentieth-century intellectual/political formation known as Western Marxism, albeit itself somewhat contested territory,[13] functioned to define the field of relevant theorists. The variations on the theme of experience were more broadly located on both sides of the Atlantic, which allowed me to contrast the legacy of American pragmatism with its European counterparts.[14] *Downcast Eyes,* while sketching earlier debates about visuality, focused on the denigration of vision in twentieth-century French theory, while *Reason after Its Eclipse* homed in on the first and second generation of the Frankfurt School. *The Virtues of Mendacity,* although less spatially and temporally circumscribed than the other works, was intended to speak to concerns in contemporary American politics.

All of these efforts tried to cut the historical universe at its joints and honor what I thought would be the self-understanding of my protagonists. I did, to be sure, heed the warning of the intellectual historian and anthropological theorist James Clifford that discourse analysis "is always in a sense unfair to authors. It is interested *not* in what they have to say or feel as subjects, but is concerned merely with statements as related to other statements in a field."[15] But it was nonetheless gratifying, as it had been when the surviving Frankfurt School members recognized themselves in my reconstructions, to receive reassurances from several of their later counterparts that I hadn't entirely misconstrued their arguments.[16]

Although history is not philosophy and the world it recreates is not composed of eternal universals or abstract objects, it shares with philosophical realism the premise that what is revealed by its sources and represented by its narratives can be measured, at least hypothetically, against a prior reality. Such is, after all, what distinguishes the stories historians tell from those invented by writers of imaginative fiction, no matter how much, *pace* Hayden White, they may overlap. The telos of historical writing—and perhaps this is what is shaken when "lateness" arrives—is an asymptotic congruence between *res gestae* and *historia rerum gestarum*, the things or actions that happened in the past and the stories told or written about them.

Without my consciously intending it, the study before you rests on a subtle departure from these assumptions. Rather than seeking to illuminate a previously acknowledged intellectual tradition, trace the history of a self-identified group of thinkers, and respect given contextual boundaries, it invites the reader to entertain the ungrounded existence of an intellectual formation that has hitherto been unnamed and only dimly perceived, if at all, by its adherents. Instead of tracing the history of an established concept whose usage over time has changed in significant ways, it employs a post facto category of its own invention, which would not have been recognized as such by its putative exponents. While many of the figures I have analyzed before reappear here—Adorno, Benjamin, Kracauer, Blumenberg, Barthes, Duchamp, Foucault, Lyotard, Derrida, and Ankersmit, to mention the most prominent—it is uncertain they would embrace the roles I now assign them. Although conceding a certain overlap between magical nominalism and what the eminent Polish professor of Jewish studies Agata Bielik-Robson has called "Jewish nominalism,"[17] it makes no claims about the contextual origins, religious or otherwise, that would situate it firmly in a specific cultural tradition.

For these reasons, *Magical Nominalism* might at first glance appear to be the product of an overheated historical imagination, which has violated the imperative to hew closely to the evidentiary record. Imposing a novel conceptual framework on the messy contingency of his material, its author may seem to have embraced a bit too eagerly Hayden White's claim that all historians are tacit metahistorians, refracting their narratives through rhetorical and ideological lenses instead of reconstructing the past "as it actually was." Rather, that is, than carving the past at its proverbial joints, he may appear to be treating it as if it were an undifferentiated slab of flesh indifferent to the naturally guided placement of his butcher's knife. Congruence between *historia rerum gestarum* and the *res gestae* of the past would thus no longer provide even an asymptotically desired telos.

Were this the case, however, *Magical Nominalism* would performatively contradict what it sets out to explain. For it would serve as a sterling example of moving from realism—or rather the historian's traditional version of it—to what we will call *conventional* rather than *magical* nominalism. Taking seriously the implications of late style may allow us instead to move in a very different direction, which brings us closer to the latter than to the former. For while eschewing the realist goal of a congruence between subjective knowledge and objective reality, it nonetheless honors the irreducibility of the object to the constitutive power of the subject. It thus puts limits on the willful self-assertion that, as we will see, underpins the conventional nominalist challenge to realism.

Characterizing Beethoven's last works, Adorno writes, "Touched by death, the hand of the master sets free the masses of material that he used to form; its tears and fissures, witnesses to the finite powerlessness of the I confronted with Being, are its final work."[18] That is, instead of acting like an autonomous creator who confidently fashions his materials into an organically unified aesthetic whole, the composer unflinchingly confronts their recalcitrant resistance to assimilation and integration. "No longer does he gather the landscape, deserted now, and alienated, into an image. . . . His late work still remains process, but not as development; rather as a catching fire between the extremes, which no longer allow for any secure middle ground or harmony of spontaneity."[19] Rather than expressing creative mastery and the exercise of an artist's will ex nihilo, a late work evidences the limits of his controlling powers: "Objective is the fractured landscape, subjective the light which—alone—it glows into life. He does not bring about their harmonious synthesis."[20]

Aside from the patently risible nature of any comparison with Beethoven's musical genius, the leap from the creation of works of art to the writing of works of scholarship may well seem one more of faith than of reason. But if *Magical Nominalism* can be recognized as a "late work" in an expanded sense that transcends the difference between the two, it would forestall misreading its argument in terms of the conventional nominalism that so often enables the imposition of subjective categories. "The formal law of late works," Adorno notes, "is, at the least, incapable of being subsumed under the category of expression."[21] Mutatis mutandis, a similar limit would apply to the constitutive power of the scholar, even when he or she no longer abides by the self-effacing protocols of realist reconstruction. Or to anticipate one of the leitmotifs of the book, acknowledging the "lateness" of a work implies that its author lacks sovereign authority over the material assembled in it.

Perhaps the familiar distinction Kant made about two types of judgment in his third *Critique* will help clarify the point. The logical structure of an a priori general rule subsuming specific instances, underpinning what he called determinant judgments, would not really apply to late works.[22] The paradigmatic reasoning of his reflective judgments would be more apposite, for they begin with concrete instances rather than transcendental rules and support a more provisional "as if" conclusion about their common or at least overlapping properties through analogical comparisons. Significantly, Kant applied the latter to aesthetic *judgments*, which were very different from the *creation* of an artwork. As such, they more easily translate into the late work of an intellectual historian than that of a creative artist per se.

The contemporary Italian philosopher Giorgio Agamben suggestively teases out the implications of precisely this distinction for nonaesthetic purposes in his essay "What Is a Paradigm?"[23] Agamben cites Michel Foucault instead of the American philosopher of science Thomas Kuhn as the source for his use of the term and illustrates it by Foucault's influential interpretation of Jeremy Bentham's panopticon. Noting its etymological origins in the Greek *para-deiknymi* (beside itself),[24] Agamben argues that its intelligibility is more horizontal than vertical, more circular than linear, more egalitarian than hierarchical. Rather than a particular example of a general rule, whether the latter is derived deductively or inductively, a paradigm, he writes, is "a singular case that is isolated from its context only insofar as, by exhibiting its own singularity, it makes intelligible a new ensemble, whose homogeneity it itself constitutes."[25] The cases in that new ensemble relate to each other allegorically rather than symbolically or metaphorically, with each case manifesting a different moment in a dynamic relational system. There is no transcendental origin prior to the singular cases, no abstract principle that is already immanent in each of them. They are comparable chords in an atonal composition that lacks the hierarchically leading tonic or keynote in a diatonic scale. The conventional opposition between generality and particularity is jettisoned, as is the telos of a dialectical "higher synthesis." What remains instead, Agamben concludes, is a "force field traversed by polar tensions, where (as in an electro-magnetic field) their substantial identities evaporate."[26]

The metaphor of a force field, as it happens, is one I have found helpful in identifying certain explanatory strategies in my prior work,[27] and it was striking to discover Agamben invoking it in his account of paradigmatic reasoning. But what makes it especially appropriate in connection with the relationship between a late style and magical nominalism is his insistence that the force field is not merely an epistemological or interpretative model introduced by a subject but rather inherent in the world itself. "The intelligibility in question in the paradigm," he writes, "has an ontological character. It refers not to the cognitive relation between subject and object but to being. There is, then, a paradigmatic ontology."[28] How might this ontology be described? For Agamben, the answer seems to be something on the order of the similitudes, affinities, or likenesses that the natural philosopher Paracelsus called signatures, and which are manifest in a premodern world of astrological correspondences and sacramental transubstantiations. As such they draw on the tradition of sympathetic magic, which will occupy us in a later chapter. "Knowledge of celestial signatures," Agamben acknowledges, "is the magician's science, in the sense that producing an *ymago* [*sic*] means sympathetically imagining and reproducing in a signature (which can also be a gesture or a formula) the signature of the planet in question."[29]

While not as bewitched by the legacy of sympathetic magic as was his friend Walter Benjamin, Adorno was nonetheless intrigued by its implications for appreciating the value of mimetic behavior. Despite the qualms he had about the survival of correspondences in astrological or other guises, Adorno's notion of late style does therefore comport with Agamben's argument in one significant way. Although the subject can cast light on an objectively fractured landscape, even the most talented of geniuses cannot render it coherent or order it hierarchically by his or her constitutive fiat. If there is any coherence revealed when that light is cast, it is not that of generic rule and specific illustrations or of common essence and different appearances but rather that of a cluster of analogically comparable but nonidentical moments in a dynamic constellation. The existence of the latter paradoxically depends on the gravitational or magnetic pull of the paradigmatic elements in its field whose apparent isolation and integrity it at the same time undermines. The observing subject can illuminate such a field but does not constitute it out of whole cloth.

The antimethodological method encouraged by Agamben's paradigmatic reasoning might be fruitfully compared with Benjamin's celebrated ruminations on translation, which Adorno found so compelling.[30] The normal belief that translations strive for commensurable renditions of prelinguistic intended meanings or equivalent ways to designate a given world assumed that a transcendent signified existed prior to the act of signification. Benjamin argued instead that each language expresses in itself a partial meaning that can then be supplemented in the process of translation. The rendering of one into another does not produce a simple one-to-one equivalence, in which comparable words merely correspond to the same prelinguistic objects, thoughts, or actions. Each language is a fragment of a semantic whole that is asymptotically approachable but can never be fully realized. Absent the recovery of an Adamic or primal urlanguage, the process of translation analogically reveals a richer medley of overlapping meanings than can ever be expressed by constructing an artificially contrived, transcendental metalanguage. Significantly, Benjamin points out, the Greeks identified no Muse or goddess of translation, as in the case of the other arts, who can benignly inspire the practitioner to get it right. In Étienne Balibar's gloss of Benjamin's position, "The idea of this language is one of community rather than substitutability—in other words, the *common fulfillment* of languages grounded in their irreducible diversity."[31]

In the spirit of Agamben's thoughts on paradigms and Benjamin's on translations—and we might add Wittgenstein's celebrated notion of "family resemblances"[32]—this book eschews a strong, a priori definition of magical nominalism posited by a sovereign authority in favor of a nonsynthesized series of heteroclite, only quasi-commensurable exemplars. Inevitably, this will produce impatience on the part of those who expect the rigorous clarification of disambiguated terms at the outset of an argument traditionally urged by logical reasoning and analytic philosophy.[33] I ask for their indulgence for reasons that I hope will become clearer as the argument develops. Nor should readers hope for a final "chase" to which I can now "cut," because the intervening scenes have equal weight with any putatively cumulative conclusion. But by the end of the book, if the experiment is successful and the reader patient enough to stick with it, the ensemble should serve as the stars in a constellation or forces in a field that will imbue the term with whatever multifaceted meaning it may have. Some forbearance will therefore be necessary before magical nominalism begins to reveal its unstipulated, aggregated, multifaceted meaning, enabling what was initially only virtual to become increasingly—but never entirely—actual.

The reader may, however, justifiably wonder how the paradigmatic cases or translatable "languages" of magical nominalism have been chosen, absent a preestablished criterion of selection, either already manifest in the historical record—those "joints" where cutting would come easiest—or imposed by my a priori schematic imagination. Perhaps the best answer, or at least the only one I can come up with, is that after my initial intuition that magical realism had a nominalist counterpart, I began an effort to draw on prior intellectual experiences to suggest examples that might both illustrate the insight and flesh out its meaning. The result was a ragged and uneven process of analogical comparison that was anything but methodical, and which ultimately produced the seemingly anomalous exemplars explored in the book. Because the great lesson of nominalism is to value singularity, it seemed permissible to compare apples and oranges (and perhaps bananas as well) while still hoping to cast light on their nonidentical similarities.

A final way *Magical Nominalism* may be said to typify late style is that in presenting its case for those similarities it often draws on the negativity we have seen Said highlight in his reading of Adorno on Beethoven. Rather than confidently identifying the concrete singularities whose ontological priority to universals and abstractions nominalism typically endorses, it frequently falls back on the apophatic tradition of negative theology to claim that they are better understood as limits on what can be known or posited. And while giving as charitable a reading to the legacy of magic as its author's incurable Enlightenment sympathy for rational discourse will allow, it raises objections at various points in the book to the more questionable implications of taking it too seriously. This exercise, in other words, is not intended as a triumphalist historical account of a hidden tradition whose rediscovery will somehow guide us all into a better future.

But nor should it be taken as a record of its author's disaffection with his earlier ideals and interests, which might be implied by a hasty reading of his passage from, say, examining ambitious universalizing concepts like totality or experience to the deflationary alternative of particularizing nominalism. For it is, after all, inevitable that someone's "lateness" will overlap with the fresh starts of a new generation. As is often remarked, the rhetoric of decadence, whatever the scale of its application, can hint at the possibility of renewal. Whatever unreconciled fragments are left behind can always be fashioned into unforeseen constellations that can illuminate a new cultural landscape and reconstitute force fields that crackle again with energy. "In the history of art," so Adorno may have darkly concluded his essay on Beethoven, "late works are the catastrophes."[34] But in the writing of intellectual history, they may avoid that fate if they stimulate future generations to ask previously unposed questions and come up with innovative and arresting answers. Or at least that seems a plausible justification for attempting this kind of risky exercise. Whether or not it will be validated in the long run is, to be sure, unlikely for its author to find out. But while "lateness" may signify the waning of many capacities, I am happy to report that hope is not among them.

Introduction

Modernity's paths, the irreversible eruption of its mystical nominalism, have to be followed through to the end.

ERNST BLOCH

The Nominalist Revolution

There are few riskier temptations for a historian than selecting a key moment in the onrushing flow of events and calling it the hinge of an epochal shift.[1] When Virginia Woolf famously proclaimed in her essay "Mr. Bennett and Mrs. Brown" that "on or about December, 1910, human character changed,"[2] she was both adopting and mocking a convention that was already well established. In accounts of the arrival of something called "modernity," the game has long been and still is often played. Whether assigned to Copernicus's overturning of the geocentric view of the cosmos, Gutenberg's invention of the printing press, the fall of Constantinople to the Turks, Columbus's voyage to "the new world," Descartes's gesture of starting philosophy afresh, or the Peace of Westphalia, not to mention such symbolic events as Petrarch's discovery of Cicero's letters and Poggio coming upon Lucretius's *De Rerum Natura*, there is no dearth of candidates for the honor of ushering in something called "the modern age."

In all of these cases, later commentators select an event and bestow upon it an honorific name: the threshold of modernity. A tipping point, they claim, was reached, small quantitative changes turned into a qualitative leap, and the historical equivalent of a violent shift in tectonic plates occurred. Or more precisely, historians designate a specific episode, never experienced as such by participants when it occurred, as a turned page ushering in a new chapter in the grand narrative of history. The act therefore is one of post facto naming rather than simple recognition of what happened in the conscious, felt experience of those to whom it was happening (or even on the level of unconscious structural changes). It tacitly reveals, in other words, a nominalist rather than realist historical ontology, one that expresses the posterior subjective judgment of the historian rather than merely recording objective historical fact. If you were a member of the elite Bloomsbury circle writing in 1924 about changes in the British novel, "on or about December, 1910," human character may seemed to have changed, but, let's be honest, it pretty much stayed the same for the other 99.999 percent of the inhabitants of the planet living through that unremarkable month.

Acknowledging the role of subjective naming rather than objective discovery in the designation of a putative threshold moment for modernity is particularly apt. For adopting a nominalist rather than realist interpretation of assigning epochal thresholds is arguably itself one of the earmarks of modern consciousness.[3] Thus, it is perhaps fitting that one of the most suggestive candidates for occupying the "hinge moment in Western history" position, at least from the point of view of intellectual history, is the arrival—or rather, the triumph—of the late-medieval philosophical/theological school of thought that came to be called *nominalism*. Although a more sustained attempt to tease out its multiple implications will have to await our opening chapters, suffice it to say now that it indicated an erosion of belief in the ontological reality of timeless universals or essences, which can then be instantiated by singular exemplars. "Man" was not an a priori, eternally valid category but an inductively derived approximation based on generalizing from specific cases. Nominalism also questioned the existence of abstract objects prior to their concrete appearance in time and space. There was no ideal triangle as such, only the actual triangles fashioned by human skill, whose congruent features allowed post facto generalizations about their shared qualities. All such generic terms were linguistic conventions, merely arbitrary names, or concepts imposed by humans on a world of unique and contingent particulars. More than just a quarrel over the relation of words to things, the debate between realism—in the sense of the ontological truth of universals and abstractions—and nominalism thus raised fundamental questions about the nature of reality itself and the limits of human knowledge.

Significantly, soon after its emergence, nominalism earned the sobriquet the *via moderna* in opposition to the *via antiqua* of Scholasticism.[4] Anticipations of its arguments can be found, to be sure, in the atomism of classical Greek philosophers like Leucippus and Democritus, as well as among Cynics like Antisthenes, who was said to have objected to Plato: "I see a horse, but I don't see horseness."[5] Boethius had raised questions about the status of universals in his *Second Commentary on Porphyry's Isagoge*, which he translated into Latin in the early sixth century.[6] His concerns were revived in the heterodox Christian theology of Roscelin of Compiègne (ca. 1050–1125), and Peter Abelard (1079–1142), which challenged many of the reigning assumptions of the day.[7] But the gathering strength of nominalism did not really reach a tipping point until the influential work of the English Franciscan William of Ockham (1287–1347),[8] which had a profound impact among leading theologians in Oxford and Paris.

For those who like a more punctual turning point in their threshold narratives, a particular event has served as the epochal hinge moment in which nominalism came into its own and the hegemonic Scholastic worldview began to fade: the prohibition in 1277 by Étienne Tempier, the bishop of Paris, of 219 theses in theology, natural philosophy, and logic. The late thirteenth century, to be sure, may well seem premature as the beginning of the modern age, especially if the mark of modernity is a radical break with the past (a self-image promoted by Descartes's method of doubting everything except the doubting self). But as a momentous shift away from the neo-Aristotelian Scholastic orthodoxy of the High Middle Ages, most extensively developed by St. Thomas Aquinas, who had died just three years earlier, the Condemnation of 1277, as it came to be known, presaged a radical shift in Western consciousness. As in the case of all so-called threshold events, the causes, meaning, and effects of the prohibition are more nuanced and complicated than any straightforward before and after narrative would suggest.[9] Ironically, the Condemnation has even been called "a concerted effort by conservatives of all camps" to overturn the radicalism of extreme rationalists.[10] But it has nonetheless functioned for such later interpreters as Pierre Duhem, Anneleise Meier, Hans Blumenberg, and Michael Allen Gillespie as a turning point in the intellectual history of the West.[11]

What was so crucial about this particular episode in the never-ending dispute over theological matters that so exercised the Middle Ages? In the words of Blumenberg, "This document marks the exact point in time when the interest in rationality and human intelligibility of creation cedes priority to the speculative fascination exerted by the theological predicates of absolute power and freedom."[12] Much is packed into this bold assertion, and a good deal of it will seem counterintuitive to anyone with a certain image of modernity. That is, modernity is often understood as an era of increasing secularization, rationalization, and what Max Weber famously designated "the disenchantment of the world." What then can the decline of an "interest in rationality and human intelligibility of creation" in favor of a "theological premise of absolute power and freedom" have to do with the onset of the modern age? Is it not an embarrassment, as the literary critic C. D. Blanton has wryly observed, that "the legitimation of modernity . . . depends not on nominalism's anticipation of rational subjects or empiricist methods, but rather on its most recognizably medieval aspect, the strict theological insistence on the divine capacity to elude the strictures of human logic, including the substantial existence of universals?"[13]

The answer to these questions lies in the way in which reason, revelation, and creation were all intertwined in the Scholastic worldview.[14] Why, it might be asked, was the integration necessary in the first place? Blumenberg suggests that when the early Christian expectations of an imminent Second Coming were disappointed, it was no longer appropriate to continue the denigration of the actual world promoted by acosmic, radically dualist gnosticism. Instead, a world-affirming theology needed to incorporate a more stable notion of a secure, rule-bound cosmos, which was then provided by adopting Greek philosophy.[15] Drawing on the Platonic explanation of cosmogenesis, this "first overcoming of gnosticism" was based on the belief, expressed in its most extreme form as explicit pantheism, that all that existed had emanated from God's essential being, rather than being created separately from him. It was thus possible to avoid the gnostic choice between investment in the salvation of souls at the end of time and investment in the world before its time was up.

God's created cosmos, it was assumed, operated according to the rules of reason, intelligibility, and harmony. Those rules were, moreover, revealed to humans in scripture and could be explicated and elaborated by dogmatic theological speculation. But created as they were in the image of God (*imago Dei*), humans also possessed the ability to contemplate the heavens or read the cosmos as if it were a legible book. Although angels were above humans in the great chain of being, sharing a higher "intelligence" with God, while humans were less favorably endowed, human reason was still a formidable faculty.[16] It was capable of discerning the similitudes and analogies that allow us reliable access to God's creation. As the historian Amos Funkenstein explains: "To the degree in which the essence of a thing is known to us, our concept of it represents that thing, is a true picture of it. But things resemble God to the degree in which they have perfections, because each perfection in them, however incomplete, reflects—and therefore represents—its paradigm in God, the source of all perfections. The various perfections (essences) constitute a mutual order that again reflects and represents—however vaguely—the unity and simplicity of God."[17]

Reason was thus not in conflict with faith but in accord with it, and theology and philosophy—in particular, that developed by Aristotle—were fully compatible. Reason could be used to prove the existence of revealed truths, such as the ontological existence of God. Universal essences could be understood as either inherent in objects (*in re*), as in Aristotle, or prior to them (*ante rem*), as in the Platonic doctrine of forms, or ideas, where they were immaterial, permanent, and mind-independent. What in a later age would become a burning issue—the uncertain relationship between a theory of knowledge or epistemology and a theory of reality or ontology—was not yet troubling enough to cast doubt on the system as a whole. For universal truths were both in the real world and in the minds of men. Thus, it was possible for mere mortals to know the rational principles, say of geometry or optics, which God had followed in building reality, and then construct the great Gothic cathedrals of the High Middle Ages by following them to create symbolic microcosms of the cosmos as a whole.[18]

Why, we might wonder, was such a harmonious and balanced worldview the object of enough doubt and suspicion to lead the bishop of Paris to challenge it in 1277? Students of the Condemnation have acknowledged the uncertainty of Tempier's motives, and struggled to discover full coherence in the welter of theses that were challenged (along with others attacked in similar measures in 1270 and later in 1277 by the archbishop of Canterbury). Some have pointed to the competition between monastic preaching and teaching orders, Franciscan versus Dominican, for hegemony in the church.[19] Others have looked to the local debates at the University of Paris, pitting the arts faculty, who were more often secular than regular clergy and taught logic and dialectics, against the theologians.[20] Still others have speculated about anxiety over the threat of Islamic influence, indirectly posed by the role of the Andalusian philosopher Averröes (1126–98) in transmitting, promoting and developing Aristotle's legacy.[21]

Whatever the contextual causes of the challenge to neo-Aristotelian Scholasticism, there was an immanent cause as well, a theological tension within the system itself that could not be permanently contained. The integration of pagan philosophical rationalism and cosmology—whether Neoplatonic, Aristotelian, or Stoic[22]—into a theology based on the power of faith in revelation began in earnest during the Hellenistic period with figures like Philo of Alexandria, a Jewish thinker much influenced by Plato and Stoicism, who sought to reconcile the Hebrew Bible with Pythagorean mathematics and musical harmonies.[23] But it was from its onset inherently unstable.[24] How to reconcile the virtues of pagan philosophers, who had had no chance to accept Christ as their redeemer, with the unlikelihood of their salvation remained a nagging problem.[25] The pointed questions posed by the church father Tertullian in 198 CE—"What indeed has Athens to do with Jerusalem? What concord can there be between the Academy and the Church? What between heretics and Christians?"[26]—were never satisfactorily answered in the millennium that followed. The creator

God of the Hebrew Bible, capable of making a covenant in time with a chosen people and punishing them when they failed to honor its terms, required substantial reinterpretation to be reconciled with the unmoved mover, the eternal source of motion rather than a providential intervener in human affairs. The drama of contingent human redemption dependent on the acceptance of the Gospel (the "good news" of scripture), belief in the Incarnation, and eschatological hope for a Second Coming, was an uncomfortable fit with a cosmological vision of eternal, unchanging order. The Scholastic expedient of distinguishing between a higher cosmic harmony, evident in the eternal orbits of celestial spheres, and the messier sublunary world inhabited by sinning mortals, was hard to maintain for long. The nagging problem, flagged as early as Plotinus, of reconciling infinity, understood either spatially or temporally, with a static and eternal cosmos was never satisfactorily solved. And perhaps most stressful of all, the Aristotelian God was too beholden to the constraints of reason—a residue of Plato's belief in the priority of ideas, or forms—to be equated with an omnipotent Christian divinity who was under no obligation at all, not even to give reasons or justifications for his actions.[27]

From its inception, medieval thinkers struggled mightily to resolve these tensions. As Arthur Lovejoy noted in his classic study *The Great Chain of Being*, theologians, at least since Augustine, sought to reconcile a notion of God as the Good, which implied "an apotheosis of unity, self-sufficiency, and quietude" and God as goodness, which suggested "diversity, self-transcendence, and fecundity."[28] The principle of plenitude, which certified the cosmological great chain as complete in its perfection, clashed with the ideal of divine creativity producing ever new marvels in the world and beyond. Scholasticism produced ingenious efforts, such as those of John Duns Scotus (1266–1308), to concede certain positions, while holding on to others. Aquinas was more moderate than the extreme followers of Averröes and sought a compromise in which composite substances are made up of matter and form, existence and essence, without giving priority to one over the other.[29] But it seemed increasingly clear to many that Athens had dangerously eclipsed Jerusalem. According to Blumenberg, "The Middle Ages' symbiosis with Aristotelian philosophy had depended on an inequality in the attention given to God's attributes: on neglecting omnipotence, and still more omnipresence, in favor of spiritual self-sufficiency and of the world's continual and constitutive dependence on the divinity's inner life."[30]

With the passing of Aquinas, the time was ripe for redressing the balance, as the door was open again for those who had worried that positing an inherently rational cosmos implicitly undercut the omnipotence of a God who had an unfettered ability to choose, and could even use it to overturn the choices he had made in the past. When God had asked Abraham to sacrifice his son, had he not shown that his moral laws were not absolutely binding? When Christ had said "with God all things are possible" (Mark 10:27), had he not indicated that his natural laws could be suspended? A distinction first introduced by Peter Damian in the eleventh century and elaborated in the thirteenth-century *Summa Halensis* between God's *potentia absoluta* and his *potentia ordinata,* God's absolute power at all times and the binding power of what he had already ordained, gained increasing currency.[31] Although the nominalists were not the first or only school of thought to employ the distinction, they gave it special force. For William of Ockham, it did not mean two separate powers but rather two facets of the same power: "*Absoluta* considers power alone, without regard to divine action or will. *Ordinata* considers God's power from the standpoint of his decrees, his revealed will."[32] It introduced an inevitable temporal dimension into the question of divinity, which fit poorly with the eternal image of Aristotle's unmoved mover, who "embodied the principle of universal, immutable order, self-contained and without any desire; he is in need of nothing."[33]

Theologians wrestled mightily with the implications of the distinction. Did God's omniscience mean he knew the future, and if so, how could it be understood as contingent? Did God's omnipotence mean he could change past events, as Damian had speculated, allowing him, say, to restore the virginity of a "fallen" woman? Or would doing so be a sign of his weakness, as St. Anselm argued, because it revealed he had made prior mistakes? Did the acts of God called miracles show that God could change his mind and suspend his previous legislative decisions? But why did he have to do so if he were by definition perfect? How could the cosmos be understood as rational if it allowed the contradictions that Aristotelian logic had banished from reason? However these questions were answered, the inevitable upshot of the distinction was a nonnecessitarian ontology and an awareness of the difference between actuality and potentiality (or the even less constrained "possibility," as not everything can be construed as inherently potential). As Blumenberg puts it, "because the Creation is uncaused, because it does not require a preexisting model for more demiurgic implementation, it demonstrates the radicalness of the groundless will that is the ground of everything; it is the maximum of causality and the first in the sequence of pure acts of grace that constitutes the real theme of theology."[34]

The implications for the self-understanding of mere mortals were no less perplexing. Believing that humans were able to partake of the same rationality attributed to God, and thus able to use their finite reason to know the order he had created, now seemed evidence of a hubris ill-befitting a creature burdened by "original sin" and dependent on divine grace for salvation. Rashly assuming that this actual cosmos was inherently the best and most rational one God could have made, and therefore perfect and eternal, implicitly denied the power of divine will to make other possible worlds, both in the past and in a future stretching into infinity.[35] Expecting rational justifications for God's ineffable choices was a sign of human arrogance, which had been scornfully rebuked as early as the book of Job in the Hebrew Bible. God owes nothing to anyone, Ockham liked to say, including revealing the truth to us. For all we might know, God might be a deceiver, deliberately filling our minds with nonsense, a disturbing implication whose consequences continued to trouble leading thinkers as late as Descartes.[36] All of these qualms underlay the Condemnation of 1277, which cleared the ground for the nominalist alternative that flourished in the century that followed, and whose reverberations continued well into the modern era, when its theological origins were by and large forgotten.[37]

Once the priority of divine will over reason was reaffirmed, human epistemic humility could follow, at least as far as knowing the allegedly rational order of the cosmos was involved. A contingent reality, subject to the unpredictable whims of the Creator, meant the erosion of its intelligibility as an ordered hierarchy or chain of being, and with it the power of mere humans to read the world as if it were a legible text.[38] Natural theology, the "argument from design" that claimed the world manifested the rational intentionality of its creator, lost much of its allure. If creation were no longer an open book and the firmament—the word itself coming from the Latin *firmus*, which implied solidity and stability—no longer a visible manifestation of cosmic harmony, even more uncertainty could cloud human understanding of God's attributes and actions. Concomitantly, the long-standing contest between kataphatic (the way of affirmation) and apophatic (the way of negation) theology—the former believing God can be positively described, the latter only negatively—could tip once again in the latter direction.

For some, faith was sufficient to fill the void and overcome the skeptical implications of radical nominalism; rationalist argumentation, such as Anselm's ontological proof for God's existence, was not necessary for those who trusted in their experience of his living presence.[39] In many respects, the Protestant Reformation launched by Martin Luther followed this path.[40] Luther had, in fact, studied with Gabriel Biel, the chief German interpreter of the *via moderna*.[41] Rather than deciphering the rational cosmological order of creation, he taught that it was better to read scripture—*sola scriptura* rather than *sola ratione*, as Anselm had claimed—to access the revealed truths of the word.[42] Rather than the Scholastic *theologia gloria* (theology of glory), celebrating creation as the emanation of the divine, it was better to a follow a *theologia crucis* (theology of the cross), in which the violence of God's separation from the world was foremost, a violence that did away with the sinful "old Adam." Rather than the corrupt order of the medieval Catholic Church, with its hierarchy mediating the sinner's access to God, Christians should seek an intimate, personal relationship with the Redeemer. If simple faith were not enough for some, then the raptures of mystical experience, sometimes nurtured by a residual belief in the Platonic idea of *methexis* or participation in ideal forms, might help restore contact with divinity.[43]

But for others, the result of the dissolution of the uneasy equilibrium between philosophy and theology, cosmos and creation, Athens and Jerusalem, was a vertiginous feeling of abandonment.[44] As Maurice Blanchot observed, the very word "disaster" betokens "being separated from the star . . . the decline which characterizes disorientation when the link with fortune from on high is cut."[45] For its victims, the menace of "demonic skepticism" outweighed the comfort of fideism.[46] Not only was the emotional comfort of being at home in a meaningful cosmos lost, so too was the reassurance that a loving God was committed to its smooth running. Increasingly "hidden" or "absent" from the world—a *deus absconditus*[47]—God seemed to have left the sinning, flawed human race pretty much to its own devices. "The absolutism of the hidden God," Blumenberg noted, "freed the theoretical attitude from its pagan ideal of contemplating the world from the divine point of view and thus ultimately sharing in God's happiness. The price of this freedom is that theory will no longer relate to the resting point of a blissful onlooker but rather to the workplace of human exertion."[48]

Rather than a rational, predictable figure, beholden to the laws, both natural and moral, he had himself promulgated, God appeared to be impelled to act by little more than arbitrary caprice and unfathomable whim. Indifferent to the injustice of human suffering, he had created a world without any inherent telos or, to use Aristotle's term, final cause. Even if certain theologians came to argue he had predetermined which people were to be saved and which not, they ruefully conceded that the knowledge of who belonged to the elect of the redeemed was kept from man, whose good works could never suffice alone to bring about salvation. Perhaps no less unsettling was the thought that a capricious divinity might even enjoin men to commit deeds that were evil by the moral standards already ordained by that very same God.[49] In short, the threat of a gnostic rejection of such a world of inexplicable evil, a threat that the early Middle Ages had met by adopting the classical cosmos and Augustine's blaming the human abuse of their freedom to sin, once again loomed, allowing Blumenberg to claim that modernity had the task of overcoming gnosticism once again.

It is perhaps not surprising that such an ineffable, indifferent, and unapologetically cruel God, aloof from the suffering of his creation, could have gained in plausibility during the terrible fourteenth century, a period of pandemic disasters (the Black Death in particular), economic depression, political disorder, climate change, famine, and growing institutional crisis in the church.[50] The rise of cities, some have also argued, helped erode the secure boundaries of the feudal hierarchy that had underpinned, or at least mirrored, the cosmological and theological order of Scholasticism. A static or cyclical cosmological order was, moreover, hard to maintain in the face of a new appreciation of the open-ended infinity of time.[51] On a practical level, the endless standardized units of spatialized time artificially produced by the newly invented mechanical clock—prepared by the regularities of monastic life and necessitated by the demands of commercial trade—replaced the familiar cyclical biorhythms of rural life.[52] With traditional social roles increasingly in flux, the late-medieval / early-modern self was compelled to reflect on its increasingly problematic interiority or construct new stratagems for negotiating the uncertainties of a social world whose behavioral norms were no longer absolutely binding.[53]

Many of these expedients seem to have been effective, and, as the historian William Bouwsma noted, "postmedieval culture achieved substantial success in reducing anxiety. Its creation of new boundaries focused anxiety on their maintenance and converted it into relatively manageable fears."[54] But the vertiginous implications of the collapse of the cosmological order of the High Middle Ages were never entirely overcome, even for those who continued to find comfort in renewed versions of faith. Tellingly, before placing his famous wager on the existence of God in the late seventeenth century, Blaise Pascal could confess that "when I consider the short duration of my life, swallowed up in the eternity before and after, the little space which I fill, and even can see, engulfed in the infinite immensity of spaces of which I am ignorant, and which know me not, I am frightened, and am astonished at being here rather than there; for there is no reason why I am here rather than there, why now rather than then. . . . The eternal silence of these infinite spaces frightens me."[55] For those less prone to gambling (or, to name its more respectable intellectual analog, probability theory), the anguish resulting from that silence would stubbornly remain a live threat even into the twentieth century, allowing the Hungarian philosopher Georg Lukács to call "transcendental homelessness" the prevailing existential condition of modern men and women.[56] Although some could celebrate the liberation of the individual encouraged by the nominalist destruction of given hierarchies and resist the temptation of nostalgic yearning for a lost past, others continued to lament it as the erosion of integrated community, shared meaning, and enduring rootedness in a world bereft of orientation.[57]

We have to be careful, to be sure, before concluding that nominalism as a coherent ideological movement was the sole or even primary source of all these changes, which may well have been the result of other deeper, material causes. It may have been a genuine "revolution" in philosophy and theology, as some have called it,[58] but ideas alone are, after all, rarely sufficient to bring about epochal transformations. It would, however, be no less problematic to go to the other extreme and automatically turn them into mere superstructural epiphenomena. In this case, it seems safe to say that there was a strong elective affinity linking and mutually reinforcing the waning of the Scholastic faith in real universals, the collapse of the pre-Copernican cosmic order, the emergence of modern science and technology, and the transformation of the feudal order into nascent capitalism. And no less clear is the powerful, if mixed affective impact—at times exhilaration, at others dread—that nominalism had on those who understood its existential implications.

The Realist Counterrevolution

The unsettling challenge of nominalism is perhaps nowhere more apparent than in the rapid response it elicited from those who felt threatened by it. Even later commentators who have questioned its momentum as a coherent, enduring movement have conceded that it was taken as such by its critics.[59] In fact, it soon spawned, as revolutions tend to do, a counterrevolution, or rather a series of them, which sought to revive universalist realism in one form or another. During the Counter-Reformation, a spirited defense of Scholasticism was launched by the Spanish Jesuit Francisco Suárez and the School of Salamanca, which had a powerful impact on Baroque Catholicism.[60] Platonism returned in the fifteenth-century Italian Renaissance among humanists like Marsilio Ficino and Giovanni Pico della Mirandola, and in seventeenth-century Cambridge with Henry More and Ralph Cudworth.[61] A "cosmotheist" belief in the enchanted harmony of a heliocentric, spherically organized solar system, as the historian

Josef Chytry has pointed out, still informed the worldviews of Copernicus, Bruno, and Kepler in the years between 1540 and 1620.[62]

Even after the waning of residual faith in cosmotheism as the Scientific Revolution proceeded, the Enlightenment still struggled to jettison all of its implications. The great chain of being, as Lovejoy demonstrated, retained its influence well into the eighteenth century and was then temporalized in the next.[63] Trust in God's providence in the world continued to provide comfort for some religious believers, and found a secular, self-organizing counterpart in the idea of an economic "invisible hand" coordinating self-interested private actions and the public good.[64] Putative cosmic correspondences like the star that accompanied the birth of Jesus or the eclipse of the sun that accompanied his death could continue to resonate for some believing in comparable coincidences—the storms that occurred at the hours of Napoleon's and Beethoven's deaths—even into the nineteenth century.[65] The so-called argument from design for the existence of God was revived in the British theologian William Paley's influential *Natural Theology* (1802), and indeed pockets of anti-Darwinist belief in a teleological "intelligent design" persist in our own.[66] Neoplatonism also continued to inspire the German Romantics, for example in Novalis's "magic idealism" and Friedrich Schelling's *Naturphilosophie*.[67]

The counterrevolution appeared in other ways as well. Whereas the nominalist challenge to Scholastic realism had been fueled in part by dismay over the lingering power of pagan ideas, the classical world's cultural legacy enjoyed a revival of interest with the waning of the Middle Ages and the rise of the Renaissance.[68] Its continuing influence could be felt during the Enlightenment, which Peter Gay could call "the rise of modern paganism."[69] Although Gay's own sympathies were with the later phase of the Enlightenment, culminating in the strongly nominalist David Hume, the earlier period, which more justly deserved the label of the "age of reason," saw the return of speculative metaphysics on a grand scale with philosophers like Descartes, Malebranche, Spinoza, and Wolff. Optimistic philosophers like Leibniz employed the "principle of sufficient reason" to claim that although there were other possible worlds, this was surely the best of all. His theodicy sought to justify what might seem like the irrational imperfections of existence, even the seemingly unjust evils suffered by innocent people, as ultimately functional in the service of a greater good. Although famously ridiculed by later Enlightenment thinkers like Voltaire, the faith in universalist rationalism expressed by Leibniz and other metaphysicians of his era never entirely lost its appeal. As the continuing attraction, despite all the efforts to refute it, of Spinoza's pantheism throughout the modern period demonstrates, a strong ontological rationalism could continue into our own era a live option.[70]

To be sure, there were also contrary figures in the Enlightenment, such as the seventeenth-century Port-Royal Jansenist Antoine Arnauld, who carried on the tradition of stressing God's will over his reason in debates with Leibniz and Malebranche.[71] In addition to questioning the assumption of a preexisting ideal cosmic harmony, he also stressed the importance of human free will in moral decisions. And uncertainty about our ability to know God's reasons for creation and the laws ruling what he had created could still vex thinkers like Descartes, who worried that God might be a deceiver. The idea of divine perfection could be marshaled to provide him at least some reassurance that we could not, after all, be the victims of such deception.[72] But many later modern thinkers remained unable to land with confidence on one or another side of the realist/nominalist divide, a shining example being Ralph Waldo Emerson, whose 1844 essay "Nominalist and Realist" has been called bipolar in its indecisiveness.[73]

Efforts to revive a realist metaphysics continued, however, with German idealism, especially when it sought to move beyond the self-limiting strictures of Kantian critique or Fichtean subjectivism, albeit taking into the historical change to which Scholasticism had been indifferent. Although Hegel considered the nominalist critique of realism a necessary negation of contentless abstraction, he considered it only a sublatable "moment" in a dialectical process that ultimately negated that negation.[74] His objective idealism pushed past the subjective idealism of Kant and Fichte to restore the ontological reality of universals beyond the positing of a transcendental, constitutive subject. Later antirationalists with little use for Hegel, such as Martin Heidegger, could also spurn nominalism as inherently nihilistic and seek to revive a pre-Socratic reverence for the most abstract of all categories—or from his perspective, the most concrete—Being.[75]

Nor has the counterrevolution to nominalism waned with the passing of time. There have even been sporadic efforts to rebuild the "heavenly city" of the High Middle Ages through the revival of neo-Thomism, which began in earnest after Pope Leo XIII's encyclical *Aeterni patris* in 1879. Twentieth-century Catholic theologians such as Jacques Maritain, Étienne Gilson, and Hans Urs von Balthasar sought to apply Scholastic teachings to a wide variety of contemporary issues, social, political, cultural, and aesthetic.[76] Pope Benedict XVI's more recent plea for the "rehellenization" of theology expressed the same urge to restore the balance between Athens and Jerusalem.[77] The antinominalist crusade has been continued in our time by non-Catholic theologians like John Milbank and Conor Cunningham, who defend an unapologetically "Radical Orthodoxy" and seek to reenchant the world by reversing the effects of secularization.[78] In addition, other strains in medieval philosophy—especially the Neoplatonism developed by Plotinus, the Pseudo-Dionysius, and Nicholas of Cusa based on a dialectic of identity and difference—have been credited with anticipating Hegel's dialectics and its various offshoots in contemporary theory.[79] Ironically, criticizing the modern age as nominalist has even been a tactic of postmodernist critics of modernity, who want to go beyond it.[80]

After acknowledging all of these examples of a realist counterrevolution, it would clearly be misleading to say tout court that "modernity" both originated in nominalism and remained in its thrall until this day, as if no potent alternatives existed and modernity were a monolithic epoch. Indeed, we can still see the resiliency of realist universalism in one of the most heated public debates of our time, which concerns the relative weight of biology and culture in the determination of gender—and, or sexual—identities. Staunchly realist defenders of "natural" sexual differences often accuse their opponents of falling back on the simplistic nominalist belief that merely declaring one's identity as such should suffice to justify it in the eyes of others. A natural kind is thus reduced to an arbitrarily chosen cultural role.

Their opponents often respond that what may seem natural is merely the result of accumulated, conventional practice, and that it is really role-playing all the way down. The sides in the debate do not, however, always line up in the same direction. For although it is the case that some transgender activists argue nominalistically that gender is nothing but an artificial construct and reassignment a matter of personal decision, others ironically fall back on a realist essentialism of their own. That is, they claim that despite their outward physical appearance and the gender assigned them at birth, some people cannot help psychologically identifying with their "true" gender, which is not experienced as a choice, but rather as a hard-wired given. They demand the right to align their outward appearances with their inner, essential selves. In response, transgender skeptics sometimes adopt the constructivist logic of nominalism to insist that to the contrary, they can and should choose otherwise. There is obviously a great deal more that can and will be said about these issues, but for our purposes, the lesson to be learned here is simply that it would be mistaken to characterize nominalism as having swept all before it in the modern world and that universalizing realism, even without its religious underpinnings, has been vanquished.

And yet, what is no less clear is that despite the best restorative or palliative efforts of its critics, the enduring provocation of nominalism has continued to trouble even the most apparently self-confident exponents of realist ontologies, especially when they are understood as implicit onto-theologies. Arguably, the main sticking point for those resisting the full implications of secularization has remained the inscrutability of God's omnipotent will, which, it will be recalled, was the motivating premise of the nominalist revolution. But even for those who operate entirely within what Charles Taylor called "the immanent frame,"[81] the impact was no less powerful. With no way of compensating for divine inscrutability, modern science had to abandon any hope of understanding the ultimate reasons or purposes behind creation, even if it might still seek the proximate causes that made it function. Although it is sometimes argued that modern science "rests upon a new notion of man as a willing being, modeled on the omnipotent God of nominalism and able like him to master nature through the exercise of his infinite will,"[82] no exercise of mastery could imbue what was mastered with the ultimate meaning previously attributed to the cosmos. Nor was modern science really able to justify satisfactorily the project of mastery itself. With the loss of belief in nature as replete with cosmic significance went the estrangement of humans from their natural "home" that became such a constant source of lament in the modern world.

It is telling that even when early-modern philosophers returned to speculative metaphysics, the nominalist challenge to the reality of universals remained a pressing issue.[83] For all their rationalist system-building, they focused primarily on the epistemic and semantic nature of universals, rather than their allegedly ontological status. The lingering influence of nominalism on Descartes has, for example, been argued by later commentators.[84] Leibniz's ontology of individual monads has also been seen as evidence of the effects of the nominalist critique of universals and abstractions.[85] Even Spinoza's debts to the nominalist tradition have not gone unremarked.[86] In science as well, nominalism continued to prevail. When Charles Darwin presented to an astonished world his pathbreaking evolutionary account of "the origin of species," he explicitly denied the ontological realism of his categories: "it will be seen that I look at the term 'species' as one arbitrarily given, for the sake of convenience, to a set of individuals closely resembling each other, and that it does not essentially differ from the term variety, which is given to less distinct and more fluctuating forms."[87]

If we fast-forward to another contemporary public controversy vying for prominence with the one mentioned above on gender identity, which concerns the validity of racial categorizations, we can see how nominalism can still serve as a powerful solvent of realist universals. Here biological evidence is now marshaled mostly by the nominalists. Despite countless attempts at isolating genetic differences for racial groups, biologists seem now skeptical of finding conclusive evidence that they are natural kinds.[88] Indeed, as the notorious "one-drop rule" so long dominating American racial thinking shows, the culturalist explanation of identity seems far more plausible than the naturalist alternative.[89] Tellingly, the rule applies only to Black/white relations and is not in force for other groups. It also fails to acknowledge mixed race identities, often registered in the categorizations of other cultures, at least since "mulatto" was dropped from the United States census in 1930. If in our tortured reasoning about race, to put its implications crudely, a white mother can have a Black child, but a Black mother cannot have a white one, it is clear we are not carving nature at the joints.

Thus, although it would be wrong to ignore the resilience of universalist realism in one form or another, we have to concur with Blumenberg, Gillespie, and many others in stressing the powerful, enduring impact of the *via moderna* on the modern age. But what then must be next addressed—and this is really the larger purpose of the book before you—is whether nominalism as traditionally understood should itself be treated as a coherent whole. Was there, in fact, a significant difference between the dominant variant normally identified with it as such, and a previously unnamed subordinate alternative, whose implications have been largely ignored? If so, what are the inadequacies of reducing the drama of modernity to a struggle between the revolution of nominalism and the counterrevolution of realism? For was the only alternative to that disenchantment of the world so often attributed to the deflationary effects of nominalism the restoration of confidence in the existence of real universals in a harmonious cosmos? Or was there a version of nominalism that provided a different choice?

It is the ambition of this book to offer an answer to these questions, and in so doing, unsettle the opposition of realism and nominalism, conventionally understood, as the exclusive options in the modern age. Instead, we will draw on the paradigmatic method adopted from Agamben and Benjamin to explore a hitherto unappreciated third alternative, whose existence may help explain those features of modernity that cannot be grasped in terms of a simple realism/nominalism binary. The goal is not to supersede or sublate their perennial oscillation by exorbitantly claiming that what we will call *magical nominalism* is somehow the primary *impensé* of modernity. Nor is it even to urge us, following Bloch's metaphor in the epigraph to this introduction, to travel down its path all the way "to the end,"[90] as our inconclusive conclusion will performatively make clear. Rather, it merely hopes to arouse curiosity about where that path has already led, and encourage future attempts to carry on paradigmatic comparisons and the work of translation in new and fruitful directions.

* * *

Chapter 1 will explore in greater depth the effects of the nominalist challenge to Scholastic realism developed within Christian theology. Rather, however, than attempting an encyclopedic overview including everything from theology, philosophy, and science to political theory and art—even nominalism in mathematics would have to be considered, a task well beyond this author's ken[91]—we will offer instead only an "ideal type" of what can be called conventional nominalism. The adjective has a double meaning: not only has this version become the prevailing notion of the concept in general, but it also it stresses the role played by convention in the process of naming. The chapter will conclude with a quick glance at the legacy of conventional nominalism in political theory from Thomas Hobbes to Carl Schmitt, focusing on its implications for the idea of sovereignty.

After reflections on the relations between magic and both science and religion, the second chapter will begin the task of revealing the alternative to the conventional nominalism derived from Ockham's theological challenge to Scholastic realism. But it will do so not by constructing an "ideal type," which is appropriate for conventional nominalism, but rather by exploring the first in a series of paradigmatic examples, which accrue meaning cumulatively and analogically. While acknowledging its overlap with what has been called "Jewish nominalism,"[92] it will seek to foreground its "magical" features by focusing on the esoteric speculations of Walter Benjamin about a lost Adamic view of language "as such" prior to the plurality of human tongues. Rather than the human self-assertion attributed by Blumenberg to the nominalist undermining of the realist cosmos, the magical alternative, we hope to show, challenges the power of the constitutive subject by lending the affective aura so often accompanying magic to unique particulars irreducible to the essentializing categories imposed on them.

Following an intermezzo to consider some of the qualms voiced by critics of nominalism in whatever guise and explore the links between magical nominalism and negative theology, we will build on our analysis of Benjamin's *Sprachmagie* to examine an unlikely trio of paradigmatic examples of magical nominalism. The first is located in the contemporary theoretical discourse reflecting on the premises of historical narrative and explanation, which sometimes influences, albeit indirectly, actual research into and writing about the past. The impact of conventional nominalism has, of course, already been widely remarked following "the linguistic turn" in twentieth-century philosophy of history.[93] But we hope to show that the palpable echo of magical nominalism can also be discerned in recent exaltations of "sublime historical experience" and the "event," with their muffled, often ambivalent redemptive implications. The latter was particularly prominent in the mélange of theoretical provocations that came to be called, for better or worse, French poststructuralism, although, as we will see, it culminated in the work of Alain Badiou, who explicitly rejected that label.

We will next turn to the perennial conflict in aesthetics between realism and nominalism, or, as the philosopher Nelson Goodman liked to call the latter, "irrealism." After a rapid account of the history of that struggle from Ockham to the present, we will then home in on Marcel Duchamp's embrace of "pictorial nominalism" and its relation to the still controversial intervention in visual art he called the readymade. Although Duchamp may have been too ironic and deflationary to assign a redemptive mission to art, his work unexpectedly betrays the symptoms of a nominalism that has both conventional and magical traits. The latter are even more evident in the ruminations on nominalism in the realm of music found throughout Theodor W. Adorno's oeuvre, to which the chapter then turns. Wary of the weaknesses of conventional nominalism as a ground for critique, Adorno hesitated to go as far as his friend Walter Benjamin in seeking to reenchant the world through sympathetic magic and the quest for a lost Adamic language. And yet, he shared the magical nominalist resistance to the domination of the self-asserting subject, defended what he called "the preponderance of the object," and appreciated the noncommunicative function of musical language that, like the proper name, was beyond communicable meaning.

Our final major paradigm will be that quintessentially modern invention called the photograph, as filtered through the extensive discourse that has tried to make sense of it. The debates over photographic indexicality and contingency, along with Roland Barthes's celebrated distinction between the *studium* and *punctum* of a photograph, will orient the discussion. We will also explore the complicated relationship between the historical discourse of the "event" and the photographic image, which captures discrete moments isolated from the flow of time, as well as the ways photographs have been compared to readymades and proper names. The chapter will conclude with a consideration of Siegfried Kracauer's early thoughts on the relationship between photographs, memory, and history.

In a final, "inconclusive" conclusion, we will return to the question of the implications of nominalism for political theory. Against the conventional nominalist version, culminating in Carl Schmitt's decisionist concept of sovereignty, we will move quickly through a selection of magical nominalist alternatives, often inspired by the heterodox surrealist Georges Bataille. Drawing on some of the reservations voiced in the intermezzo, we will end without a ringing crescendo, reflecting the belief that magical nominalism is better understood in terms of negative theology than as the source of positive answers to the provocative questions it continues to raise.

1
Conventional Nominalism

No one [today] says that he is a nominalist, because nobody is anything else.

JORGE LUIS BORGES

The Via Moderna

Surveying the state of his field in 1983, the eminent medieval intellectual historian William Courtenay concluded, "For the moment at least, the nominalism of the fourteenth century, if we are to really understand it, must be studied nominalistically."[1] That moment drags on today. For not only would it be philosophically problematic, indeed a performative contradiction, to essentialize a theory that explicitly challenged abstractions, but it is also historically questionable to force all of those thinkers who might be grouped together into one homogeneous camp. "For much of its history," notes the philosopher Deborah Brown, "the term 'nominalism' has been used with so much variety of meaning that it is difficult to pin it to any single doctrine."[2] "Unfortunately," adds another commentator, "the term 'nominalism' is very imprecise, covering a great multitude of rather different philosophic sins and perhaps even a few philosophic virtues."[3]

From Roscelin and Abelard through Duns Scotus and William of Ockham to John Buridan and Gregory of Rimini, there are too many discrepancies and even disagreements to allow a scrupulous scholar to forge their ideas into a unified, common program remaining consistent over time. Some of nominalism's most prominent exponents, such as Buridan, were acceptable to the church, while others, including Duns Scotus, Ockham, Nicolas d'Autrécourt and Jean de Mirecourt, were officially censured[4] Even the categorical opposition between realism and nominalism begins to waver once their commonalities are acknowledged within a broader definition of Scholasticism that is capacious enough to include competing subschools of thought. And when the discussion is expanded to include the role nominalism played in late-medieval literature, for example in the work of Geoffrey Chaucer, the uncertainties expand with it.[5]

Faced with the challenge of making the fine discriminations that might satisfy serious scholars of medieval thought and literature, a student of modern European history might well hesitate before entering such disputed territory, littered as it is with unresolved controversies over the legacies of a number of subtle and complicated thinkers.[6] It would, moreover, be a daunting task to sort through all of the arcane theological polemics generated by their ideas for the proper understanding of, say, natural law, the Trinity, predestination, the Eucharist, transubstantiation or the role of icons as opposed to idols in devotional practices. For unlike in the debates over nominalism and realism roiling contemporary analytic philosophy, the entanglement of religion and philosophy in the late Middle Ages meant that one cannot be adequately understood without grappling with the other.[7]

Only the examples of predecessors like Hans Blumenberg, Michael Allen Gillespie, and Jürgen Habermas, who have courageously explored the impact of nominalism on modern thought, suggest that crossing the border by a nonspecialist may nonetheless be worth taking the risk.[8] Or rather, it will be only if he or she explicitly adopts what Max Weber made famous as "ideal types." Differing from statistical averages, these are hypothetical, fictional models, ideal not in the sense of normative perfection but rather of mental images. They are consciously constructed as heuristic tools to help us find our way through a welter of particular examples and orient ourselves in a world with no clear directions. In Weber's words: "An ideal type is formed by the one-sided *accentuation* of one or more points of view and by the synthesis of a great many diffuse, discrete, more or less present and occasionally absent *concrete individual* phenomena, which are arranged according to those one-sidedly emphasized viewpoints into a unified *analytical* construct. In its conceptual purity, this mental construct cannot be found empirically anywhere in reality. It is a *utopia*."[9] It is telling that this last term was used by Theodor Adorno in *Negative Dialectics*, a work of philosophy that sought to go beyond Weber's neo-Kantianism without adopting a fully Hegelian alternative, when he called "the utopia of cognition" the use of "concepts to unseal the non-conceptual with concepts, without making it their equal."[10]

Understood in the sense of being nowhere real in all of their qualities—thus justifying Weber calling them "utopias"—ideal types are themselves indirect products of what is normally taken to be the nominalist mentality, which denies the knowability of real essences enduring over time.[11] As such they avoid the performative contradiction entailed by subsuming various instances of nominalism under an abstract universal assumed to have prior ontological existence.[12] And at the same time, they instantiate one of the main lessons normally learned from nominalism itself: the need for the subject to generate the concepts and categories that we use to master the contingency of a no longer legible world.[13]

Or to be more precise, this necessity is at the heart of presenting what we will call conventional nominalism, which has been at the center of virtually all discussions of the discourse, serving as the primary model in any account of nominalism's putative role in enabling the onset of what we call modernity. As indicated in the preface, the elaboration of magical nominalism, however, will necessitate a different methodological strategy, which will depend on comparing paradigmatic exemplars rather than positing an ideal typical version of an essential concept. Rather than a unified analytical construct, generated by the conceptualizing imagination of a synthesizing social scientist, it will emerge only through the cumulative process of analogizing overlapping but not identical cases. To tie it down prematurely with a prescriptive definition or ideal typical reconstruction might alleviate a reader's understandable impatience, but it would violate the imperative to honor the heterogeneity and singularity the term has been introduced to suggest.

Because there is a better fit between the fictionalist method of ideal types developed by Weber and the presentation of conventional nominalism, that is how we will proceed here. The adjective "conventional," it must first be made clear, is meaningful in two ways. First, the nominalism in question has come over long usage to be the more or less conventional interpretation of the word. The essentializing of the idiosyncratic nominalisms produced by late-medieval thinkers is thus not merely a function of a contemporary historian's attempt to bring post facto order into chaos by positing an ideal type, or at least not that alone. It also reflects the ways complex clusters of ideas can often be reduced, packaged, and disseminated over time. That is, certain terms survive their often disparate origins and imprecise usages to acquire the illusory quality of coherence and become shorthand brand names or umbrella labels for a cluster of different positions whose nuances are then lost to posterity. Often beginning as polemical insults hurled by their opponents, they are ultimately adopted by friends and foes alike. Call it "hypostatization," "reification," "commodification," or just simply "standardization," it is the almost inevitable fate befalling all fluid discourses that congeal into "-isms" and enter the memory bank of a culture.

And so it was with nominalism, a term that Ockham himself never actually used to describe his own position.[14] Nor did he have many direct disciples who formed a coherent school, possibly because when he died in 1347 in exile at the emperor's court in Munich, he was still under a ban of excommunication. But by the fifteenth century, so one commentator notes, "the very labels 'nominalist,' 'realist,' 'Scotist'" had now hardened from the inchoate movements of the earlier period into names hurled in battle."[15] In the case of nominalism in the postmedieval world, this meant, among other things, a gradual forgetting of the theological stakes involved in the debate over divine omnipotence that had originally sparked the challenge to Scholastic realism, and an erasure by all but the most serious students of medieval thought of the nuances that once distinguished variants of nominalism. Nor did its tacit links with living in a certain way—the Franciscan order's life of simplicity and poverty—survive, as it was turned entirely into a theoretical or methodological principle in a contest of ideas.[16]

Granted that in the technical considerations of later analytic philosophers new discriminations have been developed, such as predicate, concept, class, resemblance, and priority nominalisms.[17] Some modern nominalists deny only the ontological reality of universals (e.g., greenness, density, or courage), while others only abstract objects (e.g., shapes, numbers, lengths, or groups).[18] Some are nominalists when it comes to natural kinds and others only with reference to historical institutions. Some argue nominalism is psychological, others ontological.[19] And on occasion, some have invented new variations, such as "trope" or "mereological" nominalism.[20] Even the apparent oxymoron "essentialist nominalism" has been coined to characterize one of its oldest hybridized instantiations.[21] And terms like "ostrich nominalism," which began as a pejorative, have gained their defenders.[22]

But by and large in the greater world beyond the rarefied confines of contemporary analytic philosophy, "nominalism" has come to function as a generic concept with a more or less settled meaning. Take, for example, Richard Rorty's characteristically crisp, no-nonsense definition in a 2000 essay on Hans-Georg Gadamer's hermeneutics:

> Let me define "nominalism" as the claim that all essences are nominal and all necessities *de dicto*. This amounts to saying that no description of an object is more true to the nature of that object than any other. Nominalists think that Plato's metaphor of cutting nature at the joints should be abandoned once and for all. . . . A consistent nominalist cannot countenance a hierarchical organization of the kingdom of the thinking mind which corresponds, as Plato's organizational charts did, to an ontological hierarchy. So struggles for priority between metaphysics and physics, or between techies and fuzzies, look ludicrous from a nominalist perspective. So does Heidegger's distinction between metaphysics and Thinking, as well as his claim that "in the end, philosophy's business is to safeguard the power of the most elementary words."[23]

Understanding nominalism in this condensed and reduced form may well blur the complexities of late-medieval thought or ignore the arcane nuances of contemporary analytic philosophy, and can thus be justifiably targeted by serious students of their intricacies. But when nominalism is appreciated as a diffuse, ubiquitous, and hypostasized "-ism" that began in medieval theology and thrives in modern secular thought, transcending its distinct variations, its abiding power cannot be denied. Indeed, even one of its strongest foes, the pragmatist C. S. Peirce, could ruefully conclude a survey of modern thinkers in 1903: "There was a tidal wave of nominalism. . . . In one word, all modern philosophy of every sect has been nominalistic."[24]

The second sense in which "conventional" modifies this variant of nominalism is its foundational role in the development of what philosophers have come to call conventionalist epistemologies. From the time at least of William of Ockham and extending to the present, nominalism has been identified, grosso modo, with the denial of the ontological reality of universal categories and abstract objects. Extrapolating from the insistence on divine will that we have noted spawned medieval challenges to Scholasticism, it has come to imply the post facto imposition of generic names or abstract concepts on a world of inherent contingency. It is thus conventionalist in the sense of necessitating a mutually constituted agreement on the meaning of a word, derived from the Latin *conventionem*, or "a meeting, assembly, or agreement." In addition to the universal signs that were natural—for example, smoke signifying fire—Ockham argued there were artificial ones that are "conventional signs meant to signify many things. Therefore, just as the word is said to be common, so it can be said to be universal. But it is not so by nature, only by convention."[25] Nominalist premises were to a greater or lesser degree foundational for such modern conventionalists as the mathematical theoretician Henri Poincaré; the analytic philosophers A. J. Ayer, Rudolf Carnap, W. V. O. Quine, and Nelson Goodman; the historian and philosopher of science Pierre Duhem; and the structural linguist Ferdinand de Saussure.[26]

Conventionalism, to be sure, can be divided into a more explicitly voluntary practice in which categories are consciously coined by common agreement, and a comparable effect produced without deliberate design, which gradually solidifies into a binding tradition over time.[27] The latter come to be embedded in and reproduced by what Ludwig Wittgenstein would call a form of life, Michel Foucault a discursive practice, and Christian Metz a scopic regime. The conventional categories and ways of thinking they perpetuate may, in fact, have a greater hold over those who are in their thrall than ones deliberately posited, even coming to seem natural or inevitable because they seem to have existed "since time immemorial." There is, as the philosopher of science Ian Hacking argued, a "looping effect" in which bestowing a name works over time to reinforce a practical identity, leading to what he called "making up people."[28] Conventionalist linguists who insist on the arbitrary origins of signs do not therefore contend that languages are invented ex nihilo by their speakers, despite the occasional coining of neologisms. And even champions of nonidentity and *Unbegrifflichkeit* (nonconceptuality) like Adorno, whose magical nominalist sympathies we will encounter later, concede that general concepts contain sedimented meanings, so it would be "a nominalist error to believe that every concept we employ is a *tabula rasa* which can be transformed into a richly furnished table only by virtue of human definitions."[29]

But whether a product of time-honored usage or a conscious invention, the terms employed by a conventional nominalism cannot be understood as referencing real universals prior to their coinage or the reifying solidification resulting from their repetitive application. Retreating from the volatile synthesis of Greek cosmology and Jewish/Christian Creationism that had culminated in Scholasticism, the nominalists accepted the limitations on human reason and the uncertainty about the contingency of the world implied by divine omnipotence and inscrutability. As Blumenberg puts it:

> The impotence of reason, as deduced by William of Ockham from the principle of omnipotence, consists in the inapplicability of the principle of economy to the classical questions of metaphysics: The nature that does nothing in vain is no longer a definition of divine activity, to which the detours and superfluous expenditures cannot be ascribed. What is given, the actual world as well as actual grace, is never the maximum of what is possible. The thesis of the possibility of infinitely many worlds is only the equivalent of an assertion of the powerlessness of finite reason.[30]

Even when not carried to the extremes of skepticism or fideism, the nominalists' abandonment of belief in a rationally ordered, teleologically determined, fully legible cosmos presented an enormous challenge for subsequent thinkers. But it could also offer a no less exorbitant opportunity. Stressing the priority of possibility over actuality meant that what had already been created was diminished in favor of the as yet uncreated.

If repeating the wholesale gnostic denial of the value of creation, and with it a total withdrawal from worldly affairs, were to be avoided,[31] however, some orienting principles would be necessary to fend off the nihilism that critics of nominalism often warned was the consequence of believing that only God was necessary and everything else contingent. One such strategy was the principle of parsimony—or of economy, in Blumenberg's usage—that came to be called Ockham's razor.[32] It contended that it was methodologically prudent to eliminate extraneous explanatory elements in accounting for phenomena, for "plurality should not be posited without necessity."[33] Relinquishing those terms that were superfluous would help secure the credibility of those that were not. Against the realists who argued for the ontological existence of universals, whether Platonic forms or Aristotelian essences, it was better to remain on the more modest level of concrete particulars, if, that is, they can play the same explanatory role. Metaphysical entities, objects of thought without spatiotemporal coordinates and prior to sensual experience, should be eliminated from cognition, although they might remain as articles of faith. Ockham still had great respect for "the Philosopher," as Aristotle was known, and steadfastly upheld the principles of logical reasoning,[34] but he resisted the attempt to understand theology as a systematic "science" based on metaphysical principles. He eliminated eight Aristotelian ontological categories, leaving only substance and quality.[35]

Thus, even Duns Scotus's attempt at a middle ground in which a common nature was understood to be identical with an individual particular, although formally distinct from it, failed to acknowledge that particulars can only be identical with themselves.[36] Forms, either *ante rem* as in Platonism or *in re* as in Aristotelianism do not exist; only things that can be treated independently of others do. Simplicity is preferable to complexity, sensual experience to rational inference, the perception of singularities to general categories, and hypothetical conjectures to syllogistic deductions.[37] Intuitive cognition apprehends objects immediately in their contingency and can judge them to exist, whereas abstractive cognition, expressed for example in concepts, eludes existential judgments.[38] Substances refer only to the individual substratum of sensible qualities and not to any abstract essence inherent in them or prior to them. There is no need to explain a process of individuation from a prior generic category, for particulars are always already isolated.[39] Only they, moreover, can be confirmed to exist through direct experience and not by ratiocination alone. The distinction between essence and existence is only grammatical, not substantial.

Without the realists' belief in the congruence between cosmic harmony and human reason, the nominalists elevated the evidence of the senses, which provide our only access to a world of individual objects. Rejecting the confusion of logical categories or tautological terms with physical realities,[40] they favored an empiricist epistemology that grounded knowledge of the world, and especially scientific knowledge, in inductive generalizations confirming hypotheses rather than deductive assertions leading to syllogistic proofs. What the Aristotelians had confidently classified as categorical, assertoric, self-evident propositions, nominalists like Ockham understood only as conditional possibilities. The premise underlying the inductive method, the uniformity and homogeneity of nature, could only be a working hypothesis rather than a metaphysical certainty because of God's ability to intervene capriciously.[41] But it was one that was justified pragmatically by the results it enabled.[42]

For other reasons as well, historians of science routinely acknowledge the role played by nominalism in the early-modern Scientific Revolution, including the Copernican challenge to the long-standing geocentric view of the cosmos.[43] Among them was the denial of the teleological goals that Aristotle had claimed were inherent in the world. The claim, still sometimes repeated by those seeking solace for inexplicable misfortune, that "things happen for a reason" was at best only a consoling fantasy. *Pace* (in advance) Leibniz, contingent facts did not have inherent purposes or "sufficient reasons." Because belief in such purposive, or final, causes assumed that the future was constrained by the past, at least to the degree that they posited potentials that were necessarily realized, they limited the absolute power of God's will in fashioning an open-ended future. As Blumenberg puts it, "Teleological elements in natural philosophy contradicted the fundamental theological position of voluntarism, which did not permit one, in explaining nature, to have recourse to a knowledge of the purposes God meant nature to serve. Knowledge of acts of God's will must be reserved for revelation. If the Creator's intentions cannot be known, neither can the goals of natural processes."[44]

The abandonment of final along with formal causes accelerated the erosion of belief in a harmonious and complete cosmos understood as a great chain of being. Rearguard efforts by late Renaissance Neoplatonists to salvage cosmotheism through a heliocentric system of perfect spheres faltered.[45] The new cosmology replaced it with a universe infinite in duration and extension, which, as Alexander Koyré demonstrated, accompanied the technologically enabled discoveries in astronomy of the sixteenth and seventeenth centuries.[46] No longer understandable as the rational emanation of God's being or organized in a hierarchy of similitudes and analogies, that universe lacked essential substances or timeless quiddity. Instead of fixed stars in an eternal hierarchy of geometrically perfect, celestial spheres, the heavens were turned into a vast, acentric, and endless void, only sporadically occupied by galactic matter. Space had gained in depth and the scale of time extended, but harmonious order and coherent structure were lost. Even before the first definitive measurement of stellar parallax by the German astronomer Friedrich Bessel in 1838, the solid cosmic carapace known as the firmament had been pierced to let the light in from a bewildering array of far distant and nonsynchronous stars.

The "de-limitation" of the cosmos was furthermore matched by a comparable expansion of the ecumene—the known lands of human inhabitation—by the voyages of terrestrial discovery, which happened at roughly the same time.[47] It was not by chance that the frontispiece of Francis Bacon's *Novum Organum* (1620) depicts a ship boldly passing through the Pillars of Hercules flanking the straits of Gibraltar, trailed by a second poised to follow.[48] Discoveries in both scientific and geographic exploration hastened the weakening of the traditional religious suspicion of curiosity, long distrusted for distracting the faithful from absorbing the wisdom of scripture. They also violated the prudential taboo on venturing into dangerous, unknown territory, defying the Latin motto *nec plus ultra* (nothing further beyond).[49] One possible outcome of these new de-limited understandings of both the universe and the world was, to be sure, that unease on the part of a humanity now faced with an opaque disorder of random contingency we have already noted. Nihilism and the return of the gnostic denigration of the value of creation always remained a threat. If there were no guarantee that an omnipotent God was always telling us the truth—a frightening possibility that still haunted Descartes and Mersenne in the seventeenth century—corrosive skepticism could easily follow.[50]

But an alternative conclusion could also be drawn, which helped make the voyages of discovery and the Scientific Revolution possible. Significantly, after Columbus's voyages, King Charles I of Spain (Charles V of the Holy Roman Empire) changed the motto of his country's coat of arms, which had the Pillars of Hercules on them, to *plus ultra*. Among scientists, final causes or sufficient reasons may no longer have seemed plausible, but efficient causes, explaining how things worked rather than what they inherently were or intended to be, might still be sought through experiential observation and experimental repetition.[51] Although paradoxically, this quest could ultimately lead to a new ontology, the mechanistic materialism that expressed the hubris of what later came to be called scientism, it was also possible to bracket metaphysical or purposive questions entirely and focus instead just on how things were caused and how they functioned. Our knowledge might always be conditional rather than absolute, but it was still useful in dealing with the challenges of contingency.

There were, to be sure, persistent traces of the theological origins of nominalism, which never entirely disappeared, no matter how secular the context. Gillespie, for example, draws our attention to the hidden connection between medieval notions of divine omnipotence and modern science: "In nominalistic terms, God is pure willing, pure activity, or pure power, and the world in its becoming is divine will, is this God. Or in more modern terms, the world is the ceaseless motion that is determined by divine will understood as efficient or mechanical causality."[52] Rather than static being, expressed in terms of eternal forms or rational essences, as the most prominent Greek philosophers had thought, the infinite universe is always moving, if without a predetermined goal or final cause. "To discover the divinely ordered character of the world, it is thus necessary to investigate becoming, which is to say, it is necessary to discover the laws governing the motion of all beings. Theology and natural science thereby become one and the same."[53]

But because God's will could also be exercised in the miraculous suspension of these laws, the quest for certainty was destined to falter.[54] It was thus incumbent on humans to exercise what a later age would call epistemic humility and recognize that science would never really understand creation with the same confidence of those who had once believed they shared in divine intelligence. Becoming less content with ruminative, participatory *contemplation*, which then often came to be redirected toward an internal spiritual landscape, modern scientists turned instead to technologically enhanced, hypothetically informed *observation* of the world from the outside.[55] No longer securely embedded in an allegedly objective analogical order in which macrocosm and microcosm mirrored each other and infinity duplicated on the level of finitude, modern humans came increasingly to accept their precarious situatedness in an immense universe without fixed coordinates.[56]

Giving up our privileged place in a geocentric cosmos as the origin point of a series of concentric spheres soon led to the realization that humans could only have a particular, situated view of the universe. Realizing that comets and then planets had elliptical, eccentric orbits and then that the Milky Way was merely an effect of our peculiar place in an immense disk of stars in our galaxy hammered home the lesson that even if there were a God's eye view of it all, we did not share in it.[57] Three-dimensional, perspectival space depicted on a flat two-dimensional canvas had, of course, already been developed in European painting as early as Filippo Brunelleschi and Leon Battista Alberti in the fifteenth century, and soon blossomed into what has been recognized as the dominant "scopic regime of modernity."[58] The visual metaphor of perspective soon made its way into scholarship as well to figure the limits of partial knowledge, for example among historians.[59] "More than a form of thought," Blumenberg noted, "perspectivism becomes a form of life, if the passion for reflecting on one's own standpoint can be styled in this way."[60]

Acknowledging the inevitability of perspectival situatedness reinforced the epistemic humility that followed the abandonment of the maximalist realist belief that the cosmos was organized according to universal essences that were also accessible through human reason.[61] An increasingly hidden God (*deus absconditus*), whose ineffability defied rational explanation, went along with an increasingly opaque creation.[62] The comforting metaphor introduced by Plato in the *Phaedrus* that the best theories are ones that "carve nature at its joints" lost its power when the joints were increasingly hard to find. Whatever glimpse of creation might be granted to us was always partial and skewed by the particular location we occupied in observing it. Because that location was always in flux and relative to the rapidly moving other parts of the universe, orientation, let alone a secure feeling of groundedness, was lost. Either fideism or skepticism, as we have seen, could easily follow from this disorienting loss of confidence in human reason and its alleged congruence with an intrinsically rational and legible world.

But there was also another, more positive inference that might be drawn, which was the inadvertent consequence of the underlying stress on divine will in the formation of nominalism. "Raising theology to its maximal pretension over against reason," Blumenberg notes, "had the unintended result of reducing theology's role in explaining the world to a minimum, and thus of preparing the competence of reason as the organ of a new kind of science that would liberate itself from tradition."[63] That new science relied less on a metaphysical notion of reason than one that was more functional and instrumental, and it sought to explain only how things worked rather than their ultimate purpose or essential meaning. As Elizabeth Brient has argued, the replacement of a closed cosmos by an infinite universe in astronomy was mirrored in the immanent infinitization of nature, which modern science could never hope to know in its entirety, settling instead for an endless quest with no possibility of ultimate certainty.[64] For all its affirmation of unshackled curiosity, the modern knowledge regime was based on acknowledging the limits of what could be known, an attitude already foreshadowed in the late Middle Ages with Nicolas of Cusa's defense of *docta ignorantia* (learned ignorance). Although the idea of divine providence survived into the seventeenth century, indeed even grew in strength with the Calvinist doctrine of predestination, it was attributed to a God whose purposes were inscrutable to those who were ruled by it.[65]

In the place of eternal forms, the nominalist-inflected new science now operated on the assumption—better put, working hypothesis—that nature was ruled by dynamic forces.[66] These, moreover, could be harnessed by humans for their own purposes. Ironically, the vacuum left by the loss of faith in a rational cosmos was filled by humans who could assert their own will, pursue their own ends, and mobilize the power of nature for what they construed as their own benefit. Nominalism, as the philosopher Gerhard Schweppenhäuser notes, "turned away from the contemplation of creation and developed into a concept of productivity. It could not be the goal of science to recognize the whole of nature in its being-in-itself. It would be important to describe the features and phenomena of nature to handle and alter them in line with the purposes and needs of humankind. This was the prerequisite of modern technology that focused on production."[67]

The putative displacement of voluntarism from a divine to a human subject may seem, to be sure, a questionable leap. Even if the will is favored over reason, it is always possible, after all, to deny, as Schopenhauer famously did, that it is a *free* will based on undetermined human choice. But arguably, the groundwork for the shift from divine to human was already laid when the balance between Athens and Jerusalem, Greek cosmology and Hebraic Creationism, was being tipped in favor of the latter. What contributed to the tipping was an increased scrutiny of the implications of the Incarnation in such works as the great Scholastic dialectician St. Anselm's *Cur Deus Homo* of 1094–98.[68] If God were indeed present in the human form of Jesus, then God had taken on himself human characteristics, including the capacity to succumb to or resist the temptation to sin. "All power follows the will," Anselm wrote,

> For, when I say that I can speak or walk, it is understood, if I choose. For, if the will be not implied as acting, there is no power, but only necessity. For, when I say that I can be dragged or bound unwillingly, this is not my power, but necessity and the power of another; since I am able to be dragged or bound in no other sense than this, that another can drag or bind me. So we can say of Christ, that he could lie, so long as we understand, if he chose to do so. And, since he could not lie unwillingly and could not wish to lie, none the less can it be said that he could not lie. So in this way it is both true that he could and could not lie.[69]

For Anselm, in other words, Christ is not compelled by an external necessity, such as a binding moral law, to avoid sinning but rather chooses freely not to do so.[70] His ability to make such decisions—and this is the crucial point—is part of his *human* nature. Although his divine goodness explains why he always makes the right choice, the fact that he can choose is what is critical. Extrapolated upward, as it were, from the Son to the Father, from humans to the divine, it underpins the distinction between *potentia absoluta* and *potentia ordinata*.

If the power to choose had migrated from Christ because of his half-human qualities to God the Father, it was also possible for it to migrate down again from God all the way to humans themselves. Augustine was already struggling with its implications—Hannah Arendt called him "the first philosopher of the Will"[71]—but it was not until Duns Scotus that its full primacy was established. According to Arendt, "the idea that there could be an activity that finds its rest within itself is as surprisingly original . . . as Scotus' ontological preference for the contingent over the necessary and of the existent particular over the universal."[72] Ironically, this outcome was an inadvertent result of the nominalists' insistence on God's absolute will, free from any constraints, rational or otherwise. For it left humans in the uncomfortable position of utter dependence on a deity whose will might not only be capricious, but even malicious from a human point of view, what Descartes came to call in his initial *Meditation on First Philosophy* the *deus fallax*, or "devious God."[73] Rather than enduring the anxiety engendered by this possibility or being fully comforted by the thought that by definition God was benevolent, Descartes retreated into the only certainty left, which was in the existence of the subject who felt the dread. This was a finite subject who could no longer count on the metaphysical reassurances of benevolent transcendence, a subject fully immanent in a world without absolute guarantees. But it was also a subject, able to be understood in species-wide as well as individual terms, who no longer would passively accept his or her fate.

What Blumenberg called "self-assertion" thus served as a strategy to avoid disillusionment with a meaningless creation,[74] which might have just as easily generated another gnostic attempt to escape from it into acosmic indifference.[75] The will expanded from a moral faculty allowing fallible but free human beings to honor or defy moral imperatives to a practical determination to explore and control their often opaque and hostile environment. Ironically, epistemic humility with regard to the limits in ability to share in divine intelligence about essential truths could promote instead a compensatory confidence, slowly encouraged by the results it produced, that humans could at least master contingency through action or fabrication. The powers of creativity and productivity, which had been reserved for God, were now thinkable as human attributes as well.[76]

A concrete example of the shift, which chanced to happen at virtually the same time as the nominalist theological revolution, concerned the devices by which time was measured in the late Middle Ages.[77] Like the sundial, the remarkable instrument so important for oceanic navigation called the astrolabe, invented by the Greeks but perfected by Arab astronomers in the tenth and eleventh centuries, was dependent on measuring celestial movements to tell the time. It was in tune, in other words, with the rhythms of the cosmos. The mechanical clock enabled by the invention of the escapement in the late thirteenth century, on the other hand, produced a regular, uniform and reliable temporality that was entirely a result of human technological ingenuity. Independent of the rotation of the stars in the sky, changes in seasons or hours of daylight, it allowed the imposition of artificial, homogeneously uniform time not only on natural phenomena, but also on human experience. It could even be understood, much to the chagrin of later philosophers like Henri Bergson, as the spatialization of temporality itself, as the hands of the clock relentlessly swept around its face dividing time into quantifiable units of equal distance.

Perhaps the most triumphant theoretical realization of human self-assertion in cultural rather than technological terms came in the celebrated *verum-factum* formula of the eighteenth-century Italian philosopher of history Giambattista Vico's *New Science*: "The truth is what has been made." The maker could be the species as a whole, a privileged group or the gifted individual. And what was made could be more than just mundane history. Although medieval aesthetics had favored the imitation of transcendent forms or organic unities, agreeing with Aquinas that *solus deus creat*, the way was opened to the later exaltation, reaching its heights with the Romantics, of the inspired genius, whose creative gifts and originality imitated God's.[78]

What this bold exaltation of human creativity did not ultimately resolve, however, was what might be called a secular continuation of the struggle between the two modes of God's power. Not everyone, after all, was equally unnerved by the possibility that God could be maliciously deceptive and the world entirely contingent; in fact, as we have noted, Descartes had tried to quiet his doubts by reasoning it would contradict God's perfection. Understanding the world as determined by a concatenation of efficient causes discoverable by inductive reasoning was equivalent, mutatis mutandis, to the religious belief in the abiding *potentia ordinata* of a God who had already willed certain law-like regularities in nature. Understanding it, per contra, as a contingent manifold of as yet unrealized possibilities, which only awaited our initiative to realize them, might be understood as a human arrogation, writ small, of God's *potentia absoluta*. In other words, an intensification of the perennial quarrel between determinism and voluntarism, passive analysis of the world's objective processes and subjective intervention to change or harness them, can be derived, at least in part, from the multiple implications of the nominalist undermining of Scholastic realism.

It was therefore not a matter of simply replacing divine omnipotence with its human counterpart, as a reductive secularization theory might assume. Instead, the unstable balance between heteronomy and autonomy, which still reverberates in countless current debates about the human condition, was intensified by the nominalist demolition of the Scholastic system. Played out within a still religious framework, even the most resolute nominalists took pains to avoid reviving the old heresy of Pelagianism—the belief that salvation could come from good works alone—that Augustine had so vigorously attacked.[79] Some, such as Jean de Mirecourt and Nicholas d'Autrécourt, went so far in the other direction that they read God's omnipotence as the reason to believe in predestination, which made even the apparently human decision to sin ultimately his responsibility.[80] But even in a more putatively secular context, there was ambivalence about the hubristic divinization of man. As Blumenberg notes, the origin of human autonomy "lies not in man elevating and aggrandizing himself but in answering the need imposed by his essential strangeness in this world and his falling short of its truth that is founded in God. What is primary is not the excess and ardor of power but rather an exercise of power that submits to *necessity*. Since the world God created cannot become mankind's property, man is now compelled to build his own world by his own efforts."[81] Modern self-assertion could thus be seen as a heroic response to the loss of an increasingly absent God and the concomitant illegibility of the world he had created. But the cost, it has often been lamented, was the increasing estrangement of humans from the natural world, which was then treated as raw material to be dominated entirely for our purposes. Although there were many other sources for this epochal transformation—new technologies, the rise of capitalism, demographic expansion, increased urbanization, the exploitative colonization of new lands, to name a few—the diffuse impact of the nominalist revolution cannot be ignored.

Nominalism and the Turn toward Language

One prominent manifestation of its impact was a heightened interest in the conundrums of semiosis in general and language in particular, which had been a special focus of the nominalist challenge to Scholastic realism.[82] By shifting attention from universals as things (*res*) inhering in objects and derived from divine ideas to mere names (*nomina*) imposed by humans, Ockham and his followers provoked what has been called one of the major linguistic turns in the history of philosophy.[83] From the time of the Greek Sophists to twentieth-century analytic, hermeneutic, and structuralist philosophers, there have been successive waves of interest in the role language plays in our encounter with and understanding of the world. Each one, however, had divergent understandings of what language might be and which aspects of it were significant for philosophy, and so it is necessary to clarify the salient linguistic implications of conventional nominalism. As we will argue, they were very different from those characterizing its magical counterpart, which sought to overcome the divide between word (or more precisely, name) and thing.

Prior to Scholasticism, the dominant medieval approach to language was derived from Augustine's considerations of signs, symbols, and sacraments.[84] Drawing a distinction between natural and conventional signs—*signa naturalia* conveying meaning without intention and *signa data* invented to convey the meaning of something sensed or understood by an interpreting subject—Augustine acknowledged a gap that might exist between word and thing. He stressed the ultimate priority of the latter over the former, and took pains to warn against the confusion of signs with their referents, which would lead to the idolatry of words. Ultimately, reality presented itself to believers through direct mental contact with God's truth, which appeared silently. Adherence to the letter of words rather than the spirit was, for Augustine, characteristic of the Jewish attitude to language, which put words over the things to which they referred. For as Paul had said in 2 Corinthians 3:6, while comparing the gospel with the Hebrew Bible, we are "ministers of the New Testament; not of the letter, but the Spirit. For the letter kills but the Spirit gives life."[85]

There was, however, one profound alternative to the assumption that a gap necessarily existed between word or symbol and thing—or at least spiritual things—that had yawned since the Fall and only intensified in the aftermath of the vain attempt to build the Tower of Babel. For Augustine, the Incarnation and the sacraments that reenacted it meant the literal transformation of the word into flesh. With the appearance of Jesus, what might be called semiotic exile ended and the unity of sign and referent was achieved. The sacraments, in particular the Eucharist, overcame the gap through a communion with the real presence of the divine. Rather than symbols external to the objects or essences they signified, the sacraments enjoyed an immanent relationship between signs and the spiritual ideas they expressed. The Scholastics built on this argument to claim that "signs were effective on the basis of inherent or infused virtue."[86] Aquinas also stressed the value of analogical language, which hovered between univocal and ambiguous terminology, as especially meaningful when speaking of God, whose attributes could not be adequately described through straightforward denotations of descriptions.[87]

The Eucharistic host was, of course, an object not only to be consumed, but also to be seen, along with other devotional images and holy relics. In the twelfth and thirteenth centuries, the importance of "ocular communion," in which the sacramental wafer and wine of the Mass were understood not as mere symbolic representations of the body and blood of Christ, but as their transubstantiated presence.[88] The use of elaborately decorated monstrances or ostensoria to display the host or relics to the faithful gained in frequency. Even diplomatic seals borrowed some of the participatory immanence that spilled over from religious sacramental objects.[89] The precise status of sacred devotional objects was, to be sure, a constant source of dispute, with anxiety over idolatry always a possible stimulus to iconoclastic doubt. Fine distinctions between objects to be venerated and objects to be worshipped or adored were made to reassure the skeptics but with mixed results. In fact, throughout the history of Christianity, including its Orthodox and Protestant variants, distinguishing between idols and icons has often been a bone of ferocious contention. In other words, the nominalist critique of realism was also conducted in visual terms, a conclusion reinforced by the fact that Ockham criticized the Aristotelian notion of intelligible "visible species."[90] Although his passive notion of visual experience did not survive nineteenth-century advances in the science of vision, we will hear a distant echo of his critique in the idea of "pictorial nominalism" when we examine Marcel Duchamp in a later chapter.[91]

It is fair to say, however, that "the nominalist revolution" focused more on linguistic than visual signs in their assault on ontological realism. Although Ockham sometimes referred to universals as "only a kind of picture," or a mental image, the nominalists were more concerned with their status as conventionally posited words.[92] As early as Roscelin of Compiègne, who was described by Anselm as one of those heretics who "do not think universal substances to be anything but the puff of an utterance [*flatum vocis*],"[93] they sought to challenge any intrinsic connection between things in the world and the words that purported to embody them.[94] Unlike "natural signs" such as tracks in the snow indicating the passage of a fox, they were unmoored from what later semioticians would call their indexical function.[95] Accordingly, nominalists were often called Terminists in contemporary documents.[96]

One possible implication that might be drawn from the stress on words as conventional utterances rather than natural signs—Habermas has discerned it already in the theology of Duns Scotus, which he saw as liberating practical reason from natural teleology[97]—was a shift of emphasis from what later speech act theorists would call the locutionary function of language to its illocutionary one. That is, the use of language by a subject for the referential description of objects or speculation about reality could give way to its pragmatic use by a subject speaking to another subject, or, to put it in the jargon of J. L. Austin, from its constative to its performative role. In the case of religion, this shift meant focusing less on objective metaphysical questions about Being or creation to ones involving an intersubjective relationship between worshipper and God. Employed in private prayer or the public worship of the liturgy, language could now function primarily in the service of salvation rather than theological speculation, a tendency that culminated after the Reformation in the experiential immediacy of pietistic and evangelical devotional practices. The realization of this potential was, to be sure, a long way in the future, and medieval theologians were still primarily preoccupied with ontological and epistemological questions.

Many attempts were made to nuance their answers, as theological difficulties in dealing with the triune notion of God and the status of the sacraments prevented them from carrying their demolition of universals and abstractions too far. Some nominalists like Abelard cautiously retreated from Rocelin's more radical position. Perception, he argued, allows us to encounter a particular with a proper name, while the intellective cognition produces general terms that are a *res ficta*. In other words, they are mental images common to all the particulars named by the general term, but proper to none. Neither substantial nor an accident, they are created by the intellect's ability to abstract. Against Roscelin's debunking of them as empty words, Abelard claimed they are cognitively meaningful, even prior to their articulation in language.

As nominalism matured, however, into a full-scale assault on the Scholastic compromise, it increasingly applied the principle of parsimony to language, leading to what has been called "a program of semantic reduction."[98] Species and genera are merely concepts, natural signs within the mind, which have semantic but not ontological status. Only particulars can claim existence. The nonexistence of abstract objects is evidenced by their inability to have a causal effect on the world (we are hurt by a specific tree falling on us, not by a generic or ideal "tree as such").

One of the implications of this argument was growing intolerance of linguistic ambiguity and equivocation. A great deal of hermeneutic effort had been spent over the centuries by theologians in many different traditions wrestling with the connotative nuances, symbolic resonances, and etymological obscurities of scripture, as well as later ecclesiastical pronouncements. An elaborate system of exegetical approaches was introduced to interpret texts literally/historically, allegorically, tropologically, or anagogically. The first pointed back to events in the past; the second to events in the future; the third to moral choices in the mundane world of human affairs; and the fourth to the eternal spiritual sphere open to mystical readings. The premise underlying the application of these exegetical tools was the existence of a cosmos pulsating with rich symbolic meanings immanent in creation.

When the nominalists teased out the implications of God's omnipotence for a new understanding of an infinite universe, no longer replete with legible meanings but contingent and open to as yet uncreated possibilities, exorbitant textual exegesis lost much of its allure. As Funkenstein notes, "Of the many logically possible universes, ours is neither the best nor otherwise the product of a particular, discernible aim representative, thereby, of God's image. The Nominalists had to reject the doctrine of analogy because they had already desymbolized the universe (as well as history) almost completely."[99] Ockham distinguished between absolute mental terms, which signify each object to which they refer in exactly the same way, and connotative terms, which have both primary and secondary significations.[100] Although he acknowledged a place for figurative speech in poetry and the rhetorical expression of philosophy and theology, he distrusted the deceptive potential in polysemic terminology. The connotative, symbolic richness of words was thus sacrificed to Ockham's razor, leaving only their straightforward, unequivocal denotative meanings, yet another way in which nominalism has been credited with enabling a modern scientific approach to the world.[101]

Universals were not metaphysical realities, as the Scholastics had argued, but rather linguistic conventions. Unlike the intuitive cognition of singular entities, whose existence could be verified by the senses, they were abstractions or concepts in the mind and then expressed as precisely as possible by language. Logic, likewise, dealt with propositions in a system of signs, which allow us to make true or false judgments about them, but was not immanent in reality. Even mathematics, Ockham argued, was imposed on the world rather than ontologically prior to our reckoning. Terms of quantity, he argued, were actually connotative concepts, not unequivocal natural signs.[102] Such an attitude might seem uncongenial to the growth of quantitative reasoning in modern science, and certainly many scientists and philosophers of science remained Platonist realists.[103] But ironically, because mathematics was freed from its linkage with actual objects and turned into merely a formal language floating above the world, it was more easily available for application to a wide variety of phenomena.

By violating Aristotle's prohibition against *metabasis* (the illicit transference of reasoning from one domain to another), the nominalists opened the door to a scientific approach to society as well as nature.[104] It was the door Descartes and Leibniz walked through when they promoted a *mathesis universalis* as the foundation of all science.[105]

How one might use language to describe the infinity of individual particulars in the world remained, to be sure, a challenge,[106] and many later efforts were made to forge a workable compromise to restore a delicate balance between subjective construction and objective existence. It was, for example, possible to argue for the ontological solidity of social abstractions that had been historically created but then were reified into structures that came to seem beyond human constitution. Because they were not natural kinds valid for all time, however, they might ultimately be dismantled.[107] Such, for example was the Marxist understanding of commodity fetishism in a capitalist economy, which appeared so well entrenched that it could be compared with the Eucharist as the embodiment of universality in concrete objects.[108] Social abstractions were real enough to function like a second nature, even if they ultimately could be dissolved or de-reified by human action.

All of these efforts to nuance and soften the derealizing implications of nominalism carried to an extreme did have their effect, and continue to do so today. But it is fair to say that the pervasive influence of the conventionalist nominalist critique of real universals in shaping modern culture, in our attitude toward language and elsewhere, has been profound. Even rueful observers like the Catholic hermeneutician Jean Grondin could concede that "nominalism forms the default metaphysics of our time, our basic worldview, out of which it is quite difficult to justify anything like a religious faith," and Jorge Luis Borges observed sourly, to repeat this chapter's epigraph, that "no one [today] says that he is a nominalist, because nobody is anything else."[109]

Nominalism and Political Theory

To illustrate this point, I want to offer a swift, concluding glance at the role often attributed to conventional nominalism in the development of modern political theory and practice. There has been a very lively debate over the claim that all modern political ideas can be understood as mere secularizations of earlier theological ones, with theorists like Carl Schmitt and Karl Löwith pitted against others like Erik Peterson and Hans Blumenberg.[110] Coming down firmly on one or another side depends very much on which theology is invoked, how we interpret the vexed issue of secularization, and whether or not we want to discredit modernity by denying it the "legitimacy" of self-authorization. Without trying to resolve the dispute, it is safe to say that the nominalist assault on realism stimulated fresh thinking about politics in the early-modern era. The post-Aristotelian turn in medieval religion meant that traditional analogies between celestial and mundane orders were undone. The venerable idea of a "cosmopolis" in which the hierarchical order of the medieval polity was understood to echo the ontological great chain of being, an idea that also had similar currency in other cultures such as China, was eroded by the nominalist undermining of the Scholastic compromise.[111] Although a revival of Neoplatonic cosmological thought did occur during the Renaissance, it did not long survive the increasing prestige of modern science. Likewise, analogies between the organic human body and the body politic, classically advanced in the twelfth century in John of Salisbury's *Policraticus*, also gradually lost their force.[112] With their erosion went the rise of two fundamental, if not always fully compatible premises of modern politics: the autonomy of sovereign will and the priority of the individual over corporate or collective entities. Although often interwoven, they can also be examined in isolation, and so we will look at each in turn.

Although the tension between reason and will in politics has never been fully resolved, it is arguable that the balance tipped in favor of the latter in a wide range of modern theories ranging from the divine right of kings to popular sovereignty.[113] The nominalists' faith in divine omnipotence, so it has often been argued, was transferred by analogy to secular leaders claiming unlimited sovereign power.[114] It was not by chance that Habermas could use the contemporary word "decisionistic" to describe the nominalists' valorization of divine will over reason.[115] The term was coined by Carl Schmitt, the Nazi's "crown jurist," who was the most prominent exponent of the idea that the theology of omnipotence was secularized into the unbridled power of the political sovereign.[116] The crucial premise of Schmitt's argument about the transfer of legitimacy from a divine legislator to a secular equivalent was the identification of the former not with the rational God of the Scholastics but with the nominalists' omnipotent God, whose will is unbound by rational constraints. Schmitt denounced contemporary champions of the role of reason in politics, in whatever form, for misunderstanding the essence of "the political," which needs no justification beyond itself. Moral constraints or economic self-interest, which liberalism defended in rational terms, did not trump the exercise of sovereign will in the existential struggle to survive, which Schmitt identified with politics as inherently a contest between friends and foes. Equally problematic was the liberal insistence on the rights of individuals existing prior to the state, which might limit the unchecked power of the sovereign will at the present.[117]

There have, of course, been many critics of Schmitt's resolute attempt to cordon off the political from other values, including the imperative to base legitimacy on rational justifications rather than arbitrary will. Echoes of the dispute over the superiority of God's *potentia absoluta* to his *potentia ordinata* are not hard to hear, which created an ambiguity in Schmitt's analogy that has troubled many subsequent critics. On the one hand, God's *potentia absoluta* is a transcendental capacity, true for all time, which suggests that mundane politics is at the deepest level always already in a permanent state of emergency with no rational constraints. This is the distinction Schmitt and others have made between mere "politics" (*die Politik*) and "the political" (*das Politische*).[118] But there is also the historical moment—the contingent event—when the latter overwhelms the former, and for whatever reason the exercise of arbitrary will breaks through the facade of instituted and codified legality in the same way a miracle suspends the laws of nature. What is a transcendental potentiality becomes, we might say, a manifest actuality, and "the political" and "politics" converge. This happens when the sovereign declares a state of emergency (or exception); that is, he changes something through a performative speech act. It has even been argued a reciprocally constitutive relationship exists between asserting sovereign power and declaring a state of emergency, as one mutually implies rather than precedes the other.[119]

There is, however, a salient difference between a divine command and a human speech act, which Schmitt's identification of one with the other occludes. As commentators on Hobbes have long pointed out, a performative speech act by a mere mortal can change something—or have what linguists call a perlocutionary effect—only when it is carried out in the context of an already constituted set of rules. That is, only a licensed official, secular or religious, can "declare you man and wife" and make it binding. The most salient example of the suspension of a normative order in Schmitt's lifetime came when President Hindenburg of Germany activated the notorious Article 48 of the Weimar Constitution in 1930 to declare a state of emergency and replace parliamentary rule with government by presidential decree. If and when to activate the rule may have been only vaguely stipulated—"if public security and order are seriously disturbed or endangered within the German Reich"—but the legitimate power to do so was legally circumscribed. It was actually intended to save the Republic, not undermine it. Although supposedly temporary, the article served as a precedent for Hitler's Enabling Act after the Reichstag fire three years later, which had a much more permanent effect. The point, however, is that it was enshrined in the constitution that created the Republic, and thus part of a normative order that, paradoxically and inadvertently, countenanced its own suspension. After the war, the framers of the Basic Law of the German Federal Republic were careful to reduce the powers of the president so that he or she would be a genuine figurehead without any potential to govern.

In addition to liberal proceduralists or defenders of deliberative democracy based on rational justification, some critics of Schmitt are latter-day exponents of neo-Aristotelian politics, often refracted through a lingering sympathy for neo-Thomist theology.[120] Nominalism, they charge, may well be the main culprit for the nihilism of our Godless times. What one of their number, the conservative French political philosopher Pierre Manent provocatively called the modern "triumph of the will," even tied the hypertrophy of unconstrained political sovereignty to the rise of twentieth-century totalitarianism.[121] But as Agata Bielik-Robson observes, they have been flying against increasingly powerful headwinds: "*Potentiality opposed to actuality*—as power opposed to passivity, subject opposed to object, energy opposed to matter—creates a powerful organizing scheme in which the former is granted the advantage of infinity and originality against the finite, derivative, and mainly relative status of the latter. With this one revolutionary move, potentiality, so far characteristic of the lowest forms of existence, got translated into an infinite power/potency, which became so suggestive that no Thomistic attempt to return God back to the highest form of actuality could ever succeed."[122]

Ironically, however, attribution of a politics of sovereign, irrational will to nominalism tout court would do violence to the actual political implications drawn by Ockham himself. Deeply involved in the political disputes of his day, in particular the struggle between the papacy and the Holy Roman Emperor, he advocated the separation of church and state rather than the absolute claims of either. Ockham also defended internal limits on the absolute sovereignty of the heads of either institution, which has allowed him to be called a forerunner of constitutionalism and a defender of subjective rights against the state and church.[123] Unlike other critics of papal power, such as Marsilius of Padua, he did not invest sovereign power in church councils either. There is, in other words, no direct line connecting the political views of medieval nominalists and the politics of unconstrained, undivided sovereign will in Schmitt, whose essentialist notion of an ontological "concept of the political" is, moreover, contrary to nominalist thinking. In fact, Blumenberg's contention against Schmitt's political theology, to quote Hannes Bajohr, was that "it was precisely the unbearable omnipotence of the 'decisionist' God against which modernity was founded and which disqualified this structure as a model for politics."[124] That is, rather than a straightforward secularization of religious content, modern politics—at least its pluralist, rhetorically grounded "liberal" version[125]—was a reaction against the potential for tyranny in a simple transfer of substance from divine to human. There is, after all, an important distinction between sovereignty located in a state or a constitution rather than in an actual person (despite efforts from Louis XIV to claim "*l'état, c'est moi*" or Rudolf Hess to assert that "*Hitler aber ist Deutschland, wie Deutschland Hitler ist*").

But whether or not nominalism can be justifiably taxed with the rise of a modern politics of unchecked voluntarism and undivided sovereignty, it certainly had a powerful impact on the rise of another typically modern invention: the individualist political theory that questioned organic notions of the body politic and sacramental ideas of kingship. In his classic study *The King's Two Bodies*, a powerful political metaphor that drew on the distinction between the earthly body of Jesus and the *corpus mysticum* of Christ, Ernst Kantorowicz discerned a shift away from the sacramental veneration of monarchy in Shakespeare's *Tragedy of Richard II* (1595): "A curious change in Richard's attitude—as it were, a metamorphosis from 'Realism' to 'Nominalism'—now takes place. The Universal called 'Kingship' begins to disintegrate; its transcendental 'Reality,' its objective truth and god-like existence, so brilliant shortly before, pales into a nothing, a *nomen*."[126] In other words, belief in monarchy as a sacramental office transcending the creaturely flaws of whomever held it was weakening, a premonition of what would soon follow in the Puritan Revolution of the coming century.

The change was most extensively elaborated in the political theory of Thomas Hobbes, whose extensive debts to nominalism are often acknowledged.[127] As early as 1670, Leibniz even referred to him with alarm as a "super-nominalist" because he reduced truth to a function of human will.[128] Although there are the inevitable debates about the full consistency of his position, Hobbes generally expressed an epistemological skepticism about real universals reflected in his full-throated defense of materialist atomism. A long distance needed to be traveled, to be sure, between the Franciscan theologians who had launched the "nominalist revolution" and the monistic, antispiritualist materialism of an early-modern theorist like Hobbes, whose emphasis on the primordial right to self-preservation owes nothing to Christian doctrine.[129] But however attenuated, the filiation is hard to ignore. It begins with his contribution to the theoretical underpinnings of natural science. Endorsing the nominalists' stress on endless movement over eternal stasis and dynamic force over enduring form, he identified causation in nature with God's initial activity producing bodily motion without a telos. But against the idea of occult forces of any kind, he argued that particular bodies caused particular motions. Lacking any purposive direction or inherent rationality, the world for Hobbes was unremittingly bleak, reflecting, it has often been conjectured, the social and political chaos of his own times in ways reminiscent of the origins of nominalism in the tumultuous fourteenth century.

The nominalist undermining of the harmonious and rational order underlying prior cosmologies has sometimes been understood as leading to a new reliance on sense data over a priori reason as the basis of scientific knowledge. But because the unaided senses often proved unreliable—a realization that was intensified with the discovery of astronomical hindsight[130]—it was necessary to correct direct contemplation by indirect experience through instruments and imaginative construction. As Nicholas of Cusa, among others, understood, empirical data had to be processed methodologically rather than taken at face value. According to Blumenberg: "Hobbes will intensify the nominalistic tendency of this thought experiment dramatically by making the standpoint of natural philosophy independent of the actual existence of the world. He bases its possibility on something that to Descartes could only have appeared as a source of insecurity for reason, namely on mere recollection or representation in imagination."[131]

And as was also the case with the nominalists, Hobbes sought an antidote to contingency in the human capacity to use language to create order where none existed in prior nature.[132] "One still finds the echoes of Ockham's semantics," Calvin Normore writes, "at the beginning of Hobbes' *Leviathan*."[133] Although we lack access to ultimate truths, we manage to assure our self-preservation—our most fundamental right, according to Hobbes—through the conventional imposition of linguistic signs on the chaos of the world, pragmatically producing general words and concepts that yoke together particulars. Even the mathematical language that underpinned scientific inquiry, which Hobbes identified primarily with Euclidean geometry, was as much a human construct as an expression of ontological truths or literal representation of what is the case. Although not always fully consistent in his own usage, he shared the nominalist distrust of the rhetorical use of language, which introduced metaphoric imprecisions and enabled emotional rather than prudential responses to the challenges of self-preservation in a hostile world.[134]

Hobbes's skeptical distrust of the ontological reality of universals and belief in the constructive power of linguistic convention was mirrored in his political theory. Against any notion of an essential political order, which had been disturbed by the vicissitudes of history and might be regained, he posited a prepolitical state of nature—darkly characterized, in the celebrated phrase, as a "war of all against all"—whose chaotic unpredictability necessitated the artificial construction of an expedient to protect individuals from its dangers: the establishment through a voluntary contract of a powerful sovereign state. Once established by a covenant whose actual origins were less historical than the result of a thought experiment, that state promulgated laws that were their own legitimation. Rejecting the Aristotelian belief in laws and rights as relations of equity sanctioned by nature, he argued that they were solely the product of command (or in the oft-quoted phrase, *auctoritas non veritas facem legum*).[135] Thus, "No law can be unjust. The law is made by the sovereign power, and all that is done by such power, is warranted, and owned by everyone of the people."[136] The traditional Roman distinction between authority (*auctoritas*) and power (*potestas*) was for all practical purposes collapsed. Here is where, despite Ockham's own political inclinations, the attenuated filiation with nominalism gains some traction. For a parallel with the nominalist God whose willed acts are by definition good, rather than open to judgment according to a higher ethical standard, is not hard to discern. The sovereign is, in general, the chief stipulator of meanings, imposing binding definitions on the polysemic disorder of the state of nature.

Because the protection of individual safety was that state's ultimate function, Hobbes has sometimes been seen, to quote Leo Strauss, as "the founder of liberalism. The right to the securing of life pure and simple—and this right sums up Hobbes's natural right—has fully the character of an inalienable right, that is of an individual's *claim* that takes precedence over the state and determines its purpose and its limits."[137] Strauss's reading of Hobbes, like so much else in his oeuvre, has been controversial.[138] Liberalism, after all, has often been understood as upholding the value of reason against the irrational exercise of unfettered will, which it identifies with the demagogic potential in raw democracy. But, to cite Sheldon Wolin: "Hobbes, as a good nominalist, rejected an hypostasized reason on the same grounds as he rejected an hypostasized experience: there existed only individual reason and individual experience. And consistent to the last, Hobbes distrusted individual reason as he had individual experience."[139]

How, one might wonder, did the alleged founder of liberalism, come to defend a strong, authoritarian state as a bulwark against anarchy? How did he think the sovereign individual should alienate his power and surrender his subjective rights to an absolute ruler?[140] Rather than hazard yet another answer to these perennial questions, it will suffice for our purposes merely to highlight what have been seen as the nominalist premises allowing him to offer the Leviathan as an antidote to chaos. As Gillespie puts it: "At the root of Hobbes' preference for an absolute monarch is a nominalist understanding of human relations. He believes that humans cooperate and keep their covenants only because it is in their interests to do so and that they will break them when they can achieve some benefit by doing so. Thus they must be forced to keep their promises. This argument rests on Hobbes' assumption that human beings are absolute individuals."[141] There is, moreover, an echo of the nominalist conceptualization of God in Hobbes's postulation of the absolute sovereign who protects the individual, while at the same time expropriating his autonomy. His power may not be an ontological given, as it had been for the omnipotent God of the Franciscans, nor bestowed directly by God, as postulated by the divine right of kingship doctrine. But once he has been granted it by the people through the artificial covenant that creates the Leviathan, he is just as unaccountable to the individuals who agreed to it: "Like the nominalist God he is no man's debtor."[142]

Much more can be said about the ambiguous implications of the conventional nominalist legacy in Hobbes's political theory, which continued to reverberate in the thought of many of his successors. We might turn, for example, to John Locke, who developed the individualist implications of nominalism, while softening Hobbes's advocacy of a strong state sovereign on the model of an omnipotent god-like law-giver.[143] Or we could investigate the importance of nominalism for the liberal tradition in general, which, in fact, has gained renewed currency in the work of recent commentators like Larry Siedentop.[144] It would, moreover, be fruitful to examine the nominalist impulse in nonliberal traditions as well, for example anarchism. In fact, whenever collective political concepts like "the state," "the nation," "the people," "the community," or "the proletariat" are criticized as essentialized reifications and shown to be historical rather than natural constructs, the impact of the nominalist legacy is apparent.

* * *

Having established the central importance of conventional nominalism and explored some of its implications in philosophy, language, science, and politics, we can now turn our attention to the real subject of this exercise: the nonhegemonic variant of nominalism that has hitherto attracted far less attention, which we will call its "magical" counterpart. Existing, at least virtually, at the margins of medieval thought and far from the mainstream of Christian theology, it has been ignored even by those historians who want to stress the central role played by nominalism in the origins of modernity. But as we hope to show, it has led a remarkable underground existence with important consequences in our own time.

Unlike conventional nominalism, its shadow "magical" cousin cannot be understood by employing Weber's neo-Kantian method of heuristic "ideal types" or unified analytic constructs created by imagining a singular representative exemplar. Nor can it be revealed by tracing a cumulative semantic essentialization over time in the self-labeling usage of those who will come to serve as unwitting stars in the paradigmatic constellation that will gradually reveal its meaning. For they were not protagonists in a story they consciously experienced themselves. Instead, magical nominalism will have to appear retrospectively through the analogical elaboration of overlapping exemplars or cases, which show facets of what cannot be posited in advance by a stipulative definition.

It would, of course, be disingenuous to pretend there is no agency on my part, at least in the coinage of the term, which draws on the more familiar notion of "magical realism." The latter was introduced by the German art critic Franz Roh during the Weimar Republic to characterize the *Neue Sachlichkeit* (new objectivity or sobriety), the postexpressionist art movement that depicted objects and people with uncanny, if detached matter-of-factness. His 1925 book *Nach Expressionismus: Magischer Realismus: Probleme der neuesten europäischen Malerei* was translated into Spanish by Fernando Vela two years later, making the term also available for literary appropriation in the Hispanic world. As a genre blurring the distinction between realism and surrealist fantasy, which depicted a world charged with the marvelous in a matter-of-fact way, magical realism came into its own in the mid-twentieth century. Although retroactively applicable to writers like Kafka, it emerged as a recognizable literary movement in Latin America led by like Miguel Ángel Asturias, José Marti, Gabriel García Márquez, and Jorge Amado, who were soon joined by such Anglophone authors as Toni Morrison, Salman Rushdie, and Angela Carter.[145]

In an aesthetic setting, the concept of realism has, of course, long since lost its association with the medieval belief in the ontological reality of universals. It would therefore be misleading to posit magical nominalism as an antonym to magical realism, and it is not being introduced here with that intention. We are displacing it instead into a different semantic context: as an alternative to the conventional variant of nominalism we have just outlined. Doing so will lead to several valuable insights. It will help us avoid the frequent, but reductive identification of nominalism tout court with the "disenchantment of the world" that inexorably led to the positivist mentality.[146] It will allow us to sever the connection of nominalism with the hypertrophy of subjective human will and self-assertion that abetted the domination of nature, underpinning instead what can be called "anthrodecentrism."[147] And it will alert us to the endurance in the modern world of the Middle Age's capacity for wonder (*admiratio*), which, so argues the medievalist Carolyn Walker Bynum, served as the appropriate response to what John of Salisbury called "marvelous singularity."[148]

The impulses that fed into magical nominalism may be found in ways of thinking that were as nonrational—a term that avoids the negative connotation of "irrational"—as conventional nominalism with its debt to Franciscan notions of God's absolute, unlimited will. They exceeded, however, those that remained within the bounds of Christian theology, whether rationalist or voluntarist. Some were Jewish in origin, in particular the heterodox traditions that emerged outside of traditional rabbinic teaching. Others must be derived from sources that often intersected with religion, Christian or Jewish, but need to be appreciated on their own terms. That is, we have to take seriously the "magic" in magical nominalism and address its abiding role in our putatively postenchanted world.

2

Magical Nominalism

God's language has no grammar, it consists only of names. The oldest Kabbalists—Nahmanides, for example—profess to have received as tradition this understanding of the structure of the Torah. It is clear, however, that this was originally a tradition of a magical character, now transposed into a mystical tradition.

GERSHOM SCHOLEM

Magic and Science

Before exploring the underground tradition of magical nominalism, we have to pause for a moment and reflect on the name we have imposed on it, a name that was not chosen by the participants themselves. "Magical," after all, is an adjective freighted with millennia of controversy. The word comes from the Greek *mageia*, which the ancient Greeks used to describe the priests (*magai*) of their Persian enemies.[1] Whether modifying "realism" or "nominalism," the adjective "magical" invites resistance from many different quarters, at least when it refers to more than an aesthetic movement. Although we still invoke it figuratively to register delight and enchantment, its literal meaning has, at least for most of us, lost its allure. Even those who refrain from dismissively identifying it with deliberate charlatanry or sleight-of-hand legerdemain often damn it as a dangerously illusory belief system and inefficacious array of practices. Along with myth and superstition, it often serves as the stigmatized "other" of reason in its various forms, and "magical thinking" has come to be synonymous with irrational fantasy and imaginative delusion. If no longer provoking the cultural panic that could lead to the burning of witches or exorcism of demons, it remains a powerful term of opprobrium in our own day.[2]

Magic's often pejorative connotation is a result of its being long engaged in a two-front war, which shows no signs of ending.[3] On one front, it faces the combatant called "science," which distances itself from magic by promoting methodological protocols and institutional accountability that can verify or at least falsify truth claims about the natural—and sometimes social—world. Science, at least aspirationally,[4] rests those claims on the replication of results by anyone who can test them through controlled experiments, while magic, it is often assumed, remains an elite enterprise practiced by adepts with the esoteric knowledge of secret techniques that remain hidden from the uninitiated. Understood as an ideal type, the modern scientist, educationally credentialed, professionally certified, and subject to correction based on ongoing testing, is worlds apart from the shaman, wizard, or magus, whose "research" is never vetted by peer-reviewed journals or practical results confirmed through disinterested evaluation. Whereas the former seeks collaboratively approved and exoterically shared knowledge, while scorning the authority of ancient texts, the latter restricts the circle of initiates, jealously guards the esoteric status of their knowledge, and honors the arcane wisdom in "hermetic" sources or *prisca magia* preserved from the distant past, typically ascribed to the Egyptians.[5]

There is, in addition, an important difference between a scientific and magical conception of the world, which shows the former's debt to conventional nominalism. In *Dialectic of Enlightenment*, Max Horkheimer and Theodor W. Adorno argue that the scientific notion of uniform matter underlying reality worked to make everything indifferently fungible. As a result, "The manifold affinities between existing things are supplanted by the single relationship between the subject who confers meaning and the meaningless object, between rational significance and its accidental bearer."[6] In contrast, magic preserved a memory of those affinities, as "dream and image were not regarded as mere signs of things but were linked to them by resemblance or name. The relationship was not one of intention but of kinship. Magic like science is concerned with ends, but it pursues them through mimesis, not through an increasing distance from objects."[7]

The differentiation of science from magic (sometimes then stigmatized as "pseudoscience") in medieval and early-modern Europe was, to be sure, an uneven process, with many now seemingly incommensurable traditions of thought and practice—astronomy and astrology, chemistry and alchemy, probabilistic futurology and geomantic divination—originally overlapping and intertwined.[8] The magical sympathies of figures like the thirteenth-century Franciscan Roger Bacon, who is often lauded as a pioneer of empirical science, have been acknowledged.[9] The differential in efficacy between legitimate medical practices and magical healing—ranging from the "king's touch" to the potions and charms of "cunning men"—was not very wide at a time when the former was not yet based on rigorous science and the latter could draw on what we now call a "placebo effect." It has also been easy to show that the heroes of the early-modern Scientific Revolution—Copernicus, Paracelsus, Galileo, Bruno, Francis

Bacon, and even Newton—held on to beliefs that we would now clearly reject as residues of an earlier magical way of thinking. In fact, after the alchemical papers of the last of these figures were opened in 1936, John Maynard Keynes could say that "Newton was not the first of the Age of Reason. He was the last of the magicians."[10] Even the categorical distinction between exoteric science and esoteric magic did not always obtain, as a publicly available literature for aspiring adepts of the latter has been found as early as the Greco-Egyptian papyri handbooks for apprentice magicians.[11] An extensive corpus of demonological writings circulated among early-modern practitioners of witchcraft and drew on the categories of Aristotelian natural philosophy.[12]

The practice of what came to be called natural magic during the revival of Neoplatonism in the Renaissance, spelled out in such works as Marsilio Ficino's *De Vita* (1489), sought to explain occult phenomena without reference to the alleged agency of demonic or spiritual forces, which was denounced as "black magic." As a result, it could be understood as continuous with the protoscientific natural philosophy of its day.[13] Both rejected the medieval attitude of contemplative awe of God's creation in favor of an experimental and inductive testing of the natural world. A similar relationship can be discerned between such magical belief systems as astrology and social science, for example in the way the former's elaborate mathematical calculations of recurrent celestial events anticipated the algorithmic study of big data by the latter.[14] As Keith Thomas put it, "In their confident assumption that the principles underlying the development of human society were capable of human explanation, we can detect the germ of modern sociology."[15]

It would, however, be hard to deny that in most respects the ultimate differentiation of science from magic was successful, with the latter surviving in large measure only as harmless popular entertainment. Although a transitional figure like Francis Bacon was indebted to Renaissance hermetic magicians like Cornelius Agrippa, he differed from them in insisting that the secrets of nature be shared and tested rather than guarded, as it so often was, as the possession of a privileged elite.[16] Affixed to that already mentioned image of the ship passing through the Pillars of Hercules on the frontispiece to Bacon's *Novum Organon* was a motto from the Vulgate: *Multi pertransibunt & augebitur scientia* (many shall pass through and knowledge shall be increased.)[17]

The cumulative achievements that resulted from the renunciation of esoteric knowledge soon had an impact on popular attitudes toward magic. Beginning with the Enlightenment, menacing folk stories were domesticated into children's fairy tales, ghosts could be technologically simulated by phantasmagorias (also called magic lanterns), demonic possessions replicated by ventriloquists, and witches, once feared as genuine rivals in the struggle to master the world, turned into little more than harmless Halloween characters.[18] Astrological beliefs may still have been held by Galileo and Kepler, but philosophes like Pierre Bayle and Pierre Gassendi rejected them outright, ending with their survival for the most part only as daily horoscopes to give dubious guidance to gullible newspaper readers. Although "the age of reason" still grappled with the lure of esotericism—Masonic lodges with their hermetic traditions were an important site of contestation[19]—the wind was blowing mostly in one direction. With the increasingly impressive achievements of science in the nineteenth and twentieth centuries, its superiority was conclusively established. If you are diagnosed with a life-threatening disease, after all, it seems for most of us today wiser to entrust your fate to modern medicine than to consult a shaman or witch doctor.

And yet, as in the comparable case of "secularization,"[20] in which religion was likewise supposed to be vanquished but now enjoys a new resurgence in many quarters, the victory of science over magic has never been fully complete. Some scholars have even spoken approvingly of the flourishing of new modes of enchantment in both esoteric and exoteric forms in the modern world.[21] We may, for example, no longer respect traditional geomancy, but it has returned through the back door, as it were, with the semiserious popularity of Chinese feng shui. As a result, the absolute contrast posited between magic and science has weakened. Both, we now appreciate, require the suspension of naive belief in raw, unmediated experience and a willingness to doubt common sense. Both often employ mathematical procedures to reveal patterns that may not be available to empirical verification, or at least not immediately.[22] Both frequently rely on modes of analogical thinking, if in different ways.[23] Both are often keen to move from knowledge of the world to power over it.[24] And both claim they operate by following the procedural dictates of "method," however one defines that highly contested term, to get access to a hitherto occulted reality unreachable through immediate sense experience or raw intuition.[25]

The traffic between science and magic, it is also now widely acknowledged, has gone in both directions. For not only have scientific claims once deemed respectable been debunked as akin to magical thinking, but much that we now accept as scientifically valid—natural phenomena like magnetism, for example, or technological achievements like space travel—would have once been deemed closer to magic. The confusion between magic and science appeared not only early in their relationship, and especially flourished in the Renaissance, but also arguably continues in the most advanced recesses of modern science in our own day. Or so it would seem from the oft-quoted observation of the celebrated twentieth-century science writer Arthur C. Clarke that "any sufficiently advanced technology is indistinguishable from magic."[26] Even when it comes to the "human sciences," the popular linear narrative of inexorable disenchantment in the modern world seems no less vulnerable to question.[27]

Magic and Religion

If one unstable front in the war between magic and its opponents is with science, another, earlier in origin, is with religion, where boundary maintenance may be even harder to justify than in the case of science. Here too, uncertain terms of engagement and shifting lines of demarcation have produced a vast literature that defies easy summation. There is, in fact, no simple consensus on what the generic term "religion" may mean, or whether or not generalizations from the history of Christianity can be imposed on the other traditions that fall under that rubric.[28] But broadly speaking, it seems safe to say that those who distinguish between magic and religion fall into two camps. The first consists of religious believers intent on justifying the validity of their faith and policing its borders, which are threatened with infiltration from without or reinfection from within. The second includes scholars—typically, anthropologists, sociologists, and historians—who may well be indifferent to the validity claims of specific religions but agree that religion and magic constitute two distinct, albeit sometimes overlapping, belief systems, institutional traditions, and ritual practices.

The theological struggle to distinguish between genuine religion and its abjected others, magic in particular, has taken many different forms. During what has come to be called the axial age, the era around 500 BCE when the major world religions arose,[29] the moral dimension of religion emerged into prominence as ethical prophets and rule-enforcing priests shunted aside charismatic magicians. Committing a "sin" replaced the breaking of a "taboo" as the primary religious transgression. An essentially transcendent notion of divinity, albeit with a God who could intervene at his pleasure in human affairs, supplanted a pantheon of gods whose lives often intersected with those of mere mortals. Monotheism, in particular the religion of the Israelites (or Judaism, as it later became known),[30] sought to eliminate competition from alternative claimants, magicians as well as other gods, to control the natural and historical world.[31] Whereas the line between magic and religion had often been blurred in polytheistic "pagan" cultures, a jealous monotheistic God determined to delegitimize all rivals recognized the dangers in sharing supernatural powers with them.[32] The development of theology itself—the rational "logos" using argumentation rather than mythical narration or gnomic pronouncements to understand God and his workings in the world[33]—and the designation of certain texts as sacred "scripture," often codifying ethical commands and presenting exemplary parables, was introduced to debunk the irrational secrets of magical rituals. Condemnations of idolatry, classically expressed by the prohibition on images of divinity in the Hebrew Bible, had a similar target. As Jan Assmann has explained: "Images are media of a 'magical' representation of an absent divine power and therefore imply or presuppose the idea of divine absence. The 'living God' hides and reveals himself as he chooses and forbids any attempt at a magical summoning of his presence."[34] And perhaps most important of all, religions ambitiously explained the riddles of human existence, offered hope for an afterlife, and provided meaningful rituals to regulate daily life in ways that magic never seriously attempted.

In both the Jewish and Christian campaigns to quarantine genuine religion away from the contagion of deceptive magic, the positing of God's ability to reveal himself at his discretion allowed the category of "miracle" to be distinguished from an act of magic. Thus, in the book of Exodus in the Hebrew Bible, God miraculously turns Aaron's rod into a serpent, which then swallows the serpents created from Egyptian rods by their sorcerers, an act which demonstrates his greater power.[35] The New Testament similarly identifies a man named Simon

> who had previously practiced magic in the city and amazed the nation of Sama'ria, saying that he himself was somebody great. They all gave heed to him, from the least to the greatest, saying, "This man is that power of God which is called Great." And they gave heed to him, because for a long time he had amazed them with his magic. But when they believed Philip as he preached good news about the kingdom of God and the name of Jesus Christ, they were baptized, both men and women. Even Simon himself believed, and after being baptized he continued with Philip. And seeing signs and great miracles performed, he was amazed.[36]

Whether Jesus was himself considered by his contemporaries more as a magician than the son of God remains an open question even until our own times, if Morton Smith's controversial *Jesus the Magician* is any indication.[37]

For the pious believer, however, divine miracles are distinct from acts of magic, even when the latter are more than fraudulent tricks, not only because of their superior potency, but also because of their source and aim. Miracles are gifts that come only from God or his holy delegates—saints and the like—and are signs and wonders meant to reveal his glory; they suspend the laws of nature and testify to his omnipotent will, as we noted in discussing the role played by the God's *potentia absoluta* in challenging Scholastic realism. Magic, is contrast, involves either colluding with demons or the manipulation of already existing occult forces rather than creating new ones, and typically seeks to bring only the magician glory and profit.[38] Although both magical and religious rituals are performative acts, which are intended to bring about a desired result, the former do so by transferring the power of the supernatural force to the magician, while the latter are acts of supplication or placation in which God remains the ultimate source of the outcome. Whereas miracles reinforce the sense of man's dependence on God, magic asserts human power over occult forces (which helps explain its affinity to science).[39] Spells are supposed to function automatically, if the correct formula is used, whereas prayers are answered entirely at God's discretion. The first summons up and harnesses occult forces, the second intercedes with and supplicates a (hopefully) merciful God.

The criteria for distinguishing magical events from miracles, however, have not always been fully clear or persuasive. In fact, according to the historian Richard Kieckhefer, "The terms 'magic' and 'religion' were both current in medieval discourse, but they would not usually have been viewed as opposites or even as essentially distinct categories."[40] Instead, they were more like points on a spectrum in what one historian has called "a system of the sacred" than diametrically opposed.[41] Some Christian ceremonies, in particular the Mass, were somewhere in the middle.[42] Often magical charms were employed side by side with prayer as a means to bring about desired changes.[43] And when attempts to distinguish between magic and religion were made, it was not always clear what standards were being employed. Was it the discrepancy in power that mattered, as if God's advantage over his competitors were merely a test of their comparative virility? Or did a true miracle only involve a benign rather than malevolent purpose, and if so, who was to decide between them? Pharaoh's minions may have had, after all, a different evaluation of the superior power of Aaron's rod cum serpent. Why, moreover, did God's commandments, spelling out the right way to live a moral life and express pious devotion, need the added support of a suspension of natural laws to secure their observation? Why did a person who has genuine and abiding faith even need the testimony of his senses to convince him that his devotion to an omnipotent deity is justified (an argument often aimed as well at an apparently self-interested desire for eternal salvation)?

One perennial response to questions like these, prominent for example in the Protestant Reformation, has been the effort to cleanse religion of excessive reliance on awe-inspiring displays of God's glory in his exercise of supernatural power, displays which invite the reproach of being continuous with pagan magic. Some of the religious disdain for such magic, we might say, spilled over into a comparable suspicion of miracles and loss of faith in the efficacy of the sacraments. Of the seven consecrated by the Catholic Church—baptism, confirmation, marriage, the Mass, ordination, penance and extreme unction—only baptism and the Eucharist consumed during the Mass, but now understood only symbolically, survived among Protestants. A driving impulse of the Reformation, historians have long argued, was explicit hostility to the excessive reliance on miraculous powers, especially those allegedly exercised by saints, in the traditional church.[44] For their critics, they were merely displaced expressions of superstitious magic. Although in its struggle with pagan competitors, the early church had sought to win converts by incorporating still potent practices, symbols, holy places, and even objects in its own sacred arsenal, it now seemed time to purify Christianity of such dubious residues of the past. In fact, historians have located growing unease with magical practices in the church even in the centuries before the Reformation.[45]

Late fifteenth-century Renaissance humanists like Pico della Mirandola and Johannes Reuchlin had inspired a brief quickening of interest among learned men in the magical implications of the Jewish Kabbalah. But it was soon driven underground by the campaign against witchcraft initiated by the Dominicans, which reached a crescendo with the influential *Malleus Maleficarum* (*Hammer of Witches*) written in 1486 by Heinricus Institoris and Jacobus Sprenger. Often that campaign was fueled by a literal demonization of the Jews, which led, among other things, to the notorious "blood libel" in which Jews were accused of sacrificing Christian children to make unleavened matzoh.[46] As shown by the cautionary tale of Faust's pact with the devil, which gained widespread currency after the publication of Johan Spies's *Faustbuch* in 1587, seeking to master the occult arts had become a sure path to damnation.[47]

For Protestants, the word of God in scripture took precedence over signs and wonders, which could easily be the work of the devil or his earthly minions, such as witches (not by chance, usually identified as women, the gender typically accused of deviously practicing black magic).[48] Although Luther did allow room for the efficacy of some miracles and held on to the idea of Christ's "real presence" in the Eucharist (albeit through consubstantiation rather than transubstantiation),[49] he railed against the supposed bleeding of Communion wafers, the fetishism of holy relics, and the performing of miracles by statues of the Virgin Mary. Often these were merely excuses for the gullible to give offerings and buy amulets and indulgences from corrupt sellers.[50] The widespread and indiscriminate practice of sacramentalizing objects through blessings, along with its opposite, the exorcising of demons, was now understood to be driven as much by mundane, instrumental purposes as soteriological ones. The esoteric powers of priests were radically curbed with the leveling of the church hierarchy in the Reformation. In addition, the indirect effect of praising the value of hard work and self-help, especially among Calvinists, was to undercut the appeal of what, according to Keith Thomas, were "the cheap solutions offered by magic, not just because they were wicked, but because they were too easy."[51]

Ironically, however, the Reformation also enabled the inadvertent return of magical thinking in a new guise. As Robert Scribner has noted, the Protestant campaign against the medieval church's transformation of residues of pagan magic into the allegedly miraculous actions of a benevolent God could open the door for their reappearance:

> Deprived of the protective means inherent in the Catholic sacramental system, Protestants found themselves prey to anxiety that was hardly allayed by invoking the Protestant doctrine of providence. Indeed, anxiety may even have been increased by awareness of the omnipresence of a sacred order in and among the secular. I do not mean just the activity of God, his Word and his Spirit, or of the Devil. Protestant belief allowed for a whole range of supernatural beings to be active in the world, especially angels, demons, and various kinds of spirits, such as those of the revenant dead.[52]

In such a frightening world, where benign ecclesiastical magic no longer could be counted on, nonreligious sorcery could flourish, leading to hysteria about witches accused of gaining their power through a sinister pact with the devil.[53] The countermagic needed to combat it was also outsourced to nonreligious actors, who often filled the vacuum left by a clergy no longer able to summon sacramental powers. Scribner thus concludes:

> Protestantism was as caught up as Catholicism in the same dilemmas about the instrumental application of sacred power to secular life because it was positioned in the same force-field of sacrality. For this reason, Protestants experienced the same difficulties as Catholics when accusations of maleficent magic (and sometimes even of "white" magic) were laid in ways that turned them into accusations of witchcraft. The possibility of consorting with, and becoming implicated in, demonic activity was as real for Protestants as for Catholics.[54]

It may, in fact, have only been with the arrival of the coldly rational God of Enlightenment Deism that Christianity found a way to purge itself of magical residues, which could now be seen as merely irrational superstitions rather than the improper use by demons of legitimate religious rituals.[55]

Faced with the difficulty of abjecting magic entirely from religion properly understood, some observers came grudgingly to acknowledge the inextricable intertwining of the two. For example, in *The Idea of the Holy* (1917), the early twentieth-century German theologian Rudolf Otto conceded: "It must be admitted that when religious evolution first begins sundry curious phenomena confront us, preliminary to religion proper and deeply affecting its subsequent course. Such are the notions of 'clean' and 'unclean,' belief in and worship of the dead, belief in and worship of 'souls' or 'spirits,' magic, fairy tale, and myth, homage to natural objects, whether frightful or extraordinary, noxious or advantageous, the strange idea of 'power' (*orenda* or *mana*), fetishism and totemism, worship of animal and plant, daemonism and polydaemonism."[56] He then added: "Different as these things are, they are all haunted by a common—and that a numinous—element, which is easily identifiable."[57] By "numinous" Otto meant a nonrational, uncanny feeling of awe and wonder inspired by the object and not merely a subjective projection of the believing self on to it, and which is the *mysterium tremendum et fascinans* of all religious experience, even today. Accordingly, Otto could argue that there are inevitably magical elements in all great religious art—"The magical is nothing but the suppressed and dimmed form of the numinous, a crude form of it which great art purifies and ennobles"[58]—and see divination not only in primitive Christianity but continuing in its contemporary manifestations. Rather, in other words, than seeing magic and religion intertwined only in the earlier stages of their development, he concluded that the former remained a force even in the latter's mature stages. Here Otto overlapped with certain nonreligious commentators on the relationship between the two, who came at the distinction from an anthropological or sociological point of view.

Magic and Social Science

If attempts within theology to build a firewall between religion and magic were never fully successful, the same might be said of comparable efforts made by allegedly neutral social scientific commentators on the issue from the outside.[59] Some, to be sure, echoed the narrative of increasing purification derived from the Reformation critique of the medieval church. Max Weber, for example, adopted it in his famous study of *The Protestant Ethic and the Spirit of Capitalism*:

> That great historic process in the development of religions, the elimination of magic from the world [*die Entzauberung der Welt*] which had begun with the old Hebrew prophets and, in conjunction with Hellenistic scientific thought, had repudiated the magical means to salvation as superstition and sin, came here to its logical conclusion. The genuine Puritan even rejected all signs of religious ceremony at the grave and buried his nearest and dearest without song or ritual in order that no superstition, no trust in the effects of magical and sacramental forces on salvation, should creep in.[60]

Weber's celebrated argument about the influence of the Protestant ethic on the capitalist spirit, and the accumulation of capital it inadvertently enabled, presupposed that religion—or at least the Protestant tradition in which he had been nurtured—had indeed been purified of its magical residues. "The radical elimination of magic from the world," he wrote, "allowed no other psychological course than the practice of worldly asceticism."[61] In comparative terms, this distinction divided the Protestant Christianity of the developed Western world from its counterparts elsewhere. "Only ascetic Protestantism completely eliminated magic and the supernatural quest for salvation, of which the highest form was intellectualist, contemplative illumination. It alone created the religious motivations for seeking salvation primarily through immersion in one's worldly vocation [*Beruf*]."[62] Thus, for example, China, so Weber claimed, was blocked in its development of natural science as well as economic rationalization by the persistence of animistic magic.[63]

Weber's narrative of progressive disenchantment in the modern, secularizing West was, however, challenged by a very different "dialectical" notion of the ways in which the capitalist version of modernism was understood to be itself imbued with the very magical and religious forces it claimed to have left behind. In the Marxist tradition, capitalism, for all its reliance on materialist self-interest, is understood to be haunted by what it purports to have overcome. As the historian Michael Saler contends, Marx's "writings on modernity abound with metaphors and similes of enchantment—specters, ghosts, fetishes, etc., linking the modern world with the religious world it supposedly had surmounted."[64] In a similar vein, Horkheimer and Adorno detected strong residues of myth, magic, and other signs of demonic irrationality in the modern world of instrumental rationality and the capitalist "culture industry" in their *Dialectic of Enlightenment*.[65]

Other sociologists and anthropologists, while sharing a skepticism about the "disenchantment [or more literally, demagification] of the world" and the linear, supersessionist narrative posited by Weber, also kept their distance from the dialectical alternative posited by Marx and his followers.[66] Rather than characterizing magic as an outmoded cultural set of beliefs and practices thankfully left behind by modernization or one that, alas, still haunted capitalist modernity in problematic ways, they offered a more nuanced, even forgiving, appreciation of its virtues. For example, Sir James Frazer concluded his celebrated study of *The Golden Bough* (1890) on a proto-Weberian note by asserting: "Whereas the order on which magic reckons is merely an extension, by false analogy, of the order in which ideas present themselves to our minds, the order laid down by science is derived from patient and exact observation of the phenomena themselves."[67] But then at the end of his great work, Frazer could not resist qualifying his faith in the superiority of science by adding that it too may itself be supplanted in the future, as "in the last analysis magic, religion and science are nothing but theories of thought."[68]

Paradoxically, the extraordinary time and effort spent by Frazer in comparing the varieties of magical thought throughout "primitive" human cultures—he was an armchair anthropologist synthesizing the original research of other ethnographers and folklorists—resulted in a new fascination with, even respect for what he had collected. The impact of *The Golden Bough* on leading aesthetic modernists, such as James Joyce, William Butler Yeats, D. H. Lawrence, and T. S. Eliot, is now widely acknowledged.[69] So too is Frazer's influence on Freud's speculations on the ur-history of the species and the survival of many "primitive" impulses in the unconscious of modern men and women. Despite his avowed skeptical intentions and evolutionary assumptions, Frazer's work thus encouraged some to seek the aesthetic reenchantment of the world and others to acknowledge the abiding power of "primitive" impulses in the unconscious of modern men and women.[70] Even in our own day, despite all of the attempts to discredit his scholarship, challenge his universalist ambitions, and even condemn his implicit colonialist mentality, Fraser still can find his defenders.[71]

On the issue of magic in particular, Frazer's contributions still merit recognition. *The Golden Bough* begins with an account of the ways in which magic was a fundamental attribute of priestly kingship in many cultures throughout history, enabling the king endowed with supernatural powers to assure the fertility of the tribe and the natural world that feeds it. Frazer underlined the widespread connection between early kingship and the use of magical powers to master the forces of nature, such as rainfall and fertility, for the benefit of the community. In other words, he showed that magicians could be more than members of a selfish, maleficent elite working for their own benefit (or to serve the devil's agenda), but also seek to serve the people over whom they ruled. Before the differentiation of secular and sacred realms, a process that was uneven and often contested, a king/priest could enlist the powers of magic for benign purposes. Indeed, his legitimate authority was often based on the successful exercise of such powers.

Frazer's second contribution was the distinction he drew within magic itself, which "rests everywhere on two fundamental principles: first, that *like produces like*, effect resembling cause; second, that *things which have once been in contact continue ever afterwards to act on each other*. The former principle may be called the Law of Similarity; the latter that of Contact or Contagion."[72] Following the first law, what he called "homeopathic" magic drew on the power of imitation or likeness to bring about a desired result (or prevent an undesired one). The mimesis, for example, of a man by an image or a miniature doll worked through a sympathetic connection to produce an effect in the intended target. The cosmos, in short, contained occult correspondences, which could be manipulated by a skilled magician. Contagious magic worked less by likeness than by enduring contiguity, in which a severed part of a man, say his nails, teeth or hair, could also act as a conduit back to the target through a sympathetic connection. A great deal of attention has been paid to Frazer's pioneering analysis of sympathetic magic, both mimetic and contagious, over the years, as well as its echoes in the thinking of modern artists and theorists.[73] We will encounter it again while discussing figures like Walter Benjamin and Theodor W. Adorno.[74]

Frazer, however, also listed other modalities of magical thinking, including the magic of proper names, which as we will discuss shortly, was a crucial component of magical nominalism. This particular variant of magic admittedly was not foregrounded in Frazer. Nor did it play a central role in the work of another early theorist of the overlap between religion and magic, the pioneering French sociologist Émile Durkheim. Durkheim, in fact, was an explicit critic of nominalism in general, and its social scientific expression in methodological individualism in particular. Society, he insisted, is ontologically real and irreducible to an aggregate of its members. He was, in the jargon of a later era, a methodological holist rather than a methodological individualist.

It is nonetheless valuable to include Durkheim in any consideration of the relationship between religion and magic, because he approached the question from a very different direction from Weber and departed in significant ways from Frazer. In his seminal work on *The Elementary Forms of Religious Life* (1912), Durkheim included both religion and magic in his discussion of "the sacred" as a displaced expression of the social community as a whole. An array of prohibitions set it radically apart from the realm of "the profane," where base material interests and utilitarian motives prevail. Humans are *homo duplex*, living in both worlds. "Sacred things," Durkheim contended, "are those which the interdictions protect and isolate; profane things, those to which these interdictions are applied and which must remain at a distance from the first."[75] Both religion and magic have rites and beliefs, dogmas and myths, ceremonies and sacrifices, and both often invoke the same sacred forces, such as the souls of the dead.

But there are crucial differences, which often lead to an explicit conflict between them. Whereas religions show devotion to the sacred and its symbols, "magic takes a sort of professional pleasure in profaning holy things; in its rites, it performs the contrary of religious ceremony."[76] Religion, moreover, finds sustained institutional expression in an organized church, a manifestation of common worship and moral community, which includes the laity as well as clergy.[77] Magic, on the other hand, is more episodic, lacks moral gravity, and never creates a lasting fellowship that embraces both magicians and their clients. Rather, in other words, than expressing a positive devotion to the social community, it operates on its fringes, tacitly working to subvert its cohesive solidarity.[78] Although never entirely crossing the threshold between the sacred and the profane, it betokens a privatization of spirituality that undercuts its public function. Whereas religions are inherently normative, affirming in displaced form social unity, magic is thus more utilitarian and individualist in nature.[79]

Durkheim also challenged Frazer's assumption that magic antedated religion. "Quite on the contrary, it was under the influence of religious ideas that the precepts upon which the art of the magician is based were established, and it was only through a secondary extension that they were applied to purely lay relations."[80] Drawing on the study of magic by his colleagues on the journal *Année sociologique*, Henri Hubert and Marcel Mauss, Durkheim further argued that Frazer's discussion of "sympathetic magic" was imprecise. "There are sympathetic rites, but they are not peculiar to magic: not only are they to be found in religion, but it was from religion that magic received them. . . . We are now able to understand how it comes that magic is so full of religious elements: it is because it was born of religion."[81]

This is not the place to sort out all of the implications of Durkheim's work on religion and magic, which has stirred a century of controversy.[82] It is only important to note that he contributed in lasting ways to the ongoing debate on the persistence of both in a world that Weber prematurely called "disenchanted."[83] By following Frazer in raising the question of the survival of "primitive" impulses in the most advanced versions of religion and then including magic in the larger category of the "sacred," Durkheim called into question a simple evolutionary model of progressive disenchantment. Like Rudolf Otto with his notions of "the holy" and "the numinous," Durkheim posited "the sacred" as a fundamental impulse in all religions, with importance for magic as well.[84] Despite the bureaucratization of churches over time—what Weber would have called the "routinization of charisma"—a residue of the collective "effervescence" of the elementary forms of religious life survived. But by flagging the disruptive and marginalized implications of magic in contrast with religion's reinforcement of communal devotion to the social whole, Durkheim also opened the door—against his own intentions—for those who might be attracted to magic as a practice with critical rather than conservative potential.

A final seminal contribution to our understanding of the relationship between magic and religion was made by the Polish-born, British anthropologist Bronisław Malinowski, who unlike Frazer, Weber, or Durkheim, had the advantage of extensive fieldwork experience, which he gained in the Trobriand Islands in Melanesia. In his influential paper "Magic, Science and Religion" (1925), Malinowski acknowledged his debts to Frazer, whose analyses of totemism, sacrifice, initiation, and communion he extended, and whose stress on sympathetic reasoning in magic he embraced. Magic, he agreed with Frazer, is often practiced by a prominent community leader, and is functional in the integration of that community.

But Malinowski rejected the assumption that magic was a feature of "primitive" cultures to be supplanted by religion and then science.[85]

Against the claims that the mentalities of early or "backward" peoples were "prelogical," superstitious, and mystical, made most famously by the French philosopher and anthropologist Lucien Lévy-Bruhl, he insisted that they too could infer from empirical evidence to analyze the world and solve problems.[86] When that failed, magic would then be the next resort. All cultures have practices that might be construed as fitting into each category, if in different proportions. All need stratagems to deal with the threats of an unforgiving environment and the fear of death, and have to compensate when they fail to thwart them. Magic, he argued, is a practical response to more individual needs in the face of personal uncertainty, whereas religion addresses larger social questions with more transcendent answers. There are, however, exceptional conditions when magic returns: "Wherever there is great danger, uncertainty, great incidence of chance and accident, even in entirely modern forms of enterprise, magic crops up. . . . The richest domain of magic, however, is, in civilization as in savagery, that of health."[87] It is like religion in being a response to "the curse of forethought and imagination, which fall on man once he rises above brute animal nature."[88] Ultimately, its function is to give a ritual form to human optimism, the triumph of hope over fear, the ability of men to control, at least to some extent, their destinies.

In addition to the mixed messages conveyed by sociologists and anthropologists, historians have also helped blur the boundary between religion and magic. Following the pioneering work of Keith Thomas's *Religion and the Decline of Magic* of 1971, which contended that the church in the Middle Ages "appeared as a vast reservoir of magical powers,"[89] many medievalists challenged the traditional view of Christendom as an integrated community of unalloyed faith, which included virtually all under its sway.[90] Instead, they noted the residual power of pagan ideas and practices, especially among the common folk or laity who had been imperfectly Christianized despite the best efforts of the clergy, who could now be implicitly understood as religious colonists imposing their ideas on an indigenous people.[91] "Pagan" in this context did not mean the sophisticated philosophies of Plato or Aristotle but rather the popular beliefs and rituals of pre-Christian cults. Historians came to understand many Christian holy places or saints as transfigurations of previously sacred sites or local divinities. Others acknowledged the infusion of "magical" powers into the church's sacraments, whose performative efficacy was reminiscent of Neoplatonic theurgy, a genealogy that continues to generate controversy to this day.[92] Many embraced Thomas's conclusion: "Even in the years after the Reformation it would be wrong to regard magic and religion as two opposed and incompatible systems of belief. There were magical elements surviving in religion, and there were religious facets to the practice of magic. This could make it difficult for the clerical opponents of magic to know where to draw the line."[93]

Jewish Nominalism

The uncertain boundary between religion and magic was not only a vexing issue for historians of Christianity but also appeared in the history of Judaism. Notwithstanding its stress on scripture, suspicion of images, and lack of sacraments, Judaism never fully freed itself from the temptations of magic.[94] According to the literary critic Barbara Johnson, "The religiously embarrassing presence in the Bible of God's magic tricks has always called for some explanation."[95] Gershom Scholem provided one: "In this area there was always a powerful reciprocal influence between Jews and non-Jews, for nothing is more international than magic."[96] The exchange began, it seems, during the Jews' captivity in Egypt, when Moses—who some have claimed was himself originally Egyptian—employed it in his competition with the Pharaoh's magicians. Despite the best efforts of commentators from Maimonides to Herman Cohen to read Judaism as inherently rational, especially in moral terms, magical beliefs and rituals long survived, especially in the quotidian world of folk religion.[97] Significantly, *The Golden Bough* included many Jewish examples, comparable to those in other traditions, in its compendium of magical practices. Durkheim and his followers also rejected the typical Christian characterization of Judaism as a desiccated, legalistic relic of a once-robust community of faith and argued that modern Talmudic Judaism still contained the vital energies—what they called the "dynamogenic" power—of its ancient Hebrew predecessor. The persistence of magic was an important indication of this continuity. As Ivan Strenski notes in his study of Durkheim and French Jewry: "Mauss argued that magic was one sure sign of the vitality of a religion. But if so, and since it survived into Talmudic Judaism at the highest levels in the magical use of the tetragrammaton, Talmudic Judaism too must embody the dynamogenic qualities usually attributed only to 'primitive' religions. Talmudic magic was employed, for example as a countermagic and thus as an integral part of the struggles of Talmudic Judaism against opposing forms of religious magic."[98]

Beyond religious practices, Jews were often taxed—or occasionally credited—with employing the magical arts in their "profane" life. Well into the modern era, Jewish doctors, for example, were suspected of employing occult practices in their healing of illnesses. Although often accompanied by the anti-Semitic accusation they were adepts in diabolic black magic, the suspicion was well founded.[99] According to the historian John Efron: "Jews, like their Christian neighbors, did believe in demons and their ability to affect human behavior and health. They considered illness to be evidence of demonic forces at work. In order to counteract the evil doings of malign spirits, medieval Jewish medical practice, like its Christian counterpart, resorted to magic and superstition. Indeed, despite biblical injunctions against the use of incantations, Judaism, often with rabbinic sanction, permitted the use of magic and sorcery to combat illness believed to have been caused by evil spirits."[100]

The branch of the esoteric, mystical Kabbalist movement within Judaism that came to be called "practical" most explicitly demonstrated the persistence of magical elements in the Jewish tradition.[101] According to Scholem, the practice it implied "simply means magic, though practiced by means which do not come under a religious ban, as distinct from black magic, which uses demonic powers and probes into sinister regions."[102] At times, scholars have sought to distinguish the "practical Kabblah" from the more subtle mystical ideas developed in Kabbalistic "theology."[103] But in general, to repeat the observation Scholem makes in this chapter's epigraph, "this was originally a tradition of a magical character, now transposed into a mystical tradition."[104]

The earliest Kabbalistic writings, known as Merkabah mysticism and developed from about the first century BCE to the tenth century CE, include examples of theurgic magic, attempting to enlist the powers of beneficent spirits. Scholem cites an example known as "putting on, or clothing, of the name," which he calls a "highly ceremonious rite in which the magician impregnates himself, as it were, with the great name of God—i.e. performs a symbolic act by clothing himself in a garment into whose texture the name has been woven."[105] He also notes the similarity between the "practical Kabbalah" and the writings of the great medieval Spanish mystic Abraham Abulafia (1240–ca. 1291): "This consecrated form of magic, which calls out the tremendous powers of the names, is not very far removed from Abulafia's method; if the sources from which he drew the elements of his doctrine are investigated more closely . . . it becomes plain that all of them, both the Jewish and the non-Jewish, are in fact closely connected with magical traditions and disciplines."[106] A similar judgment can also be made, Scholem suggests, of the founder of the Hasidic movement in the seventeenth century, the Baal Shem Tov (ca. 1698–1760), "a master of the great Name of God, a master of practical Kabbalism, a magician."[107] In other words, mysticism and magic are as interwoven at the end of the tradition as at the beginning. Even the Star of David, the abiding symbol of the Jewish people, is derived from the hexagon on the Shield of David, which was supposed to have given him extraordinary protective powers.[108]

It is, however, the particular Jewish belief in the numinous power of names that is most pertinent for the possibility of a nominalism—a label, it bears repeating, derived from the Latin *nomen*, or "name"—that can be called magical rather than conventional.[109] Greek philosophy, Hans-Georg Gadamer, has noted "more or less began with the insight that a word is only a name, i.e., that it does not represent true being,"[110] exemplified by Plato's refutation in the *Cratylus* of the argument for a natural connection of names with their objects. In contrast, Jews more frequently sought truths in the names themselves, or at least argued that a deep connection existed that needed to be recovered. A rich tradition of speculation on precisely what that connection might be began as early as the Second Temple period (516 BCE–70 CE), flourished in medieval Kabbalistic circles, and was revived by certain theologians and their fellow travelers in the twentieth century.[111]

It is thus not surprising that Bielik-Robson, as mentioned earlier, has posited a distinct variant of nominalism, different from the one developed by Ockham and other Christian theologians, and dubbed it "Jewish nominalism."[112] Her argument differs from Hans Jonas's earlier claim that the Hebrew Bible's account of a creator God, who called the world into existence ex nihilo, was the ultimate source of the stress on will, contingency, and particularity in nominalist theology, which would only help explain its conventional version.[113] If one had to point to Jewish nominalism's most significant difference from its conventional counterpart, it would be in its attitude toward names. Whereas for Ockham and his followers, universals were "mere names" with no ontological weight, for Jewish nominalists, names could have revelatory significance, performative power, and, in their proper form, the ability to imbue particulars with inherent value. The persistent underground effect of this belief through what Bielik-Robson calls a cryptotheological "Marrano strategy," first adopted by the secret Jews of early-modern Spain, means it has had an impact well beyond its initially overt religious expression.[114] Identifying Spinoza as its first explicit philosophical exponent, she traces its influence through Hermann Cohen up to Rosenzweig, Benjamin, and Adorno.

Bielik-Robson is reluctant, however, to acknowledge that the Jewish tradition may have had potent magical underpinnings.[115] And this is not without some justification, for it largely, if not entirely, avoided the sympathetic magic that Frazer and Durkheim found so ubiquitous in the "primitive" cultures they examined. Nor did Judaism usually embrace a "participatory" notion of creation, elaborated in particular by

Neoplatonism, in which the world was understood to be an emanation of the divine, and thus hierarchically arranged by generic orders of existence. As Scholem argued: "The insights of the Kabbalah concern the structure of what exists. Nothing would be more disastrous than to confuse the connections of this structure with the doctrine of emanantism," which led to the "intellectually lazy" doctrine of pantheism.[116] Unlike classical Greek poetry, which often projected human traits onto the nonhuman world, the Hebrew Bible rarely committed what came to be called the "pathetic fallacy."[117] Aside from the odd Jewish Neoplatonist like the French Kabbalist Isaac the Blind (1160–1235), there was little in the Jewish tradition of the macrocosm/microcosm parallel found in Aristotle or the correspondences of sympathetic magic and Renaissance Neoplatonism.[118]

Instead, the Jewish notion of creation was based on a model of radical separation in which God and the world, composed of a multitude of unique singularities, are not one.[119] According to the influential theory of *tsimtsum* advanced by Isaac Luria, the sixteenth-century Kabbalist from Safed in the Upper Galilee, the world was created by God's contraction or withdrawal.[120] The infinite vacated a space for the finite, transcendence was separated from immanence, the brilliance of divine light was restricted in the created world to occasional sparks. At times, this creation myth has been compared with the Christian notion of "kenosis," the emptying out of the divine enacted by the Incarnation.[121] At others, it has been differentiated from the latter because of its resistance to the sacrificial logic of Christian redemption, which implies a circular restitution of what was once whole, and "does not liberate its recipients but enslaves them by a perverse gesture of sovereignty."[122]

This gesture of sovereignty reflects what we might call a proto-Hegelian divinity ultimately committed to the negation of negation, the overcoming of alienation and the *restitutio ad integrum* promised in the New Testament, Acts 3:21. Not only did this pattern follow a logic of sacrifice and demand the indebtedness of those for whom the sacrifice was made, it also implied a generative subject who would once again become one with the object it had created as its transcendence is fully immanentized. As we have seen, when a secularized version of conventional nominalism was derived from Duns Scotus and Ockham's stress on God's omnipotent will, it could lead to a strong notion of a political sovereign whose power over the contingent world was deemed absolute. Jewish nominalism, as Bielek-Robson portrays it, is less susceptible to this secularized notion of an absolute sovereign, because it never seeks to reunite the other with the same. The sparks of light in the created, finite world never explode into the full radiance of infinite glory.

Distinguishing between Christian and Jewish traditions of nominalism is thus very fruitful. However, all expressions of magical nominalism would be difficult to attribute to the influence, direct or indirect, of esoteric Jewish theology. Moreover, for those less confident than Bielik-Robson that the boundary between religion and magic is watertight, it is hard to deny a prior magical impulse in at least one corner of Jewish nominalism itself: its elaborate and abstruse theology of names. As a result, it would be impossible to posit a threshold event, comparable to the Condemnation of 1277 in the Christian narrative of the advent of conventional nominalism, to mark the inaugural appearance of its Jewish counterpart. Its magical origins are too diffuse and lost to historical memory to be located with any certainty.

In fact, not only the origins but precisely what the magic of names might mean is an unsettled question. In *The Golden Bough*, for example, Frazer not only explores sympathetic and contagious magic, but also ponders the importance of names, not only in the Jewish tradition but for "primitive thought" as a whole. Here, he speculates, "The name of a person is not merely an appellation, but denotes what he is to the world outside of himself—that is, his 'outer' as distinguished from his 'inner being.' Thus, the 'name of God' in the Bible is His outward manifestation in the world, and in the Semitic languages, 'name' and 'posterity' are virtual synonyms. To bless or curse the name is therefore more than to invoke verbal benediction or malediction; it is to compass or invoke the prosperity or ruin of a person in his human relations."[123]

This practice by itself would not, however, indicate the presence of magical nominalism. In *Work on Myth*, Blumenberg suggests a somewhat different function for what Franz Rosenzweig called the "name's breaking into the chaos of the unnamed": "It is a piece of mastery of—of giving shape to and bringing into view—something that went before and that is beyond our reach. What was produced can be called 'the capacity to be addressed.' It prepares the way for the exercise of influence through magic, ritual or worship."[124] In other words, the transformation of the impersonal, menacing forces that confronted primitive humans into gods or a single God—a "thou" with whom an "I" might converse[125]—allowed the personal interactions that we call religious prayer or magical invocation.[126] No one, after all, can direct praise or supplication to Aristotle's "unmoved mover," who lacks a name that can be called to summon it. To name something is an invocation; as Gadamer notes, it is "always to call it into presence."[127] As such, the act of naming or of invoking the name can be understood as enabling a communicative event, a temporal experience of "being-with," not the expression of a changeless state of being. As we will see, when transferred to the discourse of history, magical nominalism ascribed a special role to events as active interruptions of structural or narrative continuity.

But to complicate the story, at least in Judaism too much intersubjective reciprocity was deemed problematic, too much familiarity with God a sign of insolence, and so a taboo was quickly established against uttering the divine name.[128] There was therefore no easy passage in Judaism, as Blumenberg suggests for Christianity, from the ability of an omnipotent God to will what he wanted to the idea of human self-assertion in conventional nominalism. Despite the tradition that developed of arguing with God, especially when human suffering seemed unjustifiable, he could only be addressed through circumlocutions.[129] And to address was not self-assertively to command or to call into being ex nihilo.[130] Prohibited from being written or uttered directly and completely, God's name could appear only as the four-letter, vowelless Hebrew word יהוה, which has come to be called the tetragrammaton, a term derived from the Greek word τετραγράμματον or "consisting of four letters." This expedient, so it is now widely accepted, is a condensed form of *Yaweh* or *Yehovah*.[131] Observant Jews are loath to utter it in any form, preferring circumlocutions such as *Adonai* ("My Lord"), and *hakadosh baruch hu* ("The Holy One, Blessed Be He"), and simply *Hashem* ("The Name"). Nor do they address another manifestation of God, as do Christians when they call out his son's name, or one of his plenipotentiaries, as in the case of saints or his son's mother. Jews may honor Moses and the Prophets, but they do not, certain exceptions aside, pray to them.[132]

There has been no dearth of attempts to explain or justify these prohibitions, and I am the last person equipped to hazard an informed answer. The Third Commandment brought back by Moses from Mount Sinai explicitly enjoins the Hebrews not "to take the Lord's name in vain," which suggests extreme caution in uttering it, but in the Psalms, they are told to "chant praises to His Name" (Psalms 68:5), albeit using the circumlocutions mentioned above. The tetragrammaton is a device for avoiding an indiscrete utterance of the full name, while still allowing ways of honoring it, a caution that extended to written expressions as well.[133] The expedient of employing a condensed version of a sacred name, it should be noted, was not confined to Jewish practice, but was also present in medieval Christian *nomina sacra*.[134]

And yet, there is something more at stake in the Jewish prohibition than merely avoiding disrespectful or casual utterances in favor of ones that praise an oddly insecure God who seems to need constant reassurance of his glory and power. In the Kabbalistic tradition, those larger stakes were made clearer.[135] Once again Gershom Scholem helps us appreciate a plausible version of them. Revelation, he argues, was manifest in language, which preceded creation and indeed brought it into being ("Let there be light"). Language not only works performatively through what later linguists would call a speech act to produce something new, as in the more mundane "I pronounce you man and wife." It can also, to repeat the passage employed as the epigraph to this chapter, manifest divinity through revealing God's name or names, which may be modes of his being: "God's language has no grammar, it consists only of names. The oldest Kabbalists—Nahmanides, for example—profess to have received as tradition this understanding of the structure of the Torah. It is clear, however, that this was originally a tradition of a magical character, now transposed into a mystical tradition."[136] Tacitly arguing against Frazer, Scholem points out, "this conception has nothing to do with any rational understanding of the possible social function of a name; this Name cannot, after all, even be pronounced."[137]

Nor, to compound its mysterious power, can it function as a meaningful semiotic element in the profane linguistic exchange of mere humans who try to communicate with each other through linguistic acts of representation, designation, translation, and symbolism. Nor does it play a role in the intersubjective process of justification.[138] "This absolute word is originally communicated in its limitless fullness, but—and that is the key point—this communication is incomprehensible!"[139] Or to put it differently, as an absolute, the name of God is itself without meaning because it cannot be translated into other terms in human language(s), which is (are) finite and profane. As such, it shows an obvious affinity with the nonsensical language of magic—"abracadabra," "hocus pocus," "bibbidi-bobbidi-boo," etc.—which is semantically empty, but performatively powerful.[140] God is thus not definable by his putative attributes, which suggest the interchangeability of terms but is rather ineffably revealed—and mysteriously concealed—through an unspeakable, unpronounceable name. Relative to nothing else, more than a mere metaphor or trope, his name does not mean or expresses anything but is the divine essence itself. And yet, paradoxically it can unleash the infinite torrent of interpretation that characterizes commentary on the Torah. For, as Scholem puts it, "Itself without meaning, it is the very essence of interpretability. For mystical theology, this is a decisive criterion of revelation."[141]

But because the endless hermeneutic quest, carried out as it is through human language(s), can never reveal the ultimate meaning of the divine name, expressed in a language forever beyond our ken, it implies the opposite of that conventional nominalism generated by the followers of Franciscans like William of Ockham with their stress on divine will. The latter ultimately led, as we have seen, to an emphasis on human self-assertion, in which universals are understood to be merely generic signs arbitrarily imposed on the contingent world by humans who employ them to deal with the uncertainties of a no longer rational and legible cosmos.

Magical nominalism, whether expressed in Jewish terms or not, places the human subject in a far more humble position, forever unable to know or even pronounce a name with absolute ontological power, combining essence and existence, well beyond any bestowed by mere human convention.[142] As Michael Miller notes in discussing the onomatological doctrines developed in the Hekhalot literature of the third to fifth century CE, the name "is a metaphor for presence, something which always must be particular. Presence must always be presence-to and cannot be removed from the subject. The name brings the object into the world of the subject and presents a particular face."[143] If as Megan O'Connor has insightfully observed, nominalism has always manifested "a tension between two fundamental counter-tendencies—between an emphasis on language, on the one hand, and a concern for things, on the other,"[144] magical nominalism has been more intent than its conventional counterpart on somehow overcoming the distinction. The Jewish theology of the divine name does not, in fact, assume an originary assertive act of naming on anyone's part, as there can be no one prior to God who gives him his name (or to put it differently, no one who creates the Creator). When Moses asks God what he is to tell the Israelites when they ask his name, the answer reveals a God existing in an eternal present outside of temporal change: "I AM WHO I AM. This is what you are to say to the Israelites: 'I AM has sent me to you'" (Exodus 3:14).

As uniquely ineffable as God's unpronounceable name may be, its tautological power could nonetheless be delegated, at least in part, to a plenipotentiary. Or more precisely, to the original human in the Garden of Eden, who had the honor, for reasons never really spelled out, of naming the animals for the first time.[145] What has come to be called an "Adamic" view of language meant that before the Fall, and the subsequent shattering of a single language as revenge for the hubris of building a tower to heaven in the city of Babel,[146] the names bestowed by the original man on the other creatures created by God were more than arbitrary signs. In the words of the historian of language Hans Arsleff: "It held that languages even now, in spite of their multiplicity and seeming chaos, contain elements of the original perfect language created by Adam when he named animals in his prelapsarian state. In the Adamic doctrine the relation between signifier and signified is not arbitrary; the linguistic sign is not double but unitary. Still retaining the divine nature of their common origin, languages were in fundamental accord with nature, indeed they were themselves part of Creation and nature."[147]

Whether or not Adam was a genuine "nomothete" (name giver) or merely uttered the true names the animals already had been given, and so was only channeling God's power, is uncertain.[148] It does seem clear that he was denied God's full linguistic performative power expressed in the momentous declaration "let there be light" dividing day from night; the Bible does not suggest, after all, that Adam creatively brought the animals into being. Perhaps, as Gilad Sharvit has speculated, Adam was both inventing the names and recognizing them, a kind of dynamic repetition with a difference, which has messianic implications.[149] But the main point is that the names themselves were ontologically right rather than the product of an arbitrary decision. Through a kind of semantic onomatopoeia, words and things before the Fall were somehow identical, and nature was not yet rendered a mute victim of competing vernacular conventions.

There have been many attempts over the years to identify and even recover that "original perfect language"[150]often inspired by the Kabbalah when it came to the attention of a wide range of Christian thinkers after the expulsion and dispersion of Iberian Jewry in 1492. What the Germans came to call an *Ursprache* was identified with Hebrew or Sanskrit, and other more obscure candidates like the Aymara spoken by Indigenous Peruvians were also occasionally promoted.[151] Some found the answer in images or numbers rather than words. Even pioneers of the scientific method like Francis Bacon were hopeful of gaining power over nature by uncovering its hidden names.[152] Although the overcoming of linguistic confusion was sometimes linked with the ending of tribal strife, searching for the "language of paradise" could lead many scholars down the garden path to dubious theories of cultural or racial priority or even superiority.[153] But at other times, as in the case of Scholem's friend Walter Benjamin, they could inspire the hope to approximate the *Ursprache* progressively through the translation of existing languages, which compensates for what each individual tongue lacks.[154] We will finish this chapter by focusing on Benjamin's efforts, which were among the most radical attempts to enlist its powers for what he explicitly called the "redemption" of human history.[155] They will serve as a kind of initial instance of the paradigms—or if you prefer, stars in the constellation or forces in the field—that will emerge over the course of this book to flesh out the meaning of "magical nominalism."

Walter Benjamin and Magical Nominalism

According to Adorno, "Benjamin undertook a metaphysical rescue of nominalism,"[156] partly through the eccentric practice of induction he exercised in his historical works. But the full extent of what can better be called his magical version of the tradition can be appreciated only by examining his no less eccentric thoughts on language. Although Eric Downing has recently made a strong case that Benjamin can be placed in an occluded lineage of "divinatory reading" that animated realist German literature in the nineteenth century, Benjamin was unique in spelling out its magical foundations.[157] Even Alexander Stern, who seeks to situate him in an "expressivist" tradition that harkens back to Hamann and Herder in the eighteenth century and anticipates Wittgenstein in the twentieth, agrees that Benjamin's point is "not that the connection between language and the world is magic, but that language has its foundation in a magical understanding of the world."[158]

In 1916, Benjamin composed an essay "On Language as Such and the Language of Man," which has lost none of its unsettling audacity. Witness the contemporary visual artist and filmmaker Hito Steyerl's recent remark that "of all weird texts by Benjamin, this is definitely the weirdest."[159] It remained unpublished in his lifetime, but has since become one of the most widely discussed in his remarkable oeuvre.[160] It spelled out the premises of his later contention that translation might help overcome the isolation of "fallen" individual languages, which came into existence after the expulsion from paradise and the destruction of the Tower of Babel.[161] Such languages function instrumentally in the profane world to communicate human thoughts and feelings, and to designate or refer to objects assumed to exist prior to their names. Anachronistically calling them "bourgeois," Benjamin asserted that they hold "that the means of communication is the word, its object factual, its addressee a human being."[162] In contrast, language "as such" is intentionless and expressionless, at least when it comes to human subjectivity, communicating only itself in what Benjamin explicitly called a "magic circle."[163] Meaning is not communicated by it, either literally or metaphorically; but it is more than the utterly self-referential, hermetic language sought by modernist poets like Stéphane Mallarmé or Paul Valéry.[164] Rather than the earmark of a separate realm called literature or art, transcending the mundane, it is somehow at one with the substance of reality. Or more precisely, language completes the mute communication among material things, which is imperfect, by adding sound: "Things are denied the pure formal principle of language—sound. They can communicate to one another through a more or less material community. This community is immediate and infinite, like every linguistic communication; it is magical (for there is also a magic of matter). The incomparable feature of human language is that its magical communication with things is immaterial and purely mental, and the symbol of this is sound."[165]

The contribution of humans to overcoming the muteness of nature, which he calls the source of its "deep sadness" and "great sorrow,"[166] is, however, more than just the adding of sound. For Benjamin, the primary link between human language(s) and language as such is the ability to name, which, *pace* Blumenberg, he did not primarily identify with the power to address the other (divine or not). "The theory of proper names," he writes, "is the theory of the frontier between finite and infinite language."[167] For Adam's naming of the animals in the Garden of Eden is followed by his naming Eve, which is the prototype of the human bestowal of proper names on children. "The proper name is the communion of man with the *creative* word of God."[168] In addition to the translation of one language into another, which helps overcomes the effects of Babel through a continuum of gradual transformations,[169] there is also a translation of "the language of things into that of man," which "is not only the translation of the mute into the sonic; it is also the translation of the nameless into names."[170] The different languages of men, however, cannot accomplish the job individually, as "things have no proper names except in God. For in his creative word, God called them into being them, calling them by their proper names. In the language of men, however, they are over-named. . . . The deepest linguistic reason for all melancholy and (from the point of view of the thing) of all deliberate muteness."[171]

In addition to the plurality of different tongues leading to the overnaming of things, a second source of melancholy is the abstraction of language, which loses touch with the immanent particularity of proper names.[172] It has to resort instead to the transcendent language of general concepts based on the "average" case and the commensuration of different exemplars.[173] The fall of language is also manifest in the resort to rule-bound normative judgments, under which qualitatively distinct cases have to be subsumed.[174] For "good and evil, being unnamable, nameless, stand outside the language of names, which man leaves behind precisely in the abyss opened up by this question."[175] In other words, both the real universals attributed to the world by prenominalist philosophies and the arbitrary linguistic signs imposed on the world by conventional nominalism fail to do what is done by uttering the right name, which communicates nothing but itself and is not a case of any abstraction under which it can be subsumed. They fail to redeem the qualitative uniqueness of creation in which prelapsarian grace is restored. They rely instead on the alienated rule of law—grammatical as well as moral—which necessitates the judgment that singular cases can be subsumed under general rules.

Benjamin did not shy away from acknowledging that this redemptive hope was magical at its core. Glossing Benjamin's remark to Scholem that "the notion of the magic of language refers to something else at the same time: its infinitude," Eric Jacobson writes: "In the concept of magic, it seems we are dealing with a reflection of a living, eternal immediacy—an immediacy that could only be conditioned by God. This is the idea that linguistic eternity is measured by nothing other than the immediate expression of the substance inside a given thing."[176] By shifting the emphasis from the subjective name giver to the thing whose substance is named, Benjamin was suggesting one of the key implications of "magical nominalism," what Adorno would call a nonpositivist "preponderance of the object,"[177] an object which was not inherently inert or irreparably mute. Against the domination of the subject over the object expressed philosophically in all forms of idealism, or the value of mere intersubjective communication, the goal was to restore nature's ability to be heard, which had been weakened still further by the conventional nominalist demolition of Platonic, Aristotelian, or Scholastic realism.

Even when Benjamin had moved in an explicitly materialist direction, spurred on by his friendship with Bertolt Brecht, his magical nominalist yearnings remained potent. They continued to inform his investigations into the modern city in his unfinished *Arcades* project, where he marveled at the "magic of the corner" where street names intersect.[178] In "Antitheses Concerning Word and Name," a 1933 fragment composed while he was collecting his thoughts on mimesis, his early theory of language maintained its power: "In the things from which it shines back silently and in the mute magic of nature, God's word has become the communication of matter in magical community."[179] The restoration of this community, to be sure, did not imply a mystical unity in which difference and particularity are obliterated by wholeness and words immediately express the essences of things. As Jacobson notes: "This appears to be magic: that God's revelation is embedded in the still language of things and His insignia corresponds to human naming. Magic is the incidental reception of revelation, or the appearance of revelation in the incidental thing, but it is not the mystical oneness within which all distinction is collapsed."[180] There is, however, a connection that Giorgio Agamben claims Benjamin suggested between the magic of names and human happiness, when the latter is uncoupled from the idea that it is somehow deserved through effort rather than inexplicably bestowed by chance. He notes Kafka's claim that "if we call life by its right name, it comes forth, because that is the essence of magic, which does not create but summons," a definition he traces to "kabbalists and necromancers, according to which magic is essentially a science of secret names" known only to a magus. Agamben then turns to what he calls "a more luminous tradition" where "the secret name is not so much the cipher of the thing's subservience to the magus's speech as, rather, the monogram that sanctions its liberation from language. The secret name was the name by which the creature was first called in Eden. When it is pronounced, every manifest name—the entire Babel of names—is shattered. That is why, according to this doctrine magic is a call to happiness."[181]

Much more can be said about Benjamin's bold ruminations on translation and language "as such," which continue to excite interpretive interest, despite their often obscure formulation and reliance on sources he may not have fully mastered.[182] Indeed, in whatever form, the magical quest for a pure *Ursprache* may seem utopian and even deluded, allowing Umberto Eco to call it "the story of a dream and a series of failures."[183] It would, in fact, require a sustained suspension of disbelief to continue searching in the face of modern linguistics, which is overwhelmingly conventionalist and believes that atomistic semantic units make sense only within a larger structural or hermeneutic framework. And it would take an even greater leap of faith to believe that discovering the *Ursprache* would help humankind restore a state of prelapsarian grace, redeem a mute (and mutilated) nature, or bring about world peace. Like the alchemists' quest for a universal philosopher's stone that would turn base metals into gold or provide an elixir guaranteeing eternal life, it remains one of those quixotic ambitions that keep us from collapsing magic into science, however much we may acknowledge the overlap between them.

In addition, even for those who remain in its thrall and want to avoid the wholesale rejection of magic, there may be another obstacle to accepting Benjamin's audacious attempt to harness its power for a critique of the modern world. There is an apparent tension between the magic of names and the sympathetic magic that Frazer claimed was the dominant form of magical ritual and Durkheim discerned more generally in elementary forms of religion. Whereas the former implied ontological isolation and singularity, resisting metaphoric or other modes of semantic transfer, the latter asserted analogical correspondences and a certain form of relationality.[184] The tension, we might say, expressed two different notions of creation, the Jewish "separatist" and the Neoplatonic Christian "participatory" or "emanantist."

Their competing logics, in fact, seemed to vie for prominence in Benjamin's own speculative ruminations. For in addition to his debts to the Jewish nominalist quest for Adamic proper names, he also evinced nostalgia for the Greek notion of an eternal cosmos, ruled by harmonious correspondences (albeit ones he did not identify as necessarily rational). His frequent evocation of Baudelaire's poem "Correspondences" evinces his longing for the restoration of a lost cosmic relationality. In the final section of *One-Way Street*, "To the Planetarium," Benjamin wrote: "Nothing so distinguishes ancient from modern man as the former's submission to a cosmic experience of which the latter is scarcely aware. The decline of that experience began with the flowering of astronomy at the start of the modern period." It relied on instrumentally enhanced visual observation, which reified the distinction between subject and object. In contrast, "Classical dealings with the cosmos took a different form: intoxication. . . . The sole experience in which we grasp the utterly immediate and the utterly remote, and never the one without the other." Such intoxication, immersing the subject in the object, was an inherently collective experience, as "communicating ecstatically with the cosmos is something men do only communally. Modern man is in danger of mistakenly dismissing such an experience as trivial, dispensable, and leaving it to the individual—a rush of enthusiasm on fine, starry nights."[185] Only the discredited remnants of once-potent practices of sympathetic magic, like astrology and graphology, hinted at what has been lost in our disenchanted world, and yet might, despite everything, still be regained. Here Benjamin hoped to revive what has been called the early-modern "cosmopoetic understanding of the imagination,"[186] which drew on alchemical practices and hermetic traditions to bring about the mystical fusion of self and world, mind and nature, the human and the divine.

The discrepancy between "On Language as Such and the Language of Man" (1916), which draws on the Jewish magic of names, and Benjamin's subsequent essays on "The Mimetic Faculty" (1933) and "The Doctrine of the Similar" (1933),[187] which, like "To the Planetarium," espouse the correspondence theory of sympathetic magic, may, however, be possible to resolve. Benjamin himself insisted there was a continuity between the recovery of authentic ur-names and sympathetic magic, and referred to his two later essays in a letter to Scholem as an "addendum to the larger essay and . . .

by no means as a commentary." They represented, he insisted, "a new turn in our old tendency to show the ways in which magic has been vanquished."[188]

Umberto Eco notes that in the Christian integration of Kabbalah in the Renaissance, exemplified by the German scholar of the occult Heinrich Cornelius Agrippa von Nettesheim (1486–1535), who had continued the pioneering and controversial work of Johannes Reuchlin: "The Kabbalah of the names suggested that the same sympathetic links holding between sublunary objects and celestial bodies also apply to names. According to Agrippa, Adam took both the properties of things and the influence of the stars into account when he devised his names; thus 'these names contain within them all the remarkable powers of the things that they indicate.'"[189] Benjamin's knowledge of the Kabbalah, however much he learned from Scholem, was also indebted to Christian Kabbalists like Franz Joseph Molitor, whose interpretations were often eclectic.[190] Significantly, in a letter written to Scholem in 1919, Benjamin revealed his excitement at a gift from his father-in-law, a Latin edition of the works of Agrippa von Nettesheim, "which, however, I will be able to read only with a German translation," and referred to him positively on several later occasions.[191] Whether or not he was directly indebted to Agrippa, he reached a similar conclusion in his advocacy of "nonsensuous similarities" in language as the ultimate repository of the correspondences of sympathetic magic: "Language may be seen as the highest level of mimetic behavior and the most complete archive of nonsensuous similarities: a medium into which the earlier powers of mimetic production and comprehension have passed without residue, to the point where they have liquidated those of magic."[192]

The mediation between names and nonsensuous similarities posited by Benjamin, Giorgio Agamben has speculated, might best be understood in the doctrine of signatures developed by thinkers like the German Renaissance philosopher, natural magician, and physician Paracelsus, who called Adam the "first *signator*" and argued that "the signatory art teaches how to give true and genuine names to all things."[193] More than an arbitrary semiotic signifier, the signature has efficacious power, like the religious notion of the sacrament, to make something happen. Images and charms could be blessed and even baptized in the Middle Ages to endow them with magical powers. The curative ability of plants that have similarities with the organ whose illness they supposedly can heal or causal astrological links between the macrocosmic course of the heavens and the microcosmic fate of individuals manifest the same logic. "Both the theological doctrine of the sacramental character and the medical doctrine of signatures in all likelihood owe their origin to this kind of magical-theurgic tradition."[194]

One way in which the magic of names and that of correspondences might overlap was manifested in the Catholic practice of celebrating name days, whose difference from birthdays Benjamin noted. Imaginatively extrapolating from Benjamin's argument, James McFarland writes:

> The birthday celebration has a negative theological status, visible in its contrast with the name day. Coordinated with baptism, not birth, the name day has no complement, but lifts the infant through onomastic identity into an endless order of salvation. With the name, a correspondence is established between this particular human animal and the transformed human saint, bathed in the glory of God, a relation of patronage that on the one hand dignifies the child by emphasizing those few aspects of its being that are already on the road to salvation, and on the other protects if from those many aspects of its being that are not. By contrast, the birthday celebrates the infant's entry into the natural order.[195]

There is yet another wrinkle to Benjamin's argument. In "Antitheses Concerning Word and Name," he pointed to "the magical function of the alphabet: to provide the nonsensuous similarity with the enduring semiotic ground on which it can appear."[196] That is, the sympathetic magical connection may well have occurred on a level beneath that of proper names themselves. In the Kabbalah, for example in the writings of Abulafia, names were sometimes dissolved into their constituent letters.[197] These could then be rearranged or organized in numerical patterns that allegedly corresponded to the essence of things. These numerical patterns, in contrast with the conventionalist nominalist belief that mathematics was a human creation imposed on a contingent world, were understood to be ontologically real. One commentator has called this belief an expression of "hypostatic nominalism,"[198] but we might just as well call it the mathematical variant of magical nominalism. Although Benjamin did not follow Scholem in pursuing the deeper implications of mathematics, his speculations about the possible correspondences between letters, numbers, and the truths of creation show how keen he was finding some way to overcome the weaknesses of human languages after the fall.[199] And, as shown by the historical method he later practiced of destroying conventional narratives and assembling the debris into new patterns, or "dialectical images," he could also apply the Kabbalistic method of reassembling the letters of a word into new constellations to provide "profane illuminations" as well.[200]

Whether or not Benjamin's attempt at reconciling the Jewish nominalist belief in Adamic names with the sympathetic magical idea of correspondences in a harmonious cosmos was successful, it showed that a strong residue of magical thinking informed his speculations.[201] Whereas traditional religious thinkers lamented secularization as a threat to the realm of the sacred, Benjamin was more concerned with reenchanting the world than resacralizing it. Thus, he specifically celebrated transfigurations of the everyday—a program that tied him to the early Romantics and the Surrealists of his own time—through materialist epiphanies that somehow broke through the crust of convention and revealed, if only momentarily, a realm of the marvelous beneath. In ways that he never successfully demonstrated, they were connected with the revolutionary Marxist politics he embraced at the same time. Although their compatibility with the theory of historical materialism and the praxis of the workers' vanguard has been difficult to demonstrate,[202] raising it as a possibility at least suggests that like conventional nominalism, magical nominalism might also have certain political implications, however attenuated.

To be sure, it would be easy to scoff at Benjamin's exhortation "to win the energies of intoxication for the revolution," as he famously asserted in his 1929 essay on surrealism.[203] Indeed, for many, magical nominalism in general will seem like a castle built in the air and any talk of an Adamic view of language or mimetic cosmological correspondences in the quotidian world an invitation to sloppy thinking or worse.[204] Enemies of the "culture of redemption" like the literary critic Leo Bersani scoff at Benjamin's "magical and nihilistic belief that immersion in the most minute details of a material content will not only reduce that content but simultaneously unveil its hidden redemptive double."[205] Even before Benjamin defended it, the idea of "language as such" had come under attack by critics of "word magic" like Gottlob Frege and C. K. Ogden.[206] Bridling at the ambiguities of rhetoric, they sought a prosaic language that would be rigorous and logical, helping to launch what became the variant of the "linguistic turn" associated with Anglo-American analytic philosophy.

And yet, in many respects, the often underground tradition—or better put, sporadic eruption—which kept alive the alternative version of that turn we have been calling magical nominalism did succeed in raising doubts about the limits of both ontological realism with its belief in universal essences and conventional nominalism with its reliance on the constitutive power of the subject. It was able to draw on the affective aura so often accompanying magic—wonder, enchantment, marvel, delight—which has been conspicuously absent from conventional nominalism.[207] And it draped that aura around unique particulars—whether understood as proper names, spatial objects, or temporal events—that were irreducible to the essentializing categories or englobing contexts which sought to contain and master them.[208] Blumenberg's contention that human "self-assertion" filled the vacuum left by the *deus absconditus* helps us understand the importance of conventional nominalism, which projected conceptual coherence onto a contingent world that was understood to lack inherent universals. Magical nominalism, in contrast, celebrated the counterassertion of the infinite world of nonfungible particulars against the subsumptive logic of both realism and conventionalism. In so doing, it challenged the semiotic disenchantment—Weber's *Entzauberung*—wrought by conventional nominalism and sought to recover language's capacity for *Zauber*, and not it alone.

Not only can manifestations of magical nominalism be discerned in the obscure recesses of heterodox Jewish theology, and their appropriations by modern interpreters like Benjamin, they have also been sighted elsewhere, for example in certain texts of medieval French Arthurian literature.[209] But it is their appearance, often unannounced and unacknowledged, in a wide variety of later and still potent phenomena, aesthetic, historical, and even technological, that will concern us in what follows. We will not, however, link them by tracing linear filiations of influence, perhaps the most widely applied method of the traditional history of ideas. Nor will we attempt to reconstruct them as intentional acts by thinkers with specific audiences in mind, as another influential approach stressing the importance of contexts of genesis and reception has urged us to do. Instead, we will offer a series of what Agamben, as noted in our introduction, called paradigmatic exemplars, which can be related only through a kind of analogical reconstruction. Rather than instantiations of an overarching, generic concept or abstract category under which they can be subsumed, they invite comparison through similarities that are congruent but not identical. Like those translations without a transcendental signified whose revelatory effect Benjamin so admired, they are repetitions, but with differences, of a hitherto hidden impulse in a modern world that is richer and more varied than conventionally assumed.[210]

INTERMEZZO
Magical Nominalism and Negative Theology

Before turning to the paradigms that will flesh out what we mean by magical nominalism, it will be useful to pause for a moment to summarize where we are in the general argument and to consider potential objections to it. All variants of nominalism, it is clear, were suspicious of the claims made by Greek philosophers and their medieval inheritors in Neoplatonic and Aristotelian/Scholastic traditions that universals were ontologically real and abstract essences prior to or even equiprimordial with their particular instantiations. Applying Ockham's razor, they pared away putative entities like generic species or ideal forms as extraneous fictions. They equally spurned the idea of a rational cosmos whose harmonious ordering of such universals could be known by humans sharing in the intelligibility of God's creation. They accepted instead the limits of human knowledge and the gap between subjects and objects in an infinite universe without orienting guideposts. And often they developed early versions of what later would be known as the linguistic turn in philosophy, challenging the assumption that thought can encounter the external world without the refracting mediation of language.[1]

The responses of conventional and magical nominalism to the collapse of belief in a harmonious cosmos knowable by human reason, however, radically diverged. For the former, the universe is a disenchanted, intrinsically unintelligible place, which can no longer be infused with meaning by the comforting nostrums of metaphysical cosmology or rational theology. For those without residual faith in the argument for God's existence from the alleged design of his creation, all that is left are functional instruments that allows us to cope with and survive uncertainty. Prime among these is language. Nominalism in its conventional form often adopted what might be called a linguistic version of self-assertion, arguing that the general terms we use to make sense of the world are fashioned, deliberately or not, to deal as best we can with the challenges of contingency. Although the more cautious among its exponents sometimes conceded that natural kinds may exist, or at least that we have to be agnostic about their existence, they argued that our epistemological tools are inadequate to identify them with full assurance. Concepts are merely stratagems for yoking together particulars that can have at best only probabilistic comparability. Metaphors function to reveal overlapping commonalities that resist subsumption under a generic category. Analogies locate parallels in disparate phenomena, but ones that are not ontologically prior to our discerning them. Even the language of mathematics might be understood as based on the human need to bypass the qualitative distinctness of phenomena in favor of quantifiable aggregations or patterns imposing fungibility on the unique, but there is no compelling reason to assume that mathematical formulas perfectly map on to a prior reality.

Taken to an extreme in the famous Sapir-Whorf hypothesis,[2] the constitutive role of language implies that different languages produce different realities, which can lead to cognitive and moral relativism and even cultural incommensurability. The more alarmist critics of nominalism worried, in fact, that it began the slide down the proverbial slippery slope to outright nihilism.[3] For, as Agata Bielik-Robson puts it, when Ockham, "uses the word *nomen* to express the ultimate ontological status of fragmented reality, he does so in a radically skeptical and negative manner—as a token of our ignorance in the face of the multitude of particulars, which does not imply any natural order in itself. It is only we who impose order on the anarchy of beings; concepts, therefore, have no metaphysical reality, they are—as Francis Bacon will say a few centuries later—mere tools."[4]

Conventional nominalism, to be sure, could also support a more transcultural conceptualism, in which universals are validated as necessary cognitive expedients prior to their expression in different languages. Subjective idealists like Kant, positing hard-wired transcendental mental structures, were thus able to support a nominalist ontology while blunting the threat of epistemological relativism.[5] Kant, to be sure, broke with the medieval nominalists over God's will as the source of the binding laws of morality, which he interpreted in the spirit of universalist realism.[6] But when it came to epistemological issues, he remained agnostic about the ultimate nature of the world beyond the existence of particular objects, attributing whatever universal patterns might be found to the constitutive power of the human mind as such, thus mitigating the effects of cultural and linguistic difference. And when the application of the results had successful outcomes—at least measured by pragmatic or utilitarian criteria of "success"—ultimate questions of correspondence with the "real world" could be avoided by brushing them aside as irrelevant.

Whether interpreted linguistically or transcendentally, conventional nominalism has since its inception raised many troubling questions. Some, as previously noted, were posed by "counterrevolutionary" philosophers or theologians intent on restoring one or another version of a realist ontology in which universals, despite all efforts to dismiss them, do exist outside of human constitution.[7] Others challenge the plausibility of adopting a radical constructivist epistemology to explain the constitution of *all* realities, natural as well social.[8] They point out that even if nominalism denies the reality of abstract universals, its continuing faith in the existence of concrete particulars means that objects or things in the world—and the structures that connect them—stubbornly resist being turned into mere effects of the conceptual categories under which they are subsumed. Although they admit that the questions we ask may be contingent and arbitrary, the answers we receive, especially when it comes to nature, are not. Thus, the replacement of one conceptual scheme by another is not a random event but rather motivated by the better fit one may have with the evidentiary record or the greater power they have in explaining it.[9] In addition, however much we stress the mediating function of language as a semiotic system, we must also acknowledge that it can draw on ostensive reference, in which objects are indicated not through the use of other words, but rather by mutely pointing to them.

Other critics have been troubled by the collateral damage of the nominalist revolution beyond its undermining of epistemological certainty, in particular its robbing the world of inherent or even potential rationality in substantive terms. Here Kant's insistence that moral obligations reflect laws that are prior to divine will is a leading example. He and other critics of ethical nominalism charge it with reducing reason to little more than an instrument enabling the realization of ends derived from nonrational sources. The theological stress on the will over substantive reason inspiring the original nominalist critique of Scholasticism, some commentators claim, was echoed in the human determination to master—whether epistemologically or practically—a universe of random contingency.

Although the de-ontologization of real universals, understood to be eternally binding, might be applauded for opening the door to an infinity of possible futures, other critics lament instead its abandonment of any substantive standard against which an imperfect actuality might be measured and found wanting (or by which the best of those possible futures might be consciously chosen). When it leads to value-free positivism in particular, they worry that it tacitly affirms the status quo, in which a stubborn actuality blots out the latent potentiality that dialecticians like Hegel had argued was also immanent in reality. Reason is reduced to an empty shell of itself, unable to motivate critique of a world that does not measure up to the promise it objectively harbors. What is left is merely contingent, open-ended possibility, which provides no tension, beyond human desire for something different, between what is and what might be.

Marxists, in particular, have been troubled by the irrationalism they see implied by the nominalist denigration of real universals. Although Marx had once praised nominalism as "the first form of materialism,"[10] because of its challenge to ideal essences, many of his followers came to fear that its undialectical character diminished its critical potential. A typical Marxist lament was expressed by the Frankfurt School philosopher Max Horkheimer, who claimed that "the triumph of nominalism goes hand in hand with the triumph of formalism. In limiting itself to seeing objects as a strange multiplicity, as a chaos, reason becomes a kind of adding machine that manipulates analytical judgments."[11] Theodor Adorno would make a similar point in claiming that nominalism, despite its initially enlightening function in demystifying conceptual realism, had degenerated into a pedantic exercise in defining terms, which "deprive[s] others of the use of whatever true, substantive elements are contained in concepts, of the essential, structured aspects of phenomena that lie within concepts."[12] Put in reason's place as a normative standard, so such critics of conventional nominalism often charge, is the unfettered will, whose political embodiment we have noted in the theory of unconstrained sovereignty promoted by decisionists like Carl Schmitt.

Although troubled by conventional nominalism's role in dominating nature, amplifying the power of the constitutive subject, and abetting political decisionism, some of its detractors were nonetheless unwilling to revive ontological realism and universal rationalism. They were drawn instead to what we have called its magical counterpart, if often implicitly and without being fully aware of its sources. While denying traditional realist assumptions about the rational cosmos, latter-day magical nominalists—our first example here has been Walter Benjamin—balked against "the disenchantment of the world" (*die Entzauberung der Welt*). Reassessing the individual, qualitatively distinct particularities that push back against their domination through formal, subjective categorization, they wager that magical nominalism, more than its conventional counterpart, can reenchant a world of random contingency that no longer should be condemned for lacking intrinsic value. They often seek to rescue traces and prefigurations of such reenchantment lurking in the ruins of the old metaphysical systems or discover them in unexpected places in modern experience (as we will see, for example, when we examine the photograph). Although remaining nominalist in refusing to restore faith in the discredited universals of those systems, they seek more direct contact with the real in a multitude of numinous singularities beyond the grasp of subjective construction or mediation. There are pigeons, they claim, that can defiantly fly out of the holes in which we have placed them.

For our purposes, it is important to note two aspects of this quest for reenchantment. First, magical nominalism questions the epistemological turn promoted by conventional nominalism and reopens ontological questions. While sharing the conventional nominalist resistance to attempts, such as those of post-Kantian German idealism, to resurrect belief in the ontological reality of the *Begriff* (the notion or concept), its adherents refuse to equate the real with unformed, inert, base matter, which they scorn as the simple inverse of ideal essences or forms. Rather they locate it in particulars that somehow—and this is where the "magic" comes in—combine existence and essence, what Duns Scotus would have called their haecceity, or a nonqualitative, individuating "thisness" (from the Latin *haec*, meaning "this"), with their generic or essential quiddity or "whatness" (from the Latin *quid*, meaning "what").[13] If magical nominalism could thus be said to support a version of "immanent critique," it would not be based on the gap between abstract rational principles latent in reality and the contingent particulars of the status quo but on the distinction between the impoverished "actuality" of particulars that did not combine essence and existence and the higher "reality" of those that could. The latter somehow maintains the auratic power that Benjamin defined as the ability to return our gaze. Or to put it in different terms, they have overcome the muteness of fallen nature and are "things that talk."[14]

How that higher reality reveals itself by gazing back at us and to whom it may talk are, of course, questions that magical nominalists have struggled to answer. Disputing the constitutive power of subjects and making an end run around epistemological issues to engage more directly with ontological ones may be applauded as a repudiation of the arrogance of human self-assertion. But it arouses the suspicion that it smuggles in a belief in an omniscient view from nowhere that fails to acknowledge the limited perspectival situatedness of all observers. Dismissing this worry, as Heidegger famously did, by rejecting the "enframing" that turns the world into a picture of external objects viewed by observing subjects may thus reveal an even greater arrogance than the humanism it is supposed to supplant. For it suggests that it is somehow possible to inhabit—or is it, ventriloquize?—the nonperspectival place of Being or mystically unite with divinity.

A second issue concerns the magical nominalist search for a language that goes beyond a conventional semiotic system radically distinct from reality, based on the belief that words are only arbitrary signs for the objects and events they designate or the meanings they signify. If recovered, some magical nominalists hope, the lost "language as such" or primeval *Ursprache* spoken before the catastrophe of linguistic pluralism would heal the wounds and overcome the mute suffering of a nature that no longer resonated with palpable meaning. More than a tool employed by subjects to dominate objects or a means of intersubjective communication, more than a conventional semiotic system, the recovered "language of paradise" could once again become the locus of ontological truth. For it would not be imposed on things but somehow be one with them.

Precisely how this linguistic magic might actually work has, to be sure, never been easy to demonstrate. A universal grammar may not be the royal road to overcoming conventionality but rather, as we have seen in examining the Jewish mysticism of names in general and Benjamin in particular, proper names might. Or at least so it seems with the ones given by Adam before the fall into the "overnaming" of different human tongues. Such names claim ontological truth on their own terms, without being subsumed under a general rule or given meaning through translation into other words, which themselves need to be defined through still others. Adamic names are not symbolic representations of something else, nor are they generic concepts or propositions about a state of affairs.

Such names, moreover, do not advance validity claims that require verification through a process of what Kant would have called determinant judgments, which applied syllogistic logic to subsume particulars under schematic generalities or abstract concepts. Nor are they really amenable to the reflective judgments that operated through analogy and paradigmatic cases, which Kant had identified with the way we judge aesthetically.[15] As in the case of naming, there is a distinction between human judgment and divine judgment. Whereas the former is imperfect and approximate, whether based on the subsumptive logic of determinant judgments or the analogical logic of reflective judgments, the latter is based on a qualitative consideration of the unique merits of each particular case. Their incomparable truth is somehow beyond the human power to judge tout court.

But after Babel (or according to the hints in Genesis 10, perhaps even before), it has been a daunting task—indeed most commentators would argue, little more than a pipe dream—to recover such true names amid the cacophony of "fallen" vernacular tongues spoken by a disunited humankind. There is, moreover, an ambiguity in the types of names involved, left unresolved in the Bible. They might, after all, themselves be generic, referring to a collective group, or they might be uniquely singular.[16] God's unpronounceable name, whatever it might be, was of course fully proper, his and his alone, and not generic (the jealous God of the Israelites is most definitely not merely *primus inter pares* in a pantheon of gods). But it is unclear if the animals named by Adam were given individual names or ones that apply to them as a species.[17] This ambiguity persists in the still-widespread practice of giving proper names to some animals, such as the dogs and cats in our domestic households but not, say, to the squirrels scampering through our trees.[18] Whereas the former are instances of naming in the service of individuation and intersubjective address—dogs, to be sure, are more likely to come than cats—the latter merely subsume those who are so named under a generic category, which serves human interests and not those of the squirrels.

Can any case be made for the plausibility of magical nominalism's Adamic view of ontologically proper names? *Pace* Benjamin, there are few serious defenders of it in its literal form. There is, however, a robust contemporary philosophical discussion mulling over the implications of proper names per se. At one end is Saul Kripke's discussion of proper names as "rigid designators" indicating just the object they actually designate in all possible worlds in which that object exists, assuming it does exist, but nothing else in any other possible world.[19] Although his personal religious identity as an orthodox Jew can only be speculatively connected to Kripke's philosophy, some commentators have found that his evocation of Maimonides's thoughts on names suggests that it might have been important.[20] Even though he never endorses an Adamic view of an original *Ursprache*, Kripke's contention that proper names can function via reference without meaning comports with the antisemantic impulse of magical nominalism.

At the other end of the spectrum are structuralist and poststructuralist theorists of language, who deny to names any significance on their own. In *The Savage Mind*, Claude Lévi-Strauss argued that "Proper names are an integral part of systems we have been treating as codes: as a means of fixing significations by transposing them into terms of other significations" and thus always meaningful relationally.[21] Maurice Blanchot dismissed any etymological search for original meanings for fixating "the attention upon the *word* as the seminal cell of language, and thus revert[ing] to the ancient prejudice according to which language would be essentially made of names: a nomenclature."[22] Jacques Derrida described proper names in even more highly charged terms as the "originary violence" of language. According to his deconstructionist reading, they seek to reverse the "loss of what has never taken place, of a self-presence which has never been given but only dreamed of but always already split, repeated, incapable of appearing to itself except in its own disappearance."[23]

While Kripke can be enlisted in the cause of pure naming, at least for proper names, the structuralist and poststructuralist linguists would insist instead on their eternal impropriety because of their inevitable mediation through an intrusive context—at once outside and inside them—that dissolves their impermeable solidity. They push back against both the quest for the ontological truth of pure names and the conventional nominalist claim that they are the product of subjective self-assertion without remainder. Instead, such names are better situated in a dynamic field of linguistic forces beyond the intentionality of speakers. Although they can temporarily congeal into isolated moments of solid designation, like the reification of ongoing practices into completed products, they then dissolve again into their fluid state.

Nostalgia for an Adamic language before the fall into multiple human tongues may also be vulnerable to another objection. As we have noted, there is an ambiguity in the role Adam allegedly played as the nomothete of the animal kingdom. Unlike God who performatively created the universe through his speech acts, Adam gives the names to animals *already* created, and indeed may only be articulating the names they already have. According to certain commentators, he was therefore *completing* creation, not *generating* it. Once we stress language's ostensive function, we are granting that the objects it designates exist prior to their names. The distinction is apparent, as Peter Fenves notes, in Walter Benjamin's ruminations on Adamic names:

> As Benjamin develops his treatise beyond its exegesis of Genesis, the double character of human language begins to characterize language as such. The names Adam "gives" the animals turn out to be improper, after all: "Things have no proper name except in God. For in the creative word God of course calls them forth with their proper names." Every created thing, then, finds itself in a situation similar to that of Eve and her children: they are named by someone who did not create them in first speaking their names.[24]

In other words, even the purest language cannot claim absolute, immanent self-referentiality because it depends on the existence of something prior to the act of naming. The perfect unity of creation and naming belongs only to God. Skepticism toward the absolute singularity and self-referential immanence of proper names, even those allegedly bestowed by Adam in the Garden, thus remain hard to dispel.

A final question, which is raised not only by magical nominalism but by its conventional counterpart as well, asks how thin should Ockham's razor slice? Although the word "individual" draws on the Latin word for "indivisible," the search for absolute rock bottom in any descending analysis of ontological units remains inconclusive. Ockham, it will be recalled, relied on what he called "intuitive" rather than "abstractive" cognition to identify what was "simple and proper to [a] singular thing."[25] With the invention of the microscope, historians tell us, a whole new world of hitherto invisible particulars was revealed, but along with it came vexing ontological questions about the play of appearances rather than certainty about reality.[26] Just to speak in physical terms, we learned that smaller than anything we can immediately sense are molecules, which are themselves made up of atoms, which consist of subatomic particles (most notably neutrons, protons and electrons).[27] Although electrons are now considered indivisible, neutrons and protons are understood to be themselves made of smaller particles called quarks. And then there are neutrinos, which are so small that physicists for years thought—apparently erroneously—they have no mass, only energy.[28] Ever since Leibniz invented infinitesimal calculus, mathematicians have worked with the idea that numbers can be smaller than any real number but still larger than zero. And contemporary physicists seem to discover an ever more "nano" reality that is running an endless race to the bottom.[29] How far down must we go, in other words, before Ockham can put down his razor?[30]

Nominalists might respond that true individuals are not identified by their irreducibility to instantiations of more general classes of being but rather by the realization that they cannot be broken down into the same constituent elements as other individuals. In an influential paper of 1940 titled "The Calculus of Individuals and Its Uses," Henry L. Leonard and Nelson Goodman postulated that "an individual or whole" is "whatever is represented in any given discourse by signs belonging to the lowest logical type of which that discourse makes use."[31] They then claimed that two individuals are discrete if and only if they share no part in common. Here the arrow points down rather than up in establishing the uniqueness of particulars. What distinguishes individuals from generic classes is that the former eschew subclasses that create a hierarchical schema of subdivisions and instead offer no account of how the discrete parts might be organized.

In his later *Ways of Worldmaking*, Goodman would make the same point: "Although a nominalistic system speaks only of individuals, banning all talk of classes, it may take anything whatever as an individual; that is, the nominalistic prohibition is against the profligate propagation of entities out of any chosen basis of individuals, but leaves the choice of that basis quite free." Thus, it is a just as plausible to call an atom or molecule an individual as a singular entity perceived by the senses, if one consistently sticks with that level of identification. But there is no correct level ontologically. Atoms in this reckoning are not composed of subatomic particles but are defined instead—and the key here is the act of defining—as individuals that are irreducible to their putative components. To posit such components in addition is to violate the nominalist injunction against multiplying unnecessary entities. "In contrast," Goodman alleges, "the typical physicalism, for example while prodigal in the platonistic instruments it supplies for endless generation of entities, admits of only one correct (even if unidentified) basis."[32]

This is an ingenious argument that resists the infinite regression of theories that look for the smallest possible entity, but it does so at the cost of applying Ockham's razor solely to discursive and logical terms, which are relative to the discourses and logical systems in which they are located. Goodman tacitly brackets ontological questions, which contravenes Ockham's belief that universals do not exist but particulars do.[33] Typically, these have been treated in physicalist terms by other nominalists who are reluctant to embrace the claim that it is language all the way down.[34] In contrast, for Goodman, the positing of individuals is not a metaphysical assertion but rather a methodological principle.[35] There may be, however, potential arbitrariness in an explicitly antiphysicalist account, which is flagged by the aesthetic theorist Gérard Genette when he writes sarcastically: "Nelson Goodman, whose ontology is apparently a kind of nominalism tempered by cheek, is happy to say that he means to recognize individuals, but that he reserves the right to take anything whatsoever (that is to say, necessarily, classes as well) as an individual."[36]

In the case of magical nominalism, particulars are held to have ontological weight, but, as we have seen, they sometimes identify the fundamental building block of analysis with the proper name, which is not the same as a physical object. Inexorably following the logic of Ockham's razor, differentiating among an increasing proliferation of smaller and smaller particularities, each with its own proper name, would ironically undermine the principle of economy underlying the nominalist critique of unnecessary entities.[37] Does each flea, after all, deserve its own proper name? Moreover, why stop at names, even proper ones, as the ultimate indivisible particle of ontological meaning? According to some Kabbalists, it will be recalled, the more significant unit was even smaller. "For Abulafia," writes Umberto Eco, "each letter, each atomic element, already had a meaning of its own, independent of the meaning of the syntagms in which it occurred. Each letter was already a divine name."[38]

But what if the letters are understood to work their magic only when they are given numerical equivalents whose combinations somehow reveal their most profound truth, as some Kabbalists argued? Here another irony intervenes, as the semiotic relationality supposedly avoided by elevating proper names to exemplars of pure, self-referential immanence returns through the back door. For if names are truly proper, why do they need mathematical equivalents? In addition, the introduction of such alleged equivalents opens up the question of mathematics as itself contested territory, with many different implications capable of being drawn from it. We have already seen that the attribution of mathematical regularities to a harmonious cosmos comes into question when irrational numbers or the implications of infinity are fully registered, an issue that we will encounter again when we examine the aesthetic variants of nominalism. What is sometimes called the privative nature of mathematics, understood in negative terms, suggests that any attribution of indivisible individuality, let alone divine presence, to a proper name or positive number is problematic.[39]

A further question is raised if we consider the well-known distinction made by Nelson Goodman between differentiated and replete symbol systems, with the former dependent on discrete signs, like positive numbers and letters, and the latter on continuous and dense notation. The opposition is often mapped on to digital and analog representations or on language and images. Although Goodman's own bias may have been for language over images, which he thought can be read digitally, the distinction suggests that any simple privileging of alphabetical letters as ultimate ontological particulars would be hard to maintain.[40]

Not only has it been difficult to identify an integral singularity as the most granular unit of analysis, whether we call it an atom, a name, a letter, or a number, but it is also not clear that it is always practical to slice as thinly as we might. Although a strong realist ontology of universal essences may be hard to defend, it can be argued that in methodological terms—ones consonant more with conventional than magical nominalism—a kind of pragmatic "as if" approach may produce more useful results than endless slicing. In chemistry, for example, the distinction between molecular and molar mass remains significant, which shows that for science the most relevant units may not always be the smallest.[41] The same has been argued by philosophers of mathematics, who argue that classes allow far less cumbersome equations than ones that try to eliminate them entirely and are therefore more useful for scientific inquiry.[42]

The same might be said of socially or culturally meaningful units, whose proper scale and abstraction from their mediating contexts are perennial issues.[43] For sociologists in the methodologically holist Durkheimian tradition, the metalevel of society itself cannot be dissolved into its component elements. Only a method that honors the structural or relational functioning of a system will be able to register the stubborn irreducibility of its levels. Probability theorists accordingly employ stochastic methods to show that despite randomness on the level of the particular, there are patterns that hold for aggregates, which suggest that causality may be systematic or relational, albeit not for every case. They thus challenge methodological individualists, for example liberal economists, who insist on the ontological priority of singular agents acting on their own, and understand collective outcomes as always the aggregated result of individual actions, choices, and desires.[44]

The only choice, however, may not be between stubborn physicalists who search for the most basic particular reality, on the one hand, and linguistic conventionalists like Goodman who can arbitrarily chose what level to call the relevant individual, on the other. It may, in fact, be plausible to go beyond the methodological strategy of treating such higher level realities only as "as if" hypothetical expedients for social scientific or cultural analyses. That is, although not natural kinds or eternal universals separated at the objective "joints" where cutting should take place, social or cultural patterns can congeal over time into relatively stable structures that defy even conscious attempts to transform them. They act as if they are what Hegel famously called "second nature."

Marxism, for example, argues that at a certain point in history capital became a structural reality, which can be holistically analyzed as a dynamic, self-reproducing system irreducible to the intentions, acts, or beliefs of the people who are its beneficiaries or victims. Reification means that fluid processes become like solid objects, which function as if they are part of a "second nature" as stubbornly resilient as the first. "Real abstractions," to cite a term made famous by Alfred Sohn-Rethel, have ontological existence in a world dominated by fungible money and commodities.[45] What is sometimes called strong emergence theory argues that "the 'higher' levels of a complex system are ontologically irreducible to their 'lower'-level parts. The emergent properties of a system do not just exceed the aggregated properties of their components even in principle, the emergent properties cannot be explained by reference to the behavior of their components."[46] Although conventional nominalism makes us justifiably suspicious of the naturalization of the social, its overly arbitrary subjectivism can also blind us to the intransigent "reality" of humanly created social structures, especially those given to us by the past rather than consciously constructed in the present. *Pace* radical social constructivists, they have more than just discursive weight and will resist efforts to change them merely by inventing new linguistic usages.

What Alfred North Whitehead famously called the "fallacy of misplaced concreteness" can serve as a reproach to dogmatic holistic and individualist approaches alike. Reductionism, in which the complexity of a fluid reality is reified into solidified, discrete entities, can go in either direction. You can too hastily reduce, that is, wholes to their component parts, but also too quickly dissolve those parts into fleeting moments in relational wholes. In fact, the very distinction between abstract and concrete itself can lend itself to different interpretations. Although our commonsense attitude—and that of most philosophical nominalists—is to identify the former term with capacious general categories or formal patterns (as in "abstract" modern art) and the latter with substantive singularities irreducible to anything smaller, a very different definition of the distinction informs the dialectical tradition stemming from Hegel and adopted by Marx. For them, "concrete" means being situated in a complexly mediated whole, where relational and structural forces surround, penetrate, and set into motion apparently isolated elements. "Abstract," in contrast, means being removed from that context, forcibly "abstracted" from the whole, given a dubious self-sufficient integrity, and isolated from its mediations. The classic example for Hegel was the data of immediate sense experience, and for Marx, the commodity form under capitalism, in which objects produced for exchange in the market were abstracted from the production process that created them. Thus, Marx's ambivalent appreciation of nominalism as the "first materialism," which was not yet dialectical or even relational. In short, the oft-quoted reproach of the Romantic Wordsworth to the reductive impulse of the Enlightenment—"We murder to dissect"[47]—suggests that in their zeal to slice away extraneous entities, overly zealous wielders of Ockham's razor might do violence to the complex objects they are subjecting to analysis rather than experiencing as integral wholes.

These objections remain still cogent today, and cannot be cavalierly dismissed as we turn in the second part of this book to explore further paradigms of magical nominalisms. There may, however, be a promising way at least to sidestep the question of how thin our razor should slice. It would be to redescribe the nominalist challenge to the realism of universals and abstractions not in positive terms but in negative ones instead.[48] That is, rather than looking for the smallest possible indivisible unit and then assigning it a unique name or arbitrarily identifying individuality with a specific entity and calling it an irreducible whole, it would be better to identify nominalism with what Adorno would later call the "nonidentical" or Blumenberg the "nonconceptual."[49] Defined by *what it is not* rather than positively by *what it is*, it serves as a warning against the collapse of all ontological and categorical levels into a system of subsumptive categories, analogies, or macro/micrological parallels. Refusing to posit the absolute ground of the real in indivisible particulars, agnostic about what might constitute the most granular unit of analysis, it eschews the search for firm foundations or concepts without remainders. Instead, it points to the resistance of an unassimilable other to its reduction to the same, an excess that goes beyond the attempt to keep it within boundaries, a surplus that exceeds any system. Like Kant's "thing-in-itself," particular objects can be assumed to exist, but because our understanding is incapable of ever capturing or representing them as they really are, they are best understood as limiting concepts—or better put, they show the limitations of concepts while at the same time gesturing beyond their limits.

Nominalism, especially in its magical guise, can perhaps be understood less as a coherent philosophical position making positive ontological or even epistemological claims than as a protest against all attempts at universalization, conceptualization, and abstraction, whether understood ontologically, epistemologically, or linguistically. It alerts us to a negation that resists being recuperated, assimilated, or sublated and always defies subsumption under an abstract category. Here we see the relevance of positioning proper names as the meaningless other of concepts, resisting the reduction of particularity to generality and language to a semiotic system of relations among fungible terms.

Nominalism understood in this sense comports with other negative traditions of thought. Theologians have long debated the virtues of wordless, imageless, apophatic notions of divinity, as opposed to their kataphatic counterparts, which rely on positive lists of attributes, linguistic analogies or images.[50] Ever since the discovery of irrational numbers, which cannot be expressed as a fraction or a ratio of two integers, mathematicians have acknowledged that they can be only symbolized in indirect, nonnumerical ways.[51] Sometimes the religious and the mathematical have been brought together, for example, when infinitesimal calculus was invoked by theologians like Franz Rosenzweig to signify the ineffability of redemption.[52] Even some utopian social theorists have eschewed positive descriptions of the society they desire in order to honor the *Bilderverbot* (prohibition of images) they have borrowed from religious sources.[53] In short, rather than nominalism interpreted as generating a positive notion of the particular, the granular, or the individual, it can also be understood as an impulse to disrupt generic categories, subsumptive judgments, dialectical sublations, and narrative emplotments.[54] The magician's characteristic reluctance to show how the trick works may be discerned, we might say, in magical nominalism's refusal to bare the device, offer firm grounds, and in so doing dissolve its aura of mystery. It is thus not surprising to find some of the figures whose work we will be considering as paradigmatic examples of our general argument, such as Jacques Derrida, situated at the crossroads between nominalism and negative theology.[55]

The second part of the book will focus on the manifestation of the nominalist impulse, both conventional and magical, in three apparently distinct arenas of human endeavor. The first is the discourse of history, devoted to recovering, interpreting, and representing/narrating the past. The second is the discourse of aesthetics, the attempt to make sense of the disparate activities, objects and experiences that we group under the rubric of art in terms of "irrealism." The third is the theory and practice of the photograph, the culturally charged, technologically enabled capture of ephemeral moments in images that endure after time has moved on. More precisely, we will examine a finite and idiosyncratic selection of these three enormously complex human endeavors to demonstrate how an attentiveness to nominalism, especially in its magical guise, can reveal some of their more salient, if stubbornly puzzling characteristics.

3
History, Sublime Experience, and the Event

The distinction between historian and poet is not in the one writing prose and the other verse—you might put the work of Herodotus into verse, and it would still be a species of history; it consists really in this, that the one describes the thing that has been, and the other a kind of thing that might be. Hence poetry is something more philosophic and of graver import than history, since its statements are of the nature rather of universals; the statements of history are singulars.

ARISTOTLE

Conventional Nominalism and the Idiographic Method

Virtually all of the philosophical and theological issues generated by nominalism, both conventional and magical, have also played out in the register of reflecting about the past and fashioning narrative accounts of it—and appropriately so, as the rise to prominence of historical consciousness in modern culture may well have been due in large measure to the ramifying influence of the nominalist revolution. The replacement of a closed cosmos governed by harmonious regularities with an infinite, unbounded universe prepared the ground, it can be argued, for the waning of a classical notion of cyclical history in favor of the linear, open-ended alternative we associate with modernity. Or to invoke the dichotomy made famous by the conceptual historian Reinhart Koselleck, the static "space of experience," in which past patterns were assumed to repeat themselves, lost ground in favor of a moving "horizon of expectations," in which future possibilities loomed ever larger.[1] And if what was to come diverged ever more drastically from what repetitively happened before, curiosity about the unique singularity of past occurrences, rather than their typicality, could also blossom.[2] The historicist age, it has been claimed, is "the age of nominalism that permits no repetitions."[3]

The story, to be sure, is a bit more complicated. First, it is not entirely clear that the ancients consistently identified historical time with repetitive cycles, although they were often understood by posterity as having done so.[4] Nor is it the case that medieval Christianity prior to the rise of nominalism and the undermining of the cosmic natural order embraced a comparable understanding of history as cyclical, which carried with it a problematic pagan connotation. For at least since Augustine, sacred history, which prevailed in the invisible City of God, was taken instead to be linear and providential.[5] Although not random or open-ended, this salvational view of history was processual rather than cyclical, and looked forward with eschatological conviction to a momentous future event. Although paradoxically, that event might be construed as the incursion of the eternal into human temporality, it was not, *pace* Nietzsche in advance, an eternal return.

The temporality of the profane City of Man, however, might be another matter. When the Renaissance humanists rediscovered the virtues of classical culture, they could find renewed inspiration in writers like Aristotle and Polybius for a cyclical reading of secular history. As befitting an age that called itself a rebirth of the pagan past, analogies and allegories established patterns of repetition. Machiavelli, for example, pondered the rise and decline of nations in terms of moral decay. Some like Jean Bodin and Louis Le Roy were even attracted to the astrological cosmic order that seemingly had been left behind by scientific astronomy and sought to read secular history accordingly.[6] As late as Giambattista Vico's *New Science* (1730 and 1744), it was possible to discern perennial *corsi e ricorsi* (cycles and countercycles) in the "ideal eternal history" of the nations of "the gentile world."[7] In fact, as is often noted, the quintessentially modern metaphor of revolution, which came to signify a radical break with the past—and which we have seen applied retrospectively to the nominalist challenge to Scholastic realism—emerged out of an astronomical discourse of repetition and return, which initially implied the restoration of an earlier state of harmony.[8]

As the latter example shows, modern historiography could be haunted by the ghosts of past typologies, providential Christian as well as pagan cyclical; the Enlightenment idea of progress, for example, has sometimes been seen as a secularized version of Christian eschatology.[9] Even historians with less grandiose ambitions have sought structural regularities beneath the flux of occurrences or discerned repetitive patterns of development over time.[10] Comparative analyses of putative similarities in, say, economic development, revolutionary upheaval, or modern state-building have retained a place in the study of the past. Some modern historians, while eschewing rigid structural regularities, fall back on analogical reasoning to yoke together what may otherwise seem incommensurable.

Even when they eschew substantialist continuities in favor of functionalist ones—and here the historian on whose analysis of modernity we have liberally drawn, Hans Blumenberg, is a prime example—they have posited a certain repetition of "answer positions" that need to be "reoccupied" to respond to perennial questions.[11]

But for all that, what must be acknowledged is that most modern historians ultimately weaned themselves from essentialist or typological thinking, at least on a self-conscious level. Ironically, while the Italian humanists' exaggerated reverence for classical models combined with the Christian tradition of prefigural typifications to produce narratives aspiring to universal exemplary status, their research also helped undermine belief in repetitive or providential patterns. For by stimulating a rigorous scholarly interest in the reliability of the sources that were mined for the exemplification of those preordained patterns, they inadvertently created doubt about simplistic analogies.[12] The resulting honing of "scientific" research skills contributed to the waning of history as a rhetorical art seeking to impart perennial wisdom, that exemplary ideal of *historia magistra vitae* assigned by Cicero.[13]

While it was still possible as late as the mid-eighteenth century for the Tory politician and political theorist Viscount Bolingbroke to assert that "history was philosophy teaching by examples,"[14] he was clearly rowing against the tide. "The histories of the period," William Bouwsma could write of late sixteenth- and early seventeenth-century Venice, "illustrate in their particularity the age's nominalist mind-set. [They] not only discerned no general pattern in history but rejected the feasibility of imitating ancient models, pointing in this way to a new kind of historicism based on the uniqueness of each event, each moment."[15] Although it would be wrong to assume that all subsequent writers eschewed universal or generic claims, most practicing historians became tacit nominalists.[16] In Siegfried Kracauer's concise phrasing, history came to concern itself only with "the last things before the last" rather than the ultimate truths of religion or metaphysical philosophia perennis.[17]

By the nineteenth century, historians were, in fact, broadly understood to employ "idiographic" rather than "nomothetic" reasoning, to apply the terminology introduced in the 1890s by the neo-Kantian German philosopher Wilhelm Windelband.[18] While the former strives for assertoric judgments that consider unique objects in their singularity, the latter seeks universal apodictic judgments that treat particulars as exemplars of types or generic concepts. In the nomothetic camp are what came to be called the social sciences, which seek to ape the natural sciences by discovering general laws, whether structural or developmental, in various realms of human experience. They strive to move beyond description or narration to explanation, which often involved the reading of discrete occurrences as "cases" of more general causal laws.[19] Despite the occasional effort to turn history into a social science, for example by economic historians promoting "cliometrics,"[20] the majority of practicing historians share the nominalist preference for the unique instance over the typical exemplar, the singular occurrence over the perennial pattern, the particular exception over the universal rule.[21]

The nominalist revolution influenced not only historians' understanding of the subject matter of history, the *res gestae* (things done), but also their writing about them, *historia rerum gestarum* (the representation of things done). In the passage from his *Poetics* cited as the epigraph of this chapter, Aristotle had famously considered poetry as "something more philosophic and of graver import" than history, "since its statements are of the nature rather of universals; the statements of history are singulars."[22] Poetry, like philosophy, dealt with enduring essences, whereas the writing of history was a lesser genre because it narrated only ephemeral appearances. With the nominalist challenge to real universals and eternal abstract forms, however, the Aristotelian generic hierarchy could be reversed. Rather than "saving the appearances" by ever more ingenuous ways of making them compatible with purported ideal essences, as had been urged by Plato in arguing for the circular orbits of heavenly objects, they could attract legitimate attention on their own without an ulterior motive. Rescuing them from oblivion through recounting their unique stories was justification enough.

There was, however, more than one way for historians to express the nominalist elevation of the singularities of historical occurrences over universal essences. Two were the offshoots of what we have called conventional nominalism. If we wanted to identify them with modern philosophical positions, we might call one Humean and the other Kantian.[23] The first derived from the positivist faith in—some would argue fetish of—discrete facts, the granular building blocks of every historical analysis.[24] To be sure, Auguste Comte himself, for all his antimetaphysical rhetoric, had posited a progressive stage theory of human development, which his sociological method—he was that discipline's founding father—claimed were universally applicable. But later positivists, at least those who were proper historians rather than historical sociologists, were often wary of any speculative developmental pattern valid for all humankind. Not only did they reject any universal essences underlying the contingencies of historical occurrences, but they also minimized the constitutive role of the historian in interpreting the past, seeking instead to allow reliably validated sources to speak for themselves and reveal "what actually happened" in all its motley variety.[25] Although acknowledging that history was not strictly speaking an empirical science based on direct sense experience, they minimized the mediating role of generalizing concepts in the inferences drawn from the "evidence" left by the past.[26] Even philosophers of history unconvinced by the verificationist optimism of the mainstream positivist position, such as Karl Popper who preferred the falsification of inaccurate narratives, were antiessentialist nominalists.[27]

The second historiographical variant of conventional nominalism was more in tune with its conceptualist version. Although agreeing with the positivists that history as *res gestae* consisted of singular, contingent occurrences or acts surviving in the record as discrete facts, its exponents argued that the writing of history or *historia rerum gestarum* inevitably imposed generalizing concepts, ideologically inflected values, or a finite menu of formal tropes onto the narratives fashioned by historians from the traces left by the past. The last of these shifted the emphasis from historical explanations of causes to interpretations of meaning, which were often subtly conveyed by the rhetorical strategies underpinning the telling of stories. The most influential tropological formalist was the American historian Hayden White (1928–2018), who contended that, consciously or not, all historians emplotted their stories as tragedies, comedies, satires, romances, or in an ironic mode.[28] Despite their desire to be disinterested observers, producing accurate reconstructions and compelling explanations of the past, cutting, as it were, history (like nature) "at the joints," they were unconscious "metahistorians" filtering their narratives through a screen of tropes. These were the rhetorical equivalents of the transcendental categories imposed by the Kantian subject in fashioning synthetic a priori judgments about our experience of the world.[29]

Whether understood in epistemological or rhetorical terms, the ability to spin a narrative out of the contingent occurrences of the past gave historians considerable power. For although their narratives were informed by the factual evidence left in their sources, they were never entirely verified or falsified by it. "Facts," rather than being the inert, granular particulars of the *res gestae* revealed through the archival or material residues of past actions and experiences, were themselves always already "under a description."[30] And descriptions could change, as the ones intended by actors at the time of the action could be reinterpreted by later historians, who perceived other, perhaps less explicit, intentions or had a wider perspective on unintended consequences. For conceptually or tropologically inclined nominalists, the delicate balance between the descriptions of past actors and those made by present writers of *historia rerum gestarum* tilted in the latter direction. That is, the interpretations of the historical actors of their own stories could be trumped by those writing their histories, as, for example, what seemed a positive development at the time turned out with hindsight to produce an ironic reversal of intentions. Although not eschewing the "scientific" methods employed in researching the past, which were so important for the positivist inheritors of nominalism, they focused more on the reconstructive imagination of historians who wrote the narratives that drew on that research. While eschewing the essentialist realism underpinning earlier *prefigural* models of historical repetition, they nonetheless advocated a *figural* model of historical narration in which the constitutive role of the narrator predominated.[31]

Taken to their extreme, the conceptualist or tropological variants of conventional nominalism might lead to a historiographical version of that self-assertion and domination of nature that some commentators claim was implied by the denial of universal essences in the knowable world. Or as Voltaire cynically remarked, "History is after all nothing but a pack of tricks that we play upon the dead."[32] It might be called the historian's version of the Sapir-Whorf thesis writ small in which the rhetorical and ideological commitments of different narrators or narrative traditions create distinct and perhaps even incommensurable historical universes, which could then become the "truth" of different communities.

Many attempts have been made to refute this conclusion, which inevitably arouses fear of the relativization of historical knowledge. Arguably the most persuasive rests on faith in the scrutiny of the larger guild of professional historians, who are trained to judge the plausibility of competing accounts in a disinterested way. Although a full consensus is always an aspiration rather than a reality, full objectivity an impossible ideal, and the guild of historians only an "imagined community," what can be called institutional justification can serve as an ideal toward which historians should strive. At least, it encourages them to value truthfulness as a virtue, even if absolute or total historical truth is always beyond their reach.[33] This means, *pace* Voltaire, that whatever trick on the past might be played by an individual historian, it will be scrutinized and judged by an open-ended jury of his or her peers.

For those who find this answer insufficient, there is also a third alternative, which seeks to go beyond the subjectivism of conventional nominalism, as well as the intersubjective judgment of the ideal community of credentialed historians. It may not have been as frequently advocated as the others but is nonetheless of special importance for the argument of this book. It seeks to overcome the limitations of the positivist and conceptualist variants of conventional nominalism, by drawing, if often tacitly rather than explicitly, on the legacy of magical nominalism. Although it follows nominalism's "linguistic turn" in spurning a naively objectivist notion of the relationship between *res gestae* and *historia rerum gestarum*, it nonetheless resists interpreting language as a post facto imposition of an arbitrarily conceived narrative on a randomly contingent historical past. It thus distances itself from both the positivist and conceptualist versions of conventional nominalism and stresses the power the past still has over those who are its inheritors. Because its implications have never been adequately explored, it will be the major focus of this chapter.

I want in particular to examine two independent exemplars of what can be called the influence, albeit unacknowledged, of magical nominalism in historical discourse, each in a different key. Violating strict chronology, we will take them in order of increasing importance and influence. The first is what I have called elsewhere the "new experientialism," which designates in particular the work of two contemporary Dutch historians, both teaching at the University of Groningen, who advocate what Frank Ankersmit (1945–) calls "sublime historical experience" and Eelco Runia (1955–) the "presence" of the past. They developed their ideas respectively in two remarkable books, *Sublime Historical Experience* (2005) and *Moved by the Past* (2014).[34] Although the evocation of experience may imply the subjectivity of the actors of history or of those who narrate it, Ankersmit and Runia are more interested in the way the past is able to impose itself on the present without the mediation of subjective categories of meaning, rhetorical tropes, or theories of explanation. They share the ontological impulse of magical nominalism and eschew the epistemological emphasis of conventional nominalism, whether positivist or conceptualist, as well as the narrativist stress of its tropological cousin. Against generalizing or universalizing tendencies, which seek repetitive patterns in the past, they value unique encounters with its palpable traces, which produce a sense of ineffable wonder in those lucky enough to experience their power.

The second example is the discourse of "the event" adopted by a wide range of late twentieth-, early twenty-first-century French theorists after 1968,[35] often grouped together as poststructuralists (with the salient exception of Alain Badiou [1937–]). Its members, it should be acknowledged, were predominantly philosophers rather than working historians, with one important exception. Michel Foucault (1926–84) may have been trained as a philosopher and psychologist, but many of his most important works were devoted to illuminating previously occluded dimensions of the past. Whether he called himself an archaeologist or genealogist—to cite his most celebrated self-designations—he has often been appreciated as a "historical nominalist," a label he also in fact explicitly endorsed.[36]

Usually adopted to describe his rejection of essential categories operating across historical periods—perhaps his most notable target was sexuality, although he was no less critical of others like sovereignty, which he rejected in favor of analyzing the microphysics of power—it can be expanded to include an unannounced attraction to magical nominalism as well. More precisely, his thoughts on the event in particular reveal how much he shared with those nonhistorians of his generation who were touched by its legacy.

The New Experientialism

Although initially attracted to the conventionalist nominalist emphasis on the historian's constructive figuration of the past—Frank Ankersmit in particular originally came to prominence as an ally of Hayden White in the antipositivist "narrativist" camp[37]—the new experientialists grew suspicious of its basic premise. Rather than focusing on how we constitute the past, it was better to understand how it can constitute us. As Eelco Runia was to put it, "Historians like to believe that *if* there is any interaction between themselves and their objects, then it is surely a 'Kantian' interaction, an interaction, that is, in which the research object is prefigured by what they, as subjects, bring to bear on it." But, he argues, "Historical knowledge may be determined—to a degree that is barely imaginable—by the object of research."[38] Ankersmit, for his part, came to criticize the fallacies of "linguistic transcendentalism," which he detected in such postmodernist thinkers as Richard Rorty,[39] in favor of a prelinguistic encounter with the past. He came to acknowledge the inspiration of Leibniz's monadology in his approach to the past.[40] Linguistic constructivism of the kind advocated by many conventional nominalists, he argued, is based on a dubious dualism between present subject and past object. The metaphor of proximate touch and immediate contact is superior to that of distancing perspectival sight or rhetorical imposition in defining an experience of the past prior to the very split between subject and object.

Although admittedly rare, such encounters are triggered by unmediated contact with certain objects of research, material as well as textual, which defy attempts to narrate or represent them in intelligible terms, for example Lord Byron's excitement at seeing the architecture of Venice or Goethe's response to ancient Roman statues. Ankersmit mentions his own encounters with an eighteenth-century capriccio painted by Francesco Guardi and the rococo ornaments he came to know as a child.[41] The experiences they generate come to us unbidden and unprovoked by the questions we put to the past or the hypotheses about it that we test by carefully weighing evidence. Against the method of "reexperiencing" (*nacherleben*) or "reenacting" the original subjective experience of past actors, promoted in the nineteenth century by Wilhelm Dilthey and R. G. Collingwood in the twentieth as the most fruitful way of revealing historical meaning, Ankersmit and Runia have advocated a more direct communion with the past in the present.[42] Such experiences somehow overcome temporal distance rather than empathetically rehearse the putative experience of past actors. They generate what the great Dutch historian of the early-modern period Johan Huizinga called a "historical sensation," an epiphany manifest in rare but life-altering encounters with the past unfiltered by conceptual mediations or interpretative prefigurations.[43] He often liked to compare them to the experience of listening to music. They allow what Ankersmit calls fissures "in the temporal order so that the past and the present are momentarily united in a way that is familiar to all of us in the experience of déjà vu."[44] Akin to Bergson's "involuntary memory," which Walter Benjamin had linked to the unassimilated residues of trauma, a sublime experience historical "suddenly presents itself like a meteoric invasion by the past into the present. Everything surrounding us in the present is pushed aside and the whole of the world is reduced to just ourselves in this specific memory—where the memory sees us, so to say, and we see only it."[45]

Their sublimity lies precisely, as such celebrated students of the sublime as Burke and Kant had argued, not only in their emotional power but also in their resistance to all representations or explanations, their being beyond the capacity of mere language to redescribe them in communicable terms. They cannot be domesticated, *pace* Hayden White, by locating them in stories guided by prefigural tropes of emplotment. They thwart all efforts, *pace* Quentin Skinner, to reduce them to illocutionary actions in particular historical contexts, which are then available for present reconstruction. Runia calls them "fistula," "abnormal passageways" between two topoi or historical eras, and compares them with the emotionally powerful but ineffable *punctums* that Roland Barthes saw disrupting the conventional *studium* of most photographs.[46] "Historical reality," he suggests, "travels with historiography not as a paying passenger but as a *stowaway*. As a stowaway the past 'survives' the text; as a stowaway the past may surprise us."[47] Neither scientific history with its penchant for causal explanations of past events nor historical narration imbued with tropologically inflected meaning can contain and normalize such disruptive experiences, both marvelous and traumatic.

We can now perhaps begin to see in what ways the new experientialism is indebted to the spirit, if not the letter, of magical nominalism. A certain affinity is evident in its rejection of the epistemological turn of conventional nominalism in favor of a return to ontology—one, however, shorn of the universalist ambitions of realism—in which prepredicative experience gets us in direct touch with the presence of the past, not its second-order narrative representation or post facto conceptual explanation. Unapologetically anticognitivist and freely acknowledging his debts to Romanticism, Ankersmit confesses that what he seeks is "closer to moods and feelings than to knowledge; like them it is ontological rather than epistemological; and sublime experience is to be defined in terms of what you *are* rather than in terms of what knowledge you *have*."[48] Runia, for his part, elevates the role of noninterpretative metonymy over metaphor as the master trope of historical experience and contends that it "has no interest in creating meaning—it draws attention to the fact that something *is* and by zooming in on what may be called 'existential givenness' it establishes 'presence.' So, whereas metaphor tried to do away with strangeness, metonymy *makes* things strange."[49]

Valorizing meaningless strangeness goes along with the magical nominalist resistance to domestication and familiarization through subsumption under universal categories, abstract concepts, or tropologically figured narratives. Significantly, Runia argues that the priority of metonymy over metaphor was already apparent in the work of one of the most significant historical thinkers of the early-modern era—namely, Giambattista Vico, in particular in his interest in etymology. This interest derives from what we have seen is one of the abiding concerns of magical nominalism: "Vico doesn't use words and things to illuminate other words and things—instead he isolates them, descends into them, and 'finds' in them everything he possibly can. He is particularly fond of *names*. . . . For Vico, names are beyond meaning. His idea is that in names we can descend to the point where things are taken up in language, to the point, that is, where their reality, their nature, their sublime individuality still stood out."[50] Names, Runia then explains, are thus the most "primordial metonyms." It is their ability "to establish some kind of contact with a reality beyond words that explains the popularity of the commemorative practice of naming, or reciting, the names of the dead."[51]

Although contact between past and present may suggest a kind of unbroken continuity, the new experientialists are keen on stressing the disruptive, even vertiginous, effect of getting in touch with traces of a past that had been smoothed over by overly coherent stories and pat causal explanations. "This anomalous variety of discontinuity," Runia writes, "includes all instances in which we, as subjects, are overwhelmed by the presence of the past—as in *Sehnsucht* and nostalgia, in Johan Huizinga's 'historical sensation,' in what Frank Ankersmit calls 'sublime historical experience,' and . . . in the mind-boggling cases where the object of their research controls and prefigures the histories historians write."[52] Our embeddedness in the apparent continuum of history, the homogeneous, inexorable development historicism championed, need not determine the way in which we interact with the past.

How does all this comport with the magical nominalist yearning to overcome the "disenchantment of the world" resulting from the conventional nominalist revolution? Might not a penchant for "strangeness" betoken an acceptance of the estrangement and alienation that is so often linked with that disenchantment? Runia argues, however, otherwise: "Because a sublime historical event adds complexity and is, by definition, a break with what we took for granted, one might say that it brings about a re-enchantment of the world."[53] Thus as the title of his book suggests, we can be genuinely "moved" by the past, rather than have a coldly dispassionate, objective relationship to it.

Significantly, Runia ends *Moved by the Past* by citing Walter Benjamin's famous interpretation of Paul Klee's painting *Angelus Novus* as a protest against the force of "progress," a violent storm that blows us relentlessly into a future that can only continue the catastrophic historical narrative of the past.[54] The angel of history seeks to "stay, awaken the dead, and make whole what has been smashed," a fantasy of "apocatastasis" or the redemption of all souls that complements the restoration of an Adamic tongue before the Fall into the Babel of overnaming. This would heal the wounds caused by the increasing domination of nature, which is the sinister collateral damage of "progress" (and which, as we have noted, was abetted by the human self-assertion that Blumenberg saw unleashed by the nominalist revolution in its conventional guise). The saturnine Benjamin concluded that the angel's quest is in vain.

Sublime historical experiences, the new experientialists concur, are likewise only isolated oases of reconciliation, temporary moments in the rush of ongoing forces that continue to push us into a future that is all too continuous with the past. Ankersmit claims that when it is sublime, "historical experience pulls the faces of past and present together in a short but ecstatic kiss,"[55] ecstasy being understood, as it was by Huizinga, as the penetration of the boundaries of the self and an openness to the outside. But he too knows the experience will be short-lived—in an earlier version of his book, he had compared it with the ill-fated romance of Romeo and Juliet—and we should be aware that "*Historical experience is not the return to a state of primeval innocence, to a state preceding all historical writing—it should be situated, instead, in a state after or beyond all historical writing.*"[56]

He nonetheless spurns any hope for future redemption, and explicitly distinguishes his position from Walter Benjamin's.[57] Nor does he think the search for sublime experiences can somehow replace traditional historical scholarship.[58] And yet, however fragile, they still provide hope that something akin to magical vitality—like those sparks of divine light that Jewish nominalists believed were present in our mundane world—can break through, if only for a moment, the crust of convention.

The new experientialists have been most concerned with sublime historical experiences in the present, those fleeting moments of ecstatic self-transcendence in which past and present somehow connect for the historian. But they also acknowledge that a similar disruptive intensity can be attributed to moments in past history itself. Tellingly, Runia identifies the capacity to disrupt the ongoing flow of historicist change, which he calls "rhetorical *Kairos*," "with the 'event' (as Alain Badiou would say) of discontinuity. . . . It implies that the 'new'—that which is literally unimaginable—is invented out of 'what has been superseded.'"[59] Ankersmit also argues that "Only a radically decontextualized past can be an object of historical experience. And precisely this is what [Jacob] Burckhardt wanted to achieve with his cross-sectional *Querschnitt*, for this was an attempt to liberate the event from its ties with what surrounds it (and from what historiographical tradition has been saying about this)."[60] There are what he explicitly calls "sublime historical events," such as the French Revolution, which "may completely dissolve the historical identity of a previous period and replace it with a new one."[61]

This casual slippage from sublime historical *experience* to sublime historical *event* is very revealing, as is Runia's glancing acknowledgment of Badiou. It demonstrates the ability of the magical nominalist impulse to inform different dimensions of historical discourse, with varying degrees of focus on the present or past (or interpenetration of the two). There is, in fact, much more evidence of its lure in the discourse of the event that captivated so many late twentieth- and early twenty-first-century French thinkers, including the heterodox historian Michel Foucault, than in the far less widely known work of the new experientialists. We can therefore only fully appreciate the unacknowledged importance of magical nominalism by turning next in their direction.

Magical Nominalism and the Post-1968 Exaltation of the Event

What exactly happened in May 1968 in France? Or more precisely, how can we characterize what happened? Was it a revolt, a rebellion, maybe even an unsuccessful revolution? Or was it perhaps merely a harmless festival of transgression in political garb, a carnival of temporary release from the constraints of normal life? Baffled by the answer, contemporary observers fell back on the vague and undefined term *les événements*, "the events," and the name has somehow stuck.[62] Historians have continued to speak of "the events of May" to refer to the student and worker strikes and the anarchic cultural efflorescence that accompanied them, as well as the response by the forces of order that maintained President Charles de Gaulle in power.

What makes the choice of terminology so ironic is that for the previous twenty years the most influential historical school in France associated with Fernand Braudel and his colleagues at the *Annales* had been denigrating the importance of a narrative history of discrete and ephemeral events (*histoire événementielle* as François Simiand had called it) in favor of a search for the deep structures that endured for long periods of time.[63] Braudel put the reason succinctly in his classic work *The Mediterranean*: "An event is explosive, a '*nouvelle sonnante*' ('a matter of moment'), as they said in the sixteenth century. Its delusive smoke fills the minds of its contemporaries, but it does not last, and its flame can scarcely ever be discerned."[64] Imitating the social sciences with their penchant for comparative analysis, enduring patterns, and statistical regularities, the *Annales* school eschewed traditional historical narratives of the lives of great men, the chronicle of political regimes, and the tactical accounts of decisive battles. The disdain of the sociologist Émile Durkheim and his school for individualist, psychologist models of social explanation echoed in the *Annales* program.[65] Enduring or only slowly changing socioeconomic systems and the collective *mentalités* of a culture were the primary focus of their attention. Disentangling temporalities, they bypassed the rapid flux of daily happenings for the more permanent rhythms of lasting structures conditioned as much by geography as culture. Scorning vulgar empiricism, they sought to reveal glacially evolving forms of life instead of mere ephemeral surface appearances. The writing of history, they contended, should focus on perennial problems and serial patterns, rather than contingent occurrences. Its method was, *pace* Windelband, more nomothetic than idiographic.

During that same era, French Marxism in the hands of theorists like Louis Althusser and Étienne Balibar also rejected the primacy of discrete events in diachronic succession in such works as *For Marx* and *Reading Capital*, which appeared only a few years before May 1968. Jean-Paul Sartre's attempt to restore the dignity of the event in his ungainly marriage of Marxism and existentialism they scornfully repudiated.[66] Drawing on Spinoza with his hostility to linear temporality, they bemoaned the historicist reduction of the past to "the sequence of events [*à l'événementiel*], and to the effect of this sequence of events on the structure of the synchronic: the historical then becomes the unexpected, the accidental, the factually unique, arising or falling in the empty continuum of time, for purely contingent reasons."[67] Although they conceded that one might meaningfully talk of historical events, "What makes *such and such* an event *historical* is not the fact that it is an *event*, but precisely its *insertion into forms which are themselves historical* . . . [and] . . . are perfectly *definable* and *knowable*."[68] Because events are "assessed according to the single criteria [*sic*] of *brevity* (suddenness)," history is "almost of necessity confined to the sphere of political events."[69] Rather, however, than embracing the structuralist stress on enduring essences, Althusser and Balibar saw the event/structure opposition as itself grounded in a problematic notion of unfolding time based on the linear succession of discrete and homogeneous periods: "From this movement we get the determination of the historical object as an *event*, present even when it is doubted., i.e., the idea that there are *not only* events, i.e., not only 'short-term phenomena, but also non-events, i.e., *long events, long-term permanences* (which are wrongly christened 'structures')."[70]

Whether or not they were called "structures"—and Althusser ultimately came to admit that "the accidental byproduct of my theoreticist tendency, the young pup called structuralism, slipped between my legs"[71]—these nonevents were still the fundamental explanatory focus of his historical analysis, albeit not primarily because of their lengthy endurance. In his special vocabulary, radical change did occur with the "conjuncture" of forces that were to be understood in systemic terms, most notably modes of production. Their uneven development, however, could produce a contradictory "articulation," always overdetermined by many different structural pressures, which might be contained through a process of displacement or fuse into a revolutionary rupture.[72] But whatever the precise nature of the uneven social formations that led to these outcomes, they were prior to the discrete historical episodes that might be called events and far more central to a "scientific" analysis of the past.

In the wake of 1968, however, the structuralist conjuncture, including its Marxist variant, was itself soon over, and many French thinkers began to reconsider their hostility to the role of the event in history.[73] Although controversy over the importance and meaning of the event can be traced as far back as the earliest recorded accounts of the past, the term suddenly gained new urgency.[74] Sociologists like Edgar Morin and historians like Pierre Nora were quick to speak of the "return of the event."[75] Theorists once identified with structuralism like Roland Barthes would now address the challenge of "writing the event,"[76] and even Althusser himself would come in the 1980s to urge us to "think the openness of the world towards the event, the as-yet-unimaginable, and also all living practice, politics included."[77] The revival of interest in events as pivotal moments in a meaningful story signaled for many a renewed faith in diachronic narrative as the essential mode of historical presentation. As such, they could be understood as playing a role similar to "facts" for positivist historians suspicious of general patterns, as granular singularities serving as the foundational elements in the idiographic reconstruction of the past.

But ironically, when elevated to a more exalted status, events—sometimes even written with a capital *E*—could also challenge the primacy of meaningful narratives even more radically than structures and gain a more profound significance than mere facts. They could be pitted against both what Hayden White called formalist and contextualist strategies of explanation.[78] It was this dual negation that allows us to discern the shadow of magical nominalism in the poststructuralist discourse of the event. No longer confident in the teleology of dialectical development that had inspired orthodox Marxism or willing to embrace the liberal alternative associated with modernization theory, a significant number of French theorists looked elsewhere for the spark of redemption. Soon, the "event" gained an exorbitant meaning that lifted it beyond the conventional understanding of the term, as the marker of something so profound, so ineffable, that no coherent story could contain it. By the late twentieth century, it had assumed an exceptional aura manifest in the almost worshipful way a number of leading social theorists and philosophers came to evoke it. It continued to do so into the twenty-first century with post-poststructuralist theorists like Alain Badiou and the Slovenian philosopher Slavoj Žižek, who sought to leave any residues of conventional nominalism behind.[79]

Although there was no direct or self-conscious filiation, this exaltation of the event was uncannily reminiscent of the magical nominalist belief in qualitatively unique singularities, which were more than instances of real universals or exemplars of conventionally constituted categories. Expressed in the register of temporality rather than spatiality, genuine events were like those unique objects that defied subsumption under universal rules or essential types. Dimly echoing the Ockhamists' elevation of God's *potentia absoluta* over his *potential ordinata*, the celebrants of the event minimized the power of the past to determine or limit the effervescent contingency of the present. In historical terms, the event served as the chief placeholder of the disruptive excess that poststructuralists saw in language per se, the unrepresentable and irreducible obstacle to communicative transparency that characterized the experience of the sublime.

At its best, it could engender that wonder, awe, enchantment, marvel, and delight distinguishing magical from conventional nominalism, which Benjamin had identified in profane illuminations. In the spirit of magical nominalism, it held out hope against the permanent disenchantment of the world. And if sometimes its apocalyptic, antinomian force could imply catastrophe as much as redemption, trauma as much as ecstasy, this was perhaps the inevitable outcome of the demonic potential that always lurked in any invocation of magic.

Not surprisingly, philosophers rather than working historians were among the most avid proponents of the event in the spirit of magical nominalism.[80] Perhaps the first to challenge the structuralist dismissal of events in early 1968 was Jean-François Lyotard (1994–98), who did so in an introduction to a book on what was then called the "March 22 Movement."[81] Lyotard was not a historian, but he often reflected on the assumptions of historical narrative, especially when they led to a single, normative *grand récit*.[82] The latter, in fact, became the primary target of his influential critique of the triumphalist and teleological story of global modernization in *The Postmodern Condition: A Report on Knowledge*, where he famously defined postmodernism as "incredulity towards metanarratives."[83]

His earlier essay was written to introduce an ultimately unpublished study of the students at the university in Nanterre who had occupied the administration building to protest the arrest of six leaders of the National Vietnam Committee on March 22, 1968. In this short piece, Lyotard distinguished between "the system" and the "event." The former was designed to regulate "the entry, distribution, and the elimination of the *energy* that [an ensemble of persons] spends in order to exist,"[84] and was manifested in institutions that bind the energy in a field of circulating objects, such as an economy, a language, or a kinship network. A structuralist analysis based on Saussurean linguistics, Lyotard, argued, was inadequate to define its workings, for it lacks the ability to explain revolutionary eruptions, which involve a "dimension of *force* that escapes the logic of the signifier."[85] History is precisely the discipline—as opposed to political economy, social anthropology and linguistics—that takes seriously the consideration of such forces, which it understands as events. "One could call an event," Lyotard explained, "the impact, on the system, of floods of energy such that the system does not manage to bind and channel this energy; the event would be the traumatic encounter of energy with the regulating institutions."[86]

The self-regulating system that is capitalism, Lyotard continued, is confronted with such events either when its attempts to colonize previous modes of social life are resisted or when energy in the present cannot be fully regulated and tamed. In the latter case, which most interested him in the wake of May 1968, there were two orders of events, which he called quantitative and qualitative, the latter being more "enigmatic."[87] The first involved those traditional Marxist favorites: overproduction and technological unemployment. Although Lyotard, not yet past his Marxist phase, did not deny their importance, he was more interested in the second, "when the very forms through which energy is rendered circulable (the institutions, in the sense that I have given to the term) cease to be able to harness that energy—they become obsolete. The relationship between energy and its regulation undergoes a mutation. This enigma is thus the only event worthy of the name, when the regulator encounters energy that it cannot bind."[88]

To make sense of that unbindable energy, Lyotard turned to the theory of "libidinal economy," which he was elaborating around the same time.[89] "The event, as a qualitative force, is an inexplicable mutation in the position of desire: for example, where desire was *repressed* in the object (in religious societies where debt is acknowledged), it will appear *foreclosed* (in the scientific, economic, political, etc. 'positivism' of post-Renaissance and capitalist society)."[90] The March 22nd movement, Lyotard concluded with an optimism that would soon wither, is an event in all senses, but insofar as it belongs to the qualitative type, "it has performed a work of unbinding, an antipolitical work, that brings about the collapse rather than the reinforcement of the system."[91]

Lyotard's fantasy that the events of May had shaken the system to its foundations was short-lived, but his commitment to the notion of an event as a radical challenge to the status quo, an uncontrollable discharge of libidinal energy, a gathering of intensity, lingered. Thus, one of his most trenchant commentators, Bill Readings, could still describe it in 1991 as "the occurrence after which nothing will ever be the same again. The event, that is, happens in excess of the referential frame within which it might be understood, disrupting or displacing that frame."[92] He could then add, drawing on Lyotard's later theory of postmodernism, that it also means "the radical singular happening which cannot be represented within a general history without the loss of singularity, its reduction to a moment. The time of the event is postmodern in that the event cannot be understood *at the time*, as it happens, because its singularity is alien to the *language or structure* or understanding to which it occurs. The pure singularity of its occurrence, the 'it happens' which cannot be reduced to a representation, cannot be identified with 'what happens.'"[93]

Such a notion of the event is far more heavily freighted than the straightforward use of the term in mainstream historical parlance, at least in the Anglo-American world.[94] Even after it lost its meaning as a revolutionary rupture threatening the system, as it did when Lyotard turned from Marxism to postmodernism, it nonetheless remained for him a figure of radical disruption and incommensurability. In fact, it came to function as a marker of nothing less than absolute freedom.[95] In his 1982 discussion of Kant in "The Sign of History," Lyotard focused on the German term *Begebenheit,* translated as "event," which when "delivered in human historical experience must indicate a cause the occurrence of which remains undetermined with respect to time—and we recognize in this rule the clause stating the independence of causality by freedom from the diachronic series of the mechanical world."[96] In connection with the French Revolution, Lyotard claimed, the event was understood by Kant as related to the sublime because of its resistance to subsumption under cognitive categories and its accompaniment by the emotion of "enthusiasm." In the present, he concluded, a *Begebenheit* eludes both the constraining power of the dominating subject and the attempt of capitalist rationalization to contain it. Not surprisingly, at the end of *The Postmodern Condition,* he could even invoke, without identifying its provenance, one of the key features of Benjamin's magical nominalism: "Let us wage war on totality; let us be witness to the unpresentable: let us activate the differences and save the honor of the name."[97]

While Lyotard was elaborating his notion of the event as a mark of radical freedom, sublime unrepresentability, and irrecuperable libidinal energy, it was also being idiosyncratically developed in the work of another thinker whose contribution to what became known as poststructuralist thought was no less profound: Gilles Deleuze (1925–95).[98] In *The Logic of Sense,* published in 1969, Deleuze gave the paradoxically anticonceptual concept of the event (sometimes even spelled with a capital letter) special attention. Significantly, *The Logic of Sense* begins with an evocation of the enigmatic works of Lewis Carroll, which "involve a category of very special things: events, pure events."[99] These, Deleuze defines as "the simultaneity of a becoming whose characteristic is to elude the present. Insofar as it eludes the present, becoming does not tolerate the separation or the distinction of before and after, or of past and future."[100] Paradoxically, events affirm both directions at once, "active and passive, cause and effect, more and less, too much and not enough, already and not yet. The infinitely divisible event is always *both at once.* It is eternally that which has just happened and that which is about to happen, but never that which is happening."[101] Operating on the surface rather than on some putatively deeper level, not even the rabbit hole into which Alice first tumbles in Lewis Carroll's tale, events have no sense beyond themselves, no latent meaning into which they can be translated. They are the folds in being that interrupt states of affairs like flashes of lightning in a darkened sky, virtual potentialities or counterfactual possibilities immanent in what is actual.

Although absolute singularities, events are nonetheless not entirely antithetical to structures. In fact, Deleuze was careful to say that singularities can be arranged in series, which intersect with other series. "And for this reason," he conceded, "it is imprecise to oppose structure and event: the structure includes a register of ideal *events*, that is, an entire *history* internal to it. . . . The two heterogeneous series converge toward a paradoxical element, which is their 'differentiator.' This is the principle of the emission of singularities."[102] These singularities are involved in a process of endless transformation, redistribution, and displacement, which is what we might call their history.

There is, however, a distinction that Deleuze drew between a proper event, which he calls pure and ideal, and a mere accident, which he defined as a "spatio-temporal realization in a state of affairs."[103] Here the argument gets explicitly metaphysical, with echoes of Nietzsche's eternal return reverberating through the text. "Events are ideational singularities, which communicate in one and the same Event. They have therefore an eternal truth, and their time is never the present which realizes them and makes them exist. . . . To reverse Platonism is first and foremost to remove essences and to elucidate events in their place, as jets of singularities. A double battle has the objective to thwart all dogmatic confusion between event and essence, and also every empiricist confusion between event and accident."[104]

Deleuze's critique of transcendent Platonic forms or essences suggests his attenuated debt to nominalist anti-universalism, but what is perhaps even more significant is his opposing of singular events rather than particular objects to those essences. For it demonstrates the importance of temporal as well spatial questions in his thought,[105] in particular the distinction between Chronos, the time of history within which events occurred, and Aion, the totally distinct time of the event itself, which was unbounded, sacred, even eternal: "Chronos is the present which alone exists. It makes of the past and the future its two oriented dimensions, so that one goes always from the past to the future—but only to the degree that presents follow one another inside partial worlds or partial systems. Aion is the past-future, which in an infinite subdivision of the abstract moment endlessly decomposes itself in both directions and once and forever sidesteps the present."[106]

Deleuze was clearly a philosopher with no intention of turning his theory of the event into a tool for the writing of history in any plausible sense of the term, even if he came to characterize May 1968 as "of the order of the pure event."[107] Indeed, as Daniel W. Smith points out, "Deleuze distinguishes between the actualization of an event in a state of affairs, that is, in history; and the pure event, which is irreducible to its actualizations—the event in its becoming, in its specific consistency, which escapes history and is 'utopic,' both nowhere and no-where."[108] The ideal of purity, as many poststructuralists insisted, was, to be sure, always already polluted, and so the desire to differentiate pure events from their historical counterparts was destined to be thwarted.

Deleuze's philosophical idea of the event was, in fact, soon incorporated into the thinking of another poststructuralist luminary, Michel Foucault (1926–1984), whose archaeological and genealogical methods were intended to make sense of the past.[109] Although a student of Althusser and initially grouped among the structuralists,[110] Foucault by the 1970s was rapidly moving away from many of their most fundamental assumptions.[111] His new position has often be identified with nominalism, but understood in conventional terms as a linguistic practice. Thus, for example, according to John Rajchman: "Nominalism was more than a methodological or philosophical preference for Foucault. His histories are *themselves* nominalist histories. They are not histories of things, but of the terms, categories, and techniques through which certain things become at certain times the focus of a whole configuration of discussion and procedure. One might say he offers a *historical* answer to the philosophical question of how such things are 'constituted.'"[112]

That Foucault may also have gone beyond conventional nominalism is, however, suggested by his 1970 review of Deleuze's *The Logic of Sense* and *Difference and Repetition*, in which Foucault explicitly interpreted the philosopher's work as a repudiation of structuralism's disdain for "the event."[113] Deleuze, Foucault hastened to make clear, had defended it in his own unique fashion. To explain Deleuze's complicated and challenging defense required, however, careful unpacking. For there were, Foucault argued, three other recent attempts to understand the event that were less persuasive than Deleuze's. These he identified with neopositivism, phenomenology, and what he called "the philosophy of history."[114] Neopositivism, he charged, confuses an event with "a state of things," which means lodging "the event within the density of bodies, to treat it as a material process, and to attach itself more or less implicitly to a physicalism."[115] Because it is antitranscendental, rejecting what is outside the world as it is, it fails to understand the "pure surface of the event and attempts to enclose it, forcibly—as a referent—in the spherical plenitude of the world."[116]

Phenomenology, in contrast, "reoriented the event with respect to meaning: either it placed the bare event before or to the side of meaning—the rock of facticity, the mute inertia of occurrences—and then submitted it to the active processes of meaning, to its digging or elaboration; or else it assumed a domain of primal signification, which always existed as a disposition of the world around the self, tracing its paths and privileged motivations, indicating in advance where the event might occur and its possible form."[117] The first version was Sartre's, the second, Merleau-Ponty's. Because both claim that the significance of the event exists only for a subjective consciousness, phenomenology "places the event outside and beforehand, or inside and after, and always situates it with respect to the circle of the self."[118] In other words, it understands the event only in terms of its being experienced as meaningful by a conscious subject.

The third inadequate approach, that of "the philosophy of history," a category Foucault did not identify with specific thinkers, "encloses the event in a cyclical pattern of time." Treating the present as a previous future, in which its form was already prepared, and the past as a future whose content is already predestined, it "requires a logic of essences (which establishes the present in memory) and of concepts (where the present is established as a knowledge of the future), and then a metaphysics of a crowned and coherent cosmos, of a hierarchical world."[119] Because it stresses the temporal context of events, the philosophy of history, Foucault concludes, "defines its identity and submits it to a solidly centered order."[120] In short, the philosophy of history dissolves the specificity of the event in an already narrativized temporal pattern, which obscures its singular irreducibility.

Deleuze, noted Foucault approvingly, introduced a more radical version of the event. It is freed from its subjection to the world, as in the neo-positivist reading, to the self, as in the phenomenological reading, or to God understood as a cyclical pattern of eternal return, as in the philosophy of history. Rather than defining the event on its own, however, Deleuze situated it in a tense relationship with another key term, which is the "phantasm." The latter, according to Foucault's gloss, forms "the impenetrable and incorporeal surfaces of bodies; and from this process, simultaneously topological and cruel, something is shaped that falsely presents itself as a centered organism and that distributes at its periphery the increasing remoteness of things."[121] If the phantasm is the site of false organismic wholeness, cruel in its relegation of what escapes it to insignificance, does the event reach a more profound truth? For Deleuze, as we have seen, it does not. As "pure difference," the event resists subsumption under a concept or a category; it refuses to be judged as commensurate with the real; it defies analogical similarity; it remains infinitely indefinite, always a singular universal that cannot be absorbed into a dialectical process of negation negating itself. What recurs is only difference, which is manifest in the unsublatable event. We are clearly not far, in other words, from that apophatic reading of magical nominalism described earlier.

Deleuze's antiphenomenological philosophy, a nomadic affirmation of theatrical surfaces rather than cognitive or meaningful depths, was a heady mixture of Nietzsche and Spinoza, and as such might seem scarcely applicable to actual historical analysis.[122] Foucault, nonetheless found inspiration in it for his own recovery of the importance of the event. But it was, to be sure, a version of the event well beyond what had been understood by the traditional narrative historiography so disdained by structuralists in the 1960s. Whereas the latter situated events in an emplotted story as critical turning points or sites of heightened meaning in larger transitional stories of development or decline, Foucault followed Deleuze in stressing their idiosyncratic and irreducible singularity. In a 1977 interview titled "Truth and Power," Foucault claimed that his interest in the event could justify his saying, "I don't see who could be more of an anti-structuralist than myself." He then added: "But the important thing is to avoid trying to do for the event what was previously done with the concept of structure. It's not a matter of locating everything on one level, that of the event, but of realizing that there are actually a whole order of levels of different types of events differing in amplitude, chronological breadth, and capacity to produce effects."[123]

Foucault, to be sure, implied that because such events belong to differentiated networks and levels, operating as layers of systematic regularity, Deleuze's notion of pure difference, like Lyotard's celebration of undetermined freedom, may have gone too far. But he nonetheless shared their hostility to the phenomenological search for meaning based on the priority of the subject, as well as the structuralist belief in systems of signification: "From this follows a refusal of analyses couched in terms of the symbolic field or the domain of signifying structures, and a recourse to analyses in terms of the genealogy of relations of force, strategic developments, and tactics. Here I believe one's point of reference should not be to the great model of language [*langue*] and signs, but to that of war and battle . . . relations of power, not relations of meaning."[124]

These relations, as he had previously explained in *The Archaeology of Knowledge*, might be understood in terms of a correlation between new statements in a discursive field, governed by a system of what can and cannot be said, and "external" events. In fact, the task of archaeology "is to show on what conditions a correlation can exist between them, and what precisely it consists of (what are its limits, its form, its code, its law of possibility). It does not try to avoid that mobility of discourses that makes them move to the rhythm of events; it tries to free the level at which it is set in motion—what might be called the level of 'evential' engagement."[125]

Foucault's notion of "engagement" did not mean, however, that each event was an irruption of utter incommensurability and absolute freedom. In his inaugural lecture at the Collège de France in 1970, Foucault emphasized the importance of seeking to reveal new ensembles of events on all levels of the decentered historical totality. "What is significant," he insisted with an implicit bow to Deleuze, "is that history does not consider an event without defining the series to which it belongs, without specifying the method of analysis used, without seeking out the regularity of phenomena and the probable limits of their occurrence, without enquiring about variations, inflexions and the slope of the curve, without desiring to know the conditions on which these depend."[126] There is certainly no "subject of history," either actual or potential, whose intentionality produces events. Nor is there any unified process of historical evolution, dialectical mediation, teleological purpose, or a single cause-and-effect determinism, as some earlier historians had assumed. But history did not abandon this quest "in order to seek out structures anterior to, alien or hostile to the event. It was rather in order to establish those diverse converging, and sometimes divergent, but never autonomous series that enable us to circumscribe the 'locus' of an event, the limits to its fluidity and the conditions of its emergence."[127] Such series out of which events emerged had to be understood as discontinuous from each other, undetermined by a master code, and possessing a certain unmotivated randomness of their own.

In a 1978 interview later published as "Question of Method," Foucault further elaborated his reasons for adopting what he called the "eventialization" of history. "First of all," he explained, it means a "breach of self-evidence. It means making visible a singularity at places where there is a temptation to invoke a historical constant, an immediate anthropological trait, or an obviousness which imposes itself uniformly on all."[128] As such, it undermined the assumption that things had to happen in the way they happened. Second, it means "rediscovering the connections, encounters, supports, blockages, plays of forces, strategies and so on which at a given moment establish what subsequently counts as being self-evident, universal and necessary."[129] Rather than utterly ineffable, however, the event should be understood as the effect of multiple causes, what he called a "'polyhedron' of intelligibility, the number of whose faces is not given in advance and can never be properly taken as finite."[130] *Discipline and Punish*, his then recently completed work on the birth of the modern carceral system, was based on this method: "eventializing different ensembles of practices, so as to make them graspable as different regimes of 'jurisdiction' and 'veridication': that, to put it in exceedingly barbarous terms, is what I would like to do."[131] For Foucault, the event remained, as Thomas Flynn has noted, "a functional concept which serves to introduce differential relations and chance occurrences into the very core of historiography. The structure/event dichotomy is simply replaced by the series/event relationship, and series are conceived as events of a higher level, enjoying their own duration and succession."[132]

To summarize our argument so far, whether understood as an irruption of freedom, as in Lyotard; pure, singular difference, as in Deleuze; or as a nodal point of multiple series of converging and diverging phenomena allowing the unexpected to happen, as in Foucault, events were no longer banished to the margins of historical discourse, as they had been during the heyday of the *Annales* school before 1968. Like the sublime historical experiences cherished by the new experientialists, they invite being understood in terms of the magical nominalist stress on numinous particulars, which are not constituted by subjective or intersubjective will. To make this affinity even clearer, however, we need to explore the role of the event in the work of two other French thinkers of the era, Jacques Derrida (1930–2004) and Alain Badiou (1937–), for whom it served as much as what can be called a philosopheme, a potent philosophical category, as a tool of historical analysis.

Understanding the full implications of their arguments will require opening up a brief parenthesis to consider the impact of yet another celebrant of the event from across the Rhine, Martin Heidegger, who was profoundly influential in France.[133] Heidegger, to be sure, was no friend of nominalism, at least in its conventional form, nor can we easily assimilate him to the tradition that Bielik-Robson calls Jewish nominalism.[134] His central notion of Being would not easily survive the slices of Ockham's razor. And yet Heidegger's ontological resistance to the priority of the epistemological subject and fascination with the numinous power of language puts him in contact with many of the impulses we have been attributing to magical nominalism.[135] It is in part for this reason that despite their obvious political differences and attitudes toward the Jewish legacy, he has often earned a comparison with Walter Benjamin.[136]

The Heideggerian term of art that is most often rendered in English as "event" is *Ereignis,* which has a number of meanings and connotations not present in *Begebenheit.*[137] Although more closely linked with *sich ereignen* (to happen or to occur), its sedimented implication of "owning"—from the word *eigen*—has also allowed it variously to be translated by "appropriation," "the event of appropriation," or even the awkward neologism "enowning." Heidegger himself wrote that it was untranslatable, like the Greek *logos* or the Chinese *tao*, and it certainly has many connotations that the English word "event" lacks.[138] At certain points in his career, Heidegger seems to have emphasized some meanings and at different moments others.[139]

At the risk of simplification, let me focus on a few of the salient implications of his complicated argument. First, it is closely linked with Heidegger's mature notion of "experience," which he differentiated sharply from the notion of "lived experience," or *Erlebnis*, which his earliest French readers had mistakenly conflated with subjective inwardness.[140] Whereas the latter implies a world of prereflexive meanings that were located in the interiority of a subject, endowed with intentionality, the experience of *Ereignis* is more fundamental, passive, and impersonal. Second, it is also very different from the disinterested experience that a subject has of an external object in the service of mastering the world, which is conveyed by the word *Vorgang*. It is, to cite one commentator, "not just an occurrence within the domain of beings, such as a sunrise, an auto accident, or a battle. *Ereignis* is not a being but that which enables beings to manifest themselves as such."[141] Nor does it invite the historical *Nacherleben* (reexperiencing) advocated by Dilthey, but spurned by Ankersmit's in describing a "sublime historical experience."[142]

Third, *Ereignis* suggests the appropriation of Being, as opposed to the trivial happenings of the beings of daily life, which take place on the more superficial level of the ontic rather than the ontological. The appropriation that takes place is, however, not that *by* man (or Dasein) of Being, but rather *of* man (or Dasein) *by* Being. It is thus far more, Heidegger contended, than mere *Begebenheiten*, which are "visible, dramatic, but superficial public events."[143] In contrast, genuine events are like flashes of lightning that reveal deeper truths. In the gloss of Charles Bambach, "Truth is not subordinate to value, Heidegger claimed; it is a primordial 'worlding' or 'eventing' (*es ereignet*) whose grammatical structure follows neither the subject nor the predicate but takes the form of the 'middle voice.'"[144] In other words, whereas garden variety historicism leads to a relativism of values and focuses on mere ontic stories rather than revealing absolute truths, for Heidegger, it was precisely an *Ereignis* that opens a window on a deeper truth beyond mere subjective judgments, ethical or cognitive. It was thus related to the grammatical middle voice, in which no distinct subject perceives or judges an external object.

But fourth, Being's appropriation of man does not imply its positive presencing in a moment of fulfilled time, a kind of secular parousia in which alienation ends triumphantly in reconciliation and homecoming. It is more a partial disclosure than a full possession. It would be wrong, Robert Bernasconi explains, for it "to be understood simply as a power of revelation. Heidegger has not become a victim of the urge to bring everything in the light so that it can be made subject to examination. *Ereignis* also bears within itself its own withdrawal, which Heidegger announces with the word *Enteignis*. . . . *Ereignis* is not a word for Being. *Ereignis* is the word that arises from the experience of *the lack of a word for Being*."[145]

With all of these convolutions, it is not surprising that Heidegger's critics have doubted, and with reason, that his ruminations on *Ereignisse* or indeed historicity in general have any link whatsoever with real historical events in their more conventional sense.[146] When he did invoke it in specific circumstances—for example, in extolling the *Frontgeist* (the communal spirit of soldiers in the trenches) of World War I as essential preparation for Nazism[147]—the link seems not to have troubled his admirers, if they registered it all.

But despite the controversies surrounding his notion of *Ereignis*, Heidegger provided three crucial lessons for the French celebrants of the event we are now examining. The first concerns the extraordinary importance imputed to it, elevating it beyond the realm of mere ontic happening or superficial occurrence and connecting it with something as profound as Being itself. Although distancing themselves from Heidegger's exorbitant understanding of Being, both Derrida and Badiou absorbed his lesson that an event was an unusual and profound thing that opened up a tear in the fabric of everyday, mundane life. We have already seen Lyotard argue something similar, although from the Freudian perspective of a libidinal economy filtered through a Kantian notion of the causality of freedom. Unlike Lyotard, and this was the second lesson, they took seriously Heidegger's stress on the essentially passive nature of an event, so that it was not a human appropriation of the world, an imposition of our meaning on it, or the mastering of objects that lay before us. An event was not caused by intentional praxis, individual or collective, although it did involve a certain delayed response on the part of those who recognized it as such.[148] And finally, they accepted Heidegger's understanding of events as having a complicated temporal dimension that prevented them from being simple momentary punctuations of a continuum of time, incarnations of what Derrida famously was to damn as the "metaphysics of presence."

For Derrida, although the event is not the hinge episode of a meaningful, coherent narrative, let alone a "moment" in a Hegelian dialectical development, it is also not a punctual interruption in an ongoing continuum or the revelation of an ontological truth hidden by trivial ontic occurrences.[149] Instead, it is the intensified expression of the time out of joint that he called "hauntological" in his *Specters of Marx*.[150] That is, it perpetuates the spectral trace of past traumas as well as the promise of a future, or *avenir,* that is perpetually *à venir,* always destined to be delayed in arriving.[151] In *Specters,* he speaks of the inheritance of the Marxist tradition in terms of an event that cannot be absorbed into a mythological, religious or scientific narrative. "The form of this promise or of this project remains absolutely unique. Its event is at once singular, total, and uneffaceable—uneffaceable except by a denegation and in the course of a work of mourning that can only displace, without effacing, the effect of a trauma. There is no precedent whatsoever for such an event."[152]

The pure singularity of an event, Derrida explained, cannot be anticipated by what Kantians would call a regulative idea or contained in what hermeneuticians like Hans-Georg Gadamer would call a horizon of expectations. Arriving utterly unannounced, "it would suppose an *irruption* that punctuates the horizon, *interrupting* any performative organization, any convention, or any context that can be dominated by conventionality."[153] Although performative action is often said to produce events, "where there is the performative, an event worthy of the name cannot arrive. If what arrives belongs to the horizon of the possible, or even of a possible performative, it does not arrive, it does not happen, in the full sense of the word."[154] Instead, it has the quality of an unexpected surprise, which cannot be then easily recuperated by the subject or subsumed under a concept.[155]

But the surprise, Derrida cautioned in the apophatic spirit of magical nominalism, cannot be turned into an apocalyptic tearing of the veil in which truth is positively revealed. "This thought of the event," he insisted in a conversation with the feminist philosopher Hélène Cixous, is "without truth unveiled or revealed, without phallagocentrism of the greco-judeo-paulino-islamo-freudo-heideggeriano-lacanian veil, without phallophoria, that is, without procession or theory of the phallus, without veiling or unveiling of the phallus, or even of the mere place, strictly hemmed in, of the phallus, living or dead."[156]

In one of his last essays, published in 2003, "A Certain Impossible Possibility of Saying the Event," Derrida compared the event to the unanticipated and unreciprocated gift that disrupts the smooth workings of an economy of exchange. When it happens, it has the oxymoronic quality of an impossible possibility, something that comes from on high, a vertical intervention in the horizontal flow of time. It also defies efforts to represent, record, indeed merely to "say" it, at least before it happens—to "predict" it.[157] Indeed, despite its having happened, it never entirely sheds its impossibility, or better put, it shows the entanglement of possibility and impossibility. For this reason, Heidegger's *Er-eignis* is at the same time an *Ent-eignis*, which Bielik-Robson glosses as "a de-propriating erasure and a secret that blocks a trope of reversal, attempting to *trace back* the path leading to *das Frühste* [the earliest]."[158]

After an event happens, Derrida claims, "The saying of the event or the saying of knowledge regarding the event lacks, in a certain manner *a priori*, the event's singularity simply because it comes after and it loses the singularity in general."[159] Precisely because we insist on saying it, its singularity is always already undermined. "Repetition must already be at work in the singularity of the event, and with the repetition, the erasure of the first occurrence is already underway—whence, loss, mourning, and the posthumous, sealing the moment of the event, as the originary. Mourning is already there."[160] Thus, the hauntological rather than ontological status of the event as a ghost of a presence that can never be, indeed never was, fully present. As we have noted, Derrida did not share what often seems Benjamin's quixotic hope to restore an Adamic language prior to the fall or celebrate the purity of the proper name as totally beyond meaning.[161] Here we see how the overlapping paradigms of magical nominalism do not necessarily align into perfect congruence.

Not only do events themselves lose their absolute singularity in their post facto recounting, so too does the rhapsodic discourse of "the event," which remained potent even after the poststructuralist moment had passed in French thought. Its repetitive survival, albeit with a difference, is best shown if we turn now in conclusion to the work of the Marxist philosopher Alain Badiou, who adamantly separated himself from deconstruction, indeed from all poststructuralist philosophies because of their relativist disdain for unequivocal truths. He also explicitly differentiated his interpretation of the event from that of thinkers like Deleuze.[162] According to one commentator, Badiou "celebrates the pure event or arrival of innovation in the spheres of politics, cosmology, art and eros. Compared with Deleuze, this event of arrival is given no ontological underpinning—not even the contradictory underpinning of emergence from a virtuality that it simultaneously cancels or contradicts."[163] Nor does Badiou's event have the pluralist pathos of Derrida or Deleuze, as it reveals instead a univocal meaning.

One of a number of continental philosophers who sought to revive speculative metaphysics, Badiou disdained the linguistic turn that was indebted to the legacy of conventional nominalism.[164] As Laurent Milesi put it, "Badiou's anti-nominalism and anti-relativism leaves no place in philosophical investigation for linguistic issues: these are 'sophistics' and subordinate the question of truth to that of expression in language conceived as resistant and non-transparent."[165] Nor did he seek the revelation of that truth in the *Sprachmagie* of recovered Adamic names that had so intrigued Walter Benjamin.

Nonetheless, Badiou's exuberant reading of the event does share many of the characteristics of those we have already encountered among the poststructuralist legatees of magical nominalism. In fact, it has also been compared to the religious idea of the miracle, which was so critical in the medieval nominalists' undermining of Scholastic realism.[166] Badiou once explicitly admitted that "under the rubric of event, my philosophy is also a secularization, a rationalization, of the religious notion of miracle. In this sense, yes, I believe in miracles."[167] Developed throughout his voluminous oeuvre, his idea of the event is most extensively discussed in his magnum opus *Being and the Event*, published in 1988.[168] As his title indicates, there is a certain amount of Heidegger in Badiou, even if his mathematical interpretation of Being—based largely on his controversial reading of Georg Cantor's set theory—distinguishes him from the German philosopher who privileged language, in particular poetry.[169]

When it comes to the event, however, there are clear echoes of *Ereignis*, at least in the broad sense of a tear, or opening, in the fabric of everyday, routine existence. The event for Badiou transcends as well normal knowledge of Being, or what he calls "the encyclopedia," revealing instead a deeper insight into the truth. As he puts it in *Infinite Thought*: "Knowledge as such only gives us repetition; it is concerned only with what already is. For truth to affirm its newness, there must be a supplement. This supplement is committed to chance—it is unpredictable, incalculable: *it is beyond what is*. I call it an event. A truth appears in its newness because an eventful supplement interrupts repetition."[170] For Badiou, a genuine event only happens in history and not nature, and is an unfounded, haphazard, evanescent expression of pure random chance.[171] It "brings to light a possibility that was invisible or even unthinkable. An event is not by itself the creation of a reality; it is the creation of a possibility, it opens up a possibility."[172] Being appears in mathematically legible terms, but the event is "supernumerary" and thus outside of the order of the normal, more therefore than a breakthrough of Being in Heidegger's sense of *Ereignis*.[173] It is not part of "the one," but an "ultra-one," which can never be folded back into the set from which it has departed. Significantly, "one of the names of the Outside is 'event.'"[174] Because the conventional nominalists are wrong to claim that mathematics is imposed on the world rather than ontologically inherent in it, the "ultra-one" event creates, at least as a possibility, a new reality.[175]

Although events happen at what Badiou calls an "evental site" (*situation événementale*) in the conventional order of things, an abnormal place on the cusp between order and the void, they are not the product of discernible forces working to bring them about. Nor are evental sites evident as such before the event occurs. There is thus no role for virtuality in Badiou's radical contrast between events and what they punctuate, no ontological weight to what Hegel would have called potentiality or Ernst Bloch the "not yet."[176] "An event," he insists, "is never the concentration of a vital continuity, or the immanent intensification of a becoming. It is never co-extensive with becoming. It is, on the contrary, on the side of a pure break with the becoming of an object of the world, through the auto-apparition of this object."[177] Rather than emerging out of or forming a new immanent unity, a Leibnizian harmony of monads, the event is the principle of decomposition of the rigid unities that already exist. "To break with empiricism," Badiou rhapsodizes, "the event must be thought as the advent of what is subtracted from all experience: the ontologically un-founded and the transcendentally discontinuous. To break with dogmatism, the event must be released from every tie to the One. It must be subtracted from Life in order to be released to the stars."[178]

Utterly unprepared and not the product of human will or intention, the event for Badiou nonetheless also needs to be recognized as such by what he calls an intervener. "Everything will depend on the way in which the possibility posed by the event is grasped, elaborated, incorporated and set out in the world. This is what I name a 'truth procedure.'"[179] At times, he suggests it is the actors closely involved with it who are the ones who must carry it out. The recognition of an event, he writes in his 1998 *Metapolitics*, is "simply at one with the political decision. . . . The point from which a politics can be thought—which permits, even after the event, the seizure of its truth—is that of its actors, and not its spectators."[180] Elsewhere, the recognition seems to come from those who remain faithful to it after the fact. "Fidelity," he writes, is "the name of the process: it amounts to a sustained investigation of the situation, under the imperative of the event itself; it is an immanent and continuing break."[181]

Badiou's initial treatment of this issue in *Being and the Event* invited the reproach—made among others by Lyotard—that fidelity meant a kind of purely decisionist choice about which occurrences could be called authentic events. Giorgio Agamben even argued that Badiou drew on Schmitt's notion of a state of exception:

> His central category of the event corresponds to the structure of the exception. Badiou defines the event as an element of a situation such

> that its membership in the situation is undecidable from the perspective of the situation. To the State, the event thus necessarily appears as an excrescence. According to Badiou, the relation between membership and inclusion is also marked by a fundamental lack of correspondence, such that inclusion always exceeds membership (theorem of the point of excess). The exception expresses precisely this impossibility of a system's making inclusion coincide with membership, its reducing all its parts to unity.[182]

In arguing that a genuine decision is made outside any binding legal structures, Badiou would thus seem to be echoing the conventional nominalist prioritizing of the medieval *potentia absoluta* over the *potentia ordinata,* which was transfigured into human self-assertion, and in so doing tacitly undermined his anti-nominalist stress on objective truth. Acknowledging the force of this criticism, Badiou would later concede that "I now think that the event has consequences, objective consequences and logical consequences. These consequences are separated by the event. The effect of the event is a profound transformation of the logic of the situation—and that is not an effect of a decision. The decision is to be uniquely faithful to the transformation."[183] And, moreover, he admitted, it need not always be a transformation in a progressive direction, but might lead instead to the revelation of emptiness instead of fullness beneath the surface of quotidian existence, an example being what recently has been called "the fall of Marxism."[184]

Unanswered Questions

A great deal more might be said of the pivotal role of the event in Badiou and the other thinkers we have treated, and we might add younger figures like the phenomenologist Claude Romano and Badiou's student Quentin Meillassoux.[185] But by now enough examples have been introduced to illustrate how the spirit of magical nominalism infused its unique role in recent French thought. Despite the important nuances separating different theorists, a number of more or less common themes emerge. All of them reject the structuralist search for deep-seated repetitive patterns that endure over long periods of time. All invest the event with the pathos of disruptive innovation, either as a moment of freedom, radical surprise, libidinal energy, the appropriation of Being, or the undermining of conventional meaning. Virtually all understand the temporality of the event as not simply a punctual bisection of the flow of routine time, but as preserving traces of an unfulfilled past and signaling the emergence or at least promise of a radically new future. In this sense, an *e*-vent is also an *ad*-vent, a connotation, it might be noted, already suggested by Merleau-Ponty in *The Prose of the World*.[186] Or to put it in more colloquial terms, no event is ever a "current event," let alone one entirely prepared by the past. If it has any basic temporality, it is that of the future anterior (sometimes called the future perfect), the time of what will come to be a completed past in what will be the future, the time of "this will have been."[187]

The very singularity of the event, its resistance to being recuperated by contextual or conceptual meaning, serves for them all as a marker of distinction. Lyotard may call the events of May 1968 antipolitical in their unleashing of desire, while Badiou may link the event with his version of a genuinely militant politics, which has all the profundity of what the French call *le politique*. But both see it disrupting politics as usual or *la politique*.[188] Although Foucault distanced himself from the claims of "pure difference" made by some of the others and situated events relationally at the crossroads of regular series, he too positioned the event against both structuralist and phenomenological quests for explanatory or interpretive plenitude. For all of them, it stood for the ineffable, the unexpected, the surplus that always exceeds any attempt to contain it. Fidelity to the event, we might say expanding a bit on Badiou's term, involves a certain humility before its excessive, disruptive, unforeseen force, comparable to the magical nominalist awe before the power of proper names or numinous objects.

Humility, however, might also be warranted before celebrating the magical nominalist impulse in both the idea of sublime historical experience and the poststructuralist exaltation of the event. A number of troubling questions linger. Let us begin with Ankersmit and Runia. The "short, but ecstatic kiss" that unites a current historian with the past may be a suggestive metaphor, but it implies that the rest of us are left out of the encounter. The new experientialists give us, alas, little guidance in translating such magical moments into shared insights with lasting value for the community of historians as a whole. Although acknowledging their sublime unrepresentability may offer a useful corrective to the hubris of those who think they can narrate the past "as it actually was" or even master it through post facto tropological emplotments, it cannot be elevated to the rule rather than the exception in our encounters with the past.

A desire for the "presence" of the past in Runia's terms, moreover, invites the reproach that it yearns for precisely what the poststructuralist celebrants of the temporal disjointedness of the event would damn as "the metaphysics of presence." We may recall Gadamer's claim that to name something is an invocation "always to call it into presence."[189] But what if what is summoned is itself always already temporally disjointed, hauntologically spectral in Derrida's sense? That is, while keeping an eye out for those "stowaways" that somehow survive the voyage from past to present, we have to acknowledge that the past itself may have been temporally fractured rather than integrated, a condition which the ruptures in historical continuity that have be called events make especially clear.

If sublime historical experiences are rare and atypical, so too are the "genuine" or "pure" events extolled by the French theorists we have examined. Indeed, it is precisely because of their extraordinary role in interrupting the flow of historical time that they warrant such attention. But an event will be surprising only against the expectation that the ongoing narrative will go on longer. Without the ground of normal historical flow, the figure of the abnormal, unique event cannot stand out. Every rupture in that flow is, moreover, followed by a certain restoration in which the wound is sutured and the inauguration of a new normal in which a ground for future possible events follows. Although events may break through the crust of mundane historical change and allow something new to enter the world, their aftermath often involves, as Max Weber famously said of charismatic leadership, routinization. No revolution, *pace* Leon Trotsky, is permanent.

In addition, for all the rhetoric linking the event with an explosion of freedom, the unleashing of libidinal desire, or the appropriation of Being, what counts as its "genuine" or "authentic" version is never self-evident, nor is it clear who gets to decide in the rare cases when it does happen.[190] This problem is perhaps particularly glaring in Badiou. As Peter Dews wonders:

> How do specific happenings in the socio-historical world come to be nominated as events in his privileged sense? Badiou tends to draw his examples from a rather conventional repertoire of scientific, aesthetic and political innovations: the French, Russian and Chinese Revolutions, Mallarmé's poetry, Schoenberg's serialism, the cubism of Braque and Picasso—and of course Cantor's mathematics. Not only is this very much the world viewed from the *rive gauche*. In many of these cases one can contest the implication that the event concerned is an unequivocal, irreversible advance, a breakthrough that calls for the unconditional fidelity of its inheritors.[191]

Or as another skeptic, Bela Egyed, complains:

> the lack of a set-theoretical account of the event obliges Badiou to rely on historical examples in order to make his case. But, these examples, such as the French Revolution, or St. Paul's radical intervention in Christianity, are too easy. They are too obvious. They all emerge at the point where the actual is the noisiest. But as Nietzsche has warned us: "(T)he greatest events, they are not our noisiest but our stillest hours."[192]

Badiou himself acknowledged the possibility of mistaken fidelity to pseudoevents like the Nazi revolution, which is inevitable considering that identifying a putatively genuine event always involves a hazardous, or risky, decision about its endurance and ultimate effect. Nor will waiting for something called posterity to judge assure any certainty, as the now discredited legacy of the Russian Revolution, still defiantly celebrated by Badiou, makes clear. Alternately, if the best way to differentiate between genuine and false events is, as one commentator argues, "the degree to which they break from the past,"[193] we are not really any closer to a normative criterion of judgment, at least if we equate the degree of separation with something as portentous as the arrival of freedom, the unleashing of desire, the appropriation of Being or the revelation of the Truth. There is also no plausible reason to wager on the ultimate judgment of posterity about events, any more than there is on the likelihood of their sudden and unexpected arrival. What Zhou Enlai is said to have remarked about the historical effect of the French Revolution—"it is too soon to tell"—may well apply to all other candidates for the category of an event.[194]

Several of the issues we have identified in looking at nominalism in general can also be discerned in its manifestation in historical discourse. First, there is the question of scale or how thin we should expect Ockham's razor to slice, which troubles magical as well as conventional nominalism. To translate it into historical terms, how do we decide on the smallest, most meaningful temporal unit that qualifies as an event? How do we calculate its duration, especially if it can be applied from everything as punctual as 9/11 to the decade of rapidly changing conditions and forces that we call the "French Revolution?" These questions are difficult to answer because by definition the event is not *quantitative* in nature but rather the interruption of the ongoing sequential flow of time by something *qualitatively* distinct. More than an isolated, ephemeral instant or abstract point on a continuum, it has been compared to an eddy or hiccup in the flow of time, a pause before a threshold is crossed, a caesura in a metrical line of poetry.[195] But however it is metaphorized, the length of its duration is never self-evident.

We have already encountered this issue in Deleuze's imbuing the event with the time of the Aion, eternal, sacred, and without any connection to the chronological present. Others turned, if implicitly, to the distinction, which also derived from Greek thought, between Chronos, normal flowing time, homogeneous and quantitative, and Kairos, its qualitative interruption, which opens an opportunity to act decisively. The Christian tradition, in fact, had found the latter more compatible with its incarnational theology than the eternal time of the Aion.[196] The New Testament distinguished between sequential, quantitatively measurable chronology and the qualitatively unique "appointed time in the purpose of God."[197] Modern theologians like Paul Tillich interpreted kairotic time in terms of an existential crisis in which decisions for or against Christ have to be made.[198] In his "Theses on the Philosophy of History," Walter Benjamin gave this religious distinction a political twist by invoking the idea of *Jetztzeit*, a time detached from the continuum of history and ripe with revolutionary possibilities. It is time at a standstill, exploding with energy, and poised to take a 'tiger's leap' into the past in order to prepare a very different, perhaps redeemed future.[199]

It has not been hard to locate the French discourse of the event in this religious context of kairotic time, which is ironically most explicit in the work of the militant Marxist Badiou, who, Žižek tells us, "repeatedly refers to the Event as the laicized grace."[200] We have already cited Eelco Runia's identification of "rhetorical Kairos" with Badiou's notion of the event, which was manifest in his book on St. Paul, whose sudden conversion was a gift of grace, an undeserved and unjustifiable donation by God.[201] Echoes of Kierkegaard's antihistoricist, antinomian faith in the ability of the Absolute to interrupt the course of mundane history are not hard to hear when Badiou says the Christian message is "Christ is coming, he is what interrupts the previous regime of discourses. . . . We are relieved of the law."[202] Accordingly, one commentator has called Badiou's version of the event the "twentieth-century avatar" of divine revelation, an apocalyptic moment of unveiling.[203] Another has argued that while Badiou's event is not strictly speaking kairological, it can be enriched by introducing that concept as a way to describe the prepolitical conditions that allow the event to appear.[204] The idea of "fidelity to the event" has also generated the accusation that Badiou's notion of action "consists in a decision to invest faith into a contingent event (by which the subject is only touched in a moment of grace). Politics is thus replaced by an ethical relation towards the event, a relation that subjugates all questions of strategy and tactics to a form of quasi-religious adherence to what we have 'encountered.'"[205] Not surprisingly, Badiou's analysis of the event has been easily adopted to explain other religious experiences, such as the ecstatic possession of Brazilian Candomblé initiates by the spirits of orixás.[206]

But invoking the distinction between Kairos and Chronos, qualitative versus quantitative time, fails to help us answer the question of how we can demarcate a distinct event in history, fix its duration, and locate its boundaries. Something like the conversion of Paul or the terrorist attack on 9/11 seems a punctual interruption in the on-flowing course of history, sudden, precise, and literally or metaphorically violent. But what do we do with events like the French, Russian, and Chinese revolutions or the Holocaust, which lasted much longer and whose precise temporal limits are hard to fix with any certainty?[207] Taking years to play out, they themselves inevitably acquire the shape of mininarratives, and indeed can be compared with each other as following similar patterns of development.[208] As M. C. Lemon suggests, "An event is an individuated ordering of occurrences; it is not a single occurrence, nor a sequence of occurrences which follow on from each other as in the basic narrative form but have no beginning and ending—that is, constitute no overall individual phenomenon. . . . The 'content' of an event has the 'form' of a narrative."[209] "The very notion of an event," Hayden White likewise objected, "is so ambiguous that it makes no sense at all to speak of an *event per se* but only of *events under description*. In other words, the kind of descriptive protocol used to constitute events as facts of a particular sort determines the kind of fact they are considered to be."[210]

If, as often seems the case, the Incarnation is taken as the Ur-type of "the event," the most kairotic intervention possible in the onrushing Chronos of mundane occurrences, it is important to remember that Jesus of Nazareth walked the earth for something like thirty-three years (and perhaps even longer if we count the forty days between the Resurrection and the Ascension). When an event lasts that long, it can contain narratives within itself rather than being simply the interruption of one. In fact, not only are there many stories told about Jesus's life, but his teachings also included parables, some thirty of which are recorded in the New Testament. In short, if we understand the event as a temporal example of the magical nominalist stress on the most granular object that remains when Ockham's razor's work is done, it is as difficult to know when to stop slicing sustained events into their component moments.

The task of circumscribing an event is made even more difficult when the Christian expectation of a Second Coming or its treatment of the

Hebrew Bible as an Old Testament filled with anticipations of a New Testament are taken into account. For here a very nonnominalist idea of prefiguration and fulfillment, albeit with some differences, complicates the story. When Badiou extols fidelity to events like the French or Russian revolutions on the part of those who remember it in the hope of their future realization, he is smuggling in an attitude that we saw informing the magical ideal of cosmic convergences and recurrences that the nominalist stress on absolute singularity denied. As Reinhart Koselleck once observed: "The law of the repeatability of biblical expectations rested upon the belief that with every unfulfilled prophecy, the probability increases of it coming to pass all the more certainly in the future. Non-fulfillment in the past made the prophecy's fulfillment in the future all the more likely."[211] To accommodate this pattern, we would have to add another master trope to those suggested by Hayden White—tragedy, comedy, satire, romance, and irony—which we might call *prefiguration*, in which the seemingly discrete events of history that interrupt the narratives spun by the other tropes themselves form a rhetorical pattern imposed on not only the past but on the expected or desired future as well.

There is also a further question that arises when we put a little pressure on the analogy between the magical nominalist belief in the power of proper names, meaningless in terms of relational semiotic systems but containing ontological power in themselves, and the event as a singular interruption in conventional historical narratives. Here Badiou helps us see the connection. According to one of his interpreters, "The event can come to exist only if it inspires subjects to wager on its existence. Intervention is thus an active process involving the 'naming' of the event and a sequence of 'enquiries' or investigations to flesh out a referential space of elements connected positively to the event."[212] The act of bestowing a proper name, so important for the magical nominalist tradition, is thus critical. As Meillassoux explained in the case of the May events:

> What exactly do we mean, when we say that "May 68" was an event? In this expression, we are not merely designating the set of facts that have punctuated this collective sequence (student demonstrations, the occupation of the Sorbonne, massive strikes, etc.). Such facts, even when joined together in an exhaustive way, do not allow us to say that something like an event took place, rather than a mere conjunction of facts without any particular significance. If "May 68" was an event, it is precisely because it earned its name: that is to say that May 68, produced not only a number of facts, but also produced May 68. In May 68, a site, in addition to its own elements (demonstrations,

> strikes, etc.), presented itself. What is the meaning of such a tautology that characterizes all political events (in 1789, there was "1789," etc.)? It means precisely that an event is the taking place of a pure rupture that nothing in the situation allows us to classify under a list of facts (strikes, demonstrations, etc.).[213]

But ironically, although May '68 may be unique, the event is itself a generic category, an abstract concept under which specific examples are subsumed, a paradoxical set composed of unique elements, not an Adamic ur-name ontologically at one with what it designates. Despite the nuanced differences we have noted in its usage among recent French thinkers, the numinous word is used to indicate a class of occurrences with similar characteristics. As Jean Baudrillard remarked in a discussion of the relationship between events and virtual reality, "the abstraction of information is the same as the abstraction of the economy. And, as all commodities, thanks to the abstraction of value, are exchangeable one with another, so all events become substitutable one for another in the cultural information market. The singularity of the event, irreducible to its coded transcription and its staging, which is what quite simply constitutes an event, is lost."[214] How, in other words, can we distinguish, to borrow the terminology of Robin Wagner-Pacifici, between "event singularity" and "'eventness,'" which indicates their essential commonality?[215] Nor is the identity of the nomothete who bestows the privileged title of event on potential candidates, or gives them their proper names, self-evident. Is that act one of recognition or of designation? Even Badiou seems to be uncertain whether it is a historical agent who makes the decision to seize the opportunity provided by a kairotic moment or the post facto recognizer who is faithful to it through an act of pious belief.[216]

There is, moreover, an ironic implication in the choice of those who described what happened in the streets of Paris in 1968 as *les événements de Mai* or who later designated the destruction of the World Trade Center towers and attack on the Pentagon by al-Qaeda "9/11". Derrida once noted the very act of naming events after chronological dates indicates that we lack a meaningful concept or coherent narrative in which to situate them.[217] This is true enough, but it also suggests that they also cannot be given a proper name that is theirs alone, a rigid designator that distinguishes them from other events.[218] In fact, the very date 9/11 was already meaningful in another historical calendar of radical interruptions in the course of history—it was the day in Chilean history in which the American backed right-wing coup against Salvador Allende brought Augusto

Pinochet to power[219]—which suggests this kind of chronological naming may be inadequate to mark a unique event.

But, to give the screw one final twist, it can also be argued that singling out a date in a calendar for commemoration after the original event is precisely because of its iterability a kind of resistance to the inexorable flow of historical continuity. Repetitive calendrical time is, after all, not the same as the mechanical, relentless time of a clock, especially if it includes holidays that are singled out for celebration—or mourning—every year. As Rebecca Comay suggests in discussing Benjamin's notion of *Eingedenken* (a kind of unreconciled remembrance that challenges the conciliatory effect of *Erinnerung* associated with Hegelian dialectics), "At once both singular (or unrepeatable) and, in this very singularity, repeatable, the date is the very possibility (but by this very token, the impossibility) of commemoration as such. Like every idiom, proper name or signature, the date is both utterly unique and profoundly iterable."[220] By virtue of its undecidability, it may open up a space for the unexpectedly new, whether we call it kairotic and messianic or not, to appear in a future that will do more than merely continue the past.

With all of these ambiguities and uncertainties, we may come to doubt if the historical expression of magical nominalism that we have been tracing in the new experientialism and the French discourse of the event can really advance our efforts to come to terms with the past and anticipate the future. If "the philosophy of the event (or events) can be as abstract as anything in philosophy,"[221] we may well wonder how it can inform our actual attempts to understand the past and our relationship to it. There may be no easy transition, after all, from a philosopheme to what we might call a historiopheme, a concept that can fruitfully inform the practice of workaday historians.[222]

There is, however, one consideration that may nonetheless justify our taking it seriously, which draws on the interpretation of magical nominalism in negative rather than positive terms whose implications we examined in the intermezzo. Rather than seeking to give proper names to events that symbolize their historical importance or imbue them with redemptive meaning, even as they disrupt the conventional meaning of evolutionary narratives, it might be better to treat them as instances of the nonidentical that cannot be positively recuperated, represented, or symbolized.[223] In other words, they are not mere moments of transition in an immanent development but rather gaps in a story that may, just may, gesture toward an imminent opening to something radically different. As we noted in the cases of Deleuze's linking of the event with pure difference and Derrida's denial of their role as apocalyptic revelations (in particular of the phallus), they are like historical versions of the apophatic notion of the divine, or at least like irrational numbers that cannot be expressed as a ratio of integers.

If we recall the impact of the tradition of Jewish nominalism on the development of magical nominalism, Žižek's speculation on the importance of the alleged murder of Moses by the Jews as the primal event in Jewish history becomes intriguingly suggestive: "Judaism's stubborn attachment to the unacknowledged violent founding gesture that haunts the public legal order as its spectral supplement enabled the Jews to persist and survive for thousands of years without land or a common institutional history: they refused to give up their ghost, to cut off their link to their secret, disavowed tradition. The paradox of Judaism is that it maintains fidelity to the founding violent Event precisely by *not* confessing, symbolizing it; this repressed status of the Event is what gives Judaism its unprecedented vitality."[224] Žižek's ambitious explanation of Judaism's extraordinary resilience over the centuries may not be fully persuasive (based as it is on his blithe acceptance of Freud's dubious speculation about the murder of Moses). And his insistence on the violent nature of the primal event in Judaism has aroused suspicion that he and Badiou are a bit too eager to identify genuine events with literal violence.[225]

What is perhaps more valuable in Žižek's account is the identification of fidelity to an event with the refusal to symbolize it in positive terms. A similar conclusion is suggested by Maurice Blanchot in *Writing the Disaster*, where he recalls that "Jewish messianic thought (according to certain commentators) suggests the relation between the event and its nonoccurrence." The messiah may be among us, but his being there is "not the coming. With the Messiah, who is there, the call must always resound; 'Come, Come.' His presence is no guarantee. Both future and past (it is said at least once that the Messiah has already come), his coming does not correspond to any presence at all."[226] Or to put it in the more general terms of the philosopher Andrew Benjamin in *The Plural Event*, "The event can never be commensurate with itself since the 'itself' will already have been a plural possibility. . . . What it can never have is absolute finality, the end as completion."[227]

In short, reading the magical nominalist impulse in history in negative rather than positive terms suggests that the quest for narrative coherence, meaningful contextualization, and tropological emplotments as explanatory devices may be ultimately futile. Here we might say the ambition of conventional nominalism to impose a meaningful story on the contingency of history—the post facto shaping of the *res gestae* (things done) by *historia rerum gestarum* (the representation of things done)—comes up against the magical nominalist obstacle to the constitutive mastery of the storyteller. Like the "derealized" events of modernist literature, to borrow a term Hayden White appropriated from Fredric Jameson, it strips "the event of its traditional narrativistic function of indexing the irruption of fate, destiny, grace, fortune, providence, and even of history itself into a life."[228] For if events are understood as ragged and unexpected ruptures with temporalities that are neither punctual bisections of the evolutionary flow of history nor climactic episodes in meaningful narratives of transformation, then we have to acknowledge the inevitable insufficiency of our post facto reconstructions, which cannot read events as hinge moments in the development of a coherent plot.

It may well, however, be no less problematic, *pace* its more exuberant enthusiasts like Badiou, to understand an event as a kairotic moment of redemption, which bring a positive truth into the world on the model of the Incarnation. It might even be wrong to turn events into prefigurations of a redeemed future, which demand the fidelity of those who hope they anticipate a positive truth still to come. Instead, they may better be appreciated as limit experiences that thwart our desire for a replete and conclusive representative of the past as it actually was. Rather than a source of despair, understanding them in this more negative way may, in fact, allow us to appreciate their role in clearing a space for the possibility of the radically new to enter the world. It is this link between "event" and "advent" that opens the future to adventures unfettered by the weight of the past but never achieving the redemptive closure that precludes future disruptive events.[229]

Is this true of other arenas in which magical nominalism has had a subterranean effect? White's passing allusion to modernist literature alerts us to another realm in which the nominalist legacy, both conventionalist and magical, has been enormously influential: art and the aesthetic discourse surrounding it. Significantly, Ankersmit develops his notion of sublime historical experience in dialogue with Gadamer's and Dewey's treatments of aesthetic experience.[230] And Badiou included art in the inventory of those practices with "truth procedures" that emerged in the aftermath of artistic events. He defined the latter as "great mutations that almost always bear on the question of what counts, or doesn't count, as form. . . . The artistic event is signaled by the advent of new forms."[231] Nominalism, to be sure, has long been identified with the challenge to form, at least in the guise of ontological universals. Exploring its role in modern aesthetics, both in its conventional and magical guises, will be the task of our next chapter, which will focus in particular at Marcel Duchamp and the visual arts and Theodor W. Adorno and music.

4

Irrealism in Aesthetics

CONVENTIONAL OR MAGICAL NOMINALISM?

By demolishing the security of forms, nominalism made all art plein air *long before this became an unmetaphoric slogan. Thinking and art both became dynamic.*

THEODOR W. ADORNO

The Decline of Aesthetic Platonism

From their inception, the practices, objects, institutions, traditions, and experiences that have in one way or another earned the honorific title of "art" have been the site of an unresolved battle between realism and nominalism. The discourse about them that came to be called aesthetics—the term came into common use back only in the early eighteenth century with writers like Alexander Baumgarten, but what it named can be found as far back as the ancient Greeks[1]—often reflected on the implications of the dispute. To do justice to the results of those reflections, which are still very much ongoing today, would require a sizable volume of its own, if indeed only one would suffice. Instead, I want to focus on the nominalism side of the divide, with special attention to the distinction between the aesthetic versions of what we have been calling its conventional and magical variants. To make this still formidable task somewhat more manageable, I will explore the legacies of two paradigmatic exemplars, whose work helps us understand the differences between them. One is an artist with a philosophical bent, Marcel Duchamp; the second is a philosopher who was also a practicing artist, Theodor W. Adorno.

Before contrasting their versions of aesthetic nominalism, however, it will be necessary to provide at least an abbreviated account of its realist counterpart.[2] What has to be understood at the outset is that the term "realism" is meant in the sense we have already encountered in the medieval debates over the ontological status of universals, in which those who supported their existence were called realists. The later adoption of "realism" as a way to characterize artistic styles or genres, especially in literature and the visual arts,[3] on the basis of their accurate representation of "the real," historical, social, psychological, or natural, is something very different.[4]

Whether understood to be a faithful rendering of what it depicts—Stendhal's concise definition of the novel in *The Red and the Black* as "a mirror carried along a high road"—or the result of the aesthetic device that Roland Barthes famously called "the reality effect,"[5] realism in this sense earns its title by representing, narrating, or describing the world "as it is," either in terms of surface appearances or deeper structural dynamics. The former is identified more with a positivist worldview and sometimes called naturalism rather than realism, the latter with a dialectical alternative. Both, however, assume there is a rough fit between what is depicted, described, or narrated and the "real" world beyond the art.[6] Accordingly, realism in this sense often takes as its subject matter the banal experiences of everyday life and the historical transformations that affect them. It tilts the balance between simulating a real world and imagining a possible one in the direction of the former, or so it is normally understood.[7]

There are endless discussions of what mimetic representation might mean and the techniques used to produce it, as well as of the debts of novelistic realism to a complicated dialectic of individuality and typicality.[8] Comparable debates rage over the extent to which visual images are natural rather than conventional signs. Going as far back as Pliny's famous account of the birds that were fooled by Zeuxis's painted grapes, a belief in the referential validity of images became what one skeptic, W. J. T. Mitchell has called "the fetish or idol of Western culture."[9] Discussions of aesthetic realism can also focus on the existence of response-independent aesthetic qualities in objects, which transcend the subjective experiences they stimulate.[10]

Wherever one comes out on these issues, it is important to distinguish the version of realism they are contesting from the one that harkens back to the ontological universalism of the prenominalist worldview.[11] The significant antonyms in the semantic field of latter-day realism understood as mimetic verisimilitude might include imagination, fantasy, or idealism but not nominalism. In fact, to the extent that the modern novel can be understood to grow out of an antigeneric celebration of individuality, particularity, and heterogeneity, which challenged traditional literary forms, its "realism" might well be paradoxically labeled nominalist in disguise.[12]

The earlier version of realism that concerns us can, in contrast, be called aesthetic Platonism, because of its assumption that there are eternal forms or ontological essences that play a generative or normative role in the creation of works of art. Plato's own qualms about the distractions and illusions of art are well known, as is his distrust of imperfect sense experience and the inferiority of mimetic copies to the original.[13] But once mobilized in support of the medieval affirmation of creation, his account of cosmogenesis in the *Timaeus* as the product of intelligent design could underpin a positive version of the cosmos as itself like a work of art. Through the writings of Plotinus, Pseudo-Dionysius the Areopagite, and Augustine, its implications for a Christian aesthetics were developed. God's creation—indeed at times, even God himself[14]—was understood as inherently beautiful. The Pythagorean belief in the parallel between musical harmonies and mathematical regularities continued to inform what Boethius called *musica universalis* or *musica mundana*.[15] In the twelfth century, the Abbot Suger drew on the "light metaphysics" of the Pseudo-Dionysius to install the large stained glass windows in the Abbey Church of Saint-Denis, often seen as the prototype of Gothic architecture. In fact, Gothic cathedrals in general sought to imitate the ontological harmonies of the cosmos manifest in geometry and music, a legacy of Platonism already influential a century before Aquinas in the school of Chartres. Its master Thierry saw God as drawing on geometry to create a cosmos from chaos.[16] In short, as Umberto Eco put it: "A constantly recurring theme in medieval times was the beauty of being in general. . . . It was the Scriptures, then, extended and amplified by the Fathers, which produced this pancalistic [all-beautiful] vision of the cosmos. But it was confirmed also by the Classical heritage. The theory that the beauty of the world is an image and reflection of Ideal Beauty is Platonic in origin."[17]

Instead of pitting the aesthetic against the rational, the Platonic notion of beauty reconciled them by turning it into a mediation between the supersensible realm of ideal forms—*eidos* has also been translated as essence, type, or species—and sensuous appearances. Although "lower" in the great chain of being, the latter were understood to "participate" in the former, revealing the artistic genius of the master creator in all of his creations. *Methexis*—a term also used for audience participation in a theatrical production—trumps mere mimesis.[18] Plato was indebted to Pythagoras and his followers, who had discovered that when plucked, a string exactly half the length of another will play a pitch that is exactly an octave higher.[19] What became known as the overtone or harmonic series in music was also a feature of physics in general, which was ruled by comparable mathematical regularities. Indeed, so Pythagoras believed, the planets and other heavenly bodies, depending on their orbits and the distance between them, produced vibrating notes that created a music of the spheres. What came to be called the golden ratio (sometimes the golden section or the divine proportion) was taken to be a natural model for aesthetic beauty.[20]

Rather than hovering above their concrete embodiments in a sphere of ideal transcendence (*ante rem*), forms, however, could also be understood, as they were by Aristotle, as immanent in the objects themselves (*in rem*). This alternative was embraced by Scholastic philosophy during the High Middle Ages, when the Platonic notion of transcendent, eternal forms was relocated within discrete beings understood as inextricable composites of matter and form. Aristotle had distinguished between matter (*hypokeimenon* or *hyle*) and form (*eidos* or *morphe*), with the former understood as an undifferentiated primal element, whose potentiality is actualized by the latter. The formal "cause" of an object's existence introduced a teleological element into his ontology, in which the final shaping of an object was as determinate in its coming to be as the undifferentiated matter out of which it came. Although it might be said that Aristotle's revision of Plato contained "the seeds of what is called nominalism"[21]—or at least so Adorno once argued—he continued to uphold the metaphysical reality of universals, as he did the analogy between aesthetic and mathematical notions of beauty.[22]

Whether in its Platonic or Aristotelian versions, aesthetic realism accorded to universal forms enduring ontological validity that survived their ephemeral concrete embodiments or instantiations. Its echo can still be occasionally found in the modern era, as exemplified by Hegel's pronouncement that "art is the most immediate self-gratification of absolute mind. Its truth is the absolute as an object in sensuous form, which is for art the only adequate form."[23] Perhaps its primary expression was belief in the objective quality of beauty, which might be attributed to all creation—that "pancalistic" cosmos of which Eco speaks—or only to certain objects within it. Indeed to this day, aesthetic realism continues to hold, to quote a recent account, that "there is a property of beauty independent of judgments which ascribe it that grounds and explains those judgments."[24] Often this meant identifying inherent models of beauty in nature that were allegedly universal in their scope. Organic wholeness or proportionality were favorite examples, and works of art that imitated them were deemed beautiful as a result. Clarity could also be highly valued, because it reflected divine illumination. As Aquinas argued in his *Summa*,[25] a beautiful thing had three primary characteristics: *integritas* (it must not be deficient in what it needs to be most itself); *consonantia* (its dimensions should correspond to other physical objects as well as to a metaphysical ideal), and *claritas* (it should clearly radiate intelligibility, the logic of its inner being, and be able to impress this knowledge of itself on the mind of the perceiver).

Aesthetic realism could also mean ranking arts that followed a putatively natural hierarchy of the human senses with vision, "the noblest sense," at its apex.[26] In fact, as the philosopher Wolfgang Welsch has conjectured, the ocularcentrism of Greek culture may well be linked to the aesthetic realist notion of eternal forms "because of [vision's] hallmarks of distance, precision and universality, because of its capacity for determination and its proximity to cognition." It was only at a much later date that another sense like hearing could be "appreciated anew because of its anti-metaphysical proximity to the event instead of to permanent being."[27] The arts that corresponded to the alleged hierarchy of the senses were ranked accordingly, with painting above, say, the culinary or olfactory arts.[28] A similar argument, made by the twentieth-century American philosopher Susanne Langer, attempted to ground different arts, especially music, painting, dance, and sculpture, in the a priori modes of time and space posited by Kant.[29]

Aesthetic realism could also inform considerations of what counted as "art as such" when that generic category came into being, probably for the first time during the Enlightenment.[30] Serving for some as a surrogate for traditional religions, art-for-art's-sake aestheticism generated an essentialist notion of what it worshipped.[31] When the discourse of art as autonomous (unbeholden to utilitarian, devotional, or ethical functions) gathered momentum, echoes of aesthetic Platonism could often still be heard. Thus, it was not by chance that Keats's celebrated affirmation that "Beauty is truth, truth beauty,—that is all ye know on earth, and all ye need to know" came in an ode on a Grecian urn.[32] Later devotees of the cult of art like Walter Pater were also enthralled with Platonism.[33]

"Art as such" claimed to overcome the differences observed by the traditional muses of Greek mythology, and was the inspiration for efforts like those of Richard Wagner to turn opera into a *Gesamtkunstwerk* or for painters like Wassily Kandinsky to draw on the experience of synesthesia. But aesthetic realism could also designate the allegedly normative telos of the distinct arts that were differentiated from each other. Thus, for example, the criteria for "absolute music" laid down by Eduard Hanslick in the nineteenth century or for "medium-specific" painting legislated by Clement Greenberg in the twentieth were premised on the existence of objective, universal standards that transcended any particular culture or individual viewpoint. The evolution of distinct artistic genres could thus be understood as a progressive approximation of their inherent essences or concomitantly, a process of purification that rid them of extrinsic elements (for example, "program music," evoking ideas, events, or narratives competing with the formal agenda of absolute music, or the illusion of perspectival depth on a flat canvas). Modernist art was often, to cite the philosopher Arthur Danto, "a pursuit of essence, of what solely and truly is, hence of a kind of pure art, very much as if the art which resulted was like an alchemical precipitate, from which impurities had all been purged."[34]

In these and other ways, the legacy of aesthetic realism could continue to inform both artistic creation and the interpretation of its results.[35] There were, in fact, numerous explicit revivals of aesthetic Platonism, for example in the Renaissance philosophy of Marsilio Ficino, and even the great chain of being did not entirely lose its hold on the European imagination until its temporalization into an infinite quest during the Romantic era.[36] The Gothic may have lost its latent justification as an architectural instantiation of Scholastic order to become an emblem of barbaric irregularity, but neoclassicism in the hands of theorists like J. J. Winckelmann was able to inherit its normative role as a model of aesthetic realism. The religious argument from design, a residue of the Christian incorporation of Platonism, was stubbornly maintained into the eighteenth century by theologians like William Paley and Samuel Clarke, and did not entirely give up the ghost until Darwin. A faint echo might be found in our own day in attempts to identify aesthetic universals in the cognitive responses allegedly aroused in everyone by objects that transcend cultures.

The nominalist revolution in the late Middle Ages presented, however, a powerful challenge to aesthetic realism in both its Platonic and Aristotelian guises.[37] When the Scholastic faith in the rational order of the cosmos legislated by a benign deity and accessible to human reason was undermined by respect for God's unfettered will, so too was the idea of a pancalistic harmony of the spheres and their sublunary equivalents. Although the Middle Ages had known examples of what later became known as sublime rather than beautiful art—the awe surely generated by the experience of entering a magnificent Gothic cathedral justifies that conclusion—it was not really until nominalism that the cosmic order itself was called into serious question.[38] The fourteenth century, as we have already noted, was a particularly bleak period in the daily lives of medieval men and women, and it would have strained credulity to insist that despite everything, the world radiated a divine notion of beauty. As Eco puts it: "The concept of proportion is thus impoverished, although Ockham did speak of the proportion of part to the wholes. The reality of universals, which was necessary to the concept of *integritas*, was dissolved by nominalism. The problem of the transcendental status of beauty, and of the distinctions which specify beauty, can scarcely be posed in a system in which there are no such distinctions, neither formal nor virtual. All that remains is the intuition of particulars, a knowledge of existent objects whose visible proportions are examined empirically."[39]

Denied their teleological purpose in a coherent system of final causes, individual works were set free to transgress rather than merely ratify normative aesthetic ideals, or even to establish new ones on their own. Rather than being situated in a network of cosmic correspondences, in which their value derived from their embodiment of universal principles, artworks came increasingly to be considered the expression of their creators' subjectivity. The mere talent of a skilled craftsman following already-established rules no longer seemed sufficient, and the inspiration of genius came to replace it. Originating in the Latin verb *gignere,* to beget or generate, it was anticipated by what the Greeks called a personal *daimon.* The modern idea of artistic genius as the inspired creator of works of art emerged in the Renaissance, although it was perhaps not widely appreciated until the eighteenth century.[40]

Only then could an artwork's imitation of creation be replaced by the artist's imitation of the Creator—or more specifically by the nominalist version of a voluntarist divinity unbound by any rules or ordering principles—as the source of aesthetic value. By the time of Kant, to cite the literary historian Jonathan M. Hess, "what art imitates is not the cipher-writing of nature's beautiful forms but the intentionality that the interpretive activity of aesthetic judgment posited (and could only post behind these aesthetic forms)."[41] In short, the ultimate effect of what Blumenberg has called the human self-assertion enabled by the nominalist revolution made artworks the product of human agency and human purpose, even if the role of inspiration—which implies an infusion of spirit—could imply the genius served more as a vehicle than an ultimate source. A similar evolution led to heightened appreciation of the performative gifts of the virtuoso and the hermeneutic/forensic talents of the connoisseur.

In addition to the displacement of emphasis from the intrinsic value of an art object in a world of cosmic convergences to the value placed in it by its human creators, there was another shift in the way that such value was ascertained and appreciated. Rather than merely subsuming it under allegedly universal norms of beauty, such as Aquinas's *integritas, consonantia,* and *claritas,* the object came to be recognized as art and then praised (or not) as "good" art by the noncognitive faculties of taste and judgment. Whether considered subjective or intersubjective, intuitive or reflective, interested or disinterested, they were understood to be exercised outside the logic of subsumption in which a specific case was subordinated to a general rule. Nominalism's undermining of the authority of real universals meant that other criteria had to be sought.

As a result, aesthetic experience, combining sublimated sensual pleasure with cultivated judgment, began to crowd out artworks as the focus of attention.[42] At times this meant acknowledging the ineffability of a "certain something" that solicited that experience, which was expressed in Petrarch's oft-cited *non so ché* or *je ne sais quoi* during the Renaissance.[43] At others, it suggested concentrating on the cultivated sensibility that allowed art to be fully appreciated and shrewdly judged. Through the metaphorization of what had previously been denigrated as a "lower" sense, it came to be called taste, or better still, good taste.[44] It was not by chance that the elevation of a proximate sense over the distancing role of vision, often credited with a theoretical belief in the ontological permanence of what is seen, accompanied a new focus on the embodied subjectivity of aesthetic experience.

However, as in the case of other nominalist demolitions of the ontological pretensions of traditional norms, anxiety often ensued. Because gustatory preferences are idiosyncratic and unamenable to rational persuasion—the Romans had already postulated that *de gustibus non disputandum est*—the threat of an unregulated anarchy of responses to art grounded only in taste loomed large. Thus, in his 1757 treatise "The Standard of Taste," Hume ruefully acknowledged that "beauty is no quality in the things themselves. It exists merely in the mind which contemplates them, and each mind perceives a different beauty."[45] To avoid the "anything goes" implication of this observation, he fell back on an inductively derived claim that the "standard of taste" was shared by most people based on habitual learning and accumulated experience. Individual taste might be indisputable, but the exercise of "good taste" was amenable to cultivation over time, what Friedrich Schiller would later expand into the philosophically, morally, and politically motivated project he called the "aesthetic education of man."

Not everyone was satisfied with Hume's inductive, historicist solution, and the history of eighteenth-century aesthetic theory is replete with attempts to restore more binding standards of aesthetic judgment to refute the truism that "beauty is in the eye of the beholder."[46] Some unreconstructed realists, like Lord Kames, William Hogarth, and Edmund Burke, still hoped to define beauty through a list of intrinsic attributes, while Baumgarten sought to bring the beautiful under rational principles. Lord Shaftesbury's Neoplatonist aesthetics, equating beauty with the good, drew on the legacy of the seventeenth-century Cambridge Platonists, who channeled the universalist realism of Ficino and Renaissance humanism.[47] But others—and here Kant is the canonical example—sought an answer in an aesthetic judgment that acknowledged the nominalist critique of realism, while yet somehow transcending the idiosyncrasies of individual taste.

Kant's general attitude toward the realism/nominalism controversy has been difficult to pin down, as he did not address it at length. When it concerned ontological questions, a recent commentator concludes that "Kant is a nominalist about universals but a realist about tropes. So, he is ultimately a modest nominalist; and when he rejects nominalism, he rejects either an extreme form of nominalism or a certain way of formulating it."[48] In other words, although accepting the existence of logical universals, he was skeptical about their counterparts where the natural world was concerned, even if our judgments about physical objects in time and space were generated in part by a universally shared set of a priori categories in the mind.

When it came to aesthetics, Kant attempted to get beyond the radical nominalism of British empiricists like Hume without falling back on ontological universals or transcendental epistemological principles. In his *Critique of Judgment* (1790), he introduced a distinction between determinant and reflective judgments, the former employing general ideas or a priori rules under which particular cases might be subsumed, the latter analogical comparisons between particulars and the use of paradigms to illustrate shared properties. Aesthetic judgments are of the second variety, and are always singular rather than general ("this song is beautiful," not "all songs are beautiful"). If they draw on concepts, they are of the "indeterminate" kind, freer than the a priori schemata Kant attributed to cognitive judgments or even the a priori intuitions of time and space he had called the "transcendental aesthetic" in his first *Critique*.[49] But rather than being dependent on mere habit and the cultivation of taste, as they were for empiricists like Hume, they are based on the assumption of an intersubjective sensus communis that supports aesthetic judgments. The pleasures produced by aesthetic experience are thus more contemplative and disinterested than the merely "agreeable" gratification of individual desires. They are grounded in reflections rather than immediate sensual responses, which suggest they are warranted, not capricious. The judgments they solicit are based on the expectation that others will share the same delight in the apprehension of beauty, which will be generated through communicative interaction as well as direct sensible experience, rather than based on mere idiosyncratic taste or unreflective habit. Although not in accord with a transcendent notion of timeless and universal reason, such judgments are shared and justified through the persuasiveness of the reasons and analogies given to support them.

All of this is well known, and much more can be said about Kant's struggle to find a way to avoid the extreme realist and nominalist alternatives. But what is crucial for our purposes is to note that he never fell back on a full-throated realist belief in either the inherent qualities of objects or innate mental capacities. Instead, he argued that although aesthetic judgments often took the form of universal claims—"the ceiling of the Sistine Chapel is beautiful," not "I think the Sistine Chapel is beautiful"—their objectivity was really an "as if" strategy rather than an ontological truth.[50] His concept of beauty, to cite the philosopher Jane Kneller, is "a relation of formal purposiveness (harmony) of the object for cognitive powers of the subject."[51] Although aesthetic, cognitive, and moral judgments are not entirely distinct, Kant denied the Platonic unity of reason and beauty. The artistic genius—and Kant was crucial in the elevation of "his" creative importance—may imbue his works with aesthetic ideas, but they are original and produced by imagination rather than the imitation of ones provided by innate reason. Like nature, when understood from beyond the perspective of causal determination, works of art may be charged with teleological meanings that transcend instrumental utility, which Kant famously called their "purposiveness without purpose." The imitation that produces them is therefore not of nature as a harmonious cosmos but rather of the divine creator who imbues nature with teleological meaning. Here too an "as if" fiction is implied—the artistic genius as a designing god—rather than an ontological claim about the inherent, objective quality of an artwork. In fact, the disinterestedness of aesthetic judgment implies that the actual existence of the object producing aesthetic pleasure is irrelevant, unlike in the case of the objects of interested desire that can deliver direct corporeal gratification.

Kant's ruminations on the relationship between artistic and natural beauty, complicated still further by his thoughts on the distinction between the beautiful and the sublime, continue to generate considerable discussion.[52] Although his starting point seems to have been the human capacity to appreciate natural beauty, Kant also paradoxically insisted that "nature is beautiful because it looks like art; and art can only be called beautiful if we are conscious of it as art while yet it looks like nature."[53] However we interpret this claim, it rests on the assumption that although intricately intertwined, natural and aesthetic beauty are not equivalent. It further indicates that the appreciation of natural beauty is not produced by the object itself but by its culturally mediated resemblance to art, which itself, however, can only cast its spell through appearing to be natural. This hall of reflecting mirrors suggests many things but not that beauty ontologically exists in objects, whether they are natural or produced by the talents of an artistic genius. That is, not only is the pancalistic assumption that the cosmos is a product of the

Creator's design held by aesthetic Platonists called into question, so too is the more modest realist contention that certain objects, natural or artificial, are intrinsically beautiful.

Kant can therefore be said to gravitate more toward the nominalist than realist side in their perennial struggle. His legacy helped loosen the identification of aesthetics with "callistics," which concentrated only on questions of beauty. "There is no science of the beautiful," he insisted, "but only a critique of it."[54] Art, it increasingly came to be appreciated, need not be tied to an ideal of beauty, whether understood as ontologically intrinsic in objects or as projected on to them by the judgments of those who experience them. As we will see when we turn to Duchamp's assault on "retinal art" in the name of visual indifference, even the connection between the senses, which were the traditional avenues of aesthetic pleasure, and art as such could be entirely severed, and with it any remaining overlap between aesthetics and callistics.

* * *

Not only was this uncoupling expressed in aesthetic theory but also practically instantiated by art which departed from classical models of organic harmony, balance, and proportionality. Umberto Eco argues for the influence of nominalism in the origins of one such movement in particular. "The philosophical critique of the Ockhamites," he writes, "was the prelude to the aesthetics of Mannerism."[55] Derived from the Italian *maniera*, or "style," the label first appeared in Giorgio Vasari's *Lives of the Most Excellent Painters, Sculptors, and Architects* and came to define European—or more precisely, Italian—art between the Renaissance and the Baroque, that is, from around 1520 to 1600.[56] Inspired by Michelangelo's late works, it was typified by the sculpture and painting of such artists as Bronzino, Parmigiano, and Tintoretto. Valuing complexity, artificiality, and virtuosity rather than naturalistic representation, its practitioners eschewed the clarity, balance and proportionality of Renaissance painters inspired by the revival of aesthetic Platonism. Instead, it flattened perspectival space, favored ornamental and decorative effects, and distorted the human figure, twisting it in serpentine shapes and elongating its limbs. Subtlety and intricacy were its watchwords, not simplicity or clarity.

It would be a stretch to say that the nominalism of Ockham and his followers was the direct source of Mannerist art, which has itself not always been understood as a unified movement. And yet, its aesthetic reverberations are not hard to find in such descriptions of the Mannerist challenge to aesthetic Platonism as that of the Marxist art historian Arnold Hauser, who calls it "the first conscious revolt in history against the prevailing artistic conventions." He writes:

> This epoch-making turn of events, the real beginning of modern art, was the outcome of an experience that the world is not at all so well-ordered, meaningful and "beautiful" as the Renaissance masters, following the conventions of their aristocratic culture, portrayed it; that it is, on the contrary, an insoluble riddle, an equivocal tragi-comedy, a sensual-spiritual, rational-irrational, divine and demonic middle realm. In line with this experience, the mannerists, in all that they take as the subject of their art, stress contradictions, double meanings, the inseparable unity of reality and dream, of the common and the fantastic, of the intoxicating and the sobering.[57]

Significantly, the transition in early-modern astronomy from a finite cosmos to an infinite universe, for which nominalism was in part responsible, has been assigned a role in the shattering of spatial order on the canvases of Mannerist (and then baroque) artists.[58] Not surprisingly, latter-day defenders of classical notions of intrinsic beauty reacted by investing Mannerism with the pejorative connotation that the label carries to this day. Although in the early sixteenth century, so the musicologist Don Harrán tells us, it could imply "the poise and refinements of courtly behavior," by its end it had gained the meaning of "hollow virtuosity, of graces carried to precious or capricious extremes."[59]

Mannerism was, of course, not the last movement that explicitly challenged the resilient pieties of aesthetic Platonism, nor would the reactions to it be the last *rappel á l'ordre* in the history of art. A narrative of Western art and the aesthetic theory that attempted to make sense of it could be written as a displaced contest between the champions of realism and nominalism. It would be a story with lots of unexpected twists and turns. For example, the Gothic style of medieval cathedrals initially conceived as Scholastic philosophy writ in stone and thus reflecting a rational cosmic order became instead the emblem of unregulated barbarism during the Renaissance. It remained so through the Enlightenment before its positive reassessment in the writings of Horace Walpole, Goethe, and others in the late eighteenth century.[60] Conversely, the idea of the grotesque, which came to be attributed helter-skelter to a wide variety of contradictory, inorganic, "confused" exemplars, emerged during the Renaissance. It was inspired by the excavation of Nero's Domus Aurea, or Golden Palace, in Rome, where hybrid forms of irregular ornamental decoration were found on long buried frescoes. From the original *grottesche*—referring to underground caves—came the grotesque, which, among other things, valorized art, which in the spirit of nominalism, lacked inherent meaning and challenged the ideal circular form emblematizing cosmic perfection.[61] Although its models may have come from nature, it was nature understood in its abnormal, defective, even monstrous guise.

Examples like these can be given to demonstrate that new, unconventional criteria of beauty can replace older ones and that even what was initially considered ugly could somehow be recuperated for an expanded notion of beauty.[62] But they also suggest that beauty however defined was losing its privileged place in aesthetic theory and the evaluation of new works of art.[63] Despite rearguard attempts by critics like Roger Fry and Clive Bell to posit a universal source of aesthetic emotion in what Bell called "significant form,"[64] essentialist criteria of beauty were on the wane. According to Hans-Robert Jauss, "In the experience of art in the modern era, the emancipation of the aesthetic experience occurs in the explicit turning away from the Platonic metaphysics of the beautiful."[65]

By the twentieth century, the rejection had gained increasing momentum, and overt hostility to beauty often came to seem one of the salient characteristics of modernist art.[66] The aesthetic redemption of the commonplace, which had emerged with Romanticism, could end by tacitly conceding that the everyday world was, alas, stubbornly resistant to its sublimating transfiguration. Concomitantly, modernism often denied aesthetic equivalents of the Christian notion of the "real presence" of divinity in the material world, most clearly instantiated by the Eucharist.[67] When beauty was invoked, as it was by the Surrealists, it was modified by the very non-Winckelmannian adjective "convulsive."[68] Although modernist art often quested after the exceptional and miraculous, it acknowledged that it could no longer be found in eternally valid generic forms.[69]

Modern art could even value formlessness—what the heterodox surrealist Georges Bataille called the *informe*—over beautiful forms, however they were understood.[70] New respect for the unrepresentability of the sublime and an ascetic denial of any sensual pleasure in artistic experience, carried to an extreme in the de-materialization of conceptual art, meant that not only realist theories of objective beauty were in decline, but so too were those based on intersubjective reflective judgments in Kant's sense. Often political and ethical criteria came to dominate both the practice and critique of art, while questions of beauty, much to the chagrin of its indignant defenders, were seen as unwelcome distractions from weightier issues.[71] These, it was often felt, were better addressed by art that shocked, disturbed, and even deliberately alienated, rather than by beautiful forms that provided soothing consolations.

Some skeptics of aesthetic realism in its Platonic guise went so far as to reduce art to little more than an effect of its supporting institutions in the "artworld."[72] But even many who resisted a sociological approach to art were reluctant to fall back on essentialist notions of beauty. In *Languages of Art*, often regarded as the most important philosophical defense of aesthetic nominalism in the twentieth century, the American analytic philosopher Nelson Goodman (1906–98) forcefully denounced the idea that aesthetics was at all dependent on locating an essential notion of beauty: "Folklore has it that a good picture is pretty. At the next higher level, pretty is replaced by 'beautiful,' since the best pictures are often obviously not pretty. But again, many of them are in the most obvious sense ugly. If the beautiful excludes the ugly, beauty is no measure of aesthetic merit; but if the beautiful may be ugly, then 'beauty' becomes only an alternative and misleading word for aesthetic merit."[73]

What might a full-throated nominalist aesthetics scornful of essentialist notions of beauty, indeed of "art as such," look like? In the tradition of analytic philosophy, Goodman was its most prominent exemplar.[74] In fact, his towering role in that tradition would have to be acknowledged in any account of the realism/nominalism debate staged in its highly specialized and often forbiddingly esoteric idiom. We have already alluded to his seminal essay of 1940, with Henry L. Leonard, on the calculus of individuals, which presented a "mereological" argument for particulars as discursively constructed rather than ontologically given. But it was perhaps an even more influential piece coauthored with Harvard's W. V. O. Quine seven years later, "Steps towards a Constructive Nominalism,"[75] that announced Goodman's allegiance to the nominalist tradition. It begins with the defiant assertion: "We do not believe in abstract entities. No one supposes that abstract entities—classes, relations, properties, etc.,—exist in space-time; but we mean more than this. We renounce them entirely."[76] Focusing on mathematics, they concluded that "the formulas of platonistic mathematics are, like the beads of an abacus, convenient computational aids which need involve no question of truth."[77] Although Quine later had second thoughts about the necessary role of classes in the discourse of science, Goodman remained a steadfast nominalist throughout his long and influential career, which ranged well beyond the philosophy of mathematics. Even the stars, he provocatively argued, are in an important sense "made" by our representations of them.[78]

To do justice to Goodman's oeuvre would require far more attention than we can devote here (as well as greater philosophical acumen than this author can boast), but a few observations about his thoughts on aesthetics are in order. Himself an accomplished player in the world of modern art—he directed an art gallery, was a private collector, and helped produce three multimedia-performance events—Goodman made many seminal contributions to aesthetics, which had been languishing as a branch of mainstream analytic philosophy. Rejecting notions of mimetic representation as well as essentialist idealism, he argued that art was a system of symbols, linguistic as well as visual and aural, with cognitive intentions comparable to those of science.[79] Both function constructively to make worlds, albeit not ex nihilo, rather than merely duplicate them. The plausibility of scientific induction and the realism effect of art depend alike on the fit between our constructs and the established systems of symbols in which they are embedded, rather than with natural kinds. "Realism," he baldly asserted, "is relative, determined by the system of representation standard for a given culture or person at a given time."[80] Goodman was also a resolute conventionalist when it came to the emotional effect of art, which he argued reflects the particular cultural context out of which it appears and into which it is inserted. Nor did he accept the distinction between types and tokens that some other aestheticians have embraced to characterize the hierarchical relationship between an ideal version of a work and its particular instantiation.[81]

Goodman's contributions to aesthetic theory went well beyond his conventional nominalist understanding of art as a semiotic rather than natural system. He introduced many suggestive distinctions that have been widely adopted while generating vigorous debate. These would include replete and discrete signs, such as respectively colors of the rainbow and letters of the alphabet; autographic and allographic artworks, the first a work that exists in one definitive embodiment, the second a work that allows infinite, equally viable realizations or performances; and referential symbols that are denotations and others that are exemplifications, the former applying a new label to something, the latter where something already exists to which the label applies. Magical nominalism, it might be argued, is closer to Goodman's denotation than exemplification. He has also had important things to say about arts with notational systems and ones without, and the reasons for positing the unique identity of even allographic works that necessarily invite different interpretative performances.[82]

All of these issues would repay careful consideration, but I want to concentrate on only one of Goodman's contributions to a nominalist aesthetics or what he called "irrealism." The term has been adopted as everything from an antonym to realism understood as mimetic verisimilitude to a descriptive term for "a mode of postmodern allegory" resulting from biological mutations run amok.[83] The Marxist theorist Michael Löwy, a defender of the utopian impulses in Romanticism and surrealism, has even advocated "critical irrealism" as an alternative to the "critical realism" of Lukács.[84] Goodman's target, however, is explicitly the medieval sense of ontologically real universals. Because he argued for the existence of multiple actual worlds rather than multiple possible alternatives to our already existing one,[85] he did not defend an antirealist position, strictly speaking. Although allowing that there are certain symptoms of the presence of "art" in our culture—syntactic and semantic density, relative repleteness, exemplification, and multiple and complex reference[86]—Goodman remained, as W. J. T. Mitchell has put it, an "arch-conventionalist."[87] To be sure, the makers of the artistic worlds whose ways he explored were not as free as the divinity in Ockham's theology with his *potentia absoluta*. For they had to work with the residues of previous worlds, rather than create *ex nihilo*.[88] But there was no normative model of inherent rationality like the Scholastics' *potentia ordinata* to bind them, either genetically or teleologically.

Accordingly, Goodman insisted that the very question "What is art?" is an essentialist error, based on a vain search for perfect synonymy, and thus unanswerable. The purist quest for, say, the medium-specificity of painting—and here Susanne Langer and Clement Greenberg were implicit targets—was bound to fail. Instead, in *Ways of Worldmaking*, Goodman argued that the better alternative is to ask "When is art?" because "the real question is not 'What objects are (permanently) works of art?' but 'When is an object a work of art?'"[89] That is, the symbolizing function of an object can change and there are no a priori criteria to define it as art for all time. Context and usage is more important than inherent quality or authorial intent. Even a Rembrandt canvas can cover a window or serve as a blanket rather than remain an art object. "That an object functions as art at a given time, that it has the status of art at that time, and that it is art at that time may all be taken as saying the same thing—so long as we take none of these as ascribing to the object any stable status."[90] Both life and art, contrary to ancient wisdom, are transient. Only when objects function symbolically in a certain way can they be construed as making new worlds, which is what art *does* (not what it *is*). Here, in other words, was a nominalism, like that of the historical event we encountered in the previous chapter, that focused more on temporal than spatial particularity, on contingent actions rather than enduring objects.

Marcel Duchamp and "Pictorial Nominalism"

Nelson Goodman may never have been genuinely historical in accounting for the conditions allowing the transitions back and forth from non-art to art,[91] but his acknowledgment of the temporal contingency of that distinction provides a convenient transition to the first of our paradigmatic cases of aesthetic nominalism, Marcel Duchamp (1887–1968). Duchamp's interventions in the art world, which Lyotard punningly called his "transformations of the field [*du champ*]"[92] of its possibilities, have been compared with the event extolled by Badiou and others. An even more explicit link with the larger argument we are trying to make appears in Duchamp's own cryptic evocation of "pictorial nominalism" to describe his departure from painting and turn to alternative modes of artistic production, in particular what came to be called the readymade. In a note dated 1914 from the mixed-media portfolio of his work known as the *White Box* (also called *Á l'Infinitif*), Duchamp jotted down the phrase: "a kind of *pictorial nominalism* (Check)."[93]

Following this hint, the Belgian art historian Thierry de Duve titled his influential account of Duchamp's career, centered on the years he spent in Munich before World War I, *Pictorial Nominalism*.[94] In it, he cited another posthumously published note from the same period which fleshed out Duchamp's meaning:

> *Nominalism* [literal] = No more generic specific numeric distinction between words (tables is not the plural of table, ate has nothing in common with eat). No more physical adaptation of concrete words; no more conceptual value of abstract words. The word also loses its musical value. It is only readable (due to being made up of consonants and vowels), it is readable by eye and little by little takes on a form of plastic significance; it is a sensorial reality, a plastic truth with the same title as a line, as a group of lines.[95]

Duchamp then added that a grouping of such words is "without significance, reduced to literal nominalism, is *independent of the interpretation*." Stubbornly defying hermeneutic translation, the grouping "*finally* no longer expresses a work of art (poem, painting or music)."[96]

What did Duchamp mean by "pictorial nominalism," this enigmatic concept that paradoxically designates precisely what cannot be interpreted as meaningful? As much else in the remarkable legacy left behind by this wily trickster and master of disguise, it defies simple explanation. Still, armed with the insights produced by our analysis of conventional and magical nominalisms and their variations, and drawing on previous accounts such as that of de Duve, we can take a stab at understanding at least some of its implications.

As a first approximation, the term has been taken to signify the denigration of the pictorial in favor of the linguistic, the abandonment of the image for the word. It is thus defined by the literary critic Antoine Compagnon as "the substitution of the linguistic for the plastic in art, or of the discourse on art for the art object."[97] Duchamp did in fact come to distrust what he called "retinal" art, which aimed at sensual pleasure, and chose his readymades not for their formal qualities, but out of "visual indifference, and, at the same time, on the total absence of good or bad taste."[98] He minimized the importance of the experiencing body in traditional aesthetics, allowing his work to seem ascetic or even anesthetic instead.[99] Duchamp's very public renunciation of his creative practice as a painter who had produced works of extraordinary impact, most notably *Nude Descending a Staircase, No. 2* (1912), also came to be understood as a challenge to the master narrative of modernism as a Greenbergian quest for the purified essence of the medium.[100] As a result, Duchamp has often been called the father of the totally dematerialized "conceptual art" of the later twentieth century.[101]

What perhaps makes one hesitate before accepting this lineage is the explicitly anticonceptual intent of Duchamp's ruminations on language. In the note "*Nominalism* [literal]" cited above, he explicitly banished "the conceptual value of abstract words" and suggested that words are most powerful when they become semantically meaningless and syntactically disaggregated, no longer able to express an idea or instantiate an aesthetic genre. Here he differed from Goodman, who argued for the semantic density of art, and claimed that allographic art in particular depended on notational systems that required interpretation.[102] According to the literary critic Carol P. James, Duchamp's notes on nominalism indicate that he "spent his life trying to escape the Principle of Contradiction, looking for literal nominalism, He uses music to pull visual art beyond its conceptual boundaries and in the process expands the horizon of music." But "when words are deprived of their musical value and music can no longer be semantically interpreted, we are left with the literal letter shapes and sound values, zero degrees of signification, a state of openness where a urinal occupies the same plane as the Trevi Fountain by virtue of nominalism, of being named *Fountain*."[103]

We will return to the implications of music's resistance to full semantic interpretation when we examine the magical nominalist moment in Adorno's aesthetic theory, but for now what needs to be stressed are the ambiguous implications of Duchamp's apparent privileging of the linguistic over the plastic. On one level, it suggests the role words might play to resist the abstraction of concepts, shedding their referential or semantic functions, and slowly taking "on a form of plastic significance. . . . [as a] sensorial reality, a plastic truth with the same title as a line, as a group of lines." This was, of course, typical of some modernist art, notably cubism, whose practitioners often incorporated meaningless letters or fragments of texts into their compositions. Its adoption established Duchamp as a critic of the communicative function of language as a transparent medium between two or more minds. In fact, in a letter to a friend many years later, he confirmed the designation:

> I do not believe in language, which instead of expressing subconscious phenomena in reality creates thought by and after the word. (I willingly declare myself a "nominalist," at least in that simplified form). All this twaddle, the existence of God, atheism, determinism, liberation, societies, death, etc., are pieces of a chess game called language, and they are amusing only if one does not pre-occupy oneself with "winning or losing this game of chess." As a good nominalist, I propose the word "patatautology," which, after frequent repetition, will create the concept of what I am trying to explain in this letter by these execrable means: subject, verb, object, etc.[104]

As the philosopher Piotr Schollenberger rightly observes, this "opens up a zero degree of language; it points to the realm where language (what is made of consonants and vowels that are readable), and nonlanguage (what has been deprived of any intentional meaning) meet."[105] Instead, that is, of signaling the denigration of images in favor of words, pictorial nominalism, might therefore have the opposite implication: the pictorialization of desemantized words, which no longer function linguistically. To cite Schollenberger again, "in contrast with Goodman's radical conventionalism, which carefully separates and differentiates linguistic and pictorial systems, Duchamp's 'pictorial nominalism' is a means to trace, in the sphere of language, a place where discourse and figure intertwine. Duchamp stresses here the lack of referential function of the word."[106]

And yet, however much Duchamp challenged the semantic and referential functions of language and sought to isolate words from their syntactical order, he also used language performatively to bring about something new into the world. Thus an upturned urinal put on a pedestal can be called "fountain" and made into the nominal equivalent of its literal counterpart in Rome. Here the larger discursive and institutional context where the choice of an object to be so named is given legitimacy would also have to be acknowledged, as it always is in speech act linguistics. Words need not *mean*, but they can *do* (an argument echoed in Goodman's refusal to say what art *is* in favor of what it *does*). Nothing *is* art, but anything can *become* it through the act of naming (both as "art" and as "fountain").

But before concluding that we have found the basic meaning of pictorial nominalism, yet another complication has to be faced. For at the same time that Duchamp was celebrating the semantically empty but performatively potent power of words, he never entirely abandoned his fascination with actual objects situated in space and time in favor of mere discourses about them, what Duns Scotus had called the *haecceitas* (thisness) of things, not their *quidditas* (whatness).[107] To be sure, he rejected any single spatiotemporal order in which they might be securely located, such as the illusory three-dimensionality of Cartesian perspectivalism.[108] He did so, however, while also resisting the two-dimensional flatness of the modernist canvas, which no longer pretended to be a window on the world but still sought to stimulate visual pleasure. Duchamp was instead intrigued by the non-Euclidean geometry and four-dimensional physics of relativity theory that were roiling the waters of science at the time. As Jean Clair puts it: "Although he too was fascinated by the visual pyramid and the rules of the golden section, his concern was not to illustrate a *Divina Proportione* but to apply them to the highly improbable physiology of his *Mariée*, both in the 1912 painting and in the preparatory study for his *Étant Donnés*. . . . Rather than being interested in the Neoplatonic theories of Marsilio Ficino. . . . He pondered on the uchronias and utopias developed by Hinton and Pawlowski."[109] The result was works, such as *The Large Glass* and *Étant donnés*, that, according to Clair, were "the latest embodiment of mannerism, whose methods corresponded to a pure nominalism of thought—'a sort of pictorial nominalism,' Duchamp was to say—[that] lastingly undermined the idea that the mind can be anchored to a truth, the body to a form, the subject to a definition, history to a meaning."[110] Thus, the substantive integrity of objects was left behind along with the absolute space and linear time of traditional realism. Although in a dynamic relationship to the subjects observing them, they were nonetheless never fully dematerialized or turned into nothing but discursively constituted phantoms, as they might have been were Duchamp simply a conventional nominalist. Such objects endure, even if often in a state of perpetual transmogrification, "definitively unfinished," as Duchamp called *The Large Glass* when he stopped working on it in 1923.

"Pictorial nominalism," in other words, could suggest several distinct, even contradictory things. First, it could mean the power of words, isolated from their grammatical order and semantically empty, to challenge not only ontological universals, but also the abstracting power of concepts. The *nomen*, or names, in nominalism, as we will see shortly, were thus vital for Duchamp. Second, it could imply the constitutive subjectivity of conventional nominalism, through which "art" could be created by symbolization in certain privileged contexts, where discursive (and institutional) legitimation was more important than the intrinsic aesthetic quality of an art object. The designative or enunciative fiat of the "artist," who is not a creative genius,[111] indeed not even someone with the skills or talent to fashion something of formal beauty or mimetic resemblance, could result in that wresting of order from the chaos of contingency Goodman called worldmaking.

But third, "pictorial nominalism" could also suggest that the full discursive sovereignty of the worldmaking artist is always limited by the resistance of the objects he or she has capriciously chosen. Duchamp, in fact, often undercut his own identity as a master artist—with its explicitly masculinist assumptions—and proudly proclaimed his laziness in refusing to produce new works.[112] In addition to the role of the designator, who is more like a baptizer than a creator or fabricator, he understood that the spectator also plays a crucial part in validating the designation, allowing a signed urinal, a hitherto profane object, to be taken, as it were, out of the men's room in a museum and put on a pedestal in one of its galleries.[113] And Duchamp also knew, as did Goodman, that worldmaking is not ex nihilo, but dependent on what has already been made. The tautological implications of art as nothing but designation or enunciation—"I call this a work of art" equals "this is a work of art because I call it one"—is interrupted by the stubborn materiality of the already existing object so designated.[114] Duchamp himself hints at this distinction when he adopts the Jarryian neologism "patatautology" to define his goal. In fact, he insisted that not only readymades but all paintings were dependent on the prior existence of paints, brushes, canvases and the like, which were necessary for the execution of a work of art.[115]

The provocation of his audacious gesture has been understood in many different ways. Not only did it evidence Duchamp's antiretinal exercise of "visual indifference," but it also showed a comparable disdain for the sense of touch.[116] Against the traditional exaltation of the artist's talented hand, verified in the case of a unique painting by his or her signature, the readymade is the result of anonymous mass production, which was only signed, if at all, in the spirit of parodic mockery.[117] Chosen from among modern technologically produced objects—inviting its placement in a constellation with Walter Benjamin's celebrated discussion of "The Work of Art in the Age of Mechanical Reproduction"[118]—it also denigrated the artisanal skill of the premodern craftsman.[119] Despite occasional post facto attempts to justify it in formal terms as unintentionally beautiful—the upturned urinal called *Fountain* was perhaps the most frequent example of this effort[120]—the readymade stubbornly resisted being transfigured into just another formally beautiful artifact. As Rosalind Krauss put it: "Faced with a readymade object, we can make no attempt at formal decoding. For, as we have been made to feel again and again, since it was not Duchamp who 'intended' the formal relationships of the urinal, the work cannot be understood as having encoded the meanings carried by formal decisions. Duchamp's strategy has been to present a work which is irreducible under formal analysis, which is detached from his own personal feelings, and for which there is no resolution of one's efforts to decode or understand it."[121]

And yet at the same time, through being disembedded from its original context where it had functioned for a utilitarian purpose, the readymade undergoes a subtle but momentous transformation essentially through discursive redefinition. Duchamp liked to talk of the "infrathin" (*inframince*), a barely perceptible difference, often ephemeral, undecidable and indefinable, between two or more objects or the same object from one moment to another.[122] In an infrathin interval, a banal snow shovel, bottle rack, urinal, or bicycle wheel can become an artwork, or perhaps better put, a found art object. Sometimes "assisted" by being signed, upturned, put on a pedestal or hung from the ceiling, it undergoes a subtle shift in orientation through its aesthetic framing. But the opposite process can occur as well, with traditional works of art being used for more mundane purposes as "reciprocal readymades," a Rembrandt, for example, being refunctioned into an ironing board (or as Goodman would later say, into a window covering or blanket).[123] Further complications ensue if you take, as Duchamp famously did, a reproduction of a work of art like the *Mona Lisa*, draw a mustache and beard on it, give it a punning scatological name (*L.H.O.O.Q.*, which sounds in French like "she has a hot ass") and then ironize the irony by exhibiting the work later without the mustache as a "rectified readymade."

The objet trouvé soon, in fact, became a staple of surrealist art, which was inspired by, among other sources, the moment of aleatory passivity in Duchamp's practice.[124] Because of this link and the Surrealists' fascination with what they liked to call "the marvelous," it would be tempting to say that Duchamp's readymades are more typical of what we have been calling magical than conventional nominalism. By being already made, as we have already noted, they resist the full sovereignty of the self-asserting subject of conventional nominalism, whose performative speech act allegedly summons up a new world out of the chaos of contingency.

But is that summoning up in any way like the conjuring of a magician, which, if so, would strengthen the case that Duchamp could be enlisted in the ranks of the magical nominalists? It has been in fact argued that Duchamp was much influenced by the world of pseudoscientific occultism in the France of his youth, a world in which symbolist artists sought to find tap into a spiritual reality beyond the normal experience of modern men and women.[125] His tireless experiments in exploring the boundaries of conventional art—even after he allegedly gave up painting for playing chess, he was secretly working on the installation that became *Étant donnés*—earned him a comparison with a medieval alchemist, "transforming" not only his field, but also base objects into artistic gold.

And yet, it is clear that Duchamp was also suspicious of the quest for spiritual meaning that animated artists like Kandinsky, whose metaphysical theories of color he vigorously rejected. As de Duve notes: "Klee, Kandinsky, Mondrian, Malevich each wanted in his own manner to lay the cornerstone of a new language that they hoped would be universal, effectively unspeakable since it would be mute by nature, and yet speaking to everyone since the 'rendering things visible,' which gave itself as a goal, meant that it would make the visual speak, and speak in the language of pure painting. There is nothing like this in Duchamp."[126] Or to put it in a somewhat different register, Duchamp was not really interested in the spiritual reenchantment of a world left bereft of inherent meaning by conventional nominalism. His sensibility was too ironic, deflating, and playful, his wit too cynically mocking, to take on the solemn role of artist as shaman. Not surprisingly, later would-be artistic shamans like Joseph Beuys would explicitly turn against him.[127]

Another way to address this issue would be to focus on the objects themselves subtly transformed by Duchamp's infrathin recontextualizations. For all the auratic authority they may have gained when exhibited in a museum, they were always chosen from multiple copies of the same mass-produced object and often replaced by substitutes after their initial selection. In other words, they depart, in Goodman's terms, from the autographic singularity of traditional painting or sculpture, which can imbue the "original" with almost fetishistic power, and enter instead the less immediately enchanted realm of allographic art.[128] Gérard Genette correctly notes that the symbolic resonance that readymades amplify is severely limited: "If we look to the Goodmanian criteria to define the aesthetic object as a locus of infinite (active) contemplation, thanks to the inexhaustible character of its symbolic functioning, it becomes hard to see how an object of thought as peremptorily defined as the concept of a ready-made could inspire such contemplation."[129] That is, there is a world of difference in the response we may have to, say, the Isenheim Altarpiece or the Rothko Chapel, whose immersive experience is as close to enchantment as many of us will ever experience, and the one we have when looking at a signed urinal. The possibility of "reciprocal readymades," traditional works of art being turned into commonplace use objects, shows that the profanation of the sacred is always a live possibility. In short, unlike Walter Benjamin, Duchamp had no role to play in what Leo Bersani was to call "the culture of redemption."[130]

It would, nevertheless, be problematic to situate Duchamp completely in the conventional nominalist camp and deny certain affinities with its magical counterpart. For there are two intriguing parallels that suggest otherwise: his elevation of the role of the proper name and his affirmation of the interruptive temporality of the artistic "event." De Duve alerts us to the importance of the former when he writes: "I intend the world *nominalism* in its Duchampian sense and not in the philosophical sense established since the time of Abelard and Ockham. But it might someday be necessary to ask whether these various nominalisms do not in fact all deal with the same problem, that of universals, while at the same time asking if there is not a fundamental difference: whereas for the medieval thinkers, names are signs, generally speaking, the words *art* or *painting* as they appear in the nominalism of Duchamp are always proper names."[131] In a chapter titled "Art Was a Proper Name" in his ambitious treatise *Kant after Duchamp*, de Duve attempted to flesh out this contention.[132] In so doing, he implicitly challenged the lament of philosophers like Jean-Luc Nancy that the healthy plurality of arts represented by the separate muses had been replaced during the Romantic period by an abstract generic concept.[133] "The word 'art' is a linguistic sign," de Duve admits, "no one would deny it. But it is not a logical concept. It is thus not a common noun, even though it is common to all the things you call art. This commonality results from the namings you have brought about through your judgments; it is not prior to them in the manner of a linguistic denotation or a conceptual extension."[134] Works or objects designated as art share a name in the way all of the Peters and Pauls of the world share a proper name, which does not describe or signify but only designates them.[135]

Drawing on Saul Kripke's discussion of proper names as rigid designators, which we have encountered before in our discussion of Benjamin's theory of language, de Duve argues that "even though rigid designators might have a meaning, and this meaning might consist of a list or cluster of properties, essential or not, what makes them proper names is their use: they serve to fix the reference and not to pronounce a meaning."[136] To call something a work of art is thus not to subsume it under a concept or assign it an essential meaning but to exercise what Kant would have called a reflective judgment, comparing it to other cases of what has been called art in the past, "a comparison by analogy, an 'as if-comparison.'"[137]

Although proper names can be transmitted from generation to generation, the actual judgment "this is art" involves an experience in the here and now—de Duve calls it the "deictics of experience"[138]—that involves a contingent decision about a particular object. But implicit in that decision, as in the case of Kant's putatively universalizing judgment of taste, is the assumption, however dubious in reality, that a sensus communis would come to agree about the designation.

Seeking to avoid any suspicion that he is smuggling in a generic concept of art despite his protestations to the contrary, de Duve argues that it is better to avoid saying "art is a proper name" in favor of "art was a proper name," because the latter offers "an archaeological description of the tradition regulated by the idea of art as a proper name. This tradition, congruent with the history of the avant-garde, is modernity."[139] It began when art was understood as autonomous, following no inherent rule, and independent of the quality of beauty. And it continues today, whether in the guise of modern or postmodern art. For de Duve, the readymade is a critical moment in clarifying that tradition, and he even goes so far as to argue it might best be understood "as neither an object or a set of objects nor a gesture nor an artistic intention, but rather, as a statement. It is the sentence 'this is art,' art such as it is pinned to absolutely any object whatsoever, *given* (I say 'given,' and not 'provided') that it was recognized—that is, judged—as art."[140]

De Duve's reading of Duchamp's substitution of the proper name "art" for the conceptual category of art and employing it according to Kant's idea of reflective as opposed to determinant judgments is suggestive. By invoking Kripke's notion of meaningless, rigid designators, he provides an intriguing link with the Jewish nominalist tradition Bielik-Robson and others have identified as distinct from the mainstream alternative we have been calling conventional. His argument, however, has not been universally accepted. According to Diarmuid Costello, equating shared proper names—the Peters and Pauls of the world—with different objects designated as art is problematic, "given that what distinguishes proper names from concepts is that they are conferred *without* regard to the other bearers of the name, it is hard to see how art can be a proper name when the judgment that confers it is essentially comparative."[141] Jason Gaiger similarly points out:

> that the term "art" cannot possibly function as a logically proper name, equivalent to "Paul" or "Harry," and that even in the most problematic cases of its extension it carries with it an elaborate, even if never fully determinate, descriptive content. In judging something to be a work

> of art, we refer it to other instances of objects which we have similarly designated by the same term and seek to establish some common or overlapping feature or set of features. If "art" were a logically proper name, the judgment "this is art" would remain unproblematic and devoid of interest. It is precisely because the judgment is comparative, relating the object in question to other similar objects, that the question of art status is an issue for us.[142]

J. M. Bernstein, building on Gaiger's critique, adds that "sameness is the last thing one wants for art."[143] The term "art" may therefore be better understood as an honorific title, like Doctor or Professor, than a proper name rigidly designating its referent.

De Duve might answer that he is favoring the taxonomic rather than individual version of the proper names bestowed by Adam in the Garden of Eden, the one that designated the species "cow" rather than its exemplars "Bessie" or "Buttercup." From the point of view of magical nominalism, however, a further problem then arises. Duchamp's proper names—whether they be "art," "readymade," or "Fountain"—are all bestowed by a mundane nomothete, who has somehow gained the legitimacy to baptize them. But as we saw when looking at the Jewish tradition of Adamic naming, it was not clear whether Adam had the performative power to bestow names ex nihilo or was merely recognizing the names already given by God. To the extent that the latter informed such magical nominalist quests for an *Ursprache* as Walter Benjamin's belief in "language as such," the proper name was given ontological weight as a "true" or "right" name. For Duchamp, in contrast, it was an arbitrary designation lacking both meaning and ontological truth, the effect of a contingent performative act.

If we cannot then fully identify Duchamp with a magical nominalist paradigm because of the way he bestows proper names, what can be said of his exemplification of Goodman's claim that the real question is not "What is art?" but "When is art?" Does, in other words, the act of designation constitute an "event" comparable to what we have seen was a magical nominalist impulse in the poststructuralist reading of history? Does it have the same ability to produce that burst of freedom, release of libidinal energy, or the appropriation of Being that the event did for them? Is it an event as an "advent," in which something new enters the world, with unanticipated adventures to follow? Or is it merely a mundane occurrence without the transformative potential that magical nominalists attribute to a handful of genuine historical breakthroughs?

A great deal of visual art in the modern period, including the painting that survived Duchamp's attempt to abandon it, has sought to highlight the temporal act of creating as much as the enduring creation that ensued. American "action painters," for example, were praised by critics like Harold Rosenberg for turning their canvases into "an arena in which to act—rather than as a space in which to reproduce, re-design, analyze or 'express' an object, actual or imagined. What was to go on the canvas was not a picture but an event."[144] Although critics such as Mary McCarthy may have sourly responded that "you cannot hang an event on the wall, only a picture,"[145] many artists soon rejected the need to hang anything anywhere for any length of time, preferring instead a finite event shared by creator and audience. What in a seminal article published in 1968 Lucy Lippard and John Chandler called "The Dematerialization of Art" meant a new emphasis on aesthetic experience over the objects that engendered it, as well as on textuality over visuality.[146] The various "happenings," "auto-destructive art," "performance art," "ephemeral art," and the like that exemplified dematerialization were not only intended to thwart the commodification of artworks in the commercial marketplace but also to turn intensity, interruption, transgression, and shock into primary aesthetic values.[147] Action painting was replaced by direct "actions" in themselves.[148] Often this meant collapsing the distance between contemplative subject and contemplated object in the name of immersive immediacy.

A comparable discursive elevation of the transient aesthetic event, often interpreted in Heideggerian or poststructuralist terms, followed.[149] In a 1991 essay called "On What Is 'Art,'" Lyotard argued: "What the writer, composer, painter, or filmmaker (or even the reader, listener, or spectator) waits for is for 'it to come along.' What is waited for is the event of the 'decision' that serves as act for and end to the infinity of possibles. . . . The act that decides is not an *action* in the strict sense of the term—it is an event."[150] In a work titled *The Historicity of Experience: Modernity, the Avant-Garde and the Event*, the critic Krzysztof Ziarek further explains that "art taken as an event is not a scene of subjective contemplation or aesthetic relishing of *poeisis*. . . . It becomes a 'thoughtful' action of turning the historicity of experience against the metaphysical substantialization of being with the technological organization of life. . . . The event describes life not in terms of a self but as a field and an occurrence which exceeds the space of consciousness or the symbolic realm of social experience."[151] A more concrete version of this argument appeared in Josette Féral's depiction of the role played by an event in contemporary theater, which was tantamount to a normal dramatic performance being suddenly interrupted by a happening:

> It appears as a moment that surprises the spectators and causes the real to emerge onstage outside of any process of representation, illusion, or stage fiction. This event . . . seizes upon the spectators' senses and addresses itself directly to their emotions, creating a quasi immersion in the action that prevents all critical distance. The spectators find themselves, if only for a few moments, constrained by the event itself and forced into renouncing the "suspension of disbelief" that theatrical research and theories of communication have defined as the basis of the credulity necessary to theatrical action. To put it differently, one might say that a theatrical event is the moment when the theatrical illusion is interrupted and the stage is shaped by an action that emerges without mediation (but not without a frame), leaving room for chance or risk.[152]

Other examples can easily be given, but suffice it say that by 2012, the idea of "evental aesthetics" was so well established that a new journal was devoted to its exploration.[153]

Inevitably, the discourse of the aesthetic event was soon applied retrospectively to Duchamp's various provocations. In 1985, Lyotard noted that "*The Large Glass* and *Étant donnés* refer to events, to the 'striping bare' of the Bride, and to the discovery of the obscene body. . . . The two works are two ways of representing the anachronism of the gaze with regard to the event of stripping bare."[154] That is, the first portrays an anticipation of the event, the time of "not yet," while the second reveals what has already happened, the time of "no longer." They both refer to "that instant itself, the flash of light which dazzles the eye, an epiphany. But, according to Duchamp, the occurrence of 'femininity' cannot be taken into account *within* the time of the gaze of 'virility.'"[155] Or to put it somewhat differently, the Cartesian perspectivalist order in which objects can be securely located—an order that in some sense corresponds to the male gaze—is undone by a mannerist or baroque disorder that produces spatiotemporal disorientation. Here Lyotard was drawing on—with a special gender twist—his general argument about the temporal dislocation of the event, "the 'it happens' which cannot be reduced to a representation, cannot be identified with 'what happens.'"[156] Although the two works treat a singular object, it lacks ontological solidity: "that object is still *a name* (Duchamp is a nominalist), the name of the bride stripped bare."[157]

The readymade was an even more inviting candidate for an example of the event, because it eschewed all pretense of narrative representation. In his introduction to the English translation of de Duve's *Pictorial Nominalism*, the philosopher John Rajchman, who had already identified Foucault as a historical nominalist, argued that the readymade was also an event in the sense that it ruptured the history of painting, signaling a moment of abandonment. But, "as De Duve uses the term, to 'abandon' something is not just to discard it. It is to register the moment of its loss or 'impossibility' within a work in such a way as to open up, or call for, another history. The invention of the readymade would be an event of this sort."[158] That is, it is an event as "advent."

In 2003, the French critic Barbara Formis turned to Badiou to interpret Duchamp's provocation in an insightful essay titled "Event and Ready-Made: Delayed Sabotage."[159] According to Formis:

> First, it emerges within a historical situation at a specific point—theorized by Badiou as an "evental site." Second, like the event, its appearance in the situation is that of a disappearance: the mode in which it occurs is that of an "effacing inscription" in which the object, the spectator and the artist are all effaced. Third, the ready-made has a unique structure that inevitably entails it being designated as illegitimate: its emergence corresponds to its prohibition by the situation. Fourth, the ready-made lead [*sic*] to a major transformation of the situation within [which] it emerged—the world of art.[160]

The "evental site" is at once historical and ontological. The historical is the exhibition of the *Society of Independent Artists*, whose hypocritical pretension to being nonjudgmentally inclusive was exposed by its refusal to show the urinal. Although strictly speaking, *Fountain* was not the first readymade, it was the first that sought acceptance—if initially in vain—by an official art exhibition.[161] The ontological is the tradition of the artist as creator, whose claim to being an imitator of divine creativity ex nihilo is debunked by revealing that it is always dependent on materials that are already made (paints, brushes, canvases, etc.). Significantly, after its scandalous disruption of business as usual, the actual object—the first urinal signed R. Mutt—was lost, to be preserved only by a photograph, and then replaced later by other iterations of the mass-produced object.

The disappearance of the object matches the effacement of the "artist" who designated it. As Formis notes:

> The ready-made's sabotage of the artistic procedure thus proceeds by erasing the object, effacing the spectator's gaze and finally it also erases the artist's role. This is the third effacing gesture. The artist is not the

> 'creator' of the ready-made and so he or she does not entertain an active relationship to the artistic procedure in the case of ready-mades. The ready-made is not an object produced by a subject. The artist's activity is submitted to a chance procedure, which reduces artistic choice to its minimal level. Duchamp says that it is not the subject that chooses an object—the ready-made—, but the opposite; "it chooses you in a manner of speaking."[162]

Although there is something excessively melodramatic in Formis's identification of *Fountain* with Badiou's notion of the event as an illegitimate sabotage "forbidden by the state,"[163] it did challenge the received norms of the art world, and took a while—perhaps not even until the 1950s and 1960s—to have its full effect. Like many other provocations that produce artistic scandals, its enduring power was enhanced by the notoriety it generated, even if what was an unprecedented "advent" soon became recuperated by the art world that knew how to absorb its challenge.[164] What Badiou would have called fidelity to the original event was thus blunted by attempts to duplicate its disruptive effect, which inadvertently subverted the singularity of its intervention.

Formis makes, however, another salient point about the paradoxical undecidability of the object itself, which remains an object of everyday life even when it is elevated into an art object. It becomes, she tells us, "intervallic," never settling into one or the other identity, at once a presentation and a representation, both a rupture and a continuity, sabotaging whatever category tries to contain it. Duchamp's undermining of the boundary between art object and the everyday became, in fact, one of the main sources of the mainstream modernist suspicion of his provocation. Witness Greenberg's critique as described by Rosalind Krauss: "What Clem detests in Duchamp's art is its pressure towards desublimation, 'Levelling' he calls it. The attempt to erase distinctions between art and not-art, between the absolute gratuitousness of form and the commodity. The strategy, in short of the readymade."[165]

Against this reproach of leveling, we might say the readymade embodies the magical nominalist impulse to escape not only ontologically real universals as well as artificial ones promoted by the self-asserting subject of conventional nominalism but also a flatly positive affirmation of quotidian objects in all their banality. By 2005, W. J. T. Mitchell could sense that something different was happening as a result of Duchamp's effect: "We find ourselves talking about physical things today with a new tone of voice. 'Things' are no longer passively waiting for a concept, a theory, or sovereign subject to arrange them in ordered ranks of objecthood. 'The Thing' rears its head—a rough beast or a sci-fi monster, a repressed returnee, an obdurate materiality, a stumbling block, and an object lesson."[166]

Expressing it in Badiou's terms of the event, Alex Ling offers a similar observation: the readymade-event clearly demonstrates the indiscernibility between art and non-art, an "acknowledgment that the base material of art is, first and foremost, non-artistic. The 'evental' status of Fountain therefore lies foremost in the fact that it managed (metaontologically speaking) to elevate certain voided—and, fundamentally, common—elements from the level of non-presentation to that of re-presentation, or (on a phenomenological level) to raise that which had inexisted in art to a level of maximal existence."[167] That is, rather than leveling art down to the everyday, the readymade raised the everyday to the status of art.

By stressing "maximal existence" without fleshing out what that might mean, Ling unintentionally expresses what we have previously identified as the negative impulse in magical nominalism, its valorization of whatever exceeds categories and principles, natural or conventional, without giving it positive embodiment. Whether or not a secular version of apophatic theology, which defines divinity only through negative attributes, it shares a refusal to rest content with positively described singularities. Instead, it revels in the ambiguous and the undecidable, the suspension of laws of contradiction with their rigid either/or logic. Pictorial nominalism—forever needing to be "checked"—resists being equated decisively with either conventional or magical nominalism. Duchamp's various provocations never settle into a coherent program. Instead, they roil the waters of art without ever allowing them to restore the calm before the storm. The advent they promise never fully arrives, even if the adventure they take us on may well be worth the journey.

Adorno and the Ambiguous Implications of Musical Nominalism

Can similar impulses be discerned in Adorno's negative dialectics of musical nominalism? It surely could never be said of him, as Rajchman says of Duchamp, that his "hilarity would be a sort of nominalist humor, a laugh at the expense of categorical identity."[168] Adorno's "melancholy science" was, after all, not easily amused by anything in the modern world. But in challenging categorical identity, indeed identity theory in general and in aesthetics in particular, he shared with Duchamp a recognition that conventional nominalism need not be the final word in the reckoning with universalist realism.

Although their exile in America overlapped, Duchamp and Adorno never in fact traveled in the same circles or met personally. Duchamp moved permanently to New York only in 1942, by which time Adorno had decamped for Los Angeles. The delay in the reception of Duchamp's provocation, which meant it paradoxically became a true event when it was on the verge of being absorbed by the institutions and discourses it sought to sabotage, also diminished its impact in the Germany to which Adorno returned after the Second World War. The first solo exhibition of Duchamp's work occurred only in 1965 at the Haus Lange Museum in the small city of Krefeld, a few years before Adorno's death, while important German artists like Beuys, as previously noted, were alienated by Duchamp's trivialization of the solemn mission of art.[169] Adorno's interest in the visual arts was, moreover, never as keen as in music or literature,[170] and he was more resistant to Dadaism and surrealism, which sometimes claimed Duchamp as a fellow traveler, than to other modernist movements such as expressionism. Although a possible connection might have been made through John Cage, a friend of Duchamp and a composer whose work Adorno knew and ambivalently admired, nothing came of it.[171] So it is not surprising that in all of his voluminous writings on modernism, Adorno never seriously engaged with Duchamp's legacy.

The reason for his neglect was, however, as much substantive as adventitious. As the literary critic Gerald Bruns puts it:

> The difficulty is that it is precisely the thesis of aesthetic nominalism (in which anything goes as a work of art) that Adorno wants to contest (perhaps without hope of defeating it). Marcel Duchamp's name is nowhere mentioned in *Aesthetic Theory*, but there is no doubt that Duchamp would play Adorno's nemesis, precisely because what Adorno seems to reject is the very idea that a work of art can simply be a "found object," that is, something merely empirical or a mere social product, like the urinal of Duchamp's *Fountain*.[172]

That Adorno shared Clement Greenberg's alarm at the flattening of the distinction between art and non-art or artworks and everyday objects (even in their noncommodified state) is clear; he was invariably suspicious of the valorization of the actually existing world, the world of equally binding "facts," as all there is or might be. If nominalism had meant nothing but positivism, he would have clearly been opposed to it, whether in its pictorial or other guises. Adorno was no less distrustful of the conventional nominalist elevation of the constitutive subject, whose imposition of categories on a contingent world he associated with the domination of nature, which included the excesses of idealism at its most subjective. To be sure, while defending what he called "the predominance of the object," he did recognize the necessity of at least some subjective projection on to the world as inevitable for human self-preservation, and perhaps even in some ways ultimately salutary. But, and this is the vital point, he never saw constitutive subjectivity as a sufficient response to the absolute contingency of the world left behind by Ockham and the conventional nominalists.

At the same time, Adorno was never tempted to fall back on a Platonic version of aesthetic realism as a compelling alternative. "It is self-evident," he asserted in the oft-cited opening sentence of *Aesthetic Theory*, "that nothing concerning art is self-evident anymore, not its inner life, not its relation to the world, not even its right to exist."[173] That is, although at one time it might have been thought that art followed immutable rules reflecting cosmic harmonies, we have long since been disabused of that dubious assumption. "Art has no universal rules," Adorno insisted, "though in each of its phases there certainly are objective binding taboos. Their very existence defines what forthwith is no longer possible."[174]

If Adorno rejected universalist aesthetic realism, while criticizing the positivist version of nominalism for affirming existing facts, and its conventional alternative for granting too much constitutive power to the self-asserting subject, can we then place him in the magical nominalist camp? Do his manifold debts to Walter Benjamin at least allow us to call him one of the Jewish nominalists identified by Bielik-Robson as the more religiously respectable counterparts of their magical cousins? Might he therefore be accurately described, in Hent de Vries's terms, as a "minimal theologian?"[175] Or can we instead, as in the case of Benjamin, find powerful residues of magical thinking in his incorporation of theological motifs in his negative dialectics? And if so, can we say that Adorno shared with Duchamp some of the same impulses—most notably, an interest in proper names and the event-like quality of aesthetic disruptions of the status quo—that would allow us to put them in productive conversation, despite the obvious differences separating them?[176]

To address these questions, we first have to consider Adorno's nuanced attitude toward magic in general, which may have played an implicit role in his refusal to gravitate to either pole of the traditional realism/nominalism opposition.[177] Walter Benjamin, as we have seen, cannot be understood without taking into account his unapologetic openness to magical thinking, in particular in its linguistic guise. He was also drawn to modern survivals of magical techniques, such as graphology and astrology, and sympathetic to the efforts of their modern defenders such as Ludwig Klages. Adorno, however, for all his debts to Benjamin, was much more skeptical of anything that explicitly smacked of the occult, whose contemporary manifestations in, for example, popular horoscopes he mercilessly ridiculed.[178] Whatever the merits of situating Duchamp in the culture of European occultism, it would be very difficult to discern its power on the young Adorno. When he criticized an early draft of Benjamin's *Arcades* project in a frequently cited letter of 1938, Adorno pointedly warned: "The theological motif of calling things by their names tends to switch into the wide-eyed presentation of mere facts. If one wanted to put it rather drastically, one could say that your study is located at the crossroads of magic and positivism. That spot is bewitched. Only theory could break this spell—your own resolute and salutarily speculative theory."[179] By the time of *Minima Moralia*, published in 1951, Adorno could denounce occultism in no uncertain terms as "a symptom of regression in consciousness. . . . By its regression to magic under late capitalism, thought is assimilated to late capitalist forms."[180] Even worse, it was comparable to the fascist modes of thought that were still dangerously alive in postwar America. "Occultism," in short, "is the metaphysics of dunces."[181] It was the task of critique, he often insisted, to free us from the "spell" (*Bann*) cast by modern capitalism.[182] Here he was echoing Marx's critique of the "whole mystery of commodities, all the magic and necromancy [*all der Zauber und Spuk*] that surrounds the products of labor on the basis of commodity production."[183]

And yet, at the same time, Adorno understood the costs of the one-dimensional "disenchantment of the world" identified with relentless secularization.[184] As David Kaufmann puts it, for Adorno, "the negation of mere magic has in turn been demystified, has been revealed in history to be a false positivity, a myth. The prohibition on magic, on the attempt to harness divine power, leaves one smack in the middle of an unchangeable world."[185] The process of disenchantment began, paradoxically enough, with the attempt of primitive magicians to master their mysterious and often hostile environment. They often did so, he and Horkheimer argued in *Dialectic of Enlightenment*, by imitating what they feared in order to participate in its power. But significantly, mimesis had a benign as well as malevolent potential. The latter may still have been evident, for example, in the way modern fascists mocked their victims by imitating them, but the former was preserved in the nondominating mimesis of the natural world at its most nurturant.[186] Because this mimesis was behavioral, as is still often evident in the play of children, it involved the body and the senses, even if nonsensuous similarities in language could also develop.[187] As such, it went beyond the mere imitative verisimilitude of the world as it is, which inspired typical aesthetic "realism" in its non-Platonic guise.

In complicated ways, the benign mimetic impulse found one of its last refuges in works of art, whose aura, to borrow Benjamin's words, cannot be entirely dissolved if the artwork is to retain its emancipatory promise. Responding to Benjamin's hasty advocacy of that dissolution in a draft of "The Work of Art in the Age of Mechanical Reproduction," Adorno composed a lengthy letter in March of 1936 in which he reminded Benjamin of his earlier appreciation of the aura and suggested his turn against it may have reflected the influence of his problematic recent friendship with Bertolt Brecht:

> I now find it somewhat disturbing—and here I can see a sublimated remnant of certain Brechtian themes—that you have now rather casually transferred the concept of the magical aura to the "autonomous work of art" and flatly assigned a counter-revolutionary function to the latter. I do not need to assure you how aware I am of the magical element that persists in the bourgeois work of art. . . . However, it seems to me that the heart of the autonomous work does not itself belong to the dimension of myth—but is inherently dialectical, that is, compounds within itself the magical element with the sign of freedom.[188]

The explicit point of Adorno's reproach is to salvage the emancipatory potential in aesthetic autonomy, a sign of his high modernist sympathies, which separated him from Benjamin and Brecht (and we might add, Duchamp). Thus, later in the letter, he affirms Benjamin's observation of the decline of the aura, which he attributes not only to mechanical reproduction but also to the fulfillment of formal aesthetic laws, and adds, "The autonomy of the work of art, and therefore its material form, is not identical with the magical element in it."[189]

But while Adorno is at pains here to defend the autonomy of the work from Benjamin's dismissive equation of it with its "magical element," his remarks paradoxically suggest something else, which is even more significant for our purposes: an acknowledgment that there is a residue of magic in artworks, however self-referential and autonomous they may pretend to be. It is this residue that can be associated with the benignly mimetic moment in art, which is a crucial source of its utopian potential. Believing in its vital importance allowed Adorno to claim in one of the most frequently cited aphorisms in *Minima Moralia*, "Art is magic delivered from the lie of being truth."[190]

One plausible gloss of this gnomic assertion would be that magic cannot claim to satisfy the verification procedures of modern science, and attempts to defend its veracity on other grounds would also be in vain. But another is that something of what has made it so potent in human culture for so long is still preserved in works of art, artifacts of imagination and fictionality that can never be entirely reduced to their "truth content" when it is equated with cognitive propositional assertions.[191] Nor can they be identified entirely with absolute autonomy, understood either in terms of authorial sovereignty or the self-referential integrity of the work as an organic whole. For the "magical element," especially if it is understood to contain a trace of mimetic comportment, preserves a moment of irreducible otherness that resists the immanent self-sufficiency of the work. Only in its magical element, he writes, "is art's mimetic character preserved. . . . Emancipated from its claim to reality, the enchantment is itself part of enlightenment: its semblance disenchants the disenchanted world."[192] As he and Horkheimer put it in *Dialectic of Enlightenment*:

> Both reason and religion outlaw the principle of magic. . . . Art has in common with magic the postulation of a special, self-contained sphere removed from the context of profane existence. Within it special laws prevail. Just as the sorcerer begins the ceremony by marking out from all its surroundings the place in which the sacred forces are to come into play, each work of art is closed off from reality by its own circumference. The very renunciation of external effects by which art is distinguished from magical sympathy binds art only more deeply to the heritage of magic.[193]

The persistently enigmatic quality of works of art attest to magic's enduring presence. As we will see, Adorno's defense not only of the nonpropositional but also the nonsemantic dimension of music suggests his unannounced affinity for a nominalism that is more akin to its magical than conventional variant.

In fact, even Adorno's attitude toward conventional nominalism was hardly straightforward. Although he has sometimes been portrayed as unremittingly hostile,[194] he also appreciated its progressive possibilities, which had been realized in certain historical contexts. As he made clear in his 1958 introductory lectures on dialectics: "Dialectic is not a form of nominalism, but nor again is it a form of realism. For these twin theses of traditional philosophy . . . must both be subjected to dialectical critique."[195] In what follows, we will try to follow the twists and turns of Adorno's critique, first in philosophy in general, then in aesthetics, and finally in music in particular. In so doing, we will work with the assumption that critique does not mean simply negative fault-finding but rather a nondogmatic evaluation of the merits and costs of what is being analyzed.

In their critique of the reduction of the Enlightenment to instrumental reason in *Dialectic of Enlightenment*, Horkheimer and Adorno accused nominalism of going too far in its denigration of conceptual realism and the metaphysical tradition of substantive rationalism. "Enlightenment finally devoured not only symbols but also their successors, universal concepts, and left nothing of metaphysics except the abstract fear of the collective from which it had sprung." As a result, the critical impulse in the rationalist tradition had been undermined. But then they added, "Enlightenment as a nominalist tendency stops short before the *nomen*, the non-extensive, restricted concept, the proper name."[196] What this cryptic remark may suggest we will explore later when we return to that link with proper names already mentioned in connection with Duchamp. Elsewhere, in his 1959 lectures on Kant's *Critique of Pure Reason*, Adorno noted the presence of a nominalist impulse in the idea of synthetic a priori judgments: "This concept of synthesis is nothing but the theory of nominalism brought to the highest pitch of abstraction because it declares not merely concepts, but everything that can be meaningfully discussed, to be the consequence of mental activity. Moreover, in the criticism Kant directs at metaphysics, we can still hear the echo of the old nominalist critique of universals. . . . We can say that the foundation of Kantian philosophy is still nominalist."[197] He then, however, adds, "but Kant stands on the threshold of a development in which the considerations that led to a radical nominalism begin to turn against themselves. . . . He is the first to have conceived of the relation of universals to the particulars subsumed under them as *dialectical*."[198]

Crossing that threshold is Hegel, who is described in Adorno's *Hegel: Three Studies*, first published in 1963, as having developed a dialectical method, "which is the approach of a consistent nominalism awakened to self-consciousness, an approach that examines any and every concept in terms of its subject matter and in so doing convicts it of its inadequacy."[199] But then he adds that Hegel's reflection on the self moves beyond the claim that truth is merely a function of the constitutive subject, the claim of subjective idealism, to "an objective idea, an idea that is no longer nominalistically reducible."[200] His version of truth is based on a kind of dynamic Platonism in which temporality is included. Or more precisely, "Hegel's truth is no longer in time, as nominalist truth was, nor is it above time in the ontological fashion: for Hegel time becomes a moment of truth itself."[201] That is, the temporality of contradictions, which emerge, sharpen, and are then sublated, is part of the truth, which is the process as a whole.

From this perspective, nominalism is itself a moment of the truth, but certainly not all of it. Later in *Hegel: Three Studies*, Adorno makes a direct connection between the nominalist impulse and the social forces of modern bourgeois society: "Nominalism is part of the bourgeois bedrock; it accompanies the consolidation of urbanism across all its phases, and in the most diverse nations the ambivalence of that process is sedimented in it. Nominalism helps to free consciousness from the pressure of the authority of the concept that had established itself as universality; it does so by disenchanting the concept and making it a mere abbreviation for the particularities it covers."[202] But once again, Adorno continues, it goes too far, for "such enlightenment is always also its opposite: hypostasis of the particular. To this extent, nominalism encourages the bourgeoisie to be suspicious of everything that would restrain isolated individuals in their 'pursuit of happiness,' the unreflective pursuit of their own advantage, as being mere illusion."[203] Thus, Adorno darkly concludes, "nominalism, which is anti-ideological, has been ideology from the very beginning."[204] Hegel, in his attempt to go beyond it, is thus a powerful weapon in the struggle to overcome bourgeois society.

Not surprisingly, when Adorno turned to the anti-Hegelian tradition of *Existenzphilosophie*, from Kierkegaard to Heidegger, he discerned a regression to unmediated nominalist premises. In *Negative Dialectics*, he contends that "nominalism, one of the roots of the existential philosophy of the Protestant Kierkegaard, gave Heidegger's ontology the attractiveness of the nonspeculative. Just as the concept of existence is a false conceptualization of existing things, the complementary precedence which these things are given over the concept allows the ontological concept of existence to profit in turn."[205] In other words, despite the nominalist critique of realist metaphysics, it offered existentialism an alternative that dulled the critical edge that had impelled Enlightenment nominalists: "Where consistent enlighteners absolutize nominalism—instead of dialectically penetrating the nominalist thesis too—they recoil into mythology. Their philosophy becomes mythology at the point where, believing in some ultimate datum, they cut reflection short."[206]

Ironically, the positivist fetish of individual facts and distrust of abstract concepts was in tension with its elevation of mathematics to a universal sign system, which smacked of the very Scholastic realism that nominalism had sought to undermine.[207] The juxtaposition of isolated facts and formal universals—what Michel Foucault would later condemn mutatis mutandis as the "empirico-transcendental-empirical doublet" in Kant's epistemology[208]—meant a dual abstraction from a concrete whole in which historically generated generic categories and the concepts that made sense of them were still at least temporarily "real."[209] As a result, so Adorno told his students in his 1960 lectures Philosophy and Sociology, "Theory in the emphatic sense is not really possible at all under expressly nominalist conditions, i.e. when concepts are deprived of all substantiality and regarded simply as *flatus vocis*."[210]

In summary, in critiquing nominalism—or more precisely, what we have been calling conventional nominalism—as a philosophical impulse with social implications, Adorno leveled the following accusations. Although he appreciated the value of its challenge to the absolute authority of generic, subordinating concepts over particulars, he balked at the nominalist fetishizing of those particulars—whether in existentialist or positivist guise—as utterly unmediated by concepts. Despite its theological origins, he saw nominalism as really coming into its own with the secular disenchantment of the world wrought by bourgeois modernity, in which individual self-interest and self-preservation trumped any claims to collective solidarity. While admitting that it fostered an active subjectivity, he charged it did so at the cost of obliterating the integrity of the objects dominated by the constitutive subject. Although that subject, at least in its transcendental guise, could itself be undermined by a nominalist critique of universals, the stress on the will as opposed to reason in the nominalist tradition, whether divine or human, meant tacit complicity with the domination of nature abetted by the dialectic of enlightenment. Likewise, the nominalist emphasis on linguistic constructivism led to the problematic exaggeration of the sovereignty of language over the world of recalcitrant materiality. In short, in many respects, Adorno echoed a time-honored anxiety about the implications of nominalism that extended back to theological debates in the Middle Ages.

What then is the role of nominalism in the realm of the aesthetic in general, and music in particular, for Adorno? Did he merely repeat his philosophical critique in, as it were, a different key? Did he disdainfully identify it, as Rose Rosengard Subotnik, has written, with a musical condition "obviously antithetical to interaction and consequently to meaning?"[211] Or were there ways in which nominalism, understood more in magical than conventional terms, served less dubious purposes when art rather than philosophy or science was involved, thus allowing observers such as Peter Uwe Hohendahl to go so far as to speak of the "radical nominalist stance that Adorno adopts with regards to art."[212] In Adorno's posthumously published *Aesthetic Theory*, the first mention of nominalism comes in his crucial discussion of aesthetic semblance (*Schein*), in which he argues that "the truth of artworks depends on whether they succeed at absorbing into their immanent necessity what is not identical with the concept, what is according to that concept accidental. . . . The illusory quality of artworks is condensed in their claim to wholeness."[213] It is this illusion, he claims, that nominalism challenges. According to Adorno, "Aesthetic nominalism culminates in the crisis of semblance insofar as the artwork wants to be emphatically substantial. The irritation with semblance has its locus in the object itself."[214] Reflecting on such passages, Shierry Weber Nichelson writes, "this emphasis on the importance of the nonidentical and nonsubsumable detail is, by another name, Adorno's aesthetic nominalism, and it is part of the dialectic of illusion or semblance (*Schein*)."[215]

Nominalism, so Adorno contended, organizes works of art "from below to above, not by having its principles of organization foisted on it,"[216] which suggests its affinity with a democratic rather than authoritarian culture. It allows art to breathe, as the epigraph of this chapter from *Aesthetic Theory* suggests, *en plein air*, without the constraints of generic forms.[217] But, drawing on his critique of philosophical nominalism, he hesitated before fully endorsing the wholesale demolition of universals: "The philosophical critique of unreflective nominalism prohibits any claim that the trajectory of progressive negativity, the negation of objectively binding meaning, is that of unqualified progress in art. . . . Though it is nominalism that helped art achieve its language in the first place, still there is no language without the medium of universality beyond pure particularization, however requisite the latter."[218] The danger we have seen Clement Greenberg warn against also alarmed Adorno: nominalism at its most corrosive ultimate liquidates "all forms as a remnant of a spiritual being-in-itself. It terminates in a literal facticity, and this is irreconcilable with art."[219]

There has been, Adorno noted with concern, a relentless trend toward the elevation of the particular over the universal in the history of Western art, which is best evidenced in what he called "the decline of artistic genres as such. Art has been caught up in the total process of nominalization's advance ever since the medieval *ordo* was broken up."[220] Benedetto Croce, he noted, was perhaps the first philosopher of aesthetics to understand that each work had to be judged on its own merits, rather than as an exemplar of a given type, a conclusion that had escaped Hegel in his blithely optimistic history of aesthetic progress.

And yet, Adorno argued, it would be mistaken to miss what remained of the older faith in generic forms, indeed ironically in the universal concept of art itself. A dialectical approach registers the tensions in that concept, at once abstractly universal and yet performatively yearning for concrete particularity. For, Adorno writes: "The drive towards nominalism does not originate in reflection but in the artwork's own impulse, and to this extent it originates in a universal of art. From time immemorial, art has sought to rescue the special; progressive particularization was immanent to it."[221] But when it entirely forgets its generic universality, it risks effacing the very boundary that separates art from the random particularities of everyday life, what Adorno calls "unformed, raw empiria." The history of the bourgeois novel, "the rise of the nominalistic and thus paradoxical form par excellence," illustrates the danger in this effacement, and anticipates the fate of later art as well, for "every loss of authenticity suffered by modern art derives from this dialectic."[222]

In art, formal generic types are thus more than exhausted conventions to be discarded with scorn. Here the aesthetic realists were right to protest against the corrosive effect of undialectical nominalism, even if they erroneously universalized what were only historical constructs. Such types are necessary as the constraint against which particular works always measure themselves, for without them the latter lapse into pure contingency. Although often abetting authoritarian social norms, conventional genres can also serve to resist the status quo, because of their distance from the pseudonaturalized givens of quotidian existence. They also serve as a healthy check on the arbitrary willfulness of the aesthetic subject, the alleged genius who invents entirely out of thin air. As a result: "The relation of the universal and the particular is not so simple as the nominalistic tendency suggests, nor as trivial as the doctrine of traditional aesthetics, which states that the universal must be particularized. The simple disjunction of nominalism and universalism does not hold."[223]

Modernist art, which in general was championed by Adorno, might be understood as the culmination of the process of nominalization.[224] But here too his dialectical instincts discerned the counterpressure of formal universalization: "That in nominalistically advanced artworks the universal, and sometimes the conventional, reappears results not from a sinful error but from the characteristics of artworks as language, which progressively produces a vocabulary within the windowless monad."[225] Expressionist poetry, for example, adopted some of the color conventions that were promulgated by the visual artist Wassily Kandinsky. "Expression, the fiercest antithesis to abstract universality, requires such conventions in order to be able to speak as its concept promises."[226] And yet, Adorno concluded pessimistically, the trend was moving inexorably away from the creative dialectic of convention and transgression, and not because of the internal aesthetic pressure of nominalization alone: "The crisis of meaning in art, immanently provoked by the unstoppable dynamism of nominalism, is linked with extra-aesthetic experience, for the inner-aesthetic nexus that constitutes meaning reflects the meaninglessness of the world and its course as the tacit and therefore all the more powerful apriori of artworks."[227]

With these general considerations about Adorno's dialectical relationship to nominalism behind us, we can now turn to the real matter at hand: the ways in which the issue was treated in his writings on music. What first has to be acknowledged is that the application of a philosophical category, developed in a context that was explicitly theological, to the very different realm of music can only be an exercise, suggestive but imprecise, in analogical imagination. As in the case of other such transfers, for example Duchamp's notion of "pictorial nominalism," the results cannot be held to very rigorous standards of definitional clarity. Thus, for example, there may be a rough parallel between universals, concepts and generic forms, but it would be wrong to equate them entirely. And although Adorno shared Nelson Goodman's interest in the issue of performance—he attacked the goal of "perfect, immaculate performance" as preserving the work "at the price of its definitive reification"[228]—he did not reduce the question of nominalism to the distinction between pure and impure renditions of an original. For Adorno, all art was the site of productive, if always unstable tensions between concept and material, semblance and truth, generic form and concrete instantiation, wholeness and what transgresses it.

Totalized integrity, to be sure, might be a regulative ideal, but, ironically, only works that failed to achieve it could be understood as "authentic" works of art, at least until the society out of which they emerged was itself a reconciled totality.[229] Thus, as Lydia Goehr has noted, Adorno kept his distance from the Platonic notion of *Werktreu* and "thought that the cost of listening to works only as they are offered in final or perfect aesthetic appearance or as perfectly performed is that we lose sight or hearing literally of the construction (form) and work (labor) that makes the works the masterworks they sometimes are." Moreover, so he also argued, "to consider works as made, as opposed to their being perpetually in the making, tends to play into a deadening or industrialized desire not really to experience the works at all."[230]

What must be understood as well is that Adorno was always enough of a Hegelian to think historically and eschew essentialist arguments about music or any other art. Thus rather than positing eternal definitions of artworks, understood as either categorically Platonic or nominalist, he spoke of a process of nominalization, a secular trend away from essential forms since the end of the Middle Ages, but one that could be disrupted or perhaps even reversed. And as we saw when citing his claim that "nominalism is part of the bourgeois bedrock; it accompanies the consolidation of urbanism across all its phases," he tied it, albeit somewhat loosely, to the larger socioeconomic context in which the history of art had to be situated, even as it could also be understood as well in terms of its immanent developmental logic.

When does nominalization really come into its own in Western music, tipping the balance away from working within received forms to their tacit abandonment or even explicit subversion? Adorno could never definitively say. In *Aesthetic Theory*, he notes that "the sense of form in Bach, who in many regards opposed bourgeois nominalism, did not consist in showing respect for traditional forms but rather in keeping them in motion, or better: in not letting them harden in the first place; Bach was nominalistic on the basis of his sense of form."[231] He then continues shortly thereafter to argue that "in an artist with the comparable level of form of Mozart it would be possible to show how closely that artist's most daring and thus most authentic formal structures verge on nominalistic collapse."[232] But it then seems that it was really Richard Wagner who was

> the first case—if this philosophical expression be allowed—of consistent aesthetic nominalism: his work is the first one in which the supremacy of the individual work, in the individual work that of the concrete, thoroughly constructed form, becomes, as a matter of principle, completely realized against all kinds of schemata, against every externally pre-given form. He was the first to draw the conclusions from the contradiction between inherited forms, indeed the inherited form of the language of music, on the one hand, and the concretely arising artistic tasks, on the other.[233]

Elsewhere, however, Adorno would grant the same honor to Mahler, whose work he compared to the bourgeois novel.[234]

It was, at long last, in the atonal music of Schoenberg and the second Vienna School, the music whose impact on Adorno's own practice as a composer and ideas as an aesthetic theorist was profound, that one might locate the most powerful culmination of the nominalist impulse in modern art. What Schoenberg had famously called "the emancipation of dissonance" meant the end of the tyranny of traditional tonal hierarchies. In *Philosophy of New Music*, Adorno tells us that Schoenberg's school "obeys without excuse the actuality of an accomplished nominalism. Schoenberg draws the consequences from the dissolution of all binding types, in music, as was implicit in his own laws of development: in the emancipation of ever-broader levels of the material and in the progression toward absolute musical domination of nature."[235] For Adorno, the greatness of the early Schoenberg was precisely his unflinching embrace of the nominalist dissolution of form, which allowed him to avoid the dubious search for organic wholeness and reconstituted authenticity he decried in Stravinsky.

It was because of Adorno's identification with the early Schoenberg that commentators such as Hohendahl and Nichelson were able to discern a positive version of aesthetic nominalism in his position.[236] Max Paddison helps us understand Adorno's distinction between a destructive and constructive version of nominalism by foregrounding his two concepts of form: the first, "from above to below" and the second, "from below to above": "The first kind of form can be understood in relation to the handed-down pre-given genres and formal types, imposed on the material 'from above.' These represent a level of universality (what Adorno calls *schlechte Allgemeinheit*) and are normative, the form being organized from totality to detail. The second can be understood as form which emerges out of the 'inner necessity' of the material, 'from below.' It represents the nominalism (i.e. 'self-identity') of the particular, is critical, and moves from detail towards totality."[237]

But for all of his praise for Schoenberg's expressionist atonality as a weak form emerging from below, the final ominous phrase in the citation above from *Philosophy of New Music*—"progression toward absolute musical domination of nature"—reveals one of Adorno's long-standing fears. Both a philosophy, such as conventional nominalism, and an artistic practice that sees the world as a chaotic manifold open to the unbridled power of the subject whose will can impose an arbitrary new order on it, are complicit with the instrumental rationality that has emerged from the dialectic of enlightenment.

Such an outcome, Adorno charged, was manifested in the next stage of Schoenberg's career, a stage Adorno did not find as congenial as its atonal predecessor: that of the twelve-tone row. Schoenberg, he writes, "was the first to detect the principles of universal unity and economy in the new, subjective, emancipated Wagnerian material. His works adduce the evidence that the more rigorously the nominalism of musical language—inaugurated by Wagner—is pursued, the more completely this language allows itself to be rationally dominated. . . . It is this rationality and unification of the material that makes the initially subordinated material entirely compliant to subjectivity."[238] Paradoxically, by regularizing that subordination through rigid rules of composition, the pendulum swung too far in the opposite direction, and the healthy subjective moment in musical expression was in danger of being snuffed out in favor of an impersonal method. The problematic implications of this shift he discerned in Anton Webern's last works, which smacked of reification. By the time he wrote his dark rumination on "The Aging of the New Music" in 1955, Adorno could both protest against the dangers of unconstrained nominalism—"as a result of the atomistic disposition of musical elements, the concept of musical coherence is liquidated, a concept without which nothing like music really exists"—and also warn that "the effort to rationalize music completely has something useless and frantic about it; it applies to a chaos that is no longer chaotic. It is time for a concentration of compositional energy in another direction; not toward the mere organization of material, but toward the composition of truly coherent music out of a material however shorn of every quality."[239]

What that other direction might be was not easy to see, but the dialectic of form and formlessness, that inexorable process engendered by the ruthless nominalist subversion of universals of any kind, was not entirely over. As many observers have remarked, it was now apparent in what Adorno called *musique informelle,* a term he introduced in a seminal essay of 1961 included in his collection *Quasi una Fantasia.*[240] He defines it as "a type of music which has discarded all forms which are external or abstract or which confront it in an inflexible way. At same time, although such music should be completely free of anything irreducibly alien to itself or superimposed on it, it should nevertheless constitute itself in an objectively compelling way, in the musical substance itself, and not in terms of external laws."[241] Comparing it to the atonal music breakthrough that occurred around 1910, but noting the intervening serial revolution, Adorno says that *musique informelle* must deal with the contradictions and problems "facing music at a stage when an unconstrained musical nominalism, the rebellion against any general musical forms, becomes conscious of its own limitation."[242] It cannot therefore go back to the early Schoenberg, the music of expressionist atonality, as the dialectic of music and society has moved on. Now the challenge is to face the fact that "the more urgently the structural arrangements insist through their own shape on their own necessity, the more they become guilty of acquiring contingent matter, external to the composing subject."[243]

The stress on the exigency of this "contingent matter, external to the composing subject" means that older notions of nominalist art which "had always imagined that it could locate its enduring core and substance in the subject" are wrong, for "this subject now stands exposed as ephemeral."[244] The old Romantic and expressionist subject whose interiority was objectively realized in artistic form is a thing of the past, as antiquated as the ideal of organic wholeness in the work. What now demands to be acknowledged is the fact that the musical material of today "is not simply the subject in its own right; it also contains the element of what is alien to the subject, the element of otherness."[245] Thus John Cage's music, to take an example Adorno appreciatively cited, has to be applauded "as a protest against the dogged complicity of music with the domination of nature."[246]

This does not mean, to be sure, an undialectical privileging of that contingent otherness, which would invite the positivist flattening out of aesthetic semblance which is always a danger in nominalism unchecked. For all the importance of sonority, music cannot be reduced to nothing but noise or sound. "It would be wrong," Adorno argued, "to believe in the critical function of the note as opposed to the configuration, as if it were an immediate good, as opposed to a superstructure, and to imagine that the note from which all meaning had been removed, could nevertheless supply its own meaning."[247] Meaning, on the other hand, should not be entirely ascribed to the relations among notes—especially a constructed relationality imposed by the composer—as the material is often in excess of any such attempt to master it. Without abstractly negating any and all subjectivity, music must somehow find a way to open itself up to what the subject cannot spin out of itself or intend with no remainder. That is, "It must become the ear's form of reaction that passively appropriates what might be termed the tendency inherent in the material,"[248] which is not turned into a dead "object" to be dominated by a sovereign "subject." In short, a *musique informelle* must avoid the "hostile extremes of faith in the material and absolute organization."[249] If it succeeds, "it would emancipate itself both from projects which are purely subjective and from thing-like objectifications.... It would present itself not as an object to be described, but as a force-field to be decoded."[250]

In that force field—and this is why the final twist in Adorno's argument about nominalism suggests its affinity with the variant we have been calling magical—there is a claim made by material that is always in excess of conceptual or structural or compositional control. To make this point clearer, Adorno suggests a comparison expressing an important lesson of much modernist art, which invokes the element of surprise that results from the process of composition not being entirely controlled by the subject: it is, he says, "much as a chemist can be surprised by the new substance in his test-tube."[251] As a result, it has something in common with the radically unexpected and unprepared event whose importance we have seen in historical discourse and applied to Duchamp's readymades. In fact, the explicit comparison has been recently made by Vangelis Giannakakis, who argues that Adorno's negative dialectics is a philosophy of the event.[252]

In certain respects, Adorno's awareness of the unexpected difference between a nominalism that valorizes what is the fact and a nominalism that surprises us with what is new invites an intriguing comparison with

Duchamp's pictorial nominalism. There is, we might say, an "infrathin" distinction between the object understood in conventional nominalist terms and the object in magical nominalist ones. One way to capture the difference is to return to Duchamp's focus on the proper name, which was individual rather than generic and somehow expressive of the essence of that individual, what philosophers like Kripke would call a rigid designator rather than a collective name or shifter that can serve as an interchangeable term for many different qualitatively distinct entities.[253] Adorno, as we know, was deeply indebted to Benjamin in many ways, among them his fascination with the utopian impulse in proper names.[254] As we noted earlier, in *Dialectic of Enlightenment* he and Horkheimer acknowledged that the corrosive power of Enlightenment "stops short before the *nomen*, the non-extensive, restrictive concept, the proper name." Shortly after this observation, they added that in Judaism "the link between name and essence is still acknowledged in the prohibition on uttering the name of God. The disenchanted world of Judaism propitiates magic by negating it in the idea of God."[255] Such a negation, like the famous *Bilderverbot*, or prohibition on images of God, is always in the service of a utopian possibility that cannot be realized now but must not be entirely abandoned as a future redemptive hope.[256] That possibility is of a world in which the endless displacement and deferral of meaning is stilled, the subsumptive logic of general terms is undone, and individual names and the essences they designate are finally—or once again—one.

In what sense can we identify his position as a defense of a nominalism that has a magical coloration? A useful way to approach this question would be to address the plausibility of putting him in the tradition Bielik-Robson has called Jewish nominalism, which we have argued was the more respectable religious version of its magical counterpart. Significantly, Bielik-Robson is herself keen to include him in her account of "Jewish cryptotheologies" following a "Marrano strategy" of masking their true beliefs.[257] Tracing a lineage of "positive nominalism" that goes back at least as far as Spinoza, she argues that it continues with figures like Hermann Cohen, "who also regards the defense of the singular, possessing a unique name of its own, as the most advanced ethical imperative, and the next generation of 'Cohen's children'—Rosenzweig, Benjamin and Adorno—will see this imperative as particularly urgent in a late modernity whose enlightened, purely instrumental reason threatens to reduce everything individual to the formal order of general concepts."[258] Disdaining both the extremes of transcendental idealism and negative nominalist empiricism, Adorno, she writes, "would come as close as possible to what we call here 'Jewish nominalism,'" which can be understood as combining "three dialectical moments":

1) The name is the true call of language whose role is to guard the process of individuation, which can never be assumed as safely given;
2) yet, such naming can only be an attribute of "revealed language," and remains inaccessible to human language that is forced into the economy of general concepts;
3) still, the language of concepts should be used in such a way as not to absolutize the moment of conceptual generality but rather employed in a "utopian" manner, i.e., as "utopia of cognition [that] would be to open up the non-conceptual with concepts without making it the same as them."[259]

Bielik-Robson's argument is largely persuasive, even if it may assume that Adorno was more conversant with Jewish thought than he actually was.[260] She reminds us that Adorno used the term "inverse theology" to describe his position as early as his letter of December 17, 1934, to Benjamin in referring to Kafka.[261] But several elements in Adorno's position suggest that "magic nominalism" might well be an even more accurate description than "Jewish nominalism." However often he may have invoked "theology" as an authority in defending his positions, it is striking how limited were the lessons Adorno took from it. The prohibitions on picturing or naming God were, after all, only a small fraction of the 613 commandments recorded in the Hebrew Bible, and Adorno does not seem to have been worried about observing any of the others. Although he loosely talked about "redemption" as the point of view from which critique should be carried out, he never really fleshed out what it might mean. What he often found most congenial in Jewish theology was obliquely derived from the magical impulses that remained in it. As Scholem pointed out in his discussion of the Kabbalistic theology of names, "this was originally a tradition of magical character, now transposed into a mystical tradition."[262]

Magic, as we have seen, is itself a very unstable signifier with many different denotations and connotations. Although its characteristics defy easy essentialization, a recent study by Christopher Lehrich, largely informed by Claude Lévi-Strauss's rumination on the bricolage of "savage thought," suggestively argues that magical thought tends to favor the particular over the universal. "Thought that turns resolutely towards the concrete," he writes, "requires qualities at odds with historical and scientific abstractions. In particular, by deferring to natural things, magical thought constructs a system whose anchors lie in nonhuman stabilities."[263] In his study of *The Name of God in Jewish Thought*, Michael T. Miller adds, "The lack of sense which for Kripke defines names is also derivative of language in its magical function; nonsense words are 'the symbol par excellence of magical language.' This being the case, naming is an essential magical action, for it literally creates identities."[264]

While Adorno certainly never valorized magic in most respects, his general attitude comported with these attributes of magical thought. In addition, and this is a consideration Bielik-Robson neglects to take into account, his insistence on the continuing importance of mimesis alerts us to Adorno's fascination with the residues of what is often called sympathetic magic. Although insisting that the cliché about the "magic of art" ignores its complicity with the rationalist disenchantment of the world, he nonetheless concludes that it "has something true about it. . . . The aporia of art, pulled between regression to literal magic or surrender of the mimetic impulse to thing-like rationality, dictates its law of motion; the aporia cannot be eliminated."[265]

How does all this manifest itself, if at all, in musical terms? There is, as stressed earlier, no simple translation of philosophical or theological concepts into aesthetic equivalents, and a fortiori into music, where language is at its most indirect and attenuated. And yet, without understanding the theoretical sources of Adorno's dialectical attitude toward nominalism, we cannot make sense of how it operates in his writings on musical matters. The issue is raised in Gianmario Borio's essay on the question of meaning in Adorno and the musical avant-garde, which flags the importance of Benjamin's theological notion of language: "Transferring these ideas to the realm of music, Adorno works along the path of secularization: the linguistic gesture of music mimes that impulse with which man seeks to enter into communication with the Supreme Being by means of prayer, as 'the human attempt, futile, as always, to name the name itself, not to communicate meanings.'"[266] The citation at the end of this sentence comes from Adorno's 1956 essay "Music, Language and Composition," in which he claims that "in comparison to signifying language, music is a language of a completely different kind. Therein lies music's theological aspect. What music says is a proposition at once distinct and concealed. Its idea is the form [*Gestalt*] of the name of God. It is demythologized prayer, freed from the magic of making something happen, the human attempt, futile, as always, to name the name itself, not to communicate meanings."[267] Music, to be sure, cannot do without its meaningful elements, the relational patterns that somehow signify, its striving for coherence. But it also conveys something in excess of meaning, something beyond intention or expression, something that, like the proper name, just is and cannot be interpreted in other terms. As a result, music cannot be decoded without remainder, reduced entirely to language or notation of any kind.

Or as he put in another essay of the same era, "On the Contemporary Relationship of Philosophy and Music" (1953), "in music, what is at stake is not meaning, but gesture. . . . As language, music tends toward pure naming, the absolute unity of object and sign, which in its immediacy is lost to all language. In the utopian and at the same time hopeless attempts at naming is located music's relation to philosophy, to which, for this very reason, it is incomparably closer, in its idea, than any other art."[268] In music, Adorno continued, getting the name right is equivalent to "the absolute as sound," but it cannot appear without the mediation of the compositional rationality and intended meaning that thwarts its direct appearance. "It is the paradox of all music," he concludes, "that, as an effort towards that intentionless things for which the inadequate word 'name' was chosen, it unfolds precisely only by dint of its participation in rationality in the broadest sense."[269] The riddle of music, its eternally enigmatic character, is due to the fact that "it does not possess its object, is not in command of the name; rather, it longs for it, and in so doing, aims at its own demise."[270]

In short, the magical nominalist impulse in music, its striving to get beyond intelligible real universals to the qualitatively unique particulars beneath, while also thwarting the sovereign constitutive power of the dominating subject, is the reason it can be said to function like a secular version of prayer. It manifests a yearning for a bliss beyond the interminable displacement and deferral of meaning, for an absolute that overcomes the tension between subject and object, for a state in which aesthetic semblance is no longer needed as an illusory antidote to a fully administered world. As such, it prefigures that utopian alternative to the current disenchanted world for which Adorno never lost hope.

There is one final twist to Adorno's argument. Through the gesture of multiple performances, the mark of an allographic art in Nelson Goodman's sense, music gives us a glimpse of utopian bliss as an infinity of mimetic repetitions and similarities, echoes and resonances, and not the death-like stasis of a Platonic perfect order. As such it is a constant rebuke to the aesthetic realist hope for the recovery of timeless universals. But it also challenges a nominalism in the service of bourgeois disenchantment, the positivist affirmation of the status quo, and the subjectivist domination of nature. Instead, it draws on the power of an apophatic nominalism imbued with the unsettling spirit of art as "magic delivered from the lie of being truth."

5
The Photograph

Photography reinforces a nominalist view of social reality as consisting of small units of an apparently infinite number—the number of photographs that could be taken of anything is unlimited. Through photographs, the world becomes a series of unrelated, free-standing particles; and histories, past and present, a set of anecdotes and faits divers. *The camera makes reality atomic, manageable, and opaque. It is a view of the world which denies interconnectedness, continuity but which confers on each moment the character of a mystery.*

SUSAN SONTAG

Indexical Traces: Realist or Nominalist?

The final paradigmatic instance of magical nominalism we will consider is "the photograph," to employ a convenient, if inevitably simplifying, locution to stand for the vast, inexorably expanding universe of actual photographs. At first glance, it may seem an odd choice to include with the Adamic notion of the name, the historical/philosophical discourse of the event, and the pictorial and musical exemplars previously examined. At the crossroads of technological invention, cultural phenomenon, documentary instrument, and aesthetic medium, the photograph defies placement on a flat, two-dimensional map that would comfortably situate it alongside the others. Instead, it demonstrates why it is better to visualize the discursive landscape in which magical nominalism plays a meaningful role as multidimensional, populated by heterogeneous exemplars that are nonetheless somehow related. They remain singularities but ones that analogically share significant traits without being reducible to fungible instances of an overarching concept. If we want to maintain performative consistency, the nominalist allergy to categorical identity-thinking allows us to compare paradigmatic exemplars that overlap, revealing mimetic similarities, only if we respect their irreducibly unique qualities.

The photograph is an excellent case in point. Despite its unique qualities, it has elicited interpretations that are strikingly reminiscent of those we have been putting forward in other contexts as indicators of magical nominalism. One would be the frequent evocation of magic itself, understood both literally and metaphorically, to explain its genesis and account for its effects. Another would be its ability to register idiosyncratic particularity rather than generic typicality (although, as we will see, this characterization has occasioned some debate). A third would be its resistance to the full constitutive control of the subject who never creates it ex nihilo, a resistance that is often explained in terms of the semiotic functions classically developed by C. S. Peirce as an indexical trace rather than a symbolic representation or iconic imitation of whatever is captured by its apparatus. A fourth would be the interpretation of the photograph's distinctive temporality as a complex event that interrupts and complicates the normal onrushing, unidirectional flow of occurrences. A final indication of the plausibility of its inclusion in any account of magical nominalism is the way in which the photograph can be compared with readymades and proper names, whose emblematic roles in the tradition we have already encountered.

Before exploring the implications of these multiple similarities, it will be necessary to distinguish the photograph from its proximate generative and receptive contexts, which extend from the technical apparatuses making it possible to the larger social and cultural institutions in which it can be situated.[1] The latter might be called, broadly speaking, "photography."[2] Its distinction from the photograph per se parallels one often made between, on the one hand, "the cinema," which includes all the stages of production, theatrical and other spectatorial venues, critical reviews, box office receipts, and remediation on television or streaming platforms, and an individual film, on the other.[3] It is the photograph as such, rather than the larger institutional contexts or collective practices of photography as a cultural/technological/social apparatus, that we can plausibly consider a paradigmatic instance of magical nominalism.

Distinguishing the photograph from photography in this way may court the reproach of fetishistic abstraction from dialectical holists and of regressive formalism from critics of ideological naturalization.[4] But the nominalist imperative to wield Ockham's razor also suggests something will be gained by focusing our attention on a more granular level, distinguishing a particular element from the general form of life in which it is normally embedded. The singular integrity of the discrete photograph may be in danger of immersion in social media's ongoing rush of disposable images—a recent commentator talks of the transformation of frozen, framed "scenes" into flowing informational "streams"[5]—but they result more from an atomizing "art of stillness" than do their cinematic cousins.[6] Even when their digital dematerialization undermines their status as discrete objects in the world, they retain their link with the singular moment of their capture.[7] Even when they are entangled with other visual practices, for example as elements in photomontages or combined with painting, they survive the apparent violation of their "medium-specificity" and stubbornly retain their link with the moment they were clicked and the specific objects or events revealed to the camera eye. Even when they gain added resonance by being placed in a series of other photos or in the oeuvre of a specific photographer, they can be looked at on their own. Although it may well be that the "meaning of any photographic message is necessarily context-determined," as the photographer and critic Allan Sekula once argued,[8] the ability of the isolated photograph to disrupt and challenge settled meaning and perhaps even negate meaningfulness as such, as we have seen in other examples of magical nominalism, must also be taken into account.

It will, of course, be quickly objected that "the photograph" can itself be construed as a generic category or class term hovering above its individual instantiations, as well as subsuming opposing subcategories such as black-and-white / color, analog/digital, studio portrait / snapshot, and tiny daguerreotypes / immense light boxes, to mention only a few. Here we are confronted with the perennial difficulty that nominalists of whatever stripe often have in identifying the smallest particular unit, at least when it is understood ontologically, and we have to fall back on the prudent methodological reasons Goodman and other nominalists adduce to prevent Ockham's razor from slicing ever smaller units ad infinitum.

Perhaps a more troubling objection can be drawn from the endless iterability of photos from negatives and the later process of digital duplication, which Walter Benjamin famously called their "mechanical reproducibility."[9] Doing so would suggest that the photograph is intrinsically plural rather than singular. Or to borrow the opposition we have already encountered in Nelson Goodman's analysis of works of art, it is essentially an "allographic" rather than "autographic" phenomenon. The objection would follow that were iterability taken to be an essential quality of the photograph as such rather than an external one added by its contextual placement in photography, it would thwart any attempt to discern its magical nominalist qualities. For it would lack what Benjamin had called an aura, a concept, as Gunter Gebauer and Christoph Wulf note, that he specifically coined "to designate the experience of magical enchantment."[10] Benjamin argued that the auratic quality of paintings and other unique images, which had reflected their ritual, cultic functions, had been superseded by the "exhibition value" of lithographs, photographs, and films. This replacement, he conjectured, might well have an ultimately progressive political potential because of its anti-elitist implications and undermining of the fetish of authenticity.

However one judges his hopes for the new media, Benjamin's enthusiasm for the new nonauratic technologies in "The Work of Art" essay—and this is its real importance for the argument of this chapter—would seem to signal a reversal of his lament over the disenchantment of the world so evident in his earlier work on language. But like much else in his elusive oeuvre, Benjamin's attitude toward the apparent loss of the aura was by no means as straightforward as it might seem at first glance. If we turn to his earlier essay "Little History of Photography" of 1931 a very different implication can be drawn from "The Work of Art in the Age of Mechanical Reproduction." For here he makes an invidious distinction between an original photo and its reproduction in the mass media, which suggests iterability comes from the outside: "The difference between the copy, which illustrated papers and newsreels keep in readiness, and the original picture is unmistakable. Uniqueness and duration are as intimately intertwined in the latter as are transience and reproducibility in the former."[11] In this essay, de-auraticization, rather than an admirable precondition for the arrival of a progressive exhibition value, signals a crisis in the human capacity to experience the power of unique particularities. "The peeling away of the object's shell, the destruction of the aura," Benjamin warns, "is the signature of a perception whose sense for the sameness of things has grown to the point that the singular, the unique, is divested of its uniqueness—by means of its reproduction."[12]

It is perhaps meaningful, although the wording may not be intentional, that elsewhere Benjamin does not state that the photograph per se but rather "*photography* is decisively implicated in the phenomenon of the 'decline of the aura.'"[13] Does this word choice allow us to assign reproducibility to the englobing category of photography rather than see it as intrinsic to the isolated photograph itself? Perhaps we can do so if we acknowledge that its iterability can be thwarted by destroying the negatives of analog photos or the creation of non-fungible tokens (NFTs) for digital ones. And of course, photographs can be made by direct-positive processes, as was the case with daguerreotypes. So if we take seriously the distinction between photography and the photograph, Benjamin's earlier ruminations on *Sprachmagie* may still have comparable resonance for the latter.

From its inception in the 1830s, in fact, the aura of magic has been routinely invoked to name the process that produces photographs as well as the effects they have on those who are enchanted and astounded by them.[14] Drawing on what one observer has called "a magical urge to capture and preserve permanently what we know to be a transient existence"[15] classically expressed in the ancient legend of the Corinthian maid, the photograph seemed for many the realization of a perennial yearning. As early as 1839, one of its fabled pioneers, William Fox Talbot, expressed his wonder at the "marvelous" thing he had just wrought: "The most transitory of things, a shadow, the proverbial emblem of all that is fleeting and momentary, may be fettered by the spells of our '*natural magic*,' and may be fixed for ever in the position which it seemed only destined for a single instant to occupy."[16] Fox Talbot had, in fact, already mused in 1830 in a poem called "The Magic Mirror" about a future technology that would capture nature in a permanent image.[17] Later Victorians often adopted the same phrase to describe that technology when it became real.[18] Across the Channel, the great early twentieth-century French photographer Jacques-Henri Lartigue similarly enthused: "photography is a magic thing. A thing that has mysterious odors, a little strange and frightening, something one quickly grows to love."[19]

A wealth of examples can be adduced to show the enduring temptation to link the photograph with magic, even among the most sophisticated analysts of the phenomenon. For example, according to Berenice Abbott, herself an eminent photographer of the first half of the twentieth century: "Great photographers have 'magic'—a revealing word that comes from [Edward] Steichen. I believe the 'magic' photographers are documentarians only in the broadest sense of the word."[20] In *Camera Lucida*, a text to which we will return shortly, Roland Barthes (1915–80) argues that "realists" like himself "do not take the photograph for a 'copy' of reality, but for an emanation of *past reality*: a *magic*, not an art."[21] Susan Sontag likewise remarks that photographs "have the status of found objects—unpremeditated slices of the world. Thus, they trade simultaneously on the prestige of art and the magic of the real."[22] In *Towards a Philosophy of Photography*, Vilém Flusser contends that "like all images, they have a magical effect; and they entice those receiving them to project this undecoded magic onto the world out there. The magical fascination of technical images can be observed all over the place. The way in which they put a magic spell on life, the way in which we experience, know, evaluate and act as a function of these images."[23] He then adds that they work against the hegemony of textuality to "liberate their receivers by magic from the necessity of thinking conceptually, at the same time replacing historical consciousness with a second-order magical consciousness and replacing the ability to think conceptually with a second-order imagination."[24]

Even when Barthes's distinction between art and magic is ignored, as in the 2015 collection of statements by contemporary photographic artists titled *Photography Is Magic*, the metaphor remains potent. In her introductory essay to the collection, Charlotte Cotton invokes the tricks of what she calls "close-up magicians": "Photography is a form of magic—or to put it another way, the photographer provides cerebral experiences for the viewer that are equivalent to magic. Just as sleight of hand facilitates, but does not fully materialize, the magical experiences that resides in the dynamic of our own imaginations, so too photography—when liberated from a pedestrian definition as the sum of its mechanics and materials, its chemistry and software—can spark the occurrence of magic in our minds."[25] Here magic implies an imaginative state of mind elicited in the viewer rather than anything objectively true about the process of producing the images that do the eliciting, but the aura of something ineffably marvelous beyond normal experience remains. In short, as the historian Eric Rosenberg puts it, "*Pace* Baudelaire, photography has always been about the re-enchantment of the world."[26]

There have, to be sure, been skeptical responses to these evocations of the photograph's putatively magical aura. The Marxist cultural theorist John Tagg, for example, answers Barthes by insisting that "the photograph is not a magical 'emanation' but a material product of a material apparatus set to work in specific contexts, by specific forces, for more or less defined purposes. It requires, therefore, not an alchemy but a history."[27] The British critic and curator David C. Blight likewise dismisses Cotton's *Photography Is Magic* as "a book about trendy photographic art, swaddled in equivocal definitions of magic." But tellingly, he concludes by conceding that "photography's magic lies not in its aesthetic preoccupations, but in its digital spirit as algorithmic information, with, or ideally without, an image."[28]

As this last remark illustrates, it has been difficult for even hard-headed skeptics to avoid responding to photographs as somehow more than the sum of the mechanical, chemical, or digital technologies that produces them, more than the result of artistic talent, more than a mere duplication of what the unaided human eye can see. What needs to be demonstrated, however, is that if there is magic in the photograph in more than a loose metaphorical sense, it resides at least in large measure in its nominalist implications, whose widespread acceptance is reflected in the title of a recent collection of essays on contemporary photography, *Occam's Razor*.[29] But if its nominalism is to be understood in more than conventional terms, that "character of a mystery"[30] surrounding it noted by Susan Sontag in the epigraph chosen for this chapter will also have to be confronted and, as best is possible, explained.

Before tackling that task, it has to be acknowledged that in the now almost two-century long history of photography, there have been efforts to situate it on the opposite side of the nominalism/realism divide. As Allan Sekula pointed out in his seminal essay "The Body and the Archive" of 1986:

> For nineteenth-century positivists, photography doubly fulfilled the Enlightenment dream of a universal language: the universal mimetic language of the camera yielded up a higher, more cerebral truth, a truth that could be uttered in the universal abstract language of mathematics. For this reason, photography could be accommodated to a Galilean vision of the world as a book "written in the language of mathematics." Photography promised more than a wealth of detail; it promised to reduce nature to its geometrical essence. Presumably then, the archive could provide a standard physiognomic gauge of the criminal, could assign each criminal body a relative and quantitative position within a larger ensemble.[31]

Influential social scientists like the Victorian Social Darwinist and pioneer of eugenics Francis Galton sought to find in superimposed, composite images a parallel to the quantitatively measured "average man" proposed by pioneer statisticians like Adolphe Quetelet.[32] Their efforts were fueled by a desire to discover a way of making what was often invisible on an individual level apparent on a collective one, thus providing templates for generic identification. Sekula explicitly identifies this quest with what he calls "the 'realist' approach," and says that by realism he means "that venerable (medieval) philosophical realism that insists upon the truth of general propositions, on the reality of species and types."[33]

Whatever its scientific merits, the ideological underpinnings of this putatively universalist realism soon became evident. Carried into the twentieth century by anthropometric scientists like Rudolf Martin or Nazi pseudoscientists like Hans F. K. Günther, it often led to composing images of racial or "degenerate" types, frequently Jews. Galton had in fact already expressed anti-Semitic views. Even if ironically, as Amos Morris-Reich has demonstrated, some Zionist writers and photographers like Arthur Ruppin, Erich Brauer, and Helmar Lerski could continue this quest in twentieth-century Palestine, it never shed its dubious pedigree.[34]

The ambition to use photography for realist ends—realism understood in the medieval sense—also inspired less putatively scientific efforts. During the Weimar Republic, especially the middle years dominated by the cool, detached mood of the *Neue Sachlichkeit* (New Objectivity), photographers themselves often sought to capture representative examples of generic types, drawing on the authority of the then popular discourse of physiognomy to justify their quest.[35] Albums of such photographs, the most influential of which was August Sanders's *Antlitz der Zeit* (*Face of Our Time*) of 1929, contained images not of stigmatized races or deviants but of characteristic rural and urban residents, bankers and beggars, artists and students, bohemians and fraternity members, children and the elderly, to present a cross section of German society. Clinically photographed in homogenously centered formats with standardized focal lengths and uniform lighting rather than captured through casual snapshots, they were intended to provide objective knowledge about the real world. Although the taxonomic categories employed were understood as historical rather than natural kinds, the goal was to reveal, as impassively as possible, collective types rather than the psychological interiority of idiosyncratic individuals.

These efforts at exploiting the realist rather than nominalist potential of photography almost always produced disappointing results. Galton's "pictorial statistics" foundered when its more sinister implications became clear in the work of avowed racists like Günther. Ironically, Sander's album could be both taken out of print by the Nazis and faulted by a leftist critic for lacking "a sharper and clearer sociological formulation in regard to classification. Here the goal must be a herbarium, so to speak, of human existence."[36] Even if Walter Benjamin found much in Sander's work to appreciate, it was not because it imposed typological categories from above.[37] In fact, it has been argued by later commentators that despite his taxonomic intentions, Sander's portraits invoke "a psychological register of an inner self which disturbs the authority of the social register of the image."[38]

Whatever the ideological motives of its advocates, there was a problem in the realist ambition itself. To cite Sekula again, the promise of a taxonomic archive was frustrated "both by the messy contingency of the photograph and by the sheer quantity of images. The photographic archive's components are not conventional lexical units, but rather are subject to the circumstantial character of all that is photographable. Thus it is absurd to imagine a dictionary of photographs, unless one is willing to disregard the specificity of individual images in favor of some model of typicality, such as that underlying the iconography of Vesalian anatomy or of most of the plates accompanying the *Encyclopédie* of Diderot and d'Alembert."[39] Other positivists attempted to use photographs for forensic purposes, the most frequently cited example being the French criminologist Alphonse Bertillon, who also pioneered the use of fingerprints. They were not driven, however, by a quest for innate characterological universals but rather for tell-tale evidentiary idiosyncrasies, such as the shape of an ear, of specific individuals.[40] Here the typical nominalist elevation of contingency over necessity could be turned into a virtue, at least for the trained eye able to discern the smallest of differences.

Significantly, Walter Benjamin's physiognomic inspired enthusiasm for the revelatory effect of the photograph, expressed in his admiration for Sander's album of types, was based on a recognition of precisely this potential. As Sekula notes:

> This emphasis on the telling detail, the metonymic fragment that points to the systemic crimes of the powerful, would be repeated and refined in the writings of Walter Benjamin. Our tendency to associate Benjamin with the theory and practice of montage tends to obscure the degree to which he built his modernism from an empiricist model, from a model of careful, idiosyncratic observation of detail. This model could argue both for the photographer as monteur, and for the photographer as revolutionary spy or detective, or, more "respectably," as critical journalist of the working class.[41]

Drawing on this tradition of regarding the photographer, wittingly or not, as "revolutionary spy or detective," defenders of the critical potential of the medium, like the British art historian John Roberts, have argued that more than merely revealing individual idiosyncrasies for criminological purposes, photographs can lay bare larger social patterns: "What capitalism dislikes about the photographic document is precisely this uncontrollable volatility of the photograph, in which even images that are supposedly secure within the very heart of the system spill out to be used and reframed by others to defame and embarrass the state, particularly in a world now dominated by instant image transmission."[42]

Here we might say a conventional nominalist premise still partly informs the argument—an image is available to be redescribed and recontextualized by a subject who can use it to subvert prevailing wisdom—but there is also a more strictly magical nominalist potential as well. For photography, as Sontag noted, "is the paradigm of an inherently equivocal connection between self and world—its version of the ideology of realism sometimes dictating an effacement of the self in relation to the world, sometimes authorizing an aggressive relation to the world which celebrates the self."[43] For the former, which, *pace* Sontag, is better called magical nominalism than realism, the subject, whether understood as the photographer or the later interpreter of the image, is less crucial than the unexpected and unintended trace of an object that exceeds subjective domination. Once again, Benjamin was among the first to acknowledge its importance in his "Little History of Photography":

> No matter how artful the photographer, no matter how carefully posed his subject, the beholder feels an irresistible urge to search such a picture for the tiny spark of contingency, of the here and now, with which reality has (so to speak) seared the subject, to find the inconspicuous spot where in the immediacy of that long-forgotten moment the future nests so eloquently that we, looking back, may discover it. For it is another nature that speaks to the camera rather than to the eye: "other" above all in the sense that a space informed by human consciousness gives way to a space informed by the unconscious.[44]

There is much to consider in Benjamin's packed argument here: the tension between the artistic and documentary potential of the photograph, the beholder's quest for the unexpected detail that thwarts the photographer's total control, the photo's capturing of a deictic moment of hic et nunc uniqueness, the dual temporality of that moment and the later moment(s) of beholding the image, the distinction between the human and camera eye, and the revelation of a spatial reality that was previously inaccessible to human consciousness.[45]

Let us focus for the moment on Benjamin's phrase "a tiny spark of contingency," which will help us appreciate the link between the photograph and magical nominalism. Significantly, according to Samuel Weber, Benjamin had already defended "the irreducible element of the 'contingent' or 'accidental' in the work of art" in his critique of German Romanticism.[46] It may be because it fostered the experience of an unbridgeable distance between object and subject that generated an aura, which could result not only from the accidental detail in art that exceeded the intention of the artist but also from an unintentioned moment of contingency in a photograph.

Consider, for example, the famous self-portrait taken in 1946 by the American photographer Fred R. Archer (1889–1963), known for his unconventional, theatrical, and even abstract images.[47] It shows his face melting into the front of a large format camera. But despite his best efforts to determine the outcome, a "tiny spark of contingency," against which even the meticulous Archer could not guard, appeared on the developed image. A fly had chanced to land on his trigger finger as he snapped the shutter, an arresting and unexpected intrusion, which he was ultimately delighted to leave in the final print. The serendipitous presence of the fly expresses the limits of the subjective control of an image produced by a photographer as opposed to one created by a painter.[48] Although later changes can, of course, be made in the dark room or through digital manipulation, comparable to the alterations often made to painted canvases, there is something unique about the unintended intervention of objects that leave the trace of their presence on the photographic image at the moment when it is taken. The very locution of "taking" a photograph, rather than "making" it in English suggests the importance of a prior reality that is recorded, not made out of whole cloth, as do the metaphors of "capturing" or "shooting" an image.[49]

Translated into the influential semiotic vocabulary introduced by C. S. Peirce, what is produced in the act of photographic recording is more an index than icon or symbol.[50] Where the icon is a sign that imitates or resembles what it represents and the symbol is a culturally legible, conventionally meaningful substitute for it, the index signifies by the physical trace or imprint left behind by an event or object. Common examples are the smoke produced by a fire, the tracks in the snow made by a passing fox, a death mask, and a weathervane blown by the wind. The celebrated Japanese photographer Hiroshi Sugimoto was thus able to compare photographs to fossils, which are physical residues of the life they once embodied.[51]

The indexical sign functions like a finger—usually, in fact, the forefinger that in English we call the index finger—pointing to an object accompanied by the ostensive designations "this" or "there."[52] As Mary Anne Doane suggests, because the index asserts nothing beyond such designations, "it is evacuated of content; it is a hollowed-out sign."[53] Although it presents itself to the eyes of the beholder in the here and now, it is, moreover, usually caused haptically at an earlier moment and in a different place.[54] Or to put it differently, the unique "touch" of the painter's hand, which is the guarantee of a work's authenticity, is replaced in a photograph by the causal "touch" of the object on the recording apparatus of the camera. When an image is altered in postproduction, it is tellingly called retouched (or at least it was before it came to be known as digitally photoshopped).

The applicability of Peirce's categories of signs to photographic images has been a source of vigorous controversy in the burgeoning literature on the medium.[55] Although occasionally the claim is made that photographs can be understood entirely in terms of one or another, the real issue is the salience of each in making sense of all the ways specific photos convey meaning—or work to defeat it. The most heat has been generated in polemics over the role of indexicality, pitting "indexophiles" like Rosalind Krauss against "indexophobes" like Joel Snyder.[56] Roughly speaking, there is an overlap between those who minimize indexicality and those who advocate the artistic rather than documentary function of photographs.[57] A powerful recent example is the eminent art historian Michael Fried's *Why Photography Matters as Art as Never Before* (2008). He argues that certain contemporary art photographers, among them Jeff Wall, Thomas Struth, Alexander Gursky, Thomas Ruff, and Thomas Demand, elevate their carefully staged images meant to be hung in large format on a museum wall into genuine works of art by eliminating as much as possible the accidental touch of the real world that might disrupt their creative sovereignty. They swat, as it were, the fly from Archer's finger.[58] That finger is once again part of an artist's skilled hand, which leaves its distinguishing mark on the image it creates. Displaying his characteristic interpretative panache, Fried reads these art photographs as latter-day instances of the antitheatrical absorptive painting he has long championed.[59] Even the works by Wall that seem to be in the tradition of street photography, exemplified by Gary Winograd's work in New York in the 1960s and 1970s, purge all spontaneity and serendipity from the image.

What is important for our purposes is that along the way, Fried downplays the indexical origins of photographic images, which Peirce himself had acknowledged as entangled with iconic resemblance in establishing their truth-showing authority. There is nothing "candid," Fried points out, about the cameras of these art photographers, whose digitally generated images are well-wrought, self-referential artifacts that attempt to snuff out Benjamin's "spark of contingency."[60] Rather than seeking that miraculous "decisive moment" when a revealing image is taken, all the effort goes into its preproduction staging and postproduction manipulation.[61] An apparent exception like Demand's analog photographs of constructed scenes of his own making, Fried argues, are actually pictures that "*represent or indeed allegorize intendedness as such*."[62] In the terms of our distinction between the two traditions of nominalism, his is resolutely conventional, asserting the constitutive intentionality of the subject over the resistance of the unintended world to its sovereign control.[63]

At the opposite end of the interpretative spectrum are theorists who stress the epistemic or evidentiary ability of the photograph to show the world, or at least an aspect of it, as it is, whatever the intention of the photographer may be. Although some defenders of the importance of indexicality, for example Rosalind Krauss, contend that contemporary art has itself incorporated the "uncoded event" that characterizes the photographic image,[64] most are concerned more with the ontological or social than aesthetic implications of indexicality. For them, the camera acts as a disinterested witness, whose visual testimony is compelling and able to resist challenges to its reliability. A classic example is "The Ontology of the Photographic Image" (1945) by the celebrated French film critic André Bazin, who contends: "For the first time an image of the world is formed automatically, without the creative intervention of man. The personality of the photographer enters into the proceedings only in his selection of the object to be photographed and by way of the purpose he has in mind. . . . All the arts are based on the presence of man, only photography derives an advantage from his absence. . . . We are forced to accept as real the existence of the object reproduced."[65]

Later defenders of the "transparency" of the photographic image like Kendall Walton may qualify some of Bazin's more categorical pronouncements but agree that viewers of such images are in perceptual contact, however mediated, with the world. Although both painters and photographers share beliefs about the world and are motivated by intentions in trying to capture it, Walton contends that "photographs are counterfactually dependent on the scene, even if the beliefs (and other intentional attitudes) of the photographer are held fixed. Paintings which have a counterfactual dependence on the scene portrayed lose it when the beliefs (and other intentional attitudes) of the painter are held fixed."[66] Bazin's bald assertion that photographs "automatically" record the world may not survive careful scrutiny, but his claim that they limit the artist's full sovereignty is hard to gainsay.[67] Not surprisingly, commentators like John Roberts, who insist on the critical potential of photography to disrupt prevailing ideological assumptions by disclosing inconvenient truths about the world disdain Michael Fried's attempt to celebrate the immanent formalism of absorption in recent art photography.[68]

Because defenders of the unintentional—or at best, "weakly intentional"—transparency of photographic images are often simply labeled realists, the distinction between realism and nominalism (conventional or magical) that we have been tracing since the Middle Ages often gets blurred. Its importance, however, is sometimes indirectly registered, as for example in the philosopher Stanley Cavell's claim that "a representation emphasizes the identity of its subject, hence it may be called a likeness; a photograph emphasizes the existence of its subject, recording it, hence it is that it may be called a transcription."[69] That is, in the familiar terms that extend back to Duns Scotus, the photograph, *pace* the Francis Galtons of the world, shows the *haecceitas* rather than *quidditas* of the objects whose indexical traces are preserved on its recording mechanism. Or to adopt another term from medieval Christian philosophy, the photograph is akin to an *acheiropoieton*, an image like the veil of Veronica or the Shroud of Turin in which Jesus's face and body are believed to have left a direct imprint on a cloth.[70] More than an iconic resemblance or symbolic representation, such miraculous relics show no mediation of a human hand.

Another way to draw the distinction between realism and nominalism when it comes to photographs is to assign the power to attribute universalizing identities or meanings to the englobing institutions and practices of photography rather than to the isolated photograph. These might even include, as John Tagg has argued, "certain privileged ideological apparatuses, such as scientific establishments, government departments, the police and the law courts."[71] But nominalistically disembedding the photograph from the generalizing conventions of photography—or at least attending to its idiosyncratic departures from them—might also be a valuable exercise, as demonstrated in what remains the most influential consideration of the question, Roland Barthes's *Camera Lucida*. Although its often enigmatic and elliptical arguments have been thoroughly examined from many different directions, their salience for the understanding of magical nominalism has not yet been widely appreciated.[72]

Barthes and the *Punctum*

Barthes's interest in visual culture in general and photography in particular antedated the publication of *Camera Lucida* in 1980.[73] In the essays from the 1950s collected in *Mythologies*, he had been a pioneering critic of the ideological uses of photography, the "myths" he discerned in everything from electoral portraits and pictures in illustrated magazines—the notorious image of a Black soldier on the cover of *Paris-Match*—to Edward Steichen's exhibition of *The Family of Man*.[74] By 1961 and his essay "The Photographic Message," Barthes was, however, moving in a new direction, in which he now distinguished between the sociological function of the photographic image as "a product or a channel" and what he called its "structural autonomy."[75] The latter he identified with the capacity of the camera to produce a nonarbitrary *analogon* of reality, which may reduce its referent in various ways but does not inherently transform it. The photographic image, moreover, may be called "*a message without a code*,"[76] and more precisely, a message that works through perceptual continuity rather than the discontinuity that provides meaning for linguistic codes, as Ferdinand de Saussure had shown.[77] This capacity Barthes identified with the denotative function of the photographic image, while its connotative function, or what he soon called "the rhetoric of the image," added a second, culturally invested meaning. A purely denotative image is rare, manifest perhaps only when what is shown is genuinely traumatic, which means "the 'mythological' effect of a photograph is inversely proportional to its traumatic effect."[78] But paradoxically, to add another twist to the argument, the power of the connotative message of an image is inevitably parasitic on "*the denoted message which 'naturalizes' the system of the connoted message.*"[79]

Barthes's dichotomy between connotatively coded and denotatively uncoded messages, however much he may have deconstructed their stark opposition, drew on his early hopes for a scientific semiotics. By the time he wrote *Camera Lucida*, however, his emphasis had changed.[80] Structuralism was replaced by an idiosyncratic kind of phenomenology, the rigor of scientism by a frankly personal response to photographic images driven by desire and melancholy, and the quest for meaning by a growing recognition of the limits of signification. The last of these was already anticipated in an essay he wrote in 1970 on some stills from Sergei Eisenstein's movies, in which he speculated on a third level of meaning beyond the informational and symbolic, which he called "obtuse" and defined as "the epitome of a counter-narrative; disseminated, reversible, set to its own temporality, . . . counter-logical and yet 'true.'"[81]

Camera Lucida has been called "surely the most quoted book in the photographic canon."[82] It has been subjected to an extraordinary number of exegetical exercises, focusing on everything from its debts to Lacanian psychoanalysis and parallels to Walter Benjamin's early work on photography to its implicit theological assumptions, both Buddhist and Christian.[83] Our concern here, however, is to tease out the magical nominalist moments in Barthes's analysis, which have not been previously appreciated. Barthes's approach makes the task initially appear straightforward. "In the Photograph," Barthes writes, "the event is never transcended for the sake of something else: the Photograph always leads the corpus I need back to the body I see; it is the absolute Particular, the sovereign Contingency, matte and somehow stupid, the *This* (this photograph, and not Photography)."[84] Against the Galtons of the world, Barthes refused to enlist the camera in the search for essential truths revealed by composite superimpositions: "Since every photograph is contingent (and thereby outside of meaning), Photography cannot signify (aim at a generality) except by assuming a mask. It is this word which [Italo] Calvino correctly uses to designate what makes a face into the product of a society and its history."[85]

Masks, to be sure, are often worn by those who are photographed, especially when they deliberately pose, and therefore photographs can reveal the history of a society and its current mores, as we will see shortly when we look more closely at Barthes's notion of the *studium*.

Great photographic portraitists—he mentions Sander along with Nadar and Avedon—are thus potent mythographers of their societies, giving us essentialized typifications of their subjects. In contrast, what Barthes cherished in photographs, or at least those he found most compelling, appears when the mask drops and something surprising, something unexpected, is revealed. When that happens what is exceeded are not only social conventions and preprogrammed poses, but also the intentionality of the photographer—"the operator" in his terminology[86]—who is trying, even without a conscious desire to be an artist, to create a "good" or "well-composed" picture.

In so arguing, Barthes departed from conventional nominalism with its stress on the self-assertion of the subject, as well as from proponents of an art photography that tries to use digital means to approach the sovereign control of a painter. Without employing Peirce's terminology, Barthes emphasized instead the ineradicable imprint of the real, the referent whose ghostly presence is registered on the recording mechanism of the camera. Not only can the photographer surprise the subject—here we are talking about images of people caught unawares—but the subject, whether human or not, can surprise the photographer with a "*trouvaille* or lucky find."[87]

Perhaps the best way to show how much Barthes was unwittingly speaking the language of magical nominalism is to go directly to his celebrated distinction between the *studium* and *punctum* of a photograph, which draws on but goes beyond his earlier contrast between its connotative and denotative functions.[88] Let us take them in order. Barthes defines *studium* as "application to a thing, taste for someone, a kind of general enthusiastic commitment, of course, but without special acuity. It is by *studium* that I am interested in so many photographs."[89] The emotional response it evokes in the beholder is, however, a "polite interest," more a measured "liking" than a passionate "loving." Tacitly retreating from his earlier assertion that photographs are simply messages without a code, Barthes admits that "the *studium* is ultimately always coded,"[90] and can express both the intentions of the photographer and the conventional meanings of the culture in which it reflects. He further admits that most photographs—the examples he gives are news and pornographic images—are nothing but *studium*. They are what he calls "unary" photographs, transforming "'reality' without doubling it, without making it vacillate (emphasis is a power of cohesion): no duality, no indirection, no disturbance. The unary Photograph has every reason to be banal, 'unity' of composition being the first rule of vulgar (and notably, of academic) rhetoric."[91]

If photographs were nothing but coded, rhetorically meaningful images, drawing on and reinforcing the generic conventions of their society, they would not be candidates for inclusion in a survey of paradigmatic examples of magical nominalism. But Barthes's introduction of the supplementary notion of their ability, or at least that of some of them, to contain a *punctum* opens that door. Far less frequent than the denotation without a code he had posited earlier as the opposite of culturally imbued connotation in all photos, it disturbs the smooth workings of the *studium* in a unary photograph, acting like a "sting-speck, cut, little hole—and also a cast of the dice. A photograph's *punctum* is that accident which pricks me (but also bruises, me, is poignant to me)."[92] Often an inadvertent detail comparable to what psychoanalysts call a "partial object,"[93] it can awaken powerful emotion in the beholder. Because it follows no code, the affective reaction it solicits is idiosyncratic and contingent. What Barthes calls the "*kairos* of desire" manifests itself when the photograph takes us beyond the explicit image in the frame to produce a rare moment of intense bliss (*jouissance*).[94] It distinguishes, for example a truly erotic photograph from a merely pornographic one, which conforms to the culture's banal notions of sexuality and as a result is ultimately boring.

In addition to producing a moment of bliss, the *punctum*, whose name implies a violent puncture wound, also has the capacity to traumatize. The word "trauma" is in fact derived from the Greek word for wound, which in Latin translates to *punctum*. Barthes often refers to it as a detail that detonates an explosion, ripping apart the tranquil homogeneity of the *studium*, disturbing the docile, respectable, conformist subject who affirms it. From the Lacanian perspective Barthes seems to have adopted, traumatic violence and the self-shattering of *jouissance* may well in fact be two sides of the same coin.[95] Both resist the recuperative efforts of symbolization. The *punctum* can thus defy efforts to "tame the Photograph, to temper the madness which keeps threatening to explode in the face of whoever looks at it," exemplified by the vain attempt, *pace* in advance Michael Fried,[96] to make "photography into an art, for no art is mad."[97]

The *punctum* is, however, more than just the projection of a personal desire for explosive bliss onto a detail of the image. For although it draws on that ineffable something an individual beholder adds to the photograph, it is also "*what is nonetheless already there*."[98] It is thus very much like the intransitive writing Barthes championed in his earlier defense of Émile Benveniste's analysis of the middle voice, where the subject of the verb cannot be categorized as either agent or patient, sharing elements of both.[99] The *punctum* goes beyond the simple dichotomy of active or passive, which can grant exorbitant power to the sovereign subject.

It is through this argument that Barthes's analysis opens itself to a magical rather than conventionalist nominalist reading, dovetailing with Peirce's idea of indexicality.[100] As the critic Naomi Schor puts it, "the *punctum* does not come under the sway of the will. It escapes the intentionality of both the photographer and the spectator."[101] What is already there is a referent in the world prior to the act of photographing it, which leaves a palpable trace of its having been there. "I call 'photographic referent,'" Barthes explains, "not the *optionally* real thing to which an image or sign refers but the *necessarily* real thing which has been placed before the lens, without which there would be no photograph. . . . In Photography I can never deny that *the thing has been there*."[102] There is thus a link between photographic images and "the image of Christ which impregnated St. Veronica's napkin: that it was not made by the hand of man, *archeiropoietos*."[103] It is for this reason Barthes can claim, in a passage we have already cited, that we should "not take the photography for a 'copy' of reality, but for an emanation of *past reality, a magic,* not an art."[104]

What is also crucial for Barthes is the complicated temporality implied by the astonishing capacity of past reality to "emanate" a trace, an imprint that endures in the present and indeed will continue into the future as long as the image remains to be seen. Issues of time have, of course, been at the center of theorizing about the new technology from the start—the accumulated time of long exposures versus the instantaneous time of the snapshot; the staggered time of chronophotography versus the flowing time of cinema; the frozen time of the arrested image versus the simulacral movement in a blur; the simultaneity of photomontage versus the consecutive temporality of serial viewing; the microtemporality of the "optical unconscious" versus the phenomenological *durée* of human experience.[105] Following Benjamin, Barthes was, however, especially interested in the relationship between the moment of taking the image—the "there and then"—the moment of beholding it—the "here and now"—and the moment of an implied future—the "there and when." In certain respects, what connects all of them may seem like the involuntary memories from the personal past of the beholder called up by Proust's famous madeleine, with which it has in fact often been compared. But Barthes resists the comforting thought that photos are smoothly continuous with memories, enabling a holistic, complementary unity between past and present. Although the *studium* may seem "*heimlich,* awakening in me the Mother (and never the disturbing Mother),"[106] the *punctum* is always *unheimlich,* arousing an uncanny sense of a revenant that restlessly haunts the present and foretells the future.

The recognition "that this has been" cannot be recuperated in interiorizing remembrance. "Not only is the Photograph never, in essence a memory (whose grammatical expression would be the perfect tense, whereas the tense of the Photograph is the aorist)," Barthes insists, "but it actually blocks memory, quickly becoming a counter-memory."[107] The aorist tense expresses a single and complete action in the past, whereas the perfect tense, as Barthes seems to be evoking it here,[108] expresses a past action that still affects the present. The past moment when the photograph was taken is discontinuous with the present moment when it is viewed and cannot be contemplatively recuperated in a dialectical totality, which retrospectively incorporates (or digests) all temporal moments into a meaningful whole. It is a moment of rupture, even of violence, which disrupts the narrative meaningfulness that seeks to overcome contingency. Instead, the photograph for Barthes can produce a shudder of recognition of a future catastrophe—the death of the subjects it may depict, and by extrapolation, of the subjects who behold them. "By giving me the absolute past of the pose (aorist), the photograph tells me death in the future. What *pricks* me is the discovery of this equivalence."[109] It is thus a check on fantasies of organic revitalization, more of a memento mori for Barthes than an aide-mémoire.[110] For in addition to the aorist tense evoked when viewing a photograph is another implied temporality, that of what French grammarians call the *futur antérieur*, or "future perfect" in English, the time of what will become a completed past in what will be the future. An example would be the sentence "When he looks at this picture, I will already be dead."

Much of the power of *Camera Lucida* comes from Barthes's moving personal reflections on the implications of all this for his response to an image of his now-dead mother, never reproduced for the reader, which has come to be called "the Winter Garden Photograph." But there are also larger implications for the photograph in general, and historical ones in particular, which even more vividly evoke the traumatic shudder produced by knowing the subject is already dead or will inevitably die. "The *punctum*, more or less blurred beneath the abundance and the disparity of contemporary photography," he tells us, "is vividly legible in historical photographs: there is always a defeat of Time in them: *that* is dead and *that* is going to die."[111]

The death of the subject, or at least the shattering of its sovereign integrity, was, of course, a major theme of poststructuralist thought, and brings us back to Barthes's debts to Lacan in his theory of the photograph. Lacan himself did not write extensively on its implications, but it is possible to discern aspects of his work that resonate with the argument we are making here.[112] It might seem that seeing oneself in a photograph, even before the current frenzy of "selfies," would merely reinforce the consolidation of the narcissistic image of subjective unity produced by the early experience Lacan called the "mirror stage" of development or "the imaginary," before the entrance into language or "the symbolic." But if we apply his later ruminations on the distinction in visual experience between "the look" and "the gaze" in his *Four Fundamental Concepts of Psychoanalysis*, which go beyond the specular logic of the mirror stage, a different conclusion can be drawn.[113]

Here, to reduce a complicated argument to its rudiments, visual experience is divided into being the one who sees and the one who is seen, an eye and the object of sight. The self as looking subject is a sovereign viewer situated at the apex of a perspectival, geometricalized field, whereas the self as object of the gaze is placed vulnerably within that field. Rather than seemingly integrated, as in the mirror stage, the self in this unreconciled dialectic is fractured and unstable. At one point in his argument, Lacan adduces the anamorphic skull looming mysteriously at the bottom of Holbein's famous painting *The Ambassadors* to illustrate the discordance of two visual registers in one image. At another, he recalls an actual experience he claims to have had on a boat in which he found himself mesmerized by the shining surface of a floating sardine can reflecting sunlight. Lacan experienced himself being looked at by the inanimate can: "It was looking at me at the level of the point of light, the point at which everything that looks at me is situated."[114] Conflicting with the perspectival lines of sight emanating from the subject was the light shining off the object. Here an inert thing in the world had the power—dare we call it "magical?"—to puncture the narcissistic mastery of the one who sees (or in terms of conventional nominalism, the one who dominates a world of passive contingency through visual self-assertion).

Lacan was analyzing visual experience as such and only glancingly considered the impact of modern technologies, such as photography. But at one point he does say that "the gaze is the instrument through which light is embodied and through—if you will allow me to use a word, as I often do, in a fragmented form—I am *photo-graphed*."[115] Extrapolating from remarks like these, Ruth Iskin contends that "the implication in Lacan's theory is that the scopic regimes of light-based signifying media from still photography, film and TV to the computer screen play concrete roles in reconfiguring subjectivity, just as geometric perspective is an apparatus of the Cartesian subject of certainty."[116] Putting aside the problematic validity of bunching it with other media, what this suggests is that the photograph captures and preserves the light shining off the sardine cans of the world in a way that undermines both the constitutive power of the photographer and the perspectival sovereignty of its viewer.

There may be, as the visual theorist James Elkins tells us, "something creepy about this idea of objects staring back at us. . . . If I think of the world in the ordinary way, I am much reassured. Everything is mine to command." When I resist the possibility that objects can look back, "I am also resisting the possibility that I may not be the autonomous, independent self that I claim I am."[117] But it is precisely this defense of the conventional assumption of subjective integrity that Barthes and Lacan claim the photograph disrupts. Another way to make this point is to return to Benjamin's notion of the aura, which he employed, to cite Gebauer and Wulf once again, "to designate the experience of magical enchantment." In his discussion of Baudelaire's preference for painting over photography, he defines it in the following terms: "Experience of the aura thus rests on the transposition of a response common to human relationships to the relationship between inanimate or natural object and man. The person we look at, looks at us in turn. To perceive the aura of an object we look at means to invest it with the ability to look at us in return."[118] In the essay where this appeared, Benjamin implicitly aligns himself with Baudelaire's position in concluding that photography undermines the aura. But, *pace* Baudelaire and Benjamin, if we apply Lacan's theory of the look and the gaze to the photograph, as Iskin suggests we might, then it would be plausible to come to a different conclusion.[119] Like sardine cans shining in the sun, objects in photos—or at least those that act like Barthes's punctums[120]—wound the narcissism of sovereign subjects and disorganize their visual field by asserting the uncanny power of the particular objects that magically gaze back at them.

The Photograph as Event, Readymade, and Proper Name

Our argument about the magical nominalist implications of the photograph will be strengthened if we consider possible parallels with the discourses of sublime historical experience, the event, the readymade, and the proper name. We will take them in order. It is not surprising to see that the new experientialists were themselves aware of the affinities between their search for "historical stowaways" producing "sublime historical experiences" and Barthes's ruminations on the unintentional magic of photographic *punctums*. In *Moved by the Past*, Eelco Runia explicitly cites their "autonomous power, that exists independently of [Barthes's] own receptivity"[121] to argue that they can release unfiltered residues of the past—"spots of time"—into the present. He contends that "Barthes's ideas about the ability of the past to reach out and overwhelm us in the present" are amplified in the images in W. G. Sebald's novels, which also show that certain objects from the past can have a comparable impact on us.[122]

In *Sublime Historical Experience*, F. R. Ankersmit likewise appropriates Barthes's insight that "however much a photographer may wish to manipulate his pictures, there will always be traces or reminiscences of the real escaping his control. That is simply part of the medium. And in this way the tension between what is made and what is found (which will ordinarily disappear in a painting) will always present itself in photography."[123] The photographer "returns us to the scene of the crime," as Benjamin famously said of the work of Eugène Atget, whose effect Ankersmit explicitly explains in terms of Barthes's *punctum*.[124] Paralleling the trope of objects "looking back at us" employed by Lacan and Barthes, Ankersmit, it will be recalled, argued that there are extraordinary moments in our encounter with the past "where the memory sees us, so to say, and we see only it."

Sublime historical experiences may also be triggered in other ways, as demonstrated by a very small but significant number of photographs whose importance has been explored by the French visual theorist Georges Didi-Huberman in his arresting study *Images in Spite of Everything*.[125] The four photographs in question were taken surreptitiously by a *Sonderkommando* in Auschwitz in 1944 and then smuggled out of the death camp. They are important not for the glimpses they offer of the cremation of gassed bodies and women being herded to the gas chambers, which are blurred and partly occluded, even if they can serve to bear indexical witness to the horrors they record. What makes them significant for Didi-Huberman is their preservation of the courageous acts of the photographers, whose defiance of the Nazis has the power to unsettle us today. He calls them "tear-images" in opposition to the typical "veil-images" taken by the perpetrators rather than victims, which fit too easily into our conventional narratives of the Holocaust. Not only do they subvert meaningful narratives but also trouble the integrity of the viewing subject. They "will never be reassuring *images of oneself*; they will always remain *images of the Other*, harrowing, tearing images as such, but their very otherness demands that we approach them. . . . *Identity is altered*: for an instant, the looking subject, however firm he is in the exercise of observation, loses all temporal and spatial certainty."[126] Like other stowaways from the past, they get us beyond postfact conventional reconstructions or what he calls "shield-images" to put us in touch, however fleetingly, with what in theological terms would have been called the raw, unfiltered "real presence" of the past.

Such photographic instances of sublime historical experience are, of course, extremely rare. But if we turn now to the French poststructuralist discourse of the event, the magical nominalist parallels are considerably stronger. What is preserved indexically in the photographic image may, after all, be categorized as a temporal event rather than a spatial object. This conclusion is especially compelling if iconic resemblance to such objects is de-emphasized in favor of the photons of light reflecting off their visible surfaces at a particular moment rather than testifying to their integral existence. We have already noted Mary McCarthy's sardonic riposte to Harold Rosenberg's defense of action painting, "You cannot hang an event on the wall, only a picture," to which Thierry de Duve has responded "it seems, however, that with photography we have indeed the paradox of an event that hangs on the wall."[127] Or as the novelist and critic John Berger put it, "the language in which photography deals is the language of events."[128]

There are, however, two distinct relationships between photographs and events. The first draws on the observation that what has come to be called an "historical event" is often identified by its having been captured in iconic images. Thus, Michel Frizot can write: "the photographic image has defined the concept of an event. By this I mean that the event, in the twentieth century, has progressively come to be that of which we have photographic images."[129] In other words, certain vivid *representations* of historically meaningful happenings—for example, the planes crashing into the Twin Towers on 9/11 or the Space Shuttle Challenger disaster[130]—have come to emblematize them. There are, of course, also media pseudoevents deliberately created solely for photo opportunities. And photographs used for advertising may deliberately seek to negate any relationship with genuine events, for, as Berger argued, "publicity is essentially *eventless*. It extends just as nothing else is happening. For publicity all real events are exceptional and happen only to strangers."[131]

The second relationship is, however, more pertinent for our argument about magical nominalism. It focuses on the event-like quality of any photograph, not the historical importance of what may be represented by it. At first glance, this may simply suggest the punctual disruption of a chronological flow, like a vertical line bisecting a horizontal one. Or to cite the distinction Barthes himself introduced in speaking of the *punctum*, it releases a "*kairos* of desire" into the *chronos* of normal temporal experience. Here the inexorable onrushing quality of time is taken to be frozen or paused, suspending animation, which also implies that link between photography and death posited by Barthes and others.

But, as we noted in discussing the poststructuralist ruminations on the event, the complex pluritemporality of genuine events was often stressed instead of their singular punctuality, a distinction which is also suggestive in considering those "events hanging on walls" called photographs. The German art historian Britta Hochkirchen has drawn on Gottfried Boehm's concept of "iconic difference" and Reinhart Koselleck's thoughts on historical photographs to argue that images in general are viewed relationally with different elements perceived over time.[132] An image-event is thus less a punctual unity than a constellation of juxtaposed temporalities, which is even more evident when the image is a photograph. For, as Barthes argued, although it records a moment in the aorist tense, a moment of a past that has already happened, it can also imply the "future perfect," foretelling (or better, fore*showing*) what will happen, a presentiment of mortality. Accordingly, the philosopher Andrew Benjamin, whose analysis of the plurality of historical events we have already encountered, argues that "the irreducibility and thus impossibility of a *reduction ad unam*—which, once again, is a quality of the image and thus that which is proper to the photographic image—repositions the image as a plural event."[133]

The application of the poststructuralist discourse of the plural historical event as an unexpected disruption of narrative meaning, perhaps even a sign of libidinal intensity, radical freedom or the appropriation of being, may well seem a dubious exaggeration when applied to photographs tout court. Most, after all, are entirely banal in their effect and do little, if anything, to challenge conventional wisdom and received perceptions of the world. A typical snapshot is, after all, a far cry from a world-changing rupture like the French Revolution or even the so-called events of 1968.

Mapping Barthes's distinction between *studium* and *punctum* onto the idea of the event makes the parallel seem, however, a bit more plausible. Translating the former into the vocabulary of the event would be to assign it the meaning accorded by mainstream historiography, at least in its anti-structuralist guise. That is, it implies the event as intelligible in the context of a coherent narrative, or what we might call an historicist account of meaningfully emplotted development. As such, events are understood to be explicable in terms of a linear temporality of succession in which there is a before and after, a beginning, middle and end. They capture what is sometimes called the "decisive moment" in a narrative, like a visual ekphrasis serving to highlight its overall meaning.[134] They can also function as episodes in a story with identifiable ethical implications, a classic example being what has come to be called a "Whig interpretation" based on identifying progressive and reactionary actors and interests in a general story of emancipation.[135]

Unlike the "unary" photograph, which is nothing but a *studium,* an image with a *punctum* is, as we have seen, disturbed, split, often with a singular detail that operates like a "part object." It is never entirely coded, and so impossible to render fully intelligible in a semiotic system or coherent story. Although the completed object is missing, the *punctum* nonetheless "has, more or less potentially, a power of expansion. This power is often metonymic."[136] But resisting closure in a meaningful whole, it is a "subtle *beyond*—as if the image launched desire beyond what it permits us to see."[137] As "events that hang on a wall" (or are preserved in an album or digital cloud), those photos with *punctums* invite comparison, albeit on a much more modest scale, with the poststructuralist exaltation of the historical event for resisting narrative recuperation and historicist integration. Minimizing the role of intended meaning, stressing the importance of contingency and chance, both can be deemed paradigmatic instances, if in very different registers, of the magical nominalist impulse.

There may, to be sure, be one important difference. The emotional intensity unleashed by the *punctum* in a photo would seem less likely to foreshadow some future state of bliss, happiness or completion than the one we have seen attributed to at least some historical events. It is, after all, resolutely backward looking, bringing into the present a moment that is inevitably past or traumatically foreshadowing only the future catastrophe of mortality. As such, it may comport with the more sober notion of the event we have seen in certain poststructuralists like Derrida, which preserves the spectral trace of past traumas and only gestures toward a future or *avenir* that is perpetually *à venir,* always destined to be delayed in arriving. From a very different perspective, John Roberts worries that the "after the event" effect of a photograph disconnected from the larger context in which it was taken may be complicit in the infinite delay of radical change, "precisely because the critical and cognitive link between the photodocument and the transformation of social experience is suppressed, not just in the wake of the hegemony of the nonsymbolic, but as a result of the determination of the state to decouple when necessary the 'singular event' from the political process."[138]

Whether the state is somehow to blame for the isolation of photographic events from larger processes, they do not seem to provide much incentive for Badiou's revolutionary "fidelity to the event" as a prefigural anticipation of a future truth. One passage in *Camera Lucida,* which we have already cited in part, suggests why there may be reluctance to read the photographic event as an advent: "In the Photograph, the event is never transcended for the sake of something else. The Photograph always leads the corpus I need back to the body I see; it is the absolute Particular, the sovereign Contingency, matte and somehow stupid, the *This* (this photograph, and not Photography), in short, what Lacan calls the *Tuché*, the Occasion, the Encounter, the Real, in its indefatigable expression."[139]

And yet elsewhere in that very same book, where Barthes acknowledges his own experience of photographs that have animated and impelled him into the future, a different conclusion can be drawn: "The best word to designate (temporarily) the attraction certain photographs exerted upon me was *advenience* or even *adventure*. This picture *advenes*, that one doesn't. The principle of adventure allows me to make Photography exist."[140] The unusual word "advenience" suggests something coming from without, rather than self-generated, which comports with the magical nominalist stress on that "preponderance of the object" we have noted in Adorno. But as Barthes tells us, it can also imply the adventure that might follow from contact with that object. So there is perhaps at least some potential for photographic events to transcend their fixation on the past and join their historical counterparts extolled in poststructuralist discourse as advents bringing something new and marvelous into existence.

Equating photographic events hanging on walls with momentous ruptures in historical continuity may admittedly seem like a stretch. But the case for their paradigmatic status as exemplars of magical nominalism can be strengthened if we examine two intriguing parallels that can be drawn with others we have already encountered. The first involves the readymades that Duchamp produced in the name of pictorial nominalism. The other invokes the power of proper names to resist generic categories, which the German philosopher Martin Seel has suggestively argued applies to photographs as well.

We have already noted affinities between Duchamp's readymades and "the event" as theorized by Badiou and others, which tie both to photographs. They have, however, additional similarities, which, in fact, Duchamp often acknowledged. He was himself, it should be remembered, long fascinated by photography, as evidenced by the influence of Eadweard Muybridge's chronophotographs on his most celebrated painting, *Nude Descending a Staircase* (1912).[141] Later works such as *The Large Glass* (1915-1923) have also been understood, among many other things, as "part of a materialized version of the workings of photography, or as another way of making a picture which, like a photograph, is developed on glass."[142]

The connection with the readymade, however, was very different. In a note explaining how to make one, Duchamp wrote: "Specifications for 'Readymades': by planning for a moment to come (on such a day, such a date such a minute), 'to inscribe a readymade'—The readymade can later be looked for. —(with all kinds of delays). The important thing then is just this matter of timing, *this snapshot effect,* like a speech delivered on no matter what occasion but at such and such an hour."[143] By metaphorically invoking the "snapshot effect" of the readymade, Duchamp indicated several parallels with taking a photograph. First, the readymade is produced through a momentary break in the ongoing rush of time, in which it is abruptly relocated in a different register—an object of everyday use, a banal commodity, suddenly redescribed or, to use Duchamp's term, "inscribed" as a work of art. Second, while the act of relocation or inscription, like a photographer's choice to frame and click at a certain moment, accords a measure of agency to the one who chooses the object or shoots the image, what is transfigured is always already there, an object existing prior to any subjective constitution. As such, it limits the creative sovereignty of the subject, thus drawing on a nominalism that is more magical than conventional. Third, like the *punctum* in Barthes's analysis of certain photographs, a readymade challenges the prevailing cultural meanings of the day, redefining in particular what can be called a work of art. It too is an advenience, which can produce an unexpected adventure from without.

Focusing attention on Duchamp's link between readymades and the snapshot, Rosalind Krauss summarizes its implications as follows: "The photograph heralds a disruption in the autonomy of the sign. A meaningless meaning surrounds it which can only be filled in by the addition of a text. . . . The readymade's parallel with the photograph is established by its process of production. It is about the physical transposition of an object from the continuum of reality into the fixed condition of the art-image by a moment of isolation, or selection."[144] She then adds a further claim that explains the readymade cum photograph in linguistic terms: "It also recalls the function of the shifter. It is a sign which is inherently 'empty,' its signification a function of only this one instance, guaranteed by the existential presence of this object. It is the meaningless meaning that is instituted through the terms of the index."[145]

Shifters, first identified by the Danish linguist Otto Jesperson, were incorporated into Roman Jakobson's influential semiotic theory to indicate indefinite indexical symbols such as personal pronouns. They are grammatical units with a deictic character whose meaning can only be ascertained by situating them in a specific temporal and spatial context, which also takes into account the addresser and addressee of the sentence where they are used. The arbitrary assignation of the term "readymade" to random objects can be compared to a shifter because it can be applied indifferently to an infinity of possible candidates, none of which has any greater qualitative claim on the signifier than any other. It is recognized as such only if the contextual conditions are appropriate—the declaration of the addresser is considered legitimate by the institutions to whom it is directed—and there is an actual object, which exists prior to the declaration. But, and this is crucial, that object has no property of "readymadeness" prior to the act of designation.

There may be an even better linguistic parallel for the photograph that bolsters its candidacy for inclusion as a paradigm of magical nominalism, which is suggested by Martin Seel's essay "Photographs Are Like Names."[146] Drawing on Saul Kripke's theory of the ostensive and denotative role of proper names, Seel argues that photos are not like sentences that describe or represent, but are rather like names that designate: "The photo says or characterizes nothing, but it names something. *Photographs are like names of momentary configurations of things.*"[147] They are not names of objects per se, revealing their essential meaning, but rather only of the singular, unique moment when those objects are captured by the camera. "The linguistic proper name is (as a rule) a lasting referent of an enduring object, the photographic name in contrast is always a lasting referent of a (very) ephemeral thing."[148] It records, in other words, the contingent event of capturing the appearance of an object (including human beings) at a unique moment of time.

Although Seel admits that photographs can also be situated in meaningful contexts, where they function connotatively like Barthes's *studium*, they always have the potential to be like proper names with no meaningful resonance beyond their contingent existence. Unlike films, which record ongoing, processual occurrences that normally involve active human agency in their production, photographs resist assimilation to a meaningful story. "While the photographic image gives us the freedom of a contemplative encounter with the meaningless ephemerality of a presence that is now past, the film transports us into an (often fictional) correspondence with its happening."[149] In short, photographs performatively confirm that no generic conceptual or narrative imposition can fully master or subsume the infinite world of given singularities that transcend human constructions.[150] As such, they instantiate the magical nominalist experience of ineffable particularity.

Coda: Siegfried Kracauer on the Photograph

Martin Seel's fleeting contrast between photographs and films provides a convenient transition to one final example of magical nominalism infusing the worldview of a major cultural theorist. Siegfried Kracauer (1889–1966) is remembered primarily for his pioneering work on cinema from both a historical and ontological point of view but was also a shrewd analyst of both its debts to and differences from photography. He grew up in the same German-Jewish milieu during the turbulent years before and after World War I that had nurtured his friends Benjamin and Adorno, and he joined the latter in American exile during the Nazi era.[151] Like them he fitfully incorporated both theological and materialist motifs in his cultural analyses, and struggled with the implications of a modernity that was only imperfectly *entzaubert*. Resisting the consolations of idealism or historicism—he shared Benjamin's hostility to Hegel and was even skeptical of Adorno's negative version of dialectics[152]—Kracauer defied easy efforts to situate him in a coherent intellectual tradition. He is not, for example, explicitly included in Agata Bielik-Robson's account of Jewish nominalism or Marrano cryptotheologies, although in some ways he would be a plausible candidate.[153]

The difficulty of pigeonholing Kracauer was evident in the ambivalent tribute Adorno composed for him on the occasion of his seventy-fifth birthday in 1964, subtitled *Der wunderliche Realist* and translated in *Notes to Literature* as "The Curious Realist: On Siegfried Kracauer."[154] Other renditions of the title have included "eccentric" or "whimsical realist."[155] Clearly, it has not been easy to translate *wunderlich*, which the dictionary equates with "strange" or "odd" in English. It may therefore be permissible to add yet another candidate for the troublesome adjective, based on the *Wunder* or miracle in *wunderlich*: "magical." This rendering foregrounds the capacity for wonder in Kracauer's personality, that thinking with "an eye that is astonished almost to helplessness" of which Adorno wrote,[156] especially evident in his reactions to the new media of photography and film. Benjamin noted something similar when he characterized Kracauer's interpretative practice as "solidly based on the exact study of his own most personal experience. (Just as white magic goes hand in hand with the rigorous, sober scrutiny of experience, while black magic never gets further than enchantment and mystery)."[157]

As for Adorno's noun "*Realist*," its literal English cognate is the obvious choice, but here too a little reflection may grant us some license to suggest an alternative. For the type of "realism" that Kracauer more often than not espoused was closer to nominalism in the old medieval sense of the term than many standard versions of realism, including the realism of universals. As a result, "Kracauer: The Magical Nominalist" may well be the most evocative way to translate Adorno's title and characterize Kracauer's idiosyncratic position. Although he did not share all of its typical expressions—for example, the fascination with the singularity of proper names that Seel was even to extend to photographs[158]—he shows us one final face of the elusive spirit of magical nominalism.

Kracauer's intellectual formation, to be sure, was influenced by the mood of sobriety and moderation that characterized the *Neue Sachlichkeit* during Weimar, even as he sought to distance himself from the ideology of neutral reportage that so often characterized the movement. There is indeed little in him of that mixture of overwrought anguish and utopianism infusing the expressionism of a slightly earlier era.[159] Ironic detachment and cool distance—what he liked to call his "extraterritorial" estrangement from the world[160]—marked his work of the middle Weimar years, work also inflected by the phenomenological critique of psychologism and its imperative, in Husserl's famous slogan, to return *zu den Sachen selbst* (to the things themselves) rather than *bei bloßen Worten stehen zu bleiben* (remaining with mere words).[161] These Kracauer celebrated in all their motley contingency rather than subsuming them under human categorizations.[162] As Helmut Lethen put it in his study of Weimar's culture of distance, *Cool Conduct*, "Kracauer stresses the camera's ability to undermine the conventions of the expressive arts, in order to make visible the natural foundation that exists unconsciously in the frozen gesture."[163] His film theory was likewise suspicious of the fetish of directorial control, which later spawned so-called auteur theory.[164] Trusting in the "primacy of the optical," Kracauer resisted not only the expression of subjective emotion but also the hegemony of concepts and categories.[165] Although he called himself a materialist, his was rarely, if ever, of the dialectical variety. While being a recognized master of the feuilleton form, he never narcissistically foregrounded his own sensibility in the manner of many other writers in that tradition.

This is not to say, however, that Kracauer was ever a flat-footed positivist, placing his bets on passive observation and inductive generalization. Significantly, one of the alternate ways of describing the mood of the *Neue Sachlichkeit* was "magical realism," a phrase, as noted in an earlier chapter, first coined by the art critic Franz Roh in 1925.[166] Drawing on Husserl's and Heidegger's phenomenology, Roh celebrated the miracle that allowed inchoate matter to crystallize into autonomous objects. Referring to post-expressionist art that focused on such objects coldly rendered in sharp detail and often with an uncanny, enigmatic aura, Roh may have also been channeling some of André Breton's exuberance for "the marvelous" in everyday things expressed in the first *Surrealist Manifesto* the year before. The label "objectivity," Roh wrote, fails to "acknowledge that radiation of magic, that spirituality, that lugubrious quality throbbing in the best works of the new mode, along with their coldness and sobriety."[167] In moving from expressionist to magical realist art, he commented, "It feels as if that roughshod and frantic transcendentalism, that devilish detour, that flight from the world have died and now a love for terrestrial things and a delight in their fragmented and limited nature has reawakened."[168]

In another appreciation of "magical realism" in 1928 by the historian Misch Orend, the closeness to what we have been calling "magical nominalism" was even more apparent: "The magic that things emanate from the base of their singular existence and that we see in them is not a naïve magic striving to move beyond a utilitarian existence into a higher, one, striving to force upon a person his own pre-existing judgments. This new magic is the visible existence of the things themselves as they preserve it in themselves without reference to the human world. It is their uniqueness—and therefore infinity—with the uncanny calm that surrounds them."[169]

Despite Kracauer's suspicion that in certain respects the *Neue Sachlichkeit* mirrored capitalist reification and the fetishism of commodities—a concern shared by Benjamin and Adorno—he seems to have been intrigued by its distance from naive mimetic naturalism. Many years later, in his posthumously published *History: The Last Things Before the Last,* Kracauer would write, "Naïve realism has long since gone; and nobody today would dream of calling the camera a mirror. Actually, there is no mirror at all."[170] When he investigated the situation of *Die Angestellten* (salaried employees) in Weimar, he had already acknowledged that "reality is a construction. Certainly life must be observed for it to appear. Yet it is by no means contained in the more or less random observational results of reportage; rather, it is to be found solely in the mosaic that is assembled from single observations on the basis of comprehension of their meaning. Reportage photographs life; such a mosaic would be its image."[171]

Although he resisted the fetish of form over content that sometimes led to the excessive use of montage, he never went to the opposite extreme of believing film was a purely mimetic medium. For he understood that construction involved the creative juxtaposition of the givens already produced by the world (dare we call them "readymades?"), not the imaginative expression of the interiority of the subject doing the constructing. Mosaics, after all, may be made not found, but they do not produce the elements they assemble out of thin air. Employing the oxymoron "active passivity" in his final ruminations on the craft of the historian, Kracauer sought to find a way to limit the creation ex nihilo of the observer while acknowledging the role he or she played in producing new constellations—to use a favorite terms of his friend Walter Benjamin—of the archival materials that were imposed on him from without.[172]

For all of Kracauer's stress on the sphere of the profane and resistance to utopian fantasies, he nonetheless betrayed enough residual desire for some sort of potential transfiguration to alert us to his roots in a nominalism that can still justly be called magical, a nominalism unwilling to rob inanimate objects of their latent power. The phrase "redemption of physical reality," which he could still employ as late as 1960 in the subtitle of *Theory of Film*, could not entirely shed its religious aura, even if Kracauer was far more skeptical than some of his friends about even the weak messianic power that might somehow disrupt the deadening routines of modern life.[173] What Walter Benjamin once said of the experimental method of German Romanticism found its echo in Kracauer's approach to the world: "Experiment consists in the evocation of self-consciousness and self-knowledge in the things observed. To observe a thing means only to arouse it to self-recognition. Whether an experiment succeeds depends on the extent to which the experimenter is capable, through the heightening of his own consciousness, through magical observation, one might say, of getting nearer to the object and of finally drawing it into himself."[174] In such a way, moments of revelatory power, those disruptive events that Benjamin famously called "profane illuminations," might appear.

There is evidence of these hopes in Kracauer's remarkable 1927 essay "Photography," which is often placed alongside Benjamin's "Little History of Photography" and Barthes's *Camera Lucida* in the canon of photographic theory.[175] A close reading of its argument will serve as a fitting conclusion to our discussion of the photograph as a paradigm of magical nominalism. Kracauer begins his essay with a suggestive contrast between the photograph of a popular twenty-four-year-old film diva, immediately recognizable by all who see it, and a picture of a grandmother taken sixty years ago, when she was twenty-four. In the latter, belief in a perfect likeness is far less certain, for it captured "a moment of time past that passes without return. Although time is not part of the photograph like the smile or the chignon, the photograph itself, so it seems to them, is a representation of time."[176]

But significantly, it is a temporality that is in tension with the one underpinning the dominant view of historical development, which Kracauer identifies with historicism and sees as emerging with Goethe and reaching its height with Wilhelm Dilthey. Its advocates "believe they can explain any phenomenon purely in terms of its genesis. That is, they believe in any case that they can grasp historical reality by reconstructing the course of events in their temporal succession without any gaps."[177] It is thus like that conventional version of historical narrative that we have seen challenged by magical nominalist notions of sublime historical experience and the event. Kracauer characterizes the distinction in the following way: "Photography presents a spatial continuum; historicism seeks to provide the temporal continuum. According to historicism, the complete mirroring of an intratemporal sequence simultaneously contains the meaning of all that occurred within that time. . . . The equivalent of its temporal photography would be a giant film depicting the temporally interconnected events from every vantage point."[178] Kracauer then distinguishes both photographs and historicist narratives from a third mode of interacting with the past, which he identifies with memory.[179] Unlike both historicism in temporal terms and photography in spatial ones, memory contains inevitable gaps. It is shaped by a different organizing principle, which is the search for personal significance linked with what is construed as truth content. As such, memories produce images that congeal into what he calls "the last image, since it alone preserves the unforgettable. The last image of a person is a person's actual *history*." Omitting all extraneous details that fail to conform to the alleged truth of that history, it is "like a *monogram* that condenses the name into a single graphic figure which is meaningful as an ornament."[180]

At first glance this comparison would imply that photographs are inferior to memory. From the latter's perspective, Kracauer writes, "photography appears as a jumble that consists partly of garbage. . . . In a photograph a person's history is buried as if under a layer of snow."[181] Often, in fact, Kracauer's essay is understood as elevating both history and memory over photography.[182] This interpretation is not entirely implausible if we recall Kracauer's empathy for those who experience "metaphysical suffering from the lack of a higher meaning in the world" and his invocation of Lukács's characterization of his era as one of "transcendental homelessness."[183] Insofar as historicist narrative and personal memory seem to provide meaning while photographs deny it, it would appear that he saw the latter as contributing to the problem rather than the solution of modern alienation.[184] As Adam Lipszyc notes, "In Kracauer's terms we might thus say that photography is devoid of the moment of name, which is identical with the moment of truth."[185]

However, in the next section of Kracauer's essay, which considers art photography, a subtle transition in his argument occurs. In the nineteenth century, he notes, some photographers sought to emulate traditional painting, in which an artwork "approaches the transparency of a final memory image, in which the features of 'history' converge." But "with the increasing independence of the technology and the simultaneous evacuation of meaning from the objects, *artistic photography* loses its justification." Modern painters, in fact, have themselves come to compose "their images out of photographic fragments in order to highlight the side-by-side existence of reified appearances as they manifest themselves in spatial relations. This artistic intention is diametrically opposed to that of artistic photography." Those who still seek to compose photographs that correspond to traditional artistic models of organic wholeness replete with meaning are in fact complicit with pseudospiritual efforts to cover over the material contradictions of society. "It would be well worth the effort to expose the close ties between the prevailing social order and artistic photography."[186]

Although stressing the "spatial continuum" recorded in a photograph, Kracauer was also keenly aware that it "must be essentially associated with the moment in time in which it came into existence."[187] As revealed by the distinction between the images of the current diva and of the grandmother during her youth with which the essay begins, the more a photograph ages, the less it resembles the legible immediacy of life. Nor does it have the significance of "the monograms of remembered life" that can be identified with personal memory. "The photograph is the sediment which has settled from the monogram, and from year to year its semiotic value decreases. The truth content of the original is left behind in its history; the photograph captures only the residuum that history has discharged."[188] Here it resembles fashion, which also loses its meaning with time and becomes like a comical ruin, which can engender the spooky feeling also brought on by contact with ghosts. An old photograph "conjures up anew an image of a disintegrated unity. This ghost-like reality is *unredeemed*. . . . A shudder runs through the viewer of old photographs. For they make visible not the knowledge of the original but the spatial configuration of a moment; what appears in the photograph is not the person but the sum of what can be subtracted from him or her."[189]

What appears to be Kracauer's concerns about the role photography plays in abetting the disintegration of meaning and the unified self are voiced in the next section of his essay, which pivots from a generic discussion of the medium to its increasing social role in modern life. Pointing to the radical growth of illustrated newspapers and journals, he assigns it responsibility for the loss of historical understanding and the erosion of collective memory: "The *contiguity* of these images systematically excludes their contextual framework available to consciousness. The 'image-idea' drives away the idea. The blizzard of photographs betrays an indifference toward what the things mean." The blame is not just the new technology, "for the world itself has taken on a 'photographic face'; it can be photographed because it strives to be absorbed into the spatial continuum which yields to snapshots."[190]

Kracauer explains the transformation of the world registered in its photographic face in two ways that show how much he shared positions often identified with the Frankfurt School. It expresses, he argued, the replacement of a symbolic relationship between man and nature by an allegorical one, a change from the appearance of the idea in sensuous form to one in which the two are alienated. This was, of course, the same transformation that Benjamin was simultaneously tracing, albeit at an earlier period, in his *Habilitationsschrift* on the Baroque *Trauerspiel*. "It is only with the domination of nature," Kracauer continued in an anticipation of Horkheimer and Adorno's *Dialectic of Enlightenment*, "that the image loses its symbolic power." Even more precisely, it was "a secretion of the capitalist mode of production," which had reduced nature to a mere resource for commodification.[191]

All of this may sound as if Kracauer were unequivocally lamenting the invention of photography, damning it for being yet another tool of capitalist alienation. But the final, decisive move in his essay suggests otherwise. As Andreas Huyssen observes, it is "a complete reversal of the negative take on photography in its relation to the privileged memory image with which Kracauer began his reflection in the photography essay."[192] As in the case of the paradoxical defense in "The Mass Ornament" (1927) of the emancipatory potential of capitalist rationalization,[193] he conjectures that there is no going back. For were the current order to falter, "then liberated consciousness would be given an incomparable opportunity. Less enmeshed in the natural bond than ever before, it could prove its power in dealing with them. The turn to photography is the *go-for-broke game* [*va banque*] of history."[194] Precisely because it does not present history as a coherent narrative of redemption, imitate the organic unity of a work of art, or ape the "monogram of remembered life," it is able to emancipate nature from its subjection to cultural construction (or in our terms, from the problematic way that conventional nominalism masters contingency through subjective domination). Aerial shots of cities, for example, reveal unanticipated juxtapositions of things that are distanced from the intentions of the humans who created them. Like the alienation effects or "making strange" that characterizes much modern art, photography can make us see unanticipated relations that disturb the settled cultural order. "For the first time in history, photography brings to light the entire natural cocoon; for the first time, the inert world presents itself in its independence from human beings." Not only does this mean that it helps us realize "the *provisional status* of all given configurations," but it might also "awaken an inkling of the right order of the inventory of nature." It does so through creative destruction, allowing that sifting through ruins whose value Benjamin was to show in his *Arcades* project: "The disorder of the detritus reflected in photography cannot be elucidated more clearly than through the suspension of every habitual relationship among the elements of nature."[195]

Kracauer was thus anything but a detractor of the new medium, nostalgic for a lost era of holistic meaning and organically integrated art. But his hope here is also not that of a Hegelian dialectician, either idealist or materialist, for the triumphant overcoming of alienation in a grand synthetic unity, which preserves as well as cancels what it transcends. Although registering in his own experience what he called "the tear in the world,"[196] he was never optimistic about the possibility of fully healing it. It is for this reason that one particular photograph of Kracauer himself, an incomplete montage assembled from the shards of a broken negative glass plate taken around the same time as he wrote his essay on photography, has become so iconic a symbol of his legacy.[197] As Miriam Hansen noted, "It is precisely *because* of the medium's negativity—its affinity with contingency, opacity to meaning, and tendency towards disintegration—that Kracauer attributes to photography a decisive role in the historical confrontation between human consciousness and nature."[198] Instead of taking the side of human consciousness, he shows his solidarity with the magical nominalist validation of a nature that cannot be confidently understood as possessing inherent universals and yet is more than a mere figment of the constitutive human imagination.

In later ruminations on the photograph, Kracauer reinforces the impression of his undeclared debt to the anti-anthropocentric implications of this tradition.[199] Even when shooting photographic portraits, he writes in 1932, it is disastrous to try to "realize an artistic 'conception'" in the hope of revealing the essence of the sitter's physiognomic soul.[200] In *Theory of Film*, while dismissing naive mimesis of reality and acknowledging the formative element in using a camera, he emphasizes what he calls "the outspoken affinity" photographs have for "unstaged reality," revealing "nature in the raw, as it exists independently of us." They furthermore tend "to stress the fortuitous. Random events are the very meat of snapshots." A photograph is also inclined to "suggest endlessness. This follows from its emphasis on fortuitous complexes which represent fragments rather than wholes." And finally, "The medium has an affinity for the indeterminate" because it "is bound to convey unshaped nature itself, nature in its inscrutability."[201]

Similar arguments underpin the parallels Kracauer draws in his posthumously published *History: The Last Things Before the Last* between the photographer and the historian, both of whom subordinate their formative to their realistic impulse, highlight the random contingency of their material, and accept infinite endlessness rather than seek totalizing closure.[202] Not surprisingly, his ruminations on history have been compared with those of self-identified nominalists like Foucault.[203] In both cases, the idea of a single, overarching metanarrative based on a simple chronological continuum is rejected in favor of understanding the historical universe as heterogeneous, oscillating between micro and macro levels of development that resist reconciliation, and filled with abrupt, inexplicable transitions. The very idea of a coherent period, Kracauer writes, "disintegrates before our eyes. From a meaningful spatiotemporal unit it turns into a kind of meeting place for chance encounters—something like the waiting room of a railroad station."[204] Although understood through the lens of social science, history may appear governed by law-like rules, which reflect the transformation of society into a "second nature," it "is also the realm of contingencies, of new beginnings. All regularities discovered in it, or read into it, are of limited range."[205] Like photography, history resists the attempts of philosophy and aesthetics to contain and master what exceeds conceptualization and metaphorization. The historian should adopt the attitude we have already discerned in the devotees of sublime historical experience: "a sort of active passivity on the historian's part. He must venture on the diverse routes suggested to him by his intercourse with the evidence, let himself drift along, and take in, with all his senses strained, the various messages that happen to reach him."[206]

All of this might sound very deflationary, implying that the quest for historical meaning is ultimately in vain and that hopes for the interruption of chronological aimlessness by kairotic events or profane illuminations will be defeated. And indeed, unlike Benjamin, Kracauer seems never to have believed in the possibility of restoring Adamic names or fully reenchanting the fallen world.[207] Photographs are not like the monographs of memory in which name (or at least initials) and image are symbolically united. The difference between Benjamin and Kracauer is also shown in their contrasting attitude toward the obscure theological notion of "apocatastasis." As explained earlier, it is the optimistic belief, often traced back to the church father Origen of Alexandria in the third century, that when the Last Judgment comes, all of the dead of human history, even sinners, will be redeemed. Benjamin seems to have interpreted this hope as implying a more cosmic notion of making whole of what had been burst asunder, an idea that has sometimes been compared to the Jewish notion of *tikkun olam* or the *restitutio ad integrum* lauded in the New Testament.

In *History: The Last Things Before the Last*, Kracauer also briefly alludes to this idea, albeit without calling it by its traditional religious name. In discussing the quest of "technical history" to preserve even the "smallest facts" in the vain hope of accumulating the data to verify macrohistorical generalizations, he notes in passing: "There is only one single argument in its support which I believe to be conclusive. It is a theological argument, though. According to it, the 'complete assemblage of the smallest facts' is required for the reason that nothing should go lost. It as if the fact-oriented accounts breathed pity with the dead. This vindicates the figure of the collector."[208] Some commentators have read this passage as an expression of Kracauer's reluctance, despite everything, to abandon his redemptive ambitions, or relinquish what we might call the magic in his magical nominalism. Gertrud Koch, for example, conjectures that "Kracauer deploys the figure of redemption through memory—the anamnestic solidarity with the dead—in a framework in which people and facts are to an equal extent also things."[209] Miriam Hansen similarly claims that Kracauer's idea of redemption "was conceived of in the utopian sense of a restoration of all things past and present and linked to the kabbalist concept of *tikkun*."[210]

An attenuated expression of such utopian hopes, I would agree, can be faintly discerned in Kracauer's dogged retention of the rhetoric of redemption. But it is also clear that his pessimism about the possibility of healing the world or reenchanting what had been disenchanted was far greater than even Benjamin's or Adorno's. From almost the beginning of his career, in fact, he distanced himself from the messianic enthusiasms of his more utopian peers like Ernst Bloch, Franz Rosenzweig, Martin Buber, and the young Leo Löwenthal.[211] However conclusive in theological terms, however useful in legitimating the collector's mania for complete sets of whatever he sets out to collect, the fantasy of total recall in the service of redeeming the dead is not one that Kracauer could bring himself to apply to history. The latter was, after all, no more than the "anteroom" to metaphysical or religious absolutes, containing only "the last things before the last." Nor is it clear that when he said in his 1927 essay that photography represents the "go-for-broke game" of history, he ready to place his bet on its producing a radical change equivalent to a secularized version of apocatastasis. It is thus not surprising that some commentators like Adam Lipszyc, have found his use of the rhetoric of redemption disturbingly unclear and unconvincing, reflecting "a deep intellectual confusion."[212]

Whether or not this verdict is justified, it is true that Kracauer's version of magical nominalism was always subdued and ambivalent. He only hinted at what the redemption of physical reality might really mean or fleshed out what sort of historical changes might help bring it about, however effective photographs and films might be in showing the way. In "On the Concept of History," Benjamin could contend that "the past carries with it a secret index by which it is referred to redemption."[213]Adorno could conclude *Minima Moralia* by asserting that "the only philosophy which can be responsibly practiced in the face of despair is the attempt to contemplate all things as they would present themselves from the standpoint of redemption."[214] Kracauer, however, always remained more cautious about reading the hidden messages of history or philosophizing from so lofty a standpoint.

Instead, as he made clear as early as the *Frankfurter Zeitung* essay he wrote in 1922 called "Die Wartenden," he identified with the patient, fragile hopefulness of "those who wait." Rather than responding to the crisis of "transcendental homelessness" through the decisionist leap of faith taken by "short-circuit people," political as well as religious, or retreating into an absolute skepticism that could lead to cynical resignation, those who wait adopt a stance of "*hesitant openness*."[215] Comparing this attitude to the similar defense of waiting in Samuel Beckett and Robert Musil, Harry Craver notes that it involved a kind of decision of its own: "to remain suspended between skepticism and devotion, to neither believe, nor to conclusively deny. This was a form of reluctant skepticism that desired but still resisted utopia. A view of Judaism as the faith of a people who waits is clearly relevant here, though as a religious motif it had a wider resonance of which Kracauer was well aware."[216]

But rather than acknowledging it as a self-justifying formula for impotence, Kracauer contended that this stance had its unexpected rewards. For by leaving behind the "overburden of theoretical thinking," those who wait can draw closer to "a reality that is filled with incarnate things and people and that therefore demands to be seen concretely."[217] In "The Curious Realist," Adorno recognized the sources of this hesitancy by observing that Kracauer "holds fast to the idea that what ought to be thought cannot be thought; his thinking selects this negative idea as its substance."[218] The faint utopian impulse that Kracauer, for all his protestations to the contrary, never entirely abandoned did not mean a yearning for a fully emancipated form of human life but rather a hope that "the state of innocence would be the condition of needy objects, shabby, despised objects alienated from their purposes. For Kracauer they alone embody something that would be other than the universal functional complex, and his idea of philosophy would be to lure their indiscernible life from them."[219]

Or to put it in the terms of our argument, whether writing about history, photography, or the marginal phenomena of everyday life, Kracauer is best understood as a magical nominalist in a minor key. He was more in the apophatic than kataphatic tradition, the secular analog of negative rather than positive theology. Valuing the ontological irreducibility of particular things and events that resisted subsumption under generic categories, both those assumed to be inherent in nature and those imposed by subjective conceptualization, he could only patiently wait in the anteroom of history with cautious anticipation of a redemption that might never come.

In Lieu of a Conclusion

If, as suggested in its preface, the book you have just read actually does betray the strains of a late style, and that characterization is more than a self-serving conceit to excuse its weaknesses, there can be no expectation of a full-fledged conclusion to summarize its argument or achieve narrative closure. Unlike a work of art aspiring to organic wholeness, it cannot offer a resounding cadence to bring it all to a satisfactory state of higher resolution, a final scene in which all the threads of the plot are tied together, a finished canvas in which every brush stroke has been "licked" away. Rather than an exercise in "magisterial" control of the material by an author at "the height of his powers," as a flattering reviewer's clichés might have it, it leaves the landscape it has surveyed still fractured, even if a new paradigmatic ensemble has been introduced to cast some light on it. Resisting rigorous definitions at the beginning means no claims made about a "definitive" study at the end. There is, in other words, no sovereign subject performing a retrospective, dialectical totalization to mend the fractures.

The question of sovereign authorial mastery does, however, conveniently lead us back to one thread of the argument that has been left dangling, and which might profitably be tugged again to serve as a final example of the ways in which magical nominalism troubles conventional wisdom, or better put, the wisdom of conventional nominalism. The chapter devoted to the latter tradition ended, it will be recalled, with a brief discussion of its implications for modern political theory. It noted that the theological elevation of divine will over reason, which spurred the nominalist revolution, cast doubt on the plausibility of a "cosmopolitan" homology between heavenly order and its terrestrial political counterpart. Instead, it led the world to be seen as a chaos of contingency requiring human self-assertion to authorize political legitimacy. Although Ockham himself may not have followed this logic, the voluntarist premises of nominalism opened the door for a conception of unified sovereign power unbound by rational, moral, or other constraints, introduced by Thomas Hobbes and perfected by Carl Schmitt.[1]

In its strongest version, couched in the language of political theology, this meant the transfer of a transcendent God's *potentia absoluta* to his secular, immanent counterpart, endowed with the decisionist power to make law rather than merely observe it. Like the God who can violate the natural order he has himself created through miracles, the secular sovereign can suspend the normative legal order in a "state of emergency." Such a state, Schmitt implied, was the transcendental premise of all politics, even though it might be actualized only when the facade of legality broke down, or like God's *potentia ordinata,* was suspended by sovereign will. There was, to be sure, a less authoritarian version of the political legacy of conventional nominalism in liberalism, with its stress on individual will and the importance of founding contracts, which supported a certain view of human freedom as opposed to nihilism (or that "triumph of the will" extolled by fascism). Classically expressed in Locke's dissent from Hobbes's all-powerful sovereign, this political version of conventional nominalism did not deny individuals their right to withdraw consent from a government that abused its power. But it too depended on the ability of human action—or language as a speech act—to establish order performatively rather than merely recognize it as already inherent or teleologically anticipated in the world.

Were there, we now have to ask, contrasting political lessons that might be drawn from magical nominalism? To give an adequate answer to this question would require a serious examination of the often very different political legacies of the various thinkers whose work in one way or another exemplified the tradition. Although a robust literature that would provide the tools to conduct such a comparison does in fact exist, it would be a daunting challenge to find a common denominator, if indeed one exists, underlying all of their efforts.[2] But any attempt to address the differences between a magical and conventional nominalist politics would have to begin by focusing on the specific question of their contrasting attitudes toward sovereignty.[3] I want to leave the reader with some preliminary thoughts on what such an investigation might reveal.

What first has to be acknowledged in any such account is that both nominalisms repudiate the realist premises of a cosmopolitics in which an inherent or teleological order in the world, such as the great chain of being, mirrors the harmonies of the cosmos. Both dissolve the hierarchically ordered institutions derived from Neoplatonism that claim to mediate between God and the world. Both question normative appeals to natural law or inherent political virtues in the Aristotelian sense revived by Renaissance humanists.[4] And as the discourse of the event as a rupture in the course of history demonstrates, both reject the binding power of developmental historical laws. For each tradition, the erosion of the ontological and axiological norms of the realist tradition leaves a vacuum that cries out to be filled in order to escape anarchic nihilism.

If conventional nominalism promotes the self-assertion of a sovereign subject with the legitimacy to issue commands that then function as binding laws, even if the more liberal version retains the right of individuals to challenge their validity, do the figures we have taken to be paradigms of magical nominalism offer a fully worked out alternative? Political sovereignty, as it turns out, was often one of their major concerns, linked with a generally critical attitude toward the allegedly self-asserting, autonomous subject, transcendental, communal, or individual, whose mastery of contingency they often challenged.[5] While acknowledging that religious residues—or perhaps better put, the parareligious ones we have been calling magic—remained even in the most seemingly secular expressions of sovereignty in our disenchanted modern age, they were reluctant to identify them with the omnipotent voluntarist God that Schmitt had claimed was the avatar of the modern decision-maker in the state of exception.

Walter Benjamin's baffling and controversial relationship to Schmitt would be the place to begin. Despite unsuccessful attempts by his friends Scholem and Adorno to minimize any debt Benjamin may have had to Schmitt, later efforts by commentators like Jacob Taubes to assert its importance have had a considerable impact.[6] The significant role Schmitt's political theology played in Benjamin's *Origin of German Trauerspiel* has been undeniable ever since the discovery of a laudatory letter written by Benjamin to Schmitt in 1930 that accompanied a gift of the book. His use of Schmitt's argument was not, however, uncritical.[7] Benjamin's description of the baroque worldview, to be sure, did comport with the nominalist repudiation of cosmic harmony and the "theological rationalism" later revived in vain by German idealists like Kant. Baroque thought lacked faith in innate eschatology or what Benjamin called "saturated emanationism," as reflected in the way the *Trauerspiel* eschews the unities of Aristotelian tragedy. Instead of restoring a state of grace, it squarely faces the threat of catastrophe: "Baroque extracts a profusion of things that tended to elude every formation and at its high point brings them to light in drastic form so as to clear a last heaven and to place it, as vacuum, in a condition to swallow up the earth one day with catastrophic violence."[8]

Responding to this state of lawless exception, the powers of decision are granted to the prince, who is often allegorized as the sun in the ghostly remnant of cosmological order that has a residual hold on the baroque imagination. In so arguing, Benjamin betrayed the influence of Schmitt's political theology. But in two crucial ways, he distanced himself from the latter's conclusions. "If the modern concept of sovereignty amounts to a supreme executive power on the part of the ruler, the Baroque concept develops on the basis of a discussion of the state of exception, and *makes it the most important function of the prince to avert this state*."[9] The political implications of failing to avert it are clear: "The theory of sovereignty, for which the exceptional becomes exemplary once dictatorial prerogatives are developed, makes the completion of the figure of the sovereign in the mold of the tyrant virtually obligatory."[10] For Schmitt, who was soon to become the "crown jurist" of Nazism, this completion may not have been problematic, but for Benjamin who was shortly after to become one of its most lamented victims, it assuredly was. Thus, as Samuel Weber puts it: "In emphasizing the dictatorial tendency of the sovereign, Benjamin follows Schmitt here practically to the letter. . . . But in so doing, he arrives at a result that is almost diametrically opposed to that of Schmitt: the very notion of sovereignty itself is put radically into question."[11]

A second reservation in Benjamin's adoption of Schmitt's political theology concerns the latter's argument that a voluntarist God is secularized without remainder into the figure of the mundane earthly sovereign who decides in a state of exception. As Agata Bielik-Robson has argued, Schmitt's decisionist analogy takes the form of a "*repressed cryptotheology*."[12] Here heterogeneity is dissolved into identitarian sameness, and power remains concentrated in the hands of one allegedly absolute and normatively irresponsible figure. Benjamin in contrast retains the tension between the transcendent and immanent realms, the symbolic and the material, maintaining rather than sublating the distinction between the king's two bodies later highlighted by Ernst Kantorowicz. "As highly enthroned as [the sovereign] is over his subjects and his state, his status is circumscribed by the world of creation; he is the lord of creatures, but he remains a creature."[13] That is, the mortality of the actual prince, his inclusion in the realm of created things, the natural world, prevents his ever being simply an avatar of the voluntarist deity underpinning conventional nominalism and Schmitt's secularized decisionism. In fact, he is often portrayed in the *Trauerspiel* as paralyzed by indecision. Whatever power he may exercise in promulgating mundane laws, he cannot escape the inevitability of his own death. Because of the gap between his elevated pseudodivinity and his humble creaturely vulnerability, the sovereign is also potentially a martyr. The sovereign as martyred tyrant, to cite Sigrid Weigel's gloss on Benjamin, is "the victim of a theologically founded politics, which admits of no distinction between the person and his authority and thus knows no limits."[14] If there is a figure in the *Trauerspiel* who does seem to manifest the ability to intervene in the dramatic action, it is that of the "intriguer." But his plotting produces only destabilization and not the totalizing command sought by Schmitt's tyrannical sovereign, who may assert his *potentia absoluta* but is actually incapable of decisive action.[15]

Benjamin's rejection of the Christian political theology inspiring Schmitt allowed him to draw on an alternative notion of divine violence that had messianic rather than mythological implications, leading, that is, to radical transformation rather than conservative preservation. No longer grounded in a Christian eschatological or Greek tragic narrative of fate, the Baroque *Trauerspiel* undermined the ability of a sovereign to act decisively in the service of a foreordained outcome. Instead, what we have seen as the magical nominalist prioritizing of objects in the world over subjective construction comes to the fore. As James Martel puts it: "The spirits that haunt the *Trauerspiele* are not of people but rather of 'apparently dead objects' which, unfettered from their previous (or future) eschatological significance come to subvert the grand narratives and morals these playwrights wish to convey. . . . This is another version of what Benjamin appreciates in Kafka as well: the idols, or objects that are meant to represent and promote sovereign power turn against that very thing, undermining the idolatry they would otherwise be fomenting."[16]

It was perhaps not by chance that a substantial number of the heteroclite cast of characters who have emerged in our account of magical nominalism also distanced themselves from the conventionalist voluntarism that informed Schmitt's political theological doctrine of sovereignty. Adorno, who in so many other respects was indebted to Benjamin, did not share his ambivalent appreciation of Schmitt's political theology. In *Minima Moralia*, he derided the friend/enemy logic of Schmitt's idea of the political, which he linked with the New Testament assertion "He who is not for me is against me" and mocked for exhibiting "regression to the behavior patterns of the child, which either likes things or fears them."[17] Likewise, in his frequent critiques of Kierkegaard's defense of decisionist leaps of faith, Adorno explicitly linked the Danish philosopher's notion of the existentially isolated subject, which he also extended to Heidegger's reading of Dasein, to the legacy of conventional nominalism and its stress on will over reason.[18]

Many of the French poststructuralists who stressed the singularity of disruptive events in history were also suspicious of the self-assertive decisionist subject made possible by conventional nominalism, whether in its authoritarian or liberal guise. Michel Foucault, for example, criticized the traditional notion of hierarchical or deductive power culminating in a single dominant figure in favor of a microphysics of disciplinary power.[19] "What we need," he told an interviewer in 1977, "is a political philosophy that isn't erected around the problem of sovereignty, nor therefore around the problems of law and prohibition. We need to cut off the King's head"[20] and "abandon the model of Leviathan."[21] Whereas sovereignty meant the ultimate right to "take life" by the state, disciplinary "biopower" meant the ability to "make life" or "let die." Rather than absolute and centralized, it was exercised in a dispersed and agonistic manner, both to constrain and to enable. What Foucault came to call governmentality could control populations in subtler, more indirect ways than those derived from the coercive authoritarianism of an all-powerful sovereign at the apex of a pyramid. Although his nominalist view of history may not have departed in every respect from Schmitt's, Foucault never embraced a political theology that assigned a central role to a voluntarist metasubject who assumed the powers of a secularized divinity.[22]

Lyotard likewise challenged the politics of sovereign will implied by the secularization of voluntarist monotheism. Instead, as a self-proclaimed polytheistic "pagan,"[23] he favored a perpetually agonistic politics reflecting the irreconcilable "differends" or incommensurable regimes of phrases in play at any one time.[24] No self-asserting subject had the performative power to declare a state of emergency or posit laws ex nihilo. Lyotard's celebrated definition of postmodernism as "incredulity towards metanarratives" meant, in fact, that he had no use for any unified sovereign subject who might be considered either the protagonist or narrator of a universal story.

Derrida characteristically deconstructed the binary opposition between sovereignty understood in Schmitt's sense as the power to decide in a state of emergency and the competing forces that intersect with and undermine its claim to absoluteness.[25] Although sharing Schmitt's suspicion of the ability of universal rational law to ground itself without recourse to an outside that was neither universal nor rational, Derrida did not equate it with a strong subject—either understood as singular or communal—that imposed its will. Against both the Christian narrative of kenosis and redemption as consoling fables of sacrificial reconciliation and the anamnestic totalization of its secular Hegelian version, Derrida resisted the re-incorporation of alienated otherness back into a sovereign metasubject.

As Geoffrey Bennington writes, "The matrix for the errors and stupidity of the tradition of thinking about sovereignty is the tendency to assume . . . that the sovereign is *one*, which tendency (even in Carl Schmitt) leads to all the features analyzed by Derrida in his rapprochement in *Voyous* [*Rogues*] of sovereignty and subjectivity."[26] The tension between law and exception, like those between nation and state and universality and singularity, is unbridgeable, and the realization of democratic solidarity based on popular will must always be a future ideal, never an actual reality. For there is no homogeneous "people," no community of integrated friends opposed to eternal foes, whose general will might serve as the democratic embodiment of an omnipotent God or divinely inspired monarch. "As soon as there is sovereignty," Derrida warned, "there is abuse of power and a rogue state. Abuse is the law of use; it is the law itself, the 'logic' of a sovereignty that can reign only by not sharing."[27]

Deleuze similarly rejected the traditional juridical concept of sovereignty as unified and indivisible, locating it instead in an unstable, fluid, and dynamic field of heterogeneity, difference, and multiplicity.[28] Lamenting the historical hegemony of centered, settled peoples, who created strong unified states, over the wanderings of premodern nomads, Deleuze identified the latter with a (dis)order of nature he thought ontologically superior. It may be an exaggeration to call him, as have some, the theorist of a "world without sovereignty," because he understood the need for some unified agency to thwart the crushing power of statist centralization.[29] But he was a champion of deterritorialization and the instability of energy intensities in ways that immunized him against belief in the self-assertive sovereign subject of conventional nominalism.

From a very different political perspective, Frank Ankersmit also raised questions about the compatibility between a strong notion of popular sovereignty and the idea of representative democracy.[30] Whereas one expressed the point of view from above of the ruler, the other grew out of that of the ruled from below. Without embracing it himself, he even noted that nineteenth-century liberals had sometimes resurrected the idea of the sovereignty of reason to counter the questionable identification of sovereignty with the untrammeled will of the people. There may be no obvious link between what we have called Ankersmit's new experientialist defense of sublime historical experience, which stressed the open passivity of the historian, and his reluctance to endorse the ideal of indivisible sovereign power posited by Hobbes or Schmitt. But significantly, in both instances, he kept his distance from the conventional nominalist stress on unconstrained self-assertion in the face of the absolute contingency of the world. With Claude Lefort, he argued for the void at the center of political authority, which could be filled only at its peril with a putatively concrete embodiment.[31]

To take one last example, Alain Badiou, who is included in our account of magical nominalism because of his celebration of the singular event, has at times been charged with channeling Schmitt's decisionism, in particular by Lyotard.[32] He gave some credence to the charge when he suggested his philosophy aimed "to formulate a philosophy of the singular that is, at the same time, capable of being a philosophy of the decision and of the wager."[33] Colin Wright has convincingly argued, however, that Badiou's "politics of the void" rejects the strong self-assertion of Schmitt's absolute sovereign.[34] When pressed to explain his relationship to decisionism, Badiou himself explicitly stated:

> I think there is no decisionism at all in my philosophy. There is a complete misreading on this point. Lyotard said that I was an absolute decisionist, a sort of new Carl Schmitt. But I think there's some confusion here because, after all, the crucial question is the event and the event is not the result of a decision. The difficulty is that in *L'Être et l'événement*, I say that the name of the event is the matter of a pure decision and I have to change that point. It's not very good terminology, the terminology of the nomination. I now think that the event has consequences, objective consequences and logical consequences. These consequences are separated by the event. The effect of the event is a profound transformation of the logic of the situation and that is not an effect of decision. The decision is uniquely to be faithful to the transformation.[35]

Other candidates for inclusion in our survey of paradigmatic magical nominalists may not have been as concerned with the issue of political sovereignty, but their work nonetheless often suggested a comparable disdain for a strong notion of subjective agency. It might, for example be possible to see a parallel between Roland Barthes's celebrated proclamation of the death of the author or Siegfried Kracauer's disdain for auteur theory in film studies and the evacuation of the position of absolute political sovereign. Marcel Duchamp may have foregrounded the enunciative authority of an artist able to declare a found object a readymade artwork, but he undercut the role of the genius who created the work ex nihilo. Nor is there much left of the "sovereign gaze," so often seen as a tool of political and gender power, in such works as his final installation *Étant donnés*.[36]

While their shared renunciation of the version of decisionist sovereignty endorsed by the conventional nominalist tradition from Hobbes to Schmitt is thus clear, what the magical nominalists put in its place is not. Nor should it be surprising, considering their often very different political inclinations, that they would not share a common position, or even that the question of sovereignty would not necessarily be high on their agenda. There is, however, one magical nominalist alternative to the conventional nominalist version of sovereignty that merits consideration as we end our inconclusive conclusion. It is the unique notion of sovereignty developed by the renegade French surrealist Georges Bataille, which betrayed the antinomian impulse that Jacob Taubes called "apocalypse from below" in contrast with Schmitt's "apocalypse from above."[37]

Bataille, it turns out, was friends with Benjamin during the latter's exile in Paris in the 1930s, and was entrusted with Benjamin's unfinished *Passagenarbeit,* which he hid in the Bibliothèque nationale until after the war. Although they were not in agreement on everything, both shared a suspicion of Schmitt's decisionist notion of sovereignty. Without arguing for an explicit filiation, subsequent scholarship has also discerned affinities between Bataille's celebration of formlessness (*informe*) and Adorno's embrace of *musique informelle,* both of which affirm the inability of the strong subject to master material contingency.[38]

Bataille's sustained attempts to develop a unique notion of sovereignty without a constitutive subject have also been recognized as an important influence on later poststructuralist thinkers like Foucault, Lyotard, and Derrida.[39] Foucault's 1963 "Preface to Transgression," one of the first works to put Bataille on the poststructuralist map, explicitly celebrated his subversion of "the sovereign subject."[40] In "The Idea of a Sovereign Film" (1995), Lyotard explicitly cites Bataille's *Literature and Evil* and *Inner Experience* as sources for the claim that "sovereign is an experience which is not authorized and which does not appeal to any authority; an experience or an existence which appears, happens, without relation to any law by which it could claim or demand to be 'what it is.'"[41] In *Rogues,* Derrida likewise approvingly claimed: "We have here all the makings of a counter-concept of sovereignty such as we might find in Bataille. Beyond mastery, beyond the Hegelian concept and state, beyond or contrary to the classical notion of sovereignty, the sovereignty of which Bataille speaks cultivates evil and sexual as well as poetic transgression."[42] As he added elsewhere: "One has to dissociate God's sovereignty from God, from the very idea of God. We have God without sovereignty, without omnipotence."[43]

It would be impossible to do justice to Bataille's controversial oeuvre, or even adequately reconstruct his sustained ruminations on the issue of sovereignty, in these final remarks.[44] But some general observations are in order. Although too indebted to Durkheim and Hegel ever to be attracted to nominalism in its conventional guise, Bataille was also a critic of rationalism in any form, especially if it privileged ideal essences over what he called the base materialism of existence. However attentive he may have been to residues of the sacred in the modern world, he never endorsed the secularization of a theological notion of an omnipotent God whose unconstrained power underpinned Schmitt's decisionism. Rather than following the substitutionist logic of secularization as understood by Löwith or Schmitt, he favored profanation, which more radically undermines the power it challenges.[45] Nor, for all his fascination with the nihilistic implications of Nietzsche's critique of rationalism, did he adopt the latter's stress on the self-fashioning will. As Allen Weiss has noted, Bataille renounced "the idealizing willfulness whereby we transform things, the world, ourselves. Rather than a *will to power,* he insists upon the *will to chance,* which is a counterwill, entailing the renunciation of volition."[46]

Bataille did, however, have hopes for reenchanting a world that had lost touch with its roots in myth and the sacred. He identified with the "sorcerer's apprentice" in a "secret society," who performed "strange procedures" and "ritual acts hidden from the static vulgarity of disintegrated society."[47] At times, these led to experiments in mystical limit experiences to annihilate the centered self; at others, they sought to spark the formation of an affectively imbued, sacred community with the effervescence that Durkheim had identified in primitive religions. As a founding member of the Collège de Sociologie in Paris in the late 1930s, Bataille sought to build a vital community of like-minded intellectuals outside the established academic and political institutions of his day.[48] Less esoteric than another group with which he was involved around the journal *Acéphale,* it nonetheless attracted a select audience, including émigrés like Walter Benjamin.[49] Among those who addressed its membership in 1939 was a Russian expert on Siberian shamanism, Anatole Lewitzky, later shot by the Nazis for his role in the French Resistance. Commenting on his lectures, Roger Caillois, Bataille's colleague at the College, wrote: "The question enthralled me because in my schema [Mauss's schema], there was a complete antinomy between magic and religion. I was feeling very Luciferian at that time, I regarded Lucifer as the rebel who was effective. Shamanism, consequently, was important to me as the synthesis between religious powers and the realm of infernal affairs. Bataille, for his part, was in approximately the same frame of mind. But the difference was that Bataille wanted really to become a shaman."[50]

Bataille may never have attained his goal of becoming a practicing shaman, but his idiosyncratic recasting of the idea of sovereignty allows us to include him in the magical nominalist paradigmatic force field. Sovereignty, he insisted, should be dislocated and decentered; it is "the imperative form of heterogeneous existence."[51] Against the homogenizing power of monotheism or royal absolutism, outside of the commensurating exchange of the marketplace, resisting the idealizations of beautiful form, it valorizes what is normally abjected and denigrated in traditional cultural hierarchies, "the accursed share."[52] It values a negativity that cannot be recuperated or sublated through Hegelian dialectical totalization, heterogeneous difference that can never be homogenized into sameness. Expressed in what Bataille called a "general economy" instead of the "restricted economy" of capitalism, it celebrates the useless *dépense* (waste or expenditure) exhibited in the potlatch ceremonies of northwestern Native Americans. In the place of an omnipotent Creator, it honors the dismembered God, whose violent sacrifice is the source of communal cohesion. Such a community is itself without hierarchy, having no head—in Bataille's terminology, acephalic—and not the product of intentional acts, such as a social contract. The sacred, according to Bataille, grew out of an atheological religious experience of ecstatic heterogeneity, not the commands of a willful legislator. A resacralized politics would likewise need no act of legitimating foundation.

With Bataille, needless to say, we have come a long way from the origins of conventional nominalism in the adoration of an all-powerful God by a pious fourteenth-century Franciscan theologian. His audacious defense of transgressive sexuality, base materialism, corporeal abjection, and self-mutilating violence meant he entered cultural territory that magical nominalism in most instances had only hesitantly approached. What we might call, recalling Caillois's term, his "Luciferian" sympathies and fascination with death and its release from the limitations of constrained life meant he flirted with a politics that came dangerously close for some critics to the fascism whose revitalizing power he ambivalently admired.[53] By expanding the metaphoric range of what he called violence—it included eroticism, expenditure, play, laughter and, in his unique sense, sovereignty, as well as the dissolution of the conventional self—Bataille made it hard to know when he was advocating what in normal discourse would be the real thing.

For those interpreting it more charitably, Bataille's was a "politics of the impossible," which was worth pursuing even if it had no real chance of achieving the resacralization of a fallen world (or reenchantment of a disenchanted one) Bataille had so fervently sought.[54] In comparing Derrida with Bataille, Bennington has noted the similarity of their politics to the "repeated *kairos* of the event," which "can only be that of the 'arrival' or advent, perhaps even terrifyingly that of the other that cannot be the Messiah, but without which there would be no time or politics at all." For both Bataille and Derrida, "this opening constitutively compromises the supposed sovereignty of the sovereign, the being-sovereign of the sovereign."[55]

Bataille's politics often invited comparison with Benjamin's controversial and elusive distinction between divine and mythical violence in his

1921 "Critique of Violence," a text, according to Derrida, which "can be read as neo-messianical Jewish mysticism (*mystique*) grafted onto post-Sorelian neo-Marxism (or the reverse)."[56] Mythical violence, more Greek than Jewish in origin, seeks to establish order in a world of contingency but instead abets the idolatrous ideology of repressive state power and resignation in the face of fate. Divine violence, in contrast, undoes idolatry and the hubris of those who think they can discern the truth. It also demonstrates that a belief in the absolute sacredness of bare life can be suspended in the name of a higher goal. "If mythical violence is lawmaking," Benjamin explained, "divine violence is law destroying, if the former sets boundaries, the latter boundlessly destroys them; if mythical violence brings at once guilt and retribution, divine power only expiates; if the former threatens, the latter strikes; if the former is bloody, the latter is lethal without spilling blood."[57] Whereas the principle of mythical violence is power expressed in law-making and law-enforcing, violence that founds and violence that preserves, the principle of divine violence is justice, which honors the heterogeneous singularity of the individual case. Anticipating Bataille's definition over Schmitt's, Benjamin concludes that it is this variant that deserves to be called sovereign violence.[58]

Unsurprisingly, the comparison between Bataille and Benjamin has been extended to include other figures we have already encountered in our exploration of magical nominalism and the event. Witness James Martel: "Badiou's understanding of singularities and events accords perfectly with Benjamin's own view of divine violence, and its corollary, revolutionary violence. The idea that such moments seem to come out of nowhere, unexpected even by their protagonists, are evidence—to return to Benjamin's more theological language—of the ability of God (and hence human beings) to sweep away determinism, and even the fact of impossibility itself."[59] Martel may be moving too quickly here in conflating divine and revolutionary violence and seamlessly transferring God's ability to act freely to the self-determination of mere mortals, but he is onto something in sniffing out the resemblances between Benjamin, Badiou and implicitly Bataille. In rejecting the conventional nominalist sovereign, especially when its absolute power of decision had authoritarian implications, they all adopted an alternative with magical nominalist features that came close to an anarchist "apocalypse from below."

But is there, I want to leave the reader wondering, perhaps a bit too much "magical thinking" in the pejorative sense of that phrase contained in such hopes? Rejecting the decisionist authoritarian potential of conventional nominalism, that sovereignty from above endorsed by the Schmitts of the world, may well be a salutary effect of magical nominalism's check on the unlimited power of subjective self-assertion. But the problems we grappled with in our intermezzo, which are generated when magical nominalism seeks positive alternatives, remain. Take, for example, the disturbing implications of Benjamin's bold invocation of a divine violence that does away with the law-making and law-enforcing effects of mythical violence. Some find its anarchistic implications inspiring. Martel, for instance, claims that "acts of divine violence—whether they come from Messianic sources of from our own responding acts of revolution—do not wipe away the existing world; they merely make a space for our own action, for a human judgment that is not the product of presupposition and 'facts on the ground.'"[60] Similarly, there are moments in Agamben's work on the normalization of the extralegal state of exception where he challenges Schmitt's understanding of sovereignty by invoking Benjamin's idea of divine violence. Whereas Schmitt seeks to maximize the power of the sovereign to maintain order, Benjamin embraces its destruction. Or so Agamben approvingly claims.[61]

The danger in such a celebration of apocalyptic violence is that Benjamin's confidence that it will be "lethal without spilling blood" may turn out to be misplaced. For as Derrida reminds us, we have no criteria to tell us if violence is really divine or mythic. A postscript added to his 1989 consideration of Benjamin's essay warns: "Divine violence, which is the most just, the most historic, the most revolutionary, the most decidable or the most deciding does not lend itself to any human determination, any knowledge or decidable 'certainly' on our part. It is never known in itself, 'as such,' but only in its 'effects' and its effects are 'incomparable,' they do not lend themselves to any conceptual generalization. There is no certainty (*Gewißheit*) or determinant knowledge except in the realm of mythic violence."[62] In short, we cannot calculate the odds of success when we wager on the divine pedigree of a violence that can produce an emancipatory historical event. Those who act in its name can justify, and unfortunately have, the most awful crimes.

Taking in the troubling implications of such a leap of faith, Derrida confesses that he ultimately finds Benjamin's "Critique of Violence" intolerable. For it generates a horrible temptation: "to think the holocaust as an uninterpretable manifestation of divine violence insofar as this divine violence would be at the same time nihilating, expiatory and bloodless, says Benjamin, a divine violence that would destroy current law through a bloodless process that strikes and causes to expiate." And so finally, despite all of "the polysemic mobility" of Benjamin's text, Derrida warns that it begins "to resemble too closely, to the point of specular fascination and vertigo, the very thing against which one must act and speak, do and speak, that with which one must break (perhaps, perhaps)."[63]

There is, moreover, a slippery slope that may descend from seeking the antinomian destruction of oppressive laws—call them mythic or merely made by fallible humans—to wishing for the destruction of the world as such. In other words, *pace* Martel's comforting claim that it only opens a space for human action, the temptation to restore the gnostic denigration of creation may attract those who despair of ever healing what is so badly fractured. They may adopt the nihilistic attitude that can be discerned in philosophers like Schelling and poets like Schlegel: "*bliss* to be found. . . . not in happiness *in* the world, but a joy at the annihilation of the world, at exposing the world as imposed and unfree."[64] Fortunately, this logic is rarely followed to the end, but lest it be dismissed as completely implausible, it is worth recalling the chilling reaction of Jacob Taubes to the later Schmitt's argument that the sovereign should be really understood as a "*katechon*: The retainer [*der Aufhalter*] that holds down the chaos that pushes up from below." Against Schmitt, Taubes protested:" That isn't my worldview; that isn't my experience. I can imagine as an apocalyptic: let it go down. I have no spiritual investment in the world as it is."[65]

The destruction of willful sovereign power need not, of course, imply a world-annihilating apocalypse in which all human law is seen as mythic and creation condemned as irretrievably corrupt. It is true that the harmonious cosmotheism of prenominalist Christianity may no longer be a plausible option, while conventional nominalism's delegation of divine will to the self-asserting sovereign has proven for many an inadequate surrogate. There is, nonetheless, no warrant for returning to the earlier gnostic acosmism with its blanket condemnation of creation that they were designed to overcome. For magical nominalism suggests that there is another alternative, which can preserve some investment in creation without complacently valorizing it as a whole. Eschewing any hope for total reenchantment, it savors those encounters that testify to the shards of magic still latent in the world.

That double "perhaps" at the end of Derrida's comment on Benjamin's "Critique of Violence," so characteristic of the oscillating ambivalence that runs through deconstruction, succinctly expresses magical nominalism's affinity for apophatic or negative theology. The attitude of expectant waiting embraced by Kracauer, the openness of Ankersmit to sublime historical experiences that cannot be intentionally summoned, Barthes's delight in being wounded by the *punctum* that unexpectedly pierces the conventional meaning of a photo's *studium*, Adorno's exaltation of unintended musical moments that are like demythologized prayers or the uttering of numinous proper names—the list could easily be expanded.

All of these present paradigmatic examples of a magical nominalism that operates in what we might call a minor key. It does not harbor exorbitant, ultimately vain hopes that divine violence or a revolutionary, kairotic event can bring about messianic redemption, recover the Adamic names of "language as such," or restore the full complement of sacred magic to a disenchanted, profane world. It marvels instead at the intense, fleeting eruptions of irreducible particularity—call them profane illuminations, sublime historical experiences, "sparks of contingency" in a photograph, everyday objects transfigured into aesthetic readymades, or the enigmatic quality of music that goes beyond the intentions of the composer—that always frustrate subjective attempts to master them through conceptual domination, creative fiat, the exercise of sovereign power, or narrative enclosure.

Another facet of this apophatic reticence appears in the pithy response Bielik-Robson makes to Taubes's accusation—later echoed by Agamben—that Adorno's messianic commitment was merely a weak aesthetic "as if," as opposed to the literal hope for redemption he attributed to Benjamin.[66] Adorno's version of messianism, she tells us, is "not 'apocalypse now' but 'exodus now'; not the exercise of an apocalyptic divine violence, coming down to administer a final blow to the sinful world (which, in fact is nothing but a mythic justice of retribution, the very archetypal image of nemesis), but the truly exodic practice realizing itself on an everyday basis in the ethics of singularity."[67] Here "exodus" implies an endless project of liberation from subjugation rather than a final homecoming in reconciled totalization. As such, it honors the unsublatable value of nonidentical particulars that have their own idiosyncratic resistance to domination, conceptual and literal. At the same time, it protects us from vain fantasies of total redemption or exaggerated fears of apocalyptic destruction. We can, it tells us, still feel *amor mundi*, love of the world, despite everything.[68]

Along our mundane journey, disruptive experiences of extraordinary events and unscripted encounters with objects of "marvelous singularity," to recall John of Salisbury's felicitous phrase, appear as their own reward. Releasing us from the compulsion to situate them in an endless semiotic chain of significations or subsume them under general concepts, they stand, like proper names, for themselves alone. At the very least, they fortify us against the dangerous temptations of willful anthropocentric hubris, on the one hand, and resigned capitulation to the unmagical banality of our everyday lives, on the other. While at the very best, they may produce flashes of unmediated contact with the world in all its astonishing effervescence, which can still, despite everything, arouse tremulous feelings of wonder and awe.

Acknowledgments

If there is any magic in the production of a scholarly text, it is surely in the alchemical process by which the dross of initial curiosity, preliminary research, the writing of drafts, additional research, rewriting, and rewriting again is turned into, well, not gold, but at least a publishable book. The secret ingredient is always the critical support of those who urged the author on or buoyed him up as he flailed away. In the case of *Magical Nominalism,* the process was unusually prolonged and meandering and drew on a wide and diverse company of enablers. It began in 2008, when I contributed to a special issue of *Culture, Theory and Critique* honoring W. J. T. Mitchell, which later became *The Pictorial Turn,* edited by Neal Curtis. In hindsight, many of the ideas developed in this book were already in that essay in embryonic form, although confined to the history of photography. Tom Mitchell's example of situating issues in visual culture in the largest possible historical fields, while employing maximal theoretical pressure to analyze them, was a clear inspiration.

Recognizing that a great deal of subsequent research would be required to develop and flesh out my argument, I applied for a fellowship at the American Academy in Berlin in 2010 to supplement the sabbatical I was due at the University of California, Berkeley, where I still actively taught. I benefited enormously from that opportunity, and so my first thanks go to the American Academy, its then leaders Gary Smith and Pamela Rosenberg and my stimulating cohort of fellows, Brigid Cohen, Stanley Corngold, Aaron Curry, Laura Engelstein, Catherine Gallagher (my personal favorite), Anne Hull, Kirk Johnson, Han Ong, Ken Ueno, James Wood, and John Wray. Their politely quizzical responses to my attempts to spell out the argument of the project made it clear, however, that it was not yet fully cooked.

Fortunately, I was able to leave the pot to simmer on one of those proverbial back burners that aid slow cooking when an invitation to give the 2012 George Mosse Lectures at the Hebrew University in Jerusalem compelled me to pivot to a different project, which produced *Reason after Its Eclipse: On Late Critical Theory* four years later. At virtually the same time, however, other invitations provided opportunities to consider seemingly unrelated issues that would ultimately find their way into *Magical Nominalism*. In 2010, Ezra Mendelsohn had included me in a conference, also at the Hebrew University, to celebrate my old friend Steven Aschheim's retirement, which inspired me to explore the discourse of the event in French poststructuralist theory. Herbert Tucker and Rita Felski's invitation in 2011 to join a *New Literary History* forum on the vicissitudes of "context" generated an essay called "Historical Explanation and the Event," which allowed me to deepen my understanding of the issues. The link between photography and the event came, as it were, into focus when I gave talks in 2010 and 2011 at conferences organized at Williams College by Olga Shevchenko; the University of Wrocław by Leszek Koczanowicz; and Simon Fraser's Institute for the Humanities by Samir Gandesha. Composing the afterword shortly thereafter to the American writings of Siegfried Kracauer, edited by Johannes von Moltke and Kristy Rawson, led me to connect other dots by returning to a figure I had approached very differently in previous encounters with his legacy.

After the Mosse Lectures that became *Reason after Its Eclipse*, I still remained immersed in the robust international discussion of Critical Theory, which only intensified with the impending centennial of the founding of the Institute of Social Research in 2023. In addition to the various essays collected in *Splinters in Your Eye* (2020) and *Immanent Critiques* (2023), I also wrote one on Adorno's ambivalent attitude toward nominalism for a conference organized in 2013 at Harvard by Peter Gordon, Alexander Rehding, and Michael Rosen. It was presented the following year as well, at Simon Fraser University's Institute for the Humanities, at an event on the Frankfurt School organized by Samir Gandesha and Steven Taubeneck.

The simmering pot heated up a bit more when I returned to Frank Ankersmit's notion of sublime historical experience, for a 2018 forum on his oeuvre organized by Eugen Zeleňák and Marek Tamm in the *Journal of the Philosophy of History*. I presented its argument at Oxford the same year in a lecture series on the politics of representation organized by Gautham Shiralagi and Saul Nelson. Although sublime historical experience had been discussed earlier in *Songs of Experience* (2006), I was now able to link it with photography and interpret it in terms of magical nominalism.

Participating in a symposium in 2014 at Berkeley's Townsend Center for the Humanities organized by Alan Tansman with Hayden White, Harry Harootunian, and Ethan Kleinberg, which dealt with the work of Ankersmit's Groningen colleague Eelco Runia, had alerted me to a larger context in which it might be situated. I came to call it the new experientialism in a contribution to a collection edited by Christian B. Miller and Ryan West titled *Integrity, Honesty, and Truth Seeking* (2020).

In 2018, I first encountered the remarkable work of the Polish scholar of Jewish studies Agata Bielek-Robson, whose investigations of "Jewish nominalism" opened my eyes to a tradition that dovetailed in intriguing ways with its magical counterpart. Initially through correspondence and then through personal meetings, my understanding of the issues was deepened, especially of Benjamin's contribution to the discourse explored in this book. Agata was also among those who responded to earlier drafts, either in part or as a whole, of the manuscript.

Let me acknowledge with genuine gratitude additional encouraging and constructive readings by Susan Buck-Morss, Josef Chytry, Robert Kaufman, Robert Hullot-Kentor, Anthony Long, and Michael Morgan. Special thanks go to Peter Gordon, who provided a detailed response to the final draft no less acute than the three excellent reports by anonymous readers for the University of Chicago Press. Conversations with Megan A. O'Connor, who completed an excellent Berkeley English Department dissertation in 2019 on "Nominalism, Romanticism, Negative Dialectics," also proved very beneficial. I am deeply indebted as well to Darrin McMahon, long ago an outstanding Berkeley undergraduate in intellectual history and now a distinguished practitioner in our field, for welcoming the book to his series The Life of Ideas at the University of Chicago Press, and to Dylan Montanari, Stephen Twilley, and Fabiola Enríquez for guiding it efficiently through the publication process. Thanks are owed as well to Trevor Perri for his copyediting and to Elizabeth Bartmess, the 2023 winner of the Purple Pen Contest for New Indexers for her work on *Immanent Critiques*, for preparing this index as well.

As in the past, any acknowledgment for help with work has to culminate with a recognition of the loving support I have received in life from my family. Without Shana, Rebecca, Grayson, Frankie, Sammy, Ryeland, Sidney, and Beth, I would not have known that sparks of enchantment still exist in our increasingly bleak world. And as always, I owe an inestimable debt, intellectual as well as personal, to Catherine Gallagher, for fifty years the singular companion of whatever route I may have wisely or foolishly taken, and the bright star whose light still guides me on.

Foreshadowings and preliminary versions of sections of the book have appeared in the following venues:

"Magical Nominalism: Photography and the Re-enchantment of the World," *Culture, Theory and Critique* 50, nos. 2–3 (July–November, 2009); reprinted in *The Pictorial Turn*, ed. Neal Curtis (London: Routledge, 2010), and *Transvisuality: The Cultural Dimension of Visuality*, ed. Tore Kristensen, Anders Michelsen, and Frauke Wiegand, vol. 1, *Boundaries and Creative Openings* (Liverpool: Liverpool University Press, 2013).

"Photography and the Event," in *Discussing Modernity: A Dialogue with Martin Jay*, ed. Dorota Koczanowicz, Leszek Koczanowicz, and David Schauffler (Amsterdam: Rodopi, 2013); and *Double Exposure: Memory and Photography*, ed. Olga Shevchenko (New Brunswick, NJ: Transaction, 2014); in Polish in *Tetksty Drugie* 5 (2011).

"Siegfried Kracauer: Magical Nominalist," in *Siegfried Kracauer's American Writings*, ed. Johannes von Moltke and Kristy Rawson (Berkeley: University of California Press, 2012); in French in Martin Jay, *Kracauer l'exilé* (Paris: Bord de l'eau, 2014).

"Historicism and the Event," in *Against the Grain: Jewish Intellectuals in Hard Times*, ed. Ezra Mendelsohn, Stefani Hoffman, and Richard I. Cohen (New York: Berghahn, 2014), in German in *Können Wir der Geschichte Entkommen? Geschichtsphilosophie am Beginn des 21. Jahrhunderts*, ed. Christian Schmidt (Frankfurt: Campus, 2013).

"Adorno and Musical Nominalism," *New German Critique* 129 (September 2016), published by Duke University Press; in Italian in *Aisthema* 6, no. 1 (2019); in Spanish in *Revista Iconoclasia* 2 (2020); in Chinese in *Journal of Guangzhou University* 19, no. 6 (2020).

"Sublime Historical Experience, Real Presence and Photography," *Journal of the Philosophy of History* 12 (2018); in Spanish in *Revista de Filosofía Universidad Iberoamericana* 53, no. 1 (2021).

Notes

Preface

1. Theodor W. Adorno, "Late Style in Beethoven," in *Essays on Music*, ed. Richard Leppert, trans. Susan H. Gillespie (Berkeley, 2002); Edward W. Said, *On Late Style: Music and Literature against the Grain* (New York, 2007); Linda Hutcheon and Michael Hutcheon, "Late Style(s): The Ageism of the Singular," *Occasion: Interdisciplinary Studies in the Humanities* 4 (2012); and Gordon McMullan and Sam Smiles, eds., *Late Style and Its Discontents: Essays in Art, Literature and Music* (New York, 2016).

2. Said, *On Late Style*, 12.

3. For my more positive assessment, see Martin Jay, *Genesis and Validity: The Theory and Practice of Intellectual History* (Philadelphia, 2022).

4. Hayden White, *Metahistory: The Historical Imagination in Nineteenth-Century Europe* (Baltimore, 1975).

5. For an attempt to apply the category to the great cultural historian Johan Huizinga, the author of *The Waning of the Middle Ages* (or as it has recently been retranslated *The Autumn of the Middle Ages*), see Birger Vanwesenbeeck, "Huizinga, Theorist of Lateness?," in *Rereading Huizinga: Autumn of the Middle Ages, a Century Later*, ed. Peter Arnade, Martha Howell, and Anton van der Lem (Amsterdam, 2019). He notes that for both Adorno and Huizinga "the interest in late style is apparently inseparable from their mode of writing about it. This is, of course, because both Adorno and Huizinga saw themselves as latecomers to the respective cultures in which they lived so that their late-style writings have a comparable performative quality to them, one that compels their authors to 'act out' the very late-style strategies they write about. What is to be gained strategically from such an approach is that, like their subjects, they, too, seek to stall the flow of time, if only temporarily. For what characterizes the latecomer in any given period, whether they be a musician, a painter, a historian, or a philosopher, is the implicit desire to stop or move beyond time" (256). Huizinga, however, was only forty-nine when *The Waning* was first published in 1919 and lived until 1945, so it is hard to attribute his interest in lateness to his own looming death.

6. For an account of historians who have succumbed to this temptation, see Jeremy D. Popkin, *History, Historians, and Autobiography* (Chicago, 2005).

7. The dissertation, completed for my doctorate at Harvard in 1971, was titled "The Frankfurt School: An Intellectual History of the *Institut für Sozialforschung*, 1923–1950." It was published as a book two years later by Little, Brown in Boston as *The Dialectical Imagination: A History of the Frankfurt School and the Institute of Social Research, 1923–1950*,

8. As Max Horkheimer's gracious introduction showed, he felt comfortable with the results, as did Herbert Marcuse, Leo Löwenthal, Felix Weil, and Friedrich Pollock. Erich Fromm, however, was disappointed, as he made clear after the book was published. Whether or not Adorno, who expressed skepticism about the dissertation's chances in a letter he sent to Marcuse in 1969, would have approved, can only be conjectured, as he died two years before it was completed.

9. The Kracauer project led to several individual essays, which were only assembled many years later in a French translation as *Kracauer l'exilé* (Paris, 2013); the intellectual portrait of Adorno appeared as a volume in the Modern Masters series edited by Frank Kermode in 1985. The latter, however, pushed a bit beyond the traditional limits of intellectual biography by including the teleological pull of deconstruction in the force field of "influences" in which I situated Adorno's thought.

10. Martin Jay, *Cultural Semantics: Keywords of Our Time* (Amherst, MA, 1998).

11. Martin Jay, *Marxism and Totality: The Adventures of a Concept from Lukács to Habermas* (Berkeley, 1984); *Songs of Experience: Modern European and American Variations on a Universal Theme* (Berkeley, 2004); *Reason After its Eclipse: On Late Critical Theory* (Madison, WI, 2016); *Downcast Eyes: The Denigration of Vision in Twentieth-Century French Thought* (Berkeley, 1993); and *The Virtues of Mendacity: On Lying in Politics* (Charlottesville, VA, 2010).

12. "Ocularcentrism" may have been more a term of art than the others but would easily have been understood as an object of their critiques.

13. Reduced to its essentials, the controversy involved the inclusion of nonhumanist Marxists like Louis Althusser, Galvano della Volpe, and Lucio Colletti in the category. I opted for the broad-church version of Western Marxism adopted by Perry Anderson, and included them.

14. An accompanying essay, "Experience in America," in *Experience*, ed. Nadia Tazi (New York, 2004) focused on the distinctly American history of the term. This collection in the Keywords series included comparable essays for Africa, Europe, China, India, and the Arab world.

15. James Clifford, *The Predicament of Culture: Twentieth-Century Ethnography, Literature and Art* (Cambridge, MA, 1988), 270, cited in *Downcast Eyes*, 16.

16. For my account of one such response, with all its attendant anxieties and ambiguities, see Martin Jay, "Waiting to Hear from Derrida," in *Essays from the Edge: Parerga and Paralipomena* (Charlottesville, VA, 2011).

17. See Agata Bielik-Robson, *Jewish Cryptotheologies of Late Modernity: Philosophical Marranos* (New York, 2014). As her subtitle indicates, she locates it, at least metaphorically, in an underground tradition of Jewish thought stretching from Spinoza to Derrida.

18. Adorno, "Late Style in Beethoven," 566.

19. Adorno, "Late Style in Beethoven," 567.

20. Adorno, "Late Style in Beethoven," 567.

21. Adorno, "Late Style in Beethoven," 564.

22. The parallel here is, to be sure, imprecise. The constitutive power in a reflective judgment is assigned by Kant to the a priori schemas of the transcendental mind, which informs all human cognition, whereas the constitutive power of the individual artist is his or her unique expressive imagination. But what unites both is the priority given subjective imposition over receptivity to the imperatives of what it masters or shapes.

23. Giorgio Agamben, "What Is a Paradigm?," in *The Signature of All Things: On Method*, trans. Luca D'Isanto with Kevin Attell (New York, 2009).

24. Its etymological root is often understood slightly differently as *paradeiknynai,* which is translated as "show side by side."

25. Agamben, "What Is a Paradigm?," 18.

26. Agamben, "What Is a Paradigm?," 20.

27. See, for example, *Force Fields: Between Intellectual History and Cultural Critique* (New York, 1993). It was also introduced in my intellectual biography of Adorno to identify the constellation of influences that were juxtaposed in his work. In addition, it has served as the title of the biannual column I have contributed to *Salmagundi* since 1987.

28. Agamben, "What Is a Paradigm?," 32.

29. Agamben, "Theory of Signatures," in *The Signature of All Things,* 55.

30. Walter Benjamin, "The Task of the Translator," in *Illuminations: Essays and Reflections,* ed. Hannah Arendt, trans. Harry Zohn (New York, 1969). Although Adorno did not write extensively on translation, he admired this essay. See Susan H. Gillespie, "The Possibility of Translation," *boundary 2* 48, no. 1 (2021): 54.

31. Étienne Balibar, *On Universals: Constructing and Deconstructing Community,* trans. Joshua David Jordan (New York, 2020), 77–78.

32. See Alexander Stern, *The Fall of Language: Benjamin and Wittgenstein on Meaning* (Cambridge, MA, 2019). Both Wittgenstein and Benjamin, he argues, "see the primary obstacle to clear philosophical vision as a drive to give formal definitions of general terms—concepts. Both propose to resolve this problem by way of returning our attention in some sense to the phenomena themselves. . . . Instead of the rigid, conventional understanding of concepts, Wittgenstein proposes that we understand the uses of terms as 'families,' whose instances relate to each other via various kinds of similarities, resemblances or affinities (*Verwandtschaften*) 'overlapping and criss-crossing'" (343–45). For another discussion of Wittgenstein's approach, see Renford Brambrough, "Universals and Family Resemblances," in *Universals and Particulars,* ed. Michael J. Loux (Notre Dame, IN, 1976).

33. See for example, Timothy Williamson, "Clarifying Terms," in *Philosophical Method: A Very Short Introduction* (Oxford, 2020).

34. Adorno, "Late Style in Beethoven," 567.

Introduction

1. For an earlier consideration of this question, see Martin Jay, "1990: Straddling a Watershed?," in *Essays from the Edge: Parerga and Paralipomena* (Charlottesville, VA, 2011).

2. Virginia Woolf, *Collected Essays,* vol. 1 (London, 1966), 320. What allowed her to make this retrospective claim in 1924 has been often discussed, for example, by Edwin J. Kenney Jr., "The Moment, 1910: Virginia Woolf, Arnold Bennett, and Turn of the Century Consciousness," *Colby Quarterly* 13, no. 1 (March, 1977). He points not only to the death of King Edward VII but also to the first postimpressionism Exhibition in London, which shocked British aesthetic sensibilities.

3. There were, of course, earlier post factum threshold namings, for example between BC and AD. Historians often credit the usage of *Anno Domini* to the sixth-century monk Dionysius Exiguus, with BC (before Christ) coming much later, perhaps in the seventeenth or eighteenth centuries. See Lynn Hunt, *Measuring Time, Making History* (New York, 2008). The difference is that these were not self-conscious retrospective impositions but rather understood to reflect objective changes in history, sacred as well as profane. The contemporary BCE/CE (Before the Common Era / Common Era) alternative, on the other hand, is inherently nominalist.

4. For a discussion of these oppositional terms, which emerged in the fifteenth century, see Heiko A. Oberman, "Via Antiqua and Via Moderna: Late Medieval Prolegomena to Early Reformation Thought," *Journal of the History of Ideas* 48, no. 1 (January–March, 1987).

5. The anecdote is recorded by Simplicius, who also noted Plato's reply: "No, for you have the eye with which a horse is seen, but you have not yet acquired the eye to see horseness." See W. K. C. Guthrie, *The Sophists* (Cambridge, 1971), 214. It should also be noted that nominalist arguments arose in other philosophical and religious traditions, for example, in the Buddhist critiques of Hindu realism in India.

6. Porphyry's Greek text was a third-century introduction to Aristotle's *Categories*. See Paul Vincent Spade, "Boethius against Universals: The Arguments in the *Second Commentary on Porphyry*," (unpublished manuscript, 1996).

7. For discussions of twelfth-century nominalism, see the special issue of *Vivarium* 30, no. 1 (1992). It focuses on the schools of thinkers called *Nominales* or *Nominalis*, terms used for the first time after 1140.

8. His name, which in Latin was *Gulielmus Occamus*, is sometimes rendered as William of Occam, and refers to the town in Surrey from which he came. In the citations that follow, we will adopt whichever spelling is employed by the author.

9. For the nuances, see, for example, Edward Grant, "The Effect of the Condemnation of 1277," *The Cambridge History of Later Medieval Philosophy*, ed. Normann Kretzmann, Anthony Kenny, Jan Pinborg, and Eleonore Stump (London, 1982); John F. Wippel, "The Condemnations of 1270 and 1277 at Paris," *The Journal of Medieval and Renaissance Studies* 7 (1995); J. M. M. H. Thijssen, "1277 Revisited: A New Interpretation of the Doctrinal Investigations of Thomas Aquinas and Giles of Rome," *Vivarium* 35, no. 1 (1997). Also very helpful is Thijssen's "Condemnation of 1277," *Stanford Encyclopedia of Philosophy*, published January 30, 2003; substantive revision December 18, 2023, https://plato.stanford.edu/entries/condemnation/#:~:text=On%20March%207%2C%201277%2C%20the,of%20arts%20under%20his%20jurisdiction.

10. Randall Collins, *The Sociology of Philosophies: A Global Theory of Intellectual Change* (Cambridge, MA, 1998), 47.

11. For a discussion of Duhem's interpretation of 1277 as crucial for modern science, see John E. Murdoch, "Pierre Duhem and the History of Late Medieval Science and Philosophy in the Latin West," in *Gli studi di filosofia medievale fra otto e novecento*, ed. Ruedi Imbach and Alfonso Maieru (Rome, 1991). Anneliese Meier's major contribution was *Studien zur Naturphilosophie der Spätscholastik*, 5 vols. (Rome, 1949–58), which Hans Blumenberg discussed in a long review called "Die Vorbereitung der Neuzeit" in *Philosophische Rundschau* 9 (1961). He then wrote *The Legitimacy of the Modern Age*, trans. Robert M. Wallace (Cambridge, MA, 1983) and *The Genesis of the Copernican World*, trans. Robert M. Wallace (Cambridge, MA, 1987). Michael Allen Gillespie, *The Theological Origins of Modernity* (Chicago, 2008) developed the argument further. For other accounts of the role nominalism played in the origins of modern science, see Louis Dupré, *Passage to Modernity: An Essay in the Hermeneutics of Nature and Culture* (New Haven, 1993); and Edward B. Davis, "Rationalism, Voluntarism, and Seventeenth-Century Science," in *The Role of Beliefs in the Natural Sciences, Facets of Faith and Science*, vol. 3, ed. Jitse M. van der Meer (Lanham, 1996).

12. Blumenberg, *The Legitimacy of the Modern Age*, 160. Although here he posited a specific threshold moment, elsewhere Blumenberg was aware of the conventionalist nature of such an exercise. In *Work on Myth*, trans. Robert M. Wallace (Cambridge, MA, 1985), he

admitted that "insecurity and lack of confidence, as affective aspects of the unfathomability of time, are phenomena that smolder for long periods, corrupting subcutaneously above all by constraining people to set up dividing lines, turning points, indicators, and means of orientation to which expectations and apprehensions are attached, as in the fin de siècle" (99). In *The Legitimacy of the Modern Age*, he also conceded that "the epochal turning is an imperceptible frontier, bound to no crucial date or event" (469) and acknowledged that "the Middle Ages and the modern age existed for a good bit of history intermeshed or side by side, or at any rate without the phenotypical distinction" (470). In his own work, in fact, Blumenberg generally resisted a radical incommensurability between the medieval and modern epochs. Both *The Legitimacy of the Modern Age* and *The Genesis of the Copernican World* aim at uncovering the continuities, transformations, and reoccupations that link one era to another. He was explicitly critical of philosophers like Husserl who follow Descartes in positing an "absolute beginning" founding modernity. See *The Genesis of the Copernican World*, 404.

13. C. D. Blanton, "Medieval Currencies: Nominalism and Art," in *The Legitimacy of the Middle Ages: On the Unwritten History of Theory*, ed. Andrew Cole and D. Vance Smith (Durham, NC, 2010), 205. Blanton's larger point is that modernity's attempt to distinguish itself utterly from the Middle Ages fails to acknowledge how much it is haunted by what it claims to have left behind.

14. There was, of course, considerable variation and nuance in their integration. Even Thomas Aquinas, according to David Knowles, was not uncritical in his adoption of Aristotle: "He accepts his metaphysics almost in entirety, but his world-system only with reservations, and for all the higher levels of Christian life, he repeatedly asserts Aristotle's incompetence." *The Evolution of Medieval Thought* (New York, 1962), 264–65.

15. Blumenberg, *The Legitimacy of the Modern Age*, part 2. Gnosticism, it should be noted, has itself long been a highly contested term, both historically and conceptually. For a trenchant account of the debates over its meaning and the need to overcome it yet again in the early twentieth century, focusing on the work of the German Jewish philosopher Hans Jonas, see Benjamin Lazier, *God Interrupted: Heresy and the European Imagination between the World Wars* (Princeton, 2008), part 1. Jonas did not share Blumenberg's belief that human "self-assertion" had really served as a successful response to the challenge of gnostic acosmism.

16. The distinction between angelic "intelligence" and human "reason" is discussed by Lorraine Daston in "Intelligence: Angelic, Animal, Human," in *Thinking with Animals: New Perspectives on Anthropocentrism*, ed. Lorraine Daston and Gregg Mitman (New York, 2005). The former was more intuitive, the latter more discursive. Whether or not reason and intelligence were synonymous, both were potentially in tension with the voluntarist principle of divine omnipotence.

17. Amos Funkenstein, *Theology and the Scientific Imagination* (Princeton, 1986), 52.

18. For discussions of the parallels between Scholasticism and Gothic architecture, see Hans Sedlmeyer, *Die Entstehung der Kathedrale* (Zurich, 1950) and Günter Bandmann, *Mittelalterliche Architektur als Bedeutungsträger* (Berlin, 1951); Erwin Panofsky, *Gothic Architecture and Scholasticism* (New York, 1957); and Otto Georg von Simson, *The Gothic Cathedral: Origins of Gothic Architecture and the Medieval Concept of Order* (Princeton, 1987).

19. The mendicant Franciscan Order (or Order of Friars Minor) was founded in 1209 by Giovanni di Pietro di Bernardone, who took the name of Francis of Assisi. The Franciscans were notable for their insistence on following the example of Jesus and living the humble, "primitive" life of poverty that existed before the establishment of the church, while devoting themselves to charity. The Dominican Order, also called the Order of Preachers, was

founded in 1216 by the Spanish priest Dominic of Caleruega. It was dedicated primarily to the education of the faith as well as preaching church doctrine, often understood in Thomist terms, for which its members became known as the "hounds of the Gospel." By 1300, there were some 28,000 Franciscans and 12,000 Dominicans. Not only were the Franciscans more numerous, but they also were powerful in the Roman Curia. See Robert W. Southern, *Western Society and the Church in the Middle Ages* (Cambridge, 1970), 285.

20. See, for example, Walter J. Ong, *Ramus, Method and the Decay of Dialogue* (Cambridge, MA 1983), 146–47. He notes that the arts faculty was closely associated with the medical, which stressed physical reality and quantitative calculation. He also points out that Ockham never actually finished his theological training, which led to his nickname *Venerabilis Inceptor* gently mocking his turning into a "venerable beginner" (134). Sometimes "inceptor" is wrongly taken to mean the founder of the nominalist tradition.

21. Gillespie, *The Theological Origins of Modernity*, 21. For doubts that leading Aristotelians like Siger of Brabant were closet Latin Averroists, see Knowles, *The Evolution of Medieval Thought*, 276. For a positive evaluation of the Islamic Aristotelians as more materialist and naturalist than their Christian counterparts, see Ernst Bloch, *Avicenna and the Aristotelian Left*, trans. Loren Goldman and Peter Thompson (New York, 2019). In Islamic Kalām (the speculative study of the word of God), there was also a tradition stressing God's omnipotent will, which began with Al-Ash'ari in the tenth century and culminated with al-Ghazali (ca. 1058–1111). In fact, Hans Jonas even argues that they were the first monotheistic theologians to stress will over reason. See his "Jewish and Christian Elements in Philosophy: Their Share in the Emergence of the Modern Mind," in *Philosophical Essays: From Ancient Creed to Technological Man* (Englewood Cliffs, NJ, 1974), 30–31. Contemporary Radical Orthodox theologians like John Milbank, Philip Blond, and Conor Cunningham often trace the nihilism they see latent in nominalism to the Asharite tradition.

22. For an account of the medieval reception of Stoicism, see Gerard Verbeke, *The Presence of Stoicism in Medieval Thought* (Washington, DC, 1983). Because of their materialist resistance to universal Platonic Ideas, the Stoics are often seen as nominalists avant la lettre.

23. For a recent effort to resuscitate his project, pitting it against the modern disintegration of cosmic harmonies typified by Kant, see Susan Buck-Morss, *Year I: A Philosophical Recounting* (Cambridge, MA, 2021), chap. 3.

24. The efforts of Greek philosophers to tame unruly nature, driven by instinctual desires and prone to unpredictable catastrophes, by optimistically redefining it as a cosmic harmony may have already felt forced. The attempt to incorporate that effort into a theology of divine creation only exacerbated the problem. "From its earliest beginnings," Willemien Otten has argued, "Christianity has had trouble finding a proper role for nature. . . . Throughout the early rise of Christianity, it quickly became clear that ancient *natura*, hard-pressed as it was to conform to Neoplatonic structure, would likely rebel against its newly imposed biblical Divine Maker, especially if accepting the cosmic order of Christianity meant that *natura* was forced into a role of passive confinement." In other words, the subjugation of natural materiality in pagan cosmologies was reinforced by the claim that nature was created *ex nihilo* by an omniscient divinity. Willemien Otten, "Nature as a Religious Force in Eriugena and Emerson," in *Religion: Beyond a Concept*, ed. Hent de Vries (New York, 2008), 354. She claims that a successful alternative, which neither subjugated nature nor sought to escape from it, was posited by John Scotus Eriugena (807–877) and later by Emerson, but it remained outside mainstream theology.

25. See John Marenbon, *Pagans and Philosophers: The Problem of Paganism from Augustine to Leibniz* (Princeton, 2015).

26. Tertullian, *The Prescription against Heretics*, 7, from Peter Holmes translation of 1870, available at The Tertullian Project, last modified February 3, 1998, http://www.tertullian.org/anf/anf03/anf03-24.htm. Tertullian's identification of his antirationalist version of faith with "Jerusalem" was a tendentious reading of the Hebrew Bible. See, Yoram Hazony, "Jerusalem and Carthage," *Hebraic Political Studies* 3, no. 3 (2008). He argues that the Jewish tradition was far less hostile to rationality than implied by Tertullian, and that it was in fact symbolically closer to Athens than to Carthage, Tertullian's home. The opposition he posited, however, still continues to reverberate in contemporary discussions of the relationship between reason and revelation. See, for example, Leora F. Batnitzky, "On Reaffirming a Distinction between Athens and Jerusalem," *Hebraic Political Studies* 2, no. 2 (2007).

27. For discussions of the complex theological considerations of this question in medieval thought, Islamic and Jewish as well as Christian, see Tamar Rudavsky, ed., *Divine Omniscience and Omnipotence in Medieval Philosophy: Islamic, Jewish and Christian Perspectives* (Dordrecht, 1985). Plato himself had already pondered the same issue in his dialogue *Euthyphro*, where the question is put: "Is the pious loved by the gods because it is pious, or is it pious because it is loved by the gods?" (10a). Plato could reply to Euthyphro, who argued for the latter alternative, that the gods might disagree, so that there must be an inherent quality in goodness. This ploy was, however, not available to proponents of monotheism.

28. Arthur Lovejoy, *The Great Chain of Being: A Study of the History of an Idea* (New York, 1965), 82–83.

29. As a result, Aquinas was attacked from both sides. In fact, one of the critical voices supporting the Condemnation of 1277, Henry of Ghent, had criticized him for not giving priority to God's essential Ideas before their existential creation.

30. Blumenberg, *The Genesis of the Copernican World*, 164.

31. See William J. Courtenay, "The Dialectic of Omnipotence in the High and Late Middle Ages," in *Divine Omniscience and Omnipotence in Medieval Philosophy*, ed. Rudavsky; Funkenstein, *Theology and the Scientific Imagination*, 124–52; Lawrence Moonan, *Divine Power. The Medieval Power Distinction up to its Adoption by Albert, Bonaventure and Aquinas* (Oxford, 1994); Emanuele Castrucci, *On the Idea of Potency: Juridical and Theological Roots of the Western Cultural Tradition* (Edinburgh, 2016); and Theo Kobusch, "The Possible and the Impossible: *potentia absoluta* and *potentia ordinata* under Close Scrutiny," in *The Legacy of Early Franciscan Thought*, ed. Lydia Schumacher (Berlin, 2021). The distinction continued to inform theological debates well after the end of the Middle Ages. For a fine-grained account of the controversies surrounding it since its beginnings and well into the early modern period, see Francis Oakley, "The Absolute and Ordained Power of God in Sixteenth- and Seventeenth-Century Theology," *Journal of the History of Ideas* 59, no. 3 (1998). Its political echo can be heard in the claim that a pope had a *plenitudo potestatis* putting him above civil law, forwarded by defenders of papal power like the thirteenth-century canonist Hostiensis.

32. Courtenoy, "The Dialectic of Omnipotence," 254.

33. Funkenstein, *Theology and the Scientific Imagination*, 125.

34. Blumenberg, *The Legitimacy of the Modern Age*, 152.

35. According to Blumenberg, "The contact between *omnipotence* and *infinity*, which produces the initial spark [for human 'originary creativity'], apparently occurs around

the eleventh century, when it becomes necessary to systematize the doctrine of divine omnipotence against the 'dialecticians.'" "'Imitation of Nature': Toward a Prehistory of the Idea of the Creative Being," in *History, Metaphors, Fables: A Hans Blumenberg Reader*, ed. and trans. Hannes Bajohr, Florian Fuchs, and Joe Paul Kroll (Ithaca, 2020), 345.

36. In his *Meditations on First Philosophy* of 1641, Descartes considered the possibility that either an omnipotent God or an evil demon could be the source of deception, but reasoned that as a perfect being, God could not be a deceiver. For an argument that claims anxiety over the possibility that God might deceive us was more important than Descartes's comforting conclusion in launching modernity, see Agata Bielek-Robson, "*I Hurt, Therefore I Am*: Descartes with Blumenberg (and Job)," in *Interrogating Modernity: Debates with Hans Blumenberg*, ed. Bielek-Robson and Whistler.

37. Awareness of these theological origins did not, however, entirely disappear. For a discussion of their importance for certain modernist artists, see Erik Tonning, "Modernism, Nominalism and the Hidden God in Samuel Beckett, Wallace Stevens and David Jones," *Literature & Theology* 37, no. 1 (2023).

38. Blumenberg argues that nominalism was mistakenly understood by some as the restoration of the gnostic disdain for the world. For his account of how this assumption colored the reception of Copernicus and his followers, who were accused of playing "the role of the early Christians who were suspected of wanting the world's downfall," see Blumenberg, *The Genesis of the Copernican World*, 271. He argues that modern science can be better understood as the second overcoming of gnosticism rather than its simple return.

39. The testimony of religious experience as opposed to reasoned argumentation has had a powerful appeal for many believers of different faiths over the years. For a discussion of its implications, see Martin Jay, *Songs of Experience: Modern European and American Variations on a Universal Theme* (Berkeley, 2004), chap. 3.

40. Luther was himself heavily influenced by nominalism, although critical of some of its accompanying theological doctrines. See Graham White, *Luther as Nominalist: A Study of the Logical Methods Used in Martin Luther's Disputations in the Light of their Medieval Background* (Helsinki, 1994); Thomas Osborne, "Faith, Philosophy and the Nominalist Background to Luther's Defense of the Real Presence," *Journal of the History of Ideas* 63, no. 1 (January, 2002); Heiko A. Oberman, *Man Between God and the Devil* (New Haven, 2006); and Theodor Dieter, "Luther as Late Medieval Theologian: His Positive and Negative Use of Nominalism and Realism," in *The Oxford Handbook of Martin Luther's Theology*, ed. Robert Kolb, Irene Dingel, and L'ubomír Batka (Oxford, 2014). There were, to be sure, later Protestants who resisted the lure of nominalism. See the five articles of Seth Synder, "The Myth of Protestant Nominalism," *Ad Fontes*, September 13, 2022, to December 2, 2022, https://adfontesjournal.com/church-history/the-myth-of-protesant-nominalism-pt-1-flawed-genealogies-of-modernity/.

41. Heiko A. Oberman, *The Harvest of Medieval Theology: Gabriel Biel and Late Medieval Nominalism* (Grand Rapids, MI, 2001).

42. Luther, to be sure, held on to the pre-Copernican cosmology, as we know from remarks he made in his *Table Talk*, on June 4, 1539. The antonym to scripture could also be understood as tradition, which was a pillar of the Catholic Church. The other *solae* promoted by the Reformation were *fide* (faith) and *gratia* (grace).

43. For a recent account of its abiding power, see Niklaus Largier, *Figures of Possibility: Aesthetic Experience, Mysticism, and the Play of the Senses* (Stanford, CA, 2022).

44. Perhaps the most eloquent expression of this lament is John Donne's poem "An Anatomy of the World. Wherein, by occasion of the untimely death of Mistress Elizabeth

Drury, the frailty and the decay of this whole world is represented. The First Anniversary" (1611), which contains the often quoted lines:

And new philosophy calls all in doubt,
The element of fire is quite put out;
The sun is lost, and th' earth, and no man's wit
Can well direct him where to look for it.
And freely men confess that this world's spent,
When in the planets, and the firmament
They seek so many new; they see that this
Is crumbled out again to his atomies.
'Tis all in pieces, all coherence gone;
All just supply, and all relation:
Prince, subject, father, son, are things forgot,
For every man alone thinks he hath got
To be a phoenix, and that then can be
None of that kind, of which he is, but he.

The "new philosophy" in question included the scientific revolution identified with Copernicus, but Donne was also familiar with nominalist challenges to Scholasticism. For one account of his complicated response, see Michael McCanles, "Paradox in Donne," *Studies in the Renaissance* 12 (1966).

45. Michel Blanchot, *The Writing of the Disaster*, trans. Ann Smock (Lincoln, NE, 1986), 2.

46. For a discussion of the threat of "demonic skepticism" unleashed by nominalism, see Gyula Klima and Alexander H. Hall, eds., *The Demonic Temptations of Medieval Nominalism* (Cambridge, 2011). The link with the demonic seems to have persisted into modern times. The first chapter of Paul Forster, *Peirce and the Threat of Nominalism* (Cambridge, 2011) is called "Nominalism as Demonic Doctrine."

47. The term was introduced in the Hebrew Bible in the Book of Isaiah: "Indeed, you are a hidden God, you God of Israel, the Savior." (45:15). It received especial notice during the Reformation in the works of Luther and Calvin, although it had been part of the theology of Aquinas and Nicolas of Cusa as well. For a historical materialist attempt to explore the social reasons for its special prominence among seventeenth-century French Jansenists, see Lucien Goldmann, *The Hidden God: A Study of Tragic Vision in the* Pensées *of Pascal and the Tragedies of Racine*, trans. Philip Thody (New York, 1964).

48. Blumenberg, *The Legitimacy of the Modern Age*, 200.

49. For a discussion of this fear and Ockham's attempt to answer it, see Marilyn McCord Adams, "Ockham on Will, Nature and Morality," in *The Cambridge Companion to Ockham*, ed. Paul Vincent Spade (Cambridge, 1999).

50. See William J. Bouwsma, "Anxiety and the Formation of Early Modern Culture," in *A Usable Past: Essays in European Cultural History* (Berkeley, 1990).

51. Infinity was, to be sure, already posited by certain ancient Greeks, for example Anaximander who argued that prior to the cosmos there was a primal chaos, or *apeiron*, which was boundless and unlimited. But Aristotle had argued that actual infinity, as opposed to potential infinity, was impossible, and most Greeks seem to have agreed with him. In the Hebrew Bible, God is called *Ein Sof*, which is usually translated as "the infinite" or "the boundless."

52. See David S. Landes, *Revolution in Time: Clocks and the Making of the Modern World* (Cambridge, MA, 1983).

53. See Jerrold Seigel, *The Idea of the Self: Thought and Experience in Western Europe since the Seventeenth Century* (Cambridge, 2005). He acknowledges that the premodern self was sometimes conceived as potentially split, but "these strains appeared differently, and more easily resolvable in classical theory because ancient culture gave access to a resource of which many moderns have deprived themselves, namely the belief that the world, like the self, is structured so as to fulfill intelligible moral ends" (51). And although there are medieval instances of lacerating self-scrutiny—for example, among members of monastic orders—"the Christian adaptation of ancient philosophy and cosmology provided a theoretical frame in which resolutions that would be denied to moderns were still possible" (53).

54. Bouwsma, "Anxiety and the Formation of Early Modern Culture," 180.

55. Blaise Pascal, *Pensées*, trans. W. F. Trotter, (New York, 1958), 61.

56. Georg Lukács, *Theory of the Novel*, trans. Anna Bostock (Cambridge, MA, 1971), 41.

57. See, for example, the twentieth-century Swiss theologian Hans Urs von Balthasar, who blamed what he saw as the relativist nihilism of modern life on "the catastrophe of nominalism" in *The God Question and Modern Man* (New York, 1967).

58. Gillespie, *The Theological Origins of Modernity*, chap. 1.

59. In his global study of the social networks disseminating philosophical ideas, Randall Collins notes that "it is tempting to portray a 'nominalist movement' springing up in rebellion against the metaphysical establishment, progressive thinkers unified around empiricism and taking many steps toward the eventual dominance of natural science. But William of Ockham himself has few personal pupils of significance, and his network soon peters out. Although there were henceforth many 'nominalists' and even 'Ockhamists,' these labels are loosely applied to a rather decentralized and diverse set of thinkers. Often these are terms of abuse, bestowing unity only through the ill will of opponents." *The Sociology of Philosophies*, 487.

60. For one account, see Daniel D. Novotny, "In Defense of Baroque Scholasticism," *Studia Neoaristotelica* 6, no. 2 (2009). It has been argued that the identification of Thomism as the quintessential theology/philosophy of the High Middle Ages was itself a projection backwards of the Counter-Reformation. See Knowles, *The Evolution of Medieval Thought*, 267.

61. In certain respects, however, nominalism and humanism complemented each other. As Bouwsma argues, "For both movements language ceased to link the mind with ultimate reality and so to identify the objective boundaries defining existence." "Anxiety and the Formation of Early Modern Culture," 175. The Cambridge Platonists, on the other hand, explicitly targeted nominalists like Hobbes and Calvin.

62. Josef Chytry, *Cosmotheism: Cytherean Sitings between Heraclitus and Kittler* (New York, 2020), 3–48. He notes that although Bruno, unlike Copernicus and Kepler, may have replaced belief in a closed world with an open universe containing an infinite number of worlds, he conceptualized the latter as a coherent and unified One. He contrasts their *Verzauberung* (enchantment) of the cosmos with the *Entzauberung* (disenchantment) of Galileo, Descartes, and Newton. In certain respects, cosmotheism can be considered a kind of immanentist theology opposed to the idea of a transcendent deity entirely outside of the world, and as such is at other end of the spectrum from the gnostic denigration of creation.

63. Although the great chain of being lingered, the implications for humans placed in its middle may not have always been as positive as they once might have been. Thus, in

Alexander Pope's *Essay on Man*, often seen as an emblematic example of the great chain argument, our species is defined with striking ambivalence:

> A being darkly wise and rudely great,
> With too much knowledge for the sceptic side,
> With too much weakness for the stoic pride,
> He hangs between; in doubt to act or rest;
> In doubt to deem himself a god or beast;
> In doubt his Mind or Body to prefer;
> Born but to die, and reas'ning but to err;
> . . .
> The glory, jest and riddle of the world.

64. Jacob Viner, *The Role of Providence in the Social Order: An Essay in Intellectual History* (Princeton, 1972); and Jonathan Sheehan and Dror Wahrman, *Invisible Hands: Self-Organization and the Eighteenth-Century* (Chicago, 2015).

65. Hans Blumenberg, *Work on Myth*, trans. Robert M. Wallace (Cambridge, MA, 1985), 106.

66. For a wide-ranging account of controversies over teleological design and mechanical causality, see Jessica Riskin, *The Restless Clock: A History of the Centuries-Long Argument over What Makes Living Thinks Tick* (Chicago, 2016).

67. See Pierre Hadot, *The Veil of Isis: An Essay on the History of the Idea of Nature*, trans. Michael Chase (Cambridge, MA, 2006), 247–82.

68. This phrase refers to the first translated title of Johan Huizinga's classic study, which was *The Waning of the Middle Ages*, trans. F. Hopman (New York, 1954). His quick dismissal of the importance of nominalism (p. 54) has, however, been disputed by later observers, for example, William J. Bouwsma, "*The Waning of the Middle Ages* Revisited," *A Usable Past*, 333.

69. Peter Gay, *The Enlightenment: An Interpretation*, vol. 1, *The Rise of Modern Paganism* (New York, 1966). Gay, to be sure, vigorously disputed attempts to read the Enlightenment as a secularized version of Scholastic theology, as evidenced by his sharp polemic against Carl L. Becker's *The Heavenly City of the Eighteenth-Century Philosophers* (New Haven, 1932) in *The Party of Humanity* (New York, 1964).

70. For an account of Spinoza's enduring influence in the German-speaking world, see Willi Goetschl, *Spinoza's Modernity: Mendelssohn, Lessing, and Heine* (Madison, WI, 2003). Spinoza has also been seen as the most potent source of the radical Enlightenment and modern democratic theory by Jonathan I. Israel, *Radical Enlightenment: Philosophy and the Making of Modernity, 1650–1750* (Oxford, 2001). He continued to roil the waters in Germany in the interwar period, causing what Benjamin Lazier in *God Interrupted* has called a new "pantheism controversy." Spinoza's unexpected impact on late twentieth-century French thought, so often thought to be Nietzschean or Heideggerian in inspiration, is demonstrated in Knox Peden, *Spinoza Contra Phenomenology: French Rationalism from Cavaillès to Deleuze* (Stanford, CA, 2014).

71. See Steven Nadler, *The Best of All Possible Worlds: A Story of Philosophers, God, and Evil in the Age of Reason* (Princeton, 2010), chap. 6.

72. As noted earlier, while Descartes speculated that both an omnipotent God and an evil demon could be the possible source of deception, he concluded that the former, as a perfect being, could not be a deceiver. And so our clear and distinct ideas were placed there innately through divine benevolence. In so arguing, Descartes smuggled back in a positive attribute of divinity, which a more rigorously apophatic theology had denied.

Whether or not he was himself firmly antinominalist is, however, uncertain. See, for example, Lawrence Nolan, "Descartes' Theory of Universals," *Philosophical Studies* 89 (1998), 161–80.

73. Joseph Urbas, "'Bi-Polar' Emerson: 'Nominalist *and* Realist,'" *The Pluralist* 8, no. 2 (2013).

74. In his *Lectures on the History of Philosophy*, Hegel wrote that the nominalists "grasped the true conception that individuation, the limitation of the universal, and indeed of what is most universal, Being and entity, is a negation" (80). In other words, the nominalist role in the epic narrative of the World Spirit is to negate the undialectical, abstract universalism of Scholastic rationalism and prepare the way for a more concrete, richly mediated universal in the future.

75. For a consideration of Heidegger's role in modern debates about realism and antirealism, including those in the analytic tradition, see Lee Braver, *A Thing of This World: A History of Continental Anti-Realism* (Evanston, 2008). The focus here is on the question of a mind-independent objective world more than on the reality of universals. See also Peter Eli Gordon, "Realism, Science, and the Deworlding of the World," in *A Companion to Phenomenology and Existentialism*, ed. Hubert L. Dreyfus and Mark A. Wrathall (Malden, MA, 2006). He criticizes the early Heidegger's claim that scientific knowledge can bypass the interpretive filter of cultural "worlds." In contrast, Heidegger's inspiration for what is called object-oriented ontology is praised in Graham Harman, "The Future of Continental Realism: Heidegger's Fourfold," *Chiasma* 3 (2018).

76. For a survey of the impact of neo-Thomism, see Rajesh Heynickx and Stéphane Symons, eds., *So What's New about Scholasticism? How Neo-Thomism Helped Shape the Twentieth Century* (Berlin, 2018).

77. See the discussion in Marc D. Guerra, ed., *Pope Benedict XVI and the Politics of Modernity* (Abingdon, 2014).

78. See Phillip Blond, ed., *Post-Secular Philosophy: Between Philosophy and Theology* (London, 1998).

79. Andrew Cole, *The Birth of Theory* (Chicago, 2014). Cole never mentions Ockham and nominalism.

80. See, for example, John Deely, *Four Ages of Understanding: The First Postmodernist Survey of Philosophy from Ancient Times to the Turn of the Twenty-first Century* (Toronto, 2001). He draws on C. S. Peirce's critique of nominalism to argue that postmodernism is a return to realism. See also Cornelis de Waal, "The History of Philosophy Conceived as a Struggle between Realism and Nominalism," *Semiotica* 179, nos. 1–4 (2010).

81. Charles Taylor, *A Secular Age* (Cambridge, MA, 2007), chap. 15.

82. Gillespie, *The Theological Origins of Modernity*, 40–41.

83. See Stefano Di Bella and Tad M. Schmaltz, eds., *The Problem of Universals in Early Modern Philosophy* (Oxford, 2017).

84. See, for example, Nolan, "Descartes' Theory of Universals," 161–80.

85. See Benson Mates, *The Philosophy of Leibniz: Metaphysics and Language* (Oxford, 1986).

86. See, for example, James K. Feibleman, "Was Spinoza a Nominalist?," *The Philosophical Review* 60, (1951), 386–89.

87. Charles Darwin, *The Origin of Species by Natural Selection* (London, 1910), 39.

88. See Megan Gannon, "Race Is a Social Category, Scientists Argue," *Scientific American*, February 5, 2016, https://www.scientificamerican.com/article/race-is-a-social-construct-scientists-argue/.

89. See Winthrop Jordan, "Historical Origins of the One-Drop Racial Rule in the United States," *The Journal of Mixed Race Studies* 1, no. 1 (2014). The essay was edited by Paul Spickard after Jordan's death.

90. Ernst Bloch, *The Spirit of Utopia*, trans. Anthony A. Nassar (Stanford, CA, 2000), 27. Precisely what Bloch might have meant by "mystical nominalism," a concept also later adopted by Gershom Scholem, has been difficult to say. In the introduction to Agata Bielik-Robson and Daniel H. Weiss, eds., *Tsimtsum and Modernity: Lurianic Heritage in Modern Philosophy and Theology* (Berlin, 2021), 1, the editors suggest it might have been inspired by Gustav Landauer's *Skepsis und Mystik: Versuche im Anschluß an Mauthners Sprachkritik* (Berlin, 1903), where Duns Scotus's notion of *haecceitas* is given a reading that combines mysticism with materialism.

91. For some help, see Otávio Bueno, "Nominalism in the Philosophy of Mathematics," *The Stanford Encyclopedia of Philosophy*, article published September 16, 2013; last modified June 29, 2020, https://plato.stanford.edu/archives/fall2020/entries/nominalism-mathematics/. The article begins by defining mathematical nominalism as "the view according to which either mathematical objects, relations, and structures do not exist at all, or they do not exist as abstract objects (they are neither located in space-time nor do they have causal powers)." For a discussion of its historical role in the development of a constructivist tradition in mathematics, see David Sepkowski, "Nominalism and Constructivism in Seventeenth-Century Mathematical Philosophy," *Historia Mathematica* 32, no. 1 (2005). He stresses the influence of nominalists like Pierre Gassendi, Isaac Barrow, and Thomas Hobbes even on Newton.

92. Agata Bielik-Robson, *Cryptotheologies of Late Modernity* (London, 2014), chap. 7.

93. Perhaps its most powerful impact has been in intellectual and cultural history, where vigorous debates occasioned by the work of Dominick LaCapra, Hayden White, Joan Wallach Scott, Reinhart Koselleck, David Harlan, Mark Poster, and others have roiled the waters for a generation. See, for example, John Toews, "Intellectual History After the Linguistic Turn: the Autonomy of Meaning and the Irreducibility of Experience," *American Historical Review* 92, no. 4 (1987); Anthony Pagden, "Rethinking the Linguistic Turn: Current Anxieties in Intellectual History," *Journal of the History of Ideas* 39, no. 3 (1988); Judith Surkis, "When Was the Linguistic Turn? A Genealogy," *American Historical Review* 117, no. 3 (2012).

Chapter One

1. William J. Courtenay, "Medieval Nominalism Reconsidered: 1972–1982," *Journal of the History of Ideas* 44, no. 1 (1983): 164. Included in Courtenay's many works on fourteenth-century philosophy is *Ockham and Ockhamism: Studies in the Dissemination and Impact of His Thought* (Leiden, 2008). The most substantial account of Ockham's life and thought is Marilyn McCord Adams, *William of Ockham*, 2 vols. (South Bend, IN, 1987).

2. Deborah Brown, "Hume and the Nominalist Tradition," *Canadian Journal of Philosophy* 42, sup. 1 (2012): 27.

3. Henry Veatch, *Realism and Nominalism Revisited* (Milwaukee, 1954), 60.

4. J. M. M. H. Thijssen, *Censure and Heresy at the University of Paris, 1200–1400* (Philadelphia, 1998). Their transgressions sometimes had a political as well as theological source in the tangled ecclesiastical struggles of the period, when the papacy was in Avignon (1309–76). See David Burr, "Scotus, Ockham and the Censure at Avignon," *Church History* 37, no. 2 (1968).

5. For discussions of the connections, see Richard J. Utz, ed, *Literary Nominalism and the Theory of Rereading Late Medieval Texts* (Lewiston, NY, 1995) and Hugo Keiper, Christoph Bode, and Richard. J. Utz, eds. *Nominalism and Literary Discourse: New Perspectives* (Atlanta, 1997). More specific analyses of Chaucer and nominalism include Russell A. Peck, "Chaucer and the Nominalist Questions," *Speculum* 53, no. 4 (1978): 745–60; and Holly Wallace Boucher, "Nominalism: The Difference for Chaucer and Boccaccio," *The Chaucer Review* 20, no. 3 (1986): 213–20.

6. Over the years, the issues raised by the controversy have continued to perplex philosophers and confounded historical consensus. Duns Scotus, for example, could be lauded as the "doctor subtilis" in his time, and then during the Renaissance, when humanists mocked medieval theologians for their obscurity, be turned into the prototype of the "dunce," wearing the pointed cap he had made famous. The task of sorting through all of the controversies is made even more difficult by the still incomplete editions of the leading figures' collected works, not all of which have been translated from Latin. In addition, they were theologians first and philosophers second, which meant that their contributions to philosophical issues were often interspersed in texts that had other agendas.

7. See Joël Biard, "Nominalism in the Later Middle Ages," *The Cambridge History of Medieval Philosophy*, ed. Robert Pasnau with Christina van Dyke (Cambridge, 2014), 661–73; and Gyula Klima, "The Medieval Problem of Universals," *Stanford Encyclopedia of Philosophy*, first published September 10, 2000; substantive revision February 27, 2022, https://plato.stanford.edu/entries/universals-medieval/.

8. Hans Blumenberg, *The Legitimacy of the Modern Age*, trans. Robert M. Wallace (Cambridge, MA, 1983); Michael Allen Gillespie, *The Theological Origins of Modernity* (Chicago, 2008); Jürgen Habermas, *Auch eine Geschichte der Philosophie*, vol. 1, *Die okzidentale Konstellation von Glauben und Wissen* (Frankfurt, 2020), 761–851.

9. Max Weber, *The Methodology of the Social Sciences*, ed. and trans. Edward A. Shils and Henry A. Finch (New York, 1997), 90.

10. Theodor W. Adorno, *Negative Dialectics*, trans. E. B. Ashton (New York, 1973), 10. Adorno's utopia, to be sure, always implied the faint possibility of its becoming actual, while Weber's remained only a methodological principle. That the Frankfurt School, despite its Hegelian leanings, could sometimes embrace Weber's method is illustrated by a letter Max Horkheimer sent to Franz Neumann on August 2, 1941, defending Friedrich Pollock's concept of "state capitalism": "Ideal types, in my view, should perform exactly the same function that they have in the essay [by Pollock]. . . . They create utopias, wonderful or hateful, against which reality is measured.' Max Horkheimer, *Gesammelte Schriften*, 19 vols., eds. Alfred Schmidt and Gunzelin Schmid Noerr (Frankfurt, 1985–96), 17:115–16.

11. For a discussion of Weber's nominalist epistemology, see Frédéric Vandenberghe, "Simmel and Weber as Ideal Typical Founders of Sociology," *Philosophy and Social Criticism* 25, no. 4 (1999).

12. There were, to be sure, nominalists, such as Buridan, who attempted to avoid a performative contradiction by distinguishing between "predicate essentialism," a linguistic construct, from "real essentialism." See Gyula Klima, "The Essentialist Nominalism of John Buridan," *The Review of Metaphysics* 58 (2005).

13. The concept of contingency can be traced back to Aristotle's *De Interpretatione*, where, Leszek Kolakowski tells us, it refers to judgments "which predicate of an object something which may or may not apply to it without altering its nature" and "denoted the state of a finite being that might or might not exist but was not necessary, i.e. its essence did not involve existence." *Main Currents of Marxism*, vol. 1, *The Founders*, trans. P. S. Falla

(Oxford, 1978), 12. For the nominalists, we might say it was existence without essence all the way down.

14. Paul Vincent Spade, "Ockham's Nominalist Metaphysics: Some Main Themes," in Paul Vincent Spade, ed., *The Cambridge Companion to Ockham* (Cambridge, 1999), 113.

15. Randall Collins, *The Sociology of Philosophies*, 519. What can also occur over time is a radical semantic shift in the meaning of a term. Although this did not happen in a drastic way with nominalism, "realism" turned around the seventeenth century from a term denoting belief in universal essences to one meaning a focus on the material world. It then later became an aesthetic term with various meanings, opposed at times to fantasy, at others to naturalism. In other realms, such as political theory, it came to be contrasted with "idealism" or "utopianism." Among contemporary philosophers, it still generates lively discussions, but not often about universals. See, for example, Cora Diamond, *The Realistic Spirit: Wittgenstein, Philosophy, and the Mind* (Cambridge, MA, 1995).

16. The distinction between philosophy as an aide to living a good or virtuous life and philosophy as an intellectual discipline goes back as far as the Greeks. Figures like Diogenes the Cynic and Socrates were exemplars of philosophically informed lives, while others like Aristotle were known more for their thought alone (an attitude expressed in Heidegger's famous claim: "'What was Aristotle's life?' Well, the answer lay in a single sentence: 'He was born, he thought, he died.' And all the rest is pure anecdote."). Modern thinkers like Nietzsche and Foucault sought to revive the idea of philosophy as a guide to life. The attenuation of the link between nominalism and its Franciscan roots meant it never really became a philosophy of living well or virtuously.

17. See, for example, D. M. Armstrong, *Nominalism and Realism: Universals and Scientific Realism* (Cambridge, 1978). His *Universals: An Opinionated Introduction* (Boulder, 1989) makes a case for the realism of universals. For defenses of the last two of these variants, see Gonzalo Rodriguez-Pereyra, *Resemblance Nominalism: A Solution to the Problem of Universals* (Oxford, 2002) and Guido Imaguire, *Priority Nominalism: Grounding Ostrich Nominalism as a Solution to the Problem of Universals* (Berlin, 2018).

18. See Gonzalo Rodriguez-Pereyra, "Nominalism in Metaphysics," *The Stanford Encyclopedia of Philosophy*, first published February 11, 2008; substantive revision April 1, 2015, https://plato.stanford.edu/archives/sum2019/entries/nominalism-metaphysics.

19. At times, disputes arise over whether or not the two are compatible, as in the work of the American philosopher Wilfred Sellars, normally called an advocate of "psychological nominalism." See Ryan Simonelli, "Sellars' Ontological Nominalism," *European Journal of Philosophy* (2021).

20. Trope nominalism argues that particularized properties are not instances of universals, but rather "abstract particulars," or tropes, and that complex particulars are actually bundles of tropes. For an attempt to identify Ockham as a trope nominalist avant la lettre, see Stephen E. Lahey, "William Ockham and Trope Nominalism," *Franciscan Studies* 55 (1998) and Nick Effington, "Mereological Nominalism," *Philosophy and Phenomenological Research* 100, no. 1 (January, 2020). Mereology is the study of the relationship between parts and wholes.

21. Klima, "The Essentialist Nominalism of John Buridan."

22. The introduction of the term to condemn W. V. O. Quine's nominalism for ignoring problems it could not solve can be traced to Armstrong, *Nominalism and Realism*. For recent defenses of it, see Guido Imaguire, "In Defense of Quine's Ostrich Nominalism," *Grazer Philosophische Studien* 89 (2014) and Jean-Baptiste Guillen, "A Common Sense Defense of Ostrich Nominalism,"

Philosophia 49, nos. 2/3 (2021). For those exhausted by analytic philosophical disputes, a rock group called No Ostriches has recorded a digital album with a number called "Ostrich Nominalism."

23. Richard Rorty, "Being That Can Be Understood Is Language," *London Review of Books* 22 (March 16, 2000), https://www.lrb.co.uk/the-paper/v22/n06/richard-rorty/being-that-can-be-understood-is-language.

24. C. S. Peirce, *Collected Papers of Charles Sanders Peirce*, vols. 1–6, ed. Charles Hartshorne and Paul Weiss (Cambridge, Mass, 1935–38), 19. For an account of Peirce's critique of nominalism, see Paul Forster, *Peirce and the Threat of Nominalism* (Cambridge, 2011).

25. William of Ockham, *Philosophical Writings: A Selection*, ed. and trans. Philotheus Boehner (Indianapolis, 1990), 34.

26. See, Yemima Ben-Menahem, *Conventionalism: From Poincaré to Quine* (Cambridge, 2006). The case of the historian and philosopher of science Duhem is especially interesting because of his debts to Catholic theology. See, R. N. Martin, *Pierre Duhem: Philosophy and History in the Work of a Believing Physicist* (La Salle, IL, 1991).There are, as might be expected, interpretations of these thinkers that qualify their nominalist credentials or argue for changes in their positions over time. See, for example, Paul Needham, "Duhem's Moderate Realism," in *New Perspectives on Pierre Duhem's "The Aim and Structure of Physical Theory"*, ed. A. Brenner, P. Needham, D. J. Stump, et al., *Metascience* 20 (2011). It would also be necessary to look more closely at the work of the other figures in this list and the changes in their attitudes over time before pigeonholing them. See, for example, Charles Parsons, "Quine's Nominalism," *American Philosophical Quarterly* 48, no. 3 (2011), which locates his nominalist moment early in his career and teases out only residues of it in his later work.

27. For a discussion of the distinction, see Steve Fuller, *Social Epistemology* (Indiana, 1988).

28. For a summary of his argument, which he calls "dynamic nominalism," see Ian Hacking, "Making Up People," *London Review of Books* 28, nos. 16–17 (August, 2006).

29. Theodor W. Adorno, *An Introduction to Dialectics*, ed. Christoph Zierman, trans. Nicholas Walker (Cambridge, 2017), 198. For discussions of Adorno on *Unbegrifflichkeit*, see Martin Jay, "Adorno and Blumenberg: Nonconceptuality and the *Bilderverbot*," *Splinters in your Eye* (London, 2020), and Sebastian Tränkle, *Nichtidentität und Unbegrifflichkeit: Philosophische Sprachkritik nach Adorno und Blumenberg* (Frankfurt, 2022).

30. Blumenberg, *The Legitimacy of the Modern Age*, 162.

31. According to Blumenberg, the doctrine of predestination in the late Middle Ages worked against consciously choosing withdrawal from the world, exemplified by monasticism, as the road to salvation. For although unknown to men, that road had already been chosen for each of us by God, and so our choices were irrelevant to the outcome, which could not be earned by our actions. See *The Legitimacy of the Modern Age*, 154. This helps explain why Calvinists became what Max Weber called "inner-worldly ascetic" activists intent on changing the world rather than "other-worldly mystics" seeking to leave it.

32. The term is often attributed to the Scottish philosopher Sir William Hamilton, who coined it in 1852. See Susan Borowski, "The Origin and Popular Use of Occam's Razor," *Scientia* (June 12, 2012), https://www.aaas.org/origin-and-popular-use-occams-razor. The literature on Ockham is formidable; see, for example, Gordon Leff, *William of Ockham: The Metamorphose of Scholastic Discourse* (Manchester, 1975); Rondo Keele, *Ockham Explained: From Razor to Rebellion* (McLean, VA, 2010).

33. William of Ockham, *Quodlibetal Questions*, 2 vols., trans. Alfred Freddoso and Francis Kelly (New Haven, 1991), 2:521.

34. According to Philotheus Boehner, one of the guiding principles of Ockham's work was the belief that "all things are possible for God, save such as involve a contradiction." Introduction to Ockham, *Philosophical Writings*, xix. But Ockham was careful to distinguish logic from other sciences because it deals only with mental content and not things. "The Notion of Knowledge or Science," in *Philosophical Writings*, 12.

35. The others were quantity, relation, where, when, position, having, action, and passion. Aristotle, *Categories*, 1b25. For a discussion of Ockham's "irenic separatism" between faith and reason, see Alfred J. Freddoso, "Ockham on Faith and Reason," in *The Cambridge Companion to Ockham*, ed. Paul Vincent Spade (Cambridge, 1999).

36. In Habermas's reading of the difference between Scotus and Ockham, the former in some ways anticipates Kant and the latter Hume, thus reversing the historical order of their later counterparts. He sees Scotus attempting a "transcendental ontology" that will somehow preserve a moment of epistemological universality, whereas Ockham is a more consistent empiricist. See Habermas, *Auch eine Geschichte der Philosophie*, vol. 1, chap. 6.

37. Some interpreters of Ockham have insisted, however, that he believed universal ideas were not entirely a product of linguistic convention, but had some purchase in nature. See, for example, Philotheus Boehner, "The Realistic Conceptualism of William of Ockham," in *Collected Articles on Ockham*, ed. Eligiius M. Buytaert (New York, 1958).

38. Ockham, *Philosophical Writings*, 23. The term "intuition," it should be noted has had many different meanings in the history of philosophy and theology. We have already encountered it in the claim that angels have an intuitive grasp of the truth, while mortals have to arrive at it by discursive means. In the case at hand, it involves an immediate appreciation of existence rather than of truth. According to Elizabeth Karger, however, Ockham did not assume that intuitive judgments were infallible and always produced more reliable evidence than abstract cognition. See her "Ockham's Misunderstood Theory of Intuitive and Abstract Cognition," in Spade, ed., *The Cambridge Companion to Ockham*, 204–26.

39. See Eric M. Rubinstein, "Nominalism and the Disappearance of the Problem of Individuation," *History of Philosophy and Logical Analysis* 5, no. 1 (2002). The so-called *principium individuationis*, a term coined by the Scottish theologian and minister George Gillespie in the mid-seventeenth century, became an issue again in the nineteenth century with philosophers like Schopenhauer and Nietzsche.

40. They were not hostile to logic per se but were critical of what later semantic philosophers called an "intensional" form of logic, which is confined to the internal content of a term or concept constituting its formal definition, in favor of an "extensional" one, whose range includes the particular external objects that it denotes. The distinction between analytic and synthetic judgments, famously introduced by Kant in his first *Critique*, is sometimes seen as roughly mapping onto this opposition.

41. See William A. Wallace, "Ernest Moody: Galileo and Nominalism," in *Prelude to Galileo: Essays on Medieval and Sixteenth-Century Sources of Galileo's Thought*, Boston Studies in the Philosophy of Science 62 (Dordrecht, 1976).

42. According to Ernest Moody, the hypothesis of the uniformity of nature paralleled the equally contingent hypothesis of a divine order of grace for Christian believers, whose souls could be saved, but whose salvation was not guaranteed. "Neither hypothesis is logically or metaphysically necessary, and each is, in its own domain, used as a methodological principle justified by its fruitfulness." "William of Ockham," *The Encyclopedia of Philosophy*, vol. 8 (New York, 1967), 312.

43. See Hans Blumenberg, *The Genesis of the Copernican World*, trans. Robert Wallace (Cambridge, MA, 1987), part 2, chap. 2. There are, to be sure, questions raised about

how much nominalism was the cause or merely the philosophical justification for certain aspects of the Scientific Revolution. For an example in the case of Galileo, see Jürgen Mittestrass, "Remarks on Nominalistic Roots of Modern Science," *Organon* 4 (1967): 39–46.

44. Blumenberg, *The Genesis of the Copernican World*, 154.

45. Josef Chytry, *Cosmotheism: Cytherean Sitings between Heraclitus and Kittler* (New York, 2020), part 1.

46. Alexander Koyré, *From the Closed World to the Infinite Universe* (Baltimore, 1957).

47. See Hans Schelkshorn, "Modernity as a Process of De-limitations," *Interdisciplinary Journal for Religion and Transformation in Contemporary Society* 5 (2019).

48. Francis Bacon, *Novum Organum*, trans. and ed., Peter Urbach and John Gibson (Chicago, 1994). The frontispiece faces the title page.

49. Significantly, in the sixteenth century, King Charles I of Spain (Charles V of the Holy Roman Empire) changed the motto of his country's coat of arms, which had the pillars on them, to *plus ultra* after Columbus's voyages.

50. Some historians have stressed the recovery of ancient Greek skeptical thought rather than the implications of nominalist voluntarism. See Richard H. Popkin, "Amos Funkenstein and the History of Skepticism," in *Thinking Impossibilities: The Intellectual Legacy of Amos Funkenstein*, ed. Robert S. Westeman and David Biale (Toronto, 2008).

51. Ockham's reliance on the evidence of repetitive experience in supporting his confidence in efficient causality makes him more of an anticipator of Hume than of Kant. But his critique of rational proofs for the existence of God was shared by both later philosophers. Hume, however, went further along the road to atheism than Kant who tacitly echoed Ockham when he famously said in his first *Critique*, "I have found it necessary to deny knowledge, in order to make room for faith."

52. Gillespie, *The Theological Origins of Modernity*, 35.

53. Gillespie, *The Theological Origins of Modernity*, 36.

54. The American pragmatist John Dewey made the search for absolute knowledge and eternal values the target of his 1929 study *The Quest for Certainty*, which shows that it still survived into his day. But nominalism had done a great deal to undercut its hold over Western culture well before. Among the pragmatists, Dewey himself is often placed between Peirce, who defended realist essentialism, and William James, who was more a consistent nominalist.

55. The Latin *contemplatio*, whose etymology suggests the space of a temple where slow rumination might take place, was the equivalent of the Greek *theoria*. Observation is a more empirical exercise, often entailing controlled replicability and technological precision. Frequently employed for religious purposes, contemplation is sometimes conflated with meditation, in which immersion replaces the strict split between subject and object demanded by observation.

56. On the rise and fall of the macro/microcosmic analogy, see George Boas, "Microcosm," *The History of Ideas* (New York, 1969). He notes that by the fifteenth and sixteenth centuries, it survived only among certain Christian humanists, for example, Giovanni Pico della Mirandola and Johann Reuchlin.

57. See Blumenberg, *The Genesis of the Copernican World*, part 5, chap. 1. It was not until 1750 and Thomas Wright's *An Original Theory or New Hypothesis of the Universe* that our solar system's eccentric place in the Milky Way was first appreciated. His discovery was one step in the progression from a geocentric to a heliocentric and then galactocentric view of the universe, which has itself been superseded by an acentric view (already advanced by Giordano Bruno in the sixteenth century, which contributed to his trial and execution).

58. See Martin Jay, "Scopic Regimes of Modernity," *Force Fields: Between Intellectual History and Cultural Critique* (New York, 1993). Although dominant, "Cartesian perspectivalism," as I call it there, was never entirely hegemonic.

59. The first explicit appeal to perspectivism among historians appeared in Johann Martin Chladenius, *Allgemeine Geschichtswissenschaft* (Leipzig, 1752). For a recent discussion of its general application and tacit dependence on embodiment, see Emmanuel Alloa, *The Share of Perspective*, trans. Nils F. Schott (New York, 2024).

60. Blumenberg, *The Genesis of the Copernican World*, 533.

61. There was, of course, a more modest realism that distinguished between metaphysics and epistemology, which believed in the existence of real essences, but questioning our ability to know them as such.

62. As already noted, the term first appeared in the Hebrew Bible in Isaiah 45:15. It was later cited by Aquinas, Nicolas of Cusa, Pascal, Calvin, and particularly by Luther, who compared his age with that of the prophets. But Luther also argued that it was in his apparent absence that God was also a *deus revelatus* who revealed himself through his Son to the faithful. Deist theologians of a later period, using the metaphor of a clock-maker, stressed instead his absence, at least after the initial act of creation. For them, God was also an "idle God" or *deus otiosus*, who had withdrawn from the world.

63. Blumenberg, *The Legitimacy of the Modern Age*, 347.

64. Elizabeth Brient, *The Immanence of the Infinite: Hans Blumenberg and the Threshold to Modernity* (Washington, DC, 2002). She argues, contrary to Blumenberg, that late medieval Neoplatonism, in particular Meister Eckart and Nicholas of Cusa, enabled the transition from the collapse of the medieval worldview to modern science.

65. For a discussion, see Keith Thomas, *Religion and the Decline of Magic* (New York, 1971), chap. 4. Max Weber's thesis about the relationship between the Protestant ethic and the spirit of capitalism was based on the anxiety caused by human ignorance of divine purposes, including whether or not an individual was among those predestined to be saved.

66. The belief, however, that mathematics might still be an expression of divine order did not easily lose its grip. Thus, as William J. Bouwsma notes, "Both Galileo and Kepler believed that God had created the world on a geometrical model comprehensible to human beings, who could thus understand the cosmos exactly as God had made it. Kepler thought mathematical insight close to Platonic recollection. . . . Even Hobbes, often considered an atheist by contemporaries, thought geometry 'the onely Science that it hath pleased God hitherto to bestow on mankind.'" *The Waning of the Renaissance: 1550–1640* (New Haven, 2000), 189.

67. Gerhard Schweppenhäuser, "Criticizing Nominalism and 'Negative Metaphysics'. Philosophy-historical Considerations in the Concept of 'Nature in Dialectic of Enlightenment," *Bajo Palabra* 21 (2019): 261.

68. See William J. Courteney, "The Dialectic of Omnipotence in the High and Late Middle Ages," in *Divine Omniscience and Omnipotence in Medieval Philosophy*, ed. Tamar Rudavsky (Dordrecht, 1985), 245.

69. Anselm, *Cur Deus homo*, book 2, chap. 10.

70. The realism/nominalism controversy centered on ontological and epistemological questions, but the mention of moral law and sin suggests that it had an ethical dimension as well. In fact, a parallel narrative could be fashioned focusing on the tension between the imperative to follow divine commandments and the suspension of moral laws by prophetic or messianic figures who claimed to be beyond them. It would begin with Abraham's willingness to slaughter Isaac in the Hebrew Bible, continue through medieval antinomian

movements, both Jewish and Christian, which sometimes embraced the idea of "redemption through sin," and reach its most philosophically intense expression in Kierkegaard's *Fear and Trembling*. God's ability to suspend his moral laws was sometimes assumed by self-asserting humans who claimed to be his prophets or even the messiah. The Jesus who challenged Mosaic law in written scripture by telling his followers "but I say unto you," became a model for later antinomian challengers to ethical codes. Countering those challenges was not only a concern of defenders of religious law, but also deontological moral philosophers like Kant. For an insightful treatment of this issue, see Matt Goldish, "Messianism and Ethics," in *Rethinking the Messianic Idea in Judaism*, ed. Michael L. Morgan and Steven Weitzman (Bloomington, IN, 2015).

71. Hannah Arendt, *The Life of the Mind*, vol. 2, *Willing* (New York, 1978), 84.

72. Arendt, *The Life of the Mind*, 145.

73. For a discussion of the implications of this realization, which she compares with Job's response to God's baffling actions, see Agata Bielik-Robson, "*I Hurt, Therefore I Am*: Descartes with Blumenberg (and Job)," in *Interrogating Modernity*, ed. Bielik and Whistler.

74. Blumenberg defines it as "an existential program, according to which man posits his existence in a historical situation and indicates to himself how he is going to deal with the reality surrounding him and what use he will make of the possibilities that are open to him." *Legitimacy of the Modern Age*, 138. It should be noted that self-assertion was not, strictly speaking, a direct expression of the nominalist demolition of real universals, which was still accompanied by confidence in the wisdom of God's ineffable will. It was only when that faith faltered and the anxieties of abandonment flourished that it could emerge as an expedient to fend off despair. There is thus a hiccup between the *via moderna* of Ockham and the full-throated constructivism of self-assertion. For discussions, see Jürgen Goldstein, *Nominalismus und Moderne. Zur Konstitution neuzeitlicher Subjektivität bei Hans Blumenberg and Wilhelm von Ockham* (Munich, 1998); and Adi Efal-Lautenschläger, "World-Modelling and Cartesian Method: Blumenberg's Hyperopia," in *Interrogating Modernity*, ed. Bielik-Robson and Whistler.

75. The temptation to escape or even annihilate the world did not, however, entirely disappear. For a discussion of its role in the thinking of certain German Idealists, especially Schelling, see Kirill Chepurin, "Knot of the World: German Idealism between Annihilation and Construction," in *Nothing Absolute: German Idealism and the Question of Political Theology*, ed. Kirill Chepurin and Alex Dubilet (New York, 2021).

76. According to Blumenberg, "How much room the realm of possibility already allowed for is apparent in Ockham's refutation of the claim of his predecessor, Duns Scotus, that God alone possesses creative powers. . . . This is not yet the investiture of human beings with the attribute of creating, but it releases the potential of this idea from its exclusively theological conception and makes its transfer predictable." "'Imitation of Nature': Toward a Prehistory of the Idea of the Creative Being," in *History, Metaphors, Fables*, 349.

77. See David S. Landes, *Revolution in Time: Clocks and the Making of the Modern World* (Cambridge, MA, 1983) and Gillian Adler and Paul Strohm, *Alle Thyng Hath Tyme: Time and Medieval Life* (London, 2023).

78. For a discussion of medieval aesthetics, see Umberto Eco, *Art and Beauty in the Middle Ages*, trans. Hugh Bredin (New Haven, 1986). For a history of the idea of genius, see Darrin McMahon, *Divine Fury: A History of Genius* (New York, 2013).

79. Pelagius (ca. CE 354–418) had argued against the inheritance of original sin from Adam and for the power of man's will to seek salvation without the help of divine grace. The nominalists were attacked as Pelagians by Thomas Bradwardine and others. For a

defense of Ockham, see Rega Wood, "Ockham's Repudiation of Pelagianism," in Spade, *The Cambridge Companion to Ockham*. For a discussion of subsequent efforts to refute the charge, still leveled during the Reformation, see Charles Raith II, "Scholastic Developments on Merit: A Downward Path into Pelagianism?," *The Regensburg Forum*, February 6, 2017, http://regensburgforum.com/2017/02/06/scholastic-developments-on-merit-a-downward-path-into-pelagianism/#_ednref66.

80. Gillespie, *The Theological Origins of Modernity*, 29.

81. Blumenberg, "The Relationship between Nature and Technology as a Philosophical Problem," in *History, Metaphors, Fables*, 311. The anticipatory role of nominalist voluntarism in the development of autonomy is discussed in J. B. Schneewind, *The Invention of Autonomy: A History of Modern Philosophy* (Cambridge, 1998), 21–25. Although Blumenberg is careful to pose his argument here in historical terms, elsewhere he makes clear that he thinks it is feature of the human condition per se to contrive categories or metaphors to deal with what he called the unknowable "absoluteness of reality." In *Work on Myth*, he confesses his conventional nominalist allegiances: "The 'art of living'—that primary skill, which has become obsolete even as a phrase, of dealing with and husbanding oneself—had to be acquired as a faculty for dealing with the fact that man does not have an environment that is arranged in categories and that can be perceived exclusively in its 'relevances' for him. To have a world is always the result of an art" (7).

82. Another important manifestation of the nominalist challenge to realism was the changed attitude towards money in the late Middle Ages. See David Fox and Wolfgang Ernst, eds., *Money in the Western Legal Tradition: Middle Ages to Bretton Woods* (Oxford, 2016); and D. Fox, "The *Case of Mixt Monies*: Confirming Nominalism in the Common Law of Monetary Obligations," *Cambridge Law Journal* 70, no. 1 (2011).

83. Describing Ockham's "linguistic turn," Christopher Bode writes, "In Ockham, epistemology is redefined as *criticism of language*, and since we can only talk about the existence of that which we know, ontology follows suit. The battle was about texts and meaning, and Ockham pointed the way that Hobbes, Berkeley and Wittgenstein were to explore later on: *the meaning is the usage*—and therefore it can only be *made*, and it's not there, and it's not *stable*." "A Modern Debate over Universals? Critical Theory vs. 'Essentialism,'" in *Nominalism and Literary Discourse: New Perspectives*, ed. Hugo Keiper, Christoph Bode, and Richard J. Utz (Leiden, 1997), 310. The phrase was first popularized by Richard Rorty, ed., *The Linguistic Turn: Recent Essays in Philosophical Method* (Chicago, 1967). See also Ian Hacking, *Why Does Language Matter to Philosophy?* (Cambridge, 1975) and Geoffrey Galt Harpham, *Language Alone: The Critical Fetish of Modernity* (New York, 2002).

84. See William Courtenay, *Covenant and Causality in Medieval Thought: Studies in Philosophy, Theology and Economic Practice* (London, 1984). For a succinct account of Augustine's position, see Susan A. Handelman, *The Slayers of Moses: The Emergence of Rabbinic Interpretation in Modern Literary Theory* (Albany, 1982), 113–20. See also, Brigitte Miriam Bedos-Rezak, "Medieval Identity: A Sign and a Concept," *American Historical Review* 105, no. 5 (December, 2000).

85. This often-cited passage played a central role in the supersessionist theology of Christianity, which contributed to anti-Semitic denigrations of Judaism as a legalistic, spiritually dead relic. Within Judaism, it might be noted, movements like Hasidism sought to bring more experiential immediacy to a rabbinic tradition that seemed to come dangerously close to this caricature.

86. Bedos-Rezak, "Medieval Identity," 1492. Aquinas's position was, to be sure, somewhat more complicated than this straightforward formula would suggest. See Robert

Pasnau, "Aquinas on Thought's Linguistic Nature," *The Monist* 80, no. 4 (1997). He argues that Aquinas held that words and concepts shared a semantic likeness and that there was also at least a partial syntactic likeness between language and thought.

87. For one account, see John F. Johnson, "Speaking of the Triune God: Augustine, Aquinas and the Language of Analogy," *Concordia Theological Quarterly* 67, nos. 3/4 (2003).

88. See the discussions in Hans Belting, *Likeness and Presence: A History of the Image before the Era of Art* (Chicago, 1994) and Susannah Biernoff, *Sight and Embodiment in the Middle Ages* (New York, 2002).

89. According to Bedos-Rezak, although not fully sacral, "seals were the incarnation of the *ego* of diplomatic discourse, marking the charter so that it acquired substance and body." "Medieval Identity," 1527.

90. See Katherine H. Tachau, *Vision and Certitude in the Age of Ockham: Optics, Epistemology and the Foundations of Semantics* (Leiden, 1988); Biernoff, *Sight and Embodiment in the Middle Ages*; Stuart Clark, *Vanities of the Eye: Vision in Early Modern European Culture* (Oxford, 2007), chap. 1; and Eleonore Stump, "The Mechanisms of Cognition: Ockham on Mediating Species," in *The Cambridge Companion to Ockham*, ed. Spade, 168–203. It has even been argued that the nominalist critique of visual forms spawned the later anti-ocularcentrism of Western culture. See Philip Blond, "Toward a Theological Materialism: The Politics of the Eye," in *Theology and the Political: The New Debate*, ed. Creston Davis, John Milbank, and Slavoj Žižek (Durham, NC, 2005), 446.

91. For an account of the discovery of a more active observing subject in the early nineteenth century, see Jonathan Crary, *Techniques of the Observer: On Vision and Modernity in the Nineteenth Century* (Cambridge, MA, 1990). Although the medieval notion of visible species was long discredited, he shows that a new appreciation of the constitutive role played by the eye undercut the belief that it was merely the passive receptor of external stimuli.

92. William of Ockham, *Philosophical Writings*, ed. and trans. Philotheus Boehner (New York, 1957), 41.

93. Anselm, *De Incarnatione Verbi, Opera Omnia*, vol. 1, ed. F. S. Schmitt (Edinburgh, 1938), 285. Cited in Constant J. Mews, "Nominalism and Theology before Abaelard: New Light on Roscelin of Compiègne," *Vivarium* 30, no. 1 (1992): 4. The Latin *flatus vocis* is sometimes rendered as "voices of the air" or a "breath of voice." In the sentence cited from Anselm, the Latin phrase is in the accusative case.

94. Even radical nominalists like Roscelin were not yet, however, prepared to deny any connection between words and the individual things to which they referred. It is sometimes claimed that this final untethering of language from its referential function did not really happen until modernist poetry in the late nineteenth century. Thus, for example, George Steiner argues in *Real Presences* (Chicago, 1989), that "*it is this break of the covenant between word and world which constitutes one of the very few genuine revolutions of spirit in Western history and which defines modernity itself*. . . . Mallarmé's repudiation of the covenant of reference, and his insistence that non-reference constitutes the true genius and purity of language, entail a central supposition of 'real absence'" (93–96, italics in original).

95. The tripartite distinction between the indexical, iconic, and symbolic functions of words was, as we noted earlier, introduced by the pragmatist Charles Sanders Peirce.

96. See Walter J. Ong, *Ramus, Method and the Decay of Dialogue* (Cambridge, MA, 1983), 58. This use is not to be confused with "terminism" as the theological doctrine that God has a fixed period of probation during which individuals can accept his grace or not.

97. Habermas, *Auch eine Geschichte der Philosophie*, 1:790. In so arguing, Habermas was tacitly disagreeing with John Dewey, who charged that "the defect of nominalism lies in its virtual denial of interaction and association. It regarded the word not as a mode of social action with which to realize the ends of association, but as an expression of a ready-made, exclusively individual, mental state; sensation, image or feeling, which, being an existence, is necessarily particular. . . . Interaction, operative relationship, is as much a fact about events as are particularity and immediacy." *Experience and Nature* (La Salle, IL, 1987), 153.

98. Funkenstein, *Theology and the Scientific Imagination* (Princeton, 1986), 57. For a translation of the first part of Ockham's *Summa Logicae*, where his argument is perhaps best articulated, see William of Ockham, *Ockham's Theory of Terms: Part One of the "Summa Logicae"*, trans. Michael J. Loux (South Bend, IN, 2011).

99. Funkenstein, *Theology and the Scientific Imagination*, 58.

100. For discussions, see Claude Panaccio, "Semantics and Mental Language," in *The Cambridge Companion to Ockham*, ed. Spade; and Paul Vincent Spade, "Ockham's Distinctions between Absolute and Connotative Terms," *Vivarium* 13 (1975): 55–76. They also explicate other important distinctions in his semantics between "categorematic," and "syncategorematic" terms, and the types of "supposition," personal, simple, and material, that underpin his theory of reference. There is considerable debate in the literature over the precise meaning of Ockham's semantics, whose details we will not attempt to spell out.

101. The more radical breaking of the covenant between word and thing wrought by aesthetic modernists like Mallarmé, discussed by Steiner in *Real Presences*, had a very different implication. Rather than seeking to still the connotative resonance of words in the service of denotative simplicity, it celebrated their capacity to multiply symbolic meanings.

102. For a discussion, see André Goddu, "Ockham's Philosophy of Nature," in *The Cambridge Companion to Ockham*, 150–54.

103. It is sometimes argued that Copernicus may have used a mathematical model in describing a heliocentric universe without believing it corresponded to reality, as did later thinkers like Giordano Bruno. See Christopher I. Lehrich, *The Occult Mind: Magic in Theory and Practice* (Ithaca, 2007), 36.

104. For a discussion of *metabasis*, see William T. Parry and Edward Hacker, *Aristotelian Logic* (Albany, 1991), 453.

105. The ideal of a universal mathematics has also been found in Greek thought. See David Rabouin, *Mathesis Universalis: L'idée de "mathématique universelle" d'Aristote à Descartes* (Paris, 2009).

106. It is a challenge that continues to generate discussion. See, for example, Richard B. Brandt, "The Languages of Realism and Nominalism," *Philosophy and Phenomenological Research* 17, no. 4 (1957): 516–35.

107. Or to return to the distinction drawn by social epistemologists, this meant a conventionalism that acknowledged the constraining power of unconsciously created, habitual practices, institutions, and discursive regimes.

108. For a comparison of the Eucharist and the commodity, see Andrew Cole, *The Birth of Theory*, chap. 4. Marxism also sought an emancipatory alternative to the alienated abstractions of capitalism, which would dialectically sublate the nominalist negation of universals. For a discussion of the search for a normative concept of totality, especially powerful in the tradition of Western Marxism, see Martin Jay, *Marxism and Totality: The Adventures of a Concept from Lukács to Habermas* (Berkeley, 1984).

109. Jean Grondin, "Faith in the Nominalistic Age? The Possible Theological Contribution of Hermeneutics," *Religions* 14, no. 220 (2023): 1. Jorge Luis Borges, "From Allegories to Novels," in *Borges: A Reader*, ed. Emir Rodriguez Monegal and Alastair Reid (New York, 1981), 231.

110. See Davis, Milbank, and Žižek, eds., *Theology and the Political*; and Hent de Vries and Lawrence E. Sullivan, eds., *Political Theologies: Public Religions in a Post-Secular World* (New York, 2006). Blumenberg's *Legitimacy of the Modern Age* attacks Schmitt and other secularization theorists in the name of a "reoccupation" argument that stresses the perennial existence of certain questions that are answered differently over time.

111. See Stephen Toulmin, *Cosmopolis: The Hidden Agenda of Modernity* (Chicago, 1990). He places the end of its plausibility, however, only in the early seventeenth century. It could, of course, be argued that the hierarchy of the great chain of being was in some ways a projection of earthly political and social arrangements, which were then given post facto ideological justification by their alleged mimetic origins.

112. For a claim that John's metaphor was more physiological than anatomical, see Cary J. Needham, "The Physiological Significance of the Organic Metaphor in John of Salisbury's *Policraticus*," *History of Political Thought* 8, no. 2 (1987): 211–23. The metaphor did not, however, disappear entirely with nominalism, and could still appear in the Renaissance—for example, in Shakespeare's *Coriolanus*.

113. Certain conservative political theorists criticized both reason and will—for example, Michael Oakeshott, *Rationalism in Politics and Other Essays* (London, 1981). Defined in different ways, reason has been defended by liberals who favor communicative rationality, Hegelian Marxists who think politics can ultimately be made substantively rational, and technocrats who argue for the application of instrumental reason in political decision-making. For recent considerations of the reason/will tension, see Sinkwan Cheng, ed., *Law, Justice, and Power: Between Reason and Will* (Stanford, CA, 2004).

114. This narrative of the origin of the doctrine of sovereignty should not, however, be taken as universally applicable. In fact, in the case of Jean Bodin, who is traditionally considered the originator of the modern notion of sovereignty, there was still a strong residue of humanist Neoplatonism. Although he stressed the importance of the absolute power of the sovereign to make laws, he also believed, according to Stéphane Beulac, that "the laws of God and of nature, as well as the human laws common to all peoples, are really one and the same. They refer to principles of reason and justice, to a superior moral (and nontemporal order), and thus are not strictly enforceable. This is Bodin the humanist speaking." "The Social Power of Bodin's 'Sovereignty' and International Law," *Melbourne Journal of International Law* 4, no. 1 (2003), http://classic.austlii.edu.au/au/journals/MelbJIL/2003/13.html. For a critique of a transhistorical notion of sovereignty, see Raia Porohovnik, *Sovereignty: History and Theory* (Charlottesville, VA, 2008).

115. Habermas, *Auch eine Geschichte der Philosophie*, 1:785.

116. Carl Schmitt, *Political Theology: Four Chapters on the Concept of Sovereignty*, trans. George Schwab (Chicago, 2006). There is a voluminous literature on Schmitt's political theology and notion of sovereignty. For my own take, see "The Reassertion of Sovereignty in a Time of Crisis: Carl Schmitt and Georges Bataille," *Force Fields: Between Intellectual History and Cultural Critique* (New York, 1993).

117. Carl Schmitt, *The Concept of the Political*, trans. George Schwab (Chicago, 1996), 69–73.

118. The differences are spelled out in James Wiley, *Politics and the Concept of the Political: The Political Imagination* (London, 2016).

119. Colin Wright, "Event or Exception? Disentangling Badiou from Schmitt, or. Towards a Politics of the Void," *Theory and Event* 11, no. 2 (2008): 6.

120. See, for example, Jean Bethke Elshtain, *Sovereignty, God, State and Self* (New York, 2008).

121. Pierre Manent, *The City of Man*, trans. Marc A. LePain (Princeton, 1998), chap. 5. The phrase references Leni Riefenstahl's infamous film of the Nazi Nuremberg rally.

122. Agata Bielik-Robson, "Beyond Sovereignty: Overcoming Modern Nominalistic Cryptotheology," *Journal for Cultural Research* 20, no. 3 (2016): 301.

123. For a collection of his political writings, see William of Ockham, *A Letter to the Friars Minor and Other Writings*, ed. Arthur Stephen McGrade and John Kilcullen, trans. John Kilcullen (Cambridge, 1995). For discussions, see Arthur Stephen McGrade, *The Political Thought of William of Ockham: Personal and Institutional Principles* (Cambridge, 2002); John Kilcullen, "The Political Writings" in *The Cambridge Companion to Ockham*, ed. Spade; and Joseph Canning, *A History of Medieval Political Thought, 300–1450* (London, 1996), 159–61.

124. Hannes Bajohr, "The Vanishing Reality of the State: On Hans Blumenberg's Political Theory," *New German Critique* 145 (2022): 134.

125. A salient recent example of a nominalist philosopher who scorned the nonliberal conclusions drawn by a Carl Schmitt is Richard Rorty. His pragmatic antifoundationalism made the search for an ultimate sovereign power, whose irrational commands made the rules, otiose.

126. Ernst H. Kantorowicz, *The King's Two Bodies: A Study in Medieval Political Theology* (Princeton, 1957), 29. The transformation of the king's two bodies argument into the discourse of popular sovereignty based on an ideal notion of "the people," shows, however, that it could survive the nominalist demolition of one essence in a new form. See, for example, Eric L. Santner, *The Royal Remains: The People's Two Bodies and the Endgames of Sovereignty* (Chicago, 2011).

127. For discussions of Hobbes's nominalism, see Gillespie, *The Theological Origins of Modernity*, chap. 7; G. K. Callaghan, "Nominalism, Generality and Abstraction in Hobbes," *History of Philosophy Quarterly* 18, no. 1 (2001): 37–55; and Stewart Duncan, "Hobbes, Universal Names, and Nominalism," in *The Problem of Universals in Early Modern Philosophy*, ed. Stefano Di Bella and Tad M. Schmaltz (Oxford, 2017. For a dissenting view, see Sergio H. Orozco-Echeverri, "On the Origin of Hobbes' Conception of Language: The Literary Culture of English Renaissance Humanism," *Revista de Estudios Sociales* 44 (2012).

128. G. W. Leibniz, "Preface to an Edition of Nizolius," in *Philosophical Papers and Letters*, ed. L. E. Loemker (Dordrecht, 1969), 128. *Plusquam nominalis* is sometimes translated as "ultranominalist."

129. Hobbes's own religious beliefs, which have not always been acknowledged as relevant for his politics, were not all that far removed from those of Ockham. See J. G. A. Pocock, "Time, History and Eschatology in the Thought of Thomas Hobbes," in *Politics, Language and Time: Essays on Political Thought and History* (New York, 1973). He points out that Hobbes's God, unknowable by reason, was close to a *deus absconditus*, his faith was more fideist-skeptical than deist, and that "he most rigorously separated the Hellenic from the Hebraic components of his cultural tradition and went further than any major philosopher since Augustine in rejecting the former and relying upon the latter" (200). Still, when it comes to self-preservation as the highest value, the New Testament is clear: "For whoever wishes to save his life will lose it, but whoever loses his life for my sake, he is the one who will save it" (Luke 9:24). Hobbes's religious beliefs, to be sure, remain

controversial, with some commentators even suggesting he may have been a closet atheist. See Preston King, ed., *Thomas Hobbes: Critical Assessments*, 4 vols. (London, 1993).

130. See Martin Jay, "Astronomical Hindsight: The Speed of Light and Virtual Reality," in *Refractions of Violence* (New York, 2003). Ole Roemer's discovery in 1676 of the speed of light opened up the vista of starlight reaching us from sources distant in time as well as space that were no longer actually shining.

131. Blumenberg, *The Genesis of the Copernican World*, 43.

132. For discussions of Hobbes's views on language, see Martin A. Bertman, "Hobbes on Language and Reality," *Revue international de philosophie* 126, no. 4 (1978): 536–50; Philip Pettit, *Made with Words: Hobbes on Language, Mind, and Politics* (Princeton, 2008).

133. Calvin G. Normore, "Some Aspects of Ockham's Logic," in *The Cambridge Companion to Ockham*, 51.

134. Thomas Hobbes, *Leviathan*, ed. Michael Oakeshott (New York, 1962), 44. For a discussion of his hostility, see Blumenberg, "An Anthropological Approach to Rhetoric," in *History, Metaphors, Fables*, 203–5.

135. The formula appeared in the 1668 Latin revised edition of *Leviathan*, book 2, chap. 26.

136. Hobbes, *Leviathan*, 255. Collapsing justice into positive law inevitably raised objections on the part of a wide variety of theorists who insisted that a distinction be made between them. See, for example, Stéphane Rials, "Rights and Modern Law," in *New French Thought: Political Philosophy*, ed. Mark Lilla (Princeton, 1994), 164–65. He explicitly blamed Ockham for the collapse. Lest this complaint be seen as only expressed by right-wing upholders of natural law, it should be noted that leftists like the American literary critic Fredric Jameson also criticized nominalism for a "tendency toward immanence, the flight from transcendence" that characterized the antiutopian one-dimensionality of late capitalist culture. See *Postmodernism, or, The Cultural Logic of Late Capitalism* (Durham, 1992), 250. His specific target here is the deconstructionist Paul de Man, whom he disparagingly characterizes as "not a nihilist, but a *nominalist*."

137. Leo Strauss, "Notes on Carl Schmitt's Concept of the Political," in *Carl Schmitt and Leo Strauss: The Hidden Dialogue* by Heinrich Meier, trans. J. Harvey Lomax (Chicago, 1995), 100–101. Strauss also points out that whereas Hobbes's state of war is between individuals, Schmitt's is between groups. The problem, as has often been pointed out, is that there is no mechanism in Hobbes's political universe through which individuals can successfully charge the state with violating their supposedly inviolable rights.

138. See, for example, James R. Martel, "Hobbes' Anti-Liberal Individualism," *Las Torres de Lucca: International Journal of Political Philosophy* 5, no. 9 (2016): 31–59.

139. Sheldon Wolin, *Politics and Vision: Continuity and Innovation in Western Political Thought* (Boston, 1960), 255. Wolin, to be sure, himself understood liberalism as driven more by anxiety and fear than hope in the results of rational deliberation.

140. Authoritarian does not, of course, mean totalitarian, and Hobbes's state was not intended to interfere in private economic behavior or regulate belief. His definition of freedom was closer to the negative view that is associated with liberalism than the positive one derived from republicanism. According to Ian Shapiro, "it is true that for Hobbes the power of the state is absolute, but it is important to notice that the powers Hobbes ascribes to the state are basically those which most liberals, too, regard as nonnegotiable: the guarantee of property rights and the rule of law, of territorial integrity and a workable currency system, the enforcement of contract and basic criminal sanctions, and the raising of tases for these limited purposes." *The Evolution of Rights in Liberal Theory* (Cambridge, 1986), 66.

141. Gillespie, *The Theological Origins of Modernity*, 242.

142. Gillespie, *The Theological Origins of Modernity*, 243.

143. See Nicholas Hudson, "John Locke and the Tradition of Nominalism," in *Nominalism and Literary Discourse*, ed. Keiper, Bode, and Utz; Jan-Erik Jones, "Locke on Real Essence," *The Stanford Encyclopedia of Philosophy*, first published December 19, 2012; substantive revision September 2, 2022, https://plato.stanford.edu/archives/fall2022/entries/real-essence/.

144. Larry Siedentop, *Inventing the Individual: The Origins of Western Liberalism* (Cambridge, 2014).

145. For a selection of commentaries, see Lois Parkinson Zamora and Wendy B. Farris, eds., *Magical Realism: Theory, History, Community* (Durham, NC, 1995). For a general overview, see Maggie Ann Bowers, *Magic(al) Realism* (New York, 2004). Not all commentators are enamored of the concept. See for example, Liam Connell, "Discarding Magical Realism: Modernism, Anthropology and Critical Practice," *ARIEL: A Review of International English Literature* 29, no. 2 (1998). A less celebrated alternative called itself magical idealism, coined by the German Romantic Novalis to signify his imaginative unification of philosophy and poetry. The Italian fascist philosopher Julius Evola (1898–1974) borrowed the term to characterize his own worldview. For a recent attempt to breathe life into it, see Cologero Salvo, *Introduction to Magical Idealism* (Boca Raton, FL, 2019).

146. For an example of the linkage between nominalism and disenchantment, see Jane Bennett, *The Enchantment of Modern Life: Attachments, Crossing and Ethics* (Princeton, 2001), 66–70. In *The Alienation of Reason: A History of Positivist Thought* (New York, 1969), Leszek Kolakowski identified nominalism, along with phenomenalism, the separation of facts and values, and the unity of the scientific method, as one of the cardinal "rules of positivism" (5–6). An imprecise term often serving more as a target of critique than a self-designation, positivism is generally taken to imply an epistemological subject who is more passive than constitutive, a subject closer to Hume's than Kant's. Whatever knowledge it has of the world is acquired entirely through a posteriori experience without the help of a priori categories structuring that experience. It draws on objective observation and inductive reasoning to fashion generalizations from encounters with the particulars of the world. The latter it identifies with discrete "facts," which are taken to be the building blocks of any account of reality. The basis of Auguste Comte's positivism, so Adorno argued, "is simply that of a rigorous nominalism that rejects the objectification of any concept as mere dogma, and Comte regards such objectification of concepts over against the facts as nothing but a kind of semi-secularized theology." Theodor W. Adorno, *Philosophy and Sociology 1960*, ed., Dirk Braunstein, trans. Nicholas Walker (Cambridge, 2021), 20.

147. The term has been promoted by the recent school of "object-oriented ontology" (OOO), which has Heideggerian roots. See Graham Harman, *Tool-Being: Heidegger and the Metaphysics of Objects* (Chicago, 2002) and *The Quadruple Object* (London, 2011). Harman does not dismiss subjective responses to objects—he will later distance his position from Michael Fried's controversial argument in "Art and Objecthood"—but he wants to restore primacy to objects. He is thus critical of the claim that we have entered the "Anthropocene" for giving too much credence to the idea of total human control.

148. Carolyn Walker Bynum, "Wonder," *American Historical Review* 102, no. 1 (February 1997): 13. She shows that wonder was a response, sometimes of awe and sometimes of dread, to bizarre, novel, and unique events or objects, the opposite of the urge to imitate

and generalize that accompanied the Scholastic impulse to "de-wonder" the world. For an account of the role of wonders and marvels during the Middle Ages, see Michelle Karnes, *Medieval Marvels and Fictions in the Latin West and Islamic World* (Chicago, 2022).

Chapter Two

1. Fritz Graf, "Excluding the Charming: The Development of the Greek Concept of Magic," in *Ancient Magic and Ritual Power*, ed. Marvin Meyer and Paul Mirecki (Leiden, 1995).

2. For a survey of the ways in which magic has been dismissed, see Ariel Glucklich, *The End of Magic* (New York, 1997), 17–79.

3. The metaphor of a two-front war is, of course, a simplification of the larger triangulated dynamic that so often pits religion and science against each other, and creates shifting alliances and confrontations with magic. Efforts to sort it all out continue unabated. See, for example, Peter Harrison and John Milbank, eds., *After Science and Religion: Fresh Perspectives from Philosophy and Theology* (Cambridge, 2022), especially Millbank's essay "Religion, Science, and Magic."

4. In practice, as sociologists of science have made clear, scientific inquiry was for a long time restricted to those with a certain pedigree. Only "gentlemen" had the trust necessary to be taken seriously, whereas tradesmen and women did not. See Steven Shapin, *A Social History of Truth: Civility and Science in Seventeenth-Century England* (Chicago, 1994).

5. The term "hermetic" refers to the "Hermetic Corpus" attributed to Hermes Trismegistus, but likely written by Neoplatonists in Alexandria in the first few centuries CE. It remained obscure until Marsilio Ficino's Latin translation of the *Corpus Hermeticum* in the fifteenth century. In the nineteenth century, Eliphas Lévi attempted to connect it with an idealized version of ancient Judaism. *Prisca magia* echoes the idea of a primitive universal *prisca theologia*. See Christopher I. Lehrich, *The Occult Mind: Magic in Theory and Practice* (Ithaca, 2007), chap. 1.

6. Theodor W. Adorno and Max Horkheimer, *Dialectic of Enlightenment: Philosophical Fragments*, ed. Gunzelin Schmid Noerr, trans. Edmund Jephcott (Stanford, CA, 2002), 7. As Marxists, Horkheimer and Adorno also interpreted capitalism in comparable terms. Objects produced for consumption or use were transformed into fungible commodities to be exchanged. This is why they could argue that nominalism is "the prototype of bourgeois thinking" (47), a charge that is plausible when the variant involved is conventional rather than magical.

7. Adorno and Horkheimer, *Dialectic of Enlightenment*, 7.

8. For comprehensive accounts, see Lynn Thorndike, *The History of Magic and Experimental Science*, 8 vols. (New York, 1923–58); Francis Yates, *Giordano Bruno and the Hermetic Tradition* (London, 1964) and *The Occult Philosophy in the Middle Ages* (London, 1979); Charles Webster, *From Paracelsus to Newton: Magic and the Making of Modern Science* (Cambridge, 1982); Jacob Neusner, Ernest S. Frerichs, and Paul Virgil McCracken Flesher, eds., *Religion, Science and Magic in Concert and in Conflict* (New York, 1989); Stanley J. Tambiah, *Magic, Science, Religion and the Scope of Rationality* (Cambridge, 1990); Birgit Meyer and Peter Pels, eds., *Magic and Modernity: Interfaces of Revelation and Concealment* (Stanford, CA, 2003); Randall Styers, *Making Magic: Religion, Magic and Science in the Modern World* (Oxford, 2004); Alison P. Coudert, *Religion, Magic and Science in Early Modern Europe and America* (Santa Barbara, CA, 2011); Steven P. Marrone, *A History*

of Science, Magic and Belief: From Medieval to Early Modern Europe (London, 2015); and Jeffrey H. Williams, *The Search for the Absolute: How Magic Became Science* (San Rafael, CA, 2020). On the varieties of magic practiced during the Middle Ages, see Valerie I. J. Flint, *The Rise of Magic in Early Medieval Europe* (Oxford, 1991); Richard Kieckhefer, *Magic in the Middle Ages* (Cambridge, 2014); Martha Rampton, ed., *European Magic and Witchcraft: A Reader* (Toronto, 2018); and Jennifer M. Rampling, *The Experimental Fire: Inventing English Alchemy, 1300–1700* (Chicago, 2020).

9. A. G. Molland, "Roger Bacon as Magician," *Traditio* 30 (1974).

10. John Maynard Keynes, "Newton, the Man," (1942). He went on to explain: "Why do I call him a magician? Because he looked on the whole universe and all that is in it as a riddle, as a secret which could be read by applying pure thought to certain evidence, certain mystic clues which God had laid about the world to allow a sort of philosopher's treasure hunt to the esoteric brotherhood. He believed that these clues were to be found partly in the evidence of the heavens and in the constitution of elements (and that is what gives the false suggestion of his being an experimental natural philosopher), but also partly in certain papers and traditions handed down by the brethren in an unbroken chain back to the original cryptic revelation in Babylonia. He regarded the universe as a cryptogram set by the Almighty—just as he himself wrapt the discovery of the calculus in a cryptogram when he communicated with Leibniz. By pure thought, by concentration of mind, the riddle, he believed, would be revealed to the initiate." "Newton, the Man," MacTutor, School of Mathematics and Statistics University of St Andrews, Scotland, updated March 2006, https://mathshistory.st-andrews.ac.uk/Extras/Keynes_Newton/.

11. See Christopher A. Faraone and Sofia Torallas Tovar, eds., *The Greco-Egyptian Magical Formularies: Libraries, Books and Individual Recipes* (Ann Arbor, 2022).

12. See Stuart Clark, *Thinking with Demons: The Idea of Witchcraft in Early Modern Europe* (Oxford, 1997.)

13. Laura Sumrall "Natural Magic in Renaissance Science," in *Encyclopedia of Renaissance Philosophy*, ed. M. Sgarbi, September 4, 2017, https://doi.org/10.1007/978-3-319-02848-4_956-1. It should be noted that the Neoplatonic revival was an elite affair influencing learned men like Robert Fludd or John Dee and had little impact on the practice of magic on a popular level.

14. See Alexander Boxer, *A Scheme of Heaven: Astrology and the Birth of Science* (New York, 2020).

15. Keith Thomas, *Religion and the Decline of Magic* (New York, 1971), 327. He points out that theologians were more distressed by the social-scientific than natural-scientific implications of astrology, because it challenged their belief in human free will (361).

16. See Paolo Rossi, *Francis Bacon: From Magic to Science*, trans. Sacha Rabinovitch (London, (1968).

17. Francis Bacon, *Novum Organum*, trans. and ed. Peter Urbach and John Gibson (Chicago, 1994). The frontispiece faces the title page.

18. For one account, see Leigh Eric Schmidt, *Hearing Things: Religion, Illusion and the American Enlightenment* (Cambridge, MA, 2000). There have been, to be sure, modern revival attempts. Wicca, an invented religious tradition based on pagan witchcraft, was launched in Britain by Gerald Gardner in the early twentieth century. Some estimates put its adepts as high as 800,000 around the world. But it remains a fringe phenomenon arousing little alarm among the general population. Today more critical attention is focused on the accusers of witchcraft than on the alleged practitioners.

19. For an account of the heated controversy over a popular German necromancer, see Renko Geffarth, "The Masonic Necromancer: Shifting Identities in the Lives of Johann Georg Schrepfer," in *Polemical Encounters: Esoteric Discourse and its Others* (Leiden, 2007).

20. For examples of recent objections to the conventional narrative of secularization, see Charles Taylor, *A Secular Age* (Cambridge, MA, 2007); and Hent de Vries, *Philosophy and the Turn to Religion* (Baltimore, 1999). For an insightful overview of contemporary attempts to go beyond secularization, see Agata Bielik-Robson, "The Post-Secular Turn: Enlightenment, Tradition, Revolution," *Eidos* 3, no. 3 (2019).

21. See, James W. Cook, *The Arts of Deception: Playing with Fraud in the Age of Barnum* (Cambridge, MA, 2001), chap. 4; Simon During, *Modern Enchantments: The Cultural Power of Secular Magic* (Cambridge, MA, 2002); B. Meyer and P. Pels, eds., *Magic and Modernity* (Stanford, CA, 2003); Corinna Treitel, *A Science for the Soul: Occultism and the Genesis of the German Modern* (Baltimore, 2004); George Ritzer, *Enchanting a Disenchanted World* (Thousand Oaks, CA, 2005); Joshua Landy and Michael Saler, eds., *The Re-Enchantment of the World: Secular Magic in a Rational Age* (Stanford, CA, 2009); and Leigh Wilson, *Modernism and Magic: Experiments with Spiritualism, Theosophy and the Occult* (Edinburgh, 2015). For a survey of this field, see Michael Saler, "Modernity and Enchantment: A Historiographic Review," *The American Historical Review* 111, no. 3 (2006).

22. Although the quantitative procedures of modern science cannot be equated with, say, magical numerology, precise astrological calculations of the movements of heavenly bodies were useful for the development of astronomy. But to turn the arrow around, advances in mathematics could also be harnessed for occult purposes. Ever since Pythagoras of Samos (ca. 569–475 BCE) and his followers discovered the wonders of mathematical abstraction, the difficulties of mapping them on to the world and the paradoxes in mathematics themselves have opened the door at least a crack for a more magical reading of their implications. For a provocative consideration of the inspiration certain modern critical theorists and theologians took from a postrational reading of mathematics, see Matthew Handelman, *The Mathematical Imagination: On the Origins and Promise of Critical Theory* (New York, 2019).

23. See Stanley J. Tambiah, "Form and Meaning of Magical Acts: A Point of View," in Robin Horton and Ruth Finnegan, eds., *Modes of Thought: Essays on Thinking in Western and Non-Western Societies* (London, 1973); and Lehrich, *The Occult Mind*, chap. 4.

24. According to Perez Zagorin, Francis Bacon's "activist approach to knowledge was shared by the contemporary occult sciences, which were also intent on operations and practical ends, and therefore indicates the formative presence of such studies as natural magic and alchemy in the development of Bacon's thought." Perez Zagorin, *Francis Bacon* (Princeton, 1998), 40. He further notes that "despite the fact that Bacon basically viewed science as a public, collaborative, and progressive enterprise, his earlier writings expressed a frequent interest in the esoteric principle of withholding higher truths from the unworthy" (43). In "Solomon's House," the scientific society depicted in his *New Atlantis*, secrecy, in fact, prevails. The parallel between the magical and scientific desires to dominate nature is also stressed in Adorno and Horkheimer, *Dialectic of Enlightenment*, 19.

25. There is, of course, a voluminous literature on the value of method in general, generated by such works as Hans-Georg Gadamer, *Truth and Method* (New York, 1975). For a specific history of the emergence and vicissitudes of a specifically "scientific method," which came into its own only in the late nineteenth century, see Henry M. Cowles, *The Scientific Method: An Evolution of Thinking from Darwin to Dewey* (Cambridge, MA, 2020).

26. It was the third of his "three laws" and first appeared in a footnote in his 1973 revision of *Profiles of the Future*. See Donna Lu, "Clarke's Three Laws," *New Scientist*, accessed March 1, 2024, https://www.newscientist.com/term/clarkes-three-laws/#ixzz6ZwjYlGqU.

27. See for example, Jason Ananda Josephson Storm, *The Myth of Disenchantment: Magic, Modernity, and the Birth of the Human Sciences* (Chicago, 2017).

28. See, for example, the argument that the conventional distinction between religion and magic itself carries traces of its origins in the history of Christianity, and would thus be problematically applied to Hinduism, in Veena Das, "If This Be Magic . . . : Excursions into Contemporary Hindu Lives," in *Religion: Beyond a Concept*, ed. Hent de Vries (New York, 2008). If the generic notion of religion can be condemned for homogenizing the heterogeneous, the same complaint can be lodged against an umbrella concept of magic. See, for example, Lehrich, *The Occult Mind*, 161.

29. Initially formulated by Karl Jaspers, the concept has been widely adopted by historians and sociologists of religion, for example in Robert Bellah and Hans Joas, eds., *The Axial Age and Its Consequences* (Cambridge, MA, 2012).

30. For an argument that the label was actually of Christian coinage, see Daniel Boyarin, "The Christian Invention of Judaism: The Theodisian Empire and the Rabbinic Refusal of Religion," in *Religion*, ed. de Vries.

31. See, for example, the passage in Exodus 22:17, "When you enter the land that the Lord your God is giving you, you shall not learn to imitate the abhorrent practices of those nations. Let no one be found among you who consigns his son or daughter to the fire, or who is an augur, a soothsayer, a diviner, a sorcerer, one who casts spells, or one who consults ghosts or familiar spirits, or one who inquires of the dead. For anyone who does such things is abhorrent to the Lord, and it is because of these abhorrent things that the Lord your God is dispossessing them before you." Similar prohibitions can be found in Deuteronomy, 18:10–11 and Leviticus, 19:26, 19:31, and 20:16.

32. For an account of the importance of magic in the pagan classical world, see Radcliffe C. Edmonds, *Drawing Down the Moon: Magic in the Ancient Greco-Roman World* (Princeton, 2019). The word "pagan" was a pejorative coinage of early Christians, not a self-designation. For a discussion of its origins and more positive recent adoptions, see Martin Jay, "Modern and Postmodern Paganism," in *Cultural Semantics: Keywords of Our Time* (Amherst, MA, 1998).

33. The supposed replacement of mythos by logos, which was often invoked in linear notions of Western cultural development, has itself become controversial. See, for example, Richard E. Buxton, *From Myth to Reason? Studies in the Development of Greek Thought* (Oxford, 1999) and Kathryn A. Morgan, *Myth and Philosophy: from the Presocratics to Plato* (Cambridge, 2003). See also Hans Blumenberg, *Work on Myth*, trans. Robert M. Wallace (Cambridge, MA, 1985).

34. Jan Assmann, *Of God and Gods: Egypt, Israel, and the Rise of Monotheism* (Madison, WI, 2008), 87. The connection between visibility and magic remains powerful among those who want to elevate language over images in religious experience. The twentieth-century French theologian Jacques Ellul, for example, writes in *The Humiliation of the Word*, trans. Joyce Main Hanks (Grand Rapids, MI, 1985), that "for the Church and the fourteenth century, this rush towards images, toward the 'realization' of spiritual and revealed truth, ends up of course in magic and the coarsest of beliefs" (188).

35. Exodus, 7:8–13.

36. Acts of Apostles, 8:9–23.

37. Morton Smith, *Jesus the Magician: A Renowned Historian Reveals How Jesus Was Viewed by the People of His Time* (Newburyport, MA, 2014). Christianity had been accused of relying on magic as early as the Greek philosopher Celsus in the second century, whose lost text *The True Word* is known through its refutation by Origen.

38. Or more sympathetically understood, it "enhances the magician's sense of well-being; it serves as an emotional outlet and a means of emotional support for the practitioner, the client, or both." Richard Kieckhefer, "The Specific Rationality of Medieval Magic," *The American Historical Review* 99, no. 3 (1994): 827.

39. The same distinction is often introduced to set mysticism apart from magic. See, for example, Evelyn Underhill, *Mysticism: A Study in the Nature and Development of Man's Spiritual Consciousness* (New York, 1961), chap. 7.

40. Kieckhefer, "The Specific Rationality of Medieval Magic," 821.

41. David Gentilcore, *From Bishop to Witch: The System of the Sacred in Early Modern Terra d'Otranto* (Manchester, 1992).

42. According to Keith Thomas, the increasing role of priests in consecrating the wafer and wine drew on theological subtleties too arcane for the normal congregant to understand. "What stood out was the magical notion that the mere pronunciation of words in a ritual manner could effect a change in the character of material objects." *Religion and the Decline of Magic*, 33.

43. See Hans Ulrich Gumbrecht, "The Charm of Charms," in *A New History of German Literature*, ed. David Wellbery (Cambridge, MA, 2004), which discusses the magical formulae found in a codex in the monastery of Fulda from the eighth century. He suggests that their ultimate importance may lie more in aesthetics than in religion: "While charms are far from any modern conception of literature, their magic mechanisms suggest a relationship of immediate tangibility to the things of the world which Western poetry—sometimes unknowingly—has always presupposed and cultivated, since its own Occitan beginnings in the late 11th and early 12th centuries" (7).

44. As early as 1395, the Lollards were already attacking the magical residues in orthodox rituals. See Thomas, *Religion and the Decline of Magic*, 51.

45. See Michael D. Bailey, "The Disenchantment of Magic: Spells, Charms, and Superstition in Early European Witchcraft Literature," *American Historical Review* 111, no. 2 (April 2006).

46. See Anthony Grafton, "The Mysteries of the Kabbalah and the Theology of Obscure Men," in *A New History of German Literature*. He focuses on the effects of the campaign launched by a converted Jew, Johannes Pfefferkorn, against Reuchlin. For an account of the link between the blood libel and the church's earlier attack on usury, which he calls "magical thinking" in the pejorative sense, see James A. Arieti, "Magical Thinking in Medieval Anti-Semitism: Usury and the Blood Libel," *Mediterranean Studies* 24, no. 2 (2016).

47. See Dorothea von Mücke, "To Explore the Secrets of Heaven and Earth," in *A New History of German Literature*. Goethe's retelling of the tale in which Faust, despite all his transgressions, is ultimately saved, demonstrates the resilience of the pagan legacy in the face of Christian attempts to extirpate it.

48. Thomas, however, cautions against overemphasizing the misogynist sources of the persecution of witches: "The idea that witch-prosecutions reflected a war between the sexes must be discounted, not least because the victims and witnesses were themselves as likely to be women as men" (568).

49. For a history of the disputes over the Eucharist throughout Christianity from a Catholic perspective, see Gary Macy, *The Banquet's Wisdom: A Short History of the*

Theologies of the Lord's Supper (Akron, 2005). Other, less pious critics of the Mass than Luther challenged its differentiation from magic, as shown by the adoption of the incantation "hocus-pocus" to exemplify magical mumbo jumbo. Although the evidence is uncertain, it is often speculated that the phrase was a mockery of "*hoc est corpus*" (here is the body), which accompanies the Catholic presentation of the Host.

50. For a discussion of changes in the role of signs and wonders during the Reformation, see Philip M. Soergel, *Miracles and the Protestant Imagination: The Evangelical Wonder Book in Reformation Germany* (Oxford, 2012).

51. Thomas, *Religion and the Decline of Magic*, 278.

52. Robert W. Scribner, "The Reformation, Popular Magic, and the 'Disenchantment of the World,'" *Journal of Interdisciplinary History* 23, no. 3 (Winter 1993): 486.

53. See Bailey, "The Disenchantment of Magic" and Thomas, *Religion and the Decline of Magic*, chaps. 14–18.

54. Scribner, "The Reformation, Popular Magic, and the 'Disenchantment of the World,'" 491.

55. Deism, of course, did not entirely replace more traditional forms of Christian worship or put an end to the religious incorporation of magic. For example, the enduring practice of making the sign of the cross by Catholic, Anglican and Orthodox Christians—and certain Lutherans—is sometimes seen as a residue of a magical ritual. Defenders of the practice argue that it is merely a public sign of their faith in a triune god, an act of self-sanctification or a way to bless someone else. Its continuity with such countermagical gestures as waving a cross at an alleged demon suggests for others that it remains a superstitious ritual, a suspicion given credence by its function as a good luck charm by some athletes even today.

56. Rudolf Otto, *The Idea of the Holy*, trans. John W. Harvey (Oxford, 1950), 117.

57. Otto, *The Idea of the Holy*, 117.

58. Otto, *The Idea of the Holy*, 67. It, of course, can be argued that something of the magic remains in secular art as well.

59. See, for example, Murray Wax and Rosalie Wax, "The Notion of Magic," *Cultural Anthropology* 4, no. 6 (1963), and the responses it generated in the same issue.

60. Max Weber, *The Protestant Ethic and the Spirit of Capitalism*, trans. Talcott Parsons (New York, 1958), 105. The English translation of *Entzauberung* as "disenchantment" is standard. It carries with it the connotation of disappointment and perhaps even pessimism, which is not conveyed by the more literal "demagification." Weber, it has often been pointed out, did not really offer a rigorous definition of magic itself.

61. Weber, *The Protestant Ethic and the Spirit of Capitalism*, 149. Weber's argument—that Protestants, anxious about their predestined salvation, looked for *signs* of it in their worldly success, which inspired their work ethic and the capital accumulation that followed—was itself based on a residue of magical thinking. For a judicious assessment of Weber's argument about magic and disenchantment, see Lutz F. Kaelber, *Schools of Asceticism: Ideology and Organization in Medieval Religious Communities* (University Park, PA, 1998), chap. 3. The concept of charismatic authority, which Weber contrasted with traditional and rational-legal modes of legitimation, also suggests he understood that a residue of magical thinking remains a live option even after *Entzauberung*.

62. Max Weber, *The Sociology of Religion*, trans. Ephraim Fischoff (Boston, 1964), 269–70.

63. Weber, *The Sociology of Religion*, 34.

64. Saler, "Modernity and Enchantment," 98. He is inspired by Derrida's argument in *Specters of Marx*. For a similar argument, see Eugene McCarraher, "We Have Never Been Disenchanted," *The Hedgehog Review Reader*, ed. Jay Tolson (Charlottesville, 2020).

65. Horkheimer and Adorno, *Dialectic of Enlightenment*, "Excursus I: Odysseus or Myth and Enlightenment." Adorno's critique of astrological horoscopes in *The Stars Down to Earth and Other Essays on the Irrational in Culture*, ed. Stephen Crook (New York, 1994) also shows his disdain for the occultist residues in modern culture. But, as we will see while discussing his own adoption of some of the elements of magical nominalism, his attitude was never entirely skeptical.

66. An alternative critique of Weber defended a rigid distinction between religion and magic, and argued that secular *Entzauberung* had nothing to do with the decline of genuine religion. According to the Catholic philosopher Charles Taylor, "Disenchantment is the dissolution of the 'enchanted' world, the world of spirits and meaningful causal forces, of wood sprites and relics. Enchantment is essential to some forms of religion, but other forms, especially those of modern Reformed Christianity, both Catholic and Protestant—have been built on its partial or total denial. We cannot just equate the two." *A Secular Age* (Cambridge, MA, 2007), 553.

67. Sir James George Frazer, *The New Golden Bough*, ed. Theodor H. Gaster (New York, 1959), 649. Frazer's book was first published in two volumes in 1890, but by its third edition (1911–14), it reached twelve volumes. All citations are from Gaster's condensed version, which runs over seven hundred pages.

68. Frazer, *The New Golden Bough*, 649.

69. See John B. Vickery, *The Literary Impact of "The Golden Bough"* (Princeton, 1992).

70. One example, suggested to me by Josef Chytry, would be the effect of chanting, political as well as religious, in the modern world, which can arouse through hypnotic rhythms something of the magical experience undermined by disen-*chant*-ment.

71. See, for example, Victor Kuman, "To Walk Alongside: Myth, Magic and Mind in *The Golden Bough*," *Journal of Ethnographic Theory* 6, no. 2 (2016). Among Frazer's most consequential detractors was Ludwig Wittgenstein, who attacked him along with Freud in "Remarks on Frazer's *Golden Bough*," in *Philosophical Occasions 1912–1951*, ed. Alfred Nordmann and James C. Klagge (Indianapolis, 1993).

72. Frazer, *The New Golden Bough*, 7.

73. For a recent overview, see Patrice Ladwig, "Mimetic Theories, Representation and 'Savages:' Critiques of the Enlightenment and Modernity through the Lens of Primitive Mimesis," in *The Transformative Power of the Copy: A Transcultural and Interdisciplinary Approach*, ed. Corinna Forberg and Philipp W. Stockhammer (Heidelberg, 2017). The idea of "sympathetic magic" had already been introduced by the German ethnologist Richard Andree in 1878, but *The Golden Bough* gave it widespread currency.

74. For an attempt to trace a lineage from Frazer to Benjamin and Adorno, see Patrice Ladwig, "Mimesis, Representation and 'Savages': Critiques of the Enlightenment and Modernity through the Lens of Primitive Mimesis," in *The Transformative Power of the Copy*.

75. Émile Durkheim, *The Elementary Forms of Religious Life*, trans. Joseph Ward Swain (New York, 1968), 56.

76. Durkheim, *The Elementary Forms of Religious Life*, 58.

77. As many observers have pointed out, Durkheim's belief in the existence of a church as a necessary criterion of religiosity excluded other forms of cultic or corporate solidarity, such as a sect.

78. Durkheim was alarmed by what he saw as the decline of social solidarity in his day and sought functional equivalents of traditional religion to prevent its further erosion. Insofar as magic was in the service of undermining devotion to society, he opposed it.

79. As Dominick LaCapra has noted, this distinction allowed the Durkheimians to argue that "technology secularized magic as a means of controlling seemingly desacralized and disenchanted objects in the world." *Emile Durkheim: Sociologist and Philosopher* (Ithaca, 1972), 241.

80. Durkheim, *The Elementary Forms of Religious Life,* 404.

81. Durkheim, *The Elementary Forms of Religious Life,* 405. Hubert and Mauss were the authors of *Théorie Générale de la Magie* (Paris, 1902), late republished under Mauss's name alone in 1950 and in English translation as *A General Theory of Magic,* trans. Robert Brain (London, 1972). For a comparison of their position with Durkheim's, see Wouter W. Belier, "Religion and Magic: Durkheim and the *Année sociologique* Group," *Method and Theory in the Study of Religion* 7, no. 2 (1995). He traces the variations in their theories over time, and elaborates the ambiguities and differences in their arguments.

82. For attempts to assess its legacy, see Sondra L. Hausner, ed. *Durkheim in Dialogue: A Centenary Celebration of "The Elementary Forms of Religious Life"* (New York, 2013).

83. Or to turn it on its head, it also indirectly leads us to wonder whether an entirely reenchanted world, should that ever happen, would be entirely sacralized, or whether the sacred/profane distinction would still be an abiding opposition.

84. For a comparison, see Michael Stausberg, "The Sacred, the Holy, Numinous—and Religion: On the Emergence and Early History of a Terminological Constellation," *Religion* 47, no. 4 (2017).

85. Bronislaw Malinowski, "Magic, Science and Religion," in *Science, Religion and Reality,* ed. Joseph Needham (London, 1925); reprinted in William A. Lessa and Evon Z. Vogt, eds., *Reader in Comparative Religion* (New York, 1979), from which all citations are taken. For an overview of his contribution, see Leonard Glick, "The Anthropology of Religion: Malinowski and Beyond," in *Beyond the Classics? Essays in the Scientific Study of Religion,* ed. Charles Y. Glock and Phillip E. Hammond (New York, 1973).

86. Lévy-Bruhl's *Mental Functions in Primitive Societies* was published in 1910, *Primitive Mentality* in 1922, *The Soul of the Primitive* in 1928, *The Supernatural and the Nature of the Primitive Mind* in 1931, *Primitive Mythology* in 1935, and *The Mystic Experience and Primitive Symbolism* in 1938.

87. Malinowski, "Magic, Science and Religion," 40.

88. Malinowski, "Magic, Science and Religion," 45.

89. Thomas, *Religion and the Decline of Magic,* 45. He was indebted to the insights of modern anthropologists, most notably E. E. Evans-Pritchard. He rejected, however, Malinowski's contention that magic was a response to the lack of technical solutions to real world problems and declined once they were found (656). He in turn has been criticized by some later anthropologists for overly rigid categorizations of religion and magic. See Hildred Geertz, "An Anthropology of Religion and Magic, *The Journal of Interdisciplinary History* 6, no. 1 (Summer 1975).

90. For an overview of the discussion, see John van Engen, "The Christian Middle Ages as an Historiographical Problem," *The American Historical Review* 91, no. 3 (June 1986).

91. Some historians, however, have argued that medieval clerics often deliberately encouraged the continuing practice of pagan magic as a positive supplement to their own teachings. See, for example, Flint, *The Rise of Magic*.

92. For recent attempts by Catholics to refute the stubborn charge that the sacraments are magic, see Billy Kangas, "Are Sacraments Magic?," *The Orant*, April 20, 2013, https://www.patheos.com/blogs/billykangas/2013/04/are-sacraments-magic.htmlo; and Rob Agnelli, "The Magic of the Sacraments," Catholic365.com, June 1, 2017, https://www.catholic365.com/article/6760/the-magic-of-the-sacraments.html. For an alternative argument from within the Catholic Church that the sacraments can, in fact, be used in magical ways, see "Those Magical Sacraments," *Unam Sanctam Catholicam*, January 16, 2014, http://unamsanctamcatholicam.blogspot.com/2014/01/those-magical-sacraments.html.

93. Thomas, *Religion and the Decline of Magic*, 267.

94. For discussions of Jewish attempts to abject or incorporate magic, see Jacob Neusner, "Science and Magic, Miracle and Magic in Formative Judaism: The System and the Difference," and Moshe Idel, "Jewish Magic from the Renaissance Period to Early Hasidism," in Neusner, Frerichs, and Flesher, eds., *Religion, Science and Magic*. These accounts refute generalizations about the radical difference in incorporating magic between Judaism and Christianity, for example, Assmann, *Of God and Gods*: "Christianity did not follow Judaism in its radical emigration from the world into Scripture. Rather, through its theology of incarnation, it reopened the door to images, sacramental magic, and other forms of religious life" (105).

95. Barbara Johnson, *Moses and Multiculturalism* (Berkeley, 2010), 14.

96. Gershom Scholem, *The Messianic Idea in Judaism and Other Essays in Jewish Spirituality* (New York, 1971), 263. Scholem's own attitude towards the magical impulse in the kabbalah was highly ambivalent. He had nothing but disdain for "magical Jews" like Oskar Goldberg, whom he claimed abused its implications. Among them were Erich Unger, who was held in high esteem, much to Scholem's chagrin, by Walter Benjamin. See Scholem, *From Berlin to Jerusalem: Memoires of My Youth*, trans. Harry Zohn (New York, 1980), 146–49; and Scholem, *Walter Benjamin: The Story of a Friendship*, trans. Harry Zohn (New York, 1981), 95–98.

97. The classic account remains Joshua Trachtenberg, *Jewish Magic and Superstition: A Study in Folk Religion* (Philadelphia, 2004), originally published in 1939. See also Maureen Bloom, *Jewish Mysticism and Magic: An Anthropological Perspective* (London, 2007). She points out that ancient magical practices to ward off demons and the like remain alive today in the amulets and other apotropaic devices used by orthodox Jews around the world.

98. Ivan Strenski, *Durkheim and the Jews of France* (Chicago, 1997), 109.

99. For a discussion of the typical mixture of genuine and imagined accusations of Jewish magic in the first Polish Encyclopedia, see Jerzy Kroczak, "Jews in *New Athens* by Benedykt Chmielowski," *Studia Judaica* 19 (2017): 62–65.

100. John M. Efron, *Medicine and the German Jews: A History* (New Haven, 2001), 22–23.

101. The theosophical kabbalah sought esoteric meanings underneath the textual surface of the Torah, revealed in combinations of letters read as acrostics, anagrams, or numerological symbols. The ecstatic kabbalah lost all interest in the Torah's surface meaning and claimed that each letter was itself God's name. The incantation of these letters could lead to ecstatic states, which were supposed to bestow performative powers on the Kabbalist.

102. Gershom G. Scholem, *Major Trends in Jewish Mysticism* (New York, 1974), 144.

103. Employing the term "theology" for Jewish thought might itself be questionable. As Gillian Rose once noted, "Strictly speaking, there is no Jewish theology—no *logos* of God—because Rabbinic Judaism, formed in post-biblical times, is the creation of the Rabbis, who, claiming to be the rightful heirs of the prophets, established Talmud Torah as the focus of Jewish life. Talmud Torah means the teaching of the teaching, or the commentary on the law." *Judaism and Modernity: Philosophical Essays* (Oxford, 1993), 182. She goes on to say, however, it may be necessary to use the term to talk of Jewish notions of creation, revelation, and redemption in philosophical terms.

104. Scholem, *The Messianic Idea in Judaism*, 293.

105. Scholem, *Major Trends in Jewish Mysticism*, 77.

106. Scholem, *Major Trends in Jewish Mysticism*, 144. For more on the theurgic name mysticism in Abulafia, see Moshe Idel, *The Mystical Experience in Abraham Abulafia* (Albany, 1988).

107. Scholem, *Major Trends in Jewish Mysticism*, 349.

108. Scholem, *The Messianic Idea in Judaism*, 257–81.

109. See Trachtenberg, *Jewish Magic and Superstition*, chap. 7, for a survey of the various manifestations of Jewish name-magic, including divine, angelic, and human examples. For a more extensive discussion, see Michael T. Miller, *The Name of God in Jewish Thought: A Philosophical Analysis of Mystical Traditions from Apocalyptic to Kabbalah* (London, 2016).

110. Gadamer, *Truth and Method*, 366. In ancient Greece, the Stoics came closest to the Jewish position by arguing that a primal nomothete gave original names to objects. They were especially interested in etymology, which is derived from the Greek *etymon*, or true sense of a word.

111. The tradition was, however, by no means unified. For discussions of its many variations, see Gershom Scholem, "The Name of God and the Linguistic Theory of the Kabbalah," *Diogenes* 79 (1972) and 80 (1973); Joseph Dan, "The Name of God, the Name of the Rose, and the Concept of Language in Jewish Mysticism," *Medieval Encounters* 2, no. 3 (1996); and Miller, *The Name of God in Jewish Thought*. Miller points out that there were three different traditions in Jewish linguistic thought: "The linguistic or verbal nature of Creation, the Torah as a linguistic blueprint or paradigm for the world; and the Name of God" (1). He draws in part on Jarl Fossum, *The Name of God and the Angel of the Lord: Samaritan and Jewish Concepts of Intermediation and the Origins of Gnosticism* (Tübingen, 1984) but disagrees with Fossum's belief in the importance of the doctrine in the Second Temple era. Emmanuel Levinas also notes the difference between the Kabbalistic tradition and that of rabbinic Talmudic commentaries, where God is called by his attributes—for example, "the holy one." For a discussion, see Susan A. Handelman, *Fragments of Redemption: Jewish Thought and Literary theory in Benjamin, Scholem and Levinas* (Bloomington, 1991), 282.

112. Agata Bielik-Robson, *Jewish Cryptotheologies of Late Modernity: Philosophical Marranos* (London, 2014), chap. 7. An earlier, if undeveloped recognition of the difference between Christian and Jewish nominalism can be found in David Biale's 1985 commentary on Scholem's use of the phrase "mystical nominalism": "the Kabbalah might be called a school of 'mystical nominalism' as a consequence of its notion that only names (or signs) signify essences, although, as opposed to the philosophical nominalism of William Ockham [*sic*] the Kabbalah took the divine names to be essential attributes of God rather than merely subjective significations." "Gershom Scholem's 'Ten Unhistorical Aphorisms on the Kabbalah': Translation and Commentary," in *Jewish Culture between Canon and Heresy* (Stanford, CA, 2023), 196. There is also a debate among scholars of Jewish law about its realist or nominalist foundations, but it focuses on different kinds of issues. See,

for example, Jeffrey L. Rubenstein, "Nominalism and Realism in Qumranic and Rabbinic Law: A Reassessment," *Dead Sea Discoveries* 6, no. 2 (July 1999).

113. Hans Jonas, "Jewish and Christian Elements in Philosophy: Their Share in the Emergence of the Modern Mind," in *Philosophical Essays: From Ancient Creed to Technological Man* (Englewood Cliffs, NJ, 1974).

114. See, for example, the attempt to apply it to Adorno in Jakub Górski, "Concerning Some Marrano Threads in the Aesthetic Theory of Theodor W. Adorno," *Religions* 10, no. 3 (2019). Bielik-Robson herself explores its importance for Derrida in *Derrida's Marrano Passover: Exile, Survival, Betrayal, and the Metaphysics of Non-Identity* (New York, 2023).

115. Bielik-Robson writes: "Far from fostering any kind of magical realism, which would attribute an ontological power to the act of naming, they nonetheless believe that naming as such opens the gate to a special relationship with reality, a relationship maintained not in the mute operations of Ockhamian-Baconian instrumental reason, but in the dialectical process of linguistic communication, where names and naming constitute, in Benjamin's words, in its very essence and true calling of language." *Jewish Cryptotheologies of Late Modernity*, 233. She also criticizes attempts, for example by Winfried Menninghaus, to label Benjamin's ruminations on language "*Sprachmagie*" (253). Michael T. Miller is likewise disinclined to stress the magical dimension in his history of Jewish name theology, mentioning it only in connection with the Hasidism, who inherited the Kabbalistic fascination with names and "provided an innovative interpretation according to their mores, in terms of practical and magical performance." *The Name of God in Jewish Thought*, 21.

116. Scholem, "Ten Unhistorical Aphorisms on the Kabbalah," in Biale, *Jewish Culture between Canon and Heresy*, 194.

117. The term was coined by John Ruskin in his *Modern Painters* of 1856 to denote the projection of human traits onto the natural world, for example by Romantic poets.

118. Boas does, to be sure, note some Kabbalistic evocations of micro/macrocosmic analogies. See "Microcosm," 230. In the nineteenth century it was discovered that medieval translators had Latinized the name of the eleventh-century Neoplatonist Jewish philosopher Solomon Ibn Gabriol to Avicebron and had misconstrued his work as Islamic or Christian in origin.

119. See Bielik-Robson, *Jewish Cryptotheologies*, 238–39. There were, to be sure, exceptions to this generalization, such as the thirteenth-century Kabbalist Yosef Gikatella, who developed an emanantist theology of the name. See Miller, *The Name of God in Jewish Thought*, chap. 5.

120. See Agata Bielik-Robson and Daniel H. Weiss, eds., *Tsimtsum and Modernity: Lurianic Heritage in Modern Philosophy and Theology* (Berlin, 2021).

121. See, for example, Shaul Magid, *Hasidism Incarnate: Hasidism, Christianity, and the Construction of Modern Judaism* (Stanford, CA, 2014), chap. 5. For another comparison, which stresses the ethical implications of kenosis, see Renée D. N. van Riessen, *Man as a Place of God: Levinas' Hermeneutics of Kenosis* (Dordrecht, 2007). For a recent exploration of the antiredemptive implications of kenosis, see Alexander Dubilet, *The Self-Emptying Subject: Kenosis and Immanence, Medieval to Modern* (New York, 2018).

122. Bielik-Robson, *Derrida's Marrano Passover*, 115.

123. Frazer, *The New Golden Bough*, 219–20.

124. Blumenberg, *Work on Myth*, 16. He later argues that "all trust in the world begins with names, in connection with which stories can be told. This state of affairs is involved in the biblical story of the beginning, with the giving of names in Paradise. But it is also involved in the faith that underlies all magic and that is still characteristic of the beginnings

of science, the faith that the suitable naming of things will suspend the enmity between them and man, turning it into a relationship of pure serviceability" (35). In fact, "the modern age has become the epoch that finally found a name for everything" (38).

125. It was, of course, Martin Buber who stressed the importance of this relationship, not only between humans and God, but also between humans themselves. In his friend and collaborator Franz Rosenzweig's *Star of Redemption*, trans. William W. Hallo (London, 1921), the same argument also appears: "With the proper name, the rigid wall of objectness has been breached. That which has a name of its own can no longer be a thing, no longer an everyman's affair" (186).

126. Blumenberg argues, however, that "the name that functions magically must be unintelligible, and in the gnostic art myth—indeed, in the undercurrent of magic in the modern age—it still stems from out-of-the-way or dead languages." Blumenberg, *Work on Myth*, 22.

127. Hans-Georg Gadamer, *The Revival of the Beautiful and Other Essays*, ed. Robert Bernasconi, trans. Nicholas Walker (Cambridge, 1986), 135.

128. There are, to be sure, comparable issues surrounding the naming or refusal to name God in other traditions, for example among Christian mystics like Meister Eckhardt. For a discussion, see Ernesto Laclau, "On the Names of God," in *Theology and the Political: The New Debate*, ed. Creston David, John Milbank, and Slavoj Žižek (Durham, NC, 2005).

129. See Anson S. Laytner, *Arguing with God: A Jewish Tradition* (Lanham, MD, 1990).

130. As Miller notes in commenting on Rosenzweig's stress on naming as addressing, "to name something postulates it in relation to us and makes it knowable. But, a corollary of identity is separation: that which is identified—named—must admit of a transcendence or an autonomy in not being consumed by the subject. The name, then, also *distances* the object." *The Name of God in Jewish Thought*, 77.

131. According to Miller, however, some Kabbalists came to believe that before YHWH God had another name AHYH, which was "revealed exclusively to Moses" and was "a more primal, incorporeal and interior name than the regal third-person YHWH." *The Name of God in Jewish Thought*, 109.

132. To be sure, there have been exceptional figures in Jewish history generating the devotion that can turn into prayer after their deaths. The tomb, or *Ohel*, of the Chabad Lubavitcher "*rebbe*" Menachem Mendel Schneerson (1902–1994) in Old Montefiore Cemetery in Queens, New York, is visited by hundreds of his followers every day. See Stefanie Halpern, "A Meeting of Life and Death: Ritual and Performance at the Ohel, the Grave of Rabbi Menachem Mendel Schneerson," *Journal of Ritual Studies* 29, no. 1 (2015). The Hasidic adoration of the *tsadik* (or righteous one) has even been called an example of "incarnational thinking" comparable to the Christian notion of sainthood by Magid, *Hasidism Incarnate*.

133. The complicated relationship between oral and written language, exemplified by the distinction between the oral and written Torah, would have to be unpacked in a serious examination of the taboo.

134. Daniel Heller-Roazen, *Dark Tongues: The Art of Rogues and Riddlers* (New York, 2013), chap. 8. The Kabbalah was itself important for later Christian thinkers like Jacob Boehme and Franz Joseph Molitor, the latter of whom inspired Scholem and Benjamin.

135. There were, to be sure, other Jewish interpretations of the importance of the name beyond those derived from the Kabbalah, for example, in Franz Rosenzweig's "New Thinking." Scholem argued that Rosenzweig was not much interested in Kabbalah, although his claim was later challenged by Moshe Idel. For a discussion of the dispute, see Rivka

Horwitz, "From Hegelianism to Revolutionary Understandings of Judaism: Franz Rosenzweig's Attitude Towards Kabbala and Myth," *Modern Judaism* 26, no. 1 (February 2006).

136. Scholem, *The Messianic Idea in Judaism*, 293. "The whole Torah," said a prominent Kabbalist, "is the great name of God." For discussions of Scholem's complex and evolving interpretation of this issue, which compares it with those of Walter Benjamin and Emmanuel Levinas, see Handelman, *Fragments of Redemption*, and Eric Jacobson, *Metaphysics of the Profane: The Political Theology of Walter Benjamin and Gershom Scholem* (New York, 2003).

137. Scholem, *The Messianic Idea in Judaism*, 294.

138. The denigration of discursive justification is characteristic of mystical or magical thought, which was quintessentially expressed in the seventeenth-century German mystic Angelus Silesius's famous poem "The Rose." It contains the oft-cited line: "Die Ros ist ohne warum; sie blühet weil sie blühet." This refusal to say why, to give reasons or justifications, is often celebrated by antidiscursive philosophers like Martin Heidegger. Benjamin was also an enthusiastic reader of Silesius. See his letter of July 22, 1910, to Herbert Belmore, in *The Correspondence of Walter Benjamin*, ed. Gershom Scholem and Theodor W. Adorno, trans. Manfred R. Jacobson and Evelyn M. Jacobson (Chicago, 1994), 5. Adorno as well cited him in his lectures on metaphysics as an example of the mystical tradition, including the Kabbalah, that argued that transcendence was immanent in the historical world. Theodor W. Adorno, *Metaphysics: Concept and Problem*, ed. Rolf Tiedemann, trans. Edmund Jephcott (Stanford, CA, 2000), 100.

139. Scholem, *The Messianic Idea in Judaism*, 294.

140. For a discussion of the parallels, see Naomi Janowitz, *The Poetics of Ascent: Theories of Language in a Rabbinic Ascent Text* (Albany, NY, 1989), 90.

141. Scholem, *The Messianic Idea in Judaism*, 295. As he explained to Benjamin in a letter of September 20, 1934, "You ask what I understand by the 'nothingness of revelation?' I understand by it a state in which revelation appears to be without meaning, in which it still asserts itself, in which it has *validity* but no *significance*. A state in which the wealth of meaning is lost and what is in the process of appearing (for revelation is such a process) still does not disappear, even though it is reduced to the zero point of its own content, so to speak." *The Correspondence of Walter Benjamin and Gershom Scholem, 1932–1940*, ed. Gershom Scholem, trans. Garry Smith and Andre Lefevre (New York, 1989), 142.

142. In pushing back against the hypertrophy of human self-assertion, magical nominalism may be understood as indirectly affirming what Joseph Albernaz and Kirill Chepurin have claimed is the "sovereignty of the world" rather than the constitutive subject. "Contra Blumenberg's insistence on immanence winning the existential competition," they write, "transcendence does not disappear when the position of the transcendent Deity is reoccupied in modernity, because it is *the position itself that is transcendent*: the sovereign position of a transcendent totality of possibility. The world retains the structure of transcendence 'equivalent' to that of the transcendent God, and with it, the alienation that transcendence produces." "The Sovereignty of the World: Towards a Political Theology of Modernity (After Blumenberg)," in *Interrogating Modernity*. ed. Bielik-Robson and Whistler, 96.

143. Michael T. Miller, "Chaos and Identity: Onomatology in the Hekhalot Literature," *Bamidbar* 2, no. 1 (2012), 41–42. The Hekhalot literature was a body of esoteric texts presenting visions of ascents into heavenly palaces (the name comes from the Hebrew word for "palaces"). It overlaps with Merkabah ("Chariot") literature, which focuses more particularly on Ezekiel's chariot. They are often grouped together as "Books of the Palaces and the Chariot."

144. Megan A. O'Connor, *Nominalism, Romanticism, Negative Dialectics* (PhD diss., University of California, Berkeley, 2019), 5.

145. Adam gave names to "every beast of the field and every bird of the air," but nothing is said of the fishes of the sea, a notable omission that led to voluminous Talmudic lucubrations in the years since. The ocean in general has often served as a region beyond human ken and control, not easily fit into even the Greek idea of an orderly, harmonious cosmos. Luckily for the Talmudists, they were spared having to reconcile the Biblical version of naming the animals with the implications of Darwinian evolution, which revealed the ongoing creation and extinction of innumerable different animal species.

146. Although the story of Babel, recounted in Genesis 11, is generally seen as the source of linguistic pluralism, Umberto Eco reminds us that in Genesis 10, after the Flood, the sons of Noah were given lands "every one after his tongue," which implies that the original language spoken in the Garden of Eden was already divided before Babel. See Umberto Eco, *The Search for the Perfect Language*, trans. James Fentress (Oxford, 1995), chap. 1.

147. Hans Arsleff, *From Locke to Saussure: Essays on the Study of Language and Intellectual History* (Minneapolis, 1982), 25.

148. The word *nomothete* is Greek, not Hebrew, in origin, and was introduced with the translation in the third century of the Hebrew Bible into Greek known as the Septuagint. Originally signifying "law-giver," it connotes a wise legislator of human laws or "nomos," which were differentiated from "physis" or natural laws. For a discussion of the ways in which Plato wrestled with the relationship between giving laws and bestowing names, see Nancy Demand, "The Nomothetes of the *Cratylus*," *Phronesis* 20, no. 2 (1975). If Adam is merely uttering names that already have been given, his work can be called the completion, rather than generation of creation, an interpretation favored by some commentators, for example Jarl Fossum and Michael T. Miller.

149. Gilad Sharvit, *Dynamic Repetition: History and Messianism in Modern Jewish Thought* (Waltham, MA, 2022), 180.

150. There have also been many conjectures about when the vanity of the quest was acknowledged. For example, Erich Heller claimed that "if ever a poet seemed to live by certain naïve notions the Middle Ages had about language, it was, anachronistically, Shakespeare: namely the sense that the verbal sign does not differ in any relevant degree of reality from that which it signifies. For when Adam named all things, he named them in accordance with the will of God; and thus things and names became one. . . . But then there appears Hamlet who seems to extend invitations to translators through his tormenting conviction that all words are inadequate designations of the real things or real inner states." *In the Age of Prose: Literary and Philosophical Essays* (Cambridge, 1984), 39–40. Besides homogenizing medieval attitudes towards language, Heller turns Shakespeare into a self-divided figure, both embracing an Adamic view of language and inventing a conventional nominalist hero who doubts its existence.

151. In *The Search for the Perfect Language*, Eco points out that sometimes the quest was for a future universal language, for example Ludwik Lejzer Zamenhof's Esperanto, rather than the recovery of an original one.

152. For a discussion, see Blumenberg, *Work on Myth*, 372. The idea of hidden or secret names was also important in the Jewish tradition. For ruminations on it, see Walter Benjamin, "Agesilaus Santander," first and second versions, in *Selected Writings*, vol. 2, *1927–1936*, ed. Michael W. Jennings, Howard Eiland and Gary Smith, trans. Rodney Livingstone et al. (Cambridge. MA, 1999).

153. See Maurice Olender, *Languages of Paradise: Race, Religion and Philology in the Nineteenth Century*, trans. Arthur Goldhammer (Cambridge, MA, 1992).

154. Walter Benjamin, "The Task of the Translator," (1926) in," *Selected Writings*, vol. 1, *1913–1926*, ed. Marcus Bullock and Michael W. Jennings (Cambridge, MA, 1996). The commentary on Benjamin's ruminations on translation and language is extraordinarily abundant. For valuable examples, see Beatrice Hanssen, "Language and Mimesis in Walter Benjamin's Work," in *The Cambridge Companion to Walter Benjamin*, ed. David S. Ferris (Cambridge, 2004); Jacobson, *Metaphysics of the Profane*; Handelman, *Fragments of Redemption*; Peter Fenves, *The Messianic Reduction: Walter Benjamin and the Shape of Time* (Stanford, CA, 2011); and Winfried Menninghaus, *Walter Benjamins Theorie der Sprachmagie* (Frankfurt, 1980).

155. Precisely what Benjamin understood by "redemption" is unclear. One possibility is the idea of "apocatastasis" (*apokatastasis*) the hope, initially voiced by the church father Origen of Alexandria in the third century, that at the Last Judgment, all of the dead of human history, including sinners as well as saved, will rise from the grave redeemed. Benjamin seems to have interpreted this hope as implying a more cosmic notion of making whole what had been burst asunder, which would show his debt more to Christian than Jewish nominalism, as Bielik-Robson has defined them. In fact, in one of his earliest works, he invoked the idea of *restitutio ad integrum* from the New Testament. See Walter Benjamin, "Theological-Political Fragment," *Selected Writings*, vol. 3, *1935–1938*, ed. Howard Eilend and Michael W. Jennings (Cambridge, MA, 2006), 306. For a history of the doctrine, see Ilaria L. E. Ramelli, *The Christian Doctrine of Apokatastasis: A Critical Assessment from the New Testament to Eriugena* (Leiden, 2013).

156. Theodor W. Adorno, "Introduction to Benjamin's *Schriften*," in *Notes to Literature*, ed. Rolf Tiedemann, trans. Shierry Weber Nicholsen (New York, 1992), 2:222.

157. Eric Downing, *The Chain of Things: Divinatory Magic and the Practice of Reading in German Literature and Thought, 1850–1940* (Ithaca, 2018). He shows divinatory inclinations in the work of Gottfried Keller and Theodor Fontane and argues that despite his overt disdain for predicting the future, Benjamin also shared many of their aspirations to harness the residual energies of sympathetic magic for more than just knowing the past.

158. Alexander Stern, *The Fall of Language: Benjamin and Wittgenstein on Meaning* (Cambridge, MA, 2019), 60. For a critique of Stern's application of Charles Taylor's notion of an aesthetic expressivist tradition, see Alison Ross's review in *Notre Dame Philosophical Reviews*, February 2, 2020, https://ndpr.nd.edu/reviews/the-fall-of-language-benjamin-and-wittgenstein-on-meaning/. Drawing on other works by Benjamin, most notably his study of Goethe's *Elective Affinities*, she argues for a more literal theological reading of his view of language. Ross also rejects Stern's hermeneutic analysis of Benjamin, which posits a quest for meaning immanent in the world, in favor of one motivated by a cognitive search for truth. Her critique comports with the argument advanced here that an Adamic view of names posits their substantial unity with what they name. Meaning, in contrast, is based on the distinction between signifier and signified in a semiotic view of language. Where we perhaps differ is in her stressing truth rather than reenchantment as Benjamin's goal, although perhaps in his mind they may have been synonymous.

159. Hito Steyerl, "The Language of Things," (2006), *Transversal 06/06: Under Translation*, 2006, eipcp – European Institute for Progressive Cultural Policies, https://artistsspace.org/media/pages/exhibitions/hito-steyerl/1128046083-1623172961/the_language_of_things.pdf.

160. Walter Benjamin, "On Language as Such and the Language of Man," *Selected Writings*, vol. 1.

161. Hanssen notes that the "magical communication among many layers, registers, realms, states of existence, and levels of intentionality, was translation, or translatability, a term that was to receive its earliest account not, as is commonly assumed in Benjamin's 1921 translation essay, but in the 1916 'On Language as Such and the Language of Man.'" "Language and Mimesis in Walter Benjamin's Work," 58.

162. Benjamin, "On Language as Such and the Language of Man," 65.

163. See Walter Benjamin, "Fortsetzungsnotizen zur Arbeit über die Sprache," *Gesammelte Schriften*, ed. Rolf Tiedemann and Hermann Schweppenhäuser (Frankfurt, 1989), 7:786. On the circle, Benjamin placed "God creates" at the top, "the thing is named" to the right, "mathematics thinks" at the bottom and "man knows" on the left. For a discussion, see Fenves, *The Messianic Reduction*, 130–33.

164. For a distinction between the "hermetic" language of modernist poets and the "orphic" language of those, like Benjamin, who see a link between language and creation, see Gerald Bruns, *Modern Poetry and the Idea of Language: A Critical and Historical Study* (New Haven, 1974).

165. Benjamin, "On Language as Such and the Language of Man," 67.

166. Benjamin, "On Language as Such and the Language of Man," 72.

167. Benjamin, "On Language as Such and the Language of Man," 69. How literally Benjamin took the Genesis story is sometimes disputed. Stern, for example, contends that "Benjamin's theory does not depend on the literal truth of the Biblical creation myth, nor does it require the historical or theoretical viability of the existence of a single human language. . . . The Bible is cited, in other words, as a narrative ladder that provides an initial framework for discussing the nature of language, but which can be afterwards thrown away without losing any of the insights that have been gained." *The Fall of Language*, 51.

168. *The Fall of Language*, 51.

169. Benjamin's interest in gradual transformations rather than discrete units was also expressed in visual terms in his ruminations on color. See Martin Jay, "Chromophilia: Der Blaue Reiter, Walter Benjamin and the Emancipation of Color," in *Splinters in Your Eye* (London, 2020).

170. Benjamin, "On Language as Such and the Language of Man," 70.

171. Benjamin, "On Language as Such and the Language of Man," 73.

172. Because Benjamin attributed linguistic abstraction to such a fundamental loss, he resisted the "materialist epistemology" of his friend Alfred Sohn-Rethel, who argued that the more important cause was the "real abstraction" of money in the ancient world, which was further developed by the commodity form of capitalism. When asked to comment on Sohn-Rethel's work by the Institut für Sozialforschung in 1937, he did, however, cautiously support it. See Howard Eiland and Michael W. Jennings, *Walter Benjamin: A Critical Life* (Cambridge, MA, 2014), 563.

173. In his later book on the *Trauerspiel*, Benjamin distinguished between concepts and "Ideas," which redeem particulars by fashioning new constellations out of extreme rather than average exemplars, and reveal a truth veiled by generic abstractions. For a discussion, see Stern, *The Fall of Language*, chap. 3.

174. As Stern notes, Benjamin uses *richten* as well as *urteilen* for judging, a word which also means to point and thus suggests designation rather than naming. *The Fall of Language*, 83.

175. Stern, *The Fall of Language*, 72. Dismissing questions of good and evil as mere judgments, which are inferior to knowing right names, risks antinomian anarchy and indifference to the need for moral reasoning. In his more apocalyptic moods, Benjamin seems to have been willing to run this risk.

176. Jacobson, *Metaphysics of the Profane*, 94. In a letter to Martin Buber, written in July, 1916, Benjamin indicated that he meant "magical" in the sense of "unmediated." See *Correspondence, 1910–1940*, ed. Gershom Scholem and Theodor W. Adorno, trans. Manfred R. Jacobson and Evelyn M. Jacobson (Chicago, 1994), 80.

177. Theodor W. Adorno, *Negative Dialectics*, trans. E. B. Ashton (New York, 1974), 183. Preponderance does not mean, however, total domination, as the role of the subject in the redemptive constellation Adorno sought was still vital. He would not, in other words, have agreed with the radical antisubjectivism or "anthrodecentrism" of the recent object-oriented ontology movement (OOO), launched by the Heideggerian Graham Harman. See Harman, *Tool-Being: Heidegger and the Metaphysics of Objects* (Chicago, 2002) and *The Quadruple Object* (London, 2011).

178. See Alexander Regier, "The Magic of the Corner: Walter Benjamin and Street Names," *The Germanic Review* 85, no. 3 (2010). For an exploration of the magical moments in urban experience, which recalls Benjamin's fascination with the flaneur, see Alastair Bonnett, "The Enchanted Path: Magic and Modernism in Psychogeographical Walking," *Transactions of the British Institute of Geographers* 42, no. 3 (2017).

179. Walter Benjamin, "Antitheses Concerning Word and Name," *Selected Writings*, 2:718.

180. Jacobson, *Metaphysics of the Profane*, 105.

181. Giorgio Agamben, "Magic and Happiness," in *Profanations*, trans. Jeff Fort (New York, 2015), 21–22.

182. Even one of Benjamin's most enthusiastic champions, Adorno, could confess to Scholem: "there is a peculiar analogy between the early Benjamin's relation to Jewish mysticism and the late Benjamin's relation to Marxism. In both cases, it seems as though his metaphysical-epistemological longing, as well as his insight that tradition itself is a constituent element of philosophy, led him to bind himself to quasi-authoritative texts without having fully thought them through, and without having even, in a higher sense, studied them." Adorno to Scholem, March 14, 1968, in Theodor W. Adorno and Gershom Scholem, *Correspondence 1939–1969*, ed. Asaf Angermann, trans. Paula Schwebel and Sebastian Truskolaski (Cambridge, 2021), 358–59.

183. Umberto Eco, *The Search for a Perfect Language* (Oxford, 1997), 19.

184. Benjamin contended, however, that analogy should be distinguished from relationality in general. See his "Analogy and Relationship" (1919) in *Selected Writings*.

185. Benjamin, *One-Way Street and Other Writings*, trans. J. A. Underwood (London, 2009), 113.

186. Niklaus Largier, *Figures of Possibility: Aesthetic Experience, Mysticism, and the Play of the Senses* (Stanford, CA, 2022), 175.

187. Benjamin, "On Language as Such and the Language of Man," in *Selected Writings*, vol. 1; "The Mimetic Faculty" and "Doctrine of the Similar," in *Selected Writings*, 2:188.

188. Walter Benjamin to Gershom Scholem, June 29, 1933, in *The Correspondence of Walter Benjamin and Gershom Scholem*, 61.

189. Eco, *The Search for the Perfect Language*, 120. For a more extensive discussion, see Christopher I. Lehrich, *The Language of Demons and Angels: Cornelius Agrippa's Occult*

Philosophy (Leiden, 2003). He notes that for Agrippa, all signs are divinely created as "transparent signifiers," but the Fall then created the distinction between "natural" and "arbitrary" signification.

190. See Katarina Koch, *Franz Joseph Molitor und die jüdische Tradition* (Berlin, 2012). Molitor was influenced by the romantic mysticism of Franz von Baader, and kept interest in the Kabbalah alive when the "Science of Judaism" scholars, with a few exceptions like Nachman Krochmal, tended to marginalize it.

191. Walter Benjamin to Gershom Scholem, November 23, 1919, in *The Correspondence of Walter Benjamin*, 151. Agrippa is cited twice in Benjamin's *The Origin of German Tragic Drama*, trans. John Osborne (London, 1977), 152 and 179. Benjamin also refers to him in a 1931 radio broadcast on "Dr. Faust," as a "great scholar" who "had to be defended by one of his students expressly against accusations of sorcery, based in part on the fact that Agrippa was always seen in the company of a black poodle." *Radio Benjamin*, ed. Lecia Rosenthal, trans. Jonathan Lutes with Lisa Harriet Schumann and Diana K. Reese (London, 2014), 123. Benjamin was also indebted to the work of later Christian linguistic philosophers like Johann Georg Hamann, who was often cited in "On Language as Such and the Language of Man."

192. Benjamin, "On the Mimetic Faculty," 722. For a discussion of Benjamin's idea of nonsensuous similarities, see Gunter Gebauer and Christoph Wulf, *Mimesis: Culture, Art, Society*, trans. Don Reneau (Berkeley, 1995), chap. 21.

193. Paracelsus, "Concerning the Signature of Natural Things," in *The Hermetic and Alchemical Writings*, vol. 1, ed. Arthur Edward Waite (London, 1894), 188; cited in Giorgio Agamben, "Theory of Signatures," in *The Signature of All Things: On Method*, trans. Luca D'Isanto with Kevin Attell (New York, 2009), 35. In addition to Benjamin, Agamben sees the survival of the theory of signatures in other twentieth-century figures like Aby Warburg and Michel Foucault.

194. Agamben, "Theory of Signatures," 51. He also observes that the performative power of language still has its place in the secular world: "Speech acts, in which language seems to border on magic, are only the most visible relics of this archaic signatory nature of language" (76).

195. James McFarland, *Constellation: Friedrich Nietzsche and Walter Benjamin in the Now-Time of History* (New York, 2013), 55.

196. Benjamin, "Antitheses Concerning Word and Name," 718.

197. See Miller, *The Name of God in Jewish Thought*, chap. 6.

198. Miller, *The Name of God in Jewish Thought*, 20. He also employs this term to differentiate Christianity, which ossifies, substantializes, and singularizes the name in the figure of Jesus, from Judaism, whose nominalist impulse is more relational and open-ended (58).

199. For a discussion of the differences between Scholem and Benjamin on mathematics, see Handelman, *The Mathematical Imagination*, 73–75.

200. The term first appeared in his discussion of Baudelaire and has often been invoked in treatments of his work, for example, Margaret Cohen, *Profane Illumination: Walter Benjamin and the Paris of Surrealist Revolution* (Berkeley, 1995); and Keya Ganguly, "Profane Illuminations and the Everyday," *Cultural Studies* 18, nos. 2–3 (2004): 255–70.

201. Benjamin, to be sure, could at times recognize the limits of magic. For example, in his "The Work of Art in the Age of Mechanical Reproduction," he contrasted the magician invidiously with the surgeon, comparing the former to the painter and the latter to the camera man of the cinema. Walter Benjamin, "The Work of Art in the Age of Mechanical Reproduction," in *Illuminations*, trans. Harry Zohn (New York, 1968), 233–34.

202. For a representative critique, see Peter E. Gordon, *Migrants in the Profane: Critical Theory and the Question of Secularization* (New Haven, 2000), chap. 1. For more generous analyses, see Michael Löwy, *Morning Star: Surrealism, Marxism, Anarchism, Situationism, Utopia* (Austin, 2000); and Fredric Jameson, *The Benjamin Files* (London, 2020).

203. Benjamin, "Surrealism: The Last Snapshot of the European Intelligentsia," in *Selected Writings*, 2:215. He explicitly argues that "it is as magical experiments with words, not as artistic dabbling, that we must understand the passionate phonetic and graphic transformational games that have run through the whole literature of the avant-garde for the past fifteen years, whether it is called Futurism, Dadaism or Surrealism." (212). Benjamin's debts to surrealism are widely appreciated, for example, in Cohen, *Profane Illuminations*.

204. An example is Hans Blumenberg, who wrote skeptically that "whoever can call things by their names doesn't need to comprehend them. The strength of names has thereby remained greater in magic than in every type of comprehending. The tyranny of names is grounded in names having maintained an air of magic: to promise contact with what hasn't been comprehended." *Care Crosses the River*, trans. Paul Fleming (Stanford, CA, 2010). Michael Miller adds that despite his intentions, there is a danger in Benjamin's yearning for the recovery of the *Ursprache*: "The perfect language which makes reality diaphanous, as a function of that purpose also destroys all reality; consuming and breaking down the things of the world into nothings, an inexistent chaos of which only nothing can be said." *The Name of God in Jewish Thought*, 162. In other words, the redemption of reality may be another way to say entropy. For a discussion of its role in Benjamin's thinking, see Agata Bielik-Robson, "Nihilism as World Politics: Benjamin's Theology of Entropy," in *Walter Benjamin and Political Theology*, ed. Brendan P. Moran and Paula Schwebel, eds., (London, 2024).

205. Leo Bersani, *The Culture of Redemption* (Cambridge, MA, 1990), 54.

206. See Ken Hirschkop, "Why Rhetoric is Magic to Modernism," *Affirmations: Of the Modern* 3, no. 1 (2015).

207. Here a comparison with the art of magical realism, which had a similar ability, is worth considering. See Jerónimo Arellano, *Magical Realism and the History of the Emotions in Latin America* (Lanham, MD, 2015).

208. For a suggestive comparison of magic with the Derridean idea of *différance*, see Lehrich, *The Occult Mind*, chap. 6.

209. For an examination of the thirteenth-century French prose *Lancelot*, which interprets it in terms of magical nominalism, see Jane Gilbert, "Being-in-the-Arthurian World: Emotion, Affect and Magic in the Prose Lancelot, Sartre and Jay," in *Emotions in Medieval Arthurian Literature: Body, Mind, Voice*, ed. Frank Brandsma, Carolyn Larrington, and Corrine Saunders (Cambridge, 2015).

210. For a discussion of the importance of repetition with a difference in twentieth-century Jewish thought, including that of Walter Benjamin, see Sharvit, *Dynamic Repetition*.

Intermezzo

1. Conventional nominalists did not, to be sure, always reduce mind to language, understood either as speech acts or written texts. For images in the mind might also serve the same function, at least for some generic objects. According to the historian Christopher Braider, "pictorial models of knowledge and thought begin to move to the formative center

of Western natural philosophy as early as the fourteenth century. For the via moderna of Ockhamite nominalism, the concept or 'universal' is 'only a kind of picture' (*non est nisi fictio quaedam*), a mental image constructed with a view to sorting the anarchic particulars of ordinary experience." *Baroque Self-Invention and Historical Truth: Hercules at the Crossroads* (Aldershot, 2004), 204.

2. The Sapir-Whorf hypothesis argued that a language's semantic structure determines the ways in which a speaker conceives the world. The theory is named after the American anthropological linguist Edward Sapir (1884–1939) and his student Benjamin Whorf (1897–1941). It lost popularity in the late twentieth century when cognitive psychology and Noam Chomsky's universal grammar gained adherents.

3. This concern remains potent for critics who worry about the dubious ethical implications of nominalism. See, for example, John D. Cox, "Nominalist Ethics and the New Historicism," *Christianity and Literature* 39, no. 2 (1990).

4. Agata Bielik-Robson, *Jewish Cryptotheologies of Late Modernity: Philosophical Marrano* (New York, 2017), 235.

5. See Michael Oberst, "Kant on Universals," *History of Philosophy Quarterly* 32, no. 4 (2015). He concludes that despite his overt suspicion of nominalism, Kant was a "modest nominalist," who criticized the reality of universals, but accepted them as tropes, at least when it came to our cognitive experience of the created world.

6. According to Kant, "It was the moral ideas that gave rise to that concept of a Divine Being which we now hold to be correct. . . . It is these very laws that have led us, in virtue of their *inner* practical necessity, to the postulate of a self-sufficient cause, or of a wise Ruler of the world, in order that through such agency effect may be given to them. We may not, therefore, in reversal of such a procedure, regard them as accidental and derived from the mere will of the Ruler, especially as we have no conception of such a will, except as formed in accordance with these laws. So far, then, as practical reason has the right to serve as our guide, we shall not look upon actions as obligatory because they are the commands of God, but shall regard them as divine commands because we have an inward obligation to them." *Critique of Pure Reason*, A818–19, B846–47.

7. For a bibliography of relevant works in contemporary philosophy, see Stuart Brock and Edwin Mares, eds., *Realism and Anti-Realism* (Montreal, 2007).

8. See, for example, Ian Hacking, *The Social Construction of What?* (Cambridge, MA, 1999).

9. The classic example is the replacement of a geocentric cosmos by a heliocentric solar system in an infinite universe, whose larger implications for how science works continues to generate considerable debate. Among the most heated issues is the meaning of evidence itself, as so-called facts can be understood as always already mediated theoretically rather than simply "given," and actions in G. E. M. Anscombe's famous phrase always "under a description" rather than self-evidently what they appear to be.

10. Karl Marx and Friedrich Engels, *The Holy Family*, 150.

11. Max Horkheimer, "The End of Reason," *Studies in Philosophy and Social Science* 9, no. 3 (1941): 371. Precisely what a substantive concept of "reason" meant for Horkheimer and other critics of positivism was itself a contested issue. See Martin Jay, *Reason after Its Eclipse: On Late Critical Theory* (Madison, WI, 2016).

12. Theodor W. Adorno, *History and Freedom: Lectures 1964–1965*, ed. Rolf Tiedemann, trans. Rodney Livingstone (Malden, MA, 2006), 139.

13. For a full account of the development of this distinction and its variations, see Richard Cross, "Medieval Theories of Haecceity," *The Stanford Encyclopedia of Philosophy*,

first published July 31, 2003; substantive revision January 18, 2022, https://plato.stanford.edu/archives/spr2022/entries/medieval-haecceity/.

14. See Lorraine Daston, ed., *Things that Talk: Object Lessons from Art and Science* (New York, 2004).

15. For a discussion of Benjamin's anti-Kantian thoughts on judgment, which also has a magical dimension, see Eric Jacobson, *Metaphysics of the Profane: The Political Theology of Walter Benjamin and Gershom Scholem* (New York, 2003), 111–14.

16. In *Dialectic of Enlightenment: Philosophical Fragments*, ed. Gunzelin Schmid Noerr, trans. Edmund Jephcott (Stanford, CA, 2002), Max Horkheimer and Theodor W. Adorno admit that "it cannot be established with certainty whether proper names were originally generic names, as some maintain" (17).

17. The Victorian nonsense poet Edward Lear addressed this issue in his wonderful poem "The Scroobious Pip," left unfinished at his death and later completed by Ogden Nash. It referred to a unique animal who did not fit into the taxonomic categories under which other animals were subsumed.

18. This is perhaps the least of the problems that faces a serious consideration of the Adamic notion of ontologically right names for animals. Taxonomic nomenclature, such as the binomial system invented by Linnaeus in the eighteenth century, constantly faces new challenges of classification as hitherto unknown species are discovered and traditional lineages are contested. In other words, even if we were to recover the *Ursprache*, it is not clear how it could handle a post-Darwinian understanding of organic evolution over time.

19. Saul Kripke, *Naming and Necessity* (Cambridge, MA, 1980). Kripke's target was descriptivist theories of reference, such as Bertrand Russell's, which assumed all designators were "flaccid." For an overview of current philosophical debates about naming, see Sam Cumming, "Names," *Stanford Philosophy of Encyclopedia*, first published September 17, 2008; substantive revision October 16, 2023, https://plato.stanford.edu/entries/names/.

20. Michael Fagenblat, *A Covenant of Creatures: Levinas' Philosophy of Judaism* (Stanford, CA, 2010), argues that Kripke is like Maimonides in denying semantic content to the Name (123 and 125). Bielik-Robson enlists him on the side of Jewish nominalism (*Jewish Cryptotheologies of Late Modernity*, 245–48). Kripke's understanding of the referential function of names without meaning as involving an interaction between subject and object is stressed by Michael T. Miller in his analysis of the name theory of the Hekhalot literature of the third to fifth century CE: "Chaos and Onomatology in the Hekhalot Literature," *Bamidbar* 2, no. 1 (2012): 41.

21. Claude Lévi-Strauss, *The Savage Mind* (Chicago, 1966), 172.

22. Maurice Blanchot, *The Writing of the Disaster*, trans. Ann Smock (Lincoln, NE, 1986), 96.

23. Jacques Derrida, *Of Grammatology*, trans. Gayatri Chakravorty Spivak (Baltimore, 1976), 112. For a comparison of Kripke with Derrida, see Christopher Norris, *The Deconstructive Turn: Essays in the Rhetoric of Philosophy* (London, 1983). Derrida's creative appropriation of aspects of the Jewish tradition has often been stressed, so it would be problematic to acknowledge only Kripke's debts to it.

24. Peter Fenves, *The Messianic Reduction: Walter Benjamin and the Shape of Time* (Stanford, CA, 2011), 147.

25. William of Ockham, *Philosophical Writings*, ed. and trans. Philotheus Boehner (Indianapolis, 1990), 28.

26. See Catherine Wilson, *The Invisible World: Early Modern Philosophy and the Invention of the Microscope* (Princeton, 1995), chap. 8.

27. Ockham himself did not deny that some substances were made of composites, but some of his followers, such as Nicolas d'Autrecourt, were more explicitly atomists. See André Goddu, "Ockham's Philosophy of Nature," in *The Cambridge Companion to Ockham*, ed. Paul Vincent Spade (Cambridge, 1999), 149.

28. According to the latest research, neutrinos have 0.0002 percent the mass of an electron. See Rafi Letzer, "Neutrino Experiment Reveals (Again) that Something is Missing from the Universe," *LiveScience*, September 26, 2019, https://www.livescience.com/neutrino-mass-experiment-katrin-early-results.htm.

29. In fact, there are already terms that are used for still smaller entities than nano: "pico" (million-millionth), "femto" (million-billionth), "atto" (billion-billionth), "zepto" (billion-trillionth), "yocto" (trillion-trillionth). They sound like the lost siblings of the Marx Brothers.

30. Critics of nominalism have often raised this objection. It has even been made indirectly by literary figures like Jorge Luis Borges, who sees it leading to a regressive bad infinity in Hegel's sense. See Jon Stewart, "Borges' Refutation of Nominalism in 'Funes el memorioso,'" *Variaciones Borges* 2 (1996).

31. Henry L. Leonard and Nelson Goodman, "The Calculus of Individuals and Its Uses," *Journal of Symbolic Logic* 5, no. 3 (1940): 45. They were pioneers of what came to be called mereological nominalism, which focuses on the relationship between parts and whole. See Daniel Cohnitz and Marcus Rossberg, *Nelson Goodman* (London, 2014), 92–98. For an account that suggests they were anticipated by certain medieval philosophers, see Andre Arlig, "Medieval Mereology," *The Stanford Encyclopedia of Philosophy*, published May 20, 2006; substantive revision July 25, 2019, https://plato.stanford.edu/archives/fall2019/entries/mereology-medieval/.

32. Nelson Goodman, *Ways of Worldmaking* (Indianapolis, 1978), 94–95.

33. To be fair to Goodman, this reading of his argument is contested. It informs the interpretation of his work by Dena Shottenkirk, *Nominalism and its Aftermath: The Philosophy of Nelson Goodman* (Dordrecht, 2009), but it is denied in Samuel Elgin's review in *Enrahonar: Quaderns de Filosofia* 49 (2012).

34. There are other issues raised by this argument, including the need to accept the realism of mathematical abstractions for science, which led to a split between Goodman and W. V. O. Quine, his former collaborator, and Hilary Putnam. For a discussion, see Daniel Cohnitz and Marcus Rossberg, *Nelson Goodman* (London, 2014), chap. 4.

35. For a discussion, see Lars Leeten, "What is 'Critique of Worldmaking'? Nelson Goodman's Conception of Philosophy," *Enrahonar: Quaderns de Filosofia*, 49 (2012): 34.

36. Gérard Genette, *The Work of Art: Immanence and Transcendence*, trans. B. M. Goshgarian (Ithaca, 1997), 207.

37. For a discussion of this issue, see Megan A. O'Connor, *Nominalism, Romanticism, Negative Dialectics* (PhD diss., University of California, 2019), 6.

38. Umberto Eco, *The Search for the Perfect Language*, trans. James Fentress (Oxford, 1995), 30.

39. For a discussion of this issue in the work of Franz Rosenzweig, Gershom Scholem, and Siegfried Kracauer, see *Matthew Handelman, The Mathematical Imagination: On the Origins and Promise of Critical Theory* (New York, 2019).

40. Nelson Goodman, *Languages of Art: An Approach to a Theory of Symbols* (Indianapolis, 1968). For a defense of images against Goodman, see W. J. T. Mitchell, *Iconology: Image, Text, Ideology* (Chicago, 1987), chap. 2.

41. A chemical compound's molar mass is the mass of a sample of it divided by the amount of substance in that sample. It is a bulk property of a substance, which averages many instances of the compound.

42. See, for example, John P. Burgess and Gideon Rosen, *A Subject with No Object: Strategies for a Nominalistic Interpretation of Mathematics* (Oxford, 1997).

43. See, for example, Peter Hallward, "The Singular and the Specific: Recent French Philosophy," *Radical Philosophy* 99, (2000). He distinguishes the isolated "singular," which he sees as celebrated in French poststructuralist theory, from the relationally mediated "specific."

44. That these methodological debates have policy implications in the real world is shown by the infamous retort of the British prime minister Margaret Thatcher in 1987 to people who look for governmental aide: "They are casting their problems on society and who is society? There is no such thing! There are individual men and women and there are families and no government can do anything except through people and people look to themselves first." "Interview for *Woman's Own* ('No Such Thing as Society')," in Margaret Thatcher Foundation: Speeches, Interviews and Other Statements, https://www.margaretthatcher.org/document/106689.

45. Alfred Sohn-Rethel, *Intellectual and Manual Labor* (London, 1978). He argued that conceptual abstractions were ultimately derived from real abstractions in the social world.

46. Nathan Coombes, *History and Event: From Marxism to Contemporary French Theory* (Edinburgh, 2015), 172.

47. The line appears in his poem "The Tables Turned," published in the *Lyrical Ballads* in 1798, whose last stanzas read:

> Sweet is the lore which Nature brings;
> Our meddling intellect
> Mis-shapes the beauteous forms of things:—
> We murder to dissect.
>
> Enough of Science and of Art;
> Close up those barren leaves;
> Come forth, and bring with you a heart
> That watches and receives.

48. It may also be possible to reconceptualize the realist tradition in negative terms as well. See Gerhard Schweppenhäuser, "Criticizing Nominalism and 'Negative Metaphysics': Philosophy-Historical Considerations in the Concept of 'Nature in Dialectic of Enlightenment," *Bajo Palabra* 21 (2019).

49. As Habermas notes, "The history of effects (*Wirkungsgeschichte*) of the nominalistic motif of 'saving the non-identical" extends through Hegel and Kierkegaard to Adorno's *Negative Dialectics*." Jürgen Habermas, *Auch eine Geschichte der Philosophie*, vol. 1, *Die okzidentale Konstellation von Glauben und Wissen* (Frankfurt, 2020), 789. For comparisons of Adorno and Blumenberg on this issue, see Martin Jay, "Adorno and Blumenberg: Nonconceptuality and the *Bilderverbot*," in *Splinters in your Eye* (London, 2020); and Sebastian Tränkle, *Nichtidentität und Unbegrifflichkeit: Philosophische Sprachkritik Nach Adorno und Blumenberg* (Frankfurt, 2022).

50. Initially elaborated by figures like Pseudo-Dionysius the Areopagite and Meister Eckhart, the tradition of negative theology has had echoes in secular philosophy. See, for

example, Ilse Nina Bulhof and Laurens ten Kate, eds., *Flight of the Gods: Philosophical Perspectives on Negative Theology* (New York, 2000).

51. The best known are π, φ, and e. Irrational numbers, so the legend goes, were discovered in the fifth century BCE by Pythagoras's follower Hippasus of Metapontum. Supposedly, it was so shocking that he was drowned at sea as a punishment from the gods, or at least thrown overboard by his fellow Pythagoreans for challenging the commensurability of geometry and mathematics.

52. For a discussion, see Handelman, *The Mathematical Imagination*, chap. 3. He also notes that Rosenzweig identified Judaism with irrational numbers and Christianity with rational ones because of their different relationships to time.

53. There is, for example, a robust literature debating Adorno's evocation of it. See, for example, Christopher Craig Brittain, *Adorno and Theology* (London, 2010); James Gordon Finlayson, "On Not Being Silent in the Darkness: Adorno's Singular Apophaticism," *The Harvard Theological Review* 105, no. 1 (2012); Deborah Cook, "Through a Glass Darkly: Adorno's Inverse Theology," *Adorno Studies* 1, no. 1 (2016); and Sebastian Truskolaski, *Adorno and the Ban on Images* (London, 2021).

54. Similar impulses can be found in other theoretical idioms. Thus, Jacques Lacan's notion of the Real has been interpreted by Slavoj Žižek as "not *another* Center, a 'deeper,' 'truer' focal point or 'black hole' around which symbolic formulations fluctuate; rather, it is the obstacle on account of which every Center is displaced, missed. Or, with regard to the topic of the Thing-in-itself, the Real is not the abyss of the Thing that forever eludes our grasp, and on account of which every symbolization of the Real is partial and inappropriate; it is, rather, that invisible obstacle, that distorting screen, which always 'falsifies' our access to external reality." *The Puppet and the Dwarf: The Perverse Core of Christianity* (Cambridge, MA, 2003), 67.

55. Ilse N. Bulhof, "Being Open as a Form of Negative Theology: On Nominalism, Negative Theology and Derrida's Performative Interpretation of Khôra," in Bulhof and Ten Kate, *Flight of the Gods.*

Chapter Three

1. Reinhart Koselleck, "'Space of Experience' and 'Horizon of Expectation,': Two Historical Categories," in *Futures Past: On the Semantics of Historical Time*, trans. Keith Tribe (Cambridge, MA, 1985).

2. If, as Hans Blumenberg argued in *The Legitimacy of the Modern Age*, trans. Robert M. Wallace (Cambridge, MA, 1983), curiosity about the natural world was unleashed by the nominalist revolution, we might say a similar process followed in the case of historical knowledge.

3. Adi Efal-Lautenschläger, "World-Modelling and Cartesian Method: Blumenberg's Hyperopia," in *Interrogating Modernity: Debates with Hans Blumenberg*, ed. Agata Bielik-Robson and Daniel Whistler (London, 2020), 220.

4. See Denis Feeney, *Caesar's Calendar: Ancient Time and the Beginnings of History* (Berkeley, 2007).

5. See Frank E. Manuel, *Shapes of Philosophical History* (Stanford, CA, 1965), chap. 2. He compares Augustine's version of it with the more radical alternative presented by Joachim of Fiore and notes that a linear view of history was already evident in the Book of Daniel in the Hebrew Bible. Augustine's ruminations on temporality and eternity were,

of course, extended well beyond his thoughts on linear versus cyclical historical time. See, John Doody, Sean Hannan, and Kim Paffenroth, eds., *Augustine and Time* (Lanham, MD, 2021).

6. Manuel, *Shapes of Philosophical History*, 60.

7. Giambattista Vico, *The New Science*, trans. Thomas Goddard Bergin and Max Harold Fisch (New York, 1961), 283. Significantly, he did not include the Hebrews in the nations whose cyclical history he was tracing, because they had the guidance of God. Not surprisingly, he has been admired by structuralists who look for repetition in human behavior. See Claude Lévi-Strauss, "Corsi e Ricorsi: In Vico's Wake," in *We are All Cannibals: and Other Essays*, trans. Jane Marie Todd (New York, 2016).

8. See Melvin J. Laski, *Utopia and Revolution* (Chicago, 1976); Reinhart Koselleck, "Historical Criteria of the Modern Concept of Revolution," in *Futures Past: On the Semantics of Historical Time*, trans. Keith Tribe (New York, 2004); and Martin Jay, "Mourning a Metaphor: The Revolution is Over," in *Essays from the Edge: Parerga and Paralipomena* (Charlottesville, 2011). Early revolutionaries often had as their goal the restoration of a balance that has been upset by the actions of a usurper. Ironically, although the overt meaning of "revolution" lost its cyclical connotation, the actors who appropriated the term for themselves often patterned themselves self-consciously on their predecessors. Historians have also been able to discern repetitive patterns in the trajectories of revolutions, for example, Crane Brinton, *The Anatomy of Revolution* (New York, 1965).

9. See, for example, Karl Löwith, *Meaning in History* (Chicago, 1949). His argument was challenged by Blumenberg in *The Legitimacy of the Modern Age*. For differing accounts, see Robert M. Wallace, "Progress, Secularization and Modernity: The Löwith-Blumenberg Debate," *New German Critique* 22 (1981); and Sjoerd Griffioen, "Secularization between Faith and Reason: Reinvestigating the Löwith-Blumenberg Debate," *New German Critique* 136 (2019).

10. For a subtle analysis of the role of repetition in history, which is nonetheless not as rigid or foreordained as the notion of cyclical return, see Reinhart Koselleck, "Structures of Repetition in Language and History," in *Sediments of Time: On Possible Histories*, ed. and trans. Sean Franzel and Stefan-Ludwig Hoffmann (Stanford, CA, 2018). See also Mehdi Belhaj Kacem, *Événement et répétition* (Paris, 2004), which includes a foreword by Badiou.

11. For a critique of Blumenberg's reliance on morphological patterns that have almost transcendental validity and undermine the possibility of radical novelty, see Daniel Whistler, "Modernizing Blumenberg," in *Interrogating Modernity*, ed. Bielik-Robson and Whistler. He argues for a version of modernity that conforms to Ernst Bloch's "left Aristotelian" notion of a dynamic materialism that allows for radical morphogenesis and the emergence of the new.

12. For a general discussion of the rise of "scientific" historiography, see Joyce Appleby, Lynn Hunt, and Margaret Jacob, *Telling the Truth about History* (New York, 1994), part 1. For an account of the new techniques developed by early modern historians, see Martha Howell and Walter Prevenir, *From Reliable Sources: An Introduction to Historical Methods* (Ithaca, 2001).

13. See Koselleck, "Historia Magistra Vitae: The Dissolution of the Topos into the Perspective of a Modernized Historical Process," in *Futures Past*.

14. Viscount Henry St. John Bolingbroke, "I have read somewhere or other,—in Dionysius of Halicarnassus, I think,—that history is philosophy teaching by examples," *On the Study and Use of History* (Miami, 2017), letter 2. It turns out that the reference to Dionysius of Halicarnassus was erroneous. Instead, the remark seems to have been

made in a third-century treatise on rhetoric, wrongly attributed to Dionysius of Halicarnassus, which compounded the citational error by itself mistakenly attributing it to Thucydides.

15. William J. Bouwsma, *The Waning of the Renaissance, 1550–1640* (New Haven, 2000), 45.

16. See Paul Veyne, *Writing History: Essay on Epistemology*, trans. Mina Moore-Rinvolucri (Middletown, 1984); and Cody Franchetti, "Nominalism and History," *Open Journal of Philosophy* 3, no. 3 (2013). The latter argues, however, that absolute nominalism is an insufficient ground of historical analysis.

17. Siegfried Kracauer, *History: The Last Things Before the Last* (Oxford, 1969).

18. Wilhelm Windelband, *Geschichte und Naturwissenschaft* (Strassburg, 1894). For a discussion of recent revisions of the opposition, see James T. Lamiel, "'Nomothetic' and 'Idiographic': Contrasting Windelband's Understanding with Contemporary Usage," *Theory and Psychology* 8, no. 1 (1998).

19. Casuistry has, of course, a long history in theology, and there is a complicated story that cannot be rehearsed here about the use of "cases" in other disciplines. For a probing study, see John Forrester, *Thinking in Cases* (Cambridge, 2017). For responses to his argument, see the special issue of *History and the Human Sciences* 33, nos. 3–4 (2020).

20. Cliometrics used statistical analysis and adopted neoclassical economics. Their heyday was the period from around 1955 to 1980. For an account of their lingering influence, see Michael Huppert, "The Impact of Cliometrics on Economics and History," *Revue d'économie politique* 127, no. 6 (2017).

21. It is for this reason that history is as often called an art as a science. See H. Stuart Hughes, *History as Art and as Science: Twin Vistas on the Past* (Chicago, 1975).

22. Aristotle, *Poetics* (Oxford, 1946), 1451b.

23. The legacy of nominalism, however, can be found in many other philosophical traditions. For example, Hans-Georg Gadamer, the major twentieth-century exponent of hermeneutics, which is holistic in its approach, acknowledged that "with the nominalistic break-up of the classical logic of essence the problem of languages passes into a new stage. . . . If the relationship of genus and species can be justified not only from the nature of things . . . but also in another way in regard to man and his power to give names, then languages as they have grown up historically, with their history of meanings, their grammar and their syntax, can be seen as the varied forms of a logic of experience, of natural, i.e. historical experience." *Truth and Method* (New York, 1975), 394. Even Hegel was called a nominalist by the pragmatist C. S. Peirce in a 1903 paper "On Phenomenology." For a critique of his reading, see Robert Stern, "Peirce on Hegel: Nominalist or Realist?," *Transactions of the Charles S. Peirce Society* 41, no. 1 (2005).

24. For a more elaborate attempt to spell out the premises and implications of this position and the following one, see Martin Jay, "The Truth of History and the Truth of Historians," in *Genesis and Validity: The Theory and Practice of Intellectual History* (Philadelphia, 2021).

25. The phrase *wie es eigentlich gewesen* is identified with the nineteenth-century German historian Leopold von Ranke, and was turned into the simplistic slogan of positivist historiography by its opponents. That Ranke was a much more complicated figure is often forgotten. For an analysis of the ways in which he became the patron saint of positivist historiography, despite his intentions, see Georg Iggers, "The Image of Ranke in German and American Thought," *History and Theory* 2, no. 1 (1962).

26. There is, however, a residue of the empiricist's faith in sense experience in the word "evidence," whose Latin root is *videre*, which means "to see." It was often contrasted with the unreliable testimony of "hearsay."

27. In his philosophy of science as well as of history, Popper was a realist in the sense of believing in the material reality of the world, but rejected the medieval realist notion of universal essences. For critical discussions of Popper's nominalism, see Norbert Elias, "On the Creed of a Nominalist: Observations on Popper's 'The Logic of Scientific Discovery,' in *Essays I: On the Sociology of Knowledge and the Sciences, in Collected Works*, vol. 14, ed. Richard Kilminster and Stephen Mennell (Dublin, 2009); and Wilhelm Büttemeyer, "Popper on Definitions," *Journal for the General Philosophy of Science* 36 (2005).

28. Hayden White, *Metahistory: The Historical Imagination in Nineteenth-Century Europe* (Baltimore, 1973).

29. See Ian Hunter, "Hayden White's Philosophical History," *New Literary History* 45, no. 3 (2014).

30. Introduced, as we've noted, by the philosopher G. E. M. Anscombe, the phrase was developed by Ian Hacking to indicate the ways in which the same human act could be interpreted as the outcome of different intentions. For example, a raised fist might mean a readiness to strike another person, a sign of political militancy, or a fan's response to a victory by her favorite sports team. Historical actions, rather than being straightforward "facts," were themselves the effects of intentions that needed interpretation. In his *Historical Ontology* (Cambridge, MA, 2004), Hacking argued for what he called "dynamic nominalism" to indicate the historical invention of categories to name people and their behavior, but not the natural world.

31. To be clear, "figural" here does not mean the visual representation of bodies, but rather a form of signification relying on imagery and associations rather than rational concepts and analytical explanations.

32. Voltaire, letter to de Cideville, February 9, 1757, *Oeuvres* (Paris, 1880), 39:173.

33. See Peter Novick, *That Noble Dream: The "Objectivity Question" and the American Historical Profession* (Cambridge, 1988), for a critical history of the search for objectivity in American historiography. For a more cautiously optimistic discussion of the check on relativism produced by "institutional justificationism," see Jay, "The Truth of History and the Truth of Historians."

34. Frank Ankersmit, *Sublime Historical Experience* (Stanford, CA, 2005); Eelco Runia, *Moved by the Past: Discontents and Historical Mutations* (New York, 2014). For a comparison of their work, acknowledging some minor differences, see Anton Froeyman, "Frank Ankersmit and Eelco Runia: The Presence and Otherness of the Past," *Rethinking History* 16, no. 3 (2012). The category the new experientialism is developed in Jay, "The Truth of History and the Truthfulness of Historians." Ankersmit's work is also discussed in Jay, "Sublime Historical Experience, Real Presence and Photography," in *The Journal of the History of Philosophy* 12, no. 3 (2018), a special issue of the journal devoted to his work, including Ankersmit's lengthy reply to his critics. He and the other members of their cohort have sometimes been called the new romanticists. See Jonas Grethlein, "Experientiality and 'Narrative Reference' with Thanks to Thucydides," *History and Theory*, 49 (2010). The literary critic Hans Ulbricht Gumbrecht shared their approach. See his *Production of Presence: What Meaning Cannot Convey* (Stanford, CA, 2003).

35. "The event" was also a favored term among analytic philosophers drawn to nominalism. For example, Nelson Goodman, in his critique of Peirce's distinction between

types and tokens, claimed "words and statements are utterances or inscriptions—i.e. *events* of shorter or longer duration." Cited and critically evaluated in Linda Wetzel, "The Trouble with Nominalism," *Philosophical Studies* 98, no. 3 (2000), 365, italics in original.

36. Michel Foucault, *L'impossible prison* (Paris, 1980), 56. For discussions, see John Rajchman, "The Story of Foucault's History," *Social Text* 8 (1983–84); Thomas R. Flynn, *Sartre, Foucault, and Historical Reason* (Chicago, 2005); Mary Tjiattas and Jean-Pierre Delaporte, "Foucault's Nominalism of the Sexual," *Philosophy Today* 32, no. 2 (1988); Étienne Balibar, "Foucault and Marx: The Question of Nominalism," in *Michel Foucault: Philosopher*, ed. Timothy J. Armstrong (London, 1992); Barry Allen, "Foucault's Nominalism," in *Foucault and the Government of Disability*, ed. Shelley Tremain (Ann Arbor, 2005); and Carol Bacchi, "WPR, Foucault and Nominalist Critique," parts 1 and 2, Carol Bacchi (personal website), October 1, 2020, October 31, 2020, https://carolbacchi.com/2020/10/01/wpr-foucault-and-nominalist-critique-part-i-2/ and https://carolbacchi.com/2020/10/31/wpr-foucault-and-nominalist-critique-part-2/.

37. See, for example, F. R. Ankersmit, "Hayden White's Appeal to Historians," *History and Theory* 37, no. 2 (1998). Demonstrating his abiding respect for White's challenge to conventional historiography, he coedited, along with Ewa Domanska and Hans Kellner a Festschrift for White's eightieth birthday, *Re-Figuring Hayden White* (Stanford, CA, 2009).

38. Runia, *Moved by the Past*, 48.

39. Ankersmit, *Sublime Historical Experience*, chap. 1. He did, however, credit Rorty for showing in his *Philosophy and the Mirror of Nature* how the modern mind withdrew from more direct contact with the world in favor of Cartesian or Kantian subjective interiority (87).

40. Frank Ankersmit and Marcus Tamm, "Leibnizian Philosophy of History: A Conversation," *Rethinking History* 20, no. 4 (2007).

41. For my own encounter with a historical object that jolted me out of the narrative of the past I was following, see Martin Jay, "The Manacles of Gavrilo Princip," *Cultural Semantics: Keywords of Our Time* (Amherst, MA, 1998). If this were an example of a "sublime historical experience," however, it lacked any of the nostalgia for a lost past that often seems to be the primary emotion attached to other examples.

42. For an overview of the ways in which the role of experience in historical reasoning has been defended and criticized, including Ankersmit's notion of sublime historical experience, see Martin Jay, *Songs of Experience: American and European Variations on a Universal Theme* (Berkeley, 2005), chap. 6.

43. Huizinga's idea of "historical sensation" was never fully developed, but its main elements can be discerned from the rough notes he left for an uncompleted project in 1933, which are preserved in his archive in Leiden:

- it touches upon the peculiar, silent way in which the old, that has past, has been persecuting me, since my 13th year, time and again in a different manner, but always with the same voice and color.
- first of all, and now even most, the old houses have spoken.
- I am too much in it, in history, it is no science to me, it is life itself.
- o, the protestant towns, where no bells are ringing, only the chimes.
- saint John by Geertgen [tot Sint-Jans], that grey, pensive figure in that flower-garden, there you have the Northern Netherlandish renaissance!
- use seldom the words psychological and economical, but deal continuously with the objects themselves.

- and above all, never use the word mystical, but imbue the entire representation with the object itself, the direct perception of it, leaving reason aside.
- first explorations.
- understanding just a little bit of the mystical beauty of the quotidian—In our land the Imitatio had to emerge.
- the humanists the first who were haunted by the past. But how different than the past does obsess us.
- the difficulty is that this should become a work of poetry, a piece of myself. Your case is at stake.

Anton van der Lem, "Huizinga and the Historical Sensation," Leiden Special Collections Blog, February 8, 2010, https://leidenspecialcollectionsblog.nl/articles/huizinga-and-the-historical-sensation.

44. Ankersmit, *Sublime Historical Experience*, 132.

45. Ankersmit, *Sublime Historical Experience*, 187.

46. Runia, *Moved by the Past*, 66. The relevance of Barthes's distinction between *punctum* and *studium* will become apparent when we look more closely at the magical nominalist moment in the photograph. For an analysis of the ways in which events as interruptions in the flow of historical time are like synchronic photographs, or indeed pictures in general, see Britta Hochkirchen, "Beyond Representation: Pictorial Temporality and the Relational Time of the Event," *History and Theory* 60, no. 1 (2021).

47. Runia, *Moved by the Past*, 81.

48. Ankersmit, *Sublime Historical Experience*, 225.

49. Runia, *Moved by the Past*, 90.

50. Runia, *Moved by the Past*, 150–51, italics in original.

51. Runia, *Moved by the Past*, 152–53.

52. Runia, *Moved by the Past*, 56–57.

53. Runia, *Moved by the Past*, 168. He adds "be it, of course, that the increased selectiveness makes it a re-enchantment of a rather prosaic or downright nightmarish kind," which suggests that the types of historical experiences he is describing may not always be so benign. There is, after all, a potential connection with trauma that also haunts the celebration of the "event," as we will see shortly.

54. Walter Benjamin, "Theses on the Philosophy of History," in *Illuminations*, ed. Hannah Arendt, trans. Harry Zohn (New York, 1968), 259–60.

55. Ankersmit, *Sublime Historical Experience*, 121.

56. Ankersmit, *Sublime Historical Experience*, 277, italics in original.

57. Frank Ankersmit, "Sublime Experience and Politics: Interview with Professor Frank Ankersmit," with Marcin Moskalewicz, *Rethinking History* 11, no. 2 (2007): 263.

58. In *Sublime Historical Experience*, Ankersmit is very careful to say that "the all-important lesson we must learn from Burckhardt's so strangely ambivalent attitude towards professionalized historical writing is that we should not reject or sacrifice it in favor of historical experience. The notion of historical experience makes sense only and exclusively against the background of professional historical writing" (173).

59. Runia, *Moved by the Past*, 142.

60. Ankersmit, *Sublime Historical Experience*, 167.

61. Ankersmit, *Sublime Historical Experience*, 365.

62. Precisely how the term came into common use is not clear. One veteran observer of May 1968, Dick Howard, speculates as follows: "There was a fantastic series of articles

by Edgar Morin in *Le Monde* in early May—mainly reprinted in *La brèche*. The more likely possibility is that it was journalists in general who wanted to remain neutral, not talking about revolution or anarchy . . . but be simply descriptive. That's the theory of Pierre Hassner, who recalls that in either *Je suis partout* or another right-wing paper after the war, one talked of 'events' with reference to purges of collaborators." Personal communication, September 21, 2009.

63. As Peter Burke points out, the assault on events in the name of structure has happened before in historiography, for example in the Enlightenment with Voltaire and John Millar and during the early-twentieth century with British historians like Lewis Namier and R. H. Tawney. See Burke, "History of Events and the Revival of Narrative," in *New Perspectives on Historical Writing*, ed. Peter Burke (University Park, PA, 1992), 233. A very different critique of the importance of events for the historian was made by idealists like R. G. Collingwood, with his theory of the historical reenactment of rational actions. In *The Idea of History* (Oxford, 1956), Collingwood wrote "Geology presents us with a series of *events*, but history is not history unless it presents us with a series of *acts*" (115). As we will see, an event was differentiated from both a structure and an act. In the German historiography of the same era, the so-called Bielefeld School also stressed structures over events. For a later consideration of theme, see the essays in the *Sonderheft* 19 of *Geschichte und Gesellschaft, Struktur und Ereignis*, ed. Andreas Sutter and Manfred Hettling (Göttingen, 2001).

64. Fernand Braudel, "History and the Social Sciences: The *Longue Durée*," trans. Immanuel Wallerstein, in *Histories: French Constructions of the Past*, ed. Jacques Revel and Lynn Hunt (New York, 1995), 118.

65. According to Peter Burke, "The contemptuous phrase *histoire événementielle*, 'event-centered history,' was coined at this time, a generation before the age of Braudel, Bloch and Febvre. It expresses the ideas of a group of scholars centered on the great French sociologist Émile Durkheim and his *Année Sociologique*, a journal which helped inspire the *Annales*." "Overture. The New History: Its Past and Its Future," in Burke, *New Perspectives on Historical Writing*, 7. A century later, sociologists are still hostile to events. As Elihu Katz and Ruth Katz have recently noted, "Sociologists do not find much interest in events, especially disruptive ones. . . . Events are too idiosyncratic; many are one-time affairs, at least ostensibly. Events are seen as parentheses that open and close, nuisances that interfere with the routines that deserve sociological attention. Not much attention is given, somehow, to the possibility that the exception may be the rule, or come to be the rule, or illuminate the rule; or to the idea that deviant cases also need explaining of a theory is to hold." "Life and Death Among the Binaries: Notes on Jeffrey Alexander's Constructionism," in Jeffrey C. Alexander et al., *Remembering the Holocaust: A Debate* (Oxford, 2009), 156.

66. In *Search for a Method*, trans. Hazel E. Barnes (New York, 1963), originally published in French in 1957, Sartre had written "Existentialism, then, can only affirm the specificity of the historical *event*; it seeks to restore to the event its function and its multiple dimensions. . . . For almost a hundred years now, Marxists have tended not to attach much importance to the event" (124). Althusser and his colleagues shared with structuralists like Claude Lévi-Strauss a deep distrust of Sartrean existentialism.

67. Louis Althusser and Étienne Balibar, *Reading Capital*, trans. Ben Brewster (New York, 1970), 108.

68. Louis Althusser, *For Marx*, trans. Ben Brewster (New York, 1970), 126.

69. Althusser and Balibar, *Reading Capital*, 205.

70. Althusser and Balibar, *Reading Capital*, 294.

71. Louis Althusser, *Essays in Self-Criticism*, trans. Grahame Lock (London, 1976), 125.

72. Althusser adopted the notion of an "epistemological break" from Gaston Bachelard to explain sudden ruptures in intellectual systems—for example, what he claimed was Marx's radical rejection of his Hegelian roots. The parallel with "an event" in history is not hard to discern.

73. For an account of the waning of structuralist historiography, see Lynn Hunt, "French History in the Last Twenty Years: The Rise and Fall of the *Annales* Paradigm," *Journal of Contemporary History* 21, no. 2 (1986). On the recurrent French interest in the event, see Marc Rölli, ed., *Ereignis auf Französisch: Von Bergson bis Deleuze* (Munich, 2004).

74. According to Jan Assmann, "The Egyptian word that comes closest to our concept of history is *kheperut* (events), which has negative connotations. An event is something that had best not happen. In an important work of wisdom literature one reads that God has given man magic as a weapon to ward off the blow of events. . . . However, the difference between the Egyptian and the Mesopotamian versions is obvious. In Egypt the event is a manifestation of chaos and contingency, without any meaning. In Mesopotamia the event is full of meaning, viewed as the manifestation of the punitive will of a divinity whose anger has been roused by the king." *Of God and Gods: Egypt, Israel, and the Rise of Monotheism* (Madison, WI, 2008), 23–24.

75. Edgar Morin, "Le retour de l'événement," *Communications* 18 (1920); Pierre Nora, "Le retour de l'événement," *Faire de l'histoire*, ed. Jacques le Goff and Pierre Nora, vol. 1 (Paris, 1974). The news of structuralism's decline, to be sure, took a while to come to the Anglophone world. Thus, we find the distinguished historian of ideas J. G. A. Pocock still writing in 1987: "To French historians today, of course, this would sound like *histoire événementielle*; they would want to draw attention to the *longue durée*." "Texts and Events: Reflections on the History of Political Thought," *Political Thought and History: Essays on Theory and Method* (Cambridge, 2009), 107.

76. Roland Barthes, "Writing the Event," (1968) in *The Rustle of Language*, trans. Richard Howard (Berkeley, 1986). He finishes by declaring that "the critical aspect of the old system is *interpretation*, i.e., the operation by which one assigns to a set of confused or even contradictory appearances, a unitary structure, a deep meaning, a 'veritable' explanation. Hence, interpretation must gradually give way to a new discourse, whose goal is not the revelation of a unique and 'true' structure, but the establishment of an interplay of multiple structures: an establishment itself *written*: i.e. uncoupled from the truth of speech; more precisely, it is the relations which organize these concomitant structures, subject to still unknown rules, which must constitute the object of a new theory" (154).

77. Louis Althusser, "Philosophy and Marxism," in *Philosophy of the Encounter: Later Writings, 1978–1987*, ed. Oliver Corpet and François Matheron (London, 2006), 264. It also appears on the basis of his posthumously published writings that Althusser's attitude towards nominalism itself was not hostile. Acknowledging Marx's appreciation of nominalism in *The Holy Family* as the "first expression of materialism" and interpreting Spinoza in nominalist terms, he also embraced the importance of cases suggested by Wittgenstein's claim that "the world is all that is the case." For a discussion, see Warren Montag, "Althusser's Nominalism: Structure and Singularity (1962–6)," *Rethinking Marxism* 10, no. 3 (1998).

78. Hayden White, "Formalist and Contextualist Strategies in Historical Explanation," in *Figural Realism: Studies in the Mimesis Effect* (Baltimore, 1999).

79. According to Kelsey Wood, "Žižek shows how both realism and nominalism fail to recognize that what is universal is the Lacanian Real as the incommensurability or

parallax gap that provokes the struggle for truth. Philosophical realism errs in conceiving the truth as some enduring content that serves as an infallible standard of correctness for all possible disclosures or human actions. Nominalism errs by reducing all conflicts to the different particular definitions of some term. . . . Both realism and nominalism are wrong in presuming that we have access to some unambiguous ground or thing-in-itself (conceived either as universal ideal or as individual entities) . . . Žižek points out again and again that the true universal is the Real as antagonism itself, the struggle for hegemony is itself the only sameness that permeates any possible symbolic 'reality.'" "Introduction" to *Žižek: A Reader's Guide* (Hoboken, 2012), 6–7. Nominalism is here identified entirely with its conventional usage. In his rhapsodic endorsement of the event, however, Žižek comes closer to its magical counterpart. If we wanted to cast our net still wider, we could also include the Italian postmodernist philosopher Gianni Vattimo, who often praised the miraculous power of the event in the amalgam of Heidegger, Nietzsche, Gadamer and Christianity he called "weak thought." See for example, Gianni Vattimo, *Of Reality: The Purposes of Philosophy*, trans. Robert T. Valgenti (New York, 2016), chap. 7. For Vattimo, who stressed the role of kenosis or divine "self-emptying," the key event was the Incarnation.

80. This generalization holds for non-French thinkers as well, for example the Russian philosopher Vladimir Bibikhin (1938–2004). See Artemy Magun, "The Concept of the Event in the Philosophy of Vladimir Bibikhin," *Statis* 3, no. 1 (2015). He compares Bibikhin's use of the term with Heidegger's and Badiou's, noting many similarities, but claiming it is more ironic and less moralistic than theirs, as well as more attentive to the event's aesthetic character.

81. Jean-François Lyotard, "March 23," *Political Writings*, trans. Bill Readings and Kevin Paul Geiman (Minneapolis, 1993).

82. See Sande Cohen, "The 'Use and Abuse of History' According to Jean-François Lyotard," *Parallax* 17 (2000).

83. Jean-François Lyotard, *The Postmodern Condition: A Report on Knowledge*, trans. Geoffrey Bennington and Brian Massumi (Minneapolis, 1984), xxiv. For a consideration of the costs of elevating local over grand narratives, see Kerwin Lee Klein, *From History to Theory* (Berkeley, 2011), chap. 4.

84. Lyotard, "March 23," 63, italics in original.

85. Lyotard, "March 23," 64.

86. Lyotard, "March 23," 64. The general importance of events in Lyotard's oeuvre is discussed in Geoffrey Bennington, *Lyotard: Writing the Event* (Manchester, 1988).

87. Lyotard, "March 23," 65.

88. Lyotard, "March 23," 65.

89. Jean-François Lyotard, *Libidinal Economy*, trans. Iain Hamilton Grant (Bloomington, IN, 1993).

90. Lyotard, "March 23," 65, italics in original.

91. Lyotard, "March 23," 65–66.

92. Bill Readings, *Introducing Lyotard: Art and Politics* (London, 1991), 58.

93. Readings, *Introducing Lyotard*, 58, italics in original.

94. For example, the American social historian William H. Sewell Jr. writes that an event belongs to that "relatively rare subclass of happenings that significantly transform structures." *Logics of History: Social Theory and Social Transformation* (Chicago, 2005), 100. The British intellectual historian M. C. Lemon defines it even more flatly as "a sequence of occurrences singled out for notice." *The Discipline of History and the History of Thought* (London, 1995), 71.

95. The identification of the event with radical freedom became one of the general earmarks of the poststructuralist recuperation of the concept, for example, in the work of Jean-Luc Nancy. See his "The Surprise of the Event," in *Hegel after Derrida*, ed, Stuart Barnett (London, 1998).

96. Jean-François Lyotard, "The Sign of History," *The Lyotard Reader*, ed. Andrew Benjamin (Cambridge, MA, 1989), 400.

97. Lyotard, *The Post-Modern Condition*, 82.

98. The distinction between structuralism and poststructuralism is, of course, a loose one during this period, and one can still find strong structuralist, specifically Althusserian, residues in works such as *Difference and Repetition*, trans. Paul Patton (London, 1994), original French publication 1968. For a discussion, see Paul Patton, "Events, Becoming and History," *Deleuze and History*, ed. Jeffrey A. Bell and Claire Colebrook (Edinburgh, 2009), 35.

99. Gilles Deleuze, *The Logic of Sense*, trans. Mark Lester with Charles Stivale, ed., Constantin V. Condas (New York, 1990), 1.

100. Deleuze, *The Logic of Sense*, 1.

101. Deleuze, *The Logic of Sense*, 8.

102. Deleuze, *The Logic of Sense*, 51, italics in original.

103. Deleuze, *The Logic of Sense*, 51. For a discussion of Deleuze's idea of a pure event, which tries to explain its relation to concepts, see Daniel W. Smith, "'Knowledge of Pure Events': A Note on Deleuze's Analytic of Concepts," in *Ereignis auf Französisch*.

104. Deleuze, *The Logic of Sense*, 54.

105. The spatial dimension of Deleuze's philosophy—territorialization, folds, plateaus, etc.—has been widely appreciated. But so too has his interest in temporality, evidenced in his appropriation of Bergson. For one account, see James Williams, *Gilles Deleuze's Philosophy of Time: A Critical Introduction and Guide* (Edinburgh, 2011).

106. Deleuze, *The Logic of Sense*, 77.

107. Gilles Deleuze, *Two Regimes of Madness: Texts and Interviews 1975–1995*, trans. Ames Hodges and Mike Taormina (New York, 2006), 233. Deleuze's idea of a pure event, however, has been used to make sense of an actual historical occurrence. See Tom Lundborg, *Politics of the Event: Time, Movement, Becoming* (London, 2012), which focuses on 9/11.

108. Smith, "'Knowledge of Pure Events,'" 373.

109. Thomas R. Flynn, "Michel Foucault and the Career of the Historical Event," in *At the Nexus of Philosophy and History*, ed. Bernard P. Dauenhauer (Athens, GA, 1987).

110. For a discussion of Foucault's similarities with the Annalistes in the 1960s, see Flynn, *Sartre, Foucault and Historical Reason*, chap. 1.

111. In fact, even earlier, Foucault revealed his attraction to what might be called magical nominalist impulses. In *Les mots et les choses* (1966), he traced the movement from similitudes in language to representation in the transition from the Renaissance to the classical age in terms that have been compared to the fall from Adamic language as such into the language of men in Benjamin. See Sigrid Weigel, *Body and Image-Space: Rereading Walter Benjamin*, trans. Georgina Paul with Rachel McNicholl and Jeremy Gaines (London, 1996), 36–39.

112. John Rajchman, *Michel Foucault: The Freedom of Philosophy* (New York, 1985), 51.

113. Derrida also later claimed in a memorial tribute that "Deleuze the thinker is, above

all, the thinker of the event and always of this event here [*cet événement-ci*]. He remained the thinker of the event from beginning to end." "I'll have to Wander All Alone," *Philosophy Today* 42, no. 1 (1998): 3.

114. Michel Foucault, "Theatrum Philosophicum," *Language, Counter-Memory, Practice*, ed. Donald F. Bouchard, trans. Donald F. Bouchard and Sherry Simon (Ithaca, 1977), 175.

115. Foucault, "Theatrum Philosophicum," 175.

116. Foucault, "Theatrum Philosophicum," 176.

117. Foucault, "Theatrum Philosophicum," 175.

118. Foucault, "Theatrum Philosophicum," 176. Sartre's understanding of the event evolved from the early position that Foucault criticized here. Thus in *Search for a Method*, he defined it as "the moving, temporary unity of antagonistic groups which modifies them to the extent that they transform it. As such, the event has its unique characteristics: its date, its speed, its structures, etc. The study of these factors allows us to make History rational even at the level of the concrete" (130).

119. Foucault, "Theatrum Philosophicum," 176. Perhaps Hegel was the main target, although Foucault did not make it clear.

120. Foucault, "Theatrum Philosophicum," 176.

121. Foucault, "Theatrum Philosophicum," 170.

122. For a discussion of the ways in which Deleuze explicitly distinguished his philosophical notion of becoming from history, see Patton, "Events, Becoming and History." Patton nonetheless concludes that "far from being opposed to history, or a matter of flight from the world, becoming, eventness, and lines of flight are the condition of movement or change within the world" (50).

123. Michel Foucault, "Truth and Power," in *Power/Knowledge: Selected Writings, 1972–1977*, ed. Colin Gordon (New York, 1980), 114.

124. Foucault, "Truth and Power," 114.

125. Michel Foucault, *The Archaeology of Knowledge*, trans. A. M. Sheridan Smith (New York, 1972), 168.

126. Michel Foucault, "The Discourse on Language," appendix to *The Archaeology of Knowledge*, 230. Because of Foucault's stress on situating events in series, Balibar's claim that unlike Marx, he failed to understand the relationality of events is problematic. See Balibar, "Foucault and Marx," 55–56.

127. Foucault, "The Discourse on Language," 230.

128. Foucault, "Questions of Method," 76.

129. Foucault, "Questions of Method," 76.

130. Foucault, "Questions of Method," 77.

131. Foucault, "Questions of Method," 79.

132. Flynn, *Sartre, Foucault, and Historical Reason*, 80.

133. The early French reception of Heidegger did not focus on the concept of the event. See Ethan Kleinberg, *Generation Existential: Heidegger's Philosophy in France, 1927–1961* (Ithaca, 2005). A few French interpreters, such as Michel Haar and Jean Beaufret, did begin to register its importance, which burgeoned in the 1960s. See Tom Rockmore, *Heidegger and French Philosophy: Humanism, Anti-Humanism and Being* (London, 1995). The political theological ruminations of two other German thinkers on the importance of singular events, Walter Benjamin and Carl Schmitt, also influenced the French discussion. See Bernard Flynn, "Political Theology and its Vicissitudes," *Constellations* 17, no. 2 (2010).

134. It has, however, been argued by Eliot R. Wolfson that despite his avowed anti-Semitism, Heidegger's thought shows unexpected similarities with certain Jewish

themes. See his *Heidegger and Kabbalah: Hidden Gnosis and the Path of Poesis* (Bloomington, IN, 2019).

135. Tellingly, Bielik-Robson claims his later work succumbed to *Sprachmagie*, which she tries to distinguish from Jewish nominalism. *Jewish Cryptotheologies of Late Modernity: Philosophical Marranos* (London, 2014), 27.

136. See for example, Willem van Reijen, *Der Schwarzwald und Paris: Heidegger und Benjamin* (Munich, 1998); Stefan Knoche, *Benjamin-Heidegger: Über Gewalt: Die Politisierung der Kunst* (Vienna, 2000); and Andrew Benjamin and Dimitris Vardoulakis, eds., *Sparks will Fly: Benjamin and Heidegger* (Albany, 2015).

137. In the voluminous literature on Heidegger, the word has attracted considerable attention. See, for example, the entry on "event, happening, occurrence" in Michael Inwood, *A Heidegger Dictionary* (Oxford, 1999) and Robert Bernasconi, *The Question of Language in Heidegger's History of Being* (Atlantic Highlands, NJ, 1985), chap. 6. He was not the first German philosopher to comment on *Das Ereignis*, a term used, for example, by Nietzsche in *Thus Spoke Zarathustra* in the section "Of Great Events." For general discussions, see Nikolaus Müller-Schöll, ed., *Ereignis. Eine fundamentale Kategorie der Zeiterfahrung—Anspruch und Aporien* (Berlin, 2003); Gerhard Richter, *Ästhetik des Ereignisses: Sprache—Geschichte—Medium* (Munich, 2005); and Rudolf Wansing, "Im Denken Erfahrung: Ereignis und Geschichte bei Heidegger," in *Ereignis auf Französisch*, ed. Rölli.

138. Martin Heidegger, *Identity and Difference*, trans. John Stambaugh (New York, 1969), 36.

139. As one of his most insightful interpreters, Otto Pöggeler, writes with reference to its use in the later work *Identity and Difference*, "'Ereignis' does not mean here, as it still did within the terminology of *Being and Time*, a certain occurrence of happening, but rather Dasein's complete self-realization in Being and Being's appropriation [*zueignen*] to Dasein's authenticity. The word *Ereignis* cannot be made plural. It determines the meaning of Being itself." "Being as Appropriation," in *Heidegger and Modern Philosophy*, ed. Michael Murray (New Haven, 1978), 102.

140. See Martin Jay, "The Lifeworld and Lived Experience," in *A Companion to Phenomenology and Existentialism*, ed. Hubert L. Dreyfus and Mark A. Wrathall (Malden, MA, 2006).

141. Richard Polt, "The Event of Enthinking the Event," in *Companion to Heidegger's Contribution to Philosophy*, ed. Charles E. Scott, Susan M. Schoenbohm, Daniela Vallega-Neu, and Alejandro Vallega (Bloomington, IN, 2001), 93.

142. Heidegger does not play a central role in Ankersmit's work, but he admired Gadamer "for following Heidegger when urging us to replace epistemology with ontology" (*Sublime Historical Experience*, 232).

143. Inwood, *A Heidegger Dictionary*, 56.

144. Charles R. Bambach, *Heidegger, Dilthey, and the Crisis of Historicism* (Ithaca, 1995), 228.

145. Bernasconi, *The Question of Language in Heidegger's History of Being*, 86. Jean-Luc Nancy glosses *Ereignis* in similar terms: "the appropriation of a presence and not as the (sudden) presence of a property." *The Experience of Freedom*, trans. Bridget McDonald (Stanford, CA, 1993), 113. Not all commentators, however, are convinced that Heidegger's *Ereignisse* really avoids the goal of pure presence. Pheng Cheah, for example, contends that "the deconstructive thinking of the event as something that comes from beyond the order of presence thus breaks with Heidegger's understanding of *Ereignis* as the movement

of propriation and coming into presence. Instead of being a form of presence, the true event is that which is always still to come." "The Untimely Secret of Democracy," in *Derrida and the Time of the Political*, ed. Pheng Cheah and Susanne Guerlac (Durham, 2009), 76.

146. Thus, for example, Herbert Marcuse grew suspicious of his teacher's concept of historicity. As Herman Rapaport has noted, "already in Marcuse's terms, this represented the degradation of history through a temporalized notion of Being that worked against the significance of the historical 'event' per se." *Heidegger and Derrida: Reflections on Time and Language* (Lincoln, NE, 1989), 261. He tries to defend Heidegger against Marcuse's charge.

147. Martin Heidegger, "Die deutschen Universität," in *Reden und andere Zeugnisse eines Lebensweges, Gesamtausgabe, 1910–1976*, vol. 16, ed. Hermann Heidegger (Frankfurt, 2000), 300.

148. In other treatments of the event, however, a more active reading has been advanced. For example, Slavoj Žižek, polemicizing in Leninist fashion against the fetishism of objective revolutionary conditions, writes: "We cannot establish the time of the explosion of the Event through a close 'objective' analysis . . . there is no Event outside the engaged subjective decision which creates it—if we wait for the time to become ripe for the Event, the Event will never occur." *The Puppet and the Dwarf: The Perverse Core of Christianity* (Cambridge, MA, 2003), 135. In *What Is an Event?* (Chicago, 2017), Robin Wagner-Pacifici also maintains that "all events are *made* by active agents using specific mechanisms, and these mechanisms must be recognized as universal" (8).

149. For a general account of his understanding of the event, see the entry in Niall Lucy, *A Derrida Dictionary* (Malden, MA, 2004).

150. Jacques Derrida, *Specters of Marx: The State of the Debt, the Work of Mourning, and the New International*, trans. Peggy Kamuf (New York, 1994). One of Derrida's first discussions of the event came in his early essay "Signature Event Context," where he characterized the event of the individual signature as both singular and based on what went before it and will presumably come after. "Does the absolute singularity of an event of the signature ever occur?" he asks. "Yes, of course, every day," he answers. But then he adds, "in order to function, that is, in order to be legible, a signature must have a repeatable, iterable, imitable form; it must be able to detach itself from the present and singular intention of its production." Derrida, *Margins of Philosophy*, trans. Alan Bass (Chicago, 1982), 328.

151. Derrida uses the French *futur* rather than *avenir* for a future that is continuous with the present.

152. Derrida, *Margins of Philosophy*, 91.

153. Jacques Derrida, "The University without Condition," *Without Alibi*, ed. and trans. Peggy Kamuf (Stanford, CA, 2002), 234. The word "irruption" differs from "eruption" in that it goes into something rather than is expelled by it.

154. Derrida, "The University without Condition," 234.

155. The importance of surprise is stressed by Derrida's fellow deconstructionist Jean-Luc Nancy, "The Surprise of the Event," *Hegel after Derrida*. He claims it "is not only an attribute, quality, or property of the event, but the event itself, its being or its essence. What eventuates in the event is not only that which happens, but that which surprises" (91). It is not *what* happens, the advent of something like a birth or a death, he goes on, but *that* it happens that is the event. Elsewhere Nancy links the idea of surprise with freedom in a manner recalling Lyotard. See *The Experience of Freedom*, chap. 11. The claim that events are always surprises is also made by Wagner-Pacifici, *What Is an Event?*, 2. Koselleck agrees that "every event produces more and the same time less than is contained in its pregiven elements: hence its permanently surprising

novelty" (*Futures Past*, 110). For a challenge to the assumption that "radical events" are never expected or adumbrated, see Theo Yung, "Events Getting Ahead of Themselves: Rethinking the Temporality of Events," *History and Theory* 60, no. 1 (2021).

156. Jacques Derrida with Hélène Cixous, *Veils*, trans. Geoffrey Bennington (Stanford, CA, 2001), 85. Here "the phallus" is a signifier that stands for an imaginary fullness of meaning denied the literal penis, a distinction Lacan explored in his controversial theory of sexual difference.

157. Derrida does not address the mixed cases of predictions that are accurate but not heeded. Cassandra, for example, warned the Trojans about the Greeks' gift horse, the deaths of Agamemnon and Hecuba, Odysseus's lengthy wanderings before returning to Ithaca, the murder of Aegisthus and Clytemnestra by Electra and Orestes, and the escape of Aeneas after the fall of Troy and his role in founding Rome. She benefitted from Apollo bestowing on her the gift of prophecy, but then she spurned his advances and was cursed to be never believed. There are many comparable examples of latter-day Cassandras who predict future events without being taken seriously, even without Apollo's interference.

158. Agata Bielik-Robson, *Derrida's Marrano Passover: Exile, Survival, Betrayal, and the Metaphysics of Non-Identity* (New York, 2023), 129.

159. Jacques Derrida, "A Certain Impossible Possibility of Saying the Event," *Critical Inquiry* 33, no. 2 (Winter, 2007): 446. (The original French publication was 2003, a year before his death). For a discussion, which also focuses on Reinhart Koselleck's "Structures of Repetition in Language and History," see Fernando Esposito, "Despite Singularity: The Event and its Manifold Structures of Repetition," *History and Theory* 60, no. 1 (2021).

160. Derrida, "A Certain Impossible Possibility of Saying the Event," 453.

161. Bielik-Robson, however, claims that "the name, even in Benjamin, does not capture the essence of the thing; quite the contrary, it merely secures the existential reference while guarding the thing's essence as, in Derrida's words, an 'undisclosed abyss.'" *Jewish Cryptotheologies of Late Modernity*, 249.

162. Alain Badiou, "The Event in Deleuze," *Parrhesia* 2 (2007). He describes the basic difference between them in the following terms: "In the first case [Badiou], the event is disjoined from the One, it is separation, assumption of the void, pure non-sense. In the second case [Deleuze], it is the play of the One, composition, intensity of the plenum, the crystal (or logic) of sense" (37). Deleuze, he goes on, "chooses for destiny. The event is not the risky [*hasardeux*] passage from one state of things to another. It is the immanent stigmata of a One-result of all becomings. In the multiple-which-becomes, in the between-two of the multiples which are active multiples, the event is the destiny of the One" (39). See also his *Deleuze: The Clamor of Being*, trans. Louise Burchell (Minneapolis, 2000). For discussions of their differences, see Bruno Besana, "Ein einziges oder mehrere Ereignisse? Die Verknüpfung zwischen Ereignis und Subjekt in den Arbeiten von Alain Badiou und Gilles Deleuze," in *Ereignis auf Französisch*, ed. Rölli; James Williams, "If Not Here, Then Where? On the Location and Individuation of Events in Badiou and Deleuze," *Deleuze Studies* 3, no. 1 (2009); and Andy McLaverty-Robinson, "Alain Badiou: Badiou vs. Deleuze," *Ceasefire*, April 15, 2015, https://ceasefiremagazine.co.uk/alain-badiou-badiou-deleuze/.

163. Catherine Pickstock, "The Univocalist Mode of Production," in *Theology and the Political: The New Debate*, ed. Creston Davis, John Milbank and Slavoj Žižek (Durham, NC, 2005), 312.

164. The return to speculative metaphysics was already urged by Gillian Rose in the 1980s, for example in *Hegel Contra Sociology* (London, 1981), but it only gained traction

in the early twenty-first century with what has variously been called "speculative realism," "speculative materialism," and "object-oriented ontology." Among its leading exponents are Ray Brassier, Iain Hamilton Grant, Graham Harman, and Quentin Meillassoux. See Levi Bryant, Nick Srnicek, and Graham Harman, eds. *The Speculative Turn: Continental Materialism and Realism* (Melbourne, 2011) and Maria J. Binetti, "Philosophy and the Speculative Turn in the 21st Century: New Materialisms and Realisms," *Philosophica* 52 (2021).

165. Laurent Milesi, "From Mallarmé to the Event: Badiou after Derrida," in *After Derrida; Literature, Theory, Criticism in the 21st Century*, ed. Jean-Michel Rabaté (Cambridge, 2018), 144. After stressing their differences, Milesi concludes that Derrida and Badiou share a great deal in their interpretation of "the event."

166. Daniel Bensaïd, "Alain Badiou and the Miracle of the Event," in *Think Again: Alain Badiou and the Future of Philosophy*, ed. Peter Hallward (London, 2004).

167. Alain Badiou, *Images du temps présent* (Paris, 2014), 123.

168. Alain Badiou, *Being and the Event*, trans. Oliver Feltham (London, 2006). For an overview of his argument, see Peter Hallward, *Badiou: A Subject to Truth* (Minneapolis, 2003), chap. 5. For a comparison with Deleuze, see Véronique Bergen, "The Precariousness of Being and Thought in the Philosophies of Gilles Deleuze and Alain Badiou" and Bela Egyed, "Counter-Actualization and the Method of Intuition," both in *Deleuze and Philosophy*, ed. Constantin V. Boundas (Edinburgh, 2006). See also the discussion of their work in John Mullarkey, *Post-Continental Philosophy: An Outline* (New York, 2006).

169. Badiou's complicated relationship to Heidegger has generated considerable commentary. See, for example, Jan Völker, ed., *Badiou and the German Tradition of Philosophy* (London, 2019). Along with his frequent collaborator, Barbara Cassin, Badiou explored the implications of Heidegger's toxic politics for his philosophy in *Heidegger: His Life and Philosophy*, trans. Susan Spitzer. (New York, 2016). While not minimizing his Nazi sympathies, they avoid reducing his ideas to nothing but their philosophical expression. It has also been argued that Badiou and Nietzsche, for all their many differences, shared a similar appreciation of events that defied contextual understanding and subsumption under general categories. See Aleš Bunta, "Nietzsche and Badiou: Event, Intervention, 'God is Dead,'" *Filozofski vestnik* 43, no. 2 (2022). He notes that the most significant event for Nietzsche is "the Death of God," whereas Badiou favors the "original Christian Death of the Son of God on the Cross" (194). Moments in the life of Jesus are privileged as the quintessential "event" by other thinkers influenced by Heidegger and Nietzsche, such as Vattimo.

170. Alain Badiou, *Infinite Thought: Truth and the Return to Philosophy*, ed. and trans. Oliver Feltham and Justin Clemens (London, 2005), 46.

171. Badiou does wrestle with the idea of the natural *clinamen*, the random swerve or deviation from materialist determinism posited by Lucretius and the Epicureans. See *Theory of the Subject*, trans. Bruno Bosteels (London, 2009). But insofar as the genuine event requires recognition and fidelity, it is historical rather than natural. The claim that nature is also best understood in terms of events rather than substances was advanced by Alfred North Whitehead, whose perspective has recently received a new reading. See Leemon B. McHenry, *The Event Universe: The Revisionary Metaphysics of Alfred North Whitehead* (Edinburgh, 2015) and Didier Debaise, *Nature as Event: The Lure of the Possible*, trans. Michael Halewood (Durham, 2017).

172. Alain Badiou with Fabien Tarby, *Philosophy and the Event*, trans. Louise Burchill (Cambridge, 2013), 9.

173. Badiou, *Being and the Event*, 98.

174. Badiou, "The Event in Deleuze," 37.

175. For critiques of his mathematical realism, see Ricardo L. Nirenberg and David Nirenberg, "Badiou's Number: A Critique of Mathematical Ontology," *Critical Inquiry* 37, no. 4 (2011) and John Kadvany, review of *Number and Numbers*, by Alain Badiou, *Notre Dame Philosophical Reviews*, October 2, 2008, https://ndpr.nd.edu/reviews/number-and-numbers/.

176. Badiou's distance from Hegelian dialectics in general is demonstrated in his stress, derived from Cantor, on the importance of irrational numbers, which Hegel sought to banish from analysis of infinity in his Logic. For a discussion, see Nathan Coombes, *History and Event: From Marxism to Contemporary French Theory* (Edinburgh, 2015), 34–40.

177. Badiou, "The Event in Deleuze," 39. "Auto-apparition of the object" sounds something like a miracle that defies the law-like regularities of nature, but Badiou insists nonetheless that "it's not a matter, then, of desperately awaiting a miraculous event but, rather, of following through to the end, to the utmost degree, what you've been able to extract from the previous event and of being as prepared as possible, therefore, to take in subjectively what will inevitably come about. For me truth is an undertaking; it is a process made possible by the event. The event is only there as a source of possibilities." *Philosophy and the Event*, 12.

178. Badiou, "The Event in Deleuze," 42.

179. Badiou, *Philosophy and the Event*, 10. Badiou claims that art, science, love, and politics (but not philosophy) all have distinct "truth procedures." A truth, in his idiosyncratic usage, is a particular set of statements and discourses that are set off by "an event," and follow from it. It challenges existing knowledge and conventional ways of being. Politics is the purest truth procedure because it can incorporate a collective body in a process with universal implications. But why such procedures produce something that can justifiably be called truth is unclear. Paul's conversion to Christianity, for example, may have been intended to be a universal model, but most of humankind has resisted its call.

180. Alain Badiou, *Metapolitics*, trans. Jason Baker (London, 2005), 23.

181. Alain Badiou, *Ethics: An Understanding of Evil*, trans. Peter Hallward (London, 2001), 67.

182. Giorgio Agamben, *Homo Sacer: Sovereign Power and Bare Life*, trans. Daniel Heller-Roazen (Stanford, CA, 1998), 38.

183. Alain Badiou, *Infinite Thought*, trans and ed., Oliver Feltham and Justin Clemens (London, 2005), 130.

184. Negative events are, however, rare for Badiou, allowing John Mullarkey to go as far as to claim that "what is vital for him is that events are always for the good (whether or achieved or not), they concern emancipation and, as such, equality. Hence, there is an element of self-fulfilling, Whiggish historicism in his classification of events." *Post-Continental Philosophy*, 104.

185. Claude Romano, *Event and World*, trans. Shane Mackinlay (New York, 2009); *Event and Time*, trans. Stephen E. Lewis (New York, 2013); *There Is: The Event and the Finitude of Appearing*, trans. Michael B. Smith (New York, 2015); for a discussion, see Martin Jay, *Genesis and Validity: The Theory and Practice of Intellectual History* (Philadelphia, 2021), chap. 2. For examples of Meillassoux's contribution to the issue, see his "History and Event in Alain Badiou," *Parrhesia* 12 (2011) and "Badiou and Mallarmé: The Event and the Perhaps," *Parrhesia* 16 (2013).

186. Maurice Merleau-Ponty, *The Prose of the World*, trans. John O'Neill (Evanston, 1973), 79.

187. An example of the future anterior tense is the sentence, "When he arrives I will have already left the room." The implications of anticipating a future event are discussed in Yung, "Events Getting Ahead of Themselves."

188. For an account of the distinction, which ties it to questions of the event, see Oliver Marchart, *Post-Foundational Political Thought: Political Difference in Nancy, Lefort, Badiou and Laclau* (Edinburgh, 2007).

189. Hans-Georg Gadamer, *The Revival of the Beautiful and Other Essays*, ed. Robert Bernasconi, trans. Nicholas Walker (Cambridge, 1986), 135.

190. There is another, far more trivial usage, which is part of pop culture and the marketing of unique experiences. As the sociologist Zygmunt Bauman noted, "Perhaps the most potent brands are properly advertised and hyped *events*: celebrity events, massively attended according to [Daniel] Boorstin's criteria thanks to being known for their well-knownness and selling masses of tickets because the tickets are selling well. 'Events' have an advantage over company-fixed brands which have to count on the lasting loyalty of faithful clients. Events are better attuned to the notoriously short spans of public memory and the cut-throat competition between enticements vying for consumers' attention." *Liquid Life* (Malden, MA, 2005), 61.

191. Peter Dews, review of *Being and the Event*, by Alain Badiou, *Notre Dame Philosophical Reviews*, February 19, 2008, http://ndpr.nd.edu/review.cfm?id=12406.

192. Egyed, "Counter-Actualization and the Method of Intuition," 80.

193. Amy Hollywood, "Saint Paul and the New Man," *Critical Inquiry* 35, no. 4 (Summer 2009): 275. The recent philosophical love affair with Paul often drew on the idea of the event. See the many examples in Peter Frick, ed., *Paul in the Grip of the Philosophers: The Apostle and Contemporary Continental Philosophy* (Minneapolis, 2013).

194. It turns out that this often-cited remark may itself have been misheard, as his translator now says it referred to the events of 1968, not 1789. See "Not Letting the Facts Ruin a Good Story," *South China Morning Post*, June 15, 2011, https://www.scmp.com/article/970657/not-letting-facts-ruin-good-story.

195. The metaphor of the poetic caesura—a rhythmic interruption of melodic fluidity—is mobilized in particular by Philippe Lacoue-Labarthe in his discussion of Hölderlin's challenge to the speculative closure of traditional tragedy, which he argues is the source of dialectical reconciliation. Like the event, it functions to disrupt, disorganize, and disarticulate the narrative system in which it appears. See "The Caesura of the Speculative," in *Typography: Mimesis, Philosophy, Politics*, ed. Christopher Fynsk (Cambridge, MA, 1980).

196. Deleuze's attempt to link eternal aionic time with singular events seems less plausible than Badiou's linkage with kairotic time. For it suggests timeless archetypes, which explains its attraction for mythagogic thinkers like Carl Jung, who entitled one of his books *Aion: Researches into the Phenomenology of the Self*, trans. Gerhard Adler and R. F. C. Hull (Princeton, 1979).

197. For example, Mark 1:15, which reads in the King James version, "The time is fulfilled, and the Kingdom of God is at hand. Repent ye and believe the Gospel."

198. Paul Tillich, *The Interpretation of History* (New York, 1936).

199. Walter Benjamin, "Theses on the Philosophy of History," 263. The concept of "now-time" has been much discussed in the literature on Benjamin. See, for example, Kia Lindroos, *Now-Time/Image-Space: Temporalization of Politics in Walter Benjamin's Philosophy of History and Art* (Jyväskylä, 1998); and Stefan Gandler, *Materialismus und*

Messianismus: Zu Walter Benjamins Thesen Über den Begriff der Geschichte (Bielefeld, 2008). Harry Zohn, the translator of *Illuminations,* identifies it with the mystical notion of *nunc stans* or the everlasting now of eternity. But Rebecca Comay objects that "now-time" "is nothing like a present, but rather that which undermines the very presentability of that which comes . . . not an 'occurrence' or event *in* time, but rather the opening of history (*Geschichte*) itself as the infinite responsibility of the pure event. The *Jetztzeit* is thus anything but the 'mystical *nunc stans,*' as Zohn would have it." "Benjamin's Endgame" in *Walter Benjamin's Philosophy: Destruction and Experience,* ed. Andrew Benjamin and Peter Osborne (London, 1994), 272.

200. Slavoj Žižek, "Afterword: With Defenders Like These, Who Needs Attackers?," in *The Truth of Žižek,* ed. Paul Bowman and Richard Stamp (London, 2007), 222.

201. Alain Badiou, *Saint Paul: The Foundation of Universalism,* trans. Ray Brassier (Stanford, CA, 2003). An event, he writes, "is falsified if it does not give rise to a universal becoming-son. Through the Event we enter into filial equality" (49). For all his stress on the singularity of events, Badiou seems to be arguing that only those that produce something universal are worth our fidelity. A turn to St. Paul was already advocated by the early twentieth-century German theologian Karl Barth, who stressed the otherness of a God who did not act providentially in human history but rather could demonstrate his absolute sovereignty by intervening at will. See his commentary on *The Epistle to the Romans,* trans. Edwyn Hoskyns (Oxford, 1958), written in German in 1918 and revised several times after.

202. Badiou, *Saint Paul,* 48.

203. Hollywood, "Saint Paul and the New Man," 869.

204. Antonio Calcagno, *Badiou and Derrida: Politics, Events and their Time* (London, 2007), 98–109. Not all theologically inspired commentators have been persuaded, however, by his argument. For a critique from a Thomist perspective (filtered through Nicholas of Cusa), see John Milbank, "Materialism and Transcendence," in *Theology and the Political,* ed. Davis, Milbank and Žižek. He argues for the folding in of the event into its context via a complicated ontology of mediating analogies.

205. Oliver Marchart, "Acting and the Act: On Slavoj Žižek's Political Ontology," in *The Truth of Žižek,* 105.

206. Mattjis van de Port, *Ecstatic Encounters: Bahian Camdomblé and the Quest for the Really Real* (Amsterdam, 2011), 193.

207. With reference to the last of these in particular, see Martin Jay," When Did the Holocaust End? Reflections on Historical Objectivity," *Refractions of Violence* (New York, 2003). The case of the controversial "temporal fringes" of the "storming of the Bastille" is discussed in Anna Karla, "Controversial Chronologies: The Temporal Demarcation of Historical Events," *History and Theory* 60, no. 1 (2021).

208. Not only have historians sought such patterns—for example, Brinton, *The Anatomy of Revolution*—but actors in later revolutions have been aware of the models of earlier ones. To take an obvious example, Stalin was often seen by his Trotskyist opponents as the Napoleon of the Russian Revolution. In his bitter musings on the outcome of the 1848 revolutions, Marx had already made the famously sardonic observation in connection with Napoleon III that revolutionary history can repeat, albeit in the form of farce rather than tragedy. See Jeffrey Mehlman, *Revolution and Repetition; Marx/Hugo/Balzac* (Berkeley, 1977).

209. Lemon, *The Discipline of History and the History of Thought,* 71–72. Contemporary narratology decomposes events into more fine-grained event-types, for example happenings, actions and moves. See David Herman, "Events and Event-Types" in *Routledge*

Encyclopedia of Narrative Theory, ed. David Herman, Manfred Jahn, and Marie-Laure Ryan (London, 2007).

210. Hayden White, "The Narrativization of Real Events," *Critical Inquiry* 7, no. 4 (Summer, 1981): 795. The traditional distinction between narration and description, given so much weight by literary theorists like Georg Lukács, is less important here than their common function as over-arching categories under which the apparent singularity of the event is subsumed.

211. Koselleck, *Sediments of Time*, 168.

212. Keith Bassett, "Thinking the Event: Badiou's Philosophy of the Event and the Example of the Paris Commune," *Environment and Planning D: Society and Space* 26 (2008): 898.

213. Meillassoux, "History and Event in Alain Badiou," 2.

214. Jean Baudrillard, *The Intelligence of Evil; Or the Lucidity Pact*, trans. Chris Turner (London, 2013), 94–95. Although his version of the event replicates all of the characteristics detailed by the other French thinkers discussed in this chapter, Baudrillard rejects their ontological claims in favor of locating events in a simulacral pseudo-reality where they are concoctions of the "information machine" that both produces and answers desire for their existence.

215. Wagner-Pacifici, *What Is an Event?*, 4.

216. As one skeptical commentator put it, "the true subject of historical change, it transpires, is one who possesses an intuition of the necessity of teasing out the internal possibilities of a situation in the rational construction of novelties. That is, the philosophical meta-ontologist informed by Cohen's method. That is, Badiou himself." Coombes, *History and Event*, 133. The reference to "Cohen's method" is to the semantic forcing method of the set theorist Paul Cohen, which Badiou used to provide a conceptual framework for thinking about multiplicities without relying on the concept of the one. Cohen introduced the technique of "forcing" to prove that the traditional axioms of set theory are consistent with the negation of the continuum hypothesis proved by Gödel.

217. Jacques Derrida, "Autoimmunity: Real and Symbolic Suicides—A Dialogue with Jacques Derrida," in *Philosophy in a Time of Terror: Dialogues with Jürgen Habermas and Jacques Derrida*, ed. Giovanna Borradori (Chicago, 2003), 86.

218. There is, of course, no exclusive ownership of proper names, which cannot be copyrighted like brands or trademarked like hashtags. Rigid designation, we might say, is inevitably contextual. For a somewhat tongue-in-cheek exploration of this issue, see Martin Jay, "Googlegangers and Flaccid Designators," *Salmagundi* 214–15 (Spring–Summer, 2022).

219. It happened in 1973. For my own education on the meaning of the date for Chileans, see Martin Jay, "Fearful Symmetries: 9/11 and the Agonies of the American Left," in *Refractions of Violence* (New York, 2003).

220. Comay, "Benjamin's Endgame," 268. Comay is drawing here on Derrida's argument about the paradoxical singularity and iterability of signatures.

221. Mullarkey, *Post-Continental Philosophy*, 100.

222. Some efforts have been made, however, to introduce it into historical accounts. See, for example, Shruti Kapila, "History of Violence," *Modern Intellectual History* 7, no. 2 (2010). The author discusses the radical Indian nationalist B. G. Tilak's reading of the Bhagavad Gita in terms of Badiou's notion of the event. See also, Richard Devetak, "After the Event: Don DeLillo's *White Noise* and September 11 Narratives," *Review of International Studies* 35 (2009): 795. Devetak imaginatively compares DeLillo's novel with its

constitution of events via a multitude of different narrative voices with the constitution of historical events through similar means.

223. This conclusion is especially apposite for Derrida's version of the event. As Agamben notes in discussing "signatures" that reveal meaningful similitudes, deconstruction "was intimately tied to an interpretative practice that suspends signatures and makes them idle, in such a way that there is never any access to the realized event of meaning." He contrasts this approach with Foucault's, which "means keeping events in their own proper dispersal, lingering on the smallest deviations and the aberrations that accompany them and determine their meaning. In a word, it means seeking in every event the signature that characterizes and specifies it and in every signature the event and the sign that carry and condition it" ("Theory of Signatures," 78–80).

224. Žižek, *The Puppet and the Dwarf*, 128. In *Moses and Monotheism*, Freud developed the biblical scholar Ernst Sellin's speculation that Moses was killed by the Jews. See R. A. Paul, "Freud, Sellin and the Death of Moses," *International Journal of Psychoanalysis* 75, no. 4 (1994).

225. According to Agata Bielik-Robson, "Saint Paul for Badiou and Jesus for Žižek are primarily *arch-revolutionaries*, ready to sacrifice their life and unleash an absolute inferno of global violence in the name of the 'Cause' they believe in. But what really counts is not the 'Cause' itself, but the originary destructive attitude: the readiness for the violent birth of a 'new man' on the ruins of the old and 'pathological.'" "The Post-Secular Turn: Enlightenment, Tradition, Revolution," *Eidos* 3, no. 3 (2109): 76–77. In *Derrida's Marrano Passover*, she contrasts this attitude with that of Derrida, whose positive identification as a Marrano prevents him from embracing a fantasy of totalizing redemption based on the utter destruction of a fallen world.

226. Maurice Blanchot, *The Writing of the Disaster*, trans. Ann Smock (Lincoln, NE, 1986), 141–42.

227. Andrew Benjamin, *The Plural Event: Descartes, Hegel, Heidegger* (London, 1993), 191.

228. White, "The Modernist Event" in *Figural Realism*, 74. Jameson introduced this term with reference to the novels of Sartre. White's larger point is that derealized events are typical of modernist literature in general and should be understood as informing historical discourse as well. He adopts Eric Santner's term "narrative fetishism" to define what he opposes.

229. For an argument for the value of anticipating future events, see Yung, "Events Getting Ahead of Themselves."

230. Ankersmit, *Sublime Historical Experience*, chaps. 5 and 6.

231. Badiou, *Philosophy and the Event*, 68–69.

Chapter Four

1. See Simon Grote, *The Emergence of Modern Aesthetic Theory: Religion and Morality in Enlightenment Germany and Scotland* (Cambridge, 2017), 74.

2. To avoid any confusion, the idiosyncratic theory of aesthetic realism developed by the philosopher and poet Eli Siegel, which some have seen as producing a psychotherapy cult, is outside the purview of this discussion.

3. There are, to be sure, attempts to apply the term to other artistic fields. See, for example, Carl Dahlhaus, *Realism in 19th-century Music*, trans. Mary Whittall (Cambridge, 1985). Realism in architecture is sometimes traced back to the Gothic revivalist Augustus

Pugin in mid-Victorian England, because of his stress on the use of "real" materials—stone and brick—rather than cement or stucco, as well as not masking the structure or function of a building.

4. For representative accounts of realism in literature and the figurative arts, see Linda Nochlin, *Realism* (New York, 1971); J. P. Stern, *On Realism* (London, 1973); Christopher Prendergast, *The Order of Mimesis: Balzac, Stendhal, Nerval, Flaubert* (Cambridge, 1988); Matthew Beaumont, ed., *A Concise Companion to Realism* (London, 2010); Fredric Jameson, *The Antinomies of Realism* (London, 2013); and Jens Elze, ed., *Realism: Aesthetics, Experiments, Politics* (London, 2022).

5. Roland Barthes, "The Reality Effect," in *The Rustle of Language*, ed, François Wahl, trans. Richard Howard (Berkeley, 1989). The metaphor of "holding up a mirror to nature" was introduced by Shakespeare in *Hamlet*, when the prince gives his advice to the players in the theatrical performance of "The Murder of Gonzago."

6. In the dialectical concept of realism, however, that "real world" may also contain emergent or potential qualities that move beyond it. Ernst Bloch, for example, writes, "Where the prospective horizon is continuously kept in sight, reality appears there as what it is concretely: as a network of paths of dialectical processes that take place in an unfinished world. . . . Reality without real possibilities is not complete. The world without future-bearing qualities deserves as little regard, art, or science as the world of the philistine does. *The concrete utopia stands at the horizon of every reality: the real possibilities enclose the open dialectical tendency-latency until the very last moment.*" "Artistic Illusion as Visible Anticipatory Illumination," in *The Continental Aesthetics Reader*, ed. Clive Cazeaux (London, 2000), 364.

7. This qualification has to be introduced because the development of literary fictionality, and with it the "realist novel," involved a new understanding that fictional characters were invented personae rather than coded references to real people. See Catherine Gallagher, *Nobody's Story: The Vanishing Acts of Women Writers in the Marketplace, 1670–1920* (Chicago, 1994).

8. In an oft-cited letter of April, 1888 to Margaret Harkness, Friedrich Engels wrote that "realism, to my mind, implies, besides truth of detail, the truthful reproduction of typical characters under typical circumstances," a dictum whose implications Marxists like Georg Lukács explored in numerous works. What set this tradition off from the aesthetic realism indebted to Platonic or Aristotelian aesthetic theories was its insistence that types were historical and social rather than eternal and natural.

9. W. J. T. Mitchell, *Iconology: Image, Text, Ideology* (Chicago, 1986), 90.

10. For one example of many, see Elisabeth Tropman, "How to Be an Aesthetic Realist," *Ratio* 35, 1 (2021).

11. René Wellek famously charged Erich Auerbach with confusing the two in his classic review of *Mimesis* in "Auerbach's Special Realism" in *Kenyon Review* 16 (1954). For a defense of Auerbach, which claims he was more of a historicist nominalist in his use of the term, see Barry Maine, "Erich Auerbach's 'Mimesis' and Nelson Goodman's 'Ways of Worldmaking': A Nominal(ist) Revision," *Poetics Today* 20, 1 (1999).

12. In *The Rise of the Novel: Studies in Defoe, Richardson and Fielding* (Berkeley, 1959), Ian Watt argued for the influence of individualism, economic, religious, and philosophical, in the origins of the English novel. He muddied the waters, however, by claiming that the novel's conception of mimesis derives from what he mislabeled "philosophical realism": "The distinctive narrative mode of the novel . . . is the sum of literary techniques whereby the novel's imitation of human life follows the procedures adopted by

philosophical realism in its attempt to ascertain and report the truth" (31). The method of philosophical realism, he claimed, "has been the study of the particulars of experience by the individual investigator, who, ideally at least, is free from the body of past assumptions and traditional beliefs; and it has given a peculiar importance to semantics, to the problems of the nature of the correspondence between words and reality" (12). Literary plots in novels no longer illustrated universals but "had to be acted out by particular people in particular circumstances, rather than, as had been common in the past, by general human types against a background primarily determined by the appropriate literary convention" (15). Watt, in other words, was really acknowledging the influence of nominalism on the rise of the novel.

13. See Iris Murdoch, *The Fire and the Sun: Why Plato Banished the Artists* (Oxford, 1977). For a discussion of his complicated attitude towards mimesis, see Gunter Gebauer and Christoph Wulf, *Mimesis: Culture—Art—Society*, trans. Don Reneau (1995), chap. 3.

14. The Carolingian scholar Alcuin declared that God was *aeterna pulchritude.* Cited in Władysław Tartarkiewicz, "The Great Theory of Beauty and its Decline," *The Journal of Aesthetics and Art Criticism* 31, no. 2 (1972): 170.

15. Boethius's unfinished early sixth-century treatise *De institutione musica libri quinque* provided influential instruction in the principles of music. See Gabriela Ilnitchi, "Musica Mundana, Aristotelian Natural Philosophy and Ptolemaic Astronomy," *Early Music History* 21 (2002).

16. Otto Georg von Simson, *The Gothic Cathedral: Origins of Gothic Architecture and the Medieval Concept of Order* (Princeton, 1987); Erwin Panofsky, *Gothic Architecture and Scholasticism: An Inquiry into the Analogy of the Arts, Philosophy, and Religion in the Middle Ages* (New York, 1976); Hans Sedlmeyer, *Die Entstehung der Kathedrale* (Zurich, 1950); and Günter Bandmann, *Mittelalterliche Architektur als Bedeutungsträger* (Berlin, 1951).

17. Umberto Eco, *Art and Beauty in the Middle Ages*, trans. Hugh Bredin (New Haven, 1986), 17. Pancalistic comes from the Greek *pan kalos*, "everything beautiful." See also the discussion of aesthetic Platonism in Hans Robert Jauss, *Aesthetic Experience and Literary Hermeneutics*, trans Michael Shaw (Minneapolis, 1982), where he calls it "the authoritative legacy from which and against which aesthetic experience developed in the history of European education" (37). For a general survey of medieval aesthetics, see John Haldane, "Medieval Aesthetics," in *The Routledge Companion to Aesthetics* (New York, 2013).

18. For an argument that the two are not actually binary opposites for Plato, see Jean-Luc Nancy, "The Image: Mimesis and Methexis," *Nancy and Visual Culture*, ed. Carrie Giunta and Adrienne Janus (Edinburgh, 2017).

19. See Phillip Sidney Horky, *Plato and Pythagoreanism* (New York, 2013). He argues for the importance of Hippasus of Metapontum, a student of Pythagoras, for the most important experiments in harmonics that led to the innovations in mathematics that influenced Plato.

20. Two numbers are in the golden ratio (in Latin, *sectio aurea*) if the ratio of the sum of the numbers divided by the larger number is equal to the ratio of the larger number divided by the smaller number. In 1597, the Tübingen scholar Michael Maestlin calculated that its decimal equivalent is 1.618. It is still sometimes invoked as a principle that governs everything from the largest galaxy to DNA, and can be observed in human anatomy as well (facial features and the relationship of arms and legs to torsos).

21. Theodor W. Adorno, *Metaphysics: Concept and Problems*, ed. Rolf Tiedemann, trans. Edmund Jephcott (Stanford, CA, 2000), 26.

22. For Aristotle, "The chief forms of beauty are order and symmetry and definiteness, which the mathematical sciences demonstrate in a special degree" (*Metaphysics*, in *The Complete Works of Aristotle*, ed. Jonathan Barnes, vol. 2, 1705, 1078a36).

23. G. W. F. Hegel, *Hegel: On the Arts*, ed. and trans. Henry Paolucci (New York, 1979), 7. He was, however, careful to distinguish artistic from natural beauty and argued that the former did not imitate the latter. And he sounded more like Aristotle than Plato in arguing that art unifies the universal and the particular in the way Christianity reconciles the divine and the human in Christ.

24. Allen H. Goldman, "Realism about Aesthetic Properties," *The Journal of Aesthetics and Art Criticism* 51, no. 1 (1991): 31.

25. Thomas Aquinas, *Summa Theologica*, first part, question 39, article 8.

26. See Louise Vinge, *The Five Senses: Studies in a Literary Tradition* (Lund, 1975).

27. Wolfgang Welsch, *Undoing Aesthetics*, trans. Andrew Inkpin (London, 1997), 87.

28. The precise parallels were, of course, thrown off when the role of language was considered. Nor is it clear that the correlations were ever very precise, as Jean-Luc Nancy argues in *The Muses*, trans. Peggy Kamuf (Stanford, CA, 1996), chap. 1.

29. Susanne Langer, "Deceptive Analogies: Specious and Real Relationships among the Arts," in *Problems of Art* (New York, 1957), 81–82.

30. Such categories as the "beaux arts" or "fine arts"—the term was in already in use when the École Nationale Supérieure Des Beaux-Arts in Paris was founded in 1671 by Jean-Baptiste Colbert, minister of Louis XIV—implied a distinction between arts and crafts, which had not been made during the Middle Ages, but not yet the concept of "art as such." Its full expression, in fact, may have had to wait until Marcel Duchamp, if Thierry de Duve is right. See his "The Post-Duchamp Deal: Remarks on a Few Specifications of the Word 'Art,'" *Filozofski Vestnik* 28, no. 2 (2007).

31. According to Nancy, "What is called aestheticism always had as its seed or its primary condition in a tendentious assumption of 'Art' in the singular" (*The Muses*, 37).

32. For a discussion of Plato's influence on Keats, see T. C. Kennedy, "Platonism in 'Ode on a Grecian Urn,'" *Philological Quarterly* 75, no. 1 (1996). For a different reading of the poem and much else in Keats that suggests he was devoted to "empowering the perceiver" rather than valorizing the eternal stasis of the artwork, see Wendy Steiner, *Pictures of Romance: Form Against Context in Painting and Literature* (Chicago, 1988), chap. 3.

33. Walter Pater, *Plato and Platonism: A Series of Lectures* (London, 1893). See Adam Lee, *The Platonism of Walter Pater: Embodied Equity* (Oxford, 2020).

34. Arthur Danto, "'Anything Goes': The Work of Art and the Historical Future," *Occasional Papers of the Doreen B. Townsend Center for the Humanities* 14 (Berkeley, 1998), 11.

35. There were also displaced versions of the realism/nominalism debate, for example in the controversy over whether style should be seen as generic or individual. See Andrea Pinotti, "Formalism and the History of Style," in *Art History and Visual Studies in Europe: Transnational Discourses and National Frameworks*, ed. Mathew Rampley, Thierry Lenain, Hubert Locher, Andrea Pinotti, Charlotte Schoell-Glass, and Kitty Zijlmans (Leiden, 2012), 83–85.

36. Arthur O. Lovejoy, *The Great Chain of Being: A Study of the History of an Idea* (New York, 1936), chap. 9.

37. In the visual arts, one source of the challenge came from applying Ockham's razor to those basic building blocks of medieval optics called "visible species," which allowed an object to appear as meaningful to the eyes that beheld it. Sight, according to medieval ocular theory, worked through the transmissions of these forms—or in the synonyms

listed by Roger Bacon, "similitudes, "images," "idols," "simulacra," "phantasms," and "impressions"—from the object to the eye and vice versa. Extramission meant the sending out of species from the eye, which met those coming in through intromission. Successively reproduced through a medium like air or water, they ultimately have an impact on the sensitive membranes and humors of the eyeball, which registers their pressure. Having corporeal being, they convey an object's visual form and meaning to the beholder, more along the lines of touch than what we would now understand as visual experience via light waves or particles. Ockham, however, rejected the idea of "visible species" as adding an extraneous general concept, in favor of understanding sight as an intuitive grasping of particular objects at a distance. The corporeal mediation by species, like the other abstract universals derived from ancient Greek metaphysics, was a superfluous fiction. Although there was considerable resistance to Ockham's critique of "visible species" well into the fourteenth century, in the long run his demolition was effective. However we understand sight now, it is not on the basis of the successive reproduction of iconic forms through a corporeal medium. See Katherine H. Tachau, *Vision and Certitude in the Age of Ockham: Optics, Epistemology and the Foundations of Semantics 1250–1345* (Leiden, 1988) and Suzannah Biernoff, *Sight and Embodiment in the Middle Ages* (New York, 2002).

38. For discussions of the sublime in the Middle Ages, see C. Stephen Jaeger, ed., *Magnificence and the Sublime in Medieval Aesthetics: Art, Architecture, Literature, Music* (New York, 2010). Although the recovery of the classical term *sublimitas* is usually attributed to the French translation of Longinus in the late seventeenth century, there are examples of its usage in various medieval texts as well.

39. Eco, *Art and Beauty in the Middle Ages*, 88–89.

40. For a history of its complicated fortunes, see Darrin M. McMahon, *Divine Fury: A History of Genius* (New York, 2013).

41. Jonathan M. Hess, *Reconstituting the Body Politic: Enlightenment, Public Culture and the Invention of Aesthetic Autonomy* (Detroit, 1999), 236.

42. For a discussion of its origins and implications, see Martin Jay, *Songs of Experience: Modern European and American Variations on a Universal Theme* (Berkeley, 2005), chap. 4.

43. See Paolo D'Angelo and Stefano Velotti, *Il 'non so che': Storia di un'idea estetica* (Palermo, 1997) and Richard Scholar, *The Je-Ne-Sais-Quoi in Early Modern Europe: Encounters with a Certain Something* (Oxford, 2005). They show that the term was used for more than aesthetic experiences that defied full explanation.

44. See Carolyn Korsmeyer, *Making Sense of Taste: Food and Philosophy* (Ithaca, 1999).

45. David Hume, "Of the Standard of Taste," in *Essays: Moral, Political, and Literary*, ed. Eugene F. Miller (Indianapolis, 1987), 230.

46. There have been many versions of this sentiment, but the precise wording is usually attributed to Margaret Wolfe Hungerford's novel *Molly Bawn* (1878).

47. See Ernst Cassirer, *The Platonic Renaissance in England*, trans. James P. Pettegrove (New York, 1970), chap. 6.

48. Michael Oberst, "Kant on Universals," *History of Philosophy Quarterly* 32, no. 4 (2015): 349. The term "tropes," developed by the philosopher D. C. Williams in the 1950s, means, to cite Anna-Sofia Maurin, "things like the particular shape, weight, and texture of an individual object. Because tropes are particular, for two objects to 'share' a property (for them both to exemplify, say, a particular shade of green) is for each to contain (instantiate, exemplify) a greenness-trope, where those greenness-tropes, although numerically distinct, nevertheless exactly resemble each other." "Tropes," in *Stanford Encyclopedia of*

Philosophy, first published September 9, 2013; substantive revision March 16, 2023, https://plato.stanford.edu/entries/tropes/.

49. The complexities of this concept are explored in Charles Parsons, "The Transcendental Aesthetic," in *The Cambridge Companion to Kant*, ed. Paul Guyer (Cambridge, 1992). Although the idea of "sensus communis" in *Critique of Judgment* may itself serve as a quasi-transcendental ground for aesthetic judgment, it should not be confused with the binding cognitive function of the "transcendental aesthetic" in *Critique of Pure Reason.*

50. See Eva Schaper, *Studies in Kant's Aesthetics* (Edinburgh, 1979), chap. 6.

51. Jane Kneller, "Kant's Concept of Beauty," *History of Philosophy Quarterly* 3, no. 3 (1976): 322.

52. See, for example, Eva Schaper, "Taste, Sublimity and Genius: The Aesthetics of Nature and Art," in *The Cambridge Companion to Kant*, ed. Guyer.

53. Immanuel Kant, *Critique of Judgment*, trans. J. H. Bernard (New York, 1951), 149.

54. Kant, *Critique of Judgment*, 147.

55. Eco, *Art and Beauty in the Middle Ages*, 89.

56. See John Shearman, *Mannerism* (New York, 1967). The use of the term to define a period in art history began with the art historian and archaeologist Luigi Lanzi in the seventeenth century.

57. Arnold Hauser, *The Philosophy of Art History* (Cleveland, 1965), 402. Hauser later wrote a controversial book on Mannerism, *Mannerism: The Crisis of the Renaissance and the Origins of Modern Art*, 2. vols (New York, 1965), in which he stressed its social rather than philosophical or aesthetic sources. For very different analyses of his argument, see Edwin Berry Burgham, "Marxism and Mannerism: the Esthetic of Arnold Hauser," *Science and Society* 23, no. 3 (1968); and Deodáth Zuh, "The Uncanny Concept of Mannerism: A Review of Arnold Hauser's Book on the Origins of Modern Art, and its Professional Background," *Journal of Art Historiography* 21 (2019).

58. Else Marie Bukdahl, *The Recurrent Actuality of the Baroque*, trans. Inge Tranter (Copenhagen, 2017), 36.

59. Don Harrán, "'Mannerism' in the Cinquecento Madrigal?," *The Musical Quarterly* 55, no. 4 (1969): 523.

60. See Alfred E. Longeuil, "The Word 'Gothic' in Eighteenth Century Criticism," *Modern Language Notes* 38, no. 8 (1923).

61. Geoffrey Galt Harpham, *On the Grotesque: Strategies of Contradiction in Art and Literature* (Princeton, 1982), 8.

62. For a discussion, which includes theorists like Friedrich Schlegel and Karl Rosenkranz, as well as artists like Victor Hugo, see Sasha Bru, "Politics as the Art of the Impossible: The Heteronomy of Futurist *Art-Action*," in *Aesthetic Revolutions and Twentieth-Century Avant-garde Movements*, ed. Aleš Erjavec (Durham, 2015), 24–25.

63. See Władysław Tartarkiewicz, "The Great Theory of Beauty and its Decline," *The Journal of Aesthetics and Art Criticism* 31, no. 2 (1972): 174. He claims the rise of relativizing psychological theories of beauty in the eighteenth century was a major cause.

64. Clive Bell, *Art* (London, 1927), 8.

65. Jauss, *Aesthetic Experience and Literary Hermeneutics*, 43. The key exemplification of his argument is Baudelaire.

66. See, for example Wendy Steiner, *Venus in Exile: the Rejection of Beauty in Twentieth-Century Art* (Chicago, 2001). She connects the decline of admiration for beauty with hostility to the female form and the campaign against ornamentation, which often had

a feminine connotation. The sublime, she notes, has often been figured as male, and the beautiful as female.

67. According to George Steiner, *Real Presences* (Chicago, 1989), "A Logos-order entails . . . a central supposition of 'real presence.' Mallarmé's repudiation of the covenant of reference, and his insistence that non-reference constitutes the true genius and purity of language, entail a supposition of 'real absence'" (96).

68. The phrase was André Breton's. For an analysis of its darker implications, see Hal Foster, *Compulsive Beauty* (Cambridge, MA, 1993).

69. See Eduardo Sabrovsky, *Modernity as Exception and Miracle*, trans. Javier Burden (Albany, NY, 2020).

70. See Martin Jay, "Modernism and the Retreat from Form," *Force Fields: Between Intellectual History and Cultural Critique* (New York, 1993).

71. For defenses of beauty, see Mary Mothersill, *Beauty Restored* (Oxford, 1984); Elaine Scarry, *On Beauty and Being Just* (Princeton, 1999); Ruth Lorand, *Aesthetic Order, a Philosophy of Order, Beauty and Art* (New York, 2000); Alexander Nehamas, *Only a Promise of Happiness: The Place of Beauty in a World of Art* (Princeton, 2010); Roger Scruton, *Beauty: A Very Short Introduction* (New York, 2011); and John-Mark L. Miravalle, *Beauty and Why It Matters* (Manchester, NH, 2019).

72. The claim that art is defined by the institutions of the "artworld"—museums, galleries, auction houses, art journals, etc.—that designate it as such was defended, among others, by Arthur Danto and George Dickie. For one overview, see David C. Graves, "The Institutional Theory of Art: A Survey," *Philosophia* 25, no. 1 (1997). For another that resists the conflation of Danto and Dickie, see Massimiliano Lacertosa, "The Artworld and the Institutional Theory of Art: An Analytic Construction," *The SOAS Journal of Postgraduate Research* 8 (2015).

73. Nelson Goodman, *Languages of Art* (Indianapolis, 1976), 255.

74. There is a substantial literature on Goodman's career and thought. See, for example, Mia Gosselin, *Nominalism and Contemporary Nominalism: Ontological and Epistemological Implications of the Work of W. V. O. Quine and Nelson Goodman* (Dordrecht, 1990); Mary Douglas and David Hull, eds., *How Classification Works: Nelson Goodman among the Social Scientists* (Edinburgh, 1992); Dena Shottenkirk, *Nominalism and Its Aftermath: The Philosophy of Nelson Goodman* (New York, 2009); Daniel Cohnitz and Marcus Rossberg, *Nelson Goodman*, (New York, 2014); Remei Capdevila-Werning, *Goodman for Architects* (London, 2014). For a full bibliography focusing on his importance for aesthetics, see Alessandro Giovanelli, "Goodman's Aesthetics," *The Stanford Encyclopedia of Philosophy*, first published May 7, 2005; substantive revision August 9, 2017, https://plato.stanford.edu/archives/fall2017/entries/goodman-aesthetics. For a dissenting view, see Krzysztof Guczalski, "Nelson Goodman's Aesthetics—A Critique," *Arts* 10, no. 84 (2021).

75. Nelson Goodman and W. V. O. Quine, "Steps towards a Constructive Nominalism," *The Journal of Symbolic Logic* 12, no. 4 (1947).

76. Goodman and Quine, "Steps towards a Constructive Nominalism," 105.

77. Goodman and Quine, "Steps towards a Constructive Nominalism," 122.

78. For the debates occasioned by this contention, see Peter J. McCormick, ed., *Starmaking: Realism, Anti-Realism and Irrealism* (Cambridge, MA, 1996).

79. For a critique of this assumption, see Morton White, *A Philosophy of Culture: The Scope of Holistic Pragmatism* (Princeton, 2002), chap. 8.

80. Goodman, *Languages of Art*, 37.

81. For an account of the debates occasioned by this distinction, which includes a section on Goodman, see Linda Wetzel, "Types and Tokens," *The Stanford Encyclopedia of Philosophy*, April 26, 2006, https://plato.stanford.edu/archives/fall2018/entries/types-tokens/.

82. In the case of music, the target would be the claim that only perfect compliance with a score assures a work's identity. See Lydia Goehr, *The Imaginary Museum of Musical Works* (New York, 2007), chap. 1. Gérard Genette argues that the identity of a literary work being based on a specific text is also problematic in cases where there are multiple versions of a text rather than a single authoritative one. See his *The Work of Art: Immanence and Transcendence*, trans. G. M. Goshgarian (Ithaca, 1997), 111.

83. Dean Swinford, "Defining Irrealism: Scientific Development and Allegorical Possibility," *Journal of the Fantastic in the Arts* 12, no. 1 (2001).

84. Michael Löwy, "The Current of Critical Irrealism: 'A moonlit enchanted night,'" in *A Concise Companion to Realism*, ed. Beaumont.

85. Nelson Goodman, *Ways of Worldmaking* (Indianapolis, 1978), 2.

86. Nelson Goodman, *Languages of Art*, 252–55; *Ways of Worldmaking*, 67–68.

87. W. J. T. Mitchell, *Iconology: Image, Text, Ideology* (Chicago, 1986), 55. This description was also appropriate for his attitude towards science, which Goodman argued could not provide accurate descriptions of the world as it is. Rather worlds in the plural were made, not found, and while some might seem more right than others, none was true. The quest for epistemological certainty was thus always in vain. For a recent survey of the debates this position engendered, which ends with a modified defense of Goodman, see Nicole Fišerová, "Worldmaking as an Approach to Scientific Pluralism," *Teorie Vědy / Theory of Science* 63 (2021).

88. What are worlds made of? Goodman asks. His answer: "Not from nothing, after all, but *from other worlds*. Worldmaking as we know it always starts from worlds already on hand; the making is a remaking" (*Ways of Worldmaking*, 6).

89. Goodman, *Ways of Worldmaking*, 66–67.

90. Goodman, *Ways of Worldmaking*, 69.

91. Mitchell, *Iconology*, 71. He further criticized Goodman in *Picture Theory* (Chicago, 1994), chap. 11. Goodman also was indifferent to the question of who had the power to make worlds—scientific as well as artistic—which achieved the status of being "right," if never "true." The socially constituted role of the artistic "genius" was not one he often addressed.

92. Jean-François Lyotard, *Duchamp's Transformers* (San Francisco, 1990). The French original, *Les transformateurs Duchamp* (Paris, 1977), was intended to be read, with a nod to Duchamp's love of puns, as *transformateurs du champ*. To make the point clear, the cover of the book spells his name "DUchamp."

93. Marcel Duchamp, "White Box" in *Salt Seller: The Writings of Marcel Duchamp*, ed. Michel Sanouillet and Elmer Peterson (New York, 1973), 78, italics in original. How or even if Duchamp checked to see whether this formulation was correct is not clear.

94. Thierry du Duve, *Pictorial Nominalism: On Marcel Duchamp's Passage from Painting to the Readymade*, trans. Dana Polan (Minneapolis, 1991).

95. Cited in du Duve, *Pictorial Nominalism*, 126.

96. Du Duve, *Pictorial Nominalism*, 126.

97. Antoine Compagnon, *The Five Paradoxes of Modernity*, trans. Franklin Philip (New York, 1994), 101. In *The Private Worlds of Marcel Duchamp* (Berkeley, 1995), Jerrold Seigel interprets "pictorial nominalism" in the exact opposite way: "That pictures would replace

words, perhaps with the implication that these signs, unlike verbal ones, would not encourage people to believe in the real existence of abstract relations" (265). This reading may seem less plausible because at virtually the same time Duchamp was abandoning painting. But as we will see shortly, he was intent on the pictorialization of language rather than foregrounding its semantic function, which unsettles the opposition between pictures and words rather than reverses it.

98. Duchamp in Pierre Cabanne, *Dialogues with Marcel Duchamp*, trans. Ron Padgett (New York, 1971), 48. For a discussion of Duchamp's place in the anti-ocularcentric discourse of much twentieth-century French thought, see Martin Jay, *Downcast Eyes: The Denigration of Vision in Twentieth-Century French Thought* (Berkeley, 1993), 160–69.

99. Like everything else in the reception of Duchamp, these characterizations fail to do justice to other moments in his career. In the 1930s, for example, he experimented with "optical entertainments" he called "rotoreliefs," circular patterns rotating on a turntable, often accompanied by music. These both provided an experience of optical volume and depth and had erotic connotations, which are explored in Rosalind E. Krauss, *The Optical Unconscious* (Cambridge, MA, 1993), chapter 3.

100. In the 1960s, Greenberg himself came to see Duchamp as the antithesis of the normative narrative he had fashioned. For a brief account of his response, see Florence Rubenfeld, *Clement Greenberg: A Life* (Minneapolis, 1997), 279–81. For a more substantive account, see Thierry de Duve, *Clement Greenberg between the Lines, Including a Debate with Clement Greenberg*, trans. Brian Holmes (Chicago, 2010); and Graham Harman, "Greenberg, Duchamp and the Next Avant-Garde," *Speculations: A Journal of Speculative Realism* 5 (2014).

101. Joseph Kosuth, one of the leading conceptual artists, claimed Duchamp as an inspiration. See his *Art after Philosophy and After: Collected Writings, 1966–1990* (Cambridge, 1991), 18. For a vigorous, but inconclusive discussion of this putative lineage, see Benjamin Buchloh, Rosalind Krauss, Alexander Alberro, Thierry de Duve, Martha Buskirk, and Yve-Alain Bois, "Conceptual Art and the Reception of Duchamp," *October* 102 (1994).

102. Goodman, *Languages of Art*, 148–53.

103. Carol P. James, "Duchamp's Silent Noise / Music for the Deaf," in *Marcel Duchamp: Artist of the Century*, ed. Rudolf E. Kuenzli and Francis M. Naumann (Cambridge, MA, 1990), 119. Duchamp's disdain for the logical principle of contradiction aligns him with Alfred Jarry, whose "pataphysics" was based on its rejection. See Pieter de Nijs, "Marcel Duchamp and Alfred Jarry," *RELIEF* 10, no. 1 (2016).

104. Duchamp to Jean Mayoux, March 6, 1956, cited in Ecke Bonk, *Marcel Duchamp: The Museum Valise* (London, 1989), 252. Much can be made of Duchamp's Wittgensteinian comparison of language to a game of chess, which is bound by arbitrary rules that allow winning and losing within their parameters, depending on how well you know how to play. But what I want to foreground here instead is his stress on the power of the isolated word, or more precisely, the neologism.

105. Piotr Schollenberger, "Nominalist Re-turn in Contemporary Art," *Art Inquiry: Recherches sur les arts* 17 (2015): 79.

106. Piotr Schollenberger, "Between *images* and *fromages*: Lyotard on Painting's Critical Force," *Eidos* 3, no. 4 (2019): 35. Schollenberger interprets pictorial nominalism in terms of Lyotard's arguments about discursivity and figurality, and concludes that "the critical power of painting would thus lie in its ability to grasp our attention and to show the singularity of an event 'on the edge of discourse'" (41).

107. It is for this reason that Duchamp is often considered an inspiration for minimalism as well as conceptual art, as the former drew on the belief that objects have a certain specificity that can be asserted against mental projections.

108. For a discussion of Cartesian perspectivalism as one of the three main visual paradigms of the modern era, see Martin Jay, "Scopic Regimes of Modernity," in *Force Fields: Between Intellectual History and Cultural Critique* (New York, 1993). Goodman was also critical of the naturalization of perspective as the only correct way of seeing. See *Languages of Art*, 10–19.

109. Jean Clair, "Continental Drifts," in *The Arcimboldo Effect: Transformations of the Face from the Sixteenth to the Twentieth Century* (New York, 1987), 245. Howard Hinton wrote *The Fourth Dimension* (London, 1910) and G. de Pawlowski, *Voyages au Pays de la quatrième dimension* (Paris, 1912). For a sustained account of Duchamp's fascination with modern science, see Linda Dalrymple Henderson, *Duchamp in Context: Science and Technology in the Large Glass and Related Works* (Princeton, 2005).

110. Clair, "Continental Drifts," 253.

111. Duchamp's disdain for the idea of the artist as creative genius is perhaps most explicitly expressed in his 1957 lecture "The Creative Act" in *The New Art: A Critical Anthology*, ed. Gregory Battcock (New York 1966).

112. Robert Harvey, "Where's Duchamp? Out Queering the Field," *Yale French Studies* 109 (2006): 90.

113. To be precise, *Fountain* was submitted to the Society of Independent Artists annual exhibition in New York in 1917, which was supposedly open to anyone who paid the admission fee but followed the recommendations of a hidden jury. After an extended debate, the jury (most of whom did not know Duchamp was the pseudonymous signer), decided it did not qualify as art and hid it behind a partition rather than exhibiting it. These spectators, in other words, did not have the courage of their allegedly inclusive convictions, and refused to validate Duchamp's designation as art. Duchamp, who was on the board of the society, protested by resigning, and a photograph of the signed urinal by Alfred Stieglitz and several articles about it appeared in *The Blind Man*, a journal of the New York Dadaists. One was apparently by Duchamp himself and called "The Richard Mutt Case." The "original" seems to have then been lost, but in 1935, Duchamp began making miniature reproductions of *Fountain* for his "box in a suitcase." He authorized the first full-size reproduction in 1950 for an exhibition in New York, two more in 1953 and 1963, and then eight in 1964. By then, there were plenty of official "spectators" happy to validate his choice.

114. There is another aspect of the objects Duchamp chose, which goes beyond their ontological materiality or even utilitarian function. They were also commodities in an exchange economy, which foreshadowed the explicit blurring of the distinction between art and commodity later developed by the pop artists who saw Duchamp as an inspiration.

115. Marcel Duchamp, *Marcel Duchamp parle des ready-mades à Philippe Collin* (Paris, 1998), 9. From yet another angle, the sovereignty of the designating artist is also undercut by the interference of his or her desiring body, of which Duchamp was often very aware. Despite his hostility to psychologistic interpretations of art as expressive of a creator subject, he understood that even antiretinal language was permeated by corporeality. See Rosalind Krauss, "Where's Poppa?," in *The Definitively Unfinished Marcel Duchamp*, ed. Thierry de Duve (Cambridge, MA, 1993).

116. As was often the case with Duchamp, he later suggested a different take on the value of tactility by titling the cover he prepared for the catalogue called *Le Surréalisme*

en 1947 to accompany the exhibit Exposition internationale du Surréalisme "Prière de toucher [Please Touch]." The image was of a rubber breast.

117. Duchamp's *Fountain* (1917) was signed "R. Mutt," a gesture which implied that in the art market an artist's signature could be worth more than the quality of the object signed. *Bicycle Wheel* (1913), which antedated the term "readymade" by two years, was not signed. It came to be called an "assisted readymade" because it combined two objects, a wheel and a stool.

118. See Francis M. Naumann, *Marcel Duchamp: The Art of Making Art in the Age of Mechanical Reproduction* (New York, 1999).

119. The rise of abstraction and decline of figuration in art might also seem to signal a diminution of the traditional role of craftsmanship, but the deskilling of the artist was never as total as in the case of the readymade. The ability to paint abstractly, moreover, might better be understood as demanding a different sets of skills from the ones needed to paint "realistically," rather than the loss of skills per se.

120. See William A. Camfield, "Marcel Duchamp's *Fountain*: Its History and Aesthetics in the Context of 1917," in *Marcel Duchamp*, ed. Kuenzli and Naumann.

121. Rosalind E. Krauss, *Passages in Modern Sculpture* (Cambridge, MA, 1977), 80.

122. As always with Duchamp, the relationship between "original" and "copy" was deliberately ambiguous. One of the multiplicity of identical utilitarian objects was singled out and put in an aesthetic frame (even, as in the case of *Fountain*, signed, if with a fake name), but that specific transfigured object could then itself be replaced by others of the same kind. There were, as we have noted, a number of different *Fountains*, after the first one he chose somehow got lost. Duchamp further complicated things by reproducing some of the readymades in miniature, as he did with many of his other works.

123. Duchamp, *Salt Seller*, 32.

124. Duchamp's actual relationship to surrealism is controversial. For an insightful analysis of their similarities and differences, see Harvey, "Where's Duchamp? Out Queering the Field." A similar distance can be seen in his relationship with Dada, which he also avoided to escape being subsumed under a generic label.

125. John F. Moffitt, *Alchemist of the Avant-Garde: The Case of Marcel Duchamp* (Albany, 2003). At a time when invisible forces like electromagnetism and radioactivity were first being explored, the occult and scientific worlds were often intertwined, and many aesthetic modernists were intrigued by both. See John Ramble, *Modernism and the Occult* (London, 2015).

126. De Duve, *Pictorial Nominalism*, 133.

127. In 1964, Beuys named one of his "actions" (performance pieces) *The Silence of Marcel Duchamp Is Overrated*. Its target was Duchamp's decision to withdraw from the art world in order to play chess.

128. Eric Cameron notes this connection in his contribution to the discussion of Francis S. Naumann, "Marcel Duchamp: A Reconciliation of Opposites," in *The Definitively Unfinished Marcel Duchamp*, ed. de Duve, 77. The iterations of literature, music, and drama, the main allographic arts, can, of course, produce symbolically powerful, immersive experiences with infinite symbolic resonance. But they need performances to do so, whereas autographic art does not. What makes the readymade a curious kind of allographic art is that there is no notational text, script or score that is then instantiated by an iteration or performance of the particular work. The famous letter Duchamp sent to his sister Susanne on January 16, 1919, with some instructions about how to make a readymade is generic rather than specific.

129. Genette, *The Work of Art*, 155.

130. Leo Bersani, *The Culture of Redemption* (Cambridge, MA, 1990).

131. De Duve, *Pictorial Nominalism*, 208.

132. Thierry de Duve, *Kant after Duchamp* (Cambridge. MA 1998).

133. Nancy, *The Muses*. He argues that Hegel's dialectics attempt to restore the plurality by resisting the infusion of universal divine presence into the aesthetic realm.

134. De Duve, *Kant after Duchamp*, 52.

135. Duchamp's love for words that are not only meaningless in grammatical terms but do not even designate anything is demonstrated by the addition of the mysterious "even" to the official title of the *Large Glass, The Bride Stripped Bare by Her Bachelors, Even*. He delighted in telling Pierre Cabanne, it was "an adverb which makes no sense, since it relates to nothing in the picture or title. Thus it was an adverb in the most beautiful demonstration of adverbness. It has no meaning." *Dialogues with Marcel Duchamp*, 40.

136. De Duve, *Kant after Duchamp*, 57.

137. De Duve, *Kant after Duchamp*, 62.

138. De Duve, *Kant after Duchamp*, 69.

139. De Duve, *Kant after Duchamp*, 77.

140. De Duve, *Kant after Duchamp*, 333.

141. Diarmuid Costello, "Retrieving Kant's Aesthetics for Art Theory after Greenberg: Some Remarks on Arthur C. Danto and Thierry de Duve," in *Rediscovering Aesthetics: Interdisciplinary Voices from Art History, Philosophy and Art Practice* ed. Francis Haskell, Julia Jansen, and Tony O'Connor (Stanford, CA, 2009), 123.

142. Jason Gaiger, "Art after Beauty: Retrieving Aesthetic Judgment," *Art History* 20, no. 4 (1997): 613. De Duve has continued to refine his claims about art as a proper name against other objections. For his most recent effort, see "On Wielding Ockham's Razor," *Nonsite* 33 (November 30, 2020), https://nonsite.org/on-wielding-ockhams-razor/.

143. J. M. Bernstein, "Readymades, Monochromes, etc.: Nominalism and the Paradox of Modernism," *Diacritics* 32, no. 1 (2002): 90.

144. Harold Rosenberg, *The Tradition of the New* (New York, 1965), 25. As many critics have pointed out, there was a heroic macho subtext in the celebration of action painting, which was very different from the gender-bending self-presentation of Duchamp.

145. Mary McCarthy, review of *The Tradition of the New*, by Harold Rosenberg, reprinted in *On the Contrary: Articles of Belief, 1946–1961* (New York, 1961), 24. Rosenberg replied in his preface to the second edition of *The Tradition of the New*. It is, of course, possible for a picture to be *of* an event. Thus, Robin Wagner-Pacifici can claim that Jacques-Louis David's *Rape of the Sabine Women* "neatly activates Alain Badiou's ideal of event 'recognition.'" *What Is an Event?* (Chicago, 2017), 100. But this is not the same thing as the painting itself *being* an event.

146. Lucy Lippard and John Chandler, "The Dematerialization of Art," *Art International* 12, no. 2 (1968).

147. They were, of course, also often represented in earlier artistic endeavors. In his study of *Suddenness: On the Moment of Aesthetic Appearance*, trans. Ruth Crowley (New York, 1994), Karl Heinz Bohrer argues that "dangerous moments" in the early nineteenth-century German novella show that "the narrated event claims a particular dignity that suspends the continuity of narrated time. This event-character of what is narrated implies that the history of the age is received as a sequence of unanticipated events" (39).

148. An extreme example were the violent performances of the so-called Viennese Actionists Günter Brus, Otto Muehl, Rudolf Schwarzkogler, and Hermann Nitsch in the

1960s and 1970s. For an attempt to situate their work in the context of Richard Shusterman's somaesthetics, see Martin Jay, "Somaesthetics and Democracy: Dewey and Contemporary Body Art," *The Journal of Aesthetic Education* 36, no. 4 (2002).

149. See, for example, Thomas Rathmann, ed., *Ereignis: Konzeptionen eines Begriff in Geschichte, Literatur und Kunst* (Cologne, 2003); and Gerhard Richter, *Ästhetik des Ereignisse: Sprache—Geschichte—Medium* (Munich, 2005).

150. Jean-François Lyotard, *Toward the Post-Modern*, ed. Robert Harvey and Mark S. Roberts (Atlantic Highlands, NJ, 1993), 170–71, italics in original.

151. Krzysztof Ziarek, *The Historicity of Experience: Modernity, the Avant-Garde and the Event* (Evanston, IL, 2001), 18.

152. Josette Féral, "From Event to Extreme Reality: The Aesthetic of Shock," *TDR: The Drama Review* 55, no. 4 (2011).

153. By chance, the first article in its inaugural issue was Angela Hume, "(Rescuing) Hegel's Magical Thinking," *Evental Aesthetics* 1, no. 1 (2012).

154. Jean-François Lyotard, "Newman: The Instant," in *The Lyotard Reader* (Oxford, 1989), 240. He made the same point earlier in *Les transformateurs Duchamp*, 39 and 155.

155. Lyotard, "Newman: The Instant," 240, italics in original. Newman, in contrast, does not try to represent the unrepresentable, he is able to present it successfully as a realized epiphany.

156. Bill Readings, *Introducing Lyotard: Art and Politics* (London, 1991), 58,

157. Lyotard, *Les transformateurs Duchamp*, 39. Lyotard also often stressed that "nominal definition is a designation, but designation, far from being an adequation of sign to thing is, like perspective, (in the sense of optical perspective, *but also in Nietzsche's* sense) a 'decision' that causes the sign and its referent to exist together." *Toward the Post-Modern*, 83–84, italics in original.

158. John Rajchman, foreword to *Pictorial Nominalism*, by du Duve, viii. To complicate matters, elsewhere De Duve suggests that the readymade is better understood as "an abnormal painting." *Kant after Duchamp*, 162. This allows J. M. Bernstein to argue that it can be seen as "a certain paradoxical *continuation* of modernist painting, as a response to the exhaustion of painting, and hence as a way of sustaining the stakes of painting in the absence of painting." "Readymades, Monochromes, etc.," 88.

159. Barbara Formis, "Event and Ready-Made: Delayed Sabotage," *Communication and Cognition* 37, nos. 3/4 (2004). Badiou himself soon came to acknowledge Duchamp's work as exemplifying many of his arguments about art. See his "Matters of Appearance: An Interview with Alain Badiou," in *Artforum* 45, no. 3 (2006) and "Some Remarks Concerning Marcel Duchamp," *The Symposium: Online Journal for Lacan.com* (2008), https://www.lacan.com/symptom9_articles/badiou29.html.

160. Formis, "Event and Ready-Made," 248. Later in her essay, she details some of the ways that the readymade is imperfectly explained by Badiou's elaborate theory of the event but holds to the value of applying it anyway.

161. According to Alex Ling, "the 'readymade-event'—which, just to be perfectly clear, designates the non-exhibition of *Fountain* (as opposed to the work itself)—is paradigmatic in the field of art because its effects are felt first and foremost at an ontological level, that is, it involves the 'being,' or the very 'essence,' of art." See "The Schlock of the New: Badiou, Duchamp and the Everyday Miracle," *Parrhesia* 26 (2016): 142.

162. Formis, "Event and Ready-Made," 252. Although this is not the place to develop the contrast, it is striking how fundamentally opposed all this is to the critique of alienated

labor in Marx's early manuscripts, which was so influential in the rise of Marxist Humanism around the same time as Duchamp's heyday.

163. Alex Ling notes, however, that the "state" for Badiou is simply a way of identifying whatever is in favor of preserving the status quo, and only occasionally equivalent to its political instantiation. See Ling, "The Schlock of the New," 153.

164. As Peter Bürger notes, "Once the signed bottle drier has been accepted as an object that deserves a place in a museum, the provocation no longer provokes: it turns into its opposite. If an artist today signs a stove pipe and exhibits it, that artist does not eradicate the art market but adapts to it. . . . It is a historical fact that avant-garde movements did not put an end to the production of works of art, and that the social institution that is art proved resistant to the avant-gardiste attack." *Theory of the Avant-Garde*, trans. Michael Shaw (Minneapolis, 1984), 52–57.

165. Krauss, *The Optical Unconscious*, 142.

166. W. J. T. Mitchell, *What Do Pictures Want? The Lives and Loves of Images* (Chicago, 2005), 112.

167. Ling, "The Schlock of the New," 144. Ling concludes that because the readymade remains paradoxically continuous with the mundane world, it cannot be seen entirely as a miraculous rupture, thus exposing us "not only to the shock, but also *to the schlock of the new*" (152).

168. Rajchman, foreword to de Duve, *Pictorial Nominalism*, xxi.

169. The Kunstmuseum in Krefeld recently mounted an exhibition comparing their legacies. See Magdelena Holzhey, ed., *Beuys and Duchamp: Artists of the Future* (Stuttgart, 2021).

170. Duchamp, in contrast, was himself interested in modern music, but did not come to Adorno's attention in this guise. See James, "Duchamp's Silent Noise / Music for the Deaf."

171. Cage even once played a game of musical chess with Duchamp. See Elena Goukassian, "50 Years Ago John Cage and Marcel Duchamp Played a Game of Chess," *Hyperallergic*, March 5, 2018, https://hyperallergic.com/424124/marcel-duchamp-john-cage-reunion-chess-toronto/ In 1969, Cage put together an artwork called "Not Wanting to Say Anything About Marcel" as an homage to his late friend. He was in fact quoted as saying there was only "one way to write music: study Duchamp." https://garagemca.org/en/event/la-gol-voice-theatre-sound-sculptures-marcel-duchamp-and-john-cage. Adorno worried that Cage's undialectical overreliance on contingency and indeterminacy had lost its critical edge. But he could also acknowledge that "it is Cage's contribution, which cannot be exaggerated, to have sown doubts regarding the extremes of musical logic, the blind ideal of complete domination of nature in music, hardly uninfluenced by '*action painting*.'" "Difficulties," in *Essays on Music*, ed. Richard Leppert, trans. Susan Gillespie (Berkeley, 2002), 658.

172. Gerald L. Bruns, "On the Conundrum of Form and Material in Adorno's Aesthetic Theory," *The Journal of Aesthetics and Art Criticism* 66, no. 3 (2008): 225. He backs away a bit later from the opposition, arguing that "actually, I think Adorno could have found a place for Duchamp in his aesthetics by observing that the Readymades are not just found objects but have been staged, that is, recontextualized and, therefore, implicitly conceptualized as art. Fountain may be made from a urinal, but with its signature, 'R. Mutt,' and its displacement from the world of commodities to the exhibition, gallery, studio, museum, or history of art, it has been transformed into something *other*" (233). The issue, however, would be whether or not the act of designating any object as "other" was sufficient to

perform the tasks Adorno attributed to genuine works of art, which exceeded their arbitrary placement in an aesthetic frame.

173. Theodor W. Adorno, *Aesthetic Theory*, trans. Robert Hullot-Kentor (Minneapolis, 1997) 1.

174. Adorno, *Aesthetic Theory*, 308.

175. Hent de Vries, *Minimal Theologies: Critiques of Secular Reason in Adorno and Levinas* (Baltimore, 2019).

176. For a consideration of this question, which addresses an earlier iteration of my argument about magical nominalism and has reservations about the inclusion of Duchamp, see Schollenberger, "Nominalist Re-turn in Contemporary Art," 75.

177. For an account of Adorno's complicated analysis of magic, see David Kaufmann, "Beyond Gnosticism and Magic," *New German Critique* 118 (Winter 2013); and Robert McGray, "Querying Magic as a Critical Pedagogical Activity: Theodor Adorno and the Problem of Authoritarian Irrationalism in the Culture Industry," *The International Journal of Critical Pedagogy* 7, no. 1 (2016).

178. Theodor W. Adorno, *The Stars down to Earth and Other Essays on the Irrational in Culture*, ed. Stephen Crook (London, 1994).

179. Adorno to Benjamin, November 10, 1938, in Walter Benjamin and Theodor Adorno, *The Complete Correspondence, 1928–1940*, ed. Henri Lonitz, trans. Nicholas Walker (Cambridge, MA, 1999), 283. Benjamin gritted his teeth and tried to placate Adorno in his response: "When you speak of the 'wide-eyed presentation of mere facts' you are characterizing the proper philological attitude. . . . It is true that the indifference between magic and positivism, as you so aptly put it, should be liquidated. In other words, the philological interpretation of the author should be preserved and overcome in the Hegelian manner by the dialectical materialist. Philology consists in an examination of texts which proceeds by details and thus magically fixates the reader on it." The exorcism of that fixation, Benjamin conceded to Adorno, "falls to philosophy." But then in defense of his method, he reminded Adorno that in his own book on Kierkegaard, he had acknowledged that "'astonishment' reveals 'the profoundest insight into the relationship between dialectics, myth and image.' I might feel tempted to invoke that passage here. But instead I propose an amendment to it. . . . I think one should say that astonishment is an outstanding *object* of such insight." Benjamin to Adorno, December 12, 1938, in Benjamin and Adorno, *The Complete Correspondence*, 291–92. For an attempt to show that despite this dispute, Adorno was deeply indebted to Benjamin's physiognomic method, see Vincenzo Mele, "'At the Crossroads of Positivism and Magic': Roots of an Evidential Paradigm through Benjamin and Adorno," *Journal of Classical Sociology* 15, no. 2 (2015).

180. Theodor W. Adorno, *Minima Moralia: Reflections from Damaged Life*, trans. E. F. N. Jephcott (London, 1974), 238–239.

181. Adorno, *Minima Moralia*, 241.

182. For an account of the role this key concept played in Adorno and its relation to magic, see Allan M. Hillani, "The Spell of Authority: On Adorno's Political Philosophy of the Bann," *Dissonância: Revista de Teoria Crítica* 3, no. 2 (2019).

183. Karl Marx, *Capital*, vol. 1 (London, 1976), 169.

184. For a trenchant analysis of Adorno's nuanced attitude towards secularization, see Peter E. Gordon, *Migrants in the Profane: Critical Theory and the Question of Secularization* (New Haven, 2020). What complicates Adorno's argument is that he denied the simple succession story of an enchanted world replaced by an entirely disenchanted one. Instead, he saw the latter still haunted by unacknowledged residues of the former, often

with disastrous consequences (e.g., the occultism of modern astrology). But he also saw redemptive possibilities in the traces of the world before the loss of its enchantment.

185. David Kaufmann, "Adorno and the Name of God," *Flashpoint* 1, no. 1 (1996), www.webdelsol.com/FLASHPOINT/adorno.htm.

186. Adorno's extensive treatment of mimesis has been the subject of a considerable commentary. For my attempt to make sense of it, see Martin Jay, "Mimesis and Mimetology: Adorno and Lacoue-Labarthe," *Cultural Semantics: Keywords of Our Time* (Amherst, MA, 1998). See also, Artemy Magun, "Negativity (Dis)embodied: Philippe Lacoue-Labarthe and Theodor W. Adorno on Mimesis," *New German Critique* 40, no. 1 (2013).

187. Benjamin had developed the idea of "non-sensuous similarities" in his essays on "The Mimetic Faculty" and "Doctrine of the Similar," from which Adorno took many of his ideas about mimesis. Adorno's stress on the sensuous dimension of art meant he would never have accepted Duchamp's "indifference" to retinal pleasure or the full dematerialization urged by conceptual art. Much can also be said of Adorno's fondness for children's play as a repository of benign mimetic comportment. As a spoiled only child with no children of his own, Adorno seems to have reduced children's play to their fantasy life with toys, and not considered the complications of interaction with other children, which, as experiences with rival siblings or competitive friends make clear, is not always as blissful as he imagined.

188. Adorno to Benjamin, March 18, 1936, in Adorno and Benjamin, *The Complete Correspondence, 1928–1940*, 128.

189. Adorno to Benjamin, March 18, 1936, in Adorno and Benjamin, *The Complete Correspondence, 1928–1940*, 129.

190. Adorno, *Minima Moralia*, 222.

191. This is not to say that works lack any "truth content" for Adorno, just that it is not translatable into verifiable propositions. For a discussion of this issue, see Gerhard Richter, "Aesthetic Theory and Non-Propositional Truth Content in Adorno," *New German Critique* 33, no. 1 (2006).

192. Adorno, *Aesthetic Theory*, 58.

193. Max Horkheimer and Theodor W. Adorno, *Dialectic of Enlightenment: Philosophical Fragments*, ed. Gunzelin Schmid Noerr, trans. Edmund Jephcott (Stanford, CA, 2002), 13–14.

194. See, for example, Fredric Jameson's claim that for Adorno "the term nominalism was a reproach and a critique, the diagnosis of everything suffocating about late capitalism: nominalism for him included empiricism and positivism, and the gradual extinction of the negative and the dialectical—it named a social order so absolute that no critical thinking, let alone political resistance, could take place within it: a philosopher's version, no doubt, of a postmodern dystopia." "The Aesthetics of Singularity," *New Left Review* 92 (March/April 2015), https://newleftreview.org/issues/ii92/articles/fredric-jameson-the-aesthetics-of-singularity.

195. Theodor W. Adorno, *An Introduction to Dialectics*, ed. Christoph Ziermann, trans. Nicolas Walker (Malden, MA, 2017), 205.

196. Horkheimer and Adorno, *Dialectic of Enlightenment*, 17.

197. Theodor W. Adorno, *Kant's Critique of Pure Reason*, ed. Rolf Tiedemann, trans. Rodney Livingstone (Stanford, CA, 2001), 125.

198. Adorno, *Kant's Critique of Pure Reason*, 25.

199. Theodor W. Adorno, *Hegel: Three Studies*, trans. Shierry Weber Nicholsen (Cambridge, MA, 1993), 39.

200. Adorno, *Hegel: Three Studies*, 39.

201. Adorno, *Hegel: Three Studies*, 40.

202. Adorno, *Hegel: Three Studies*, 113.

203. Adorno, *Hegel: Three Studies*, 113.

204. Adorno, *Hegel: Three Studies*, 113.

205. Theodor W. Adorno, *Negative Dialectics*, trans. E. B. Ashton (New York, 1973), 126.

206. Adorno, *Negative Dialectics*, 126–27. As Espen Hammer notes, for Adorno, "Heidegger falls behind the nominalistic critique of conceptual realism. Rather than respecting the difference, starting with Ockham and Bacon, between concept and object, *de dictum* and *de re*, Heidegger reverts to what amounts to an Aristotelian identification between language and being." But Adorno's "appeal to nominalism is not meant to suggest that only particulars have a real existence, but that there is always a non-identity between concept and object that calls for dialectical reflection." *Adorno and the Political* (London, 2006), 111.

207. Theodor W. Adorno, *Philosophische Terminologie: Zur Einleitung*, vol. 1 (Frankfurt, 1973), 43.

208. In *The Order of Things*, Foucault was talking about the Kantian subject, but the phrase is applicable in other contexts.

209. This argument, as we noted in the Intermezzo, was typical of Hegelian Marxists. Adorno often invoked it, but was less invested in the idea of a concretely mediated whole, either as a description of the current world or as a utopian telos, than were more devoted adherents of that tradition such as Lukács.

210. Theodor W. Adorno, *Philosophy and Sociology*, ed. Dirk Braunstein, trans. Nicholas Walker (Medford. MA, 2022), 140.

211. Rose Rosengard Subotnik, *Developing Variations: Style and Ideology in Western Music* (Minneapolis, 1991), 211.

212. Peter Uwe Hohendahl, *Prismatic Thought: Theodor W. Adorno* (Lincoln, NE, 1995), 203. Later in this book, however, he notes that "with Kant and Hegel, he maintained the legitimacy of reason against radical nominalism and positivism" (240).

213. Adorno, *Aesthetic Theory*, 101.

214. Adorno, *Aesthetic Theory*, 101.

215. Shierry Weber Nicholsen, *Exact Imagination, Late Work: On Adorno's Aesthetics* (Cambridge, MA, 1997), 208.

216. Adorno, *Aesthetic Theory*, 220.

217. Adorno, *Aesthetic Theory*, 222.

218. Adorno, *Aesthetic Theory*, 161.

219. Adorno, *Aesthetic Theory*, 220.

220. Adorno, *Aesthetic Theory*, 199.

221. Adorno, *Aesthetic Theory*, 201. Ironically, Adorno allows himself to use the terminology of universality here, but to indicate art's resistance to generic conventions. The stress on origins should also be noted. As Robert Hullot-Kentor has remarked in connection with Adorno's ruminations on Karl Kraus's aphorism "origin is goal," "the attention that [nominalism] brought to the individuality of the 'real particular' contributed profoundly to the development of historical perception and reasoning as well as to the scientific comprehension of nature. However, in its rejection of origin *tout court* it remains blind to the origin for which its cunning unconsciously speaks and is, as a result, ultimately no less obtuse to history than to nature." *Things Beyond Resemblance: Collected Essays on Theodor W. Adorno* (New York, 2006), 8.

222. Adorno, *Aesthetic Theory*, 201.

223. Adorno, *Aesthetic Theory*, 201.

224. During its heyday, "postmodernism," a term not yet current when Adorno was writing, seemed to some commentators to be even more apposite. See, for example, David Roberts, *Art and Enlightenment: Aesthetic Theory after Adorno* (Lincoln, NE, 1991), where he writes of "the postmodern condition of aesthetic nominalism" (133).

225. Adorno, *Aesthetic Theory*, 207.

226. Adorno, *Aesthetic Theory*, 207.

227. Adorno, *Aesthetic Theory*, 296.

228. Adorno, "On the Fetish-Character in Music and the Regression of Listening," in *Essays on Music*, ed. Richard Leppert, 301.

229. See Martin Jay, "Taking on the Stigma of Inauthenticity: Adorno's Critique of Genuineness," *Essays from the Edge: Parerga and Paralipomena* (Charlottesville, 2011).

230. Goehr, *The Imaginary Museum of Musical Works*, xxxix and xl.

231. Adorno, *Aesthetic Theory*, 221.

232. Adorno, *Aesthetic Theory*, 221.

233. Theodor W. Adorno, *Gesammelte Schriften*, vol. 16 (Darmstadt, 1998), 548–49.

234. Theodor W. Adorno, *Mahler: A Musical Physiognomy*, trans. Edmund Jephcott (Chicago, 1982), 67.

235. Theodor W. Adorno, *Philosophy of New Music*, ed. and trans. Robert Hullot-Kentor (Minneapolis, 2006), 155.

236. For another example, see Keith Chapin, who writes, "realist composers create works by relying on harmonic conventions, which they assume to be based on stable properties of nature, while nominalists create ones that avoid conventions and, because they follow the inner impulses that make them individuals, write music that is new, sui generis, and as processual as thought itself. . . . Adorno preferred nominalism but also recognized the limitations of the position." "Labor and Metaphysics in Hindemith's and Adorno's Statements on Counterpoint," in *Apparitions: New Perspectives on Adorno and Twentieth-Century Music*, ed., Berthold Hoeckner (New York, 2006), 30–31.

237. Max Paddison, *Adorno's Aesthetics of Music* (Cambridge, 1993), 181.

238. Adorno, *Philosophy of New Music*, 48–49.

239. Theodor W. Adorno, "The Aging of the New Music," in *Essays on Music*, ed. Richard Leppert, trans. Susan H. Gillespie and others (Berkeley, 2002), 192 and 191. This essay was translated by Robert Hullot-Kentor and Frederic Will. For critical remarks on Webern, see 187.

240. Theodor W. Adorno, "Vers une musique informelle," in *Quasi una Fantasia: Essays on Modern Music*, trans. Rodney Livingstone (London, 1998). For an analysis of the place of this essay in Adorno's oeuvre and the development of postwar music, see Gianmario Borio, "Dire cela, sans savoir quoi: The Question of Meaning in Adorno and the Musical Avant-Garde," in Hoeckner, ed., *Apparitions*.

241. Adorno, "Vers une musique informelle," 272. J. M. Bernstein argues that the phrase "objectively compelling" means that Adorno knew that even musique informelle "will require universals," and that a similar process occurred in abstract expressionist painting, where the limit of the monochrome painting threatened the return of something similar. See his "Readymades, Monochromes, Etc." 97.

242. Adorno, "Vers une musique informelle," 273.

243. Adorno, "Vers une musique informelle," 277.

244. Adorno, "Vers une musique informelle," 280.

245. Adorno, "Vers une musique informelle," 287. The concept of "musical material" in Adorno has generated controversy over, for example, his claims about its historical

laws of movement and the imperative to be at the cutting edge imposed by them. See Lambert Zuidervaart, *Adorno's Aesthetic Theory: The Redemption of Illusion* (Cambridge, MA, 1991), chap. 5.

246. Adorno, "Vers une musique informelle," 315.

247. Adorno, "Vers une musique informelle," 298.

248. Adorno, "Vers une musique informelle," 319.

249. Adorno, "Vers une musique informelle," 304.

250. Adorno, "Vers une musique informelle," 321.

251. Adorno, "Vers une musique informelle," 303.

252. See Vangelis Giannakakis, *Negative Dialectics and Event: Nonidentity, Culture and the Historical Adequacy of Consciousness* (Lanham, MD, 2021). He argues that "Badiou's theory of the event contains insights that can help identify and elucidate the political dimension of Adorno's thought" (38–39). To do justice to this comparison in terms of Adorno's aesthetic theory, would require a sustained reading of his thoughts on temporality. For a helpful consideration of this issue in music, see Max Paddison, "Adorno, Time and Musical Time: A Response to Stephen Decatur Smith," *The Opera Quarterly* 29, nos. 3/4 (2013).

253. The issue of whether "art" could be construed as a proper name, which generated controversy in de Duve's reading of Duchamp, did not recur in Adorno's aesthetic theory.

254. See, for example, Adorno's discussion of "metaphysical experience" in terms of a child's reverie about place names in *Negative Dialectics*, 373. As Hullot-Kentor has noted, "Benjamin's work was also conceived in opposition to nominalism, although the focus of his critique was distinct. It was concerned with nominalism's refutation of the expressive content of language . . . Benjamin developed a doctrine of ideas that attempts to recover the expressive content of language in a fashion that, with idealism, justifies thought as part of metaphysical contents." (*Things Beyond Resemblance*, 127). If, however, we distinguish between a magical and a conventionalist nominalism, Benjamin and Adorno can be enlisted on the side of the former.

255. Horkheimer and Adorno, *Dialectic of Enlightenment*, 17. For a trenchant discussion of this theme, see Kaufmann, "Adorno and the Name of God."

256. See Sebastian Truskolaski, *Adorno and the Ban on Images* (New York, 2021).

257. Bielik-Robson sometimes interprets this term to mean that Judaism is the substantive kernel and Christianity merely the external husk of the Marrano, but at other times, she suggests that it is his or her dual identity—a bit like W. E. B. Dubois's famous notion of Black "double consciousness"—that characterizes the modern split subject. The latter would comport better with Adorno's valorization of nonidentity.

258. Agata Bielik-Robson, *Jewish Cryptotheologies of Late Modernity: Philosophical Marranos* (London, 2014), 239. For a suggestive attempt to extend her argument to Adorno's *Aesthetic Theory*, see Jakub Górski, "Concerning Some Marrano Threads in The Aesthetic Theory of Theodor W. Adorno," *Religions* 10, no. 173 (2019). He follows her in situating Adorno in the tradition of "Jewish nominalism," alongside other recent thinkers like Rosenzweig, Benjamin, Scholem, and Derrida.

259. Bielik-Robson, *Jewish Cryptotheologies of Late Modernity*, 241. The final quotation is from Adorno's *Negative Dialectics*, 20.

260. For a skeptical account of Adorno's understanding of Jewish theology, including the Kabbalah, see Steven M. Wasserstrom, "Adorno's Kabbalah: Some Preliminary Observations," in *Polemical Encounters: Esoteric Discourse and its Others*, ed. Olav Hammer and Kocku von Stuckrad (Leiden, 2007). For a more generous reading, see Ansgar Martins,

The Migration of Metaphysics into the Realm of the Profane: Theodor W. Adorno Reads Gershom Scholem (Leiden, 2020).

261. Agata Bielik-Robson, "The Post-Secular Turn: Enlightenment, Tradition, Revolution," *Eidos* 3, no. 3 (2019): 65. There is a substantial literature on Adorno and "inverse theology." See, for example, Christopher Craig Brittain, *Adorno and Theology* (London, 2010); Deborah Cook, "Through a Glass Darkly: Adorno's Inverse Theology," *Adorno Studies* 1, no. 1 (2016); and Sebastian Truskolaski, "Inverse Theology: Adorno, Benjamin, Kafka," *German Life and Letters* 70, no. 2 (2017).

262. Scholem, *The Messianic Idea in Judaism*, 293.

263. Christopher L. Lehrich, *The Occult Mind: Magic in Theory and Practice* (Ithaca, 2007), 117.

264. Michael T. Miller, *The Name of God in Jewish Thought: A Philosophical Analysis of Mystical Traditions from Apocalypse to Kabbalah* (London, 2016), 92. The internal quotation is from Naomi Janowitz, *The Poetics of Ascent: Theories of Language in a Rabbinic Ascent Text* (Albany, 1989), 90.

265. Adorno, *Aesthetic Theory*, 54.

266. Borio, "Dire cela, sans savoir quoi," 57.

267. Adorno, "Music, Language and Composition," in *Essays on Music*, 114. See Matthias Martinson, "Music as Secularized Prayer: On Adorno's Benjaminian Understanding of Music and its Language-Character," *Comparative and Continental Philosophy* 10, no. 3 (2018). He cautions that "Adorno's philosophy of music is no theology of music. At most, it is a metaphysical reflection on music that preserves a theological impulse" (216). Wasserstrom, on the other hand, claims that "Adorno did develop a kind of musicological kabbalah, especially later in life." "Adorno's Kabbalah," 72. For a thorough contextualization of Adorno's thoughts on music and names in his more general defense of "nonconceptuality" and "redemption of rhetoric," see Sebastian Tränkle, *Nichtidentität und Unbegrifflichkeit: Philosophische Sprachkritik nach Adorno und Blumenberg* (Frankfurt, 2022), 111–18.

268. Adorno, "On the Contemporary Relationship of Philosophy and Music," *Essays on Music*, 139–40.

269. Adorno, "On the Contemporary Relationship of Philosophy and Music," 140.

270. Adorno, "On the Contemporary Relationship of Philosophy and Music," 140.

Chapter Five

1. The scale of the meaningful context is, of course, never easy to determine. Thus, for example, one commentator starts by stating that "on the final analysis, 'photography' does not exist at all; all that exists are photographs" but then concludes that "as a medium, photography takes part in the establishment of a particular scopic regime, at the same time, this scopic regime influences photography and determines how photographs are perceived. Scopic regimes are historically transformable, and the development of the digital photograph is the sign of such a transformation." Lars Kiel Bertelsen, "It's Only a Paper Moon. . . . Re-reading APOLLO Photography in the Light of Digital Imagery," in *Symbolic Imprints: Essays on Photography and Visual Culture*, ed. Lars Kiel Bertelsen, Rune Gade, and Mette Sandbye (Aarhus, 1999), 91 and 102. Having myself played a role in introducing the concept of a "scopic regime," I would hesitate before saying that digital imagery has meant we have entered an entirely novel one, but there are reasons to think seriously about what changes have resulted.

2. The distinction is drawn, among other places, in Roland Barthes, *Camera Lucida: Reflections on Photography*, trans. Richard Howard (New York, 1981), 4.

3. Similar points can, of course, be made about other cultural phenomena, for example, the distinction between an individual poem and "literature" as an englobing institution.

4. See, for example, the criticism made by Richard Bolton in the introduction to the collection he edited, *The Contest of Meaning: Critical Histories of Photography* (Cambridge, MA, 1989): "The accepted version of photographic practice, forged for posterity in the 1950s and 1960s, is a limited construction based in the formalist values of late modernism. Historians and curators during that time worked quite deliberately to *narrow* photography. They emphasized the autonomy of the image and set about to define the 'norms' of medium, the intrinsic technological and visual properties of the photograph." (x, italics in original). Much was, of course, gained by widening the scope of photographic criticism to include its various contexts and probing their ideological implications, but there is also a danger in reducing photographs to nothing but effects or expressions of those contexts, which we are trying to avoid.

5. Nathan Jurgenson, *The Social Photo: On Photography and Social Media* (London, 2019), 15. For reflections on the experiential implications of Jurgenson's argument, see Martin Jay, "Experiencing Otherness through Technology: The Lessons of Photography," *Ex-position* 43 (2020). The immersion of individual photos in an encompassing and dynamic visual context did not, however, start with recent social media. For example, the controversial blockbuster exhibition mounted by Edward Steichen in the 1950s, *The Family of Man*, clustered different images, often with no regard for their original scale, in order to convey an ideological message. One result was a protest by individual photographers that the integrity of their work was compromised. For discussions of the ensuing debate, see Gerd Hurm, Anke Reitz, and Shamoon Zamir, eds., *The Family of Man Revisited: Photography in a Global Age* (London, 2020). The contexts in which photos were placed from the beginning—family albums, state archives, the exhibition spaces of museums or galleries, illuminated magazines, official documents, etc.—meant that the frames around their edges were always to a certain extent porous.

6. For a discussion, which focuses on the work of Laura Letinsky, see Martin Jay, "Laura Letinsky and the Art of Stillness," *Float Photo Magazine* (2015), http://issuu.com/floatphotomagazine/docs/float_issue__3_-_fragmented.

7. For discussions of photographs as material objects, see Elizabeth Edwards and Janice Hart, eds., *Photographs Objects Histories: On the Materiality of Images* (London, 2004).

8. Allan Sekula, "On the Invention of Photographic Meaning," in *Thinking Photography*, ed. Victor Burgin (London, 1982), 85.

9. Walter Benjamin, "The Work of Art in the Age of Mechanical Reproduction," in *Illuminations: Essays and Reflections*, ed. Hannah Arendt (Boston, 1968).

10. Gunter Gebauer and Christoph Wulf, *Mimesis: Culture—Art—Society*, trans. Don Reneau (Berkeley, 1995), 279.

11. Walter Benjamin, "Little History of Photography," trans. Edmund Jephcott and Kingsley Shorter, in *Selected Writings*, vol. 2, part 2, *1931–1934*, ed. Michael W. Jennings, Howard Eiland, and Gary Smith (Cambridge, MA, 1999), 519.

12. Benjamin, "Little History of Photography," 519.

13. Walter Benjamin, "On Some Motifs in Baudelaire," in *Illuminations*, 189, italics added.

14. See the array of remarks listed in "Photography Is Magic Quotes and Sayings," Quotes Sayings (website), accessed March 4, 2024, https://quotessayings.net/topics/photography-is-magic/.

15. Anne Collins Goodyear, "The Portrait, the Photograph and the Index," in *Photography Theory*, ed. James Elkins (New York, 2007), 211. The legend of the Corinthian Maid, recounted by Pliny the Elder in his *Natural History*, refers to the effort of Dibutade, the daughter of a Corinthian potter, to preserve the likeness of her lover, who had been forced to leave her. By tracing his shadow on a wall, she provided a template that her father then filled with clay to form the exact image of her beloved. This story was often represented as "the origin of painting" in the late eighteenth century by David Allan, Joseph Wright, and others.

16. William Fox Talbot, "Some Account of the Art of Photogenic Drawing," in *Photography in Print: Writings from 1816 to the Present*, ed. Vicki Goldberg (New York, 1981), italics in original. For a discussion, see Douglas R. Nickel, "Talbot's Natural Magic," *The History of Photography* 26, no. 2 (2002). The essay was devoted to providing a sober, scientific explanation of his experimental method, and not a threnody to occult powers. But it is clear that Talbot was dazzled by the extraordinary results of his efforts. For a discussion, see Douglas R. Nickel, "Talbot's Natural Magic," *History of Photography* 26, no. 2 (2002). It is also telling that as early as 1589, the use of cameras with lenses to help make pictures, although not fix them permanently, was described in a book by Giovanni Battista della Porta called *Magica Naturalis*. See Joel Snyder and Neil Walsh Allen, "Photography, Vision and Representation," *Critical Inquiry* 2, no. 1 (1975), 149.

17. William Fox Talbot, "The Magic Mirror," in Mike Weaver, *Henry Fox Talbot; Selected Texts and Bibliography* (Oxford, 1992).

18. Amanda Henderson, "Magic Mirrors: Formalist Realism in Victorian Physics and Photography," *Representations* 117, no. 1 (2012).

19. "25 Jacques-Henri Lartigue Quotes on the Magic of Photography," Photogpedia, accessed March 4, 2024, https://photogpedia.com/jacques-henri-lartigue-quotes/.

20. Berenice Abbott, "Photography at the Crossroads" (1951) in *Classic Essays on Photography*, ed. Alan Trachtenberg (New Haven, 1980), 184.

21. Barthes, *Camera Lucida*, 88, italics in original. For an account of his identification with sorcery and even witchcraft, see John Lurz, "The Sorcerer's Apprentice: Roland Barthes and the Criticism of Magic," *New Literary History* 52, no. 1 (2021).

22. Susan Sontag, *On Photography* (New York, 1978), 69.

23. Vilém Flusser, *Towards a Philosophy of Photography*, trans. Anthony Mathews (London, 2000), 16.

24. Flusser, *Towards a Philosophy of Photography*, 17.

25. Charlotte Cotton, ed., *Photography Is Magic* (New York, 2015), 3.

26. Eric Rosenberg, "Photography is Over, If You Want It," in *The Meaning of Photography*, ed. Robin Kelsey and Blake Stimson (Williamstown, MA, 2008), 190. In his essay on "The Salon of 1859," *Selected Writings on Art and Literature*, trans. P. E. Charvet (London, 1972), Baudelaire lamented the subversion of real art based on imagination and talent by the public's fascination for photography.

27. John Tagg, *The Burden of Representation: Essays on Photographies and Histories* (Amherst, 1988), 3.

28. Daniel C. Blight, "Photography Is Not Magic: Photographic Images and their Digital Spirit," *ASX*, October 16, 2016, https://americansuburbx.com/2015/10/photography-is-not-magic-photographic-images-and-their-digital-spirit.html. A symposium on Cotton's argument was edited by Karen Spenuso and published in *Lebenswelt* 9 (2016), with a response by Cotton.

29. Bill Jay, *Occam's Razor: An Outside-In View of Contemporary Photography* (Tucson, 2000). The magical potential of the photograph can also be actualized by something else

than its indexical capturing of singular details. In discussing surrealist photography, Herbert Molderings writes: "Photographers like Man Ray, Hans Bellmer, Raoul Ubac, and Paul Nougé sought to give back to photography something of the magic that had pervaded the early days of the medium and had been lost in the course of its increasing perfection. This magic, however, no longer lay in the authenticity of an apparent self-depiction of nature . . . but rather in techniques used to alienate the automatism of the photographic process and make visible the artificiality and contingency of the process." "Photographic History in the Spirit of Constructivism: Reflections on Walter Benjamin's 'Little History of Photography,'" trans. John Bogden, *Art in Translation* 6, no. 3 (2014): 335.

30. Sontag, *On Photography*, 22–23.

31. Allan Sekula, "The Body and the Archive," *October* 39 (1986): 17.

32. See Carlo Ginzburg, "Family Resemblances and Family Trees: Two Cognitive Metaphors," *Critical Inquiry* 30 (2004). He points out that the essentialist implications of Galton's composite photographs are more successfully avoided by Wittgenstein's idea of "family resemblances."

33. Sekula, "The Body and the Archive," 18. For a response to Sekula's argument, which draws on Peirce's Aristotelian moderate realism to question the link between indexicality and nominalism, see Christoper Ball, "Realisms and Indexicalities of Photographic Propositions," *Signs and Society* 5, supplement 1 (2017). He claims that Peirce favored realism over nominalism because the former was grounded in a communitarian rather than individualist notion of signs, and argues that it is possible to think in general terms without resorting to symbolism. He also notes that Peirce wanted to overcome Cartesian dualism, which distinguished subjective consciousness, producing conceptual generalities, from a given world composed of unique particulars. Insofar as this distinction was an expression of what we have been calling conventional nominalism, his objection has merit, but magical nominalism posited a less dualistic ontology. As we will see, Barthes's notion of the photographic *punctum* sought to integrate the desire of the beholder with the existence of something already there in the image, which stimulated it.

34. Amos Morris-Reich, *Race and Photography: Racial Photography as Scientific Evidence, 1876–1980* (Chicago, 2016), chap. 5.

35. See Wolfgang Brückle, "Face-off in Weimar Culture: The Physiognomic Paradigm, Competing Portrait Analogies, and August Sanders' *Face of our Time*," *Tate Papers* 19 (2013), https://www.tate.org.uk/research/tate-papers/19/face-off-in-weimar-culture-the-physiognomic-paradigm-competing-portrait-anthologies-and-august-sanders-face-of-our-time. For a more general discussion, see Helmut Lethen, *Cool Conduct: The Culture of Distance in Weimar Germany*, trans. Don Reneau (Berkeley, 2002).

36. Franz W. Seifert cited in Lethen, *Cool Conduct*, 156.

37. Benjamin, "Little History of Photography," 520. Benjamin contends that Sanders's observational skills were akin to Goethe's notion of "gentle empiricism" rather than the imposition of generic types from above, but he also calls "the ability to read facial types a matter of vital importance." For a discussion, which situates Benjamin in the more general Weimar response, see Mary Price, *The Photograph: A Strange Confined Space* (Stanford, CA, 1994), chap. 3.

38. Celia Lury, *Prosthetic Culture: Photography, Memory and Identity* (London, 1998), 51. She is drawing here on the work of Graham Clarke, "Public Faces, Private Lives: August Sander and the Social Typology of the Portrait Photograph," in *The Portrait in Photography*, ed. Graham Clarke (London, 1992).

39. Sekula, "The Body and the Archive," 17.

40. Sekula, "The Body and the Archive," 55. Morris-Reich, *Race and Photography*, 36–41.

41. Sekula, "The Body and the Archive," 60.

42. John Roberts, *Photography and Its Violations* (New York, 2013), 10. Why "capitalism" in particular demonstrates this dislike is not very clear, especially as societies that sought to go beyond it were often no less unnerved by what photographs might reveal, as all of those images of Stalin's enemies air-brushed from official Soviet photographs amply shows.

43. Sontag, *On Photography*, 123.

44. Benjamin, "Little History of Photography," 510. When Benjamin invokes "the unconscious" here, he is talking more of "the optical unconscious" than its psychological counterpart understood in Freudian terms.

45. For an insightful consideration of the importance of the essay, as well as its many inaccuracies and flaws, see Molderings, "Photographic History in the Spirit of Constructivism." He stresses the influence of Constructivism and Moholy-Nagy on Benjamin, who tried to combine their approach with historical materialism.

46. Samuel Weber, *Benjamin's–abilities* (Cambridge, MA, 2008), 63.

47. The image is reproduced in many places, including Archer's Wikipedia entry.

48. Painters, to be sure, inevitably refract their subjective intentions through the material media or technical supports they use to realize them, which can have an impact on the results. But they are less likely to be surprised by a fly caught on their canvases.

49. One has to be careful about overgeneralizing from usage in one language, however. Although in French and Spanish, it is also *prendre* and *tomar*, in German and Italian, it is *machen* and *fare*.

50. See Charles Sanders Peirce, "Logic as Semiotic: The Theory of Signs," in *The Philosophical Writings of Peirce*, ed. Justus Buchler (New York, 1940). Although these categories have had the most influence, Peirce developed a complicated categorical system with many other coinages to define different types of signs. For a discussion of the exemplarity of the photograph in his semiotic system, see François Brunet, "'A better example is a photograph': On the Exemplary Value of Photographs in C. S. Peirce's Reflection on Signs," in *The Meaning of Photography*, ed. Kelsey and Stimson.

51. For a discussion, see Walter Benn Michaels, "Photographs and Fossils," in *Photographic Theory*, ed. Elkins.

52. This comparison is metaphorical rather than literal, as a pointed finger accompanied by a speech act is not the same as a physical imprint.

53. Mary Anne Doane, "Indexicality and the Concept of Medium Specificity," in *The Meaning of Photography*, ed. Kelsey and Stimson, 5.

54. There are, to be sure, indexes that draw on the trace left behind by other sensual experiences, such as the lingering smell of a skunk or the echo of a yodeler in the mountains.

55. See, for example, the selection of different opinions in *Photographic Theory*, ed. Elkins.

56. Rosalind E. Krauss, "Notes on the Index," *The Originality of the Avant-Garde and Other Modernist Myths* (Cambridge, MA, 1985); Joel Snyder's critique of the claims of photographic realism, whether supported by indexicality or not, began as early as his 1975 joint essay with Neil Walsh Allen, "Photography, Vision and Representation." See also his "Picturing Vision," *Critical Inquiry* 6, no. 3 (1980). David Green coined the term "indexophobia," in *Photographic Theory*, ed. Elkins, 244–48. "Indexophilia" is applied to Krauss by Michaels, "Photographs and Fossils," 435.

57. The artistic status of photography has been vigorously debated from almost the beginning of the medium. Early "pictorialist" attempts to imitate paintings may have given way to "straight" photography's objectivist alternative—whose manifesto is often identified with Peter Henry Emerson's 1890 book, *Naturalistic Photography for Students of the Art*—but the results could just as easily be evaluated on aesthetic grounds. The introduction of Peirce's categories, however, did not happen until well into the twentieth century.

58. Michael Fried, *Why Photography Matters as Art as Never Before* (New Haven, 2008). His argument is implicitly directed at earlier commentators like the British philosopher Roger Scruton who deny that photographs can ever be considered as art because they cannot represent the idealized essence of what they portray in the way painting can. See his "Photography and Representation," in *Photography and Philosophy: Essays on the Pencil of Nature*, ed. Scott Walden (Malden, MA, 2008). Both Fried and Scruton share, however, a belief that photographs differ from painting in the difficulty they have in mastering uncontrolled details, even if they draw different conclusions about their ability to be considered legitimate works of art. For a critique of both, see Diarmuid Costello, "On the (So-Called) Problem of Detail: Michael Fried, Roland Barthes, and Roger Scruton on Photography and Intentionality," in *Michael Fried and Philosophy: Modernism, Intention and Theatricality*, ed. Mathew Abbott (New York, 2018). He calls their joint concern about unintended details the "orthodox" position, and tries to argue against it by stressing the necessity of some agency in the photographic process after the initial click of the shutter.

59. Michael Fried, *Theatricality and Absorption: Painting and the Beholder in the Age of Diderot* (Chicago, 1988).

60. It may seem as if the digital revolution meant a dematerialization of the medium in which indexical traces were no longer even possible, thus undermining any last faith in the trustworthiness of photographic images as automatic records of what the camera captures. But the fact that digital images are still valid for official documents, such as licenses or passports, shows that trust has not been really eroded in most cases. In addition, it can be argued that the key to indexicality is the apparatus of exposure, which survives digitalization, rather than the fixing mechanism. See Thomas Gunning, "What's the Point of an Index, or Faking Photographs," *Nordicum Review* 25, nos. 1–2 (2004). Like many other dramatic proclamations of cultural demise, "the death of photography" has been exaggerated.

61. Whether or not they are fully successful is another matter. Referring to Jeff Wall, James Elkins notes the "'flaws' and overlooked details that persist in his tableaux despite his most meticulous efforts." "What Do We Want Photography to Be? A Response to Michael Fried," in *Photography Degree Zero: Roland Barthes's "Camera Lucida,"* ed. Geoffrey Batchen (Cambridge, MA, 2009), 180.

62. Fried, *Why Photography Matters as Art as Never Before*, 272, italics in original. Does this suggest that Demand *intended* to represent or allegorize intention or that the work can be read allegorically as such? There is, in fact, a considerable debate about precisely what Fried means by intentionality, which can be attributed psychologically to the photographer prior to the taking of the picture or ontologically to the image understood as more than the deliberate product of a creative agent. See, for example, Walter Benn Michaels, "'When I Raise My Arm': Michael Fried's Theory of Action" and Rex Butler, "Michael Fried's Intentionality," in *Michael Fried and Philosophy*, ed. Abbott.

63. Another candidate for the role Fried assigns to the art photographer is the camera itself. That is, however skillfully employed, the technical apparatus inevitably limits the creative sovereignty of the photographer, who is dependent on what it can or cannot do.

In stressing this point, Vilém Flusser goes so far as to claim that "there is no such thing as naïve, non-conceptual photography. A photograph is an image of concepts. In this sense, all photographers' criteria are contained within the camera's program." *Towards a Philosophy of Photography*, 36. By stressing the conceptual nature of the technical apparatus, he is not, however, adopting a medieval realist view that concepts are universals already in the world, which are then recorded on the photograph. The camera can both enable and undermine the ability of the particular object photographed to leave an indexical imprint. If, for example, the film is overexposed, the result may be an image without any visible trace of the object at all.

64. Krauss, "Notes on the Index, Part 2," 212.

65. André Bazin, *What Is Cinema?*, trans. Hugh Gray (Berkeley, 1967), 13. For an insightful discussion of Bazin's understanding of the photograph as demonstrative rather than expressive, and thus in tension with social and cultural meaning, see James R. Cisneros, "Imaginary of the End, End of the Imaginary. Bazin and Malraux on the Limits of Painting and Photography," *Cinémas* 13, no. 3 (2003). He compares Bazin's position with André Malraux's situating photography in the context of an "imaginary museum," which stresses its cultural function.

66. Kendall L. Walton, "Transparent Pictures: On the Nature of Photographic Realism," in Walden, ed. *Photography and Philosophy*, 38.

67. For a consideration of this issue, see the essays collected as "Agency and Automatism: Photography and Art Since the 1960s," ed. Diarmuid Costello, Margaret Iverson, and Joel Snyder, special issue, *Critical Inquiry* 38, no. 4 (2012), as well as the follow-up discussion in *Critical Inquiry*, 41, no. 1 (2014). In addition to positing differences between agency and intentionality, exploring multiple meanings of "automatic," and deconstructing the opposition of subjective inspiration and the mechanism of realization, several of the essays emphasize the important role played in much modern art, literary, musical, and visual, by aleatory disruptions of the artist's sovereign control.

68. Roberts, *Photography and its Violations*, 45–54.

69. Stanley Cavell, "What Photography Calls Thinking," *Raritan* 4 (1985): 4. The embedded writing metaphor of "transcription" inevitably invokes the "graph" in "photograph" as "the pencil of nature." Umberto Eco has argued that "we know that sensory phenomena are *transcribed*, in the photographic emulsion, in such a way that even if there is a causal link with the real phenomena, the graphic images formed can be considered as wholly arbitrary with respect to these phenomena. . . . to differing degrees, *every image is born of a series of successive transmissions*." "Critique of the Image," in *Thinking Photography*, ed. Burgin, 33, italics in original.

70. This comparison is already made in Bazin, "The Ontology of the Photographic Image," 14.

71. John Tagg, "The Currency of the Photograph," in *Thinking Photography*, ed. Burgin, 117.

72. The book has generated a small cottage industry of commentaries, for example, Jean Delord, *Roland Barthes et la photographie* (Paris, 1981); Jean-Michel Rabaté, ed., *Writing the Image after Roland Barthes* (Philadelphia, 1997); Nancy M. Shawcross, *Roland Barthes on Photography: The Critical Tradition in Perspective* (Gainesville, 1997); Geoffrey Batchen, ed., *Photography Degree Zero: Reflections on Roland Barthes' "Camera Lucida'* (Cambridge, MA, 2009).

73. For an account of his place in the larger French discourse about visuality in the twentieth century, see Martin Jay, *Downcast Eyes: The Denigration of Vision in Twentieth-Century French Thought* (Berkeley, 1994), chap. 8.

74. Roland Barthes, *Mythologies*, trans. Annette Lavers (New York, 1972).

75. Roland Barthes, "The Photographic Message," in *Image-Music-Text*, trans. Stephen Heath (New York, 1977), 15.

76. Barthes, "The Photographic Message," 17, italics in original.

77. Although Barthes was soon to distance himself from Saussure, here he held on to a fundamental tenet of structural linguistics.

78. Barthes, "The Photographic Message," 31.

79. Roland Barthes, "The Rhetoric of the Image," in *Image-Music-Text*, 51, italics in original.

80. For a helpful narrative of the transformation of his approach, see Elena Oxman, "Sensing the Image: Roland Barthes and the Affect of the Visual," *SubStance* 39, no. 2 (2010).

81. Barthes, "The Third Meaning: Research Notes on Some Eisenstein Stills," *Image-Music-Text*, 63.

82. Geoffrey Batchen, "Palinode: An Introduction to *Photography Degree Zero*," in *Photography Degree Zero*, ed. Batchen, 3.

83. For examples of these readings, see respectively Margaret Iverson, "What is a Photograph?," in *Photography Degree Zero*, ed. Batchen; Kathrin Yacavone, *Benjamin, Barthes and the Singularity of Photography* (London, 2012); Jay Prosser, "Buddha Barthes: What Barthes Saw in Photography that He Didn't in Literature," in *Photography Degree Zero*, ed. Batchen; and Sarah Sentilles, "The Photograph as Mystery: Theological Language and Ethical Looking in Roland Barthes' *Camera Lucida*," in *The Journal of Religion* 90, no. 4 (2010).

84. Barthes, *Camera Lucida*, 4.

85. Barthes, *Camera Lucida*, 34.

86. Barthes, *Camera Lucida*, 32.

87. Barthes, *Camera Lucida*, 33.

88. Although widely appreciated, Barthes's dichotomy did not persuade all commentators. Jacques Rancière, for example, grumbled that "photography, formerly accused of opposing mechanical, soulless simulacra to the colored flesh of painting, sees its image inverted. Compared with pictorial artifices, it is now perceived as the very emanation of a body, as a skin detached from its surface, positively replacing the appearances of resemblance and defeating the efforts of the discourse that would have it express a meaning. The imprint of the thing, the naked identity of its alterity in place of its imitation, the wordless, senseless materiality of the visibility of the figures of discourse—this is what is demanded by the contemporary celebration of the image. . . . What the simple relationship between mechanical impression and the *punctum* erases is the whole history of the relations between three things: the images of art, the social forms of imagery, and the theoretic procedures of criticism of imagery." *The Future of the Image*, trans. Gregory Elliot (London, 2019), 9 and 15.

89. Barthes, *Camera Lucida*, 26.

90. Barthes, *Camera Lucida*, 51.

91. Barthes, *Camera Lucida*, 41.

92. Barthes, *Camera Lucida*, 27. Barthes's string of metaphors for the *punctum* has not always been considered a strength of his argument, but rather an expression of his unsuccessful struggle to clarify its meaning.

93. Barthes, *Camera Lucida*, 43. There is some dispute over whether *objet partiel* should be translated as "part object" in accord with the standard usage in English. However

translated, the term itself has been traced back to Karl Abraham. It was given greater currency in the object relations theory of Melanie Klein, where it referred in particular to the mother's breast. When it was then adopted by Lacan, who was Barthes's reference point, it underwent a shift from referring to a part substituting for an actual whole to a universal characteristic of objects of desire, which only partially represent the function producing them. It was then folded into his complicated theory of *objet petit a*.

94. This was a talismanic word in French poststructuralist discourse with its connotations of orgasmic ejaculation, and it may well seem a stretch to apply it in the case of looking at a photograph, however powerful the experience of seeing a *punctum* might be. But Barthes clearly intended an affect stronger than mere pleasure.

95. Iverson, "What is a Photograph?," 59. See also her *Beyond Pleasure: Freud, Lacan, Barthes* (University Park, PA, 2007).

96. Fried, in fact, responded charitably to *Camera Lucida*, testing its implications against his argument about theatricality and absorption in painting. He notes that Barthes's stress on the nonintentionality of the *punctum* ties it to the antitheatrical tradition he favors. But contending that the digital revolution which made possible the art photography of Wall, Struth, Gursky, etc., had changed the rules of the game, he concludes that *Camera Lucida* is "a swansong for an artifact on the brink of a fundamental change." "Barthes' *Punctum*," in *Photography Zero Degree*, ed. Batchen, 152. For a rebuttal of this claim, see James Elkins, "What Do We Want Photographs to Be? A Response to Michael Fried," in *Photography Degree Zero*, ed. Batchen, 176–77.

97. Barthes, *Camera Lucida*, 117. He also mentions a second way in which the madness of the photograph might be tamed: "to generalize, to gregarize, banalize it until it is no longer confronted by an image in relation to which it can mark itself, assert its special character, its scandal, its madness." (118). In our society, the ubiquity of photographs serves this domesticating function.

98. Barthes, *Camera Lucida*, 55, italics in original.

99. Roland Barthes, "To Write: An Intransitive Verb," *The Rustle of Language*, trans. Richard Howard (Berkeley, 1989). Some skeptical critics claim that Barthes is waffling here between saying that what counts as a *punctum* is unique for each beholder and is yet somehow also objectively there in an unintended detail caught by the camera.

100. According to Geoffrey Batchen, "Peirce's notion of indexical semiosis collapses any sharp distinction between a referent and the psychological associations a viewer brings to it. . . . An equivalent oscillation back and forth between photograph and viewer, and between text and reader, is a central element of Barthes' discussion throughout *Camera Lucida*." "*Camera Lucida*: Another Little History of Photography," in *The Meaning of Photography*, ed. Kelsey and Stimson, 82–83.

101. Naomi Schor, "Desublimation: Roland Barthes' Aesthetics," in *Critical Essays on Roland Barthes*, ed. Diana Knight (New York, 2000), 228.

102. Barthes, *Camera Lucida*, 76, italics in original.

103. Barthes, *Camera Lucida*, 82.

104. Barthes, *Camera Lucida*, 88, italics in original.

105. For considerations of these and comparable issues, see Carolyn Gill, ed., *Time and the Image* (Manchester, 2000); and Nélio Rodrigues Conceição, "Sparks of Reality: On the Temporalities of the Photographic Image," *Aisthesis* 11, no. 2 (2018).

106. Barthes, *Camera Lucida*, 40. For a discussion of the uncanny in *Camera Lucida*, see Natasha Beaudin Pearson, "Merleau-Ponty and Barthes on Image Consciousness: Probing the (Im)possibility of Meaning," *Dainoia* 6 (2019): 12–14.

107. Barthes, *Camera Lucida*, 91.

108. Strictly speaking, as far as I can tell, *le parfait* is not a French tense. There are eight verb tenses in the indicative mood: *présent* (present), *imparfait* (imperfect), *passé simple* (simple past), *futur simple* (simple future), *passé composé* (perfect), *plus-que-parfait* (pluperfect), *passé antérieur* (past anterior), and *futur antérieur* (future anterior).

109. Barthes, *Camera Lucida*, 96, italics in original. One of the most frequently posited differences between photographs and films pits the reminder of death in the former against the simulacrum of ongoing life in the latter.

110. Prosser, "Buddha Barthes," 100.

111. Barthes, *Camera Lucida*, 96, italics in original.

112. See Ruth E. Iskin, "In the Light of Images and the Shadow of Technology: Lacan, Photography and Subjectivity," *Discourse* 19, no. 3 (1997).

113. Jacques Lacan, *Four Fundamental Concepts of Psycho-analysis*, ed. Jacques-Alain Miller, trans. Alan Sheridan (New York, 1981). There have been many attempts to unravel the complexities of this argument. For my own, see *Downcast Eyes*, chap. 6.

114. Lacan, *Four Fundamental Concepts*, 95.

115. Lacan, *Four Fundamental Concepts*, 106.

116. Iskin, "In the Light of Images and the Shadow of Technology," 58.

117. James Elkins, *The Object Stares Back: On the Nature of Seeing* (New York, 1996), 73–74. For a very different consideration of the implications of Lacan's argument, which draws on Hannah Arendt's claim that objects in the world have an aspiration to be seen, see Kaja Silverman, *World Spectators* (Stanford, CA, 2000), chap. 6.

118. Benjamin, "On Some Motifs in Baudelaire," 190.

119. Lacan, in fact, was critical of painting precisely because it of its "Apollonian, pacifying effect. . . . Something is given not so much to the gaze as to the eye, something that involves the abandonment, the *laying down*, of the gaze." (*Four Fundamental Concepts*, 101, italics in original).

120. See Iverson, *Beyond Pleasure*, 123.

121. Eelco Runia, *Moved by the Past: Discontinuity and Historical Mutation* (New York, 2014), 101.

122. Runia, *Moved by the Past*, 102.

123. F. R. Ankersmit, *Sublime Historical Experience* (Stanford, CA, 2005), 181.

124. Ankersmit, *Sublime Historical Experience*, 424. Benjamin's interpretation of Atget, which was indebted to the foreword written by Camille Recht to a 1930 German edition of his photographs, has been challenged by subsequent scholarship. See Molderings, "Photographic History in the Spirit of Constructivism," 331–33.

125. Georges Didi-Huberman, *Images in Spite of Everything: Four Photographs from Auschwitz*, trans. Shane B. Lillis (Chicago, 2008). For a fuller account of how they were taken, see Judith Lermer Crawley, "Acts of Resistance," Judith Lermer Crawley (website), accessed March 4, 2024, https://judithcrawley.ca/wp-content/uploads/2019/06/Acts-of-Resistance-2005_2.pdf. For a discussion of their implications for Ankersmit's argument, see Martin Jay, "Sublime Historical Experience, Real Presence, and Photography," in *Genesis and Validity*.

126. Didi-Huberman, *Images in Spite of Everything*, 81 and 88.

127. Thierry de Duve, "Time Exposure and Snapshot: The Photograph as Paradox," in *Photography Theory*, ed. Elkins, 109. The paradox is that it can be transformed from the recording of an event as an irreparably past moment to what de Duve calls "a picture" in which it is taken as an autonomous representation of ongoing life or the endurance of an object. He identifies the latter with time exposures and the former with snapshots.

128. John Berger, “Understanding a Photograph,” in Trachtenberg, *Classic Essays in Photography*, 293.

129. Michel Frizot, “Who’s Afraid of Photons?,” in Elkins, ed., *Photographic Theory*, 280.

130. See, for example, Dietrich Erben, “Das Ereignis und seine Bilder: Zur medialen Gegenwart des Terroranschlags auf das World Trade Center in New York,” in *Bilder machen Geschichte: Historische Ereignisse im Gedächtnis der Kunst*, ed. Uwe Fleckner (Berlin, 2014).

131. John Berger, *Ways of Seeing* (London, 1972), 153, italics in original.

132. Britta Hochkirchen, “Beyond Representation: Pictorial Temporality and the Relational Time of the Event,” *History and Theory* 60, no. 1 (2021). Boehm’s idea of “iconic difference” posited the structurally heterogeneous elements in an image that had to be read processually following a logic of contrast and oscillation rather than grasped simultaneously. In a way, this argument generalizes the effect often discerned in stereoscopic photographs in particular, which layer different planes to produce a simulacrum of three-dimensionality. For accounts of their implications, see Rosalind E. Krauss, “Photography’s Discursive Spaces,” in *The Originality of the Avant-garde and Other Modernist Myths*; and Douglas Klahr, “The Radically Subversive Narrative of Stereoscopic Photography,” *Kunsttexte.de* 1 (2013).

133. Andrew Benjamin, “What in Truth is Photography? Notes after Kracauer,” *Oxford Literary Review* 32, no. 2 (2010): 196.

134. Jaś Elsner, “Art History as Ekphrasis,” *Art History* 33, no. 1 (2010): 13.

135. See Herbert Butterfield, *The Whig Interpretation of History* (New York, 1965).

136. Barthes, *Camera Lucida*, 45.

137. Barthes, *Camera Lucida*, 59.

138. Roberts, *Photography and its Violations*, 111. His argument is based on the premise that “there is no event outside of its symbolic reconstruction—and not in any imagined identification of photographic truth with the immediacy of the ‘singular event’” (112).

139. Barthes, *Camera Lucida*, 4.

140. Barthes, *Camera Lucida*, 19.

141. To complete the circle, in 1952, the American photographer Eliot Elisofon produced a chronophotograph of Duchamp himself descending a staircase.

142. Tamara Trodd, “Thomas Demand, Jeff Wall, and Sherrie Levine: Deforming ‘Pictures,’” in *Photography after Conceptual Art*, ed. Diarmuid Costello and Margaret Iverson (Malden, MA, 2010), 148.

143. Duchamp, “Specification for Readymades,” *The Writings of Marcel Duchamp*, ed. Michel Sanouillet and Elmer Peterson (London, 1975), 32. Italics added.

144. Krauss, “Notes on the Index, Part I,” 206. For another consideration of the parallel, see Margaret Iverson, “Readymade, Found Object, Photograph,” *Art Journal* 63, no. 2 (2004).

145. Krauss, “Notes on the Index, Part I,” 206.

146. Martin Seel, “Photografien sind wie Namen,” in *Ethische-ästhetische Studien* (Frankfurt, 1996).

147. Seel, “Photografien sind wie Namen,” 88.

148. Seel, “Photografien sind wie Namen,” 94.

149. Seel, “Photografien sind wie Namen,” 102.

150. A similar conclusion is drawn by James Cisneros in his comparison of Bazin and Malraux: “The mystical quality of the photographic image stems from the indication of its limits for human understanding, which may decipher its expression but which cannot objectively grasp its enunciation.” “Imaginary of the End, End of the Imaginary,” 156.

151. The literature on Kracauer has grown exponentially in recent years. Among the most thorough treatments of his life and career are Harry T. Craver, *Reluctant Skeptic: Siegfried Kracauer and the Crises of Weimar Culture* (New York, 2020); and Jörg Später, *Kracauer: A Biography*, trans. Daniel Steuer (Cambridge, 2020). My own essays on him have been collected in *Kracauer l'exilé* (Paris, 2014).

152. In the heated polemic he conducted with Theodor Adorno in Switzerland in 1960 over the latter's work-in-progress *Negative Dialectics*, Kracauer made clear his hostility to an immanent dialectics that did not reserve a place for an ontological moment external to its relational network. Explicitly acknowledging his "life-long aversion to Hegel," he identified instead with Benjamin's resistance to the closure of dialectics, whose ability to digest into its system everything with which it comes into contact he distrusted. "I subtly implied that we [Kracauer and Benjamin] are engaged in terms of substances. We think under a sort of ontological compunction, Utopian or not, whereas Teddie is, indeed, free-hovering and does not feel any such compunction." What Adorno was to lament in his ambivalent birthday tribute to Kracauer as the absence of his friend's "protest against reification," Kracauer understood as a defense against the swallowing up of entities by processes or objects by the relational context in which they were embedded. "Talk with Teddie," in Siegfried Kracauer, *Siegfried Kracauer's American Writings: Essays on Film and Popular Culture*, ed. Johannes von Moltke and Kristy Rawson (Berkeley, 2012), 129–30. Whether or not this critique was justified is another matter, as Adorno's negative dialectics also acknowledged an unassimilable "block" that resisted self-sufficient immanence.

153. However, in a workshop Bielik-Robson organized in 2013 at the University of Nottingham on "Critical Theory and Jewish Thought," one of the papers, by the Polish scholar Adam Lipszyc, treated Kracauer's "materialist theory of photography." It was later published as "The Remnants of Grandmother, or In Search of a Materialist Theology of Photography and Film," *Bamidbar* 5, no. 2 (2015).

154. Theodor W. Adorno, "The Curious Realist: On Siegfried Kracauer," *Notes to Literature*, vol. 2, ed. Rolf Tiedemann, trans. Shierry Weber Nicholsen (New York, 1992). The original was a talk for the Hessische Rundfunk published in *Neue Deutsche Hefte* 101 (September–October, 1964). Kracauer was furious at what he saw as Adorno's implicit condescension towards him, which was by no means an unfair assessment. He bridled in particular at Adorno's charge that even before he moved to Berlin in the mid-1920s, he had begun to accommodate to reality rather than remaining at odds with it. For discussions of their highly fraught relationship, see Martin Jay, "Adorno and Kracauer: Notes on a Troubled Friendship," in *Permanent Exiles: Essays on the Intellectual Migration from Germany to America* (New York, 1985); and Martin Jay, preface to *Theodor W. Adorno et Siegfried Kracauer: Correspondance 1923–1966* (Paris, 2018).

155. The first is found in David Frisby, *Fragments of Modernity: Theories of Modernity in the Work of Simmel, Kracauer and Benjamin* (Cambridge, MA, 1986), 125; the second is my own in "The Extraterritorial Life of Siegfried Kracauer," in *Permanent Exiles*, 225. A third candidate, although not directly employed to translate the essay, is "miraculous realist," which appears in the title of Drehli Robnik, "Among Other Things—A Miraculous Realist: Political Perspectives on the Theoretical Entanglements of Cinema and History in Siegfried Kracauer," in *Culture in the Anteroom: The Legacies of Siegfried Kracauer*, ed. Gerd Gemünden and Johannes von Moltke (Ann Arbor, 2012).

156. Adorno, "The Curious Realist," 61.

157. Benjamin, "Review of Kracauer's *Die Angestellten*," trans. Rodney Livingstone, in *Selected Writings*, vol. 2, part 1, *1927–1930*, ed. Michael W. Jennings, Howard Eiland, and Gary Smith (Cambridge, MA, 199), 356.

158. As far as I can tell, Kracauer never commented on the Adamic view of language revived in particular by Benjamin, although in his 1925 study of *The Detective Novel*, he invoked Kierkegaard's notion of religion as "the highest sphere" in which "names disclose themselves." Siegfried Kracauer, *Schriften*, vol. 1 (Frankfurt, 1971), 107. Kracauer, however, argued that humans live in the realm of the profane rather than the sacred, and in his critique of Martin Buber and Franz Rosenzweig's new translation of the Hebrew Bible into German, he expressed little patience for *Sprachmagie* in any form. Referencing a famous episode in the *Nibelungenlied*, he wrote, "Language is like the spot between Siegfried's shoulder blades on which the linden leaf fell: it the only place on the body of the powerful realities that is not protected by the magic of the dragon's blood." "The Bible in German," in *The Mass Ornament*, 191.

159. In 1918, Kracauer did write an unpublished piece entitled "Über den Expressionismus: Wesen und Sinn einer Zeitbewegung. Abhandlung," in *Werke: Frühe Schriften aus den Nachlass*, ed. Inka Mülder-Bach (Frankfurt, 2004), in which he called the movement a vitalist response with religious overtones to the technological rationality of modern life. But his interest in the movement was not sustained as he deepened his commitment to the sphere of the profane rather than the sacred.

160. For an account of this metaphor, which he explicitly used throughout his career, see Jay, "The Extraterritorial Life of Siegfried Kracauer, *Permanent Exiles*.

161. Edmund Husserl, *Logische Untersuchungen*, vol. 19, part 1, of *Husserliana* (The Hague, 1984), 10.

162. Kracauer's valorization of contingency also informed his work on film. See Janet Harbord, "Contingency's Work: Kracauer's Work on Film and the Trope of the Accidental," *New Formations* 61 (2007).

163. Lethen, *Cool Conduct*, 88.

164. As Sabine Hake has noted, "The kind of individualism that required the world to be a reflection of the self undermined the original project of cinema which, according to Kracauer, involved the rediscovery of the world of objects and man's place in its changing constellation. . . . Through the equation of animate and inanimate worlds, it reinstated objects in all their power." *The Cinema's Third Machine: Writing on Film in Germany 1907–1933* (Lincoln, NE, 1993), 254–59. For Kracauer, Miriam Bratu Hansen added, "film's materialist capability not only undercuts the sovereign subject of bourgeois ideology but with it a larger anthropocentric worldview that presumes to impose meaning and control upon a world that increasingly defies traditional distinctions between the human and the nonhuman, the living and the mechanical, the unique (inner-directed) individual and the mass subject, civilization and barbarism." Miriam Bratu Hansen, Introduction to *Theory of Film: The Redemption of Physical Reality*, by Siegfried Kracauer (Princeton, 1997), xvii.

165. For a discussion of the "primacy of the optical" in Kracauer, see Gertrud Koch, "Athenes blanker Schild: Siegfried Kracauers Reflexe und die Vernichtung," *Die Einstellung ist die Einstellung: Visuelle Konstruktionen des Judentums* (Frankfurt, 1992), 133–37. The term was first used by Adorno in "Der wunderliche Realist."

166. Franz Roh, *Nach-Expressionismus, Magischer Realismus: Probleme der neuesten europäischen Malerei* (Leipzig, 1925). It is partly translated as "Post-Expressionism, Magic Realism: Problems of Recent European Painting, 1925," in *German Expressionism: Documents*

from the End of the Wilhelmine Empire to the Rise of National Socialism, ed. Rose-Carol Washton Long (Berkeley, 1993). In a letter written in March cited in the introduction to the latter, Roh wrote "With the word 'magic' as opposed to 'mystic,' I wish to indicate that the mystery doesn't descend to the represented world, but rather hides and palpitates behind it" (16).

167. Roh, "Post-Expressionism, Magic Realism," 20.

168. Roh, "Post-Expressionism, Magic Realism," 17.

169. Misch Orend, "Der magischer Realismus," *Klingsohr: Siebenbürgische Zeitschrift* 5 (January 1928); in *The Weimar Republic Sourcebook*, ed. Anton Kaes, Martin Jay and Edward Dimendberg (Berkeley, 1994), 494.

170. Kracauer, *History: The Last Things Before the Last* (Oxford, 1969), 52. In *Theory of Film*, he had already written: "Actually there is no mirror at all. Photographs do not just copy nature but metamorphose it by transforming three-dimensional phenomena to the plane, severing their ties with the surroundings, and substituting black, gray, and white for the given color schemes. Yet if anything defies the idea of a mirror, it is not so much these unavoidable transformations—which may be discounted because in spite of them photographs still preserve the character of compulsory reproductions—as the way in which we take cognizance of visible reality" (15).

171. Kracauer, *The Salaried Masses: Duty and Distraction in Weimar Germany*, trans. Quinton Hoare, intro. Inka Mülder-Bach (London, 1998), 32. In *Cool Conduct*, Lethen compares this position to Brecht's critique of mimetic realism and argues that Kracauer adopted it at the end of Weimar as a critique of his earlier "pathos of perceptual acuity" (148).

172. Kracauer, *History: The Last Things Before the Last*, 85.

173. For a discussion of the theological subtext of his desire to redeem creation, see Gertrud Koch, *Siegfried Kracauer: An Introduction*, trans. Jeremy Gaines (Princeton, 2000), 105.

174. Walter Benjamin, "The Concept of Criticism in German Romanticism" (1920), trans. David Lachterman, Howard Eiland, and Ian Balfour, in *Selected Writings*, vol. 1, *1913–1926*, ed. Marcus Bullock and Michael W. Jennings (Cambridge, MA, 1996), 148.

175. See, for example, Steve Giles, "Making Visible, Making Strange: Photography and Representation in Kracauer, Brecht and Benjamin," *New Formations* 61 (2007); and Meir Wigoder, "History Begins at Home: Photography and Memory in the Writings of Siegfried Kracauer and Roland Barthes," *History and Memory* 13, no. 1 (2001).

176. Kracauer, "Photography," in *The Mass Ornament: Weimar Essays*, trans. and ed., Thomas Y. Levin (Cambridge, MA, 1995), 49.

177. Kracauer, "Photography," 49.

178. Kracauer, "Photography," 49–50. The importance of space in Kracauer's work, reflecting his training as an architect, has been often remarked. In *The Mathematical Imagination: On the Origins and Promise of Critical Theory* (New York, 2019), Matthew Handelman shows that in his early work it was tied to an interest in geometry. In his 1922 *Soziologie als Wissenschaft*, Kracauer even toyed with Edmund Husserl's essentialist notion of geometry as inherent in the world, before concluding with Georg Simmel that society could not be reduced to logical or mathematical regularities.

179. For a discussion of the myriad ways in which memory and photography have been related, including by Kracauer, see Olga Shevchenko, "'The Mirror with a Memory': Placing Photography in Memory Studies," in *Routledge Handbook of Memory Studies*, ed. Anna Lisa Tota and Trever Hagen (London, 2015).

180. Kracauer, "Photography," 51, italics in original. For an insightful comparison of the emblematic quality of photographs and their relations to *Denkbilder* (thought images) and aphorisms in the work of Kracauer and Benjamin, see Andreas Huyssen, "Photography and Emblem in Kracauer and Benjamin's Street Texts," in *Miniature Metropolis: Literature in the Age of Photography and Film* (Cambridge, 2015).

181. Kracauer, "Photography," 51.

182. See, for example, Wigoder, "History Begins at Home": "Kracauer finds memory images far more useful. . . . The camera is capable of capturing only a brief moment that accentuates space rather than temporality. The medium of subjective memory, however, can shatter the space-time continuum in order to piece the salvaged fragments together into a meaningful order" (26).

183. For the former, see Kracauer, "Those Who Wait" (1922), in *The Mass Ornament*, 129. The latter was introduced in Georg Lukács, *Theory of the Novel*, trans. Anna Bostock (Cambridge, MA, 1974) and adopted by Kracauer in *The Salaried Masses* to refer in particular to white-collar workers in Weimar.

184. For a reading of the essay that laments Kracauer's alleged dismissal of photography "for undermining historical insights," see Christine Mehring, "Siegfried Kracauer's Theories of Photography: From Weimar to New York," *History of Photography* 21, no. 2 (1997): 132. She sees a more productive relationship between history and photography developing only after his migration to America.

185. Lipszyc, "The Remnants of Grandmother," 48.

186. Kracauer, "Photography," 52–53, italics in original.

187. Kracauer, "Photography," 54.

188. Kracauer, "Photography," 55. In his "Theory of Signatures," Giorgio Agamben includes artists' monograms along with signatures as having pragmatic as well as semiotic power, and thus sharing in the efficacy attributed to signatures by Paracelsus. See his "Theory of Signatures," in *The Signature of All Things: On Method*, trans. Luca D'Isanto with Kevin Attell (New York, 2009), 39. Kracauer's hesitation before attributing the same power to photographs testifies to the austerity of his version of magical nominalism in comparison with Benjamin's in particular.

189. Kracauer, "Photography," 56–57, italics in original.

190. Kracauer, "Photography," 58–59, italics in original.

191. Kracauer, "Photography," 60–61.

192. Huyssen, "Photography and Emblem in Kracauer and Benjamin's Street Texts," 125.

193. "The Mass Ornament," in Kracauer, *The Mass Ornament*, ends with the warning that "enterprises that ignore our historical context and attempt to reconstruct a form of state, a community, a mode of artistic creation that depends upon a type of man who had already been impugned by contemporary thinking—a type of man who by all rights no longer exists—such enterprises do not transcend the mass ornament's empty and superficial shallowness but flee from its reality. The process leads directly through the center of the mass ornament, not away from it" (86).

194. Kracauer, "Photography," 61, italics in original.

195. Kracauer, "Photography," 62, italics in original. For an insightful discussion of the implications of these observations, see Peter Geimer, "Photography as 'Space of Experience': On the Retrospective Legibility of Historical Photographs," *Getty Research Journal* 7, (2015): 102–4.

196. The phrase "der Riß der Welt geht auch durch mich, gerade durch mich" appeared in a letter he wrote to Adorno on April 5, 1923, in Theodor W. Adorno / Siegfried Kracauer, *Briefwechsel*, ed. Wolfgang Schopf (Frankfurt, 2008), 11.

197. See Maria Zinfert, "An 'Accidental Image,'" in *Kracauer: Photographic Archive*, ed. Maria Zinfert (Zurich, 2014). She points out that the glass fragments partially reassembled to make the resulting image draw attention in a literal way to the constructed nature of photographs in general, which work with the accidental residues of what the camera captures. One might add that the accidental break of the negative plate, like that of Duchamp's *Large Glass*, means that the complex temporality of this particular image includes not only a deictic index of the moment the picture was taken, but also the moment its material support was damaged, as well as the moment it was reassembled as a mosaic of fragments.

198. Miriam Bratu Hansen, "Kracauer's Photography Essay: Dot Matrix—General (An)archive—Film," in *Culture in the Anteroom*, ed. Germünden and von Moltke, 101. In his essay in the same volume, "In Kracauer's Shadow: Physical Reality and the Digital Afterlife of the Photographic Image," Lutz Koepnick comes to a similar conclusion: "Kracauer is far from arguing that photography necessarily seals our fate as inhabitants of a world fallen from prelapsarian plenitude. On the contrary, in alienating viewers from an alienated world, in making us see aspects of reality often invisible to the human eye, photography has the ability to transmit the raw and unshaped and thus open the case of nature in all its incommensurability" (118).

199. See Siegfried Kracauer, "A Note on Portrait Photography," in *The Past's Threshold: Essays on Photography*, ed. Philippe Despoix and Maria Zinfert, trans. Conor Joyce (Chicago, 2014).

200. Kracauer, "A Note on Portrait Photography," 60.

201. Kracauer, *Theory of Film*, 18–20.

202. Kracauer, *History*, 52–61.

203. See D. N. Rodowick, "The Last Things Before the Last: Kracauer and History," *New German Critique* 41 (1987): 109–10.

204. Kracauer, *History*, 150.

205. Kracauer, *History*, 31.

206. Kracauer, *History*, 84.

207. As noted above, in his critique of the Buber-Rosenzweig Bible, Kracauer was critical of *Sprachmagie* in any form. Lipszyc thus perhaps goes too far at the end of "The Remnants of Grandma," when he claims Kracauer sought "true names" in the depiction of the street in cinema (57). In a personal communication of October 22, 2022, he admits that he may be reading too much Benjamin into Kracauer but still finds attractive the possibility that "the true names are in the nameless. They are in the street (understood as the deconstructive breaking within a memorable story)." For a very different interpretation, see Carole Maigné, "Siegfried Kracauer's Radical 'Camera-Reality,'" *Archives de Philosophie* 85, no. 1 (2022): 59–60. She argues that although Kracauer shared Benjamin's belief that photographs are without expression, he was skeptical of the latter's redemptive claim that they somehow can restore Adamic names. She thus doubts that, strictly speaking, he can be called a "magical nominalist." If there were a single definitive meaning to the label, he might well fail the test, but as this book has tried to demonstrate, the term has many overlapping, but distinct exemplars, and in important respects, Kracauer earns a place as one of them.

208. Kracauer, *History*, 136. The positive reference to the figure of the collector was a nod to Benjamin, who wrote eloquently of its value.

209. Gertrud Koch, "'Not Yet Accepted Anywhere': Exile, Memory and Image in Kracauer's Conception of History," *New German Critique* 54 (Fall 1991): 98. She argues for the theological subtext of his desire to redeem creation in *Siegfried Kracauer: An Introduction*, trans. Jeremy Gaines (Princeton, 2000), 105.

210. Miriam Hansen, "Decentric Perspectives: Kracauer's Early Writings on Film and Mass Culture," *New German Critique* 54 (Fall 1991): 53. In this essay, Hansen stresses Kracauer's debts to what she calls the "discourse of secular Jewish messianism," including its gnostic alarm at the fallenness of the current world. He never, however, accepted the world-annihilating implications of gnosticism at its most dualistic.

211. See, for example, Kracauer's letter of December 4, 1921, to Löwenthal in response to the latter's ecstatic essay on "The Demonic," where he applies Max Scheler's reproach to Ernst Bloch that he is "running amok to God" to Löwenthal's essay. He then adds "Frankly, I don't *believe in the messianic time* (the 'fulfilled time' of Lukács means something else). I don't believe in *this* God and if this desperado attitude is religious, I am an entirely unreligious man and will remain so." Leo Löwenthal / Siegfried Kracauer, *In Steter Freundschaft: Briefwechsel*, ed. Peter-Erwin Jansen and Christian Schmidt (Springer, 2003), 203.

212. Lipszyc, "The Remnants of Grandmother," 51.

213. Walter Benjamin, "On the Concept of History," trans. Harry Zohn, in *Selected Writings*, vol. 4, *1938–1940*, ed. Howard Eiland and Michael W. Jennings (Cambridge, MA, 2003), 390.

214. Theodor W. Adorno, *Minima Moralia: Reflections from Damaged Life*, trans. Edmund Jephcott (London, 1974), 274.

215. Kracauer, "Those Who Wait," *The Mass Ornament*, 138, italics in original. The phrase anticipates that "active passivity" he saw as the proper attitude of the historian in his final book.

216. Craver, *Reluctant Skeptic*, 18. Craver traces the secularized residues of Kracauer's negative theology in this career.

217. Kracauer, "Those Who Wait," 140.

218. Adorno, "The Curious Realist," 64–65.

219. Adorno, "The Curious Realist," 75.

In Lieu of a Conclusion

1. Conventional nominalism did not, however, inevitably lead to a strong notion of absolute sovereignty. Some nominalists, for example, Richard Rorty, were antifoundationalist pluralists. But the lineage beginning with Hobbes and culminating in Schmitt suggests that the human self-assertion enabled by the nominalists' critique of universalist realism could easily have political theoretical consequences.

2. For a random sample, see Lutz Koepnick, *Walter Benjamin and the Aesthetics of Power* (Lincoln, NE, 1999); Tara Forrest, *The Politics of Imagination: Benjamin, Kracauer and Kluge* (Bielefeld, 2007); Andrew Benjamin, *Working with Walter Benjamin: Recovering a Political Philosophy* (Edinburgh, 2013); Espen Hammer, *Adorno and the Political* (New York, 2005); Gary A. Mullen, *Adorno and Politics After Auschwitz* (Lanham, MD, 2016); Caleb J. Bassnet, *Adorno, Politics and the Aesthetic Animal* (Toronto, 2021); Richard Beardsworth, *Derrida and the Political* (New York, 1996); Pheng Cheah and Susanne Guerlac, eds., *Derrida and the Time of the Political* (Durham, 2009); Andrew Stafford, *Roland Barthes Writing the Political: History, Dialectics, Self* (London, 2022); Chris Rojek and Brian S. Turner, eds., *The Politics of Jean- François Lyotard: Justice and Political Theory*

(New York, 1998); James Williams, *Lyotard and the Political* (New York, 2000); Stuart Sims, *Lyotard and Politics* (Edinburgh, 2020); Jon Simons, *Foucault and the Political* (New York, 1994); Thomas L. Dumm, *Foucault and the Politics of Freedom* (New York, 2002); Sandro Chignola, *Foucault's Politics of Philosophy: Power, Law and Subjectivity* (New York, 2019); Bruno Bosteels, *Badiou and Politics* (Durham, 2011); and Marios Constantinou, ed., *Badiou and the Political Condition* (Edinburgh, 2014).

3. The critique of a strong notion of sovereign will was not confined to theorists who can easily be identified with magical nominalism. Hannah Arendt, for example, famously declared that "perhaps the greatest American innovation in politics as such was the consistent abolition of sovereignty within the body politic of the republic, the insight that in the realm of human affairs sovereignty and tyranny are the same." *On Revolution* (London, 1963), 153.

Arendt's debts to Heidegger would seem to make her immune to nominalist arguments, but it is significant that she was also drawn to Duns Scotus. In "Amor Mundi: The Marrano Background of Hannah Arendt's Love for the World," in *Faith in the World: Post-Secular Readings of Hannah Arendt*, ed. Ludger Hagedorn and Rafael Zawisza (New York, 2021), Agata Bielik-Robson argues that she pushed Scotus's "nominalist teachings into a positive *directio mundi*. While most of the commentators emphasized the negative moment of the nominalist God's arbitrary and capricious infinite Will whose only justification is *quia volut*—'because he wanted it that way'—Arendt interprets the Ockhamian *quia volut* motif outside its traditional Christian context and sees it not as an existential threat to the created reality, but a moment of highest affirmation" (9).

4. See James Hankins, *Virtue Politics: Soulcraft and Statecraft in Renaissance Italy* (Cambridge, MA, 2019). Ockham is sometimes seen as a progenitor of individual human rights, but later nominalists like Jeremy Bentham would famously call them "nonsense upon stilts." In between, some theorists like John Locke could both defend epistemological nominalism and believe in innate human rights.

5. There has recently been a general quickening of interest in the crisis of sovereignty in political theory. See, for example, George Edmonson and Klaus Mladek, eds., *Sovereignty in Ruins: A Politics of Crisis* (Durham, NC, 2017).

6. Jacob Taubes, *Ad Carl Schmitt: Gegenstrebige Fügung* (Berlin, 1987); For later treatments of the issue, see Samuel Weber, "Taking Exception to Decision: Walter Benjamin and Carl Schmitt," *Diacritics* 22, nos. 3/4 (1992); Jan-Werner Müller, "Myth, Law and Order: Schmitt and Benjamin read *Reflections on Violence*," *History of European Ideas* 29, no. 4 (2003); Marc de Wilde, "Meeting Opposites: the Political Theologies of Walter Benjamin and Carl Schmitt," *Philosophy and Religion* 44, no. 4 (2011); James R. Martel, *Divine Violence: Walter Benjamin and the Eschatology of Sovereignty* (New York, 2012); Sigrid Weigel, *Walter Benjamin: Images, the Creaturely, and the Holy*, trans. Chadwick Truscott White (Stanford, CA, 2013), chap. 2; Horst Bredekamp, "Walter Benjamin's Esteem for Carl Schmitt," in *The Oxford Handbook of Carl Schmitt*, ed. Jens Meierhenrich and Oliver Simons (Oxford, 2013).

7. Walter Benjamin, *Origin of German Trauerspiel*, trans. Howard Eiland (Cambridge, MA, 2019), 49–52.

8. Benjamin, *Origin of German Trauerspiel*, 50–51. Benjamin was not always consistent in his definition of catastrophe. While here he identifies it with a cataclysmic future event, elsewhere he argues that the interminable, ongoing condition of the world is a kind of permanent catastrophe. For a discussion, see Tom Vandeputte, "Continuity as Catastrophe: Origins of a Thesis in Walter Benjamin," *New German Critique* 148 (2022).

9. Benjamin, *Origin of German Trauerspiel*, 49, italics added.

10. Benjamin, *Origin of German Trauerspiel*, 54.

11. Weber, "Taking Exception to Decision," 15.

12. Agata Bielik-Robson, "Beyond Sovereignty: Overcoming Modern Nominalist Cryptotheology," *Journal for Cultural Research* 20, no. 3 (2016): 300, italics in original.

13. Benjamin, *Origin of German Trauerspiel*, 72. For an analysis of the ways in which Kantorowicz's opposition still haunts modern notions of popular sovereignty, see Eric L. Santner, *The Royal Remains: The People's Two Bodies and the Endgames of Sovereignty* (Chicago, 2011).

14. Weigel, *Walter Benjamin*, 55.

15. De Wilde argues that in his later work, Schmitt tacitly accepted Benjamin's argument, but still contended that a sovereign can create a new order through a potent political myth. See "Meeting Opposites," 374–76.

16. Martel, *Divine Violence*, 58.

17. Theodor W. Adorno, *Minima Moralia: Reflections from Damaged Life*, trans. E. F. N. Jephcott (London, 1974), 131–32.

18. Theodor W. Adorno, *Negative Dialectics*, trans. E. B. Ashton (New York, 1973), 124–25. For a discussion of Adorno's critique of Kierkegaard's nominalism, see Peter E. Gordon, *Adorno and Existence* (Cambridge, MA, 2016), 142–46.

19. The literature on Foucault's controversial theory of power is substantial. For a recent consideration, see Eli B. Lichtenstein, "Foucault's Analytics of Sovereignty," *Critical Horizons* 22, no. 3 (2021).

20. Michel Foucault, "Truth and Power," in *Power/Knowledge: Selected Interviews and Other Writings, 1972–1977*, ed. Colin Gordon (New York, 1980), 121.

21. Michel Foucault, *"Society Must Be Defended": Lectures at the Collège de France 1975–1976*, trans. David Macey (New York, 2003), 34.

22. There is a lively discussion, however, of other similarities and differences between Schmitt and Foucault. See, for example, Mika Ojakangas, "Sovereign and Plebes: Michel Foucault meets Carl Schmitt," *Telos* 119 (2001); Annmaria Shimabuku, "Schmitt and Foucault on the Question of Sovereignty under Military Occupation," *Politica Común* 5 (2014); Sara Raimondi, "From Schmitt to Foucault: Inquiring the Relationship between Exception and Democracy," *Democratic Theory* 31, no. 1 (2016); and Regan Burles, "Exception and Governmentality in the Critique of Sovereignty," *Security Dialogue* 47, no. 3 (2016).

23. See Martin Jay, "Peter Gay and Jean-François Lyotard: Modern and Postmodern Paganism," in *Cultural Semantics: Keywords of Our Time* (Amherst, MA, 1998).

24. Jean-François Lyotard, *The Differend: Phrases in Dispute*, trans. Georges Van Den Abbeele (Minneapolis, 1988). As Elinor Darzi points out, "In Lyotardian terms, Schmitt's idea of the state of exception would describe a sovereign as an addressor uttering a reference and a sense: not a differend or an affect-phrase, but a legitimate phrase. It follows that Schmitt does not take into account a state of exception so exceptional that it cannot be named, where the person experiencing it is deprived of language." "Jean-François Lyotard," Political Theology, June 8, 2021, https://politicaltheology.com/jean-francois-lyotard/.

25. See Jacques Derrida, *The Beast and the Sovereign*, 2 vols., trans. Geoffrey Bennington (Chicago, 2009 and 2011). There is a considerable literature on the nuances of Derrida's reading of Schmitt and its implications for the question of sovereignty. See, for example, Vincent B. Leitch, "Late Derrida: The Politics of Sovereignty," *Critical Inquiry* 33, no. 2

(2007); Geoffrey Bennington, "Sovereign Stupidity and Autoimmunity" and Wendy Brown, "Sovereign Hesitations," in Cheah and Guerlac, *Derrida and the Time of the Political*; Jacques de Ville, "The Foreign Body within the Body Politic: Derrida, Schmitt and the Concept of the Political," *Law Critique* 26 (2015); Arianne François Conty, "Sovereign Power, Sovereign Justice: Carl Schmitt and Jacques Derrida on the State of Exception," *Philosophy Today* 62, no. 3 (2018).

26. Bennington, "Sovereign Stupidity and Autoimmunity," 108.

27. Jacques Derrida, *Rogues: Two Essays on Reason*, trans. Pascale-Anne Brault and Michael Naas (Stanford, CA, 2005), 102.

28. See Cerwyn Moore and Chris Farrands, eds., *On the Nature of Sovereignty: Gilles Deleuze and World Politics* (London, 2010); and Gavin Rae, *Critiquing Sovereign Violence: Law, Bio-Politics, Bio-Juridicalism* (Edinburgh, 2019), chap. 4.

29. See Julian Reid, "Of Nomadic Unities: Gilles Deleuze on the Nature of Sovereignty," *Journal of International Relations and Development* 13 (2010).

30. Frank Ankersmit, "Sovereignty and Political Representation," *Redescriptions* 17, no. 1 (2014) and "Synecdochical and Metaphorical Political Representation: Then and Now," in *Creating Political Presence: The New Politics of Democratic Representation*, ed. Dario Castiglione and Johannes Pollak (Chicago, 2018). In the latter, he distinguishes the medieval version of representation based on a part synecdochically standing for the whole from a modern one based on metaphorical identity between representatives and the represented. In either case, there is a tension between the absolutist logic of sovereignty, royal or popular, and representation of the interests of the people. For Ankersmit's general approach to politics, see his *Aesthetic Politics: Political Philosophy Beyond Fact and Value* (Stanford, CA, 1996).

31. Ankersmit, *Aesthetic Politics*, 105. For a critical comparison of their thought, see Sofia Nässtrom, "Representative Democracy as Tautology: Ankersmit and Lefort on Representation," *European Journal of Political Theory* 5, no. 3 (2006).

32. For a discussion of their tangled relationship, political as well as philosophical, see Matthew R. McLennan, *Philosophy, Sophistry, Antiphilosophy: Badiou's Dispute with Lyotard* (London, 2015).

33. Alain Badiou, "Monde contemporain et désir de philosophie," *Cahiers de Noria* 1 (1992): 28.

34. Colin Wright, "Event or Exception? Disentangling Badiou from Schmitt, or. Towards a Politics of the Void," *Theory and Event* 11, no. 2 (2008). For a further consideration of the issue, see Arne De Boever, *Against Aesthetic Exceptionalism* (Minneapolis, 2019), chap. 1.

35. Alain Badiou, *Infinite Thought: Truth and the Return to Philosophy*, ed. and trans., Oliver Feltham and Justin Clemens (London, 2003), 172. Whether Badiou escapes the charge of duplicating the absolutist inclinations of Schmitt's notion of sovereignty is not clear. For a skeptical discussion, see Peter Hallward, *Badiou: A Subject to Truth* (Minneapolis, 2003), 285–86.

36. For the importance of the gaze in the creation of absolute monarchical power in early modern France, see Jay M. Smith, "'Our Sovereign's Gaze': Kings, Nobles and State Formation in Seventeenth-century France," *French Historical Studies* 18, no. 2 (1993). Its vicissitudes were already represented by Velázquez's *Las Meninas*, as famously analyzed in Foucault's 1966 *The Order of Things*. There is no direct reference to monarchical power in *Étant donnés*, but the strong, centered, usually male gaze underlying it is left in tatters.

37. Taubes, *Ad Carl Schmitt*, 22. The literature on Taubes's own intervention in the debates over political theology is extensive. For a recent sample, see Herbert Kopp-Oberstebrink and Hermut von Sass, eds., *Depeche Mode : Jacob Taubes between Politics, Philosophy, and Religion* (Leiden, 2022).

38. Ramón del Buey Cañas, "Sobre la Ideología estética de lo Informe: Un Comentario a propósito de las Contribuciones de Adorno y Bataille," *Época* 11, no. 31 (2022).

39. Lyotard's debt to Bataille's notion of sovereignty is discussed in Gaëlle Bernard, "On the 'Postmodern' Crisis of Legitimation and the Confusion of Reasons," *Cités* 45, no. 1 (2011); for Derrida's debt, see Vincent B. Leitch, "Late Derrida: The Politics of Sovereignty" and Nick Mansfield, *The God Who Deconstructs Himself: Sovereignty and Subjectivity between Freud, Bataille and Derrida* (New York, 2010); for Foucault's, see Martin Jay, "The Limits of Limit-Experience: Bataille and Foucault," in *Cultural Semantics*. Other contributors to the discourse of the event, such as Deleuze and Badiou, had a much less positive response to Bataille's legacy. For the former, see Eleanor Kaufman, *The Delirium of Praise: Bataille, Blanchot, Deleuze, Foucault, Klossowski* (Baltimore, 2001), 189. For a recent survey of French poststructuralist thought following the distance travelled from Bataille to Badiou through the history of the journal *Lignes*, see Adrian May, *From Bataille to Badiou: Lignes, the Preservation of Radical French Thought, 1987–1917* (Liverpool, 2021).

40. Michel Foucault, "A Preface to Transgression," in *Language, Counter-Memory and Practice: Selected Essays and Interviews*, ed. Donald F. Bouchard (Ithaca, 1977), 45.

41. Jean-François Lyotard, "The Idea of a Sovereign Film," *Acinemas: Lyotard's Philosophy of film*, ed. Graham Jones and Ashley Woodward (Edinburgh, 2017), 62.

42. Derrida, *Rogues*, 68. His first appreciation of Bataille appeared in "From Restricted to General Economy: A Hegelianism without Reserve," *Writing and Difference*, trans. Alan Bass (Chicago, 1978).

43. Jacques Derrida, "Epoché and Faith," in *Derrida and Religion: Other Testaments*, ed. Yvonne Sherwood and Kevin Hart (New York, 2005), 242.

44. For earlier efforts to treat aspects of his work, see Martin Jay, "The Reassertion of Sovereignty in a Time of Crisis: Carl Schmitt and Georges Bataille," in *Force Fields: Between Intellectual History and Cultural Critique* (New York, 1993); *Downcast Eyes: The Denigration of Vision in Twentieth-Century French Thought* (Berkeley, 1994), chap. 4; *Songs of Experience: Modern European and American Variations on a Universal Theme* (Berkeley, 2005), chap. 9.

45. Giorgio Agamben makes the distinction clear: "Secularization is a form of repression. It leaves intact the forces it deals with by simply moving them from one place to another. Thus the political secularization of theological concepts (the transcendence of God as a paradigm of sovereign power) does nothing but displace the heavenly monarchy into an earthly monarchy, leaving its power intact. Profanation, however, neutralizes what it profanes. Once profaned that which was unavailable and separate loses its aura and is returned to use." *Profanations*, trans. Jeff Fort (New York, 2015), 77.

46. Allen S. Weiss, *The Aesthetics of Excess* (Albany, 1989), 8.

47. Georges Bataille, "The Sorcerer's Apprentice," in *Visions of Excess: Selected Writings, 1927–1939*, ed. Allan Stoekl (Minneapolis, 1985), 233.

48. For a history of the College, see Simonetta Falasca-Zamponi, *Rethinking the Political: The Sacred, Aesthetic Politics and the Collège de Sociologie* (Montreal, 2011).

49. For a detailed account of Benjamin's ambivalent attitude towards the members of the College and the more explicit disdain of Horkheimer and Adorno, see Michael Weingrad, "The College of Sociology and the Institute of Social Research," *New German*

Critique 84 (2001). They were troubled by both theoretical and political issues, especially the ways in which Bataille and Caillois sought to rescue the disruptive energies of fascism.

50. Roger Caillois, cited in the introduction to Anatole Lewitzky, "Shamanism," in *The College of Sociology 1937–1939*, ed. Denis Hollier (Minneapolis, 1988), 250.

51. Bataille, "The Psychological Structure of Fascism," in *Visions of Excess*, 145. For a helpful overview of his understanding of the term "heterogeneous," see Michelle H. Richman, *Reading Georges Bataille: Beyond the Gift* (Baltimore, 1982), chap. 3.

52. Georges Bataille, *The Accursed Share: An Essay on General Economy*, vol. 1, *Consumption*, trans. Robert Hurley (New York, 1988).

53. Some critics have accused of him complicity with the fascism he sought with too much sympathy to understand. See, for example, Richard Wolin, *The Seduction of Unreason: The Intellectual Romance with Fascism, from Nietzsche to Postmodernism* (Princeton, 2004), chap. 4. For a rebuttal, see Robyn Marasco, "Bataille's Anti-Fascism," *Contemporary Political Theory* 21 (2022).

54. See, for example, Jean-Michel Besnier, "Georges Bataille in the 1930s: A Politics of the Impossible," *Yale French Studies* 78 (1990); and Alexander Irwin, *Saints of the Impossible: Bataille, Weil, and the Politics of the Sacred* (Minneapolis, 2002). The valorization of "impossibility" became a temptation for many poststructuralist theorists. For one example, see Penelope Deutscher, "Loving the Impossible: Derrida, Rousseau and the Politics of Impossibility," in *Current Continental Theory and Modern Philosophy*, ed. Stephen H. Daniel (Evanston, 2005)

55. Bennington, "Sovereign Stupidity and Autoimmunity," 109.

56. Jacques Derrida, "Force of Law: The 'Mystical Foundation of Authority,'" *Deconstruction and the Possibility of Justice*, ed. Drucilla Cornell, Michel Rosenfeld, and David Gray Carlson (New York, 1992), 29. The influence on Benjamin of Georges Sorel's idea of the apocalyptic proletarian "general strike" in his 1908 *Reflections on Violence*, trans. T. E. Hulme (London, 1970) has often been remarked.

57. Walter Benjamin, "Critique of Violence," in *Reflections: Essays, Aphorisms, Autobiographical Writings*, ed. Peter Demetz (New York, 1978), 297.

58. Benjamin, "Critique of Violence," 300.

59. Martel, *Divine Violence*, 138.

60. Martel, *Divine Violence*, 146.

61. See, for example, Giorgio Agamben, *State of Exception*, trans. Kevin Attell (Chicago, 2005). For a trenchant critique that argues that Agamben's account of the relationship between Benjamin's two kinds of violence is muddled, see Malcolm Bull's review in *The London Review of Books* 26, no. 24, December 16, 2004. There is a substantial literature on this issue. See for example, Adam Kotsko's "On Agamben's Use of Benjamin's 'Critique of Violence,'" *Telos* 145 (Winter 2008); Tom Frost, ed., *Giorgio Agamben: Legal, Political and Philosophical Perspectives* (New York, 2013); and Brendan Moran and Carlo Salzani, eds., *Towards the Critique of Violence: Walter Benjamin and Giorgio Agamben* (London, 2015).

62. Derrida, "Force of Law," 55–56. For a commentary, see Robert Zacharias, "And yet: Derrida on Benjamin's Divine Violence," *Mosaic* 40, no. 2 (2007).

63. Derrida, "Force of Law," 62.

64. Kirill Chepurin and Alex Dubilet, "Introduction: Immanence, Genealogy, Delegitimation," in *Nothing Absolute: German Idealism and the Question of Political Theory*, ed. Kirill Chepurin and Alex Dubilet (New York, 2021), 19. That this temptation was more broadly felt during this period is evidenced by the need for the American Transcendentalist Margaret Fuller to proclaim with earnest solemnity that "I accept the universe," which

occasioned Thomas Carlyle's famous sardonic response: "Gad, she'd better." The exchange is reported in William James's *The Varieties of Religious Experience,* among many other places, although sometimes with differently attributed origins and wordings.

65. Jacob Taubes, *The Political Theology of Paul,* ed. Aleida Assmann and Jan Assman in conjunction with Horst Folkers, Wolf-Daniel Hartwich, and Christoph Schulte, trans. Dana Hollander (Stanford, CA, 2004), 103. In 2 Thessalonians 2:6–7, the *katechon* is introduced as the impeder of the coming of the Antichrist, whose arrival would signal the end of the world. Schmitt adopted it in *Nomos of the Earth* (1950) to characterize the Roman Empire and other later protectors against chaos and anarchy. For a discussion of the implications of Taubes' remark, see Daniel Colucciello Barber, "Relational Division" in Chepurin and Dubilet, *Nothing Absolute.*

66. Taubes, *The Political Theology of Paul,* 74. For a similar accusation, see Giorgio Agamben, *The Time That Remains: A Commentary on the Letter to the Romans,* trans. Patricia Dailey (Stanford, CA, 2005), 35–38.

67. Bielik-Robson, *Jewish Cryptotheologies of Late Modernity: Philosophical Marranos* (London, 2014), 311. She makes a similar argument for Derrida in *Derrida's Marrano Passover: Exile, Survival, Betrayal and the Metaphysics of Non-Identity* (New York, 2023).

68. The idea of *amor mundi,* love of the world, is often identified with Hannah Arendt, who originally intended it as the title for the book that became *The Human Condition.* She meant it in a positive way, which suggests its relevance for the magical nominalist faith in the possibility of "marvelous singularities" appearing in a world we should, despite all our disappointments, still love. But it has not always had that affirmative implication. When the phrase served as the title of Christina Rossetti's famous devotional poem (1865), it had a very different valence as a distraction from the love of God.

Index